Magnificent Rebels

Magnificent Rebels

The First Romantics and the Invention of the Self

ANDREA WULF

Alfred A. Knopf
New York
2022

To Saskia, my mothership

Contents

PART III: CONNECTIONS

PART IV: FRAGMENTATION

Dramatis Personae

Auguste Böhmer (1785–1800)
The oldest daughter of Caroline Böhmer-Schlegel-Schelling. She lived with her mother and stepfather August Wilhelm Schlegel in Jena from 1796 to 1800.

Caroline Böhmer-Schlegel-Schelling, née Michaelis (1763–1809)
A writer, translator, literary critic and muse to the Jena Set. She was married to Franz Böhmer from 1784 to 1788, to August Wilhelm Schlegel from 1796 to 1803, and to Friedrich Schelling from 1803 to 1809. She lived in Jena from 1796 to 1803.

Johann Gottlieb Fichte (1762–1814)
A philosopher who lived in Jena from 1794 to 1799. He moved to Berlin in July 1799. He was married to Johanne Fichte, née Rahn (1755–1819).

Johann Wolfgang von Goethe (1749–1832)
A poet and privy councillor to Duke Carl August in the Duchy of Saxe-Weimar. Goethe lived in Weimar but visited Jena regularly, often for several weeks. His lover and later wife Christiane Vulpius (1765–1816) was the mother of his son August von Goethe (1789–1830).

Georg Wilhelm Friedrich Hegel (1770–1831)
A philosopher who joined his friend Friedrich Schelling in Jena at the beginning of 1801. He lived in Jena until 1807.

Alexander von Humboldt (1769–1859)
A scientist and explorer who often visited his older brother Wilhelm von Humboldt in Jena between 1794 and 1797.

Caroline von Humboldt, née Dacheröden (1766–1829)
Wife of Wilhelm von Humboldt. She lived in Jena (with interruptions) together with her husband from 1794 to 1797.

Wilhelm von Humboldt (1767–1835)
A linguist and Prussian diplomat who lived in Jena (with interruptions) from 1794 to 1797. He was married to Caroline von Humboldt and was Alexander von Humboldt's older brother.

Novalis (1772–1801)
Friedrich von Hardenberg was a poet, writer and mining inspector who used the pen name Novalis. He studied in Jena from 1790 to 1791. His family estate Weißenfels was not far from Jena and he visited his friends regularly between 1795 and 1801. He was first engaged to Sophie von Kühn and then to Julie von Charpentier.

Friedrich Schelling (1775–1854)
A young philosopher who lived and taught in Jena from 1798 to 1803. He had an affair with Caroline Schlegel and married her in 1803.

Friedrich Schiller (1759–1805)
A playwright and poet. Schiller lived in Jena from 1789 to 1799. He moved to Weimar in December 1799. He was married to Charlotte Schiller, née von Lengefeld (1766–1826).

August Wilhelm Schlegel (1767–1845)
A writer, poet, translator and literary critic. He lived in Jena from 1796 to 1801. He was married to Caroline Böhmer-Schlegel-Schelling and was Friedrich Schlegel's older brother.

Friedrich Schlegel (1772–1829)
A writer and literary critic. He lived in Jena from 1796 to 1797 and from 1799 to 1801. He met his married lover Dorothea Veit-Schlegel in Berlin in 1799. They married in 1804. He was August Wilhelm Schlegel's younger brother.

Friedrich Schleiermacher (1768–1834)
A theologian and chaplain. Although Schleiermacher never visited Jena, he was a regular correspondent with members of the Jena Set and his views on religion became important to them. Friedrich Schlegel met him in 1797 in Berlin and shared his lodgings.

Ludwig Tieck (1773–1853)
A writer, poet and translator. He met Friedrich Schlegel in Berlin and lived in Jena from 1799 to 1800. He was married to Amalie Tieck.

Dorothea Veit-Schlegel, née Brendel Mendelssohn (1764–1839)
A writer and translator. She was married to Simon Veit from 1783
to 1799. Friedrich Schlegel was her lover for several years before
they married in 1804. She lived in Jena from 1799 to 1802.

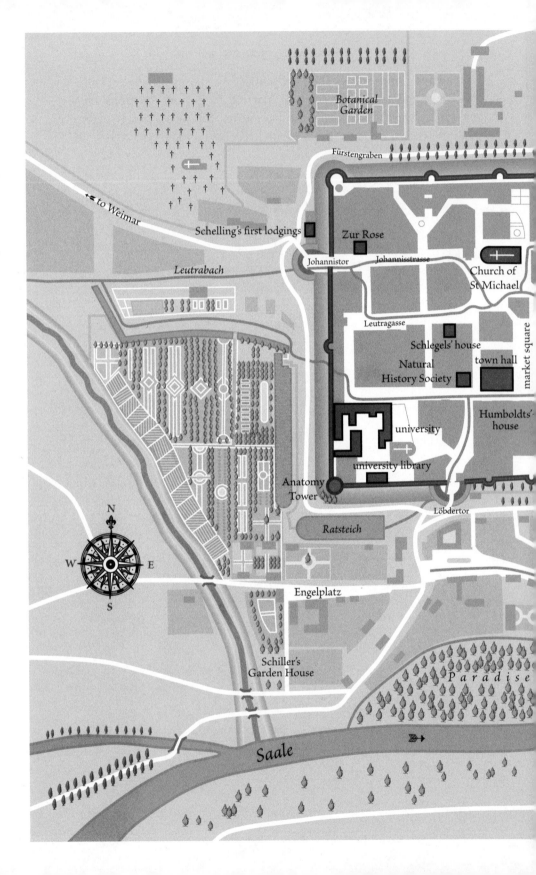

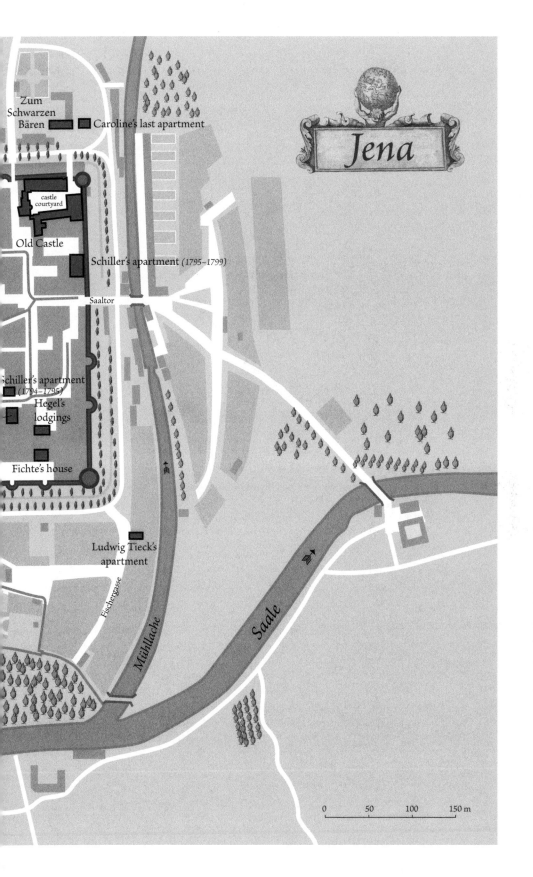

Zum
Schwarzen
Bären · Caroline's last apartment

castle
courtyard

Old Castle

Schiller's apartment *(1795–1799)*

Saaltor

Schiller's apartment
(1794–1795)
Hegel's
lodgings

Fichte's house

Ludwig Tieck's
apartment

Fischergasse

Mühllache

Saale

Jena

0 50 100 150 m

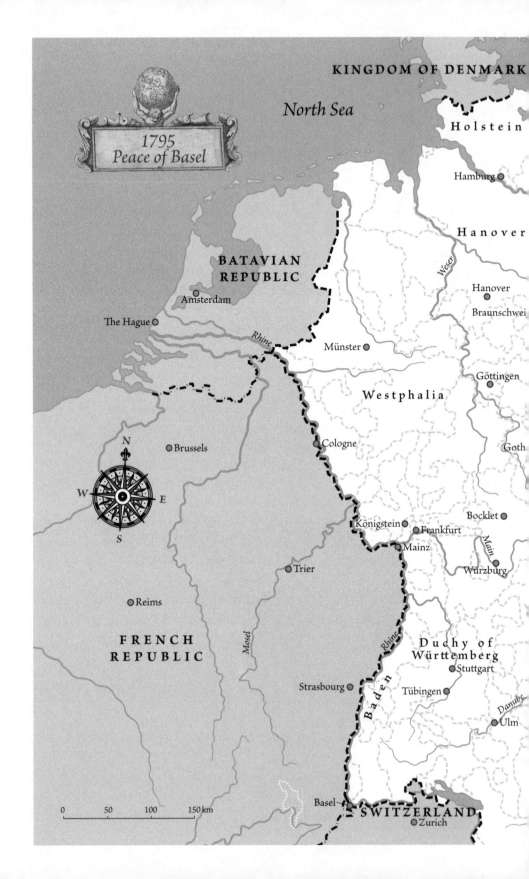

KINGDOM OF DENMARK

North Sea

Holstein

Hamburg

Hanover

Hanover

Braunschwei

1795
Peace of Basel

BATAVIAN
REPUBLIC

Weser

Amsterdam

The Hague

Rhine

Münster

Göttingen

Westphalia

N

Brussels

Cologne

Goth

W   E

S

Königstein   Frankfurt

Bocklet

Mainz

Trier

Main

Würzburg

Reims

Mosel

Rhine

Duchy of
Württemberg

Stuttgart

FRENCH
REPUBLIC

Baden

Strasbourg

Tübingen

Danube

Ulm

0   50   100   150 km

Basel

SWITZERLAND

Zurich

Attend to yourself; turn your eye away from all that surrounds you and in towards your own inner self. Such is the first demand that Philosophy imposes upon the student. We speak of nothing that is outside you, but solely of yourself.

Johann Gottlieb Fichte

From where do I borrow my concepts? – necessarily I – necessarily from myself. I am for myself the ground of all thoughts.

Novalis

I am definitely happier the freer I am.

Caroline Schlegel-Schelling

Prologue

I HAVE DONE THINGS the wrong way round all my life. Or maybe it was the right way. Or maybe it was just an unconventional way. In protest against my clever, liberal, loving and academic parents, I refused to go to university and worked instead in restaurants and bars. That didn't mean that I was not educating myself. I read. Mainly fiction and philosophy. I've always been an insatiable reader, but I wanted to decide for myself what to read and not be bound to a university curriculum. I also began an apprenticeship as a painter and decorator; I was a guide in a museum; I did an internship at a theatre. With the obnoxious confidence of adolescent selfishness, I saw the world through the prism of my own – admittedly narrow – perspective.

What was wrong with reading all day? What was wrong with changing my mind? What was wrong with dancing all night? I fell in and out of love easily. I had a daughter at the age of twenty-two. Suddenly aware that I might not be able to work in restaurants and bars forever, I began to study at a university in Germany. The only seminars I enjoyed, though, were about philosophy. In these lectures it was as if a vortex opened up, pulling me into an intoxicating world of thinking. It felt as if I had discovered the answers to the questions of life: What is evil? What does it mean to be good? Who are we? Why are we? Now, thirty years later, I can hardly remember what I read but the books and discussions with my professors and peers gave me the tools to think and question. I also began to understand history not as a sequence of events and dates that sit neatly in a row, like pearls strung on a necklace, but as an interconnected web. I began to look at the present through the lens of the past.

I took life more seriously but continued to make impulsive choices. I felt free, though, determined to be in control of my destiny. Maybe some of the choices were reckless but they were mine – or so I thought. Now, of course, I know that I was only able to behave in this way because I had the privilege of knowing that if it all went wrong, I would always have been able to knock on my parents' (middle-class) door.

After all, my parents had taught me to follow my dreams. They had done so themselves when they moved from Germany to India in the 1960s, to work for the Deutscher Entwicklungsdienst (the German equivalent of the Peace Corps). Where my parents' childhoods began in the bomb shelters of the Second World War, mine did so in the riotous colours of India. When they boarded a plane in 1966, they left behind a secure life in which my mother had been a secretary and my father had worked in a provincial bank. They returned with two small children and began again. Both in their early thirties by this point, they went to university, the first in their families to do so. My mother became a teacher and my father an eminent academic in the field of Peace and Conflict Studies.

When my own daughter was six, we moved from Germany to England. It was a snap decision. I quit my studies, sold my few possessions and moved to London. I was a single mother with a half-finished education, a trunk full of books, no income, and a seemingly never-ending supply of confidence. I moved in with a friend (the best kind of friend), applied for a fellowship and began (and finished) a new master's degree in London. I worked hard. I had my doubts. I worried. We scraped by. Just. But it was a life full of love, warmth and happiness. I might have been impulsive but I was also always very organised and structured. It wasn't chaotic impulsive, it was life-affirming impulsive.

In England I found my voice. Literally. I found it in a language that wasn't mine by birth. And I became a writer. I was older but still not wiser. One might ask, surely there are better-paid jobs? Yes, but none that I love so much. Most days my job doesn't feel like work. It's what I want to do. Every single day of my life. I write. I tell stories. I try to make sense of the past so that I can learn something about the present. I am lucky. Incredibly lucky. It could have all gone horribly wrong. But it didn't. Until now, I have had the privilege of having lived *my* life. I'm also very aware that it might not always remain like this.

There have been times when my ferocious appetite for independence became egotistical. I'm sure my daughter would have preferred not to move as frequently as we did. But despite these upheavals, she turned out to be a beautiful human being. And I became an adult as I grew up with her. That little girl grounded me and anchored my determination to be free into something bigger: to be a good person. She enabled me to find a balance between being free-spirited and being responsible.

We live in a world in which we tiptoe along a thin line between free will and selfishness, between self-determination and narcissism, between empathy and righteousness. Underpinning everything are two crucial questions: Who am I as an individual? And who am I as a member of a group and society? I live in London, a big dirty metropolis full of people, where every morning hundreds of thousands of commuters pile into the Tube to travel to their workplaces. As they push against each other in this great human wave, they share a physical space but they are also each in their own world. They stare at their small flickering screens, reading emails, checking social media accounts, playing games or scrolling through photos. It's a city where in front of Big Ben or St Paul's Cathedral tourists hustle for the best spot to take the perfect selfie. But it's also a city where people risk their lives helping others in stabbings or terrorist attacks, and where people look after their neighbours.

We've entered into a social contract with those who govern us. We've accepted the laws that frame the society in which we live – though not in perpetuity. They are negotiable. Laws can be revised or changed in order to adapt to new circumstances – but are there moments when I as an individual or we as a society can protest or even violate these laws? Mostly, these changes happen gradually – they are discussed, voted on and then implemented. And though often riddled with setbacks, frustrations and injustice, the legal scaffold is nonetheless an essential part of our democratic relationship with the state and with one another. Sometimes, the changes are more radical or only temporary. Take the global pandemic, for example, when millions of us voluntarily surrendered our basic rights and liberties for the greater good. For months, we didn't see our friends and families, and followed draconian rules because we believed it was the morally right thing to do. Others didn't. They simply refused to obey these restrictions, insisting that their individual liberties were more important.

For most of my adult life, I have been trying to understand why we are who we are. This is the reason why I write history books. In my previous books, I have looked at the relationship between humankind and nature in order to understand why we've destroyed so much of our magnificent blue planet. But I also realise that it is not enough to look at the connections between us and nature. The first step is to look at us as individuals – when did we begin to be as selfish as we are today? At what point did we expect to have the right to determine our own lives? When did we think it was our right to take what we wanted? Where did this – us, you, me, or our collective behaviour – all come from? When did we first ask the question, how can I be free?

It was while researching Alexander von Humboldt, the subject of my book *The Invention of Nature*, that I found the answers to these questions in Jena, a barely known town some 150 miles south-west of Berlin, in Germany. For it was here, in the last decade of the eighteenth century, that Humboldt joined a group of novelists, poets, literary critics, philosophers, essayists, editors, translators and play-wrights who, intoxicated by the French Revolution, placed the self at the centre stage of their thinking. In Jena their ideas collided and coalesced, and the impact was seismic, spreading out across the German states and on into the world – and into our minds.

The group was bound by an obsession with the free self at a time when most of the world was ruled by monarchs and leaders who controlled many aspects of their subjects' lives. 'A person', the philosopher Johann Gottlieb Fichte shouted from the lectern during his first lecture in Jena, 'should be self-determined, never letting himself be defined by anything external.' This emphasis on the self and the value of the individual experience became this group's guiding light.

For the roughly ten years from the mid-1790s that they were living together in Jena, the small town on the banks of the Saale River became the nexus of Western philosophy – a mere blink in time yet one of the most important decades for the shaping of the modern mind. Today, few outside Germany have heard of Jena, but what happened there in those few years remains with us. We still think with the minds of these visionary thinkers, see with their imaginations and feel with their emotions. We might not know it, but their way of understanding the world still frames our lives and being.

One of them was Caroline Michaelis-Böhmer-Schlegel-Schelling, a woman who carried the names of her father and three husbands but who also refused to be restricted by the role that society had intended for women. Caroline stands at the centre of this inspirational story.

~

30 March 1793. The carriage came to an abrupt halt. Soldiers surrounded the vehicle and one of the Prussian officers stepped forward. When he opened the door, he saw a well-dressed woman and child. He asked for names and papers, and from where they had come. 'From Mainz? Böhmer?' he said when he unfolded the pages, and with that simple question the young woman's destiny was sealed. The Prussians had heard of the young widow Caroline Böhmer and her connection with the French revolutionaries who were occupying the German city.

Incensed by the questioning and allegations, Caroline refused to cooperate and behaved so rudely, friends later said, that she was escorted screaming and shouting to Frankfurt. She and her seven-year-old daughter Auguste were placed under house arrest, under the vigilant eyes of three guards. During her interrogation she sarcastically told the officer who was recording her answers that 'he would have made a great editor, since he was so good at putting everything in such concise form'.

After that, she stood no chance. Her luggage was seized and she was charged with being a French sympathiser and imprisoned without trial. Her prison was the old fortress of Königstein, ten miles north-west of Frankfurt and twenty miles north-east of Mainz. On 8 April 1793, nine days after her arrest, she and young Auguste were forced to follow a procession of chained and shackled German revolutionaries. As they left Frankfurt in a guarded carriage, bystanders showered them with rotten eggs, stones and apples. It was even worse for the male prisoners who had to walk and were beaten till they bled.

A few hours later, Caroline made out the fortress, towering over the ruins of Königstein, which had been bombarded by the Prussians while they wrenched it out of French hands. When the prisoners arrived, they were herded through an arched gate in the high ancient walls and into the fortress's shadowed courtyard. It was a frightening sight and certainly no place for a child. No sun touched the cold stones, and as they waited they could hear the rattle of iron locks and the guards' booted steps echoing down the corridors. Once in a while, there was a distant moan. Finally, Caroline and little Auguste, along with several other women, were shoved into a dark, dirty room furnished with filthy straw mattresses, a couple of rough wooden benches and a tub of murky water. The air was stale and the walls were damp. In the days and weeks that followed, they ate potatoes without cutlery and scooped water from the tub with mugs. Soon their clothes and hair were crawling with vermin.

Prison was a far cry from Caroline's normal life. She was the daughter of a celebrated professor at the University of Göttingen, in the German state of Hanover. Her father was a respected orientalist and theologian who was known for his wit and rude jokes as much as for his learning. The family had lived in a large and elegant town house in the city centre, where their guests had included the famous German poet Goethe and the American revolutionary Benjamin Franklin, as well as the many students who attended her father's lectures in the auditorium on the first floor.

Caroline had been raised surrounded by books, intellectual conversation and knowledge. The university's library had been at her disposal and private teachers had provided an extensive education. She learned easily, spoke several languages fluently and, unlike most educated women of her age, her spelling was as accurate as any literary man's. Confident, fearless and known to be 'a little wild', she had as a fifteen-year-old declared: 'I never flatter, I say what I think and feel.' She was small and slender with blue eyes that sparkled with curiosity and brown hair that tumbled in thick curls around her face. Though beautiful, smallpox had blemished her skin, and she also squinted a little. She dressed elegantly, had many admirers, and was sure of herself. Not much frightened Caroline.

She and her daughter had attempted to flee Mainz on 30 March 1793, when almost fifty thousand Prussian and Austrian troops had approached to recapture the city from the French revolutionary army. Caroline had lived in Mainz for a little more than a year. She had been there when the French had arrived the previous October and when German revolutionaries had founded the so-called Society of the Friends of Liberty and Equality the very next day. Terrified aristocrats, clergy, civil servants and the ruling prince-elector had fled the city, but others had welcomed the invading French army and their new democratic beliefs. Those who remained pinned a red, blue and white cockade to their hats as a symbol of the revolution, and shouted 'Vivre libre ou mourir' – 'Live free or die' – as they marched through the streets.

Like other liberal Germans, twenty-nine-year-old Caroline Böhmer had welcomed the French Revolution and the French. Four years earlier, in July 1789, she had read how France's feudal roots had been ripped out by the storming of the Bastille, in Paris, and how the *Declaration of the Rights of Man and of the Citizen* had deemed all men equal. As thousands of protesters marched to the palace of Versailles, and the panicked French king and his queen fled, Caroline had told her younger sister about the glorious events in France. 'Let the wealthy step aside, and the poor rule the world,' she had said.

Liberty, equality and fraternity – the rallying calls of the revolution – promised a new world. After centuries of being ruled by despotic monarchs who favoured a few and let the rest starve, the French people had founded a republic and executed their king. Instead of a privileged few, it was now the people of France who would govern. Caroline was thrilled by the possibilities. 'After all, we are living in very interesting political times,' she wrote shortly after her arrival in Mainz. She couldn't wait to tell her future grandchildren that she was witnessing the greatest upheaval of all time. It was exhilarating, momentous and dizzying. 'Who knows when I'll end up with a bullet in the head!' Caroline said, but she wouldn't want to miss a thing.

During her year in Mainz, Caroline had spent much of her time with Georg Forster, an old friend from Göttingen and an intrepid explorer who had joined Captain Cook's second circumnavigation of the globe in the early 1770s. Forster was also one of Germany's leading revolutionaries. Every day, Caroline would walk the short five-minute stroll from her apartment to his house. In the evenings the Mainz revolutionaries met in Forster's parlour to debate, over a cup of tea, the news from France and their own plans for a republic in Mainz.

Excited to be at the very centre of the action, Caroline discussed politics and revolutions with friends and strangers, read the latest newspapers and was swept up by the turmoil. She was in Mainz when a Tree of Liberty was planted, everybody singing and dancing around it until deep into the night. She went to dinners and parties organised by the French – and soon rumours began to spread. Some

alleged an affair with General Custine, the French commander of
the troops occupying Mainz, with whom Caroline had dined several
times. Others suspected a liaison with Georg Forster. It didn't help
that Caroline was flirtatious by nature and had declared French men
more handsome than Germans.

In mid-March 1793, six months after the French had arrived, the
German revolutionaries declared the Mainz Republic, the first one
on German soil. But it was over almost as soon as it had begun. Two
weeks later, the Prussian army marched towards the city to take it
back from the French. Caroline had thought it wise to leave, but she
had only travelled ten miles before she was arrested by the Prussians.

Her imprisonment in Königstein couldn't have happened at a
worse moment. She and Auguste could endure the cold and hunger,
and sharing mattresses with strangers, but in prison Caroline was
shocked to discover that she was pregnant. Worse still, the pregnancy
was the result of a wild encounter at a ball, in early February, during
the French occupation of Mainz. The father was an eighteen-year-old
French officer whom she had met only once. At a time when women
of her standing were chastised for even being alone in a room with
a man, Caroline's behaviour was regarded as scandalous.

The combination of being widowed with a young daughter,
pregnant by a French soldier, imprisoned by the Prussians and accused
of colluding with the enemy alarmed even the formidable Caroline.
She had three, maybe four, months before the pregnancy became
obvious. If discovered, her reputation would be destroyed and the
authorities might remove her beloved Auguste from her care.

As her belly grew, she cinched her corset tighter and sent letters
to friends and acquaintances with political connections. One old
suitor had contacts at the Prussian court, and she also wrote to
August Wilhelm Schlegel, a young writer and devoted admirer from
her time in Göttingen. The Prussians, though, held firm. Caroline's
dinners with General Custine and the French were public knowledge,
and little Auguste enthusiastically chanting 'Vive la nation!' and
singing the Marseillaise didn't help the situation. With every passing
day, Caroline's despair grew. 'A long imprisonment will be life-
threatening,' she wrote to the husband of her oldest friend, finally
revealing the truth in a desperate plea for help, 'but don't tell anyone'.

Imprisoned in early April, she was still at Königstein in the
middle of June, when unseasonably cold storms froze the grapes

on the vines in the vineyards outside. In their damp cell, as mother and daughter struggled to keep warm, Auguste coped better than Caroline, who suffered from morning sickness and infected gums. Caroline felt the lack of exercise and fresh air, and her health declined steadily. She suffered from persistent headaches and a cough became chronic. She was scared. Even here, some twenty miles from the front, she could hear the thunder of French and Prussian cannon fire as Mainz was bombarded. Hundreds of new prisoners were brought to the fortress, where they were beaten by the Prussians, many dying from their injuries.

Caroline's greatest worry, though, remained her advancing pregnancy. She continued writing letters underlining how urgent her situation was becoming – 'how desperately I need to be saved soon' – only to find one friend after another turning away. Meanwhile her old admirer from Göttingen, August Wilhelm Schlegel, did his best to help, writing letters to anyone who might be able to assist. He never wavered – not when Caroline admitted the pregnancy, nor when his brother told him about Caroline's alleged affair with General Custine. If August Wilhelm couldn't get her out of prison soon, Caroline warned him, he would have to supply her with poison so that she could take her own life. Far better for Auguste to be orphaned than to live with a dishonoured mother.

~

After several months, Caroline was freed from prison in July 1793 with the help of her younger brother, who had pulled some strings with an old friend who was the mistress of the Prussian king. In November she secretly gave birth to a son. For the next two years, she zigzagged across Germany, followed by vicious rumours and treated like an outcast. Her life seemed over, but then August Wilhelm Schlegel came to her rescue. They married in 1796 and moved to Jena where Caroline became the heart and mind of a group of young men and women who hoped to change the world. She was a muse and critic who contributed to their literary works – and her home was the physical space where they met, thought, talked, laughed and wrote.

This extraordinary group of rebellious twenty- and thirty-somethings included the enigmatic poet Novalis, who played with death and darkness, the brusque philosopher Johann Gottlieb Fichte, who put the self at the centre of his work, and the brilliant Schlegel brothers, Friedrich and August Wilhelm, both writers and critics, one as impetuous and short-tempered as the other was calm. There was Dorothea Veit, a writer who scandalised Berlin's high society by her affair with the much younger Friedrich Schlegel. Also in Jena was Friedrich Schelling, a mercurial philosopher who examined the relationship between the individual and nature. There was Germany's most revolutionary playwright, Friedrich Schiller, as much a magnet for the younger generation as he was a divisive force.

At the periphery was Georg Wilhelm Friedrich Hegel, one of history's most influential philosophers, and another pair of brothers – Wilhelm and Alexander von Humboldt, the former a gifted linguist and founder of the university of Berlin, and the latter an intrepid and visionary scientist-explorer. And at the centre of this galaxy of dazzling minds was Johann Wolfgang von Goethe, Germany's most celebrated poet. Older and more famous, Goethe became something of a stern and benevolent godfather to the group. Often acting as their mediator, he was inspired by their new and radical ideas, and they in turn worshipped him. Goethe was their god and they put him on a pedestal.

Each of these great intellects lived a life worth telling. More extraordinary than their individual stories, however, is the fact that they all came together at the same time in the same place. That's why I've called them the 'Jena Set'.

~

They were born into a world so different from ours that it's hard to imagine – a Europe ruled by monarchs who determined much of their subjects' lives. The French king's palace at Versailles, with its gilded halls of mirrors and glorious gardens, radiated absolute power across France, at a time when many of the nation's people lived in abject poverty. Just as the gardens and trees were corseted into clipped topiary, laid out in rays of straight avenues and forced into elaborate patterns, so too the French people were bound to their destiny by birth and the king. Nothing was allowed to be out of place – everything was bent and shaped according to the divine right. And while the French queen Marie Antoinette played shepherdess to her flock of perfumed sheep in the small chateau Petit Trianon, peasants and labourers everywhere were starving.

Further to the east, in Russia, Catherine the Great cast herself as an enlightened monarch and modernised the country, but she too ruled with an iron fist. Here, as well as in the eastern German territories, serfdom still prevailed. This ancient feudal system bound people to land and lords. Like slaves, they had to work for local landowners and were not allowed to leave. Dues, tithes and taxes were often so high it was not possible to survive on what remained.

Across Europe, philosophers were censored for their ideas, writers were banned from writing, professors lost their jobs for speaking out, and playwrights were imprisoned for their plays. Some rulers had the right to decide their subjects' heirs or profession while others could banish them, force them to work or refuse them permission to move. And though Friedrich the Great had prided himself on being an enlightened king, even in Prussia male aristocrats could only marry the daughter of a farmer or a craftsman by special dispensation. Some monarchs could even sell their subjects as mercenaries to foreign powers, others rented out whole regiments to subsidise their own expenditures. The world in which the members of the Jena Set grew up was one of despotism, inequality and control.

Then, in 1789, came the French Revolution – an event so pivotal and dramatic no one in Europe was unaffected. It was like an eruption or a detonation. When the French revolutionaries declared all men equal, it suggested the possibility of a new social order founded on the power of ideas and freedom. 'Things are becoming reality,' Novalis wrote in 1794, 'which, ten years ago, would have gone straight to the philosophical madhouse.'

The French Revolution proved that ideas were stronger than the might of kings and queens. 'We have to believe in the *power of words*,' the writer Friedrich Schlegel declared, wielding his pen like a sword. The group was excited about the revolution. Welcoming the ideas that spread from France, Caroline, who had witnessed the birth of the short-lived Mainz Republic, believed that 'writers ruled the world'. Schelling and Hegel had enthusiastically sung the Marseillaise while studying together in Tübingen, and the philosopher Fichte wrote a pamphlet in which he declared that the 'French Revolution seems to me important for all mankind'.

Fichte placed the self, the *Ich* as it is known in German, at the centre of his new philosophy. He imbued the self with the most thrilling of all ideas: free will. This was an idea lit by the fire of the French Revolution. The empowerment of the Ich was as much about the liberation of the individual as it was a rebellion against the despotism of the state. And this radically new concept of an unfettered self carried the potential for a different life. A person 'should be what he is', Fichte told his students in Jena, 'because he wants to be it and is right to want to be it'. They all believed, as Schelling said, in a 'revolution brought about by philosophy'.

For centuries philosophers and thinkers had argued that the world was controlled by a divine hand and ruled by God's absolute truths. While humans might come to understand these absolute truths, they could not make or shape them. The eighteenth century was an era of discovery in which natural laws, such as the physics of light refraction or the forces governing the motion of the moon and the stars, had been revealed. Mathematics, rational observation and controlled experiments had paved the way towards knowledge, yet humans remained cogs in a seemingly divinely ordained machine. They were certainly not free.

But humankind began to exert some control over nature. Inventions such as telescopes and microscopes had already uncovered such secrets as planetary movements and the nature of blood. New technologies such as steam engines pumped water out of mines, physicians inoculated against smallpox, and hot-air balloons lifted people to a place where no human had ever been. When Benjamin Franklin invented the lightning rod in the mid-eighteenth century, humanity had even begun to tame what had long been regarded as God's fury.

An ever-expanding network of roads laced the German states and principalities – and new detailed maps and road signs directed travellers as they ventured beyond their home towns. The tick-tock of new pendulum clocks became the beating heart of society. Minute by minute, hands moved with predictable and increasing accuracy across clockfaces in people's pockets and parlours, and on town halls and church towers. These new timepieces told everyone when to eat, work, pray and sleep. Their rhythm became a new chorus against which people raced. Life sped up, became faster, more predictable and more rational. According to Hegel, the motto of the Enlightenment was: 'Everything is useful.'

The downside of all this scientific ingenuity, productivity and utility, the Jena Set feared, was that humankind focussed too much on reason alone. Reality, they believed, had been stripped of poetry, spirituality and feeling. 'Nature has been reduced to a monotonous machine,' Novalis wrote, turning 'the eternally creative music of the universe into the monotonous clatter of a gigantic millwheel'. Whereas the British Enlightenment philosopher John Locke had insisted in the late seventeenth century that the human mind was a blank slate which over a lifetime filled with knowledge derived from sensory experience alone, the Jena Set declared that imagination had to be given its due, along with reason and rational thought. The friends began to look inwards.

~

Jena itself was small. A university town of only four and a half thousand inhabitants who lived in around eight hundred houses, it was part of the Duchy of Saxe-Weimar, a principality headed by Duke Carl August. Geographically, the duchy was located at the centre of the German territories and at the crossroads of many postal routes – with travellers and mail bags arriving from Bohemia, Saxony, Prussia, Westphalia, Frankfurt and elsewhere, bringing letters, books and newspapers filled with the latest political and philosophical writings.

Like many old towns in Germany, Jena still had a medieval feel. At its centre was a large and open market square and just beyond, to the north, rose the huge Church of St Michael, with a tower that dominated the skyline. In the north-eastern corner of Jena, a block away from the church, was the Old Castle, once the seat of the duchy's rulers but then rarely used since the court had long since relocated to nearby Weimar, fifteen miles to the north-west. At the opposite end, in the south-western corner, was the university, Jena's centre of gravity. Housed in a former Dominican convent, it had a library of more than fifty thousand books along with a refectory, brewery and residences, although most students lodged and ate in town. Jena and its university was a transient place. People came and went, fell in and out of love, leaving behind a trail of scandals, children and broken hearts – a staggering quarter of all births in Jena were illegitimate, compared to just two per cent elsewhere in the German territories.

That Jena was dominated by its university was immediately apparent. Not only was there a thriving local economy of bookbinders, printers, tailors and taverns, but, with around eight hundred students in residence, more tea, coffee, beer and tobacco was consumed here than in other similarly sized small towns in Germany. Although the food served in Jena's taverns had a reputation for being unpalatable, the students insisted that their minds were fed with the finest fare. 'Here the torches of wisdom are burning at every hour of the day,' one student said.

Literature was everywhere. In addition to the university library, there was a lending library with more than one hundred German and international periodicals, as well as seven well-stocked bookshops. Walking through the cobbled streets on a warm summer evening, one would hear snatches of discussions on philosophy and poetry as well as the sound of violins and pianos. Then, late at night, when empty beer mugs covered the surfaces of rough wooden tables in the town's many taverns, students argued about art, philosophy and literature. After eight or nine bottles of beer, one Danish student recalled, the rowdy young men would stagger home through the streets, waking with sore heads in the early mornings to rush to the auditoriums, anatomy theatre and meeting rooms to learn from their young and radical professors. With no theatre, opera, music hall or art gallery, there were few other distractions, and students were practically forced to study for the lack of anything else to do.

Jena was a pleasant place. The town had expanded beyond the crumbling medieval walls, with more houses, gardens, nurseries and fields. To the north, also just outside the old walls, was the new botanical garden that Goethe had established and a meandering path, dubbed the 'Philosopher's Walk', for those who wanted to wander and think. Fields and vineyards crawled up the surrounding hills and rising above everything else was the Jenzig, a small mountain with a distinctive triangular shape that could be seen from almost anywhere in town.

To the south, paths snaked through a forested parkland that the locals called 'The Paradise'. Here, along the Saale River, trees fringed the gently sloping embankment and fishermen dropped their bait into the water. In spring the purple blossom of liverwort and yellow primroses carpeted the grass, and in the summer packed beer gardens did good business when revellers were serenaded by an orchestra of nightingales singing their crepuscular trills, whistles and purrs. In the winter, the town's students sometimes even glimpsed the great Goethe skating on the frozen river. How, though, did this small and decidedly rural location become the crucible of contemporary thought – a 'Kingdom of Philosophy', as Caroline called it?

~

Why Jena? Indeed, why Germany? The answer is that at the end of the eighteenth century Germany was not yet a unified nation but instead a patchwork of more than fifteen hundred states, ranging from tiny principalities to large fiefdoms ruled by powerful and competing dynasties such as the Hohenzollern in Prussia and the Habsburgs in Austria. This colourful map was the so-called Holy Roman Empire, which, as the French thinker Voltaire once said, was neither holy nor Roman nor an empire. Almost thirty million people called this their home, but only a few ruled the many.

The Holy Roman Empire was divided by an intricate web of customs barriers, different currencies, measurements and laws, and connected by terrible roads and unreliable postal services, which made communication, unification and modernisation difficult. Power was not centralised but held by princes, dukes, bishops and their courts spread across this vast jigsaw puzzle. Unlike France, Germany wasn't ruled by one king from his distant throne, but this didn't mean that rulers were any less despotic or indeed more lenient.

One unintended advantage of such fragmentation, though, was that censorship was much more difficult to enforce than it was in large, centrally administered nations such as France or England. Every German state, however small, had its own set of rules. There were also more universities in Germany than anywhere else, with about fifty such institutions compared to just Cambridge and Oxford in England. Admittedly, some were tiny, but their profusion made it much easier for poorer families to send their sons to get an education.

The Germans were also fanatical readers. Literacy rates soared, with Prussia and Saxony leading the world by the end of the eighteenth century. 'In no country is the love of reading more widespread than in Germany,' one visitor noted. Craftsmen, maids and bakers were reading just as avidly as university professors and aristocrats. The appetite for novels was huge, and in the last three decades of the eighteenth century the number of authors doubled – by 1790 there were an astonishing six thousand published writers in Germany. With the German book trade enjoying a market that was four to five times larger than that in England, the era became known as the 'Age of Paper'.

Whereas France, Spain and England had powerful monarchies and a global reach through their colonies, and the United States had the great unexplored West, everything in Germany was small, splintered and inward-looking. The German imagination was fed by words, and German readers travelled to distant countries and new worlds along the black letters on printed pages. Most German towns had lending libraries and reading societies, and cheaply printed pamphlets and novels could be bought on every corner. Books were everywhere.

But, still, why Jena? The answer, Friedrich Schiller thought, was the town's university. Nowhere else, he said, could one enjoy such true freedom. At the time of its foundation in the sixteenth century, the university and the town of Jena had been part of the Electorate of Saxony. Over generations complicated inheritance rules had led to parts of the state being divided into ever smaller parcels between the male heirs. By the 1790s the university was controlled by no fewer than four different Saxon dukes, with Duke Carl August of Saxe-Weimar the nominal rector. In reality, no one was truly in charge.*

The result was that Jena's professors enjoyed far greater freedom than anywhere else in Germany. It was no surprise that here in Jena the visionary ideas of Immanuel Kant found a fertile ground. Jena's *Allgemeine Literatur-Zeitung*,† for example, had been founded in 1785 with the express purpose of disseminating Kant's philosophy. As one British visitor remarked, Jena was the 'most fashionable seat of the new philosophy' and a town where readers discussed Kant's philosophy with the same passion as others did popular novels.

The philosopher-king argued that it was the human mind and experience that shaped our understanding of nature and the world, rather than any rules written and imposed by God. Instead of searching for absolute truths or objective knowledge, Kant turned his attention to subjectivity and the individuum. 'Dare to know', he had urged in 1784 in 'An Answer to the Question: What is Enlightenment?' In this famous essay Kant had also called for 'man's emergence from his self-imposed immaturity'. Cultivate your own mind, he wrote, 'nothing is required for this enlightenment except freedom'. And Jena's students and professors set out to do exactly that.

---

* The four Saxon states were independently ruled but politically united. They were Saxe-Weimar, Saxe-Coburg-Saalfeld, Saxe-Gotha-Altenburg and Saxe-Meiningen.
† This translates as *Universal Literary Gazette*.

The liberal atmosphere attracted progressive thinkers from the more repressive German states. 'The professors in Jena are almost entirely independent,' Schiller commented, with another scholar adding that 'here we have complete freedom to think, to teach and to write'. Of course, this didn't mean that Jena's intellectuals could do whatever they wanted – dissenting voices disliked what they regarded as a 'foolish obsession with liberty' – but they did enjoy more leeway. Thinkers, writers and poets who had been in trouble with the authorities in their home states came to Jena, drawn by the openness and relative freedoms of the university town. In consequence, the last decade of the eighteenth century saw more famous poets, writers, philosophers and thinkers living in Jena in proportion to its population than in any other town before or since.

~

Magnificent Rebels recounts one of these strangely magnified and exciting moments in history when a cluster of intellectuals, artists, poets and writers come together at a particular time and in a particular place to change the world. In this, the Jena Set resemble other influential groups: the North American Transcendentalists, for instance, comprising Ralph Waldo Emerson, Henry David Thoreau, Nathaniel Hawthorne and others, who lived in Concord, Massachusetts in the mid-nineteenth century; similarly, the Bloomsbury Set that coalesced in early twentieth-century London and included Virginia Woolf, E. M. Forster, Vanessa Bell and John Maynard Keynes; or the modernist circle of Ernest Hemingway, Ezra Pound, Gertrude Stein, and F. Scott Fitzgerald in 1920s Paris.

I believe that the Jena Set is, intellectually speaking, the most important of all these groups. In their lifetimes members became so famous that reports of their ideas and scandals filtered out through German newspapers to the wider world. Students came to Jena from all over Europe to study with their intellectual heroes – these 'Jacobins of poetry' – and then took their ideas home with them. 'We are on a mission,' Novalis wrote with unabashed confidence in 1798, because 'we are called to educate the world'. This group of writers, poets and thinkers changed the way we think about the world by placing the self at the centre of everything. In doing so, they liberated people's minds from the corset of doctrines, rules and expectations.

They became known as the 'Young Romantics'. In fact, they were the first to use the term 'romantic' in their writings, heralding Romanticism as an international movement by providing not only its name and purpose but also an intellectual framework. But what was Romanticism? Today, the term tends to suggest artists, poets and musicians who emphasise emotion and yearn to be at one with nature. Images of lonely figures in moon-lit forests or standing on craggy cliffs above seas of fog are as much associated with Romanticism as poems about forlorn lovers. Some say that the Romantics opposed reason and celebrated irrationalism; others argue that they rejected the idea of absolute knowledge. However, when we look at the beginnings of Romanticism we find something much more complex, contradictory and multi-layered.

That thinkers, historians and academics have failed to agree on one succinct definition of Romanticism would have pleased the Jena Set, who liked this indefinability of the concept. They themselves never attempted to provide rigid rules – in fact, it was the very absence of rules that they celebrated. They were not interested in an absolute truth but in the *process* of understanding. They tore down boundaries between disciplines, thereby transcending the divisions between the arts and the sciences, and pushed against the Establishment.

In 1809, long after he had left Jena, August Wilhelm Schlegel explained what the group had tried to do: they had woven together poetry and prose, nature and art, mind and sensuality, the earthly and the divine, life and death. They wanted to poeticise the increasingly mechanical clanking of the world. 'Poetry', said Hyperion in Friedrich Hölderlin's eponymous novel, 'is the beginning and the end of all scientific knowledge.' And at the centre of this Romantic project was the new emphasis on the Ich.

Today the English-speaking world celebrates the Jena Set's contemporaries, Samuel Taylor Coleridge, William Wordsworth, William Blake and the younger generation of Lord Byron, Percy Bysshe Shelley and John Keats, as the great Romantic poets. They were all of that and more, but they were not alone and they were not the first. It was the Jena Set who first proclaimed these ideas, and over the ensuing decades the effects rippled out into the world. So enthralled was Coleridge by their ideas that he travelled to Germany in 1798, determined to learn German and to meet his heroes in Jena. 'Speak nothing but German. Live with Germans. Read in German. Think in German' had been his motto. Perpetually broke, however, Coleridge ran out of money before reaching Jena, but he did learn German. Equipped with his new language, he later translated Schiller's play *Wallenstein* and Goethe's *Faust*, read Fichte's philosophy and was deeply impressed by Friedrich Schelling's ideas on the mind and nature.

Coleridge's writings introduced the Jena Set to English readers but some thirty years later also to American thinkers such as Ralph Waldo Emerson, whose own philosophy would become infused with the ideas of 'this admirable Schelling', as he called him. Inspired, many of the American Transcendentalists then set out to learn German so that they too could read the Jena Set's works in the original and learn about 'this strange genial poetic comprehensive philosophy', as Emerson described it. Kant, Fichte, Schelling and Hegel, the Transcendentalists insisted, were the 'great thinkers of the world', and as important as Plato, Aristotle, Descartes and Leibniz.

~

The Jena Set tried to understand how we make sense of the world. Questions such as Who are we? What can we know? How can we know? and What is nature? were all questions that were approached through an investigation of the self. This self-reflection became the method through which to understand the world, and in turn this inward gaze became part of the Jena Set's lived reality.

As they investigated their selves, many of them broke conventions and freed their Ichs from unhappy marriages or dull careers. They were rebellious and felt invincible. Their lives became the playground of this new philosophy. And the story of their tiptoeing between the power of free will and the danger of becoming self-absorbed is significant on a universal level. The Ich, for better or worse, has remained centre stage ever since. The French revolutionaries changed the political landscape of Europe, but the Jena Set incited a revolution of the mind. The liberation of the Ich from the straitjacket of a divinely organised universe is the foundation of our thinking today. It gave us the most exciting of all powers: free will.

At the heart of *Magnificent Rebels* is the tension between the breath-taking possibilities of free will and the pitfalls of selfishness. The balancing act that the Jena Set negotiated between the tunnel vision of individual perspective and their belief in change for the greater good remains relevant today. Their ideas have seeped so deeply into our culture and behaviour that we've forgotten where they came from. We don't talk about Fichte's self-determined Ich any more because we have internalised it. We *are* this Ich. Put another way, today we take it for granted that we judge the world around us through the prism of our self: that is the only way that we can now make sense of our place in the world. We're still empowered by the Jena Set's daring leap into the self. But we have to decide how to use their legacy.

PART I

Arrival

Now at last we've overcome all the obstacles in our path, and left them behind us too, on rails as smooth as the ones you've been on for so long. And alongside yours, too. I'm unspeakably happy . . . and this valley is already a dear friend.

Caroline Schlegel to Luise Gotter, 11 July 1796

I

'A happy event'
Summer 1794: Goethe and Schiller

ON 20 JULY 1794 Johann Wolfgang von Goethe heaved himself into the saddle and rode from his house in the centre of Weimar to Jena, where he planned to attend a botanical meeting of the recently founded Natural History Society. It was a hot summer that would soon turn into a glorious autumn – long sun-baked months during which pears, apples, sweet melons and apricots ripened four weeks early and the vineyards produced one of the century's greatest vintages.

On the fifteen-mile ride from Weimar to Jena, Goethe passed farmers scything wheat in golden fields and great haystacks awaiting storage as winter fodder in the barns. After a couple of hours of riding through flat farmland, the countryside began to change. Little villages and hamlets snuggled into gentle dips, and then the forest closed in and the fields disappeared. The land became more hilly. Shell-bearing limestone cliffs rose to the left, exposing the geological memory of the region when this part of Germany had been a landlocked sea some 240 million years ago. Just before he reached Jena, Goethe crossed the so-called Snail, the steep hill named after the serpentine road that wound up to its top.

Then, finally, he saw Jena beneath him, nestled in a wide valley and held in the elbow of the Saale River with the jagged outline of the forested mountains behind. These were more hills than mountains, perhaps, but the views were spectacular – and the reason why Swiss students in Jena lovingly called the surrounding area 'little Switzerland'.

~

Goethe was the Zeus of Germany's literary circles. Born in Frankfurt in 1749 to a wealthy family, he had grown up amidst comfort and privilege. His maternal grandfather had been the mayor of Frankfurt and his paternal grandfather had made his wealth as a merchant and tailor. Goethe's father didn't have to work and had instead managed his fortunes, collected books and art, and educated his children. Though a lively and bright child, Goethe had not shown any exceptional talents. He loved to draw, was proud of his immaculate handwriting and enjoyed the theatre. When the French had occupied Frankfurt in 1759 during the Seven Years War and their commander had been billeted at the Goethes' house, young Goethe had made the best of it by learning French from the occupying forces.

He had studied law in Leipzig and worked as a lawyer, but also began to write. In the mid-1770s he had been thrust into the public eye with the publication of his novel *The Sorrows of Young Werther* – the story of a forlorn lover who commits suicide. Goethe's protagonist is irrational, emotional and free. 'I withdraw into myself and find a world there,' Werther declares. The novel captured the sentimentality of the time and became *the* book of a generation. A huge international bestseller, it was so popular that countless men, including Carl August, the ruler of the small Duchy of Saxe-Weimar, had dressed like Werther – wearing a yellow waistcoat and breeches, blue tailcoat with brass buttons, brown boots and a round grey felt hat. Chinese manufacturers even produced *Werther* porcelain for the European market.

It was said that *Werther* had caused a wave of suicides, and forty years after its publication the British poet Lord Byron joked with Goethe that his protagonist 'has put more individuals out of this world than Napoleon himself'. *The Sorrows of Young Werther* had been Goethe's most vivid contribution to the so-called *Sturm und Drang* – the Storm and Stress movement – which had elevated feelings above the rationalism of the Enlightenment. In this period, which had celebrated emotion in all its extremes, from passionate love to dark melancholy, from suicidal longings to frenzied delight, Goethe had become a literary superstar.

The eighteen-year-old Duke Carl August had been so enraptured by the novel that he had invited Goethe to live and work in the duchy in 1775. Goethe was twenty-six when he moved to Weimar; and he knew how to make an entry, arriving dressed in his *Werther* uniform. During those early years the poet and the young duke had roistered through the streets and taverns of the town. They had played pranks on unsuspecting locals and flirted with peasant girls. The duke loved to gallop across the fields and to sleep in hay barns or camp in the forest. There had been drunken brawls, theatrical declarations of love, naked swimming and nightly tree climbing – but those wild years were long gone and Goethe had turned his back on his *Sturm und Drang* phase.

In time, both poet and ruler calmed down, and Goethe had become part of the duchy's government. The small state had just over a hundred thousand inhabitants – tiny in comparison to the five million people of nearby Prussia, or other powerful states such as Saxony, Bavaria or Württemberg. With a mostly agrarian economy – grain, fruit, wine, vegetable gardens as well as sheep and cattle – the Duchy of Saxe-Weimar had little trade and manufacturing, yet it maintained a bloated court of two thousand courtiers, officials and soldiers, all of whom had to be paid. The town of Weimar itself had a provincial feel. Most of the seven hundred and fifty houses had only one storey and such small windows that they felt gloomy and cramped inside. The streets were dirty, and there were only two businesses in the market square that sold goods which could be classed as luxury items – a perfumery and a textile shop. There wasn't even a stagecoach station.

Goethe became Carl August's confidant and his privy councillor – so trusted that it was rumoured that the duke didn't decide anything without the poet's advice. In time, Goethe took charge of the royal theatre and of rebuilding the burned-down castle in Weimar, in addition to several other well-paid administrative positions, including the control of the duchy's mines. He also worked closely with his colleague in the Weimar administration, minister Christian Gottlob Voigt. A diligent worker, Goethe was never idle – 'I never smoked tobacco, never played chess, in short, I never did anything that would have wasted my time.'

In 1794, Goethe was forty-four and no longer the dashing Apollo of his youth. He had put on so much weight that his once beautiful eyes had disappeared into the flesh of his cheeks and one visitor compared him to 'a woman in the last stages of pregnancy'. His nose was aquiline, and like so many contemporaries, his teeth were yellowed and crooked. He had a penchant for stripy and flowery long waistcoats, which he buttoned tightly over his round belly. Unlike the younger generation, who often wore fashionable loose-fitting trousers, Goethe preferred breeches. He wore boots with turned-down tops and always his tricorne. He kept his hair coiffed and powdered, with two carefully pomaded curls over his ears and a long, stiff ponytail. Knowing that everybody was watching him, he always made sure to be properly dressed and groomed when he went out. Ennobled by the duke in 1782, he was now Johann Wolfgang *von* Goethe and lived in a large house in Weimar, where he often tried and failed to work amid a constant stream of strangers knocking on his door to gawp at the famous poet. He loathed these disruptions almost as much as he hated noise, in particular the rattling of his neighbour's loom and the skittle alley in a nearby tavern.

Goethe might have turned his back on the *Sturm und Drang* era, but it seemed as if his creativity had done the same to him. For years he had failed to produce anything remarkable and his plays were no longer widely staged. He fussed over his writings for years. More than two decades earlier, he had begun to work on his drama *Faust* but only a few scenes had been published. He had rewritten and changed his tragedy *Iphigenia in Tauris* so many times – from prose to blank verse, back to prose, to its final version in classical iambic verse – that he called it his 'problem child'. And though he was the director of the Weimar theatre, he preferred to stage popular plays by his contemporaries rather than his own.

Botany was now Goethe's favourite subject, and the reason he often came to Jena. He was overseeing the construction of a new botanical garden and institute in Jena. Originally founded in 1548 as a medicinal garden, the university's existing botanical garden had been used to train physicians, but Duke Carl August had asked Goethe to extend and move it to a new location, just north of the old town walls. Goethe enjoyed every aspect of the project because it united his deep love of nature and beauty with scientific rigour. He was looking forward to the meeting of the Natural History Society.

~

As always when he was in Jena, Goethe stayed in his rooms in the Old Castle, the largely unused former home of the duchy's rulers. Set around a large rectangular courtyard in the town's north-eastern corner, the castle was a jumble of buildings of different heights and ages. The oldest part was thirteenth century, and various other buildings had been added in the seventeenth. There was also a riding hall from the 1660s and a long narrow garden, parallel to the street, which had been planted on the site of the castle's former moat.

It was sweltering when Goethe arrived in Jena on 20 July 1794, but he set out on foot to walk to the meeting, which was being hosted by the director of the botanical garden in his apartment just beyond the town hall. Goethe always enjoyed a vigorous walk, no matter the weather. He needed fresh air and exercise to counterbalance the long hours at his desk. Unless the weather was atrocious, Goethe took his coat and tricorne and walked every day.

As he left the Old Castle and walked towards the town hall, Goethe could see the spire of the imposing Church of St Michael. The Gothic church was built of the same shell-bearing limestone that he had seen in the cliff faces while riding from Weimar. The streets were lined by a patchwork of houses of different heights and periods, some ornamented with stucco, others with exposed dark timber frames. Most were taller and more elegant than those in Weimar. Unlike the more rural feel of Weimar, where cattle were often driven along the town's muddy paths, Jena had the flair of a city despite its small size. A stream had been channelled into a narrow canal that ran along the cobbled alleys through town – twice a week the sluices were opened to flush and clean the streets. Jena was compact and square within its crumbling medieval town walls, and Goethe could cross it in less than ten minutes.

It was a bustling town. During the day, the streets echoed to a cacophony of voices, rattling carts and the iron clank of horseshoes. There were more than twenty bakeries and forty-one butchers, as well as sixty-four shoemakers, sixteen wig makers and four hatters, among many other trades, such as bookbinders, tailors, bricklayers, jewellers, weavers and saddlers. At night, though, it could be pitch dark because there were no street lanterns, and all that could be heard was the sound of drunken students or the occasional splash of a chamber pot being emptied through a window.

Jena had plenty of taverns which Goethe knew from his various visits. He regularly joined the university's professors and some of the bright students at their weekly 'Professors' Club' at the Zur Rose. Next to the Church of St Michael was Der Burgkeller where the two billiard tables were perpetually enveloped in clouds of yellow tobacco smoke. Das Geleitshaus was known for its lack of light and Der Hecht for its freezing temperatures since the miserly landlord refused to stoke the oven. In Der Fürstenkeller men played boisterous card games, but in many taverns Goethe would also have been able to see groups of students sitting on benches at the wooden tables reading and discussing their lectures.

That summer all the students were talking about Johann Gottlieb Fichte, the new young professor who had arrived in Jena two months earlier, in May 1794. A philosopher, Fichte had declared the self to be the supreme ruler of the world. 'The source of all reality is the Ich,' he told his students, empowering them with the idea of self-determination and a free will. It had been Goethe who had suggested Fichte for a position at the university, and the two met regularly, but today Goethe didn't have time for a visit.

Goethe crossed the open market square. Men and women promenaded here, dressed in their best clothes and nodding at acquaintances. At its centre was a large fountain where maids filled buckets with water. Opposite, at the western side of the square, was the old town hall which dated back to the fourteenth century, its pointed arches and windows set into sturdy stone walls that had weathered into a soft sandy colour. Just beyond, in Rathausgasse, were the rooms where the meeting was being held. There Goethe greeted friends and acquaintances, then sat down to listen to the lecture. It was here that he would run into Jena's most famous inhabitant: Friedrich Schiller.

~

More than a decade previously, in the early 1780s, Friedrich Schiller had risen to prominence with *The Robbers*, a play featuring two aristocratic brothers torn between their opposing quests for power and freedom. Schiller was born in 1759, in the Duchy of Württemberg, and his early life had been overshadowed by the despotic Duke Karl Eugen – a ruler who spent flamboyantly on palaces, parties and the arts. Modelled on the French king's Versailles, the duke's court was lavish, formal and absolute. A hundred thousand gas lamps illuminated large greenhouses in magnificent gardens and the opera seated an audience of one thousand. Large hunting parties, spectacular fireworks, masked balls and other festivities devoured huge sums. The duke was famed for his extravagance, sexual exploits and volatile temper. He sold his subjects as mercenaries, imprisoned political writers and forced promising boys to enrol at the military academy. Schiller had been one such child.

Schiller's father, who was then an officer in the duchy's army, had begged Karl Eugen several times to spare his cerebral son, but to no avail. The duke demanded obedience and the father was overruled. Schiller was desperately unhappy in the harsh school environment where even reading Goethe's *Werther* was punished. At the end of 1780, aged twenty-one, he left the academy and began to work as a doctor in the duke's regiment – a profession he loathed. It was against this constraining backdrop that Schiller began to write *The Robbers*.

In the play, the younger of two brothers, Franz Moor, betrays the older Karl to get his inheritance. As a result of Franz's lies the father disowns the charismatic Karl, his favourite son, who then forms a band of robbers to fight against local tyrants. Everything ends in tragedy: Karl is torn between an oath to his robber friends and his bride Amalia, and his father – now imprisoned by Franz – dies when Karl reveals his identity as a robber. Franz commits suicide and Amalia begs to be killed if she can't be with Karl, who is bound to the robbers. In the end Karl kills her, is consumed by remorse, and offers to turn himself in. *The Robbers* was dramatic and emotional, and showed how a good person could become a criminal as a result of experiencing injustice. It was a play which spoke to the revolutionary mood of the time. The frontispiece of the second edition couldn't have been clearer, depicting a lion with the caption '*In Tirannos*' – 'against tyrants'.

At the play's premiere in Mannheim in 1782 the audience had cried, shouted and stomped, and strangers fell into each other's arms sobbing and fainting. 'The theatre was like a madhouse,' one eyewitness reported. The play's huge success made the twenty-two-year-old Schiller instantly famous. 'My God!' the English poet Samuel Taylor Coleridge exclaimed when he read *The Robbers*, 'who is this Schiller? . . . I tremble like an Aspen Leaf.' Others were less delighted. The Duke of Württemberg became so indignant about the play's revolutionary content that he had Schiller arrested, banning him from writing anything else. Released after a short imprisonment, Schiller fled Württemberg, and led an itinerant life for a few years until accepting a badly paid position at the university in Jena in 1789. There he lectured on history and aesthetics, and although money was tight, he finally had the freedom to write. Goethe, however, had kept his distance.

Both celebrated writers, the two men were very aware of each other. With Goethe in Weimar, only fifteen miles away, it seemed strange that they had never really talked. It was Goethe who had avoided contact, as he later admitted. Over the years there had been a couple of lukewarm encounters but no proper conversation. Goethe could be charming, kind and attentive when he wanted, but he could also be rude and arrogant. If he was bored or uninterested, he could abruptly change the subject. Young poets and admirers were so terrified of the 'cold, monosyllabic god' that they regularly ran out of the room to avoid having to speak to him. Christoph Martin Wieland, another famous poet in Weimar, called Goethe the 'greatest egoist I've ever met'.

Goethe certainly had no warm feelings towards Schiller. He disliked the revolutionary leanings of *The Robbers* and the incendiary effect it had had on students and the ladies at the Weimar court. The play also reminded him too much of his melodramatic and long-past *Sturm und Drang* period. Jealousy may have played a part too, because everybody was talking about the younger playwright, while Goethe himself was struggling with his own creative output.

For his part, Schiller was propelled by a mixture of admiration and dislike towards the older poet. In awe of Goethe's poetic genius, and desperately craving his recognition, Schiller also believed him to be self-obsessed and vain. To receive any kind of acknowledgement from Goethe, Schiller said, felt like seducing a prude. Ten years younger, Schiller was financially and professionally in a very different position to Goethe in 1794. Goethe was more worldly, experienced and wealthy, and his life was a visceral reminder to Schiller of how difficult his own was.

Schiller and his wife Charlotte had to live frugally. Though Charlotte came from an aristocratic family and Schiller was a famous playwright, there was little money. The yearly salary the thirty-four-year-old drew from the university was a meagre 200 thalers – roughly the annual income of a skilled craftsman such as a carpenter or joiner – and his writing wasn't particularly lucrative. Together, his salary, publishing honoraria, fees from his students and a small allowance from his wife's family only amounted to 800 thalers – enough to house and feed the family, but there was nothing extra for an elegant apartment, good furniture or clothes, or for other luxuries.

Goethe, by contrast, had already as a sixteen-year-old student received a one-thousand-thaler stipend from his father. By now Goethe drew a large salary from his many positions at the Weimar court, and he was the highest paid poet in the country. If he only had Goethe's money (or a rich wife), Schiller had told a friend in 1789, he would be able to produce as many plays, tragedies and poems as he wanted and 'the university in Jena could kiss my ass'.

The array of illnesses from which he suffered – fevers, infections, cramps, coughing, headaches and breathing problems – would prove steady companions until his death. Worried about catching a cold or other infection during the winter months, Schiller often stayed indoors for weeks on end. Each year, his mood sank during the miserable German winters, when long cold nights gave way to heavy iron skies during the day. 'Winter', he said, was 'such a gloomy visitor'. Over the past few years, Schiller had not felt optimistic. He was tall and thin – almost gaunt – with long reddish hair and pale blotchy skin. His face was dominated by a large nose and protruding cheekbones. He looked as ill as he felt. Schiller kept erratic hours, often writing at night fuelled by copious amounts of coffee and sleeping during the day. In the middle of the night, neighbours could see a lonely light in his study and Schiller pacing up and down. When the windows were open, they could even hear him reading aloud to himself what he had written.

Since moving to Jena, Schiller had worked on history and philosophy and moved away from plays and poetry. He hadn't written anything lyrical for almost six years. He had just begun to think about a new play, *Wallenstein* – set during the Thirty Years War that had convulsed Europe from 1618 to 1648 – but he was frightened of beginning. His imagination, he feared, had abandoned him. Philosophical enquiries into Immanuel Kant's philosophy had somehow eradicated his poetic sensibilities, and he felt that he was neither a poet nor a philosopher. 'Imagination disturbs my abstract thinking,' Schiller would tell Goethe later, 'and cold reason my poetry.'

That hot July day in 1794, as Goethe and Schiller walked out of the meeting of the Natural History Society, they began to talk about the lecture. Schiller remarked that botany, with all its observations and classifications, seemed a 'fragmentary way of looking at nature'. Goethe agreed, and explained that there was a different, more holistic way that saw nature as a living whole from which one could deduce the specifics. Strolling across the large open market square, they would have struck onlookers as an odd pair, the tall, thin and

perpetually ill-looking Schiller towering eight inches over the rotund
and rosy-cheeked Goethe. Once in a while they stopped, with Goethe
gesticulating and drawing plants in the air. When they found themselves outside Schiller's house at the south-eastern corner of the
market, the playwright invited Goethe in.

Goethe gladly accepted, and once inside took a quill and sketched
a plant with a few strokes to elaborate how he understood botany.
Behind variety was unity, Goethe explained, as each plant was the
variation of a primordial form. He had observed that the leaf of a
plant was this basic form from which all others developed – the petals,
the calyx, roots and so on. 'Forwards and backwards the plant is always
the leaf,' he had written in his diary after a visit to the botanic garden
in Padua during his travels in Italy a few years previously. Goethe's
thinking was wrong, Schiller objected after carefully listening. This
was not an observation from experience, it was 'an idea'.

With this one comment, Schiller summarised the differences in their
thinking and how they fundamentally disagreed on how to make sense
of the world. Goethe described himself as a hard-headed realist, as
someone who gained knowledge through the observation of nature.
Schiller, by contrast, called himself an 'idealist'. Inspired by his intense
study of Kant's philosophy, Schiller believed that our knowledge of
so-called reality was perceived through the existing categories in our
mind – such as time, space and causality. Goethe insisted that he had
come to his conclusion by *looking* at plants – an empirical and scientific
approach – while Schiller said that the 'idea' of a leaf had existed already
in Goethe's mind. Goethe 'gets too much from the world of the senses',
Schiller had told a friend, 'whereas I get things from the soul'.

The discussion was combative but also inspiring, and both agreed
that neither had won the argument. The competition between realism
and idealism, between object and subject, Goethe later said, was the
foundation on which they sealed their connection and he admitted
to not having had so much 'intellectual pleasure' for a long time.
The day marked the beginning of the most fruitful literary friendship of the age.

～

At the time both men were struggling with their writing, but over
the next ten years each inspired the other to produce some of their
best work. They collaborated closely, challenging and editing each

other. That they had such opposing temperaments only seemed to foster their creativity. 'Each of us was able to give the other something he lacked, and get something in return,' Schiller recalled. Meeting Goethe, Schiller told a friend years later, had been 'the most beneficial event of my whole life'.

Schiller had given him 'a second youth', Goethe admitted. Earlier that year, Goethe had promised to 'force himself to fasten on to something', and that something turned out to be Schiller. He had lain fallow for too long. It felt like a new spring, Goethe said, with green shoots appearing everywhere. For the previous two years Goethe had felt miserable and unproductive. In spring 1792 France had declared war on Prussia and Austria, and the brutality of mass executions during Robespierre's Reign of Terror the following year had shocked even those who had welcomed the uprising of 1789. For many, the ideals of the French Revolution – liberty, equality and fraternity – had become drenched in blood. Goethe had become increasingly disillusioned. How was he supposed to concentrate on his work or enjoy life with weekly reports coming in of 'Robespierre's atrocities'?

Unlike many other poets and thinkers, Goethe had not embraced the French Revolution. He preferred evolution to revolution – his political beliefs mirrored his scientific ideas. There were two schools of thought about the creation of Earth at the time: the so-called Vulcanists argued that everything originated through catastrophic events such as volcanic eruptions and earthquakes. In the opposing camp were the Neptunists, who believed that water and sedimentation had been the main force – a slow geological process that gradually built up mountains, minerals and land. Goethe was a Neptunist, and this was also how he envisaged social change. He believed in slow reform, not in volatile uprisings.

Goethe had also experienced war himself. The previous summer, 1793, when Caroline Böhmer had been incarcerated in the fortress of Königstein, Goethe had accompanied Duke Carl August to Mainz, the city Johannes Gutenberg had called his home in the fifteenth century. The duke's army had helped the Prussians fight the French and wrest the city back into German control. As a confidant and a member of Carl August's privy council, this was not Goethe's first military campaign, but he detested this aspect of his duties. As German soldiers had bombarded the French occupiers, Goethe remained in his tent, trying to ignore the gunfire echoing outside, and instead concentrated on work, burying his field desk under papers. He had studied optics, edited a long poem and written letters to Jena to enquire about the progress of the botanical garden. If only he could redirect the money wasted on cannon fire into plants and green-houses, Goethe lamented. At moments like these, he wrote from the battlefield, 'objects of thought' were more important than ever – he needed the distraction of ideas.

The bombardment was relentless, lasting throughout the night, and in the morning, as the sun rose behind Mainz's silhouette of broken church spires and collapsed roofs, Goethe saw the injured and dead scattered on the battlefield. The cathedral was in flames, together with its library of valuable manuscripts and documents, as were many churches, palaces, the theatre, and countless other build-ings. As the city burned, Goethe felt his 'mind had come to a standstill'. Here he was, in one of the most beautiful areas of Germany, seeing nothing but 'destruction and misery'.

When he had returned home, Goethe turned inwards. As armies marched across Europe, he focused instead on his scientific studies. Science, for him, became like a 'plank in a shipwreck'. He oversaw the construction of the botanical garden in Jena, and experimented so intensely with optics that he sometimes forgot his original purpose. As the winter of 1793 had rolled slowly into the spring of 1794, he watched the first blooms unfurl their petals in the botanical garden while involving himself in its every detail, from the gardener's housing to the decision over which plant classification system was going to be used. He oversaw the installation of new irrigation systems and glasshouses, as well as the appointment of the garden's new director and even the manuring of flower beds. Botany distracted him from the chaos of the world, and this was the reason why he had joined the Natural History Society in Jena.

~

A few weeks after meeting in Jena, Goethe invited Schiller to stay at his house in Weimar for a fortnight. Come and visit me, Goethe wrote at the beginning of September, the court would be away at another castle and no one would disturb them. They could talk, continuing their discussion, and Goethe wanted to show Schiller his collections of books, art and natural history objects. Schiller was delighted but cautioned the older poet that he was a difficult guest

– almost an invalid, in fact, suffering from chronic chest pain and stomach cramps, as well as insomnia. In return, Goethe warned that he was himself in the grip of 'a kind of darkness and hesitation' which he couldn't control. They made their plans anyway and Schiller arrived on 14 September 1794.

Goethe lived in the centre of Weimar, in a large house the duke had given him two years previously. A sweeping staircase installed by Goethe led to elegantly furnished rooms at the front of the house. The Italian greeting 'SALVE' – 'be well' – written in large black capital letters on the wooden doorstep welcomed visitors. Everywhere were Italian sculptures on pedestals, and the walls were decorated with the finest drawings, prints and paintings. Mirrors reflected the art, valuable rugs cushioned the steps of heeled shoes, and tall windows overlooked the street and square in front of the house. Guests could sit on armchairs upholstered in green and white striped silk and sip tea at dainty mahogany tables.

Towards the back of the house was a ground-floor suite of plainer rooms that Goethe had newly furnished. Here, overlooking a large garden, was his study. Unlike the front rooms, the furniture was simple and functional. Plain bookshelves and large cabinets with drawers that held Goethe's natural history objects – including his rock collection, which would eventually number eighteen thousand specimens – were placed against the walls. There were lecterns and small tables, and in the middle of the room was a large desk for writing and reading. There was neither a sofa nor an armchair, only plain wooden chairs. Comfortable furniture, Goethe explained, 'makes it impossible for me to think and puts me in a placid, passive state'.

For fourteen days, Schiller and Goethe worked, talked, ate and argued. They often sat in the large garden, warmed by that year's unusually warm September sun. They saw few people, preferring each other's company. They laid bare their ideas, beliefs, methods and theories, but were equally open about their difficulties and stagnating projects. Schiller felt so comfortable that he even slept well and Goethe wrote to a friend that his visitor had injected life into 'my sluggish thoughts'. Goethe presented his natural history findings and listened to Schiller's ideas on how beauty and aesthetic education created a freedom more powerful than any political revolution. They talked about Goethe's studies into optics as well as about possible new plays and tragedies. Goethe also recited his *Roman*

Elegies, a series of erotic poems he had written after a two-year trip he had made to Italy in the late 1780s.

In the poems, the male protagonist describes how he falls in love in Rome.

> *But at the love-god's behest, by night my business is different;*
> *Half of my scholarship's lost, yet I have double the fun.*
> *And is not this education, to study the shape of her lovely*
> *Breasts, and down over her hip slide my adventuring hand?*
> *Marble comes doubly alive for me then, as I ponder, comparing.*

A few lines down Goethe continues:

> *Often I even compose my poetry in her embraces,*
> *Counting hexameter beats, tapping them out on her back*
> *Softly, with one hand's fingers. She sweetly breathes in her slumber,*
> *Warmly the glow of her breath pierces the depths of my heart.*

Roman Elegies illustrates Goethe's philosophical beliefs – an approach where he tried to bring together the senses and the mind, feeling and observation. As such the verses evocatively unite love and sexuality with scholarly studies of antiquity. In the years since his Italian travels, Goethe had kept adding more verses and collected them in a folder entitled 'Erotica'. Occasionally he had read a few to close friends, who had all advised him to keep them unpublished because they were too lascivious. Schiller loved the verses, writing home to his wife Charlotte – 'Lolo', as he called her – that it was 'admittedly risqué, and not especially proper, but among the best things he has done'.

The poems were also Goethe's declaration of love for his mistress Christiane Vulpius. Weimar's high society had been shocked when Goethe had taken the seamstress, who worked in a small manufactory that made artificial flowers, as his lover after his return from Italy. A little more than a year later, in December 1789, she had given birth to their son August. Unlike others who either set up their mistresses and illegitimate children in a separate household or paid them off while marrying someone more suitable, Goethe moved Christiane and their son in with him.

They lived happily together, while remaining unmarried. As scandalous as the situation seemed, Duke Carl August remained open-minded and even agreed to be August's godfather. The vicious gossip, though, never stopped. People wondered why the celebrated Goethe had fallen so low. Many would have agreed with the Weimar poet Christoph Martin Wieland, who described Christiane as 'a pig with a pearl necklace'.

During Schiller's visit, Christiane and four-year-old August remained mostly invisible at the back of the large house. Like others, Schiller couldn't understand Christiane's allure and had gossiped about the relationship, but for now he accepted Goethe's domestic arrangements. Goethe's crime was not so much the affair itself as living with a woman so clearly below his social standing. Had Christiane been a member of Weimar's high society, no one would have cared. Schiller himself was no stranger to romantic complexity. Now happily settled in a conventional marriage with his wife Charlotte, he had preceded it with a rather indelicate and simultaneous courtship of both her and her sister.

For more than a year Schiller had dithered over which of the two sisters he really loved – the quiet, guarded and almost coy Charlotte, or Caroline, her older sister, who was literary, lively and unhappily married. His letters were so flirtatious and ambiguous that Caroline finally begged him to make up his mind and end this rather strange *ménage à trois*. But even after his engagement to Charlotte, Schiller continued to write letters filled with longing for both sisters. Nonetheless, all this had been more acceptable than Goethe's open relationship with the uneducated Christiane because Charlotte Schiller – then Charlotte von Lengefeld – and her sister came from an aristocratic family closely connected to the Weimar court.

Goethe didn't care what people said, nor that his works meant nothing to Christiane. She loved the theatre, dancing and nice clothes and 'managed the household efficiently', he said, running his domestic life so smoothly that nothing distracted him. She grounded him, provided him with the food he liked, with love and sex – and most importantly, she let him work whenever he wanted. She was cheerful and practical. 'What you do is easy,' she told him one early summer when she had just inspected the vegetable patch, because 'once you do something, it lasts forever'; it was different for her, because the snails had just devoured everything she had sown and planted.

Goethe's mother was one of the few who saw how the down-to-earth Christiane made her son happy, and called her 'your dear bedfellow'. Frau Goethe was glad that her son was not trapped in a terrible marriage. That there was love can be seen in the way Goethe sketched Christiane tenderly as she slept, drawing her brown

hair as it framed her round and plump face in thick waves. She
wasn't beautiful as such but she was sensual and curvaceous. Christiane
was his 'dear little one', 'dear angel' and 'dear child', and he was her
'darling sweetheart'.

~

Despite his love for Christiane, Goethe began to spend more and
more time in Jena. There, removed from the formality of his duties
at the Weimar court and the stream of visitors, he felt rejuvenated.
Instead of having to dine with the duke, Goethe shared his meals
with Schiller and his other friends. In Jena, he became carefree and
so invigorated that he soon moved into one of the most productive
phases of his life. He worked on plays, poetry and scientific writings,
as well as picking up his half-finished novel *Wilhelm Meister's
Apprenticeship*, which he had abandoned many years previously. 'The
wood gathered and put in the fireplace so long ago is beginning to
burn at last,' Goethe told Schiller, who read, commented and edited
every page. Published in eight parts, the novel describes the eponymous protagonist's journey to self-fulfilment as he escapes his destined
path as a businessman to follow his dreams of being an actor. It was
the first coming-of-age novel, or *Bildungsroman*, ever published.

Goethe's rooms at the Old Castle were just a short walk from
Schiller's apartment on Jena's market square. He was productive here,
he wrote to Christiane, 'because the quiet castle is very good for
thinking and working'. He spent the early hours of the morning in
his bed, propped up on pillows and wrapped in blankets to keep out
the cold, dictating to his assistant. The only distraction was the constant
annoying yap of a neighbourhood dog. At around four in the afternoon,
Goethe walked the few blocks to Schiller's apartment. If his friend was
still working in his study, Goethe waited patiently in the sitting room
and read or sketched. Sometimes Schiller's wild young son Karl came
running in and Goethe, who adored children, played with him.

When Schiller emerged from his study – his long hair uncombed,
wearing old yellow slippers and sometimes still in his dressing gown
because of his erratic sleeping patterns – they often talked deep into
the night. The table in Schiller's parlour was laden with books, notes
and manuscripts, but also with tea and wine. They read to each other,
discussed and scribbled down notes; only once in a while Schiller
would leave the room to get some medicine for his cramps and head-

aches. He couldn't sit still, instead pacing the room. Friends remarked how tense Schiller often was and 'how the mind tyrannised the body'.

The Schiller household soon became Goethe's second home and though he missed Christiane and son August, he left Jena only with great reluctance. When the two friends didn't see each other, they wrote letters which shuttled between Jena and Weimar several times a week. With the postal service so unreliable, they often used a maid to deliver them. They critiqued and edited each other's work, sending suggestions for improvements and changes, ranging from sweeping comments to editorial advice as detailed as 'I would add another verse after verse 14.'

They challenged each other, gossiped about friends and foes, and discussed the literary world but also the weather and other local news. Some letters were just short notes containing brief pieces of information about forthcoming visits and practical matters; others were long treatises on poetry, philosophy, commentaries on books and detailed descriptions of literary progress (or the lack of it); and some contained orders for wallpaper or fresh fish. All were imbued with deep affection. In one, Goethe wrote of his 'vivid longing' to see Schiller and hoped for good weather during the cold months to ensure a 'quick ride to see you'.

The two men were different in many respects. Goethe loved being outside in nature, whether vigorously walking in summer or skating in winter. He rarely took a carriage to Jena but instead rode on horseback. He once rode the sixty miles from Weimar to Leipzig in just over eight hours. Schiller, though, rarely ventured out, and so it was usually Goethe who travelled.

Where Goethe was easy-going, intuitive and relaxed, Schiller seemed forever to overthink things. He tried to force his creative output by working to a gruelling schedule. His illnesses danced like an evil shadow around him, a constant reminder that his time on earth was limited. With so much to do, he pushed his frail body relentlessly, never allowing himself to rest. He put so much pressure on himself that he sometimes felt paralysed with worry that he would never be able to finish something. When he wrote the last sentence of a drama or a manuscript, he felt lost, he said, 'as if I'm hanging aimless in a vacuum'. Overwhelmed by the fear that he would never produce anything again, he always needed to start a new project immediately.

But Schiller was also generous with his time, meticulously reading and commenting on Goethe's work, along with that of other writers. He encouraged young poets and his students, was an inspiring teacher, and assisted several female writers to publish their work. He was sensitive, deeply intellectual and earnest. And he looked with friendly envy at Goethe's output. Whereas everybody had to work hard to produce something tolerable, Schiller wrote, Goethe 'has only to shake the tree gently and the most beautiful fruits, ripe and heavy, fall into his hands'. No one since Shakespeare, he said, had been as gifted as Goethe.

They inspired each other, spinning the amiable conversation they had started after meeting at the botanical lecture across the years. Goethe's approach was to start with the particular and then move to the general – he would look, for example, at the specific shape of a plant leaf or animal bone and from that deduce a larger anatomical or morphological theory. Schiller, by contrast, began with the general, or with a proposed theory – the idea of the importance of art, for example – and then broke it down to a particular aspect such as how art could be utilised as inspiration.

Where Goethe's starting point was often observation or experimentation, Schiller pushed him closer to philosophical ideas. Goethe, though, checked Schiller's over-reliance on abstraction. 'Your close observation', Schiller admitted, 'never risks leading you astray.' Goethe's approach rooted Schiller, while Schiller lifted Goethe into the realm of idealistic thought. The more sensual Goethe pulled the more cerebral Schiller into the physical world, but in return gained deeper insights into theoretical concepts. And so it continued, with Goethe encouraging Schiller to write poetry and plays again, and Schiller drawing Goethe into the world of philosophy. Being with Goethe, Schiller said, was food for heart and mind.

Over the next decade Goethe would spend more time in Jena than ever before, often staying for several weeks, to see and work with Schiller – writing, plotting and talking about 'art, nature and the mind', Goethe wrote in his diary. This was, he declared, the start of a 'new era' – a period in which he would rediscover his literary voice and become once again the hero to a new generation. As the young impetuous men and women turned to him in admiration, he tried to calm their tempers and passions while becoming energised by their ideas and work. They put him on a pedestal and yearned for his approval. Goethe became their 'demi-god'.

2

'I am a priest of truth'
Summer 1794: Fichte's Ich-philosophy

THE ROOM WAS packed. Students spilled out into the corridors and stood on ladders at the windows to listen to their new professor. Even the largest auditorium in Jena was too small to hold the crowd. The young men at the back climbed on benches and tables to catch a glimpse. Everybody jostled for a seat. The air was hot and stale.

Thirty-two-year-old Johann Gottlieb Fichte stood at the lectern in riding boots with spurs and his whip. More bull than racehorse, he was of average height but muscular, with a forceful presence that could be felt throughout the room. Long hair fell to broad shoulders and dark eyes darted over a large nose. He wore a purple coat with large buttons and spoke so loudly that he was perfectly audible even from the seats at the back.

Fichte was the 'Bonaparte of Philosophy', as one student described him. Everybody wanted to hear how he redefined the relationship between the self and the external world – between the 'Ich' and the 'non-Ich', as Fichte had termed it. There was something urgent and defiant about him. Philosophy was not just the domain of philosophy students, he insisted, but important for society at large. 'I am a priest of truth,' Fichte insisted. He wanted nothing less than to incite a revolution of the mind, and to seize the torch from Immanuel Kant, the most famous living philosopher of the Western world.

~

Born in 1762, the oldest of ten children, Fichte came from humble roots. He never talked much about his childhood, but his mother had been prone to dark moods and his father had earned a meagre living as a ribbon weaver in Saxony. This upbringing hadn't destined Fichte for greatness. One day, though, a visiting baron overheard the young Johann Gottlieb reciting an entire sermon he had listened to while tending the cattle behind the church. That moment changed Fichte's life. Deeply impressed by the boy's astonishing abilities, the baron had paid for his education. Fichte was so bright that he boarded at one of the best schools in Saxony and then studied in Jena and Leipzig. He was intelligent, studious and well read, but he had no money of his own. And when the baron's financial support ended, Fichte had to work as a private tutor for wealthy families, teaching their young sons.

These posts tended to be short-lived because Fichte never managed to hide his dislike of his employers and his wards. Sometimes he insulted them, sometimes he got drunk, and sometimes concerned parents accused Fichte of letting their children become disobedient under his supervision. Perpetually broke, he regularly pawned his belongings but remained determined to learn as much as possible. He studied for long hours and enjoyed intellectual challenges. In a perfect world, he said, he would just read and write all day, and then go for a strenuous walk to clear his head, or for a boozy evening in the tavern. His life as a tutor left no room for this.

He was determined to excel and to take control of his own destiny. He dropped his heavy Saxon accent, believing no one would take him seriously if he sounded like a farmer, and he married above his social station. He had met his wife Johanne in Zurich in 1789, while working as a tutor. No beauty, as she herself said, she was the daughter of a respected civil servant and her late mother was the sister of a well-known German poet.* That Johanne was educated and her family prosperous made her an attractive match for the ambitious Fichte.

It was during their courtship that Fichte devoured the work of Immanuel Kant. 'Ever since I read the *Critique of Practical Reason*,' Fichte told a friend in 1790, 'I've been living in a new world.' This was one of the books that had made Kant famous. Published between 1781 and 1790, the *Critique of Pure Reason*, the *Critique of Practical Reason* and the *Critique of Judgement* respectively tackled the possibilities and limits of human knowledge, the moral and ethical implications of this, and our ability to judge the good and the beautiful.

~

* This was Friedrich Gottlieb Klopstock.

In the early 1780s Kant had declared a philosophical revolution as radical as Copernicus's scientific revolution more than two centuries earlier. Kant's aim was nothing less than to bridge the chasm between rationalism and empiricism, which had been the prevailing philosophical systems in the eighteenth century. Where rationalists explained that all knowledge derived from thinking and the mind, empiricists insisted that one could 'know' the world only through experience. Rationalists believed in pre-existing and absolute truths, but empiricists argued that everything in the mind came from the senses. Some empiricists said that at birth the human mind was like a blank piece of paper which over a lifetime filled up with knowledge that came from sensory experience alone. Kant took up a position *between* rationalism and empiricism.

Just as Copernicus had concluded that the sun didn't move around the Earth, Kant said, we had to redefine our understanding of how we made sense of nature. To do so, he investigated the relationship between our internal subjective world and the external world. In essence, Kant tried to answer a question: Is the tree that I'm seeing in my garden the *tree-as-it-appears-to-us* or the *tree-in-itself*? The *tree-in-itself* is Kant's famous *Ding an sich* or *thing-in-itself* – by which he meant the external world independent of human perception. According to Kant, the thing-in-itself can never be truly known because we'll always see it through the prism of our thinking. Broadly speaking, our senses, but also our mind, shape the way we see the world. They are like tinted glasses – hence, the thing-as-it-appears-to-us.

The laws of nature as we understand them, Kant wrote, only exist because our mind conceives them. Though we might think that we understand the workings of the external world through pure reason – gravity, say, or the laws of motion or classification – Kant explained that this order wasn't inherent in nature. Rather, *we* impose it on the external world, not the other way around. Time, space and causality are therefore not absolute truths but categories in our minds through which we comprehend the external world – they are the lens through which we see nature. And with this insight the 'self' became something like a lawgiver of nature, even if this meant that we could never gain 'true' knowledge of the thing-in-itself. The result was a shift towards the importance of the self – it became creative and free.

Instead of just being a cog in a mechanistic universe, Kant gave the self agency. This new thinking was so radical that reading Kant was described by some as an 'intellectual rebirth'. As Fichte studied Kant's books with a pen in hand, underlining and scribbling, he couldn't stop thinking. In a way, his own life was the proof of Kant's philosophy. Already as a young boy, tending the cattle behind the church, he had used his mind – his will – to abandon a seemingly predestined path. For Fichte, these ideas triggered a revolution in the way he understood the world. Confident and self-assured, he wanted nothing less than to teach the world how to think.

~

In the summer of 1791, Fichte decided to make a pilgrimage to meet Kant in Königsberg, the philosopher's home town on the south-eastern coast of the Baltic Sea.* Before he left, though, he broke off his engagement with Johanne. Having courted her for more than a year with tender letters and declarations of eternal love, Fichte suddenly disappeared without explanation and without leaving a forwarding address. Johanne had no idea what had happened. Marriage, Fichte told his brother, would 'clip his wings'. His Kant studies had given him a sense of purpose and he was not going to lose his new-found momentum by chaining himself to a woman.

But how to meet Kant? Would such a famous philosopher receive a penniless young tutor? Fichte decided to prove his admiration by writing a treatise on religion, the question Kant had left unanswered in his three *Critiques*. Fichte locked himself in a rented room in Königsberg and began working. He emerged five weeks later with a finished manuscript that he immediately dispatched to Kant. Five days later an impatient Fichte went to the quiet side street near the castle where Kant lived. He knocked on the door and was invited in. Kant, who was famed for his rigid daily routine, usually welcomed his guests in a room upstairs, next to his study.

The physical appearance of the sixty-seven-year-old philosopher belied the power of his intellect. 'His weak body is too tired to house such a great mind,' Fichte told a friend. Next to the big-boned Fichte, Kant must have looked even thinner and more painfully stooped than he already was. There was nothing spectacular or magnificent about the appearance of the most celebrated philosopher

* Königsberg is today's Kaliningrad in Russia, but was then part of Prussia.

of the Western world. He dressed plainly and his powdered hair was tied with a ribbon into a pigtail. His feeble voice was almost inaudible, and what he said didn't make much sense. Kant, Fichte thought, 'is beginning to lose his memory'. The philosopher seemed sleepy and had only skimmed through a few pages of the manuscript but to Fichte's surprise he liked it. Suddenly Fichte didn't care that meeting his hero had at first seemed disappointing. His doubts about the quality of his treatise evaporated when Kant advised him to publish – even suggesting his own publisher. 'Can it be true?' Fichte later wrote in his diary, 'but that's what Kant said.'

Encouraged, Fichte dispatched his manuscript and when it landed on the publisher's desk, his name was missing and its title – *Attempt at a Critique of All Revelation* – was uncannily similar to Kant's own three books. Both the omission and the similarity were deliberate. Just a few weeks later, though, Fichte was having second thoughts about this decision. He needn't have worried. The publisher saw the opportunity for financial gain and printed two cover pages, one with Fichte's name for local circulation in Königsberg, and another without it for the rest of Germany. Even the preface, dated 'Königsberg, December 1791', was deceptive – although Fichte had indeed written the book there, the city was of course deeply associated with Kant. It was a risky plan.

On 30 June 1792, three months after the publication of *Attempt at a Critique of All Revelation*, Jena's *Allgemeine Literatur-Zeitung*, Germany's most important literary journal, published an announcement that changed Fichte's life. Immanuel Kant, the journal reported, had finally written his fourth *Critique*. To the intellectual community this was seismic news. Anyone who had ever studied Kant, the *Allgemeine Literatur-Zeitung* wrote, would realise that this anonymously published book was the philosopher's long-awaited work on religion.

As excitement spread and copies of the *Attempt at a Critique of All Revelation* arrived at their destinations, one review after another reported on Kant's new work. In Jena, where many of Kant's disciples taught, people could talk of nothing else. In the smoke-filled taverns, in the university's corridors, at the weekly gatherings of the Professors' Club and during the editorial meetings of the *Allgemeine Literatur-Zeitung*, everybody discussed the great new work. In Jena alone, at least eight Kant experts agreed that only the sage of Königsberg could have been its author. It was by him, 'the great

Master', one philosophy professor declared, claiming to be so excited that for days he could hardly think. 'Read it and you will be a believer, and find salvation,' he told his colleagues. Fichte kept quiet.

Then, exactly one month later, the *Allgemeine Literatur-Zeitung* printed another startling item: Kant's correction. He was not the author of *Attempt at a Critique of All Revelation*, Kant declared. Instead, it was the work of a certain Herr Fichte who had visited him in Königsberg the year before. 'I have not contributed in any way in conversation or writing to this skilful man's book,' Kant wrote, but he was nonetheless delighted to clarify the true authorship of this important book. 'Honour upon the man to whom it is due,' Kant said, and with that Europe's most famous philosopher had anointed an unknown writer. There was no better endorsement. Those who had believed that Kant had written it were shocked yet also thrilled by the dawn of this 'third sun in the firmament of philosophy'.*

Kant's announcement made Fichte instantly famous, marking the beginning of his meteoric rise as one of Germany's most eminent philosophers. It also procured him the professorship in Jena. To hire Kant himself would have been too expensive, Goethe had told Christian Gottlob Voigt, his fellow minister in Weimar's ducal administration, but they should make Fichte an offer before it was too late. 'It's the same with Kantian theory as with fashionable factory products,' Goethe quipped, 'the first person to buy them pays the highest price, but soon everyone copies them and they're less expensive.' By the end of 1793, eighteen months after that first review of *Attempt at a Critique of All Revelation* in the *Allgemeine Literatur-Zeitung*, the Weimar government had formally offered Fichte a position. He accepted happily and then walked the almost four hundred miles from his home in Zurich to Jena, arriving in an excellent mood in May 1794. His tedious life as a tutor was finally over.

~

'My will alone . . . shall float audaciously and boldly over the wreckage of the universe,' Fichte roared from his lectern. His students were electrified. Here was a professor who made them feel alive.

---

* The 'first' sun was Immanuel Kant and the 'second' sun was Karl Leonhard Reinhold, Fichte's predecessor in Jena and a philosopher who had popularised Kant's philosophy in the late eighteenth century.

Fichte imbued philosophy with a revolutionary power and the individual with freedom. 'Act! Act! That's what we're here for,' he said at the end of his first lecture series, and when he left the auditorium onlookers described how his students accompanied him 'like a triumphant Roman emperor'.

There was nothing gentle about Fichte. He thundered, insulted and shouted, paying no attention to subtleties or refinement. He stomped rather than walked, every step an affirmation of his very existence. He ate his snuff tobacco rather than inhaling it. At parties, he would suddenly jump up in the middle of a conversation and leave with the words, 'I haven't written my Louis d'or for the day – I need to write a page or two. Good night!'* In his simple and often dirty clothes – 'filthy and disgusting', in the words of one acquaintance – he might have looked graceless next to the other professors, who dressed in colourful silk waistcoats and spotless white shirts, but the students didn't care. They were in awe of their combative professor who had climbed down from the lofty ivory tower of philosophy and seemed to be 'rooted firmly in the ground'.

By the time he walked into Jena, Fichte no longer believed in Kant's thing-in-itself. He criticised Kant's belief that the external world existed independently of the mind. The only certainty, Fichte told his students, was that the world was experienced by the self – by the 'Ich'. The Ich, he said, 'originally and unconditionally posits its own being' and through this powerful initial act the 'non-Ich' – the external world that included nature, animals, other people and so on – came into existence.

According to Fichte, this 'non-Ich' was everything 'which is different from and opposed to the Ich'. That didn't mean that the Ich creates the world, rather that it creates our *knowledge* of the world. Put simply, the world is the way we *think* it is and therefore it is knowable, unlike Kant's thing-in-itself. Fichte's starting point for everything was the Ich, not Kant's twofold view of the thing-in-itself and the thing-as-it-appears-to-us. The new focus was the self, and on the self being aware of itself – or what we now call 'self-consciousness'. And with this Fichte fundamentally recentred the way we understand the world.

---

* A Louis d'or was a French gold currency used by some publishers as payment for their authors.

As Fichte stood at the podium in Jena, he imbued the self with the new power of self-determination. The Ich posits itself and it is therefore free. It is the agent of everything. Anything that might constrain or limit its freedom – anything in the non-Ich – is in fact brought into existence by the Ich. Freedom was a spark, Fichte said, that may need to glow secretly in the dark for a long time but would soon become a raging fire burning in our souls.

His students were enthralled because Fichte's philosophy promised freedom at a time when the rulers of the German states presided over the smallest details of their subjects' lives. Only a few years previously Friedrich Schiller had been imprisoned and prohibited from writing. And the young philosopher Friedrich Schelling had to ask permission to accept a position outside his home state, the Duchy of Württemberg, filling his letter with obsequious expressions such as 'Your Serene Royal Highness' and 'pleading subserviently for most merciful dismissal'. Local rulers were the law, police and judge all rolled into one. Some might demand a cow as a death duty from a farmer while others would arbitrarily raise taxes.

Even in the more liberal Duchy of Saxe-Weimar, the duke and his administration decided who could marry, or whether someone could perform a play in the privacy of their own home (this was sometimes not permitted in Jena on the grounds that a play was not compatible with academic life). At a time when Germany's rulers expected and demanded the complete subordination of their subjects, Fichte's new ideas of an Ich as the first principle of everything were as revolutionary as any of the political changes witnessed in France.

The French Revolution had changed everything. The social order that had been the foundation of Western societies for centuries had been turned upside down by the will of the people. The French revolutionaries had declared the end of feudalism and of aristocratic privilege. They had curtailed the power of the Church, and abolished the divine right of kings. They had renamed the famous Notre-Dame cathedral 'The Temple of Reason' and the newly introduced Revolutionary Calendar began to count time and world history forward from the birth of the French Republic.

With the *Declaration of the Rights of Man and of the Citizen* in 1789, the French had enshrined the ideals of the Enlightenment into the nation's identity. 'Men are born and remain free and equal in rights,' the *Declaration*'s first article stated. Individuals had a right to liberty, property and freedom of speech, and laws had to protect them. Elected representatives should form the government the people had demanded, and the law was the expression of the 'general will' – the will of the people as a whole – a concept that was based on the writings of French philosopher Jean-Jacques Rousseau. Watching these events unfold from a distance, Fichte had written two pamphlets in response to and in support of the Revolution.* For him, it was the 'breaking dawn' of a new age.

While the Declaration announced a vision rather than a reality, it held the possibility of a better future. What had happened in France was a revolution of ideas and was vivid proof of the power of philosophy. Everybody was watching how a new state was emerging from the *idea* of a state. Fichte's Ich-philosophy built upon the spark of the French Revolution. 'My system is, from beginning to end, an analysis of the concept of freedom,' Fichte declared.

~

'Gentlemen, go into yourselves,' Fichte shouted at his students, 'we're not here to talk of anything external, but simply about the internal self.' He would then watch the young men shuffling about in their seats, some gazing intently at the floor and others closing their eyes in concentration as they pursued their Ichs. 'Gentlemen, think about the wall,' Fichte bellowed, stopping for a theatrical pause, before ordering, 'and now think of yourself as being different from the wall.' This division between the wall and the self was the first lesson in distinguishing the non-Ich from the Ich.

Older professors pitied the students who had to stare at a blank wall to see the non-Ich, ridiculing their younger colleague's eccentric attempts to explain his concept of the self. And although they attacked Fichte's 'hubris' and 'pomposity', nothing could stop him from catapulting the Ich onto the philosophical stage.

There were no absolute truths or laws created by God that shaped our understanding of the world. There was only the self. Freedom and self-determination became the underpinnings of Fichte's philosophy. Like Kant, Fichte didn't talk about a chaotic world, but of

---

* These were *Reclamation of the Freedom of Thought from the Princes of Europe* and *Contribution to the Rectification of the Public's Judgement of the French Revolution*, both published anonymously in 1793.

an ordered one where freedom and morality – or one's moral duty
– were closely connected. Whereas British empiricists had insisted
that people were driven by sensations, and by desires such as hunger,
fear or greed rather than by self-assigned moral principles, Kant had
placed rational will at the centre of his argument. Unlike animals,
humans had the ability to decide upon their actions and could set
themselves duties. We are free insofar as we can also act differently. Individuals have a choice in how they act and behave.

Choice, however, doesn't mean that we can do whatever we want.
Or rather, we *can* do whatever we want but if we do, we should
expect others to do the same. If everyone did whatever they felt
like, then that would lead to chaos. Better therefore to act in a way
we would wish others to act. Kant had distilled this idea in his
famous 'Categorical Imperative', arguing that one should act only
in such a way that one's actions can become a universal law. Unless
you want litter-dropping to become a law, for example, you shouldn't
drop it yourself. Freedom is the triumph over our base instincts and
urges. Fichte agreed, though he went further. Where Kant saw these
decisions as a responsibility, Fichte regarded them as a choice. In
other words, Kant's Ich had the burden of compliance whereas
Fichte's Ich acted from the position of free will.

Without freedom, Fichte said, morality was not possible. He argued
that only those who tried to make others free were free themselves.
The ultimate purpose of each individual was 'the moral ennobling
of mankind', and it was the task of the philosopher and scholar to
be the teacher of the human race – and to be that, he had to be
'*morally the best* person of his era'.

This concept of 'freedom' excited some and scared others. As a
new enthusiasm for democratic ideas began to spread in Jena, fathers
feared that their sons were falling under Fichte's spell. Just weeks
after Fichte's inaugural lecture, students were talking about equality
and liberty. 'Only when he abandons himself to Fichte's Ich-philosophy,'
Weimar poet Christoph Martin Wieland said of his own son's studies
in Jena, 'does he make me despair.'

Fichte's influence was growing week by week. 'Anyone who can't
learn to think for themselves under Fichte', one admirer said, 'will
never learn it.' More than half of Jena's eight hundred students came
to his lectures and many declared him their idol. Most were from
the German territories, but there were also some from France,

England, Poland, Russia and elsewhere in Europe. The most diligent were from Hungary – dressed in wide black coats and round black hats, they always sat in the first row, scribbling down Fichte's every word.

'My celebrity', Fichte noted, was 'really much greater than I imagined.' After all, it had been the great Goethe who had been instrumental in procuring his position, and even Schiller attended his lectures. Listening to Fichte's arguments, Schiller was certain that 'great things could be expected from him'. Soon thinkers across Germany were declaring the rise of a new philosopher-king in Jena.

Never a great fan of labyrinthine philosophical theories, Goethe said that Fichte's ideas reconciled him with philosophers. Though at times a little too eccentric – 'a strange fellow', Goethe said – the poet enjoyed Fichte's company. Fichte was passionate yet also unconventional and genuinely unconcerned about social etiquette. When Goethe invited him to his house in Weimar for the first time, Fichte had been so excited that he had simply marched in and dropped his hat and walking stick on a table rather than wait for the servant to take them – all the while talking without pause.

Goethe was captivated by Fichte's ideas of free will and the elevation of the creative self, not least because they seemed to connect with his interest in optics and colour theory. Optics, Goethe believed, involved more than just physics or mathematical equations because the act of seeing, the perception of the eye, was different for every individual and must therefore be subjective. With this Goethe turned against the prevailing theories that had been established by the British scientist Isaac Newton. In the late seventeenth century Newton had refracted white light through a glass prism in order to split it into colours. He had then argued that colours were contained within light, but Goethe believed that colour was in fact created by light interacting with darkness. When white was darkened, Goethe would later write, it became more yellow, and when black was made lighter, it appeared blue.

According to Goethe, the role of the eye was central because it brought the outer world into the inner. In order to understand colour, one needed to know as much about the eye itself as one did about light. What had been an investigation of the physics of light under Isaac Newton now became a study of vision in Goethe's laboratory. Goethe was not so much interested in the physicality of light as in how colours appeared to us – an approach that made Fichte's ideas on subjectivity relevant for his work. At times, though, Goethe found it difficult to follow Fichte, and admitted struggling to understand what the philosopher meant exactly. Fichte's writing style was somewhat dry but his delivery was clear and coherent. Listen to Fichte, Goethe advised, rather than read his books.

~

Perhaps unsurprisingly, Fichte's fierce determination excited amusement, and even his friends joked about his ideas. Goethe, for example, began addressing his correspondents as 'Dear *non-Ich*'. Others were more critical, worrying about what they called the 'lawless capriciousness of the current zeitgeist'. This new addiction to the Ich, they said, would destroy the world. One critic warned that Fichte's philosophy would inevitably lead to egotistical self-absorption while another accused: 'This preacher of freedom wants to rule as a despot.'

The philosopher Johann Gottfried Herder, who was head of the clergy in the Duchy of Saxe-Weimar, disliked everything about Fichte's (and Kant's) philosophy.* Vicious in his attacks, Herder accused Fichte of 'disgustingly playing with himself – a masturbation of pure-impure reason' – a pun on Kant's *Critique of Pure Reason*.

Much of the criticism was unfair because Fichte was neither advocating ruthless selfishness nor painting a world that was ruled by egoism. Some of it stemmed from his precarious balancing act between the boldly empowered self, the pitfalls of narcissism and the radical demands for an equal society; but Fichte's personality was partly to blame too. His judgement was poor and his temper easily ignited. Anyone who disagreed with him was attacked as if they were his worst personal enemy. Once he had worked himself up, little could stop him. It was, one of the students joked, as if Fichte had declared war on the non-Ich.

Instead of toning down his political convictions – for example, when Duke Carl August feared that he might be a 'wicked Jacobin' –

---

* Kant had reviewed and criticised Herder's book *Ideas upon Philosophy and the History of Mankind* in the *Allgemeine Literatur-Zeitung* in 1785. Goethe and Herder had been close friends but their relationship deteriorated when the poet became interested in Kant's and Fichte's philosophy. 'His aversion to Kantian philosophy,' Goethe said about Herder, 'and thus to the University of Jena, grew stronger and stronger.'

Fichte ratcheted up his sympathy for the radical French revolutionaries. 'It is the purpose of all governments to make government unnecessary,' he told his students at a time when rulers across Germany feared contagion from the French Revolution. Unlike Kant, who had advocated slow reform as opposed to violent upheaval, Fichte declared: 'My system is the first system of freedom: just as the French nation is tearing man free from his external chains, so my system tears him free from the chains of things-in-themselves, the chains of external influences.'

When rumours reached Duke Carl August that Fichte was telling his students that kings and princes would not exist in ten or twenty years, he became worried. Now in his late thirties, Carl August had distanced himself from his youthful exploits and had grown into his role as the ruler of the small Duchy of Saxe-Weimar. Educated in the spirit of the Enlightenment and a great admirer of his great-uncle, the Prussian king Friedrich the Great, Carl August regarded himself as an enlightened ruler.

Unlike the French Sun King, Louis XIV, who had become associated with the motto 'L'état c'est moi' – 'I am the state' – Friedrich the Great had declared that he only *represented* the state. The king was 'the first servant of his state', he had written in 1781. Instead of arbitrary despotism and divine right, in Prussia a tightly organised administration of civil servants had governed and managed a nation that had prided itself on its religious freedom and Enlightenment ideals.

Closely linked to Prussia by family ties, Carl August followed a similar line, with the result that the Duchy of Saxe-Weimar had changed dramatically since his grandfather had ruled. Back in 1736, Duke Ernst August I had issued a decree that 'he wanted no thinkers as his subjects', and he threatened anybody who dared to criticise him with six months in prison. His grandson Carl August, by contrast, encouraged a degree of frankness and rational thought which made Jena's university popular with liberal-minded professors and students. But Fichte's seditious declarations were too much even for Carl August.

Having trusted Goethe's recommendation, the duke became concerned almost as soon as Fichte arrived. It didn't help that Fichte defended the right of a people to have a revolution even if it involved violence. In one of the pamphlets that he had written in support of the French Revolution, he had demanded an end to the imprisonment of the mind. He also accused Europe's rulers of stealing bread out of hungry children's mouths and of sending soldiers into battle without giving them the right to speak their minds. 'Prince,' he wrote in his pamphlet, 'you have no right to suppress our freedom of thought.' All this alarmed Carl August so much that he sent Goethe to Jena to investigate. Goethe reported back that Fichte was 'one of the most competent personalities' one could hope to find. There was nothing to worry about, he reassured the duke.

~

Fichte had arrived alone in Jena, having thought it wise to leave his wife Johanne at home in Zurich until he knew whether the new position would work out. Their relationship had see-sawed. After suddenly ending their engagement and disappearing to Königsberg in 1791, Fichte had changed his mind two years later, conveniently just as Johanne's family had recovered from bankruptcy. He had written a sheepish letter, trying to woo her back, and spoke of a glorious future and of his important projects. It worked. Seven years older than Fichte – she was almost forty and 'abandoned by all the Graces', as one student described – Johanne said yes. She had no other suitors.

Johanne was short, her chin was long and all her upper teeth had been removed because of excruciating pain. Her face and body were covered in wrinkles, the result of having been quite overweight and then becoming very thin, she explained, but she was intelligent, well read and able to deal with Fichte's volatile temper. She could be judgemental and was parsimonious in the extreme, but she was also patient. Where he was prone to explosive outbursts, Johanne was quiet and level-headed. Even Fichte admitted that he needed her to calm him down. And with a husband who enjoyed his champagne and whose money 'took up only fleeting residence in his wallet', it was Johanne who ensured that they could pay their bills. As long as she controlled the household's purse, Fichte could concentrate on his philosophical revolution.

As Fichte continued to draw huge numbers of students, all of whom had to pay per lecture as was common at the time, his income increased and he decided that Johanne should join him in Jena. He had found a house in a quiet area of town, he told her, 'where nothing will disturb us'. Located in the south-eastern corner, next to an old tower that was part of the medieval wall, the house was at the opposite end of town from the university. It had seven bedrooms, two kitchens, a couple of parlours and other rooms, Fichte wrote to Zurich, and most importantly an auditorium for his private lectures. There was even a little garden, and from the property's upper floors they would be able to enjoy beautiful views of the Saale River to the south and the hills to the east. It was time for Johanne to come, Fichte insisted, so that they could set up their household.

Johanne, though, found it difficult to settle in their new home. Having lived all her life in Zurich, she was unhappy in Jena, and within days of her arrival, people began to talk about her and her eccentric dress sense. Fully aware of his wife's unorthodox taste and trying to avoid too much embarrassment, Fichte had told Johanne about fashions in Jena before her arrival. Most women here didn't wear elaborate clothes, he had explained, just simple white dresses. He also urged her to change her hair style – which she refused. She wasn't a shy twenty-year-old who followed her husband's every command. She walked through the streets in flowing white robes with straw flowers draped around her body. And when she pinned small wicker baskets filled with yet more blooms to her hair, people called her the 'Goddess of Abundance'.

Soon Fichte became so desperate that he thrust his purse into the hand of a colleague's wife, begging her to buy Johanne a more suitable wardrobe – only to be rebuffed. Johanne was not a bad person, the woman explained, she was honest and good but she had no taste whatsoever. It would be pointless to order her new clothes because Johanne just threw everything randomly together. Johanne's dress sense was so terrible that people pointed their fingers at her and she was often ignored at parties and other gatherings. Fichte would have to learn to live with the gossip.

In any event, Fichte was occupied with his students and working on his philosophical system, his so-called *Wissenschaftslehre** ('Doctrine of Science' or 'Theory of Knowledge'). His lecture schedule was full. From Monday to Friday, he lectured three times a day. At three and

* The term *Wissenschaftslehre* includes the words *Wissen* ('knowledge'), *Wissenschaft* (in German this applies to both the sciences and the humanities) and *Lehre* ('doctrine'). *Wissenschaft* as Fichte understood it in this context related to a 'system of knowledge', not 'science' per se. The *Wissenschaftslehre* was not a book but Fichte's philosophical system in its entirety. He revised and published many versions of it until his death.

five o'clock in the afternoon he presented his philosophical system, and at six in the evening he gave a lecture for those students who had difficulties understanding the *Wissenschaftslehre*. In addition, he also offered a more open discussion on Saturdays – which anyone could attend – where, unlike in the more formal lectures, the audience was allowed to ask questions.

Fichte's ideas were a work in progress. He didn't arrive in Jena with a fully formed philosophical system: instead, he developed and expanded as he lectured. His many students fed his imagination and thinking. He explored, found and generated his ideas, he said, '*with* the listeners, and before their eyes'. As they watched Fichte's thinking unfold, they felt that they were witnessing something momentous. They were thrilled to see their hero conjuring up this new world. Fichte's philosophy was alive – so new and so revolutionary that even its creator had to revise it as he went along. Some students established a philosophical club – the 'Society of Free Men' – dedicated to the study of Fichte's new doctrine, while others could be found late in the evenings reading Fichte's writings in dim candle-light at the rough wooden tables in the many taverns in Jena.

One of the other philosophy professors admitted to feeling obsolete. Fichte swept up every student and carried them away. The colleague liked him as a person and respected him as a philosopher, but his own students could only speak about the Ich and non-Ich. Fichte's thinking was so original and surprising that there seemed to be no space for other teachers. Life as a professor with Fichte in town, his colleague said, had become 'unbearable'.

3

'The nation's finest minds'
Winter 1794–Spring 1795:
Where All Paths Lead

A BITTERLY COLD WINTER followed the hot summer of 1794. Deep snow blanketed the Duchy of Saxe-Weimar in January 1795. Further south, the mighty Rhine froze so solid that it became a thoroughfare for French troops as they crossed the continent. Two years previously, the sovereign states of Europe had united against the French revolutionaries after the execution of the French king, Louis XVI, in January 1793. The French had then declared war on one country after another. Soon Prussia, Austria, Britain, Spain, Portugal and Holland were involved – with the French fighting on so many fronts that it was difficult to keep up with their movements. But liberally minded people who supported the Revolution and its ideals welcomed the French into their cities and states. Just as the citizens of Mainz had greeted the invading troops with celebrations back in October 1792, so too did Dutch revolutionaries in January 1795, when they declared the Batavian Republic in The Hague with the help of the French.

As the French army marched on, one victory followed the next, and the German territories west of the Rhine fell under French control. As reports came in of French attacks on the western and southern German states, Goethe worried about his mother in Frankfurt and friends elsewhere. Fighting armies didn't just mean guns and cannon fire, but also looting and hungry soldiers. Crops were ransacked, animals were slaughtered and wine cellars emptied. Occupying forces moved into private houses and had to be fed. Money and jewellery were stolen, and valuable paintings were carried away. Women were raped, the injured had to be nursed and the dead had to be buried. War was not only dangerous for soldiers.

Then, in April 1795, Prussia abandoned its ally Austria. Preoccupied with the partition of Poland in the east, Prussia had only been half-heartedly engaged in the French wars. Once large parts of Poland had been annexed, Prussia's territorial ambitions were satisfied but its coffers were empty. Instead of continuing an expensive war, Prussia signed a treaty of neutrality with France.* It haggled over its rights to the left and right banks, and then ceded the already occupied territories west of the Rhine to the French. But neutrality came with great dangers. Prussia was now a precariously situated buffer between Russia in the east and the ever-expanding territories of France to the west. Without major allies, it was isolated, clinging desperately to the observance of their treaty.

Goethe abhorred the war and the French Revolution. He also loathed being forced to choose sides. 'People always want me to take a side – all right, I'm on my side,' he later said. Schiller, by contrast, had initially been enthusiastic and was even made an honorary citizen of France in 1792 for the revolutionary leanings of *The Robbers*. But when the French National Assembly decided to execute Louis XVI, Schiller was aghast. Soon, he was refusing to read French newspapers, he told a friend, because 'these knavish executioners disgust me so'.

Schiller had changed over the past years. His wife was an aristocrat, and he had even acquired a princely patron in Denmark who so admired his work that he paid Schiller a small pension. Schiller, Goethe later joked, was far more aristocratic than he himself was. As more than fifteen thousand heads rolled from Robespierre's guillotines, Schiller became more and more horrified. Humankind was simply not advanced enough for the principles that had underpinned the Revolution, he believed. The French had not been ready for freedom and equality. They were still like 'wild animals', he now asserted, and had to be kept in 'salutary chains' by the state. In order to be truly free, one had to be morally mature – and the brutality that was engulfing France proved that the French Revolution had happened too soon. France – and with it Europe – had been catapulted back into barbarism and tyranny.

～

His was a writer's response. Schiller founded *Horen*, a journal with the explicit goal of avoiding all political discussion. Named after the

* This was the Peace of Basel in 1795.

Horae, the Greek goddesses of the seasons, beauty, order and justness, *Horen* would focus on art, culture, philosophy and poetry. First published in early 1795, at a time when the thunder of war reverberated across Europe, the journal was conceived as a 'happy distraction'. *Horen* was also an attempt to bring together the best of German culture – an organ of the German *Kulturnation*, a cultural nation independent of state lines but bound by a shared language. 'The German Reich and the German nation are two different things,' Schiller explained; 'the majesty of the Germans never rested on the crowned head of their princes.'

The Weimar philosopher Johann Gottfried Herder had long advocated this idea of Germanic cultural and linguistic kinship. 'Spit out the water of the Seine,' he had told Germans, who preferred French to their own mother tongue. Germans should speak German, he said, insisting on the importance of a shared history of language, culture and traditions. Herder believed that language embodied a particular view of the world which united Germans across borders and states. Language was the expression of shared values. This linguistic German 'nation' was not defined by wars, empires or monarchs but by words, thoughts and culture. 'A people of a language is made up of anyone who was raised in that language, poured his heart into it, learned to express his soul in it,' Herder wrote in the same year that Schiller published *Horen*.

Throughout those cold early months of 1795, Schiller's letters shuttled along icy roads and across battle lines to potential contributors. When his publisher agreed to underwrite the enterprise, Schiller was able to offer unusually generous fees for essays, poems and prose texts. Even though chronic chest pain and the freezing temperatures kept him from leaving the house, he now travelled hundreds of miles in his mind. Schiller tried to entice the best writers and thinkers to contribute. He wanted to establish a 'literary society', he told Goethe, and assemble 'the nation's finest minds'. And it was here, in the pages of *Horen*, that the Jena Set became a group for the first time.

In the first issues, published monthly from the beginning of 1795, Fichte discussed truth, and Wilhelm von Humboldt, a young aristocrat who had recently moved to Jena, examined concepts of masculinity and femininity in antiquity. Meanwhile Wilhelm's younger brother, the scientist Alexander von Humboldt, contributed an allegory set in ancient Greece, and Caroline Böhmer's old admirer,

the writer August Wilhelm Schlegel, translated extracts of Dante's
Inferno.* Goethe contributed several pieces, including his *Roman
Elegies*. Some verses, though, were deemed too salacious, such as
these lines which Goethe and Schiller withheld:

> *How can a woman embrace her lover in comfort unless she*
> *First, at his eager behest, sheds all her dainty array?*
> *Will he not want those jewels and laces, that whalebone and quilted*
> *Satin discarded at once, freeing her for his caress?*
> *We make short work of all that! – In a trice I unfasten this simple*
> *Woollen dress, and it drops, slips in its folds to the floor.*
> *Quickly, cajolingly, like a good nurse, I carry my darling –*
> *Only a light linen shift covers her now – to bed.*
> . . .
> *Ours is the true, the authentic, the naked Love; and beneath us,*
> *Rocking in rhythm, the bed creaks the dear song of our joy.*

Nonetheless, the remaining *Roman Elegies* were sensual enough to
shock Weimar's high society. Appalled by the explicit descriptions of
nudity, one local writer complained that 'all respectable women are
outraged'. Herder joked that *Horen* should swap a letter and become
Huren ('whores' in German), while Weimar poet Christoph Martin
Wieland scoffed: 'in *Horen* the great men have erected a lavatory
temple where they can answer nature's call.' But the younger generation adored the *Roman Elegies*. It was like breathing Italian air,
August Wilhelm Schlegel told Schiller, and his brother Friedrich
Schlegel thought the poems nothing less than 'divine Elegies'.

~

Among Schiller's own *Horen* contributions was *Letters on the Aesthetic
Education of Man*, a long essay composed of twenty-seven letters
addressed to his Danish aristocratic patron. Over more than one
hundred pages Schiller argued that art was the tool for an alternative
revolution to that in France. It was the Enlightenment and its emphasis
on reason rather than feeling, he explained, that had led to the
horrific excesses of the French Revolution.

All that could be achieved from reason had already been achieved,
Schiller wrote. Reason, rationality and empiricism had brought

---

* August Wilhelm Schlegel later explained that no one had ever heard of Dante
in Germany prior to his translations.

powerful knowledge, but what was missing was the refinement of moral behaviour. All the knowledge in the world could not develop a person's sense of right and wrong: maybe it would give them an understanding of the laws of gravity or allow them to invent a steam engine, maybe it enabled them to define and declare universal rights such as liberty and equality; but the bloodied metal of the French guillotines proved that this was not enough.

'Utility is the great idol of our time,' Schiller wrote, 'to which all powers pay homage.' Profit, productivity and consumption had become the guiding light of modern societies. Even philosophy, with its celebration of rational thought and scientific progress, had pushed the arts out of sight. But it was beauty that transports us towards ethical principles and makes us better people, Schiller claimed in *Letters on the Aesthetic Education of Man*. Art improves the character, and without beauty there is no sense of morality. For Schiller, taste and beauty were the bulwark against brutality, greed and immorality.

Feeling and reason had to work in tandem, and the instrument to achieve that was art. Taking his cue from Kant, whom he had studied intensely, Schiller tried to reconcile these worlds. In his third *Critique*, the *Critique of Judgement*, Kant had given imagination a vital role in human thinking – one that bridged sense and understanding. Beauty, Schiller now argued, had the ability to unite our sensual and rational sides. It directed a purely sensuous person back to thought, and a rational person back from abstractions to reality. The struggle between the sensual and the rational was a battle between the heart and the head which neither could win, Schiller explained, because the heart alone was 'just as unreliable a leader' as reason. Only art could mediate between the two.

With the shadow of the French army darkening Europe, Schiller added a political dimension to Kant's ideas, declaring that 'art is a daughter of freedom.' The French Revolution and the ensuing atrocities had shown how urgent the need for a philosophy of beauty was. In order to find a solution to political problems, he said, the path of aesthetics had to be pursued – 'it is through beauty that we reach freedom.' Schiller's *Letters on the Aesthetic Education of Man* became a founding document for a new generation of thinkers and writers called the Romantics, who would elevate imagination above reason, science and philosophy. The young philosopher Hegel declared it a 'masterpiece'.

Published in monthly instalments of around one hundred pages, *Horen*'s first issues were widely read. There were no illustrations or ornamental headers because Schiller wanted to impress his readers with the content and not with elegant frontispieces or expensive paper. Everybody was talking about *Horen*, Goethe reported, and in Weimar 'people tear the issues out of one another's hands'. With journals and newspapers ordered not only by individuals but often by reading societies, libraries and private salons, copies passed from one reader to the next, each page often turned by many dozens of hands. Well-thumbed copies were shared among family, friends and neighbours, and then posted to others who lived in towns and cities across Germany. From each issue spread the poems, essays or serialised novels into an ever-growing web of readers, reaching a far larger audience than the subscription figures alone.

~

Jena seemed to exert a magnetic pull. Nowhere else would one be able to enjoy such freedom, Schiller said, or find 'so many excellent people in such a small area'. The reason was the university's peculiar governance, in which four Saxon rulers from four different duchies had to agree on all matters, making rules difficult to enact and enforce. As a result theologians were not strictly bound to the religious canon, law professors taught revolutionary political theories, censorship was more lenient compared to elsewhere, and the scope of subjects that could be taught was broad. There was no university like it in Europe.

In France, for example, universities had been abolished in 1793 and replaced by state-run *écoles spéciales* – specialised schools for practical training. England had only two universities and they were steeped in centuries-old traditions. Whereas Jena attracted young progressive teachers and open-minded students, English professors were conservative clergymen. Being a member of the Church of England was a requirement for students wishing to enrol at Oxford or Cambridge. The curriculum was famously narrow and consisted mainly of the classics, theology and compulsory church services. Studying science there meant reading Aristotle. Oxford and Cambridge dons imparted universally approved and accepted knowledge but didn't engage in scientific or philosophical discovery. While Jena's students watched a mesmerising Fichte develop his latest ideas in front of their very eyes, the young men in Oxford and Cambridge were bored by their dull teachers' repetitious delivery. As Jena crystallised from a small university town into the centre of modern philosophy, the hallowed halls of Oxford and Cambridge exuded stifling tradition. In Jena, one of the English students observed, students were taught by 'Professors in all the various Sciences & Arts' and met real men of letters.

One such thinker was Wilhelm von Humboldt, a wealthy aristocrat who admired the ideals of the French Revolution. In late 1794 he and his wife Caroline had moved into a house on the market square that was so close to Schiller's apartment that they could wave out of the window to arrange their daily meetings. Caroline von Humboldt and Charlotte Schiller had long been friends, and one of the reasons why the Humboldts had moved to Jena. Previous visits to the small town had been filled with inspiring conversations, and had quickly led to the decision.

Caroline von Humboldt was twenty-eight when they moved to Jena. She was an intelligent and pretty woman with a head of chestnut-coloured hair, expressive lips and such large deep blue eyes that friends called her 'die Wunderäugige' – the girl with the wondrous eyes. Like Charlotte Schiller, she came from an old aristocratic family in the region with estates in Thuringia, not far from Jena. Wilhelm, or Bill as she called him, was a year younger than Caroline but looked older and more serious, his heavy-lidded eyes dominating his face. He was fascinated by ancient languages and antiquity – and so wealthy that he didn't have to work. The son of an aristocratic Prussian family with close ties to the king, Wilhelm von Humboldt had been brought up in Berlin and on the nearby family estate of Tegel.

Yet, despite their privileged upbringings, both Wilhelm and Caroline von Humboldt had felt lonely during childhood. Caroline von Humboldt had lost her mother at a young age and had been raised by an elderly French governess. Wilhelm had been only eleven when his loving and gentle father suddenly died, and his mother never showed much affection or maternal warmth. Wilhelm had escaped into books and languages, losing himself in Greek mythology and histories of ancient Rome. He was studious, guarded and earnest but adored his wife's ease and cheerfulness, as well as her kindness and perceptive mind. Caroline was well versed in all literary matters, reading and speaking French, English and Greek, but her favourite subject was art. The couple talked about everything and laughed a lot. Equal partners, she loved his mind, his knowledge, ideas and gentleness. Few would ever truly understand or know Wilhelm, she once said, because he was so reserved 'but to know you is to worship you'.

During their first months in Jena and throughout the cold winter, they spent many hours at Schiller's apartment, adjusting their rhythms to his idiosyncratic domestic habits. Many of the university's professors had the habit of meeting every week at the Professors' Club in the Zur Rose tavern as well as attending the popular concerts in the large room adjacent to it, but Schiller avoided such gatherings. Instead, he invited a select few to his house. This was his realm. He rarely ventured out and didn't like travelling. He hated disruption. Schiller had never seen the swirling foam of ocean waves or the snow-capped peaks of the Alps, nor had he walked the busy streets of Paris or admired the ancient ruins of Rome. The exciting world out there, with its large noisy cities – 'these great bustling oceans of people' – might be thrilling, he admitted, 'but I also feel comfortable in my hazelnut shell'.

Schiller travelled in his mind, reading accounts of great seafaring expeditions during sleepless nights. When Jena lay in darkness, a lamp flickered in Schiller's study as he sailed with the great explorers to tropical islands and accompanied them as they crossed mountain ranges. On the pages of these books he encountered fierce animals and deadly hurricanes, saw glistening icebergs and mirages in hot deserts. But the centre of his world would always be his study and his house where he spent long evenings with friends and visitors, discussing philosophy, poetry and art. Only at home, he said, did he find happiness.

Wilhelm von Humboldt quickly became Schiller's philosophical sparring partner and editorial adviser for *Horen*. Schiller benefited greatly from Wilhelm's sharp analytical skills and calm critical mind. 'All my ideas', he told a friend, 'develop faster and better in conversation with him.' It helped that Wilhelm was neither vain nor competitive, accepting that Schiller was the genius in their friendship. Before commenting and making suggestions, Wilhelm von Humboldt listened and scrutinised. As Schiller paced up and down, Wilhelm dissected deliberately and precisely. He had a knack for pinpointing a problem or awakening a nascent idea in others. Like Schiller, Wilhelm von Humboldt had also studied Kant's philosophy – so intensely, in fact, that his younger brother Alexander had worried that he would 'study himself to death'. Both Schiller and Humboldt were fascinated by the concept of self-determination. Schiller said that Kant's call to shape one's destiny 'from within' encapsulated everything that was important.

They discussed Kant, attended Fichte's lectures and talked about poetry – with the classically trained Wilhelm von Humboldt advising Schiller on verse metre. Wilhelm was also on *Horen*'s editorial board and diligently worked through the commissioned pieces. His own contributions, though, were dry treatises that never excited readers. Schiller tried to be diplomatic and assured his friend that his 'individual perfection' lay not in creativity but in his critical mind. To others, Schiller was more straightforward and simply said, 'I really fear that he has no talent as a writer.' And so Schiller took the lead and Humboldt happily followed, but always confident to correct, suggest and comment.

Goethe was equally impressed by the new member of their circle and enjoyed their debates. Everything was discussed but politics. Goethe had always appreciated that he didn't need to talk about the French Revolution with Schiller, and Wilhelm von Humboldt respected his friends' unwritten rules despite his own enthusiasm for the events of 1789. The trio became, as Schiller later said, 'a three-leaf clover of critical thought'.

Humboldt called these gatherings 'social thinking', and for Goethe the time he spent in Jena was 'food for the soul'. Their meetings were electrifying and even Schiller slowly cheered up. When the spring sun finally dispersed the miserable February weather, Schiller's dark mood evaporated. Wasn't it strange, he told Goethe at the end of February 1795, how they were bound to nature, no matter how much they believed in free will. A few sunbeams clarified all he had brooded over unsuccessfully for the past five weeks.

Jena was alive with possibility, inspiration and visionary ideas. It was as if the brightest minds had been concentrated in this small town like the sun's rays in a magnifying glass. Schiller was happy and told an old friend that he would 'never trade Jena and my free life here for anywhere else'.

~

The presence of such great thinkers attracted students from across Germany and Europe. In Jena they were not philosophising but 'fichticising'. Fichte himself didn't always make that easy because, unlike his captivating lectures, his writing was dense and convoluted. Students could be defeated by torturous, looping and almost incomprehensible paragraphs such as this:

> But the non-Ich can be posited only insofar as an Ich is posited in the Ich (in the identical consciousness), to which it (the non-Ich) can be opposed.
> Now the non-Ich is to be posited in the identical consciousness.
> Thus, insofar as the non-Ich is to be posited in this consciousness, the Ich must also be posited therein.

Fichte was the first to admit that his *Wissenschaftslehre* was a work in progress. 'Sparks of ideas spray out of it,' he said, 'but it is not a *single* flame.' Schiller, Humboldt and Goethe all admitted to not understanding everything, but while they had their doubts the younger generation embraced Fichte's arguments whole-heartedly. One was the twenty-four-year-old poet Friedrich Hölderlin, who had moved to Jena at the end of 1794 and who was so enraptured that he attended only Fichte's lectures. For him the philosopher was a 'Titan fighting for humanity' and the 'soul of Jena'.

However, Fichte's soaring popularity also created scheduling conflicts. With five hundred subscribed students, he needed to coordinate his packed programme with the university's wider programming if he was to secure the biggest auditorium. But when he decided to offer yet another lecture series, the only slot available was at nine o'clock on Sunday morning. Fichte's adversaries immediately accused him of holding a 'church service of Reason' in his 'temple of Reason'. And promptly, on the day of his first Sunday morning lecture, the government in Weimar received the first of several complaints. Less than a week later the university's rector informed Fichte that he would have to stop his Sunday lectures.

What was he supposed to do, Fichte asked Minister Voigt, Goethe's colleague in the Weimar administration. Fichte was willing to change the time of his lecture, but to when? He was well aware that church services were held at nine o'clock in the morning, but before then the students were still asleep. After that, at eleven o'clock, the university held its own church service, and it was pointless to lecture after lunch because the students would never be able to concentrate with a 'full stomach'. And Sunday afternoons were filled with concerts and club meetings. There was just no other time. Voigt agreed, but the Weimar department in charge of religious affairs in the duchy decided otherwise – perhaps unsurprisingly because Johann Gottfried Herder, who disliked Fichte and his radical new philosophy, was superintendent for church matters in Weimar. Arguments went back and forth, and with the support of Goethe and Voigt the decision was finally reversed. Fichte was allowed to resume his Sunday lectures, but only at three o'clock in the afternoon.

Fichte, though, had no reason to celebrate. He was now facing a new problem: a group of students had taken to smashing the windows of his house. These young men were members of the university's fraternities, secret brotherhoods who bonded through drinking and duelling – traditions that Fichte despised. When he had openly crit-icised the fraternities during his lectures, some of the students had been so in awe of their new professor that they had disbanded two of the three fraternities. The more dedicated members, however, were not happy. The first round of broken windows led to a five-month campaign of harassment in which, night after night, stones were hurled into Fichte's house.

Fichte's complaints to Duke Carl August, Goethe and Voigt had not achieved anything, and the fraternities continued their attacks. Colleagues laughed and told Fichte to get used to it because Jena's students had a reputation for being rowdy. They fought duels, drank, looked scruffy and they loved to protest – and sometimes they took their aggression to the windows of their professors.

Then, late one evening, Johanne Fichte found herself in the crosshairs when walking home from a party. Upon seeing her, a few students who were stumbling out of a tavern shouted obscenities. The incident frightened her so much that she rarely left the house after that. She shrank into a 'living skeleton', a family friend remarked, until she was just skin and bone. Fichte wrote letters to Weimar and to the university's rector asking for protection, but no one was willing to get involved.

Night after night the bombardment continued. Then, in April 1795, several months after the first stone had been thrown, Fichte was woken at two in the morning by someone banging against the gate. He opened a window and shouted: 'What do you want?' 'Fichte, we want Fichte!' a few drunken students roared. 'If you have some-thing to say,' Fichte bellowed down, 'come and see me tomorrow morning.' But the students continued to shout vile abuse. To get a better view of what was going on, Fichte went to the annexe of the house where his landlord lived. From here, he could see three young men trying to throw bricks through the windows. Failing to fling them far enough, the students grabbed smaller stones and began to smash the glass panes. Fichte snapped. Grabbing a pistol and a sword, he gulped down a glass of champagne and set off to fight the students. He was only stopped when his landlord used all of his body weight to pull him back. The students now began to threaten the landlord. 'Have him move out, he has to move out,' they demanded, 'you'll always have broken windows as long as he lives in your house.' Having smashed a few more windows, they finally stumbled off towards the market square, loudly singing French revolutionary songs.

When Fichte returned to the family's rooms, Johanne told him that a huge stone had narrowly missed her father, who had moved to Jena to live with them. He could easily have been killed. The next day Fichte went to Weimar to hand in his resignation; but Minister Voigt persuaded him to take some time off instead, at least until the situation calmed down. At the end of April 1795 the shaken Fichtes went to Oßmannstedt, a little village some fifteen miles to the north-west of Jena. The whole experience, Goethe quipped, must have been a 'most disagreeable way' for Fichte 'to have the existence of a non-Ich proven to him'.

~

There was more trouble to come. This time it came from an unexpected quarter: Friedrich Schiller, a man he trusted and respected. Fichte believed that Schiller was his supporter – and he had been. 'Fichte's supreme genius will lay waste to everything before it,' Schiller had said after he had first heard Fichte lecture, declaring him the greatest philosopher after Kant. But Schiller had quickly become weary of the increasingly abstract speculations of Fichte's *Wissenschaftslehre*. The obsession with the Ich and non-Ich was like a vortex that sucked everything in, Schiller feared, privately warning that 'this path goes towards an abyss, and all our attention will be necessary not to fall into it.' The idea of a free self appealed to Schiller, but he couldn't accept Fichte's belief that the external world didn't exist without the Ich. Fichte's world, Schiller told Goethe, was like a ball that the Ich throws and catches when it comes bouncing back.

Despite their differences, Schiller and Fichte shared many beliefs. Both had been profoundly influenced by Kant, and both insisted on the importance of education: for Schiller, it was the artist who was the true teacher of humankind, for Fichte it was the scholar. Most importantly perhaps, both men imbued the Ich with free will. None of this, though, prevented their falling out.

On 21 June 1795, while still in Oßmannstedt, Fichte submitted an article for publication in *Horen* entitled 'About Mind and Letters in Philosophy'. Leafing through the rambling manuscript, Schiller did not like what he was reading. The piece was far too long and the content didn't even reflect its title. Instead of philosophy, Fichte had written about aesthetics, a subject Schiller had already covered in *Horen*. In the reply he drafted, Schiller tried and failed to find the right tone. How should he phrase his concerns? How would the famously tetchy Fichte react? In the end, he put the sheets aside.

The next day, he tried again. But as the sheets filled with Schiller's tidy handwriting that never veered from straight and perfectly spaced lines, he found himself having to start afresh numerous times. Another sheet of paper, and another. He rewrote and rephrased. His initial expression 'dry, cumbersome and . . . often confused presentation', for example, became in the final version the less offensive 'shapeless length'.

It took Schiller two days and four drafts to craft his careful reply to Fichte, but even then there was no hiding the fact that this was a harsh rejection letter. Unless Fichte was to make a 'salto mortale' – a fateful leap – Schiller wrote, how was he to move from aesthetics to the promised subject of philosophy? It didn't help, Schiller continued, that the text bounced from 'the most abstruse abstractions straight into tirades'. No matter how much he had tried to tone down his criticism, Schiller's frustration and indignation poured from the pages. 'You're expecting me to present this to the public?' he finally asked.

Deeply hurt, Fichte replied immediately with a long letter. Surely, Schiller would trust an old friend and respected philosopher? Hadn't he until now admired Fichte's philosophical talent? How could Schiller suddenly accuse him of being the 'most confused of all confused minds'? Fichte did not appreciate being treated like a pupil, and in any case, the paper he had submitted was not particularly difficult. If Schiller had problems understanding it, the reason was the playwright's lack of philosophical competence. Fichte also suggested asking Goethe to mediate. But how would Goethe be able to resolve their disagreement, Schiller asked in his first draft of a reply, if he didn't know enough about philosophy. In fact, Goethe had asked *him* for advice, Schiller wrote, but then cut the comment in the third and final version of his reply to Fichte.

Instead, Schiller vented his frustration to Wilhelm von Humboldt who agreed that Fichte was 'like an old woman indulging her desire to nag and scold'. Still, Fichte couldn't let it go. Why not print the article and let the readers decide if the essay was as terrible as Schiller suggested? Again, Schiller refused. He was most certainly not going to give readers an editorial role in *Horen*.

'We are of two very different natures,' Schiller concluded, 'and I can think of nothing to do against that.' It would be years before Fichte and Schiller spoke to each other again.

4

'Electrified by our intellectual friction'
1795–1796: Love, Life and Literature

I T WAS A long and uncomfortable journey. From Amsterdam it was almost three hundred miles east along bumpy roads to Braunschweig in the German Principality of Braunschweig-Wolfenbüttel. August Wilhelm Schlegel was on his way to see Caroline Böhmer. Travelling across eighteenth-century Europe meant sitting in badly sprung stage-coaches where every inch was taken up by passengers and luggage. Strangers sat so close together on the narrow benches that every pothole, stone or turn of a corner tossed them like ninepins into each other. Knees knocked, arms brushed, legs bounced and bodies banged together. In winter it was freezing cold inside the carriage and in summer the air became stale. People sweated, farted, burped, smoked and ate. Some talked too much, others averted their eyes to avoid conversation. Valuables were kept close in purses and satchels – some passengers who worried about theft and highwaymen even sewed their money and jewels into their clothes.

Mailbags, boxes and trunks were piled high on the roofs and overturned carriages were a daily occurrence on the post routes, as were broken springs and wheels. Bolting horses could be a hazard, as could the deep ruts that had turned into dangerous grooves. Sometimes the coachmen fell asleep, and at other times they fought each other stubbornly over the right of way. Every fifteen miles or so the carriage came to an abrupt halt at a stagecoach station where horses were changed and passengers could relieve themselves. As some disembarked and others boarded, it could be hours before the coach was ready to leave again. With an average speed of between four and seven miles an hour – not even counting accidents, hold-ups at stations or other delays – travel was slow. There were dirty inns along the route where one could eat and sleep on bedbug-infested straw mattresses. When passengers crossed borders, they encountered customs officers who checked their papers and luggage.

Sometimes these inspections took several hours as trunks and boxes were unpacked and searched. War of course increased the hazards. Earlier that year, in the cold early months of 1795, French troops had advanced through Holland – one of the reasons why twenty-seven-year-old August Wilhelm Schlegel had finally packed his belongings in June and resigned his position as tutor for the children of a wealthy banking family after four years in Amsterdam.

The other reason was the charismatic widow Caroline Böhmer, who had moved to Braunschweig a few weeks earlier, in May 1795. August Wilhelm Schlegel had adored Caroline from the first day they met in Göttingen when he was a young student. But she had rejected him several times. 'Schlegel and me!' she had scoffed, back in 1789. 'No, nothing is going to happen between us – that much is certain.' Worse, she had been accused of several love affairs, had fallen pregnant after a brief encounter at a ball, and had been imprisoned. His patience had worn thin, but not his feelings for her.

~

Born in 1767, August Wilhelm Schlegel was the son of a respected Lutheran priest in Hanover and one of ten children. His mother was a strong-willed matriarch and his father wrote poetry in his spare time. Although not wealthy, the family lived comfortably, and August Wilhelm had been brought up in an intellectual atmosphere which had instilled in him a deep love of literature and a strict Protestant work ethic. An earnest boy who preferred books to physical exercise, August Wilhelm learned easily and quickly absorbed languages. In Göttingen, where he studied philology, he became known for his attention to detail. Calm and analytical but with a tendency to be pedantic, he knew much about languages – ancient and modern – and poetry, but also about literature in general. Though he had to work as a tutor to make a living, August Wilhelm had also published some reviews and poems and Schiller had thought them so good that he asked the young man to contribute to *Horen*.

August Wilhelm was handsome, with a strong chin and brown eyes framed by dark eyebrows which gave him a serious look. He liked fashion and was always perfectly groomed. When they had first met, Caroline had told the immaculate August Wilhelm that only in Göttingen could a student be so spotlessly dressed without being teased. He was studious, diligent and loved by his family. So in early

July 1795, on his way to Braunschweig, he stopped in Hanover to see his parents, who despaired of his decision to see Caroline. And although he was worried too, August Wilhelm ignored his mother's warnings that a connection with a fallen woman might harm his prospects. He had waited years to get Caroline's attention.

August Wilhelm Schlegel arrived in Braunschweig at the end of July 1795, just as Schiller and Fichte's fight had reached its culmination. As Schiller was writing angry letters to Goethe and Wilhelm von Humboldt about the 'great Ich in Oßmanstädt', August Wilhelm Schlegel set eyes on Caroline for the first time in two years. At thirty-two, she was four years his senior, and still pretty despite the hardship of the previous two years – with alert blue eyes, perfectly straight teeth and a heart-shaped face framed by dark curls. The daughter of Johann David Michaelis, one of the most respected professors in Göttingen, she had also been educated to a much higher standard than other girls of her time. Raised on a diet of literature, philosophy and politics in her father's house in Göttingen, Caroline had grown used to the flow of intellectual conversation.

Private tutors had instructed Caroline and her siblings in history, religion, geography, maths and languages before she was sent to finishing school in Gotha at the age of twelve. Soon fluent in English, French and Italian, Caroline became a voracious reader who raided her father's bookshelves and would read aloud to her brothers and sisters. She enjoyed Shakespeare and Milton in the original, but also philosophers such as the Scottish Enlightenment thinker David Hume, and had translated – for fun – comedies by the contemporary Venetian playwright Carlo Goldoni. Her mind was so sharp that even Wilhelm von Humboldt, a polymath who never suffered intellectual insecurity, later said he would avoid at all cost a 'contest of wit and acumen' with her. Assured and unwilling to hide her knowledge, she was a woman who knew how to deploy her weapons in a playful dance of erudition and flirtation.

It was an awkward reunion, friendly but a little distant. Nonetheless, August Wilhelm rented a room close to Caroline's apartment and they saw each other every day. Still hurt by her previous rejections, August Wilhelm revealed little emotion. Caroline was not deterred – 'I'll teach him to stop being so cold,' she promised herself.

～

It had been a long journey from her childhood in Göttingen to her new life in Braunschweig. In 1784, at the age of twenty, Caroline had married thirty-year-old doctor Franz Böhmer, the family's neighbour in Göttingen. As was common at the time, it had been her father who had chosen her husband. Caroline had then been forced to move with her physician husband to a small mining town in the mountains, some forty miles north-east of her childhood home. There she had three children in quick succession and began to feel trapped in her loveless marriage – like a 'prisoner in a dungeon', she said.

Distanced from the intellectual life she loved, she became miserable and escaped into books. Four years later, though, her husband contracted a fever from a patient and suddenly died, leaving Caroline free to move back to Göttingen. At twenty-four, she was already a widow. Then, her baby son died aged just two months, followed a year later by two-and-a-half-year-old daughter Röschen. Only her oldest child Auguste survived. Caroline drowned her pain in parties and flirtations.

A string of admirers vied for her attention, August Wilhelm Schlegel among them. When friends identified a suitable husband who could have provided social and financial security, Caroline declined without hesitation. She had no interest, she replied, in giving up her freedom and bringing up half a dozen children. Indignant, her friends cautioned against allowing these 'overenthusiastic ideas of freedom' to guide her, but Caroline had made up her mind. From now on, she would control her destiny. As long as one was willing to live with the consequences, she believed, one was allowed to do whatever one wanted. Caroline 'loves freedom and not having to justify her every move', her sister had explained to August Wilhelm.

In 1792 Caroline had moved to Mainz, the city where ideas of the French Revolution were gathering German supporters. She didn't have much money but enough to survive. 'I wouldn't leave here if my life depended on it,' she wrote to her best friend from Mainz. She just couldn't miss being a witness of these thrilling events. However, imprisonment as a sympathiser of the Revolution hadn't been quite the experience she had envisaged.

Since her incarceration in Königstein, Caroline had lived an itinerant life. After more than three months in prison, she had finally been released in July 1793, just before her pregnancy would have become obvious. Hearing the news and still undeterred by Caroline's many rejections, let alone the fact that she carried the child of another man, August Wilhelm had immediately packed his bags and travelled from Amsterdam to Königstein to help. In what became a whirlwind round trip of almost one thousand miles, he had then accompanied Caroline to Leipzig. His Dutch employers insisted on his quick return, but he had just enough time to find a family in a small village near Leipzig with whom Caroline could live during the final months of her pregnancy – even though his involvement meant people thought he was the father of the illegitimate child.

August Wilhelm had also asked his younger brother Friedrich, who was studying in Leipzig, to keep an eye on her. It was there, in early November, that Caroline gave birth to a son. When she saw the tiny face, she was glad that he looked like her rather than his father, the young French officer from that wild night at the ball in Mainz. She was relieved, Friedrich Schlegel wrote to his brother August Wilhelm the day after the baby was born, 'so that you won't heap such terrible hate on his head'. Caroline didn't tell anyone else about her child but bribed the local priest to baptise the baby. Soon, though, gossip spread in the small village and she had to leave, placing her three-month-old son with a foster family. As soon as she was settled somewhere, she promised, she would return to claim him.

But where could she live? Wherever she went, her reputation followed and doors were slammed in her face. Old friends ignored her pleas and several German cities refused her entry. Though the French might have declared all men equal, in Germany the authorities – be it duke, local government or city council – still had the right to decide who could live where. And Caroline was a fallen woman in every respect. She had not been able to escape the rumour that she was a 'revolutionary whore'. She was devastated but at the same time never lost her fierce sense of independence. Why should her life be destroyed, she asked, by 'one little foolishness', by a mistake that would have meant nothing were she a man?

For a while she had stayed with her closest childhood friend Luise Gotter in Gotha, a small town some fifty miles west of Jena. Luise had been Caroline's most trusted ally ever since they had first met as young girls at finishing school in Gotha in 1774. From the age of eleven, Caroline had shared her secrets, worries and joys with the calmer Luise but now the gossip became unbearable. 'I'm an outcast,' Caroline wrote, resolving to leave Gotha when she realised how

Luise's reputation was being dragged down by association. Berlin was an option – 'Berlin is big enough to hide one woman, isn't it?' she asked – as were Dresden and her home town, Göttingen. But all refused her. The authorities in Dresden and Göttingen rejected her pleas in the interest of protecting 'respectable families', although they didn't even know about her illegitimate child. Her imprisonment and well-known revolutionary leanings were enough to keep the city gates shut. 'My life in Germany is over,' Caroline admitted to a friend.

~

Only marriage, Caroline's mother insisted, could save her. Worried about her daughter's precarious future, Caroline's mother thought the devoted August Wilhelm Schlegel the perfect contender. Caroline had always been too independently minded to listen to her mother, but this time she agreed. Marrying August Wilhelm would never have been her first choice, nor was she a fan of the institution itself. 'Were I to be my own master,' she had announced as an eighteen-year-old, 'I would much prefer never to marry at all.' But she had little choice. Few options remained open to her, but when offered a position as a governess Caroline politely declined – a life with August Wilhelm Schlegel was much more appealing.

After all, he wasn't such a bad candidate. He was a man of moderation who enjoyed good food and wine but never too much. He liked order and tidy surroundings, preferred a daily routine to spontaneous ideas or surprises, and he longed for a secure income. He was the perfect son-in-law, if not necessarily the object of passionate love for a woman like Caroline. Yet, he was also kind, hard-working and honest, and he had proved his loyalty time and again. Caroline trusted him. Friendship, she decided, was more important than love. It helped that he was good-looking, and that they both loved art and literature. He would make a good, dependable companion, and would also provide desperately needed social security. A new name, she hoped, would herald a new beginning. All she had to do was persuade him to marry her.

But the loyal and steadfast August Wilhelm was having second thoughts. Caroline was not used to rejection. Prior to her imprisonment, she had been showered with so much male attention that some accused her of enjoying it too much. She had always been different – intriguing and strong-minded, yet still respectable – but her circumstances had changed dramatically and August Wilhelm cared about social etiquette and conventions. Could he really risk his future?

Back in spring 1795, after months of desperate travelling and banishment from several cities, Caroline had finally arrived in Braunschweig where her mother and younger sister Luise had moved from Göttingen. There, less than a week after they had settled, Caroline received a letter saying that her baby son had died of a fever in the care of his foster family. Throughout the previous year, Caroline had done everything she could to find a way to have him live with her. As a mother with an illegitimate baby, she would have ruined Auguste's future as well, but this death was the cruellest blow, having already lost two children from her first marriage. Of the four children she had borne, only ten-year-old Auguste remained – 'this child of my heart' – her strong daughter who had somehow survived prison with a big smile on her face.

It was Auguste, with her sunshine countenance, who was the only one to see her mother cry. Caroline couldn't even mourn in public because no one in Braunschweig knew about the baby, not even her own mother. But no matter how desperate she felt, Caroline tried to turn her attention to anything that might bring her a little joy: the sun on her skin, Auguste's pink cheeks, a book. Whatever life threw at her, Caroline was determined not to let it destroy her. Even during moments of the greatest distress, she was always able to find something beautiful to hold tight – 'I can make happiness even from suffering,' she said.

It was Friedrich Schlegel who had urged his older brother August Wilhelm to visit Caroline in Braunschweig. She needed him more than ever, Friedrich had said, telling his brother to ignore their family's objections. 'I'm sure you can calm them down with one or two good letters,' he wrote on 20 May 1795. Don't wait, Friedrich warned a little later. When August Wilhelm admitted that he had embarked on an affair in Amsterdam, Friedrich was upset. How could August Wilhelm inflict pain on Caroline for a few hours of joy?

During those months of mourning Caroline had lived quietly in Braunschweig, writing long letters to August Wilhelm in Amsterdam, asking him to visit as he continued to dither. His affair was nothing too serious, but it was enough to keep him distracted. Professionally, he was also considering his options. If he gave up his position in Amsterdam, he urgently needed to earn some money elsewhere. But where? Maybe he should stay in Holland after all? Or move to Rome? Or Dresden, Prague, America . . . anywhere. Friedrich Schlegel advised against America, doubting the country would suit his older brother. Everybody there, Friedrich wrote, was interested in commerce and economics rather than literature. 'Apart from the freedom,' he said, 'which admittedly is invaluable, the country seems to offer little by way of higher pleasures.' Caroline, impatient by nature, could do nothing but wait. She would have to let August Wilhelm take his time.

When August Wilhelm Schlegel finally made up his mind and travelled to Braunschweig, he remained hesitant and distant at first, but his presence gave Caroline solace. To have him with her in Braunschweig, she wrote to a friend in Leipzig, 'is truly a consolation, and one I appreciate'. With every day together in Braunschweig, their quiet friendship strengthened. Soon they were writing letters to mutual friends as a couple might, with August Wilhelm sometimes scribbling a postscript to Caroline's letters, or she adding a few lines to his. By autumn, Caroline was confident enough to send a letter to August Wilhelm's mother, who had remained opposed to the relationship. Reluctant to welcome her into the family and worried about rumours of an impending marriage, Mother Schlegel – as she was called by her children – replied to her son rather than to Caroline herself, but from now on she sent greetings to 'your Caroline' instead of calling her simply 'Böhmer'.

~

Meanwhile, in Jena, Friedrich Schiller was feeling ill, exhausted and lonely. Goethe was on vacation in Karlsbad, a spa town in western Bohemia in today's Czech Republic, and Wilhelm von Humboldt was in Berlin looking after his sick mother.

'So I am more or less abandoned here,' Schiller wrote to his old friend Christian Gottfried Körner* in Dresden, in summer 1795.

---

* Schiller had met Körner in 1785, and after the itinerant years following his imprisonment for *The Robbers*, he spent almost two years in Dresden with him. Right up until he died, Schiller counted the wealthy, refined and educated Körner as one of his most trusted friends.

The heated exchange with Fichte had made him miserable and *Horen* had turned out to be a much more onerous enterprise than he had anticipated. After the excitement of the launch, Schiller soon realised how stressful it was. It was bad enough working out the logistics of receiving and dispatching manuscripts across battle lines with the French army fighting the Austrians in southern Germany, but there were payment issues to be resolved, as well as time-consuming editorial comments. Most exasperating of all were the writers: some cautiously waited to see how the first few issues were received by the readers before agreeing to contribute, others ignored deadlines or didn't deliver what they had promised. Some were ill and others just plain lazy. 'Lord help me, or I will sink!' Schiller groaned. Fichte's flawed essay had been just one example of how difficult it was to fill the pages with good material. Wilhelm von Humboldt was a great friend and thinker, but not a good writer. Most annoyingly still, Goethe had already promised his novel *Wilhelm Meister* to another publisher – it would have been perfect for serialisation in *Horen*. The most reliable contributor of all turned out to be August Wilhelm Schlegel. He was the only writer, Schiller said, 'from whom I can expect something of considerable substance and length'.

After the first few issues were printed and sold, *Horen's* publisher carefully suggested that Schiller might add a few lighter contributions because readers were complaining about too much abstract material. Schiller was upset, but Goethe tried to calm him. He had known the antics of the German literary world for the past twenty years and there was no point fighting, Goethe said, 'let's just continue as planned.' Sometimes Schiller felt like giving up altogether, he told Wilhelm von Humboldt. There were never enough good pieces, and what was good was clearly too sophisticated for readers. Well aware of his own limitations, Humboldt suggested they commission some more palatable writers. But by the end of 1795, Schiller had worked himself into such a state that he told his publisher if readers preferred the 'watery soups' of other journals over the 'hearty fare' in *Horen*, then so be it.

To make matters worse, the literary establishment now rolled out their 'heavy cavalry' with a scathing review of *Horen* in the popular journal *Deutschland*. There was just too much of the new-fangled philosophy in *Horen*, the reviewer and editor Friedrich Reichardt pointed out. Schiller seemed to have assembled all his friends as contributors, another reviewer criticised, but just because they enjoyed talking about these ideas when they were together didn't mean they held any interest for readers in general. Schiller was furious. 'The insect just couldn't help stinging,' he wrote to Goethe about Reichardt; 'really, we need to hunt it down and swat it, otherwise we'll never have any peace.' Unlike Goethe, who often brushed off a bad review or criticism with a quip, Schiller was eaten up by them. They gnawed inside him, making him even more tense and irritable.

'We really and truly live in the age of feuds,' he announced to Goethe. It was time for their own cavalry. He would ask August Wilhelm Schlegel if he might review *Horen* in the *Allgemeine Literatur-Zeitung*, the most widely read literary journal in the German-speaking territories. Everything was arranged, Schiller explained in a letter to August Wilhelm, for he had spoken to the commissioning editor, who conveniently was a Jena acquaintance. No one seemed to care that August Wilhelm Schlegel would be reviewing a journal for which he himself wrote. All that mattered, Goethe said, was that the review would be 'in the hands of a man from the new generation'.

Schiller admired August Wilhelm Schlegel's contributions to *Horen* – a four-part Dante translation and an essay on poetry – and regularly requested more. 'Send us whatever you think is fit to print,' Schiller had begged earlier that summer. He would publish anything – a translation, a poem, a tale, a historical essay, a novel – as long as it was delivered soon. Any doubts August Wilhelm had previously felt about his literary talents disappeared. If the great Schiller praised him, who would disagree?

Schiller also wondered if their exchanges wouldn't be far more productive if August Wilhelm Schlegel lived nearby. But how to get him to Jena? Wilhelm von Humboldt volunteered some useful information. The key was Caroline Böhmer because August Wilhelm Schlegel was in love with her. Humboldt had met them both during his student days in Göttingen in the late 1780s, and when Caroline had been imprisoned in Königstein, August Wilhelm had written to him on her behalf, seeking his assistance. Humboldt had also heard that Caroline had 'had a decisive influence on Schlegel's education'. If it wasn't for her, Humboldt told Schiller, luring August Wilhelm

to Jena would be easy. And so, when Schiller heard that August
Wilhelm had left Amsterdam and moved to Braunschweig, he
enquired where he intended to live in the future.

~

August Wilhelm Schlegel had no intention of leaving Braunschweig
or Caroline any time soon. He had only just arrived and he was not
going to turn around immediately. He was not a man to be rushed.
He needed time to think and he was just beginning to enjoy his
days with Caroline. Every morning he walked over to her house to
work on their ambitious verse translation of Shakespeare. Both fluent
in English, they had begun with *Romeo and Juliet* – with August
Wilhelm translating the text and Caroline scanning the verses in a
kind of chant. She ticked syllables, tapping her fingers on the table
as she transformed August Wilhelm's text into melody and poetry.
Sometimes they went back and forth several times, adding, tweaking,
changing until they were both satisfied.

This was the first verse translation of Shakespeare's plays in German.
There had been prose translations in the past which Goethe and
Schiller thought terrible. Even if the translations had been good, the
crucial point was that Shakespeare's dramatic power was lost in prose.
'The recurring rhythm', August Wilhelm Schlegel argued, 'is the
heartbeat of life.' He sent sample pages to Schiller, explaining how
difficult the translation had been. Names could be annoying, he said,
'when they don't fit the verse metre and yet constantly recur', adding
that it often took hours to translate just one line. Schiller was so
impressed that he immediately included the pages that August
Wilhelm had sent in *Horen*'s next issue.

With her sense of language and rhythm, Caroline became essential to a project that would encompass sixteen plays in a little more
than five years. Four decades later, August Wilhelm Schlegel even
claimed that his versified Shakespeare had changed German theatre:
compare Schiller's verse metre from his earlier plays with his later
ones, he insisted, 'to see how much he learned in my school'. August
Wilhelm and Caroline's translations are still the standard edition in
Germany. They would make August Wilhelm Schlegel famous and
lead Germans to adopt Shakespeare as a national poet. To this day
Shakespeare's plays are so popular that they are more widely
performed in Germany than in England.

August Wilhelm needed Caroline as much as she needed him, and her sophisticated education was paying off. They worked together from the moment he arrived in Braunschweig, in summer 1795. She was a razor-sharp critic, dissecting poetry, plays, novels and essays with profound knowledge and literary insight. Increasingly, August Wilhelm began to rely on her. Her literary and analytical mind shaped his thinking. Dozens of the three hundred reviews and essays that were published under his name over the next years were in fact written by Caroline.* They translated, edited, worked together – with Caroline often reading aloud. Many who heard her read, commented on the melody and charming lilt of her beautiful voice and her pitch-perfect intonation. She had almost magical powers, one of their friends later wrote in a poem:

> . . . *Oh, should you wish to hear how your own song*
> *Can draw souls to itself with magic power,*
> *Have Caroline recite it to you aloud.*

Caroline was making herself indispensable.

In the midst of all this, a letter from Friedrich Schiller arrived in December 1795, urging August Wilhelm Schlegel to move to Jena. 'Why can't you live here with us in Jena?' Schiller wrote. Wouldn't it be so much easier to talk, rather than to correspond? August Wilhelm replied immediately. It was true, he wrote, there was no better place in Germany for literary activity than Jena. He had commitments at the moment – he didn't mention Caroline – but he promised to make a 'pilgrimage' to Jena in the spring and then decide. Schiller was delighted. August Wilhelm Schlegel's deep knowledge of poetry and verse – so well illustrated with his latest *Horen* contribution, 'Letters on Poetry, Metre and Language' – would be a valued addition to Schiller's and Goethe's debates.

In terms of finance, Schiller could offer the well-paid commissions from *Horen* and then there was the *Allgemeine Literatur-Zeitung*, which would be glad to have him as a regular reviewer. Schiller was also sure that August Wilhelm Schlegel would be able to lecture at the

---

* When August Wilhelm Schlegel published his collected works some three decades later, he did acknowledge some of her writings – but by no means all – by marking them with an asterisk on the contents page. In his private archive he scribbled 'Carol.' next to the titles of the many reviews that Caroline had written.

university for some extra income. 'Once you're here,' Schiller assured him, 'everything will fall into place.'

~

After years of wrestling with abstract ideas and theoretical concepts, it was time to 'close up the philosophical shop for a while', Schiller told Goethe a few days after inviting August Wilhelm Schlegel to Jena. Poetry had begun to feature more on *Horen*'s pages, including several poems by Schiller himself. In the summer of 1795, just before August Wilhelm reached Braunschweig, Schiller had written his first poem in almost seven years. Tired and ill, he had found it difficult to put the words to paper but he was determined.

In the past Schiller had struggled to find a balance between his theoretical writings and his lyrical endeavours. His philosophy was too poetic, he feared, and whenever he tried to compose a poem, his analytical mind interfered. Now, inspired by his friendship with Goethe, he was reminded that poetry had always been closest to his heart. But he feared that he might have lost his ability to compose. He hadn't felt this drawn to poetry for years, but he worried that the 'muses suck a person dry'. It was exciting but also frightening. What if he wasn't any good any more? What if his mind had become too theoretical? One thing was certain, though, Schiller thought: 'I have always been and always will be a poetic oaf compared to Goethe.' When he shared his concerns, Wilhelm von Humboldt wrote from Berlin reassuring Schiller that his ability to unite poetic and philosophical genius was unique – hence the 'restless activity' that everybody who met the playwright noticed. Humboldt was looking forward to Schiller's transition back to poetry.

Goethe, meanwhile, increasingly relied on his friend's sharp editorial comments. After a particularly fruitful session, Goethe told Schiller, he had taken scissors to his novel *Wilhelm Meister* and cut all the passages that Schiller had marked. The comments were invaluable, Goethe said, 'I cannot express how much they advanced my work.' If only he had more time. In Weimar he was too busy to get any meaningful work done, but even in Jena there were always a few administrative tasks to deal with, ranging from negotiating the gardener's salary at the botanic garden to overseeing the construction of flood defences on the Saale River. No matter what the issue was – Fichte's ongoing problems with the university or the more trivial enquiry from the landlady of the Zum Schwarzen Bären, asking if she was allowed a billiard table – the world had a way of interrupting him. By now he had worked for so long on *Wilhelm Meister*, Goethe told a friend, that 'my novel is like a stocking someone knits away at so slowly that it gets grubby'.

Schiller and Goethe spent as much time together as possible. Schiller rarely went to Weimar, so it was Goethe who came frequently to Jena. 'Only the absolute silence here in Jena, and being near you,' Goethe told Schiller, allowed him to think and work. He adored 'this lovely crazy little corner of the world' – so much so that there were months when he spent more days in Jena than at home in Weimar. Charlotte Schiller, who had known Goethe since her childhood, noted how different he was in Jena. Anyone who met him in Weimar, she said, would believe him to be formal and aloof, but here in Jena he was carefree and jovial.

The stove in Goethe's room at the Old Castle was stoked at all times because he hated the cold. He sat in his armchair wearing a white wagoner's cap, a comfortable flannel jacket and warm soft trousers. His slippers were worn and his stockings drooped around his ankles. In the mornings he often went for a walk. The fresh air and vigorous exercise cleared his head and stimulated his digestion. Depending on Schiller's health and insomnia, Goethe sometimes met him for lunch but always visited him in the evenings. Schiller had recently moved from his cramped lodgings on the market square to a larger and more comfortable apartment next to the Old Castle at the eastern edge of town. Rather than the hustle and noise at the centre of Jena, Schiller now had spectacular views across the surrounding hills and Goethe was only a few steps away. At around five o'clock in the afternoon, Goethe would put on some proper clothes and walk the short distance to Schiller's, where he often stayed until midnight, sometimes longer.

One day, as he waited for his friend to join him, Goethe sat down at Schiller's desk to make some notes. As he wrote, Goethe felt increasingly nauseated and close to fainting. It took a while to realise that a disgusting smell was coming from one of the drawers. Gingerly, Goethe pulled it open and found it filled to the top with rotting apples. He stumbled up to open a window. When Charlotte Schiller found Goethe gulping fresh air and the desk drawer wide open, she explained that her husband so loved the smell that 'without it he couldn't live or work'. Although Charlotte loathed it, Schiller insisted on always having rotting apples nearby. Somehow the sweetly fermenting aroma stimulated his creativity.

During those long visits to Jena, Goethe missed Christiane and their young son August but stayed in contact with them by writing. He regularly dispatched letters filled with declarations of love and jokes but also with household matters – from instructions on how to sow vegetables to asking Christiane to send manuscripts or books that he had forgotten. How was August, he asked, was he eating and drinking enough? Had he finally put on some weight? He sent little presents for Christiane or fresh strawberries and peaches for August. In return Christiane sent him ham, sausages, smoked fish, drinking chocolate and large amounts of beer and wine to make him feel at home.

She also made it clear that she disliked his long absences and told him how much she missed him. She teased him about flirting – 'don't make eyes at so many women' – but she also got on with her own life. She cleaned the house, did the laundry, ironed curtains, looked after August and went to her beloved theatre. She threw dinner parties for her friends, drank champagne until two o'clock in the morning and told Goethe that she had danced through a pair of new shoes at a ball with a handsome young man.

Goethe cajoled and teased her back. 'My dear child, I can't say whether I'll come back in the next few days or not,' he wrote during a particularly long stay of several weeks. It all depended whether inspiration came. If not, he would return home, but if it did he would stay in Jena and continue writing. Love oozed from his letters. 'Before I go, my darling, I have to tell you something: that I love you and am thinking of you,' he wrote. Sometimes he missed her so much that he asked her to come to Jena for a couple of days with August. 'I'm sick of working so much,' he said, 'I simply must press you to my heart once again and tell you how much I love you.' When she visited, however, she couldn't stay with Goethe in his rooms in the Old Castle because they weren't married. Instead, Goethe reserved a room for her in the Zum Schwarzen Bären just across the road while August stayed with him.

He was a loving and patient father. In Jena, August often played with other children in the courtyard of the Old Castle. Once in a while, Goethe would tie a piece of cake on a thread and let it down from the window of his study to the children below. He enjoyed

seeing their excited faces and their laughter made him smile. No
matter how hard he worked, he could always spare a moment for
August. One autumn, Goethe carved a scary grimace into a pumpkin
and put a candle inside, which delighted and frightened the boy at
the same time. Visitors often found August sitting on Goethe's lap
as he was reading, and neighbours saw the great poet feeding the
pigeons with his son in the courtyard.

They went on long walks together, sometimes marching up the
hills or exploring the meandering paths in the Paradise along
the Saale, where they caught frogs. Goethe tried to instil his love for
nature into August. As he grew older, August began to add small
notes to his mother's letters, about his little garden plot in Weimar,
a butterfly he had caught, games he played with the neighbour's
sons, or thanking his father for sweets and fruits. In winter, when
the river and the ponds froze, Goethe put on his long brown coat,
his tricorne hat and his skates and took August along. Goethe loved
gliding across the ice and despite his bulging belly, he moved rather
fast and elegantly among the crowd.

Schiller too was a doting and indulgent father. Visitors sometimes
found him on all fours playing lion with his son Karl, allowing the
little boy to climb all over him. Unlike other parents at the time,
Goethe and Schiller didn't tuck their children away in a nursery
with a governess. They didn't wield sticks or beat in manners and
knowledge with fists or belts. They let their boys roam freely in
mind and in body. Their children were a part of their lives. The boys
joined their parents at the dinner table, Charlotte Schiller breastfed
her babies and sometimes August kept Goethe up at night.

Both fathers followed the new approaches to childhood propounded
by the French philosopher Jean-Jacques Rousseau, who had turned
against the religious doctrine that children were born with original
sin. Instead, Rousseau insisted children were essentially good by
nature. 'Love childhood. Look with friendly eyes on its games, its
pleasures, its amiable dispositions,' he had written in his famous novel
Emile, or On Education in 1762, in which he told parents to give
children (by which he meant boys) 'well-regulated liberty'. Education
should be about protecting the original innocence of children. Parents
should feed their children's natural curiosity and let them learn
through discovery and play. Education should be based on freedom
and not on learning by rod and rote.

Two-year-old Karl Schiller – the 'Golden Boy', as his father called him – was a little wild, racing through the apartment with a whip in his hand and once in a while lashing out at unsuspecting visitors. Goethe never minded. He picked up the boy, ruffled his curls and jokingly scolded him. August was five years older but the boys liked each other and played together. 'August is looking forward to seeing Karl,' Goethe would write.

When Goethe's lover, Christiane, was expecting another child in late 1795, Schiller hoped it would be a girl for Karl to marry, so that he and Goethe would be united by a real family bond. When the baby was born and it was another boy, Goethe quipped that it was now up to Schiller to produce a girl in order to bring the families together. But then tragedy hit. Two weeks later the baby was dead, the third child the couple had lost in four years. Goethe rarely talked about his grief, not even to close friends, but he suffered deeply. Two years earlier, when his baby daughter had died only days after her birth, he had collapsed on the floor and lain there weeping for hours. The death of his baby son devastated him yet again, but he tried his best to keep himself occupied with work – and with six-year-old August.

At the end of 1795, only a few weeks after the infant's death, Goethe and Schiller began working together on their so-called *Xenien** – short satirical couplets in which they attacked their critics. Their humour and bite were the best possible distraction, and Goethe threw himself into the work. Over the next few months, the two men composed almost one thousand *Xenien*, mixing and combining their lines and words so much that no one could tell any more who had written what. And this strategy of concealed authorship allowed them to aim sharper and hit harder.

The *Xenien*, Schiller said, were their naughty and wild bastard children. As they composed them, they laughed so much that Schiller's neighbours could hear them. When they were particularly satisfied with their lines, they stamped their feet so loudly that the whole house noticed. Goethe 'walked around with a flyswatter', Caroline later joked, 'and every slap of it produced an epigram'. The *Xenien* pushed away the dark clouds and brought some sun and joy – at

---

* *Xenien* was a reference to *Xenia*, a collection of epigrams by the Roman poet Martial, which translates as 'gifts for the host' from the ancient Greek.

least to their authors. After every composing session, the two men emerged from Schiller's study with big smiles on their faces.

Of course Fichte was teased with several couplets about his Ich-philosophy:

> *I am I, and I posit myself, and when I posit myself*
> *As unposited – great! I thereby add a non-I.*

And they dedicated dozens of *Xenien* to *Deutschland*'s editor Friedrich Reichardt – the journalist who had reviewed *Horen* so unfavourably. 'Here are another few arrows to pierce our colleague's side with,' Schiller told Goethe as he sent another batch. This one described Reichardt as a deadly scorpion:

> *But here fluttering and flattering comes a nasty insect, from*
> *G—b—n,**
> *If you don't flee fast enough you are sure to feel his sting.*

Everybody talked about the *Xenien*. Meanwhile, Schiller had decided to publish yet another journal, as if all the problems of editing *Horen* were not enough. This *Musen-Almanach* (*Almanac of the Muses*) was to be less scholarly, more accessible, and therefore, it was hoped, more profitable. The *Xenien* would be perfect for the new journal, which was soon nicknamed 'Almanac of the Furies'. It sold out immediately.

Goethe and Schiller continued to work together on other projects too. There was *Wilhelm Meister*, of course, but Schiller was also adapting one of Goethe's plays for a performance at the theatre in Weimar. 'To a certain extent the piece is both Goethe's work and mine,' he said. By the beginning of 1796, Schiller had fully embraced his new interest in lyrical work. 'This year', he told Wilhelm von Humboldt, 'I'm going to devote myself entirely to poetry.'

~

In May 1796, six months after Schiller's initial invitation, August Wilhelm Schlegel made an exploratory trip to Jena to meet him for the first time in person. He spent several weeks in the small university town and enjoyed every minute. He saw Schiller as well as Goethe, who had been in Jena since the end of April. He brought with him the recently completed *Romeo and Juliet* translation, as well

---

* 'G—b—n' is Giebichenstein, the town where Reichardt lived.

as a story that Caroline had written.* August Wilhelm left Caroline's manuscript with Schiller and read *Romeo and Juliet* in its entirety to Goethe. The older poet thoroughly approved.

Goethe was also reminded that he had met Caroline four years previously in Mainz, at the house of the explorer and revolutionary Georg Forster. Maybe it was August Wilhelm's connection to Caroline that brought up the subject of revolutions, or maybe the general political landscape – whichever it was, Goethe became a little concerned that August Wilhelm Schlegel showed dangerous 'democratic tendencies'. But he liked the twenty-eight-year-old writer's bright mind and studious approach. August Wilhelm's presence, Goethe wrote to Wilhelm von Humboldt, made their discussions even more entertaining and spirited. For his part, August Wilhelm couldn't believe that he was among the literary titans of his age. 'You are now', his oldest brother Moritz wrote, 'at the centre of the great German literary world.' There was no better place.

The decision was quickly made. On 27 June 1796, five weeks after his arrival, August Wilhelm went to Weimar for the day for a final meeting with Goethe, who had returned home after a six-week stay in Jena. On his way back to Jena, August Wilhelm got soaked in a torrential downpour, but found he couldn't have cared less. His future would be here – with Caroline – and it would begin soon. On 29 June he left Jena for Braunschweig. Two days later, on 1 July 1796, August Wilhelm married Caroline.

In rescuing Caroline from social oblivion, August Wilhelm Schlegel gained an indispensable collaborator. The arrangement suited them both. 'His literary fame dates from that moment,' one of Caroline's old childhood friends remarked. On 8 July, a week after the wedding, August Wilhelm and Caroline arrived in Jena – and the circle that Goethe called the 'new generation' was almost complete.

---

* Nothing more is known about Caroline's story or novella. Schiller often published contributions from female writers anonymously in one of the journals he was involved in – he might have done the same with Caroline's piece.

'Philosophy is originally a feeling'
Summer 1796: Novalis in Love

O N 8 JULY 1796, the same day that Caroline and August Wilhelm Schlegel arrived in Jena, Doctor Johann Christian Stark and two of his colleagues rushed to a small house just beyond the old town walls to conduct a dangerous surgery. Dr Stark never told his patients the exact day or time of their operations. In the past, he had found that the days which patients spent thinking about an upcoming procedure only induced anxiety and dread – and that was not helpful for them or for him. Far better to surprise them.

In preparing the patient's room, Dr Stark and his team would have covered the bed with sheets and laid out their instruments: differently shaped scalpels, metal clamps to pull back skin and muscles, syringes, lancets to open veins and pierce abscesses, metal tubes for draining purulent liquids; beside them were bandages, lint, thread for ligatures and an assortment of straight and curved needles to tie blood vessels and stitch wounds. Nothing was sterilised because no one knew that germs were the source of infection.

Their patient was fourteen-year-old Sophie von Kühn. She had travelled with her family and governess to Jena from Grüningen, some forty miles to the north-west. Sophie had been ill for the past year, suffering from a liver infection and fevers. She had an abscess on her liver and a lump on her hip. She was in great pain. Common treatments for inflammatory fevers included blood-letting, oil poultices, blistering and potions made of minerals and herbs that induced sweating or vomiting – or both. In some cases, Dr Stark also recommended placing five or six leeches in the rectum, followed by an enema. Eighteenth-century medicine was a torturous round of 'cleansing techniques' to purify the body that also involved laxatives, purgatives and cupping glasses. Over the past year Sophie had endured the full weaponry of her doctor's medical chest in Grüningen but by the summer of 1796 he had run out of treatments and it was decided that surgery in Jena was the only remedy.

Dr Stark was the best in the region. He was the duke's physician as well as Goethe's and Schiller's – and he had inoculated their sons August and Karl against smallpox. He taught medicine at the university, ran a maternity hospital in Jena and had published books and articles. Yet, Sophie's surgery was extremely dangerous and the young girl must have been terrified. With no anaesthetics, the only relief a doctor could administer at the time was laudanum or alcohol – wine, brandy, rum or so on – which was perhaps useful for smaller procedures but of no real help during a major operation.

On the day of the surgery, Sophie swallowed whatever potion Dr Stark had prepared and then lay down. She would have been fully dressed but with her skirts hitched up. Doctors always wore normal street clothes – breeches, waistcoat, jacket, powdered wig – with an apron to protect them from blood, pus and other bodily liquids. Dr Stark often placed a thin cloth over the patient's face so that they wouldn't see the instruments and the blood. It was time to begin.

As the scalpel sliced through Sophie's white skin and then through the thin layer of fat into the muscle, Dr Stark's assistants had to hold down the patient with all their might. With Sophie fully conscious, Dr Stark had to work fast. Flaps of skin were pulled back, scalpels extracted the lump on the hip and blood vessels were tied off. Sophie experienced the most excruciating pain, but she did so with the endurance of a fighter, her governess thought, as she watched the gruesome spectacle. Dr Stark also inserted a metal tube into the abscess on the liver to drain the liquid, but there was so much that it continued to flow for what seemed an eternity. It was simply unimaginable 'how much stuff came out of the wound', the governess observed as she saw her beloved Sophie bleeding and oozing. The wound continued to seep so much that the bandages had to be changed constantly and even the usually confident Stark was uncertain if his young patient would recover.

That evening the governess wrote a letter to Sophie's fiancé, Novalis, urging him to come to Jena immediately. No one had told him about the procedure so as not to worry him. When he received the letter, Novalis saddled his horse and rode as fast as he could the forty miles from Dürrenberg where he worked at the salt mines, to sit at Sophie's bedside. When he walked into the sickroom he was surprised to see his fiancée cheerful and composed despite the agonising pain, even though the doctor warned him that she might not survive. That was an outcome Novalis was not prepared to accept. They had too many plans.

~

Novalis was a twenty-four-year-old poet and writer whose real name was Friedrich von Hardenberg.* Born into an ancient family of land-rich but cash-poor Saxon aristocrats, Novalis was one of eleven siblings. He had been a sickly child who had almost died of dysentery at the age of nine. Having spent months in bed fighting for his life, he had somehow emerged stronger and more determined. Previously a dreamy and almost backward-seeming boy, he had been transformed by his illness, becoming lively, impatient and forever curious. He learned Latin and Greek, loved poems and entertained his younger brothers and sisters by inventing fairy tales.

In 1790, aged eighteen, Novalis had enrolled at the University of Jena where he had fallen under the spell of Schiller who was his professor. Instead of drinking and duels – 'foolish, crazy acts', as Novalis described his early student excesses – Schiller persuaded the wild and impressionable young man to take his studies more seriously. Like so many other young men, Novalis had been enraptured by *The Robbers* and Schiller had been the hero of his youth. Schiller was, Novalis said, 'worth more than a million ordinary people'. After Jena, Novalis had studied and partied in Leipzig, where he had befriended August Wilhelm Schlegel's younger brother Friedrich. Since then he had calmed down a little and was now working alongside his cantankerous father at the salt mines, which were scattered across the Saxon states. The family lived in Weißenfels, a town some thirty miles to the north-east of Jena. And although Novalis had to work to make a living, he had the confidence that came with lineage and privilege.

Novalis was tall, lean and handsome in an almost girlish way, with

---

* 'De Novali' was the Latinised ancestral name of a twelfth-century branch of Friedrich von Hardenberg's family. It meant 'land that was ploughed for the first time' or 'from the cleared land'. As the Jena Set was breaking new ground, Novalis thought that the pseudonym was 'not entirely inappropriate'. For the sake of consistency, Friedrich von Hardenberg will be Novalis throughout this book.

a delicate face and lips. His skin was almost translucent and he wore his light brown hair long. His clothes were plain but his eyes, friends said, had an almost ethereal blaze that kept them all captivated. He talked fast, jumping from one subject to the next without taking a breath. A ravenous reader, he could absorb a book in a quarter of the time it took his friends, and then recite its contents months later. His voice was melodic, one friend said, with a natural grace and lightness. Never haughty or arrogant, Novalis was animated by an almost childish cheerfulness.

He regarded the ordinary with wonder, and the unusual with acceptance. He slept little and worked hard. Novalis claimed never to be bored and whatever he studied or learned, he did so with enthusiasm – be it studying philosophical books, reading poetry or clerking with a magistrate and tax collector to learn about administration and management in preparation for work at the family-run salt mines. Everybody agreed that there was something magical, intense and almost hypnotic about him. Women and men alike fell for him. He 'electrified me', one woman said, and another admirer admitted that 'few people in my entire life have left such a deep impression'.

In the past few years, Novalis had regularly made the five-hour ride from the family home in Weißenfels to Jena. He remained devoted to Schiller but had also met Fichte the previous year. Having seen 'the first electric sparks to burst from this fiery head', as Novalis later said, he embarked on an intense study of Fichte's Ich-philosophy in the winter of 1795/6. Reading with pen in hand, he scribbled in his notebooks, digging deep into Fichte's writings, sometimes despairing over the 'dreadful loops of abstraction'. Nonetheless, he battled on, filling more and more pages. Fichte may not have been the most accomplished player of his own instrument, Novalis concluded – others might be better at 'fichticising than Fichte himself' – but he had invented a completely new way of thinking. For Novalis, Fichte was a second Copernicus, 'the one who woke me up'.

Novalis wrote his notes in fits and starts, sometimes concentrating for long periods on nothing but Fichte's philosophy, sometimes stealing a short hour at night after a long day at work. In the course of these studies he filled five hundred pages with his notes – a long dialogue with Fichte in which Novalis asked, queried, excerpted, refuted, doubted and answered. Divided into almost seven hundred numbered sections, some of these notes were extensive philosophical discourses on subjects raised by Fichte's *Wissenschaftslehre*, while others represented just a kernel of an idea or a thought, or were simple lists of questions or reminders to himself. Many pages elaborated complex thought processes and showed a profound philosophical understanding; other notes acted as self-help maxims, such as 'practise slowness', 'if one only wills, then one can' or 'where do I exit, where do I go, and how do I proceed?' Some sections were several pages long, others just a line or two but many exhibited a fierce engagement with Fichte's ideas. His studies helped Novalis to understand himself and his place in the universe. 'From where do I borrow my concepts?' he asked himself. 'Necessarily I – necessarily from myself. I am for myself the ground of all thoughts.'

Fichte's coronation of the Ich inspired Novalis to learn about himself. 'Fichtean philosophy', Novalis jotted down, 'is a call to self-activity', but he also thought that the very foundation of the philosopher's argument was circular. If the Ich posits itself and with this act creates the non-Ich, Novalis asked, where did the original Ich come from? Neither reality nor the external world, Novalis came to believe, could have been constructed by the Ich but had to be already there. Though unknowable, we could sense it. 'Philosophy', he said, 'is originally a feeling.'

Over this year of reading and studying Novalis came to admire Fichte, but he also had reservations. Why, for example, Novalis asked, had the great philosopher ignored 'love', the most important of all topics? 'Freedom and love are one,' Novalis insisted. A child was love made visible – the living proof of the bond between two people, he said – and humanity was the expression of the love between nature and the mind.

Though Fichte's Ich was powerful and free, Novalis's criticism was that it remained separate from the non-Ich. With his self-positing Ich, Fichte might have defined a singular starting point, but it had not led to a unified world. Novalis would move away from Fichte's cold and alienating non-Ich by adding love to the equation. 'Love', he wrote, was a 'synthesising force'. Ultimately, for Novalis, that meant that Fichte's non-Ich became human – it became a 'You'. The theory of love was the highest science according to Novalis.

~

Love in his own life was very much on Novalis's mind during this time. 'The sciences and love fill my entire soul,' he admitted. Novalis had met his fiancée Sophie eighteen months earlier at the end of 1794, when she had only been twelve. Also from an aristocratic Saxon family, Sophie had grown up in a warm, loud and open-minded home that was quite unlike his own. Sophie's father may have been coarse at times, but he was also kind and affectionate. Instead of a prayer, he began meals with the toast 'To what we love'. Novalis's father, by contrast, was a former soldier and now devout Moravian who regarded religion not as a choice but as a command-ment, as the prerequisite for life. His religious instructions consisted of shouting loudly at family and servants.

Where Novalis's father was constantly on his knees praying and prohibiting any social gatherings at Weißenfels, Sophie's family loved to drink and sing while constantly teasing each other. They were good-humoured and often played cards after breakfast, lunch and dinner. Unconventional and open-minded, they also embraced the ideas of the French Revolution, something that Novalis's father rejected entirely. Revolution, reform and the Enlightenment were topics that Novalis avoided at home. The differences between father and son could not have been more obvious. The father's 'blind religious zeal and furious hostility to anything called "reform"', Novalis's younger brother observed, had created a deep chasm between them. By contrast, Novalis felt at home among Sophie's noisy and caring family. And Sophie was the centre of it all. Within the first fifteen minutes of meeting her, Novalis told his brother, his life changed. Though she was only a child, Novalis envisaged her as his wife. Wild and passionate as he had been, he suddenly wanted to be married.

None of Sophie's letters to Novalis survive, but judging from a short diary and the few sentences she added to her family's notes to him, she was a typical adolescent girl. Her spelling was erratic and phonetic, her topics the weather or family news, and her diary consisted of two-line entries that endlessly repeated sentences such as 'Again nothing happened' or listing Novalis's visits, with his name spelled in multiple ways. She liked music, food and her sisters, but despite her age she stood up to Novalis. She played him like a game of cards, his brother said. One minute she lifted his spirits, and the next she could crush him – all the while walking around the room

innocently whistling a little tune. 'I think about you too,' she told
Novalis, adding, 'when I remember to.'

None of this mattered to Novalis. He fell in love easily, and over
the past couple of years he had flirted with several young women.
The pages of his diary reveal a man wrestling with bodily urges as
he doggedly records his sexual arousal and masturbation. One day
he noted 'sensual again this morning', a few days later 'lewdness
raged from morning into the afternoon', two days later 'much lewdness', less than a week later 'took lewdness a little too far' to finally
'this morning's lewd phantasy caused an explosion in the afternoon'.
He praised himself for not giving in to his desires, 'I was rather good
today.' As an adolescent, he had written erotic poems in which rosy-
cheeked and blushing young girls played naked in streams, their
breasts mere buds.

> *We kiss and kiss those lovely mouths*
> *But only in our poems*
> *And then those rosy little breasts*
> *In violet-sweet dreams.*

Or:

> *Rosy silk wreathed her seething little body and her blushing*
> *Breasts shyly peeked out from their tight prison.*

Only a few months before meeting Sophie, Novalis and his younger
brother Karl had spent a summer in Wittenberg in Saxony – weeks
that consisted of singing, drinking, dancing and flirting. Instead of
seeing the sights of the town where Martin Luther had begun the
Protestant Reformation by posting his 'Ninety-five Theses' to the
door of Castle Church, the brothers 'preferred inspecting the pretty
girls and studying the experimental physics of their breasts and
physiques', Novalis boasted. But he had been glad when that summer
of temptations ended – how could he control himself surrounded
by women who were willing to be seduced? It was best to put some
distance between him and them. 'In the end I avoided all tête-à-
têtes,' Novalis had told his other brother, 'they were too tempting.'
Even on the day before he met Sophie, Novalis had written a letter
to a friend describing the 'Devil of Lewdness' who had aroused him
even in the old smoky office where he worked as a clerk.

At first everybody assumed that Novalis's infatuation with Sophie would peter out, but his feelings for her remained strong. Maybe only a girl as young and as innocent as Sophie could control Novalis's sexual urges? She was simply too young to be seductive. Four months after their first meeting, Sophie agreed to marry Novalis. They became engaged in March 1795, just days before her thirteenth birthday, but had kept the arrangement secret for more than a year. When his parents found out, they had been reluctant at first but had finally accepted the connection with such a young girl. After all, to be engaged this early wasn't unusual in aristocratic circles, and in any event the wedding would have to wait a few years until Sophie was older.

But then she fell ill.

~

On the day of Sophie's gruesome operation, Novalis received a letter from his old university friend Friedrich Schlegel. He informed Novalis that he was moving from Dresden to Jena, where he would join his brother August Wilhelm and sister-in-law Caroline. With Weißenfels along the route, it would be easy to meet up, Friedrich Schlegel suggested. It had been three years since they had seen each other and Friedrich's plans would permit Novalis to visit Sophie in Jena before. Come, Novalis said, and stay 'as long as you like'. Two weeks later, Friedrich Schlegel dispatched his large suitcase and set out on foot. With mounting debts, he had decided to take the stagecoach only as far as Leipzig and then walk the last twenty-five miles to Weißenfels. He was looking forward to seeing Novalis.

When they had first met in Leipzig in 1792, they had liked each other immediately. Friedrich Schlegel and Novalis made a perfect team. They debated, fought and argued constantly, often accusing each other of arrogance and pride, and then promptly praising each other's genius. Novalis complained that Friedrich was vain, easily offended and maliciously critical, and Friedrich told his friend that he was capricious, mercurial and unreliable. They urged each other to be consistent, considerate and reasonable – only to stumble into love affairs, offend each other or lose themselves in poetry. They fell out, threatened to duel and then made up again. Although only seven weeks older, the impulsive Friedrich took on the unlikely role of mentor to the equally energetic Novalis.

In a long letter to his brother August Wilhelm, Friedrich had described his new friend as having the potential to become a great poet. Novalis was still too distracted, too erratic and too immature, but his perception was original and sensuous, Friedrich said, 'he can do anything and everything – but might end up doing nothing'. Novalis talked more and faster than anyone else, with passion and with fire. And this fire was everywhere, Friedrich said – in Novalis's eyes, in his voice and in his face. Friedrich Schlegel was enthralled, writing that 'it is a sensual pleasure to dwell in your heart'. In turn, Novalis admired his friend's unconventional attitude and sharp mind. 'You introduced me to Heaven and Hell,' Novalis told him, 'through you I tasted of the Tree of Knowledge.' Friedrich was his 'high priest', and Novalis was Friedrich's 'prophet'.

But there were differences. Where Friedrich had a tendency to feel sorry for himself, Novalis was light-hearted and optimistic. While Friedrich refused even to think about a career, Novalis had spent eighteen months with a magistrate and tax collector as preparation for managing the salt mines with his father. Where Friedrich had no desire to 'shackle myself to a bourgeois yoke', Novalis longed for a 'wedding night, marriage and heirs'.

~

At the end of July 1796, when Novalis was returning from a visit to Sophie in Jena, he met Friedrich Schlegel on the road. Novalis was hopeful about Sophie's prospects of recovery, and he was looking forward to the next few days in Weißenfels with Friedrich. Like Jena, Weißenfels was situated on the Saale River and with four thousand inhabitants it was about the same size – but the two towns couldn't have been more different. Weißenfels' heyday was over. An imposing early baroque castle – where an eight-year-old Georg Friedrich Händel had once played the organ almost exactly a century earlier – towered over the town, but had long been abandoned. There was no university, and no famous philosophers or poets walked along the narrow streets. For Friedrich Schlegel, who had travelled from the bustling cities Dresden and Leipzig, it must have felt decidedly provincial.

Although Novalis came from an ancient aristocratic family, their home was no great estate with vast lands. As Friedrich Schlegel walked down Weißenfels' Klostergasse, he would have seen a plain late seventeenth-century three-storey house with no superfluous decoration. Behind it were large outhouses set around a courtyard and a small ornamental garden with a pretty stucco pavilion with windows on three sides. It was always busy here. Servants went up and down the stairs, clerks employed at the salt mines worked in offices on the ground floor, and tradesmen came and went delivering goods. Both of Novalis's parents were still alive and it could feel crowded with his ten siblings, ranging from two to twenty-five years in age, at home.

Novalis had changed since their wild student days in Leipzig. 'I'm not in such a hurry any more,' he told Friedrich, 'I've learned how to go slow.' Slow or not, the words still came gushing out. Novalis couldn't stop talking. His favourite subject, Novalis told Friedrich, had the same name as his bride. 'Sophie is her name – Philo*sophie* is the soul of my life and the key to my innermost self.' For Novalis philosophy was not an academic subject but a path into himself. We're only going to make sense of the world when we understand ourselves and vice versa, Novalis would later say, 'for we and it are integrated *halves*'. We are part of the system, he insisted, and we can 'catch sight of ourselves *as an element* in the system'.

Both Novalis and Friedrich Schlegel developed Fichte's philosophy into a more dynamic system. Instead of Fichte's opposing Ich and non-Ich, Novalis described a 'back and forth movement' in which the subjective becomes the objective, the spiritual becomes the physical, the particular becomes the general and vice versa. Philosophy had to be contradictory, Friedrich Schlegel said. Every result, every thought, every conclusion was immediately questioned and prodded. They wanted to see-saw until they were dizzy.

There was a circular feeling to Fichte's philosophy. His *Wissenschaftslehre* was based on the fundamental idea that the self observed itself as it reflected itself as a thinking self. Theoretically, though, once the self had become completely conscious of itself, the process of self-reflection was also complete. At this point Novalis and Friedrich Schlegel disagreed with Fichte, because for them philosophy was a never-ending process of thinking about thinking itself. It was an infinite reflection upon self-reflection. And because Novalis believed that we were the same as the world, that thinking ping-ponged perpetually between self-reflection and reflection upon the universe. Friedrich and Novalis were spinning into an ever greater and faster vortex that pulled the self, the world, poetry and everything else into its whirling centre.

∽

Talking with Novalis about philosophy, Sophie and love reminded Friedrich Schlegel of his own feelings. While at Weißenfels, he sent a letter to his sister-in-law Caroline, who had just arrived in Jena, recalling how they had first met, in 1793, three years earlier to the day, shortly after Caroline's release from prison in the small village near Leipzig. 'Imagine', Friedrich wrote, 'that I'm standing before you, silently thanking you for everything you've done for me and to me.' She had made him, or at least some part of him, and 'the fact that I'm like that, I owe in part to you'. No matter that Caroline had carried another man's child and was loved by his older brother, Friedrich Schlegel fell for her.

In those days, he had often come from Leipzig to see her, spending hours discussing politics, poetry, Goethe, and strong female figures in ancient mythologies. Caroline read to him and suggested books. Almost nine years his senior, she took the lead. 'Very early on, I felt the superiority of her mind over mine,' Friedrich recalled. It was as if Caroline recalibrated and channelled Friedrich Schlegel's restless energy. As they talked about the poets of ancient Greece and Rome, he began to write essays, which she edited. Her opinions about poetry, he had told his brother August Wilhelm, were new and fascinating, as was her fervent support for the French Revolution. 'She made me a better person,' Friedrich Schlegel admitted.

Until he met Caroline, he had not really been interested in the momentous upheaval that was unfolding in France. Caroline, who had witnessed the birth of the short-lived Mainz Republic, opened his mind. What happened in France, Friedrich Schlegel now said, were the first movements of the consciousness of the greater Ich – that of a nation. This didn't mean that Friedrich Schlegel was going to take to the streets, but the French Revolution had proved that words were as important as action. 'You have not just to carry out revolutions,' he wrote, 'you have to speak them too.'

At first, August Wilhelm had been concerned about Caroline's political influence on his younger brother, but soon he too was convinced by her. August Wilhelm was now 'also thinking somewhat differently about my friends, the republicans', Caroline had told Friedrich shortly after his brother arrived in Braunschweig. Of the friends who would soon be in Jena, only Caroline had experienced the Revolution in person, but they all encountered the political power of words by reading essays, treatises and newspapers. 'A word of command set armies in motion,' Novalis would soon write, 'the word freedom.'

Friedrich Schlegel was in awe of Caroline. She was thrilling, exciting and witty. He had been with her when her baby boy was born, pacing the courtyard outside like an expectant father, hearing her cries as she went through labour. Her love would be the holiest of his possessions, he said. Besotted, he nonetheless deferred to his brother's prior friendship and suppressed his feelings, but 'his passion raged, burned and gnawed deep inside him'. August Wilhelm knew nothing.

After a week in Weißenfels, Friedrich bid his goodbyes to Novalis and walked the thirty miles to Jena. As he neared the town which was to become his new home, he became increasingly worried. Only a few days previously, the latest issue of the pro-French journal *Deutschland* had been delivered to its subscribers. Within was a critical review of Schiller's new magazine *Musen-Almanach*, written by none other than Friedrich Schlegel. Unlike other reviewers, who preferred to criticise in anonymity, Friedrich had naïvely added his name. But a few days before leaving Dresden, he had suddenly been struck by the thought that Schiller might be annoyed. Shortly before his departure, Friedrich had therefore begged Christian Gottfried Körner, one of Schiller's closest friends, to plead on his behalf – which Körner dutifully did. Friedrich had also asked his brother in Jena to intercede, but he still had no idea how the famously sensitive Schiller might react.

6

'Our splendid circle'
Summer–Winter 1796: The Schlegels Arrive

WITHIN DAYS OF their arrival in Jena on 8 July 1796, August
Wilhelm and Caroline Schlegel had met everybody important.
Always immaculately dressed, they made a handsome couple. August
Wilhelm was meticulous not only in his work and his writing but
also in his clothes. Unlike his brother Friedrich, who had never been
interested in what he wore or even in cleanliness, August Wilhelm
invariably looked perfectly groomed with his coat brushed, his waistcoat straightened and tugged into place and a white silk tie knotted
around his neck. Yet, for all his propriety, he wore his curly hair short
and unpowdered – the younger generation's signal of their republican
sympathies – while most men still had their hair tied in a pigtail.

A gifted seamstress, Caroline made most of her clothes and hats
herself, often copying the latest French fashion by wearing floating
muslin dresses that were loosely draped across the breast and tied
with a silk belt just below her chest. Fortunately, neighbouring
Weimar was home to the popular *Journal for Luxury and Fashions*,
one of the world's first fashion magazines. The monthly issues
discussed dresses, hats and hairstyles as well as publishing coloured
engravings, which Caroline could use as patterns.

Fashion had changed radically during Caroline's adult years. As a
young woman in Göttingen she had worn tight corsets that held in
the waist and full skirts with wide petticoats. Since then necklines
had been lowered, waistlines had moved up and thin cotton dresses
caressed rather than imprisoned the body. These were designs inspired
by the draped dresses of classical antiquity, which Caroline would
have liked for their comfort and beauty but also for their associations
with the birthplace of democracy. Silk or woollen shawls kept exposed
flesh warm, feathers bounced in tumbling hair and tightly fitted
sleeves revealed shapely arms. Most dresses were white, sometimes a
delicate light yellow or rose but nothing too bright or loud. A few

embroidered edges, or exquisitely tied ribbons or belts, added elements of understated elegance and embellishment.

As much as she cared about her appearance, Caroline was also proud of her education. She was intelligent, erudite and charming, and she knew it. Confident in her opinions on literature, art and politics, her delivery was never dry and academic. She moved effort-lessly from one topic to the next, weaving the occasional frivolous anecdote into her literary insights. Caroline exhibited a 'bold mixture of such different qualities', Friedrich Schlegel said – she could be everything from a gentle wife to a loving mother, a flirtatious lover to a sage collaborator. Men fell easily for her. 'One look is all it takes,' Friedrich had said after meeting her.

Another admirer declared that Caroline had captivated him within fifteen minutes, but he also admitted that he wouldn't have survived an intellectual duel with her. Caroline had no interest in playing the demure and domestic wife and admitted 'a firm, almost instinctive need for independence'. It was an attitude that made her unpopular with other women throughout her life.

The day after their arrival, Caroline and August Wilhelm visited the Schillers. Charlotte Schiller was heavily pregnant, but although the baby was expected any day, she helped them find a maid and lent them tea, which they had forgotten to pack in Braunschweig. Preoccupied with the impending birth, Schiller still found time to give a warm welcome to Caroline and August Wilhelm. Two days later, as they were walking across town on a second visit, someone told them that the Schillers' baby had been born just fifteen minutes previously. News travelled quickly in Jena. Nonetheless, Schiller came downstairs for a brief chat outside his front door, before rushing back to his wife and new-born son.

Schiller was glad that August Wilhelm was finally in Jena and was impressed by Caroline. He enjoyed her company, as he wrote to Wilhelm von Humboldt a few days later, although only time would tell if there was 'some kind of thorn beneath the rose'. Goethe had not been in town but was looking forward to seeing the Schlegels. A week after their arrival, Goethe rode from Weimar to Jena. He discussed the manuscript of the eighth and final part of *Wilhelm Meister* with Schiller, and the next day he walked to the small garden villa that August Wilhelm and Caroline were renting just south of the old town walls.

Goethe had first met Caroline in 1783 at her father's house in Göttingen and then again in Mainz in 1792, a year before her imprisonment. But when the maidservant announced the arrival of the famous poet, Caroline hardly recognised him because he had gained so much weight. It was a hot summer day and Caroline was glad she hadn't taken off her stockings or wasn't just wearing her underdress, as she often did when the temperature rose.

The visit delighted her. They reminisced about the times when they had been so careless and merry. Possibly feeling a little guilty, Goethe didn't tell her that he had brushed off a request to help her in 1793, when she had been incarcerated in Königstein. One of the many letters that Caroline, August Wilhelm and her family had written during that time had landed in the hands of an old friend of Goethe's, who then forwarded the plea to him. It had reached Goethe on the battlefield during the bombardment of Mainz, just when his mood was at its lowest. With no desire to help French sympathisers, Goethe had replied that the prisoners were under the jurisdiction of the ruler of the Electorate of Mainz – he couldn't do anything for them. Caroline knew none of this and was thrilled by his attention. When he left, he 'threatened' to call at their house often on his daily walks along the Saale.

~

Over the next few weeks August Wilhelm and Caroline swept through Jena's parlours, meeting writers, professors and some of the students. There was the Professors' Club and the concerts at the Zur Rose tavern, and with no theatre in Jena, they were invited to take part in the amateur plays that were organised in private homes. They were introduced to Fichte – 'a short, stocky man with fiery eyes, very care-lessly dressed', Caroline observed – who had just named his new-born son Immanuel after his philosophical hero. After Fichte's fight with Schiller over his contribution to *Horen*, their relationship had cooled, and they now avoided each other – which in such a small town was possible only because Schiller so rarely left home. Fichte himself had resumed his lectures after a few months in Oßmannstedt the previous summer, and 'armies of young believers' continued to fill his auditorium.

Ten days after Caroline and August Wilhelm had moved to Jena, around three hundred students marched across town from the univer-sity to Fichte's house – this time not to throw stones through the windows but to serenade their professor, congratulating him on the birth of his son. When Fichte stepped outside to greet them, he was so touched that his voice broke several times. It was all a little too much. To his and everybody else's surprise Johanne, who was in her early forties, had given birth to a healthy boy and here were his students singing for him. What a difference a year could make.

August Wilhelm and Caroline also regularly saw Schiller but he didn't feel well. Editing *Horen* and *Musen-Almanach* took up much of his time, but it wasn't just work. His youngest sister had died earlier in the year, another sister and his father were seriously ill, and he was nervous about the French military advances. With the French in Italy and two other French armies advancing through Germany, everybody seemed to be holding their breath.

People in Jena 'trembled', Caroline wrote to Luise Gotter shortly after their arrival. The war put those who had embraced the ideals of the French Revolution in an awkward position. Should they support a war that threatened their own states or welcome the French? Should they be patriots and fight for their countries or hope the French would bring the Revolution to them? 'For whom do you fight, brave German people?' one German writer asked. 'For the vulgar brood of princes and nobles?'

It had been easy to admire the French and their revolution from afar; other German states had not fared so well as the Duchy of Saxe-Weimar. Armies had moved through villages and cities, leaving a path of destruction and hunger as they plundered local populations and burned houses. Until now the battles had seemed far enough away, but when neighbouring Saxony had decided to fight along with the Austrians against the French, the allied Duchy of Saxe-Weimar had followed. In May 1796, Duke Carl August's green-and-yellow uniformed infantry had marched the 250 miles to fight near Trier and Mainz. But the French army continued to gather strength, and within weeks their troops had crossed the Rhine. In mid-July they occupied Stuttgart in the Duchy of Württemberg where Schiller's parents lived.* Schiller feared for their lives.

---

* Schiller's parents lived in the grounds of the Duke of Württemberg's castle Solitude, just a few miles north-east of Stuttgart. Schiller's father was the superintendent of the gardens, orchards and forests. In July 1796, when the French came, the castle was only being defended by young inexperienced soldiers and injured veterans.

From Weimar, Goethe dispatched any news he could get through his government channels to his friend in Jena, but it was weeks before Schiller finally received a letter from his sister. French soldiers had banged loudly against their door, she wrote, and then barged in, demanding food and clothes. The soldiers stuffed shirts, shoes, silver spoons and money into their bags and tore the shawls from the women's shoulders. Reports of local women having been raped by French soldiers terrified Schiller's sister. One day the Schillers even hid in a cave in a nearby forest. They were safe for now but the situation remained precarious. 'Political matters, which I so like to avoid,' Schiller wrote to Goethe, 'have a way of coming back home to roost eventually.' With the enemy only some two hundred miles away, Schiller feared that the French could reach Jena in a matter of weeks. Even the printing of *Horen* was delayed by the war.

In July the French also reached Frankfurt, where Goethe's mother lived. An unperturbed sixty-five-year-old Frau Goethe told her worried son that she was neither afraid of the French nor going to leave the city. It was only when the bombardment started and houses went up in flames that she finally accepted that it might be too dangerous to stay – because of the fire, not the French, she said. She was back after three nights, concerned that her nice house might be plundered. Never one to panic, Frau Goethe opened her windows and played her piano so loudly that the entire neighbourhood could hear. What was the point of being despondent, she told her son. Goethe tried to be optimistic too, hoping that the Thuringian Forest mountain range just south of Jena – 'the mountains that otherwise send a cold wind our way' – would stop the French. Meanwhile friends sent their jewels, coins and precious papers from the occupied territories to Goethe for safe-keeping in Weimar. Goethe reluctantly decided to cancel a planned visit to Italy.

～

On 6 August 1796, four weeks after Caroline and August Wilhelm had moved to Jena, Friedrich Schlegel arrived from Weißenfels. Within the first forty-eight hours, he had met Fichte, paid a promised visit to Novalis's convalescing fiancée Sophie, and been introduced to Schiller. The day after their meeting Schiller told Goethe and Wilhelm von Humboldt that he quite liked the younger Schlegel brother – an assessment that would not survive reading Friedrich's harsh review.

Born in 1773, the youngest of ten, Friedrich Schlegel was the child who most worried his parents. A defiant son who either left his father furious or despairing, Friedrich had been glad to escape the parental home in Hanover to study in Göttingen and later in Leipzig. Attending lectures in mathematics, medicine, philology and law, he had also ploughed his way through an impressive reading list ranging from Kant to Goethe and Schiller to Voltaire, Dante and Shakespeare. He read so much that people were perplexed by his knowledge and originality. Friedrich Schlegel's only goal was to read, think and write. The best minds, he had told the diligent and industrious August Wilhelm, were stunted by conventional career choices. 'My goal is to live – to live *free*,' he announced, but he also wanted to be famous.

Friedrich was his older brother's opposite. Where August Wilhelm was calm and down to earth, Friedrich was short-tempered and arrogant. Where August Wilhelm was conscientious, thorough and punctual, his younger brother was careless, messy and sometimes thoughtless. Compact but not yet overweight, he had a thoughtful face and a pale complexion. His gentle appearance, though, belied a mercurial character. His Achilles' heel was that he judged quickly and imprudently, often criticising and upsetting influential patrons and friends. Even Friedrich admitted that he wasn't particularly likeable. 'People prefer to observe me from a distance,' he said, 'like a rare and dangerous beast.'

He couldn't keep, nor wanted, a job, and swung between suicidal urges and triumphant announcements. When Friedrich first read Shakespeare's *Hamlet*, for example, he identified with Hamlet's internal turmoil. 'For several days I was beside myself,' he declared, pursuing 'constant and merciless self-analysis'. He was also completely broke. Novalis had stopped lending him money and his brother had already bailed him out several times, as had their parents. Their mother had written many letters to August Wilhelm, begging him to talk sense into his younger brother. 'Fritz is bankrupting us,' she had said, urging August Wilhelm to 'give him some good advice and a warning'.

Soon the Schlegels were living together. Caroline and August Wilhelm had at first rented the small garden villa which Goethe had visited just south of the town walls, but shortly after Friedrich's arrival they moved to a bigger house in Leutragasse, one block away from the market square. Their new home comprised the rear of a large three-storey building, overlooking a courtyard rather than a public street. At least here the students would not be able to smash her windows, Caroline joked. On the ground floor were three rooms reserved for guests and a large parlour with five tall windows facing westwards onto the courtyard, which invited the evening sun into the room. On the first floor was August Wilhelm's study, the couple's bedroom and Auguste's room. Friedrich had his realm in the garret rooms under the roof.

As practical as she was elegant, Caroline soon made the house comfortable. The Schlegels had little money and the house was large, but by decorating, sewing new curtains, moving furniture and unpacking her treasured set of porcelain, Caroline created a warm, welcoming home. Her husband admired her sense of beauty – 'he isn't one of those scholars with no sense of design and elegance,' she explained to her friend Luise Gotter.

~

In November 1796 the Humboldts returned to Jena, having spent more than a year at Tegel, the family estate just outside Berlin where they had looked after Wilhelm's mother. Schiller was glad to have his friend back. It had been a difficult autumn. His younger sister had died, followed by his ailing father. Then Schiller's new-born son became so ill that everyone feared for his life. To make matters worse, Schiller was himself suffering from ulcers and cramps. As one misery succeeded another, Goethe became so worried that he delayed his departure to Weimar. He just couldn't leave him. He tried to cheer up his friend but 'it was impossible to get him out of the house, as always,' Goethe said. But slowly Schiller recovered and resumed his meetings with Wilhelm von Humboldt to which August Wilhelm Schlegel was also invited.

Wilhelm von Humboldt had looked forward to reconnecting with August Wilhelm Schlegel – they had met as students in Göttingen – but Caroline von Humboldt quickly decided that she preferred the younger Schlegel brother. Friedrich Schlegel was handsome and clever, she said, though it was a shame 'that he seems to have arrived at an exaggerated opinion of his talents too young'. She never quite warmed to Caroline Schlegel although both were strong, clever and educated women with an unconventional attitude to marriage.

Besides their two young children, the Humboldt household in Jena now also included Wilhelm Friedrich Theodor von Burgsdorff, a young aristocrat who had become Caroline von Humboldt's lover in Berlin. Wilhelm and Caroline von Humboldt had come to the unusual agreement of an open relationship when they married in 1791. In the past it had been enough for Wilhelm to visit prostitutes – a habit he had meticulously recorded, like an accountant, in his diary: '27 July in Spa 1 krone for a whore; 30 July in Brussels 7 sous for a whore; 6 August in Paris half a krone for a whore', and so on. But Caroline von Humboldt had made it very clear that she too needed freedom. Even before they married, she told him that she had to live free of all constraints. As their letters attest, finding pleasure elsewhere never affected their love for each other. 'I found what I longed for,' Wilhelm wrote to his wife, 'because I love you deeply.' Unsurprisingly, Caroline von Humboldt was one of the few who thought the gossip about Goethe, Christiane Vulpius and their son August preposterous. 'All this racket over the child! It's unbelievable,' she said. 'What nonsense!'

Gossip didn't bother the Humboldts, nor jealousy. 'When you forgo something you want, it disturbs my whole inner and outward life,' Wilhelm told his wife later, and Caroline von Humboldt's lover joined in all their activities. Burgsdorff accompanied them to Weimar to visit Goethe and spent most evenings with them in Schiller's parlour where he also met Fichte and the Schlegels.

Almost seven years her junior, Burgsdorff was passionately in love with Caroline von Humboldt, even though she was heavily pregnant with her third child. Battling with fevers and headaches, she often rested in the afternoons, but both her lover and her husband, she said, were kind enough to let her be. Burgsdorff didn't care. She was 'my dear, my great, my tender love', he said. Smitten, he observed her every move. When she poured tea during those dark winter afternoons, he stared at her, entranced by the way the glowing candlelight caressed her skin. When she looked up and smiled at him, his heart melted. 'She is the noblest most beautiful human creature in the world,' he said.

When their son was born, the Humboldts even named him Theodor after Burgsdorff. Wilhelm von Humboldt seemed content with the situation, happily leaving his wife with Burgsdorff when he had to travel. Their young children adored the young man who played with them like a friendly uncle – 'they run around and dance and ride on him,' Caroline wrote to her husband.

Caroline and Wilhelm von Humboldt's long letters were filled with deep love. They were forever intertwined, Wilhelm told her, and he wanted her to be happy because he was. 'I want to do everything, everything, that will keep you cheerful,' Wilhelm said, because 'I love you forever and always'. Guarded as Wilhelm was with everybody else, he allowed himself to be completely open with his beloved wife. There were no misgivings. 'Decide for yourself, with Burgsdorff,' he wrote to her once from Weimar, 'how you would like to handle things.' The affair lasted four years, and Burgsdorff would later accompany the Humboldts to Vienna and Paris.

~

That no one in Jena cared too much about this unusual marriage arrangement must have been encouraging for Caroline Schlegel. She and August Wilhelm had also agreed on a similar relationship. Theirs was 'an alliance that between ourselves we never regarded as anything but utterly free', Caroline later explained. And though rumours about her imprisonment at Königstein rippled through Jena's polite society, the Humboldts' open marriage gave her the confidence to ignore the hissings and whispers. When Caroline Schlegel was offered a role in one of the parlour theatre plays, she had become self-assured enough to volunteer to play a woman in a *ménage à trois*. For the first time since Königstein, Caroline felt free.

At a time when fathers and husbands determined every aspect of a woman's life, Caroline Schlegel and Caroline von Humboldt had taken control of their own destinies. It hadn't always been like this. Though Caroline Schlegel had been educated to a much higher standard than most women, her father had still been in charge of the marriage arrangements with her first husband. Religion, class and economic considerations were the determining factors for marriage. As long as they remained unmarried, women were legally bound to their father's will or that of a male relative, and with marriage their husbands took charge. Women had few legal rights. Unmarried women remained under the guardianship of their family and were often treated like servants or outcasts. Without access to money, society or a profession, marriage was often regarded as the only option. And although any assets or income were automatically signed over to the husband on the day of the wedding, at least a woman had some control over the domestic sphere once she was married.

A woman's role and domain were the children, the household and her husband's well-being. The recently codified General State Laws for the Prussian States spelled it out: 'The man is the head of the family, and his decisions about common matters shall be considered final.' Society's expectations were similarly clearly defined: where a man had to be rational, strong and assertive, the wife was to be gentle, passive and enduring. He was the oak, a contemporary book on female education explained, with the wife a twining ivy that climbed around the solid trunk. A husband was in charge of their public life while his wife's role was to create a peaceful private life.

Even newer and more enlightened approaches firmly placed women in a subordinate role. Jean-Jacques Rousseau might have had radical and progressive thoughts about childhood – from breastfeeding to letting children roam freely – but these ideas were exclusively for boys. Though Rousseau had admitted that women are born equal to men – 'she has the same organs, the same needs, the same faculties' – he nonetheless insisted that women should be completely submissive and compliant. Women should learn early on to endure injustice, Rousseau wrote in *Emile, or On Education*, 'and to bear a husband's wrongs without complaining'. Neither Caroline Schlegel nor Caroline von Humboldt agreed.

The rules in Jena seemed to be more relaxed than elsewhere, as the unusually high number of illegitimate children proved. Friedrich Schlegel had a friend who seemed 'to have slept his way through all the women in Jena', he insisted, including the unhappily married writer Sophie Mereau who lived a short walk from their new house in Leutragasse. The 'tiny beauty', as Goethe called the diminutive twenty-six-year-old, had recently published a novel – a love story advocating equality and freedom. Impressed by Sophie's poetry, Schiller had been the first to publish her poems and she was the only woman who attended Fichte's private lectures. But as if being a female writer wasn't already unusual, Sophie Mereau stumbled from one affair to the next. Half of Jena seemed to be in love with the 'adorable Miniature-Grace', as one smitten student described her. There was always a thick flock of admirers scurrying around her. Having been told that Sophie Mereau was 'an enchanting bedfellow', Friedrich Schlegel fell for her too.

Caroline Schlegel also noted that Anna Henriette Schütz, the wife of one of the *Allgemeine Literatur-Zeitung* editors, was a bit of a flirt, with a fondness for low necklines. There were rumours that Fichte had engaged in a little dalliance with her before his wife arrived from Zurich, and Caroline quipped that Madame Schütz not only served delicious apple cake at her tea party but also showed off a 'most scandalous bosom'. Similarly, Karoline Paulus, the wife of another professor, had a reputation for being rather open-minded when it came to men. Only Charlotte Schiller was indignant about the whole situation. Even their close friends, Wilhelm and Caroline von Humboldt, she told her husband, had 'trampled all propriety'.

~

There was no escaping the gossip or each other. Jena was so small that it took less than ten minutes to cross. Walking from her house in Leutragasse and across the market square, Caroline would pass the Humboldts' house, and the Paulus's house next to it within three minutes, and if she continued another hundred yards, she would see Fichte's house, slightly set back to the right, near the tower that formed the south-eastern corner of the ancient town walls. Turning left, Caroline would walk up a street that brought her to the Saaltor, one of the old gates. Walking through it and across the old moat, she faced the Jenzig mountain opposite. Now outside the medieval walls, she was on a street that ran parallel to the town's eastern border. Immediately next to the gate but within the walls was the auditorium where Fichte and Schiller had presented their inaugural lectures, and if she looked up, she might have been able to see Schiller pacing behind the windows of the large house next door, into which he had moved the previous year. Rising beyond Schiller's apartment was the silhouette of the Old Castle where Goethe had his rooms. As she walked on Caroline would see Zum Schwarzen Bären just beyond the corner tower of the castle.

The tavern was popular with students and travellers – and it was here that Christiane Vulpius stayed on the rare occasions when Goethe asked her to come to Jena. More than two hundred and fifty years earlier, in 1522, Martin Luther had also stopped at Zum Schwarzen Bären to discuss his religious ideas with students here. In 1796, when Caroline walked by the tavern, the students within were more likely discussing Fichte's philosophy than religion. In the summer, diners sat next to a pigsty in the garden, and in the winter the famously rude landlady threw out drunken students when she put down a straw mattress for the driver of the stagecoach to sleep on in the middle of the dining-room floor.

Turning left at Zum Schwarzen Bären into Fürstengraben – a broad tree-lined promenade outside the ancient walls and next to the now filled-in moat – Caroline reached the northern boundary of Jena. Walking in the dappled shade here, she would have seen tall town houses and the Church of St Michael to her left and the gently rising hills with vineyards behind the houses and gardens to her right. She passed the house where her physician Christoph Wilhelm Hufeland lived, a professor of medicine at the university and an early advocate of naturopathy who insisted on the importance of a healthy vegetarian diet.* He was also the cousin of Gottlieb Hufeland, one of the editors of the *Allgemeine Literatur-Zeitung* who lived just across the courtyard next to the Schlegels in Leutragasse.

Beyond Dr Hufeland's residence, Goethe's new botanical garden stretched along the promenade. The end of Fürstengraben lay at the north-western corner of the old wall and the highest land point of the town. There was also a crenelated round tower built from the sand-coloured local stone which had been part of Jena's skyline since the fifteenth century. From here it was just a few yards downhill to the Johannistor, one of the old gate towers. Stepping through its arched gateway, Caroline would pass the Zur Rose tavern where the Professors' Club congregated, or instead she could remain on the downward-sloping street that ran parallel along the western boundary. Staying outside the walled town centre, she walked down towards the Saale, passing houses with gardens as well as vegetable plots, orchards and fishponds to the right. To the left Caroline would have been able to see the university and the anatomy tower in the wall's south-western corner. The university itself was housed in a former Dominican convent with a large church at its centre. Here students rushed across the paths clutching their satchels and books.

Leaving the walled town behind, Caroline would pass Ratsteich,

---

* When the Schlegels had arrived in Jena, Dr Hufeland had just finished the manuscript of his book *Macrobiotics. The Art of Prolonging Life* (1797), which would become the most famous medical treatise of the age – an international bestseller that was published across Europe and even translated into Chinese.

a large pond where students skated in the winter, and then see Engelplatz to her right where Christian Gottfried Schütz, the other editor of the *Allgemeine Literatur-Zeitung*, lived. Walking south towards the Saale, Caroline would have soon reached Paradise, the popular park adjacent to the river. Here a straight tree-lined avenue invited the inhabitants to stroll in the shade or take one of the gravelled paths that dipped in gentle curves around small groves and expansive lawns. In the summer a boat would be moored down at the river to ferry noisy students and other revellers to and from the beer gardens in the neighbouring villages. The entire walk, even at a leisurely pace, would have taken Caroline no more than half an hour.

~

It was a good time to be in Jena. After a summer of worries about the French military advances, the duke had decided to ally his small duchy with Prussia, which had signed a treaty of neutrality with France back in 1795. Jena felt safe by the end of the year. The French troops who had crossed the Rhine and advanced into Bavaria had been driven back. Instead of three great French armies converging to attack Austria from Italy and Germany, the Austrians had won a few decisive battles and for now military action was concentrated on faraway Italy. 'The French Storm', as Goethe had called it that summer, seemed to have passed them by.

Having experienced the consequences, Caroline kept quiet about her political convictions. But it surprised her that Karoline Paulus openly wore the red, blue and white French revolutionary colours pinned to her hat in the streets. 'Here she's allowed to do this – and I never – never – did it in Mainz,' Caroline wrote to her childhood friend Luise in Gotha, 'that's justice for you.'

The Schlegels embraced their new life. In their large parlour on the ground floor, Caroline laid out her porcelain, poured wine, and entertained her guests. The large table seated up to twenty people, and there were a couple of sofas and a piano, which Auguste often played. With a meagre spread of gherkins, potatoes, herring and a tasteless watery soup, the food was quite the opposite of the sophisticated conversations. It seemed as if Caroline didn't know in the morning what to serve at lunch, one visitor noted. Caroline didn't care – they had little money and her cook was capable enough in her opinion. If guests grumbled about the unpalatable food, they didn't tell the hostess. The flavour, one visitor said, was not provided by the ingredients of the meal but by the intellectual menu that Caroline prepared. There was never a boring moment when she was at the table and guests quickly didn't notice the food on their plates. Caroline was so learned that one acquaintance described her as an 'intelligent god'.

That December, five months after their arrival, Caroline and August Wilhelm Schlegel went to Weimar to watch a play and to attend Goethe's 'big and entirely literary lunch'. Seated in the tasteful Yellow Room on the first floor where Goethe often welcomed his guests, they saw their host rushing around attending his visitors. Obsessed with colour theory, Goethe had chosen the bright yellow paint on the walls because, according to him, it created a cheerful and gently stimulating atmosphere. Once the servants had brought up steaming terrines and plates, Goethe himself served the food and chatted with everybody. Caroline enjoyed every minute of their visit. Goethe's house was elegant, filled with drawings, paintings and sculptures. It was the perfect expression of Goethe's artistic sensibilities.

Talking about art and literature, Caroline was in her element and those who met her in Weimar were charmed. One admirer called her the 'high-priestess' and asked August Wilhelm a few days later to greet his 'delightful wife' a thousand times for him. As always Christiane Vulpius kept away, staying at the back of the house. Caroline saw her briefly at the theatre and, like so many others, couldn't understand Christiane's appeal. Why, Caroline asked Charlotte Schiller a few days later, 'didn't he just bring back a beautiful Italian woman' from Rome? This was probably the only point on which she would ever agree with Charlotte Schiller.

~

During those first months in Jena after the Schlegels arrived, Novalis visited whenever his work schedule allowed. His fiancée Sophie von Kühn had remained in town to undergo two more operations. Amazingly, despite high fevers and infected wounds, she remained cheerful. She was still in a lot of pain, but Dr Stark continued to reassure Novalis. When Sophie rested and slept, Novalis saw Friedrich Schlegel to discuss books, poetry, philosophy and the Ich. 'I'm more and more Fichte's friend,' Friedrich told Novalis. 'I like him very much, and I believe it's mutual.'

In his study on the top floor of the house in Leutragasse, Friedrich was working at a frenzied pace. Over the past years, he had published essays on ancient Greek poetry, several reviews and an article about republicanism in which he advocated a democratic government for a global republic. Revolutions, he had said a few months before moving to Jena, were his greatest passion. 'When something inside me is at a boil like this,' he had told August Wilhelm, 'I can't calmly try to do anything else.'

He had also decided to become what he called a 'Dictator-Critic', nothing less than a literary critic with a pen as sharp as the French guillotines. Modern poetry, and German poetry particularly, Friedrich explained, was in a terrible state. It was just a jumbled-up 'geograph- ical cabinet of curiosities' because there was no unified German nation and therefore no unified voice. Opinionated as always, he declared there were only three modern poets worth reading: Goethe, Shakespeare and Dante. Certainly not Schiller.

Friedrich Schlegel divided opinion. Whereas Novalis considered his best friend destined for great things, Wilhelm von Humboldt described him as vain and spiteful, and yet also as one of the sharpest minds he had ever met. Friedrich's friends thought him unfailingly witty while Schiller claimed he had no talent as a writer. Goethe believed that the young hothead often misjudged a situation. 'It's strange', Goethe wrote to Schiller, 'how he takes the right path but still manages to get stuck on it.'

When Friedrich Schlegel had arrived in Jena, trailed by his review of Schiller's *Musen-Almanach*, the lines were drawn. Having prided himself that 'I can talk daggers', Friedrich hadn't held back. Schiller's poem 'The Dignity of Women', which had been published in *Musen- Almanach*, was so bad and monotonous, Friedrich wrote, that it was best read backwards. None of this was to diminish Schiller's return to poetry, but the truth was that the language was too opulent and the allegories ill-conceived. And as if to undermine Schiller's accom- plishments even more, Friedrich Schlegel couldn't stop praising Goethe's achievements. The two poets couldn't be compared. It would be unfair to Schiller to do so, Friedrich wrote, because Goethe was a genius. Unsurprisingly, Schiller was offended.

The animosity between Schiller and Friedrich Schlegel was mutual. Friedrich had long vented his dislike of Schiller in private. Schiller's philosophy was too dry, his prose was too formulaic, and it was clear that the playwright had to 'pump out his thoughts with the greatest effort'. All this didn't stop Friedrich Schlegel from trying to get a well-paid commission from Schiller's *Horen*. He had prepared several shorter pieces as well as some longer essays, he told his brother, 'I am merely waiting for a nod from the most gracious gentleman.' August Wilhelm Schlegel had pressed his brother's case on several occasions, but Schiller ignored the requests. Schiller was 'so childishly thin-skinned', an exasperated Friedrich wrote to Körner in Dresden, it was unlikely they would ever get on. It had been naïve to think Schiller would forgive Friedrich's critical review.

∼

Caroline, though, was glad to have her brother-in-law in Jena. They talked, wrote and went for long walks together. Friedrich 'very much entertains us with his head, which is frizzy both inside and out', she wrote to Luise Gotter in Gotha. Caroline was happy in Jena and could imagine staying here. Finally, she was once again in the company of great minds in a lively literary town rather than some little village in the middle of nowhere. And it was not just for her own sanity, she said, but also for the sake of her daughter Auguste, who might have otherwise ended up marrying a village priest.

There was no danger that Auguste was embarking on an ordinary future. In her short life, the eleven-year-old had experienced her father's death and that of her two siblings, life in a revolutionary city, imprisonment with her mother, and the birth, abandonment and death of her illegitimate baby brother. Having moved eleven times in as many years, she was, as Friedrich Schlegel commented, a 'female Odysseus'. Now it was time to focus on her education. For a long time Caroline had believed that education was not so much a matter of formal training as 'the unfolding of inborn qualities in a given environment' – in the spirit of Rousseau but applied to a girl. Caroline's teaching so far had not been so much a pedagogical 'art', she said, but 'a strategy of doing nothing' so as to allow for her natural development.

The Schlegel brothers had different ideas, and in Jena both began to teach Auguste. Knowledge was power, Friedrich Schlegel told her, and everybody, old and young, girls and boys, should learn as much as possible. Soon they had established a regime in which August Wilhelm – whom Auguste now called 'Father' – gave her writing lessons in the mornings, followed by exercises from Friedrich, her 'Uncle Fritz', in the afternoon. Maths and ancient Greek were on the timetable. Friedrich soon developed a teasing and tender relationship with her, calling her his 'little sweetheart'. Auguste felt loved by her strange patchwork family.

She was pretty and bright, her mother thought, but Caroline wasn't keen on Auguste's friendship with the daughter of the university's stablemaster. Never swayed or impressed by nobility or aristocratic titles, Caroline could still be snobbish. Auguste's friend was just so common, Caroline complained to Luise. Auguste was who she was only by virtue of having been kept 'at a distance from the ordinary', Caroline believed. Over the next few years, 'Gusteline', as Friedrich Schlegel nicknamed Auguste, became the charmed focus of the Jena Set. 'Can you believe how one can love a child this much,' Friedrich wrote to Novalis – who was perhaps not the right person to ask.

August Wilhelm Schlegel was happy too. In the proximity of his literary heroes, he was working hard and being paid, he adored his stepdaughter, and he was finally married to the woman he had loved for so long. In letters to friends he referred to 'my Caroline', almost as if he had to reassure himself that she was really his. Now happily settled, husband and wife continued their Herculean Shakespeare project. By Easter 1797, nine months after their move, they had completed and published their verse translations of *Romeo and Juliet* and *A Midsummer Night's Dream* and were in the midst of *Julius Caesar* and *Twelfth Night*. The reviews were glowing and the translations highly respected.

Often they worked side by side in August Wilhelm's study on the first floor, surrounded by piles of books as they filled sheet after sheet with different drafts of their translations. They crossed out and scribbled over lines of text, replacing words, negotiating their suggestions, and starting all over again. The pages filled with both sets of handwriting, and it proved to be a truly collaborative effort. Sometimes when they worked in the downstairs parlour, Friedrich Schlegel observed them quietly from an armchair. He loved to watch how Caroline danced her fingers along the table as they composed the verses, tapping out the metrical pattern. He joked that they should ask Auguste for help to make it a true family effort. 'You wouldn't believe how indispensable I've become to my dear Schlegel,' Caroline wrote to Luise.

A large part of their income came from August Wilhelm's well-paid articles for Schiller's *Horen* – several translations but also an essay on Shakespeare, for which he copied entire passages from Caroline's letters and notes – while she continued to edit his work and write reviews for the *Allgemeine Literatur-Zeitung* under his name. The few women who were writers often published under their husband's names or anonymously. Sophie Mereau's novel *Das Blüthenalter der Empfindung* (*First Flower of Feeling*), for example, had been published without her name on the cover, as had *Agnes von Lilien*, a novel by Charlotte Schiller's sister. Similarly, all the poems by female authors in *Horen* were printed anonymously, and although Schiller published their works, his conception of the ideal woman could not have been further from the reality of Caroline Schlegel.

In Schiller's poem 'The Famous Wife', a husband complains that he is married to a writer who has neglected her real duty as a mother and obedient wife. 'No one notices *me*, all eyes are turned / To my better half', laments the husband, continuing:

> *The day has hardly dawned to life*
> *When the stairs creak from uniforms, yellow and blue,*
> *Bringing letters, sheaves, and packages, postage due,*
> *Addressed to The Famous Wife.*
> *She is still asleep – so sweet! But I must not guard her.*
> *'The papers, Madame, from Jena and Berlin!'*
> *The noble sleeper's eyes at once fly open*
> *And her first glance falls upon . . . the new reviews.*
> *Those lovely blue eyes! – with not a glance at me! –*
> *Wander across a miserable sheet of paper,*
> *(Loud crying can be heard in the nursery)*
> *At last she puts it down and asks after her children.*

Three decades later, August Wilhelm explained that Caroline had all the talents and abilities 'to shine as a writer' but that she lacked ambition – which was a little disingenuous given her work on the Shakespeare translations and the story she had written which he had passed on to Schiller. In the end, they might have simply decided that they could command higher fees if they published under August Wilhelm's name, or perhaps Caroline was still wary of too much attention. Whatever their reasoning, close friends noticed how August Wilhelm always relied on his wife's judgement. She had such a good ear, a friend later said, that whenever August Wilhelm was unsure about a passage in his translations or poems, he allowed her the final word.

In Jena the '*esprit de* Caroline' reigned supreme. She was content for the first time in a long while.

PART II

Experiments

When I look at what you're all creating there together, it seems to me like a real magic cauldron bubbling over . . . And when I hear you talk about some work you're undertaking, there's no way to tell whether it'll turn out to be a book or not; when you talk about being in love, whether it's the harmony of the spheres or a harmonica.

Caroline Schlegel to Novalis, 4 February 1799

'Our little academy'
Spring 1797: Goethe and
Alexander von Humboldt

ALEXANDER VON HUMBOLDT and Goethe stood at a table in the middle of the anatomy theatre. Situated in the sturdy round medieval tower that formed the south-western corner of Jena's ancient town wall next to the university, the room was designed like an amphitheatre with seats in circular rows along the wall so that the students could watch their professors' every move and incision. Thick stone walls kept the room cool. On that spring day in 1797 there were no students bending over for a closer look, nor any cadavers or human body parts on display. Instead, a collection of unlucky frogs that they had cut into pieces was on the table. There was an electrical apparatus, forceps, glass plates, scalpels, tweezers, magnets and a vast array of metal wires. There were vials filled with different chemicals and sheets of papers covered in Alexander's indecipherable handwriting.

The two men cut, prodded, poked and electrocuted. Alexander von Humboldt placed a frog leg on a glass plate and connected its nerves and muscles to different metals in sequence – to silver, gold, iron and zinc – which generated only a discouraging gentle twitch. Yet when he leaned over to check the connecting metals, the leg suddenly convulsed so violently that it bounced off the table. It took them a moment to realise it had been the moisture of Alexander's breath that had triggered the leap. As the tiny droplets touched the metals, an electric current had been created that moved the leg. It was the most magical experiment, Alexander said, because by exhaling on the frog's leg it was as if he were 'breathing life into it'.

Alexander von Humboldt and Goethe were engaging with a topic that preoccupied scientists across Europe: the concept of organic and inorganic 'matter'. Unlike Isaac Newton, who had described matter as being essentially inert, or the French philosopher René Descartes, who had declared animals to be machines, some scientists were now questioning this mechanical model of nature. How could living matter be explained? Might plants and animals be governed by a different set of laws from inanimate objects? For Alexander von Humboldt, his experiments on 'animal electricity' or 'Galvanism',* as it was also called, marked the beginning of his thinking about the forces within nature. Instead of imposing a corset of classification on nature or perceiving it as a divinely ordained clockwork, he would come to describe it as a web of life. He would interpret the natural world as a unified whole animated by interactive forces.

Alexander von Humboldt had arrived in Jena on 1 March 1797, together with the news that the young general Napoleon Bonaparte was trouncing the Austrian forces in Italy. Every morning Alexander walked the short distance from his brother Wilhelm's house on the market square to the anatomy theatre. Every day he spent six to seven hours here, experimenting and dissecting, in order to complete his book on 'animal electricity'. Over the previous two years he had conducted a series of four thousand experiments involving frogs, mice and lizards, trying to discover whether animal nerves contained electricity or any other forces.

The young scientist had also tested his theories on his own body. He rubbed chemicals into incisions on his arms and torso, stuck metals, wires and electrodes on his skin and under his tongue, meticulously noting every twitch, convulsion and pain. No matter how much his wounds got infected or how many blood-filled welts covered his body, Alexander was in his element. In Jena, he placed frog hearts in oxygen and was amazed to see them continuing to pulsate for another three hours; he investigated the fluid in a human brain; and he dissected the bodies of a farmer and his wife who had been killed by lightning during a violent thunderstorm. Despite the increasingly putrid smell of death, burnt flesh and decomposing animals, he enjoyed every minute. 'I can't live without experiments,' he wrote to a friend that spring.

Goethe was thrilled by Alexander's extended visit. 'You can't get as much out of eight days of reading as he presents in an hour,' Goethe wrote to Duke Carl August a few days after Alexander von Humboldt's

---

* The term 'Galvanism' derived from the Italian scientist Luigi Galvani, who had been the first to experiment with 'animal electricity'.

arrival. In the previous three years Goethe had often stayed in Jena, but in the first half of 1797 he spent more time there than at home in Weimar. He met Schiller every day, as well as seeing Fichte and the Schlegels, but the main draw was Alexander von Humboldt. Twenty-seven and furiously curious about the world around him, Alexander slept little and travelled much. Over the previous two years, he had regularly stayed with his brother and sister-in-law in Jena. Knowing Goethe's love for the sciences, Wilhelm had introduced Alexander to the older poet during his first visit, in March 1794.

~

The brothers had a complicated relationship. Where Alexander was adventurous and needed to be outside, Wilhelm was serious and studious. Alexander was often torn between emotions while Wilhelm possessed much more self-control. Though only two years apart, Wilhelm took the role of older brother to heart. In his letters and remarks about Alexander, he sounded more like a scolding and despairing parent than a sibling. Their mother had been emotionally cold but had provided the best education then available in Prussia. The two boys had been taught by a string of Enlightenment thinkers who instilled in them a love of truth, liberty and knowledge. Wilhelm had escaped into books while Alexander found solace in nature. He roamed through the countryside, through Tegel's forests, dreaming of distant countries and the adventures of great explorers such as Captain Cook and Louis de Bougainville. When he returned in the evenings with his pockets full of plants, insects and rocks, the family nicknamed him 'the little apothecary'.

Alexander grew up a good-looking young man. He stood five feet eight, was slight and agile. He seemed torn between his urge to excel and a loneliness that never really left him. He could feel insecure and yearned for approval, but he believed in his intellectual prowess. Wilhelm was proud of Alexander's extraordinary mind but was also worried about his mental health. 'The poor boy is not happy,' Wilhelm von Humboldt told his wife; Alexander was too restless and too preoccupied dazzling everybody with his knowledge and brilliance.

Alexander himself admitted that he was driven by a fretful energy as if chased by '10,000 pigs'. He talked incessantly and jumped so quickly from one subject to the next that few could follow. Some described him as a meteor that whizzed through a room, others as an 'overcharged instrument' that never stopped playing. 'There is a drive in me', Alexander told a friend, 'that often makes me feel as if I'm losing my mind.' Caroline von Humboldt worried that he might 'snap'. Six years previously, when enrolled at the famous mining academy in Freiberg, near Dresden, Alexander quickly overtook his fellow students. Within eight months he had completed a programme that took others three years and become a mining inspector. He learned and worked so much that some joked he must have 'eight legs and four hands'.

A few months before his arrival in Jena, Alexander and Wilhelm von Humboldt's mother had died after a long illness. The sons had never been close to their mother, and neither attended her funeral. And though Wilhelm had moved back to Berlin for a few months to look after her, he had been glad when the news of her death reached Jena. The brothers inherited a fortune and Alexander immediately resigned from his position at the Prussian Ministry of Mines. A month later he announced his 'great voyage'.

Alexander von Humboldt wanted to explore the world, collect plants, seeds, rocks and animals, measure the height of mountains, determine longitude and latitude, take temperatures of water and air, and make astronomical observations, he said, but the real purpose of his exploration was to investigate how 'all forces of nature are interlaced and bound together'. But before he could embark on his great adventure, he had to finish his current projects, buy the best instruments, meet the greatest scientists to learn everything there was to know, and, most importantly, find a destination for his voyage – which proved to be more difficult than he had anticipated as much of Europe was embroiled in the French Revolutionary Wars. As gains and losses were made on all sides, and treaties signed and then discarded, Alexander von Humboldt found his movements restricted by war and armies. For now, though, he remained in Jena to finish his experiments on animal electricity.

~

Alexander von Humboldt's presence coincided with one of Goethe's most productive phases in years. Though a poet, Goethe was increasingly preoccupied with the sciences. 'I never observed the natural world for poetic reasons,' he later explained. During the bombardment of Mainz, in 1793, he had worked on his colour theory, and the previous summer he had experimented with the effect of colour and light on the growth of plants. Later, he conducted chemical experiments, wrote about the metamorphosis of plants and began to investigate insects.

Recently, he had become obsessed with butterflies and moths. Just before Alexander von Humboldt arrived in March 1797, Goethe had been observing how the caterpillars he had collected the previous autumn emerged from their chrysalises and silky cocoons. During the cold winter months he had kept the pupas warm in his parlour, where visitors must have been surprised by all the glass jars among the Italian sculpture and fine porcelain. When the pupas were finally ready to hatch, Goethe spent many days trying to catch the moments of their metamorphosis. He sat quietly for hours with journal and pen in hand, watching how the delicate wings unfolded. Minute by minute, he jotted down the development and changes. How could a living thing change so radically from one state to another? It was the 'most beautiful phenomenon', he told Schiller.

During this time Goethe also dissected insects, worms, snails and caterpillars, and prepared them as specimens. Injected with glue and wax, some were pinned to cardboard and others squeezed between two glass panes, their labels documenting the various stages of development: 'caterpillar near metamorphosis', 'caterpillar with innards removed', 'caterpillar with throat and stomach still full of food'. He prodded the minuscule eggs in the ovaries of a hawk moth, investigated the digestive systems of snails and, inspired by Alexander von Humboldt's experiments, he also turned to frogs (which he caught with his son August in the wet meadows by the Saale). Goethe compared the intestines of male and female frogs. With a scalpel, he teased out tiny organs and placed them in water, doused them in vinegar and sprinkled them with acids. He sniffed, touched and nudged.

Soon, his study resembled an anatomy theatre writ small, with miniature body parts, instruments, vials and jars everywhere. As amphibians and snails decomposed, the smell must have been overwhelming – though on one occasion after dissecting a frog's ovaries, Goethe noted in surprise: 'March 30th: still no trace of foul odour.' Everything was meticulously recorded. Caroline Schlegel joked that 'he devotes himself to his caterpillars nowadays, first killing them and then bringing them back to life'.

Goethe felt an urgent need to talk about his scientific studies. Exchange and dialogue were essential to discovery, he said. He sent Schiller regular reports – 'my recent dissections of fishes and worms have again given me very fruitful ideas' or 'I've started examining the intestines of animals more closely' – but his literary collaborator didn't understand this deep love for the sciences and rarely did more than listen politely. With Alexander von Humboldt in town, though, Goethe finally had a scientific sparring partner. 'My scientific studies', he told Schiller excitedly, 'have been brought back out of hibernation by his presence.'

Alexander was interested in everything: zoology, magnetism, geology, botany, chemistry, medicine and so much more. He had already published a book on subterranean flora – strange mould and sponge-like plants that grew in intricate shapes on the damp beams in the mines – and a treatise on the basalt along the Rhine, as well as some fifty articles. He invented a breathing mask for miners, along with a lamp that would work even in the deepest oxygen-poor shafts – yet another subject that fascinated Goethe, whose many roles included responsibility for the duchy's mines. In Jena, Alexander studied and lectured on animal electricity, conducted chemical experiments, tested a new foldable electrometer and carried his barometer up every single hill to practise how to measure altitudes. Even the duke came from Weimar to Jena to meet Alexander, telling everybody afterwards that he was enchanted by the young scientist.

During those weeks Alexander and Goethe fell into a rhythm of walks, discussions, scientific experiments and shared meals. Though twenty years younger than Goethe, Alexander often took the lead. He 'forced us' into the natural sciences, Goethe enthused, thankful to escape the endless discussions about Napoleon's daring invasion of Italy.

However, as much as he might have tried, even Goethe couldn't avoid the news entirely, for the young French general – who was exactly one month older than Alexander von Humboldt – was winning one battle after another. A short, slight man, Napoleon didn't look like a fiery military leader, but when he had grabbed the French flag and marched straight into enemy fire at the head of his troops at the Battle of Arcole, near Verona in Italy, the previous winter, his men had followed. It was on that day, Napoleon later said, that he felt his momentous destiny. Over the months that followed, the French decimated the Austrian army and pushed them out of Italy. At times the French troops marched at twice the speed of their enemies, surprising everybody. 'We do not march,' one of Napoleon's officers said, 'we fly.' The map of Europe seemed to be redrawn every few months, and every day could bring new disturbing news. 'Now I can hardly send a letter without the world having changed by the time the reply comes back,' Goethe complained.

Alexander von Humboldt was the perfect distraction. Encouraged by him, Goethe returned to his studies on comparative anatomy and the forces that shaped flora and fauna. Goethe distinguished between the internal force – the *Urform* or archetype – which provided the general form of a living organism, and the environment – the external force – which shaped the organism itself. A seal, for example, had a body adapted to its sea habitat (the external force), Goethe said, but at the same time its skeleton displayed the same general structure or *Urform* (the internal force) as those of land mammals.

Like the French naturalist Jean-Baptiste Lamarck and later Charles Darwin, Goethe recognised that animals and plants adapted to their environment rather than according to a divine plan or their use for humankind. The *Urform*, he wrote, could be found in all living organisms in different stages of metamorphosis. There were even similarities between animals and humans. And to make his point, Goethe began to fling both his arms around whenever he went for a walk. This exaggerated swinging of one's arms was a remnant from the four-legged animal and therefore one of the proofs that animals and humans had a common ancestor, Goethe explained to his neighbours who found his behaviour rather odd.

～

During that spring of 1797 the Jena Set met almost every day. 'Our little academy', as Goethe called it, was very busy. Wilhelm von Humboldt was labouring over a verse translation of one of Aeschylus's Greek tragedies, which he discussed with Goethe. Meanwhile, Goethe was working on his prose poem *Hermann and Dorothea*, for which he consulted the older Humboldt brother on verse metre, while conducting experiments with Alexander for which they set up an optical apparatus to analyse light and to investigate the luminescence of phosphorus. August Wilhelm and Caroline Schlegel worked on their Shakespeare translations, while Schiller was writing his play

Wallenstein. Interested in everything – art, science and literature – their interdisciplinary approach would become a major theme as their thinking evolved.

They went to Alexander's lectures, to Fichte's packed auditorium, to dinners and other social gatherings. That spring, one philosophy student couldn't believe his eyes when he saw so many famous men sitting in one row at a concert – Goethe, Fichte, Alexander von Humboldt and August Wilhelm Schlegel. Only in Jena, he said. Another student was similarly star-struck when he was invited to a party where all of Germany's greatest thinkers and writers seemed to be squeezed into one room.

The University of Jena 'was at the height of its success', Goethe insisted. In the afternoons or evenings, after they finished lecturing at the university or working at home, they all rushed along the cobbled streets to Schiller's apartment near the Old Castle. Here, in Schiller's parlour, Goethe recited his poems and others presented their work until late at night. Over the course of several evenings in the middle of March, Wilhelm von Humboldt read Fichte's latest edition of the *Wissenschaftslehre* aloud to everybody. After that, he read extracts from Friedrich Schlegel's publication on ancient Greece and Rome as well as August Wilhelm and Caroline Schlegel's translation of *Julius Caesar*, and Alexander von Humboldt presented the results of his animal electricity experiments. As they read, argued, discussed and laughed, time passed quickly, Goethe said, 'like a rock crashing down a mountain'. The younger Humboldt brother made him so dizzy with ideas, Goethe told a friend, 'that you sometimes don't know, or care, where your head is'.

Infected by Alexander's energy, Goethe now also worked at a frantic pace, moving easily from one topic to another. 'Morning: revised poem, then A. v. Humboldt, further optical experiments. Then Schlegel. Lunch with Schiller. Afterwards W. v. Humboldt and Prof. Niethammer; discussed Fichtean theory. Evening in the club' was a typical diary entry that spring. Goethe's diary during Alexander von Humboldt's visit covered everything from walks along the Saale to composing poems and studying scientific books. He listed discussions on philosophy, literature and geology as well as on colour theory, chemistry and magnetism. He mentioned lunches, dinners and other visits. He sorted his bone collection, read Aristotle, and examined fossilised shells. Somehow, he also found time to experiment:

'chemical experiments on insects', 'frog anatomy', 'early morning snail anatomy', and 'earthworms anatomised'.

After a few weeks in Jena, Goethe was so exhausted that he admitted to almost looking forward to a few days in Weimar in order to recover. But when he did leave Jena, Goethe missed Alexander von Humboldt so much that he immediately dashed off a letter asking his new collaborator to join him. Alexander obliged and spent a week with him – but four days after the young scientist left Weimar, Goethe was back in Jena. He was not going to lose any precious time with Alexander.

It was during Alexander von Humboldt's visit to Weimar that Goethe also received the news that Austria and France had signed a preliminary peace agreement, the Treaty of Leoben. Napoleon had evicted the Habsburg army from Italy and just as the French were readying themselves to push deeper into the German territories, a truce was agreed. 'Peace has been achieved,' Goethe reassured Schiller at the end of April 1797.

～

In the years that followed Goethe would often weave science into his literary work. For too long, he said, poetry and science had been regarded as the 'greatest antagonists'. He composed the poem 'Metamorphosis of Plants', for which he translated his earlier essay on the *Urform* of plants into verse. Similarly, *Faust*, his most famous play – in which the drama's central character makes a pact with the devil, Mephistopheles, in exchange for infinite knowledge – is packed with scientific theories, including competing geological concepts about the creation of Earth and Goethe's own colour theories. The latest philosophical ideas also fed into *Faust*, with even an idealist making an appearance:

> *The Idealist*
> *The Power of my Fantasy*
> *Today seems much augmented.*
> *I must say, if all this is me,*
> *I'm temporarily demented.*

Like Alexander von Humboldt, the scholar Faust is trying to discover 'all Nature's hidden powers'. And when Faust declares his ambition in the first scene, 'That I may detect the inmost force / Which binds the world, and guides its course', it could have been Alexander speaking. Later, for his novel about marriage and love, Goethe chose as a title a contemporary scientific term that described the tendency of certain chemical elements to combine: *Elective Affinities*. He used this inherent 'affinity' of the chemicals to bond actively with one another to evoke the changing relationships between the four protagonists in the novel.

The influence and inspiration worked both ways. As Alexander later recalled, the time in Jena 'affected me powerfully'. Goethe changed the way he understood the natural world, moving him from purely empirical research towards an interpretation of nature that combined scientific data with emotional responses. 'Nature must be experienced through feeling,' he wrote later to Goethe, insisting that those who tried to describe the world by simply classifying plants, animals and rocks would never come close. Together with a growing emphasis on the subjectivity of the Ich-philosophy, Alexander von Humboldt's perspective shifted, and almost fifty years later he would write in his international bestseller *Cosmos* that 'the external world only exists for us so far as we receive it within ourselves'. Nature, ideas and feelings 'melt into each other'.

That nature and the imagination were closely interwoven in his books was due to the 'influence of your writings', Alexander von Humboldt told Goethe later. Goethe had equipped him with 'new senses' through which to see and understand the natural world – and it was with those new organs that he would explore South America two years later. Ten years after this long spring in Jena, Alexander showed his appreciation when he dedicated his *Essay on the Geography of Plants* to Goethe. The *Essay*'s frontispiece depicted Apollo, the god of poetry, lifting the veil from the goddess of nature – making it perfectly clear that poetry was necessary to comprehend the mysteries of the natural world. In return, Goethe says through Ottilie, one of the main characters in his novel *Elective Affinities*, 'How I would like to hear Humboldt talk, even once!'

Schiller, though, began to worry that Goethe was being pulled too far away from poetry and aesthetics. In *Horen*, Schiller had warned that 'the more the frontiers of science expand, the smaller the realm of art becomes'. He was also jealous of Alexander's influence over Goethe. Schiller never expressed his concerns to either man but his letters to one of his most trusted friends, Christian Gottfried Körner, in Dresden, were filled with caustic comments. Alexander von

Humboldt would never accomplish anything great, Schiller wrote, because he was interested in too many things. The young scientist was directed only by 'naked, analytical reason', lacked imagination and sensibility, and was propelled by vanity. Put simply, Schiller said, Alexander von Humboldt had a big mouth and was a show-off.

Blinded by jealousy, Schiller failed to see any potential in the man who would become the most celebrated scientist of his age – a man who came up with a concept of nature that still shapes our thinking today. Unlike Wilhelm von Humboldt, who thought his younger brother to be the greatest mind he had ever encountered and someone with the ability to connect ideas and 'to see chains of things', Schiller believed Alexander could 'never create, only divide'. And it wasn't just Alexander von Humboldt who annoyed him. Caroline Schlegel's increasing closeness to Goethe also displeased Schiller. How was it possible, he fretted, that Caroline had already received and read the proofs of the final volume of Goethe's novel *Wilhelm Meister*, when he – who had advised, edited and commented on drafts – had not? Meanwhile, Goethe, blissfully unaware, was spending more and more time with Alexander. A few days with the young scientist, Goethe said, was like 'having lived several years'.

Then, as spring turned slowly to early summer and the temperature rose, Schiller moved into a new house. Reluctant to venture out or go for walks, Schiller nonetheless realised that some fresh air and exercise would be good for his fragile health. So when a house with a large garden was offered for a low price, Schiller bought it in March 1797 and moved in on 2 May. The 'Garden House', as he always called it, was a handsome and compact building just beyond the medieval walls to the south-west, not far from the Saale and the Paradise. Above the first floor was a light and airy mansard room overlooking the garden where Schiller could write in peace, away from the noise of the family. Still working on *Wallenstein*, he was also composing ballads, writing poems and publishing his journals *Horen* and *Musen-Almanach*. The plan was to use the house during the summer when it became hot and stuffy in town but to keep the rented apartment near the Old Castle for the cold winter months.

Goethe was happy for him, although he now had to cross town to see his friend instead of taking the few steps from his lodgings to Schiller's apartment. 'It's all very awkward and inconvenient for me,' he wrote to Christiane, but the company was too tempting to forgo the fun. And so he walked almost every day to Schiller's new house. There, at the far end of the garden, bordering an overgrown embankment that descended to a small meandering stream, Schiller and his guests would sit in a small arbour at a round stone table heaped with glasses, books, food and papers. The weather was glorious that May, and as the nightingales sang their sweet songs, the men often lingered until late, enjoying the mild early summer evenings. But the peaceful atmosphere was not to last.

～

During the three months of Alexander von Humboldt's visit to Jena, Schiller and Friedrich Schlegel's relationship had become increasingly tense. There was no point in pretending otherwise. Declare war on someone like Schiller, Friedrich Schlegel told a friend, and you have to use big guns. And that's exactly what he did. Over the past year he had reviewed and attacked Schiller's *Musen-Almanach* but also *Horen*. In May 1797, just as Schiller welcomed his friends to his new garden, Friedrich Schlegel wrote yet another caustic review of *Horen*. His main criticism was that there was not enough original content and that Schiller relied too heavily on translations of foreign drama and poetry – much of which had, in fact, been done by August Wilhelm Schlegel.

It hadn't occurred to Friedrich that his review had implications for his brother's well-paid commissions from *Horen*. Friedrich was pleased with his 'great piece of deviltry' but August Wilhelm was horrified. He had already spent too much of his adult life trying to clean up after his hot-headed brother – from calming their parents to paying off Friedrich's debts. But Friedrich was in his element. 'I like it when people say, publicly and unambiguously, what they think and what they want,' he admitted.

Reading this latest review, Schiller had finally had enough. 'This Herr Friedrich Schlegel is really just too much,' he told Goethe on 16 May. The review had struck a nerve because Schiller had struggled to fill *Horen*'s pages. His contributors were unreliable, and their material was often not good enough. The translations filled the gaps. With subscriptions declining, Schiller had been ready to give up altogether.

Disliking conflict, Goethe always tried to be diplomatic, but he never enjoyed his role as a mediator. Now, though, he took Friedrich Schlegel aside and tried to talk sense into him. But how to convince him to scale down his attacks? Goethe spoke to all parties involved and patiently listened to Schiller's complaints. At the end of May, as tensions rose, he wrote a short letter to Christiane in Weimar, in which he twice mentioned that he would much rather be at home.

It was Schiller who launched the next assault. Having failed to silence Friedrich Schlegel, he now turned on the older brother, the innocent and judicious August Wilhelm, and fired him unceremoniously from *Horen*. 'It was a pleasure to have the opportunity to welcome you into the pages of *Horen* by including your translations of Dante and Shakespeare,' Schiller wrote on 31 May 1797 to August Wilhelm, 'but since I now see that Herr. Fr. Schlegel, at the very moment I am arranging this advantageous situation for you, is publicly scolding me and saying that there are too many translations in *Horen*, you will forgive me in future [for saying no].' With this one letter, the friendship with Schiller, the main reason for August Wilhelm Schlegel's move to Jena the previous year, ended abruptly.

Shocked and distressed, August Wilhelm immediately replied and insisted he hadn't known about Friedrich's review, nor did he exert any authority or influence over his younger brother. 'Indeed, I would be very unhappy to be held responsible for all his actions,' he assured Schiller. And in any case, since Friedrich had criticised *Horen*'s over-reliance on translations, August Wilhelm was implicated. Setting pride aside, Caroline added her own postscript to her husband's letter, begging Schiller's forgiveness. 'We sincerely admire you and love you,' she wrote. Then she sent a note to Goethe, asking him to help, and August Wilhelm knocked on his door.

The following day, at six in the evening, Goethe went on a long walk with August Wilhelm, and then to Schiller for dinner. But nothing helped. He had no interest in continuing their arrangement, Schiller replied in a terse note to August Wilhelm, and he could never trust him again. How could he be August Wilhelm's friend and at the same time be insulted by his brother? It would be better to dissolve their association – which admittedly although 'an unpleasant necessity' was now unavoidable. The friendship never recovered.

In the midst of all this, Alexander von Humboldt was leaving. After three months in Jena, the young scientist bid his farewells at the end of May 1797 – together with his sister-in-law Caroline. Wilhelm von Humboldt had already left Jena at the end of April to deal with the brothers' inheritance in Berlin – their mother's furniture had to be sold, the silver and porcelain packed up, and he was even thinking of selling Tegel, the family estate. Caroline von Humboldt's lover, Wilhelm von Burgsdorff, had also departed to organise lodgings in Dresden where they would all meet.* From Dresden, Alexander, Wilhelm and Caroline von Humboldt, plus the children and Burgsdorff, planned to travel on to Italy. Caroline von Humboldt's health had never quite recovered after the birth of her third child, in January, and she always suffered during the frigid German winters. The Humboldts had decided to leave Jena for good.

Alexander joined his brother and sister-in-law to continue the preparations for his expedition. In Dresden, he had arranged to meet an astronomer to learn how to use his new sextant, and he also wanted to interview his old teacher at the nearby mining academy in Freiberg concerning some pressing geological queries. On his way south, Alexander intended to climb the Alps, he told Goethe, and explore Vesuvius, in Italy, so that he might later compare them to mountains and volcanoes elsewhere. With a new armistice signed between the French and the Holy Roman Empire, they hoped they could travel to Italy without any problems.

And though he was excited to embark on new adventures, Alexander was also sad. 'I'm leaving this town with a heavy heart,' he wrote to a friend; 'where will I find everything brought together like this again?'

~

Goethe didn't have much time to miss Alexander. The falling out between the Schlegels and Schiller kept him busy. Over the course of the following week, he saw August Wilhelm Schlegel four times and Schiller six. Until he left for Weimar, on 16 June, Goethe oscillated between the warring parties. He went on separate walks with Friedrich and August Wilhelm Schlegel, and spent the evenings with Schiller. He read August Wilhelm's draft of what would be his last contribution to *Horen*, an essay on Shakespeare's *Romeo and Juliet* commissioned before the fight, and gave it to Schiller, who then, in

---

* Burgsdorff had left Jena at the end of 1796, but Wilhelm von Humboldt asked him to return in spring 1797 to look after his wife while he was travelling. Miserable and lonely without Caroline von Humboldt, Burgsdorff immediately came at the end of March and then left Jena for Dresden on 30 April 1797.

a roundabout way, forwarded his edits to Goethe, who gave them to August Wilhelm, clarifying the changes. Schiller had had enough of the young hotheads. This whole generation was just too self-centred and highly strung, he thought. They had clearly taken Fichte's Ich-philosophy too literally.

Friedrich Schlegel had exacerbated the situation even further by accusing one *Horen* contributor, a history professor at the University of Jena, of plagiarising a famous English historian. The wording, Friedrich Schlegel claimed, was so similar that it might as well have been billed as a translation. Infuriated, the professor published a retaliation in the *Allgemeine Literatur-Zeitung* in which he rejected Friedrich's charge as an 'impertinent lie'. In the uproar that followed, Goethe advised Friedrich Schlegel to leave Jena for a while. Withdrawal seemed the only solution.

On 8 June 1797, exactly a week after Schiller had severed all contact with the Schlegels, Friedrich informed Novalis that he would be moving to Berlin later that month. His time in Jena may have been over for now, but there was growing suspicion that his criticism of *Horen* contained some truth. Subscriptions declined, and the December 1797 issue proved to be *Horen*'s last when it finally appeared in March 1798. Friedrich almost felt exhilarated by the fight with one of Germany's literary giants. Never short of self-confidence, he wrote to Novalis that he dreamed 'of somehow being the last man standing'.

The damage was done and the Schlegels and Schillers ceased all contact. As friends and acquaintances chose their alliances, only Goethe stayed neutral. When Caroline von Humboldt left Jena, just as Schiller read Friedrich Schlegel's *Horen* review, she carried the gossip to Dresden. Schiller's old friend Körner in Dresden, who knew the Schlegel brothers well, promptly turned against them – even the highly respected Shakespeare translations were now deemed to be too clunky. And he didn't like Caroline Schlegel, Körner wrote to Schiller on 10 June, having heard all the details from the Humboldts. Though Friedrich Schlegel had written the review, it was Caroline Schlegel who was the centre of the malicious rumours. She had corrupted the brothers, Körner alleged.

But Caroline Schlegel had never been one to suffer in silence. Since the Humboldts sided with Schiller, they were fair game. Their new-born baby Theodor, she wrote to her old friend Luise, was 'as ugly as the first two'. The dislike was mutual. 'I'm glad you're no longer seeing Madame Schlegel,' Caroline von Humboldt wrote to Charlotte Schiller while on the road, 'after all she's a snake.'

Relations between Charlotte Schiller and Caroline Schlegel had never been close. Initially friendly, they hadn't warmed to each other as their differences became obvious. Where Charlotte Schiller was quiet and reserved, respecting convention, Caroline was sociable, outspoken and unorthodox. Though she loved her husband, Charlotte Schiller had wearied of his bohemian literary world, and she preferred her own company to noisy parties. She was a gifted musician and an accomplished translator, but had absorbed the traditional values of her aristocratic upbringing and devoted herself to her children, household and husband. That she was religious, conservative and a little snobbish made her suspicious of a free spirit like Caroline, who had defied her destiny and prescribed place in society. As her dislike grew, Charlotte Schiller began to advise others to fumigate their rooms once Caroline Schlegel had left. 'The minute she's out of the house, you should open all doors and windows,' Charlotte Schiller told a friend, 'and fire up two pounds of incense to purify the air of every last breath from its previous occupant.'

~

Goethe was exhausted. Something didn't feel right in Jena, and it didn't help that the weather was miserable. After a gloriously warm May, it turned cold and rained so much that it felt as if it would never stop. The only answer was a holiday. In June 1797, in the middle of negotiations between the Schlegels and Schiller, Goethe wrote to Duke Carl August for permission to travel. The sight of the Humboldts packing and leaving had awakened Goethe's wanderlust. He was filled with 'the desire to look outward into the world again'. He was granted permission but was requested to delay his departure until July, when the duke would return from his own vacation.

In Weimar, while he awaited his departure to Switzerland and possibly Italy, Goethe unpacked the manuscript of *Faust*. It was 'work that's well suited to a troubled mood', he now said, having worked on it on and off for years.* Schiller had long encouraged Goethe to

---

* Goethe wrote the so-called *Urfaust* in the early 1770s, published *Faust. A Fragment* in 1790 and then worked occasionally on the play from June 1797 to April 1801. *Faust. Part One* was published in 1808 and *Faust. Part Two* in 1832.

return to it. Back in December 1794, a few months after they had first met, Goethe had explained that he didn't even dare to untie the parcel that held *Faust* imprisoned. But on 22 June 1797, just three weeks after Alexander von Humboldt's long visit in Jena, Goethe finally opened his *Faust* material. It was almost as if Humboldt's personality had inspired him. Much like Humboldt, the restless scholar Faust is driven by an unyielding search for knowledge, by a 'feverish unrest', as he declares in the play's first scene.

The same day Goethe asked his insomniac friend Schiller to spend one of his many sleepless nights thinking about *Faust* – 'so you can tell me my own dreams, and interpret them, like a true prophet'. Schiller replied immediately. Getting the play right would be difficult, he said, and Goethe would have to strike a balance between wit and seriousness, between mind and reason, and between a folk tale and a universal meaning. The play was about the 'vain attempt to unite the divine and the physical sides of human nature', Schiller thought, and *Faust* had to be both philosophical and poetic to fulfil these goals. Why Goethe wanted to tackle this now, shortly before his departure, Schiller didn't understand, 'but I've long since given up ever trying to judge you by the standards of normal logic'.

Schiller felt isolated. With Goethe in Weimar, the Humboldts gone and the abrupt end of his friendship with the Schlegels, he admitted to Körner, 'I'm quite lonely this summer' – so much so that he even went to Weimar for a week to see Goethe. The two men discussed an idea for a new ballad, Schiller's 'The Cranes of Ibycus', in which a famous ancient Greek poet was murdered. And after Friedrich Schlegel's vicious attacks, it was perhaps no coincidence that Schiller believed this to be a suitable subject. Though only a short visit, Schiller felt better afterwards. Whenever they parted, he said, it was as if something of Goethe was planted inside him: a kernel or a seedling that would grow.

Goethe hadn't abandoned the idea of a rapprochement between Schiller and August Wilhelm Schlegel. He asked August Wilhelm to contribute a poem, ballad or prose piece to Schiller's *Musen-Almanach*. Desperate to make peace and recoup some of his income, August Wilhelm agreed and sent a poem in mid-July, just as Schiller arrived in Weimar. Goethe read it together with Schiller, thanked August Wilhelm and told him that they had enjoyed it, adding his best regards to the rest of the family. Four days later, August Wilhelm went to Weimar in the hope of finding Schiller at Goethe's – but he was too late. The moment he closed the door behind his visitor, Goethe wrote to Schiller, 'it seems that the only thing that brought him here was his desire to be close to you again'.

Carefully and gently, Goethe managed to negotiate a brief truce. Schiller accepted the poem, but not without suggesting substantial changes. August Wilhelm replied with eight pages, explaining in pedantic detail what he could and could not change. Schiller conceded and published the poem as well as asking for a ballad. Relieved, August Wilhelm set to work, and two weeks later delivered 'Arion. A Romance'. There was no reply. Three weeks later and still with no news from Schiller, August Wilhelm dispatched an eleven-page letter to Goethe, who by now was in Switzerland. He had tried all he could, August Wilhelm wrote to Goethe, but Schiller still avoided him. He was at a loss. What else could he do? Surely his willingness to contribute to the *Musen-Almanach* was proof of his loyalty?

August Wilhelm Schlegel never stood a chance. Schiller had already written to Goethe that the ballad was 'cold, dry, and of no interest'. Schiller had to admit, though, that the verses about *Romeo and Juliet* were excellent, full of verve and emotion – so good, in fact, that in a letter to his trusted friend Körner, he wondered if August Wilhelm Schlegel 'hadn't stolen them from somewhere or other' – a comment Schiller would never have dared make to Goethe.

From then on, the Schlegels tried to be a little more careful. 'If we treat Schiller badly,' August Wilhelm wrote to a friend, 'we will ruin our personal relationship with Goethe.' The older poet, though, managed to avoid taking sides publicly. Schiller felt sure of Goethe's friendship, as did August Wilhelm Schlegel. 'His attentive consideration for Schiller,' August Wilhelm later said, 'which is like an affectionate husband's for a wife with delicate nerves, does not keep him from continuing to be on the friendliest terms with us.'

8

'Grasp, then, a handful of darkness'
Summer–Winter 1797: Novalis's Death Wish

NOVALIS TOOK THE long grey shift dress that Sophie had worn on the day she died and placed it carefully on her bed. He laid out the narrow sleeves just below the neckline and propped up the slim book she had been reading before her death as if she were still holding it. The skirt of the dress was stretched out on the bed. On the pillow where her head had rested, he put her bonnet, arranging the ribbons around the void where her face had once smiled at him. For the next few days Novalis stayed in Sophie's room, rereading their letters and staring at the lifeless dress. 'Without her there is *nothing* for me in the world,' he wrote.

Sophie von Kühn had died on 19 March 1797, two days after her fifteenth birthday. Having endured three harrowing operations in Jena, she had finally died at home surrounded by her family. Novalis, who was rarely allowed a day off from the salt mines, had seen Sophie nine days before but hadn't returned, unable to see the 'heavenly creature' suffer. Ever since first meeting her, in November 1794, Novalis had been consumed by love. As often as possible he had saddled his horse, riding to her family's estate, Schloss Grüningen, some fifty miles west of Weißenfels.

Novalis described her, as he did everything, in opposites. Sophie was both child and woman, he said, a woman with a 'penchant for childish games' yet a child with steadfast opinions. She could be irritable yet she had borne her eighteen months of illness and her terrifying surgeries with bravery and strength, and she held her own against Novalis. Aged fourteen, she had smoked tobacco and loved wine, but she also enjoyed more traditional female occupations such as needlework and music. Novalis described her as imperious yet charitable, as self-controlled yet wild. She wanted to please yet could be capricious. She loved reading but had no interest in poetry, and she hated gossip. She could be cold towards him, and Novalis was aware that his love smothered her, yet he couldn't stop himself. She was a free spirit yet insisted on formalities. Even though they were engaged, she wouldn't allow him to use the informal *Du* when addressing her. Her contradictions beguiled Novalis. As Sophie's sister teased, she was his 'non-Ich'.

Initially, Novalis's friends had been surprised at his love for young Sophie. They adored him, though, and over time they came to accept his feelings. Novalis had always been different. He was an aristocrat yet the only one in their group with a practical profession, getting his hands dirty in the salt mines. He wrote poetry yet he was equally fascinated by the sciences. Despite his family background, he whole-heartedly embraced the French Revolution. He wanted to live a life different from the usual expectations of the oldest son of an aristo-cratic family, yet he yearned to be married and have heirs. He was melodramatic, passionate and fell easily in love, yet his affection for Sophie had endured.

He was a man of contradictions. Often quiet in the company of strangers, he was talkative and dazzling among friends. He could be charming and gentle, but also rash, exuding 'a busy, fretful joy'. Friedrich Schlegel had always seen Novalis as the embodiment of life – 'you live, the others only breathe'. Outwardly, he lived a professional life that pleased his father, yet he tried to make sense of the world by looking inwards and practising what he called his '*Sichselbstfindung*' – the 'Finding Oneself' – inspired by his deep reading and analysis of Fichte's works.

Now, however, Novalis wanted to die. Sophie's death had plunged him into a turmoil which became even darker and deeper when, a month later, his favourite brother Erasmus had died too, after a long illness. He would follow Sophie, Novalis announced – he would take his own life and join her. Novalis began to talk about his wish for '*Nachsterben*', a word he invented that translates as 'dying after-wards' or 'following into death'. He wanted to be reunited with Sophie, declaring with a theatrical flourish that his death would be like a wedding night full of the sweetest mysteries. But he wouldn't put a pistol to his head nor string a noose around his neck. Instead, he would use willpower. His Ich was strong enough to kill him, he believed, if he committed himself to the task. Nothing could change his mind. With Fichte's Ich reverberating in Novalis's heart as an 'incessant thinking about myself', his determination to die grew.

As his thoughts kept returning to Fichte's philosophy, he wrote in his notes, 'Grasp, then, a handful of darkness.'

After Sophie's death, Novalis took Fichte's free Ich and moulded it into his own eccentric concept of *Nachsterben*. Novalis gave the mind the magical ability to move things without touching them. If our Ich can create the world, Novalis wrote, then surely it can cause an arm to regrow when amputated or revitalise an object through the power of thought alone. Just as we can direct the mind to think or do anything, so we should have the same influence over our organs and body parts. The mind can force an arm to lift or an eye to blink, so why shouldn't it be able to compel our body to produce or do whatever we ask it to do? And if that was possible, Novalis believed, then one could 'kill oneself by sheer force of will'. If he willed it enough, he would be able to die.

~

With Sophie gone, everything had stopped. 'My petrification proceeds apace,' Novalis wrote five days after her death. He was disintegrating, and as his mind crumbled, so would his body. Having taken his leave of the mines, Novalis stayed with friends near Sophie's home. He felt like a 'stranger on Earth'. He sat in her room, and in the evenings he often walked across the estate to the graveyard; past the flower gardens of the small village and up a grassy slope, it was located at the top of a small hill. Novalis entered through a simple wooden gate. Here among the crooked teeth of generations of gravestones stood a new memorial carved with Sophie's name, 'my sacred shrine', as Novalis called it. He scattered the flowers he had picked on his walks and sat beside her grave. As the sun dipped and darkness swallowed the small churchyard, he felt an intimacy with Sophie and the universe that would inspire *Hymns to the Night*, a set of six poems which made him famous.

'I walked to the grave – where I brooded at length and felt an indescribable peace,' he wrote one night, and 'I feel unspeakably lonely' after another. But there were also moments of euphoria – 'flashing moments of enthusiasm' – when he felt close to Sophie. Then, on 13 May 1797, he scribbled in his diary: 'I blew the grave away like dust – centuries were like moments – I felt her near me', a sentence that would become the nucleus of the third poem of *Hymns to the Night*. Time and space seemed to have become elastic. A blink of a moment could expand to years or centuries and solid ground could turn to dust. Emotions could become manifest in objects, and objects themselves could dissolve into nothingness. Everything was one. And as Novalis had already noted in his Fichte studies, the uniting force was love. Love was the bridge between the Ich and the non-Ich, between the real and the ideal, between the mind and the physical world of the senses.

Novalis's diary reveals his unforgiving self-examination. Day after day, he poured everything onto its pages – his physical pain, his emotional condition, his artistic approach, his recurring sexual urges, his intellectual struggles – along with his day-to-day life. The pages reveal an uncompromising investigation and meditation on the self, a search for the connections between his body and his emotional responses to Sophie's death. Everything was noted in concise, almost clinical prose, much like a doctor describing a patient's symptoms.

The entries were registered by the number of days since Sophie's death – so 30 April was simply Day 43 or 13 May was Day 56. The diary became a barometer of grief, an almost daily report on the progress of Novalis's resolution to die. One day he noted that his resolve stood firm, on another how he 'wavered and faltered', and then of becoming 'steadfast again'. He observed his mood swings as he oscillated between castigating and comforting himself, between tears and elation, loneliness and animated conversations with friends. As always, Novalis lived in extremes. Ruthlessly honest, he praised himself for crying about Sophie and scolded himself for not thinking enough of her, berating himself again and again for his sexual arousal and masturbation. 'Very lustful', he jotted down between a weather report and the title of the book he was reading, and 'much lewdness' the next day.

Sophie was everywhere. Increasingly idealised, she was 'the beginning – she will be the end of my life'. The tobacco-smoking girl who had laughed in his face when he had told her to be quiet during an argument was now mythologised. Card-playing, strong-minded, dancing Sophie was now replaced with an ethereal angel, so pious and quiet that it was 'as if she did not belong in this world'. He felt her, and yet she was absent. He had to be with her. His death would be 'true self-sacrifice', he confided to his diary two months after her death. Suicide was not an option, nor was illness. If his death was to mean anything, it had to be caused by the conviction of his Ich alone. His death wish was a sign of strength. 'Death is self-conquest,' he wrote.

During those weeks, Novalis continued to correspond with his best friend Friedrich Schlegel. Less than a month after Sophie's death, Novalis had written, 'It is obvious to me what a heavenly accident her death has been – a key to everything.' His love for Sophie, he explained, was a flame that consumed reality. He would follow her. Though a little unsure about what Novalis meant by all this, Friedrich assured his friend, 'you can count on me: I am entirely on your side.' There was a mania to the great shifts of mood in Novalis's letters, alternating between euphoric excitement about his coming reunion with Sophie and the admission that 'my insides are crumbling'. Friedrich Schlegel felt for his friend but he was almost jealous – didn't the way Novalis suffered mean that he had experienced true and reciprocated love?

Woven into Novalis's feelings was the sort of obsession and melo-dramatic yearning that characterised the suicidal young Werther in Goethe's eponymous novel, written almost thirty years earlier. They had all read the book. *The Sorrows of Young Werther* had influenced a whole generation with its exploration of forlorn love, sentimental introspection and suicide. Friedrich Schlegel had himself talked about taking his life after a failed love affair during his student years in Leipzig, five years earlier – 'I have boundless respect for the beauty of your idea,' Novalis had reassured him.

August Wilhelm and Caroline Schlegel's translation of Shakespeare's *Romeo and Juliet* – the most famous of all suicides – had also been published just a few weeks after Sophie's death. When Friedrich Schlegel dispatched a copy of the book to Novalis on 7 May 1797, he wrote: 'I think you'll be drawn to Romeo . . . this is *more than poetry*.' Novalis loved it and fell for Shakespeare. All translations were poetry, he said, and all poetry was translation. The 'German Shakespeare', he told August Wilhelm Schlegel, 'is now better than the English one'.

That same summer, poet Friedrich Hölderlin was also tackling the subject of suicide. Having abandoned his studies in Jena after only a few months in the summer of 1795, Hölderlin had found a position as a tutor for a wealthy banker in Frankfurt. He had also fallen in love with the mother of his charges. Entangled in a complicated affair, he was writing a drama about Empedocles, the ancient Greek philosopher who had taken his life by throwing himself into Mount Etna.* For

---

* Hölderlin wrote *The Death of Empedocles* between 1797 and 1800, but it was only published after his death.

all three men – Hölderlin, Friedrich Schlegel and Novalis – the act
of killing oneself had a deeply emotional dimension that was associated with love in all its shapes and forms, as well as being the ultimate
expression of free will. But Novalis was the first, Friedrich Schlegel
said, to have an '*artistic* understanding of death'.

As the months passed Novalis began to worry about the strength
of his resolve. His resolution to die remained, but sometimes even
he questioned the practicality of *Nachsterben*. He was concerned that
his pain was easing. This wound, Novalis said, had to be kept open
at all cost – 'May God preserve this dear indescribable pain forever.'
That summer he scribbled 'Christ and Sophie' into his diary, and the
words were almost her epitaph. Sophie was a sacred object. As the
real girl faded, she became his religion. Raised by a devout and stern
Moravian father, Novalis had never embraced his father's beliefs but
lamented the loss of feeling and imagination in the Christian Church.
Poetry and love, he now said, should be the centre of his new religion.
'I have religion for dear Sophie, not love,' he wrote.

~

Novalis slowly returned to reality. He began to see friends and
consider new literary projects. His style of writing changed. His
sentences became shorter and more aphoristic. He replaced commas,
semicolons and full stops with em-dashes – *Gedankenstriche* in
German, literally translated as 'a line for thinking', a pause to breathe
and think. 'He thinks elemental,' Friedrich Schlegel explained, 'his
sentences are atoms.'

On 3 July 1797, when Friedrich Schlegel left Jena after his falling
out with Schiller, he stopped at Weißenfels to see his friend en route
to Berlin. It had been almost four months since Sophie's death, and
it was clear that Novalis's resolution to die was dissolving. As they
laughed, discussed and gossiped day and night, Novalis reprimanded
himself for having fun. 'This way of life is utterly ruining me,' he
confessed to his diary on 6 July. This was the last entry that Novalis
would date by counting back to Sophie's death – 110 days since she
had died. Novalis scribbled a warning to himself: 'beware when
dealing with Schlegel.' Friedrich Schlegel's enthusiasm was pulling
him back into the clutches of the real world.

In August, and then again in September 1797, Novalis went to
Jena. With Friedrich in Berlin, he spent much of his time with

August Wilhelm and Caroline Schlegel. He liked them, Caroline in particular. Impressed by their translations, Novalis spent hours talking and reading Shakespeare with them. Shakespeare's plays appealed to the friends on many levels. For them he was the epitome of the 'natural genius' as opposed to the polished refinement of the French dramatists Jean Racine and Pierre Corneille. Racine, for example, had followed the strict rules of classical tragedy and kept to a prescribed vocabulary of four thousand words – he was famed for his economic use of images and metaphor. The French tradition, Goethe said, could never express human intimacy and passion as Shakespeare did. His plays were instinctive and emotional, his language was organic and evolving. Perhaps most importantly, the power of the creative imagination was central to his works: 'The poet's eye, in a fine frenzy rolling', Novalis wrote to Friedrich Schlegel after reading the same line in August Wilhelm and Caroline's translation of Shakespeare's *A Midsummer Night's Dream*.

The quotation not only encapsulated their understanding of the role of the poet, but would also often be used by the English Romantics, who would worship Shakespeare just as much as the Jena Set. The reason for their admiration had much to do with August Wilhelm Schlegel's book *Lectures on Dramatic Art and Literature*,* which he would publish in 1809. Despite its dry title, the book excited a whole generation by contrasting the old and the new – the classical and the romantic – as no one had done before. In contrast to the strict rules of ancient poetry, August Wilhelm defined the new romantic movement as wild, raw, mysterious, chaotic and alive. Ancient poetry might be simple and clearer, but romantic art 'is closer to the secret of the universe' – it was the expression of 'original love'. And Shakespeare, he wrote, was the quintessential romantic writer.

August Wilhelm also attacked earlier critics who had judged Shakespeare's writing to be disordered, ungrammatical, vulgar and unlearned. The French writer Voltaire, for example, had declared *Hamlet* 'the work of a drunken savage'. Far from it, August Wilhelm argued over more than two hundred pages, Shakespeare had been misunderstood by eighteenth-century commentators. It was time to celebrate this master of human emotion who stood against the insipid

* *Lectures on Dramatic Art and Literature* was published between 1809 and 1811 in Germany, then translated into French in 1814 and finally published in England in 1815.

uniformity of rules. Rather than following rigid rules, Shakespeare's writing was animated and organic, unfolding from within like a plant developing from a seed. The English playwright blended nature and art, poetry and prose, the earthly and the heavenly, comedy and tragedy. A Shakespeare play, August Wilhelm wrote, 'is the spirit of romantic poetry dramatically pronounced'.

English poets and writers, such as Percy Bysshe Shelley, William Hazlitt and Thomas Carlyle, all read and admired August Wilhelm Schlegel's book. Samuel Taylor Coleridge was so impressed that he later used entire passages verbatim for his own Shakespeare lectures in London. Coleridge's friend and fellow poet William Wordsworth believed that 'a German critic first taught us to think correctly concerning Shakespeare'. August Wilhelm Schlegel had resurrected the playwright even for the English and was nothing less than the 'discoverer of Shakespeare', one American reviewer of *Lectures on Dramatic Art and Literature* wrote.

~

After months of grieving for Sophie, Novalis emerged feeling invigorated and energised. He thoroughly enjoyed Caroline and August Wilhelm's company. 'Few are more alive than those two,' Novalis reported to Friedrich Schlegel in Berlin. His mind felt more productive than ever before. As August Wilhelm wrote to Goethe, who was still in Switzerland, 'his melancholy has thrown him back on his abstract studies with redoubled force.' Friedrich also received a report, relieved, as he wrote to Novalis, 'that you're so busy again, that you are living'.

By the end of that year, Novalis was writing and reading at a frantic pace. He was about to embark on the most creative period of his life. He had also enrolled at the famous mining academy in Freiberg where Alexander von Humboldt had studied a few years previously. If Novalis was one day to run the mines, he would need to deal with annual reports and budgets as well as find coal seams and inspect shafts. To do so, he needed to learn about geology and the latest technological advances.

Arriving in Freiberg in early December 1797, he threw himself into his studies. Like Alexander von Humboldt before him, Novalis was inspired by his charismatic professor there, Abraham Gottlob Werner, the father of German geology. Werner's teachings on the creation of Earth attracted students from across Europe. The main proponent of Neptunist theory, he believed that mountains and the Earth's crust had been shaped by gradual sedimentation of deposits from a primordial ocean. Goethe followed Werner's ideas, as did Alexander von Humboldt* and now Novalis. Most importantly, Werner was the first to understand that rocks should not be classified through mineralogy or chemistry alone but also by age. It was the formation of rocks and the fossils found within them that revealed the history of Earth, he told students. Geology had become the study of an organic process.

Every morning, Novalis climbed down the steep ladders into the mines, accompanied by the creaking sound of a large wheel that pumped the ground water up. Water was dripping everywhere. Once below, he crawled along the labyrinthine network of narrow tunnels. Even with a compass, it was easy to get lost. For five hundred years miners had chiselled and hacked at these rocks to extract ore and silver. Shafts and tunnels crisscrossed at different heights and levels, some several hundred metres deep. As part of his studies, Novalis would often spend hours down here, investigating the construction, the miners' working methods and the nature of the exposed rocks. With only the weak light of a lamp and rocks covered in damp dust, it was difficult to make out the geological history. But he loved the work. Underground was a quiet and mysterious world, Novalis would later write in his novel *Heinrich von Ofterdingen*, a world that revealed the 'path into the hidden treasure chambers of Nature'.

When he emerged from the darkness, he brushed off the dust and walked back to the Academy for seminars and lectures on minerals and geology. In the evenings he studied more, but also worked on a novel. He slept little and worked hard. The next eighteen months in Freiberg were physically and intellectually demanding, but he was so alive that a friend compared him to a spark that could ignite 'an all-consuming fire'. Novalis, however, missed his Jena friends and 'the electricity I feel with them'.

As books and papers piled high in his room, Novalis studied mathematics, geology, physics and biology. Sometimes he was frightened by all the data and figures, he said, but the sciences had 'wonderful healing powers'. Like 'opiates', they relieved his pain and

---

* Alexander von Humboldt left Europe a Neptunist in 1799, but his observations in the Andes led him eventually to become a Vulcanist – explaining that Earth had been formed through catastrophic events such as volcanic eruptions and earthquakes.

gave him comfort. In Freiberg, Novalis became convinced that physics and chemistry were as much creative endeavours as paintings and poems. 'Laboratories will be temples,' he wrote in his novel *Novices of Sais*. Science, poetry and art belonged together. It was all one.

One expression of this growing belief was his 'encyclopaedia',* a project Novalis began in Freiberg and deliberately named to challenge Diderot and D'Alembert's famous *Encyclopédie* of 1751–80. Like Diderot and D'Alembert, Novalis wanted to collect information from all disciplines and subject areas, but unlike the *Encyclopédie*'s alphabetically ordered entries, his aim was to unite everything.

His notebooks are filled with more than a thousand sections which analyse, synthesise and connect everything from music to physics, poetry to chemistry and philosophy to mathematics. And he did so with a fluidity and lightness that reveals a mind wide open to everything. Novalis began to assemble his ideas and material under conventional headings, such as archaeology, religion, nature, politics, medicine, and so on, but also under more unusual groupings, such as 'theory of the future', 'musical physics', 'poetical physiology' and 'theory of excitation'. Some of these entries were just a line or couple of sentences long, others stretched over several pages.

His encyclopaedia was the ambitious attempt to create an 'absolute universal body of knowledge', he said, a scientific system that brought together what had for too long been separated. Like light that could be refracted into a spectrum of colours, so the mind had been divided, Novalis explained. It was time to unite what had been separated. His encyclopaedia would be a scientific bible, Novalis declared, and no less than the 'seed of all books'. It was audacious, bold and eccentric.

'The sciences must all be poeticised,' Novalis wrote from Freiberg. Yes, shouted Friedrich Schlegel, yes, why not? He too would turn physics into music, Friedrich said: 'what I really want is to make Euclid singable.' A poet understood the world better than a scientific mind, the friends believed, because the language of science was too

---

* Novalis began his encyclopaedia project in autumn 1798 but never finished it. In Germany the notebooks were posthumously published as *Das Allgemeine Brouillon* – the French word *brouillon* meaning 'rough draft'. It was not the title Novalis had chosen. In English, the translators used the more palatable *Notes for a Romantic Encyclopaedia*, but it remains more widely known under its cumbersome German title.

mechanical and atomistic. 'Poetry', Novalis insisted, 'is true absolute reality.'*

For Novalis, this was 'my Magical Idealism' – his somewhat idiosyncratic idea that we can transform nature with our 'magical, powerful faculty of thought'. In his world, thoughts could become real objects, and objects could become thoughts. Put simply, one day nature would conform to our will, provided that the mind was sophisticated or poetic enough. No matter that he had failed to will himself to die after Sophie's death, Novalis continued to believe that the self had the creative power to control the external world.

This was the opposite of what other scientists believed. From the late seventeenth century onwards, the scientific community had tried to strip anything subjective, irrational and emotional from their disciplines and methods. They wanted to eliminate any vestiges of the mysticism of the Middle Ages. Enlightenment scientists had tried to bring 'light' – hence the term – into the laboratories. Rigorous experiments, accurate data, precise reports, scrupulous observations and sophisticated instruments became the foundation of this new approach. Everything should be controlled, repeatable, measurable and ideally classifiable.

The eighteenth century was the age of classification. In the 1730s the Swedish botanist Carl Linnaeus had introduced his so-called sexual system, which classified the world of flowering plants based on the number of reproductive organs in the plants – the pistils and stamens. Over time, other systems became popular and botanists declared taxonomy the king of their discipline. Animals, insects, minerals and chemicals were classified too. Linnaeus had also invented a standardised system for naming plants. Instead of scientific names that included descriptions of leaves and blooms that could be '1 foot long', he gave plants short two-word Latin names that would be the same across the world and understood in all languages. Eighteenth-century nature was ordered and neat.

And at the very moment when Novalis called for the poeticising

---

* A few years later, the English poet Samuel Taylor Coleridge also poeticised the sciences. Inspired by Humphry Davy's chemical lectures, Coleridge brought together chemistry and poetry. 'We find poetry, as it were, substantiated and realised in nature,' he wrote. But he also went to Davy's popular theatrical performances to 'enlarge my stock of metaphors'.

of the sciences, the French were introducing their new metric system, which would replace the hundreds of different units of measurements that had been used for centuries across the world. The 'metre' was not based on body parts such as an arm, finger or the 'pied du roi' (the King's foot) but on the planet itself – it was one ten-millionth of the distance between the North Pole and the Equator. The 'metre' transformed nature into a measurable unit.*

It was against this increasingly rationalised world that Novalis turned. The Enlightenment, he said, had stripped all feeling and spirituality not only from knowledge but also from life itself. Measurements, scientific data, experiments and classification couldn't provide the answers for everything. This didn't mean that Novalis was against reason or enquiry; rather he advocated synthesis. Poetic thinking, he explained, reached places where philosophy and science couldn't follow. 'The more poetical, the more true,' he wrote.

～

Novalis saw this synthesis at the mining academy in Freiberg. Here he learned about geology and mining methods, about scientific theories of Earth's creation and how to find seams of ore; but the mines also gave him a new imagery of darkness, which became a hallmark of his poetry.

For centuries – from the Bible to Shakespeare – darkness had symbolised terror, destruction, evil and death, but Novalis gave it a new meaning. Going into the bowels of the Earth became a metaphor for going inside oneself. Two years later he would turn his experience of the mines and Sophie's death into his poems *Hymns to the Night* in which the Ich and the night were the main focus. 'Downwards I turn to the holy, unspeakable, secretive Night,' declares the Ich in the first poem, and again 'Down into the earth's womb', in the last. Novalis wrote of yearning for the night – this 'quiet messenger of infinite mysteries' – and asked: 'Doesn't all that inspires us bear the colour of the Night?'

He wrote that by going inward – into the darkness – the Ich went beyond death towards a higher existence. Why dream of travels through

---

* The metric system was written into French law in April 1795. The size of a metre was measured and calculated between 1792 and 1798, and the system implemented in 1799.

the universe when the universe was *within* us, Novalis wrote elsewhere, 'inwards runs the mysterious path'. While Alexander von Humboldt paddled along the Orinoco, deep in the rainforest, where few Europeans had ever been, Novalis plunged into the wilderness of his self.

Novalis juxtaposed, jumped and transcended genres. *Hymns to the Night* was magical with strange verses that dissolved order and divisions. Once again Novalis played with opposites – of night and day, life and death, of the here and the beyond, of the personal and the universal. Using seemingly contradictory metaphors and images, such as 'And you are Death who makes us healthy at last' or 'lovely Sun of the night', he inverted conceived ideas of night and day. At the same time as the British poet Samuel Taylor Coleridge was writing his famous poem *Kubla Khan* after an opium-laced dream, Novalis wrote of feeling the joy of the eternal night in the intoxication of wine, sexual lust and opium – the 'poppies' brown juice'. *Hymns to the Night* has been hailed as the most important poem of the young Romantics, yet with its shifting lyrical point of view, its changing perspectives from auto-biography to the history of humankind, and its alternating styles of blank verse, rhyme and prose, it has an almost postmodern feel too.

Novalis's celebration of the 'longing for death' and darkness turned everything upside down. It wasn't Freud who first explored dreams and the darker regions of the mind, nor William Blake or Coleridge, but the Jena Set. Whereas Enlightenment thinkers had declared reason as humanity's path towards light, the Jena Set shone their torch into another reality. 'The world becomes a dream, the dream becomes the world,' Novalis would later write in his unfinished novel *Heinrich von Ofterdingen*.

At a time when states like Prussia were managed as though they were factories by an army of civil servants – a 'mechanical administration', as he described it – and when the industrial revolution began to turn Europe into a clanking machine, Novalis took up his pen to fight against a sense of disenchantment with the world. As steam engines, clocks and manufacturing rationalised daily life, he turned inwards. It was a reaction against the increasing materialism of the modern world; against a new reality where people became cogs in this great big machine and money ruled everything. What was the point of riches, Novalis asked, if they simply made the globe spin ever faster. To roman-ticise the world, he suggested, is to make us see the magic and wonder of the world. The mission was to see the extraordinary in the ordinary.

9

'Sublime impertinence'
Winter 1797–Spring 1798:
The Dawn of Romanticism

FRIEDRICH SCHLEGEL WAS having fun. Attending one party after another, he electrified Berlin's literary circles. With his un-powdered dark brown hair, patched old clothes and threadbare rhubarb-coloured coat, Friedrich darted through the elegant high-ceilinged rooms of airy apartments in Prussia's capital, gulping champagne from crystal glasses and eating from delicate porcelain. Standing under chandeliers that cast the flickering light of hundreds of candles across polished floors and gilded mirrors, he was thoroughly enjoying himself.

Twenty-five-year-old Friedrich made an exhilarating guest. He was outspoken and provocative, calling for a creative chaos in the arts. The old system should be torn down, he asserted, and who cared if philosophical systems, literary genres and bourgeois conventions were also swept away. His hope was that a new 'aesthetic anarchy' would incite a '*happy catastrophe*' similar to the French Revolution. Friedrich Schlegel painted in broad brushstrokes. He wasn't interested in anything subtle or gentle. He saw the world through the prism of his personality – 'an analogy of his own character', as a friend explained. Everything had to be fiery, strong and bold.

'My acquaintances multiply as quickly as my works,' Friedrich had written to his brother in September 1797, two months after arriving in Berlin. One new friend was the twenty-nine-year-old Friedrich Schleiermacher, chaplain at the city's Charité Hospital. Steeped in religion and ethics, Schleiermacher's steady moral compass impressed Friedrich Schlegel. Schleiermacher, in turn, was swept up by Friedrich Schlegel's new philosophical ideas. It was, he told his sister, as if an 'unstoppable flood of new opinions and ideas' gushed out of his friend.

Soon the two men were sharing Schleiermacher's small lodgings at the Charité. They quickly established a daily routine. Friedrich Schlegel would rise early and make coffee. Schleiermacher would usually be woken by the clinking of porcelain, and, with the door open between their rooms, the two men would begin talking while still in bed and drinking their first cup of the day. After breakfast, they worked, read and wrote until lunch, which was delivered from a nearby tavern and washed down with a few glasses of wine. Schleiermacher then left to fulfil his chaplaincy duties and to see other friends. They met again in the late evening after parties or dinners. As friends joked, they were like a married couple.

~

It was also in Berlin, shortly after his arrival, that Friedrich Schlegel met Dorothea Veit, a thirty-three-year-old Jewish woman who was at the heart of the salon culture in the Prussian capital.* Dorothea was the daughter of Moses Mendelssohn, an Enlightenment philosopher who was so revered that he was known as the 'Jewish Socrates'. Mendelssohn had written on metaphysics, literature, politics, aesthetics and theology, and was famed for championing religious tolerance. Born to such intellectual aristocracy, Dorothea had been brought up in a household of books and had met some of the greatest thinkers of the age at her father's table.

Dorothea had inherited her father's brilliant mind, along with his dark eyes, strong cheekbones and narrow nose. She may not have been pretty – even her closest friend thought her beauty lay more in her spirit than in her features – but Dorothea was fiercely intelligent, opinionated, highly educated and as witty as Friedrich Schlegel. Seven and a half years Friedrich's senior, she was also married. At the age of fourteen, and with no say in the matter, she had been engaged to Simon Veit, a twenty-four-year-old banker. Moses Mendelssohn might have been a famous Enlightenment philosopher, but when it came to his daughter's future, he had ruled his household like most other fathers at the time.

Dorothea had nothing in common with her husband, who preferred account books and balance sheets to poetry and novels. Although the Veits had two young children, Dorothea was 'unspeakably unhappy',

---

* Dorothea changed her Jewish first name 'Brendel' to 'Dorothea' around the time she met Friedrich Schlegel.

as her old friend Wilhelm von Humboldt had noted after seeing her in Berlin a few years earlier. A year or two before meeting Friedrich Schlegel, Dorothea had fallen in love with a charming aristocratic adventurer from Italy who had stopped in Berlin on a whirlwind tour through Europe. Peripatetic, independent and in search of freedom, the young man had not stayed for long and their affair had been brief, but Dorothea felt the shortcomings of her loveless marriage even more acutely.

To escape her cheerless domestic life, she became part of the Jewish literary salons, the only places in Prussia where religious, class and gender boundaries were absent. Unlike the gatherings of the bourgeoisie, where women and men kept to themselves, embroidering or talking business respectively, Jewish salons were hosted by women. Men, women, Jewish thinkers, Protestant aristocrats, famous musicians, successful businessmen, uniformed soldiers, foreign diplomats and struggling artists came together to discuss literature, concerts, exhibitions and the meaning of life. The Humboldt brothers were part of this world too, having spent much of their early twenties here to escape from 'Castle Boredom', as Alexander von Humboldt called the family estate Tegel. They also knew Dorothea well. In the salons, Dorothea experienced how people were respected for their personality and intellect rather than for social standing, fortune or gender. 'The mind is a powerful equaliser,' Henriette Herz, Dorothea's oldest friend and herself one of the great Jewish hostesses, said.

It was in one such salon that Friedrich and Dorothea first met. They liked each other immediately. Unlike Novalis, Friedrich had never cared for shy pale young girls, preferring strong women such as his sister-in-law Caroline. Just as Friedrich liked books printed in a large font, Schleiermacher explained, so he was only interested in people who had strong and bold characters. Having never enjoyed much romantic luck, Friedrich Schlegel was captivated by Dorothea's intellect. 'In daintiness she lags far behind my sister-in-law,' he wrote to Novalis, but who cared given her mind. 'She's only a sketch, but in a wonderfully grand style,' he said. Dorothea was decent and upright, he told Caroline, and soon he couldn't imagine life without her. Dorothea, in turn, fell for his unruliness, for his erudition and childlike energy. Their relationship became, as Friedrich would describe it, an 'eternal union of their minds' – although Dorothea's admiration came close to unbridled devotion. She wasn't sure if she was worthy of 'The Magnificent One', she told Schleiermacher, because everything that Friedrich did 'breathed godlike enthusiasm'.

Within weeks, they were lovers. In September 1797, Friedrich wrote to Novalis that 'I'm expecting a beautiful *notturno* tonight' – a glorious night with Dorothea. There had been 'several explosions', he said, 'during which I unburden myself of some volcanic matter'. For Dorothea, though, the relationship meant risking her marriage, custody of her two young sons, financial security, her reputation and possibly also her freedom. The new General State Laws for the Prussian States codified in 1794 made her position very clear. Adultery could be punished with prison sentences of up to a year. But, like Friedrich, she felt so stifled by convention that she was no longer willing to compromise. 'Either great or small,' she told a friend, but 'I can no longer drift around on the shabby middle way.' Her love for Friedrich emboldened her.

~

It wasn't just pleasure which propelled Friedrich Schlegel during those months in Berlin. He intended to change the world and he wanted to do so fast, with words rather than swords. 'The letter is the true magic wand,' he would later write. Like Schiller, he had decided to publish his own journal. At the end of October 1797, three months after his abrupt departure from Jena, Friedrich announced his 'great plan' to his older brother August Wilhelm. Instead of writing commissioned pieces as wage slaves for unpredictable editors – 'prostitution' to Friedrich's mind – the brothers would become their own masters and do whatever they liked.

They would fight against the division between reason and feeling. They would celebrate subjectivity and imagination. They would wage open war against the literary establishment. And above all, their journal would be of 'sublime impertinence'. But it wasn't just a love for literature that drove Friedrich and August Wilhelm, so their older and more conventional sister Charlotte Ernst* told Novalis, her

---

* Charlotte Ernst (née Schlegel) was thirteen years older than her youngest brother Friedrich Schlegel. She was married to Emanuel Ludwig Ernst, a high-ranking court official in Dresden. A calm and patient sister, she would bail out her debt-ridden brother Friedrich several times – but she was also concerned about the impropriety of his love affair with Dorothea Veit.

brothers were also vain: they simply wanted to show the world how brilliant and clever they were.

The plan was for all their friends to contribute. Although most of the content would be provided by the Schlegel brothers themselves, Friedrich hoped that his beloved sister-in-law Caroline would participate as much as possible, either independently or in collaboration. More than anyone in their group, Friedrich believed in the equality of men and women. After all, it had been Caroline who had influenced so much of his thinking when they had met shortly after her imprisonment, and he admired her mind and spirit, and her vivid letters. Together they would shape public opinion. Maybe they should call the journal *Herkules*? Surely the god of strength would convey their message to the world?

With every stagecoach, another letter arrived in Jena from Berlin – sometimes a short note, but often a dozen or more pages. Friedrich Schlegel's handwriting was like his mind. His quill rushed over the paper, with some words crossed out and others squeezed between the lines or underscored for emphasis. Whole sentences were scribbled over with looping scrawls and doodles. So much ink bled through the paper that reading the reverse side was often almost impossible. He had no patience for elegant phrases, carefully formulated thoughts or neatly copied out letters. Unlike August Wilhelm's immaculate handwriting, Friedrich's words tumbled onto the page.

There was no time. What did August Wilhelm and Caroline think about his idea? What about the title for the journal? When should they begin? Who should they ask to contribute? Was Caroline going to write? Why was August Wilhelm not enthusiastic enough? 'How impatiently – yes, with what burning hunger – do I await your reply to my last letter today!' Friedrich wrote at the beginning of November. He had so many ideas that he could neither concentrate nor work.

In the end they settled on *Athenaeum** – a title that stood for freedom, democracy and learning. Amid parties, dinners and his trysts with Dorothea, Friedrich Schlegel tried to find a publisher, and there were rumours that he had embarked on an affair with a publisher's wife to get a deal. He dashed off notes to printers and to Jena, again and again demanding pieces from Caroline. Her natural literary genre,

---

* The Athenaeum was the temple of Athena in ancient Athens where students were taught and poets recited their poems.

he told her, was the rhapsody. Peppered with jokes, myths, tales and improvisations, these epic poems, which had been performed by singers in ancient Greek, most mirrored Caroline's lively personality. Maybe she could take her rich and sumptuous letters and turn them into 'a great philosophical rhapsody'? August Wilhelm's character was better suited to longer, denser pieces, while Friedrich himself was inclined to fragments of which, he claimed, he had an infinite supply. 'My whole self', he said, was in fact 'a system of fragments'.

Fragments were the perfect expression for Friedrich but also for Novalis, who said that 'my nature consists of moments'. The friends were the first to elevate a deliberate fragment – as opposed to the accidental, say the few surviving lines of an ancient poem – to a literary genre and it became their favourite. Some fragments were a short line or two, others were several paragraphs long. They covered everything, from art and nature to the self, from law and philosophy to history. Nothing was off limits. Some were amusing, such as 'the historian is a prophet facing backwards' or 'publishing is to thinking as the maternity ward is to the first kiss'. Other fragments embraced more serious subjects: religion, society, politics and revolutions. Friedrich Schlegel, for example, wrote: 'women are treated unjustly in poetry as in life. If they're feminine, they're not ideal, and if ideal, not feminine.' Novalis anticipated Karl Marx by half a century when he wrote that 'so-called religion functions merely as an opiate: stimulating – sedating – stilling the pain of weakness'.

As easily deployed for pithy criticism as they were for snappy barbs or short bites of wisdom, fragments required little research and could be composed over a glass of wine or a meal – and ideally when the friends were together. Fragments were 'marginalia on the writings of the age', as August Wilhelm explained. Dorothea called them Friedrich's 'spoiled children' and Novalis wrote that they were 'literary seeds' – while some might be barren others would sprout. Another advantage was that incendiary sentiments could be buried among hundreds of less radical fragments. It was unlikely that the Prussian civil servants in charge of censorship in Berlin would detect them, Friedrich thought; 'if you only write for philosophers, you can be incredibly daring before the police will notice anything, or even understand the audacity.'

These fragments also allowed them to publish the greatest variety of ideas in a very few pages – as funny and witty as they were, they were also efficient and succinct. 'Friends, the soil is poor,' Novalis wrote, 'we must scatter seed abundantly for even a modest harvest.' The more fragments, the better. This was a collective endeavour to which they would all contribute – a 'giant symphonising', as Friedrich said. Together, under the umbrella of the *Athenaeum*, they would inspire each other and work better. The new journal would be their communal work of art.

Friedrich was relentless. Had Caroline and August Wilhelm heard anything from Novalis? When was Caroline sending her fragments? Where were those by August Wilhelm? And what about Auguste, his 'stubborn little girl'? Was she going to contribute? Though only twelve, Auguste had been taught well by the adults – from mathematics to poetry. She was learning Latin and Greek, August Wilhelm was giving her writing lessons every morning, and from Berlin Friedrich requested a weekly list of the books she had read. Her correspondence with Friedrich Schlegel during this time reveals a spirited girl who had no problem keeping up with her quick-witted family. Friedrich adored his 'Äffchen Augustchen' – his little monkey – but also reminded her to continue the language lessons they had started.

'Farewell, sweet child, and study your Greek,' he signed off one letter. He asked for a list of the scientific subjects she was studying and requested that she leave margins in her Greek translations so that he could insert his comments and corrections. He teased her and wrote entertaining letters about his life in Berlin. In return, Auguste sent him gossip. At home in Jena, she must have heard about Friedrich's new love affair with Dorothea and promptly enquired. There was no reason for her to be jealous, Friedrich wrote back, Auguste would always have a special place in his heart. The letters were as playful as their relationship. She was a child *and* a young woman, Friedrich said, so that he could kiss her hand but still press her to his heart. And though the youngest member of their group, Friedrich thought she would make a fine addition to the *Athenaeum*. 'Won't Auguste contribute anything?' he asked on 5 December 1797 when he still hadn't received any fragments; 'during meals you could all come up with good ones, and Auguste can just write them down on the spot.'

By mid-December, six weeks after his initial letter, Friedrich Schlegel was bombarding Caroline and August Wilhelm with so many requests for material that the couple began to turn on each other. At one point, August Wilhelm even woke Caroline in the middle of the night shouting that she had to write something. The problem for Caroline was that the house was always full of guests, added to which she had been ill most of that winter, suffering from a stubborn cough, headaches and toothaches. In desperation, Caroline began to send the household out for dinners and concerts, just to have an evening on her own. In a nagging stream of letters, Friedrich persisted in asking her (via August Wilhelm) to excerpt fragments from their letters – 'from hers, yours, mine, Hardenberg's [Novalis's], or from wherever she wants, from heaven and earth'. Caroline, Friedrich insisted, was extremely talented at sleuthing out fragments. 'Like a truffle dog', they should hunt them down.

Why hadn't Caroline helped him to write about Goethe's novel *Wilhelm Meister*, he pleaded, her analysis would be different from his. Had she dispatched more fragments? Could she compose some fragments that were unmistakably hers? Perhaps she should assist August Wilhelm with one of his reviews, or write some of her own? And in a rare moment of self-reflection, Friedrich even wondered if leaving Schiller out of their critical survey of the latest literature was a good idea. 'Won't that be rather obvious?' he asked his brother.

In Berlin, Friedrich had found a publisher to finance the *Athenaeum* project, and as the contributions began to come in, Caroline assumed the role of editor. Self-assured, well read and never afraid to speak her mind, Caroline was perfectly suited to the task. She shortened, deleted, added and rearranged. She easily roamed across subjects and disciplines. Unlike the others, Caroline didn't publish books, poems or theoretical treatises under her own name, but her many letters reveal how easily she jumped from razor-sharp literary criticism to gossipy news and political developments. Within a page or even a paragraph, she could astutely dissect a play or poem, make editorial suggestions on her husband's or friends' work and joke about their adversaries. Caroline's strikes were perfectly aimed but never bitter or aggressive. Confident in her judgement, she dispensed criticism with a smile. Her thoughts, ideas and suggestions were at the heart of the friends' work and ambitions – but while everybody else tried to claim a piece of land on which to insert their stake, Caroline was like a river that flowed through the landscape, irrigating the dry soil and turning it into fertile fields.

～

In May 1798, August Wilhelm travelled to Berlin. The Royal Theatre in Berlin had asked him to consult on its first staging of Shakespeare's *Hamlet*, using his and Caroline's verse translation, and he wanted to help Friedrich with the *Athenaeum*. But August Wilhelm was not only interested in work. He soon became enthralled by the beautiful Friederike Unzelmann, one of Berlin's most celebrated actresses. Despite her diminutive stature, elfin Friederike had a strong presence and grace on stage which captivated August Wilhelm and many other admirers. She was a 'strange fairy child', he wrote in a poem, and soon rumours reached Caroline that her husband had embarked upon an affair with the married actress.

If hurt, Caroline didn't show it – their marriage had always been a practical arrangement based on mutual respect, friendship and their shared interest in literature. If August Wilhelm was having fun in Berlin, so be it. As Caroline joked with her old friend Luise, her husband was being fêted 'even by actresses' to whom he dedicated poems filled with 'tender sighs'.

Though busy with their social lives and flirtations, the Schlegel brothers worked on the *Athenaeum*. The first issue was ready in May 1798 and the second followed a few weeks later, in July.* Like Schiller's *Horen*, the *Athenaeum* was printed on cheap paper without any illustrations, and each issue came in at just under two hundred pages. Produced as a so-called octavo size, it was not much larger than a modern paperback. Though unassuming from the outside, its content was the friends' manifesto to the world.

This was a revolution of words. Language shaped minds, August Wilhelm Schlegel wrote in a fragment about the French Revolution, and language should therefore be 'republicanised through the power of the general will'. If language carried political power, then it had to evolve accordingly. Didn't France abound with new words associated with the Revolution? *Sans-culottes*, for example, which literally meant 'without breeches', referred to the common people who wore loose trousers rather than breeches and who were the true revolutionaries. Or *terroriste*, the term coined in 1794 in the aftermath of Robespierre's brutal reign. As writers, poets and philosophers, the friends used words as their weapons. It was time to deploy what Friedrich called the 'omnipotent alphabet'.

---

* The *Athenaeum* was published in six issues from 1798 to 1800: two issues in 1798, one in March 1799 and three in 1800.

The first two issues of the *Athenaeum* were filled with contributions by the Schlegels and Novalis. There was an overview of contemporary literature, a long review of Goethe's novel *Wilhelm Meister* and a piece about ancient Greek poetry, but half the pages featured fragments. Novalis had written more than one hundred fragments of various lengths, collectively published under the title *Pollen*.* Another set of more than four hundred were simply called *Fragments* and mostly written by Friedrich Schlegel but included also several dozen by Caroline and August Wilhelm, as well as some by Schleiermacher.

Pollen and *Fragments* became the foundational texts of a new movement, launching Romanticism on the public stage – it was 'our first symphony', as August Wilhelm Schlegel said. It was here, on the pages of the *Athenaeum*, that the term 'romantic' was coined and first used in print in its new literary and philosophical meaning. The German word *romantisch* was derived from the French word for 'novel' – *roman*. *Romantisch* or 'romantic' had been used in the sense of *romanhaft* – 'like a novel', and also as a descriptive term for picturesque landscapes; but it was in the pages of the *Athenaeum* that it received a new definition. When August Wilhelm had asked his brother to send him his explanation of the word 'romantic', Friedrich had replied that it was impossible because it was two thousand pages long. In the *Athenaeum*, he managed to summarise it in one, albeit long, fragment that spread over three pages.

> Romantic poetry is a progressive, universal poetry. Its aim isn't merely to reunite all the separate species of poetry and put poetry in touch with philosophy and rhetoric. It tries to and should mix and fuse poetry and prose, inspiration and criticism, the poetry of art and the poetry of nature; and make poetry lively and sociable, and make life and society poetical; poeticise wit and fill and saturate the forms of art with every kind of good, solid matter for instruction, and animate them with the pulsations of humour . . .

But what did this all mean? To romanticise was *not* to be sentimental, lovelorn or overly emotional. To romanticise had nothing to do with candlelit dinners or declarations of love, as we often understand it

---

* Friedrich von Hardenberg began to use the pseudonym 'Novalis' in the first issue of the *Athenaeum*.

today. The term 'romantic' has metamorphosed through several stages since the mid-seventeenth century. There is the original meaning of 'like a novel' and our modern understanding that associates the word with love or romance; but for the friends in Jena it was something much more ambitious. They wanted to romanticise the entire world, and this meant perceiving it as an interconnected whole. They were talking about the bond between art and life, between the individual and society, between humankind and nature. Just as two elements could create a new chemical compound, so Romantic poetry could weld different disciplines and subjects into something distinctive and new. Novalis explained: 'By giving the commonplace a higher meaning, by making the ordinary look mysterious, by granting to what is known the dignity of the unknown and imparting to the finite a shimmer of the infinite, I romanticise.'

Though the meaning of the term 'romantic' may have been confusing, it was the unwieldiness of the concept that the group liked: their definition was never meant to be a neat entry in a dictionary. Romantic poetry was unruly, dynamic, alive and forever changing, they believed, and should not be corseted by metric patterns because it was a 'living organism'. Its essence was 'that it should forever be becoming, never perfected', Friedrich Schlegel explained. It was inherently incomplete and unfinished. And because it was incomplete, Goethe explained a few years later, it left room for the imagination of the viewer or reader.

The friends employed the same open-ended and evolving modus operandi when they thought and wrote. Fichte, for example, developed his philosophy in front of his students; Novalis shaped his ideas as he read and excerpted; and Friedrich Schlegel formed his thoughts as he spoke. Ideas were formulated, overturned and discarded. They were not interested in a closed system bound by rigid rules but in a world view that was open and in flux. In the same way they pushed the rules that society had imposed on them, so they now pushed the boundaries of philosophy and literature.

At the centre of everything was poetry – but not poetry as we understand it today. The friends turned back to the original ancient Greek term *poiētikós* – 'creative' or 'productive'. For them, romantic poetry could be anything: a poem, of course, but also a novel, a painting, a building, a piece of music or a scientific experiment. They discussed the concept in great detail. Did this mean that everything could be transformed into poetry? Yes, Friedrich Schlegel believed, as long as it 'possesses an invisible spirit'. In fact poetry was within all of us. They agreed that poetry in its original sense was the foundation of their new approach. August Wilhelm Schlegel described it as the power to create the beautiful, and Novalis simply said 'to poeticise is to create'. It was within us and in nature – it was active and productive. And most importantly, it was not bound by rules. 'Annotations to a poem', August Wilhelm quipped in one fragment, 'are like an anatomical lecture on a piece of roast beef.'

What connected all this was imagination. It was the most important faculty of the mind, they insisted, because reason alone was not enough to grasp the world. Without imagination there wasn't an external world at all. This new approach provided the bridge between Isaac Newton, who had explained that rainbows were created by light refracting through raindrops, and the British poet John Keats, who would declare twenty years later that Newton 'had destroyed all the Poetry of the rainbow, by reducing it to a prism'.

Ordinary logic was cold mechanical thinking, Novalis wrote, but imagination was creative and alive. The future world was '*rational chaos*', he said, and at the centre of it all was the unruly power of the mind to create. The '*poet* is but the highest degree of thinker', Novalis explained. This didn't mean that they turned against science or philosophy – quite the opposite, they wanted to bring together what had been separated for too long. And that could only be done through imagination, and *that* he had abundantly, Novalis said, because it was the 'most prominent feature of my identity'.

For centuries, imagination had been relegated to a subordinate role in the discipline of philosophy. Already Plato had asserted that imagination only occurred in moments of ecstasy, when an artist or poet was possessed by a divine spirit. Later, philosophers such as Descartes, Spinoza and Leibniz had regarded imagination with suspicion because they believed that it could only ever provide an illusory account of reality. The British writer Samuel Johnson had called it 'a licentious and vagrant faculty'. Imagination was unreliable and obscured the truth, those earlier thinkers had believed.

Finally in 1740, David Hume had given it a more important role in his philosophy, arguing that 'men are mightily govern'd by the imagination'. Hume, though, believed its ability was limited because it was derived from our sensory experiences and impressions.

Imagination just combined what was already in our mind. When we 'imagine' a golden mountain, he explained, we just brought together the familiar ideas of 'gold' and 'mountain'.

It had been Kant and Fichte who had declared imagination essential for the process of gaining knowledge. Kant had granted imagination the important role of mediating between the sensory and the conceptual worlds. Similarly, Fichte placed it at the centre of his Ich-philosophy when he explained that imagination brought the non-Ich into existence. 'Imagination alone is the basis of all consciousness,' he wrote. Or as Friedrich Schlegel described it: nature was like a work of art or a poem – 'we write the world as a poem, so to speak, only we don't know it at first'. Fichte's elevation of the power of imagination was a first step, but, for the Schlegels and Novalis, he didn't go far enough because he failed to incorporate art or poetry into his philosophy. Alexander von Humboldt would go even further when he insisted on the importance of imagination in the natural sciences. It was like 'a balm of miraculous healing properties', he said.

~

The *Athenaeum* never sold in large numbers but it was widely read and the literary establishment would have noticed how Schiller was punished with complete silence. Goethe, by contrast, was heaped with praise.* 'Goethe is presently the true regent of the poetic spirit on earth,' one of Novalis's fragments read.

With the exception of Goethe, the motto was out with the old and in with the new. 'Whoever is too old for rapture should avoid youthful gatherings,' wrote twenty-six-year-old Novalis in the *Athenaeum*, for 'now is the time for literary Saturnalia – the more colourful life is, the better'. The *Sturm und Drang* era and in particular Goethe's *Werther* had prepared the way for the elevation of youth and the protest against conventions, but the Jena Set provided the philosophical foundation. In *Faust*, Goethe later immortalised the cult of youth with this verse:

---

* The friends' admiration was so great that some thirty years later another great German poet Heinrich Heine said that Goethe 'owed the largest part of his fame to the Schlegels'. Though a gross exaggeration, it illustrates how much they celebrated him.

Once over thirty you're as good as dead:
We'd do better to knock you on the head
At once, and finish you off straight away.

And though today we often associate the Romantics with idealising the past, this first generation saw themselves as moderns – so much so that this was even reflected in their spelling. Their style guide for the *Athenaeum*, for example, spelled the German word for 'imagination' – *Phantasie* – with an F, because the way they used the term was 'not Greek, but in fact romantic and modern', as Friedrich Schlegel explained. This didn't mean that they were turning away from antiquity – after all, Greece was the birthplace of democracy. Caroline joked with Friedrich Schlegel that it was only the 'degree of passion' that was different between his 'old Greeks' and her 'new French'.

Friedrich Schlegel used antiquity as a prism through which to see the present. He wanted to learn from antiquity, to find answers to the issues of contemporary art, literature and life. The question was not *what* the ancients had thought but *how*, not *what* their poems were but *how* they had composed them. He was not interested in the measured, elegant order that captured Goethe and Schiller, but in the wild Dionysian element – the sensual and the intoxicating. He wanted to tear down the rules of classicism but not antiquity itself. Referring back to Plato, Friedrich Schlegel elevated the 'poetry of the frenzied' over the 'poetry of the sober'. One of the reasons why they all loved Shakespeare was his emotional and often unruly language. The 'crooked line', as Novalis said, was a 'victory of free nature over the rule'.

~

The *Athenaeum* was their attempt to work collectively as a group. They wanted to 'symphilosophise' – a new term they invented. They added the prefix 'sym' to words such as philosophy, poetry, evolution and physics – it essentially meant 'together' or 'communal' and signified the way they strived to work in a kind of intellectual symbiosis. 'Symphilosophy is our connection's true name,' Friedrich Schlegel said – a concept based on the idea that two minds could belong together. Like divided halves, they could only reach their full potential when joined.

The *Athenaeum* was 'a strange phenomenon', the eminent Weimar poet Christoph Martin Wieland said, and Friedrich Schlegel proudly reported from Berlin that everybody was talking about 'how brazen we are'. This was exactly what he had wanted. 'The Schlegels', an old but disgruntled friend claimed, 'are against everyone alive and everyone who has ever lived.' Only Goethe was delighted with the way his young friends treated him. How could he not be? When Wieland questioned how Goethe could possibly let the Schlegel brothers praise him in such an exaggerated manner – where was the modesty in that? – Goethe simply replied: 'You just have to accept it, the same way you accept full-throated criticism.' He was having a great time and was looking forward to discussing the first issue with August Wilhelm in person.

Unsurprisingly, Schiller was less impressed by the *Athenaeum*. 'This know-it-all, cutting, implacable, one-sided tone makes me physically sick,' he wrote to Goethe, after reading the first two issues. By now, Schiller hated everything connected to the Schlegels – their publications, their personalities and their influence on others. For once, though, despite his deep loyalty to Schiller, Goethe openly rooted for the Schlegels. The fragments were a marvellous 'wasps' nest', Goethe replied, and a tremendous retort to the general mediocrity and triviality of the literary world.

But Schiller was not to be placated. The Schlegel brothers were egoistical, cold, repellent, exaggerated, partisan and heartless, he replied two days later, and predicted – or maybe hoped – that they would never be of any influence. The *Athenaeum* was full of nonsense, Schiller told his wife, and anyone who claimed to understand it must surely be mentally deranged. Goethe, meanwhile, told August Wilhelm how much he liked the fragments, but warned him that the journal had placed the brothers on a war footing with the literary establishment.

As it turned out, the sales figures didn't reflect their ambition – only a few hundred copies per issue were sold. But since the journal was circulated, borrowed and handed on from one reader to the next, its long-term impact was enormous. Some of the most important texts of the Romantic project were first published in the *Athenaeum*: *Fragments* and *Pollen*, of course, but also Novalis's *Hymns to the Night*. The group's celebration of imagination, their rejection of traditional literary forms and styles as well as their insistence on the value of individual experience, would later be found in most works of the

Romantic writers and poets. These ideas came to shape Romanticism across the world.

~

In June 1798, at exactly the same time as the young friends were publishing their new ideas in the *Athenaeum*, the British poet Samuel Taylor Coleridge was preparing for what he called 'my German expedition'. A day after William Wordsworth and Coleridge's soon-to-be-famous poem collection *Lyrical Ballads* was published, in September, the two poets sailed from Yarmouth to Hamburg in the far north of the Holy Roman Empire. Within days, Coleridge realised he couldn't afford to travel the three hundred miles south to Jena and Weimar. 'Frightened at the expences [*sic*]', as he wrote in his diary, he instead spent five months in nearby Ratzeburg and studied for several months in Göttingen. He soon spoke German fluently, though he admitted that his pronunciation was 'hideous'. He left for England the following summer with a bag full of philosophical books. Coleridge's German sojourn proved a turning point in his life.

He had departed England as a poet but returned with the mind of a philosopher. 'No man was ever yet a great poet', Coleridge later wrote, 'without being at the same time a profound philosopher' – or as the Jena Set saw it, poetry and philosophy were sisters that should never have been separated. Coleridge lived and breathed the ideas that came out of Jena. He studied the works of Kant, Fichte and Schelling, and later translated Goethe's *Faust* and Schiller's *Wallenstein*. 'There is no doubt', one of his friends later said, 'that Coleridge's mind is much more German than English.'

There were many similarities between the ideas that came out of Jena and those that then developed in England. In 1800, only two years after publication of the first issue of the *Athenaeum*, William Wordsworth would write in the new preface of *Lyrical Ballads* that good poetry was 'the spontaneous overflow of powerful feelings'. Similarly, many of the other English Romantics – Coleridge, Lord Byron, Percy Bysshe Shelley and William Blake – turned against the rigorous rules of neoclassical poetry. Previously, poets such as Alexander Pope had taken famous people or topics from the public sphere as their subject matter, but now the Jena friends and then the later Romantics included their own personal experiences in their writings. Instead of reason, intellect and rules, they turned to imagination, the self and emotions – an emphasis that still shapes our world today. Imagination, Coleridge believed, bridged the subjective and the objective: it was the proof that our minds are truly free.

It was also then, for the first time, that the fragment became a favoured expression of art and literature. We can see this in the early decades of the nineteenth century, in Byron's *The Giaour: A Fragment of a Turkish Tale* or in Pushkin's poems, which he called his 'fragments'. Romantic writers across Europe, from Spain to Poland, celebrated this new literary genre.

Over the next decade the impact of the *Athenaeum*'s fragments could be seen in other art forms too. Soon, pencil drawings, sketches and studies were exhibited in galleries and museums. The reason was, the French painter Eugène Delacroix explained, that there was more room for imagination in a 'sketchy work'. In the 1830s composers like Frédéric Chopin and Robert Schumann applied the concept of a fragment to music. Chopin's preludes, for example, are only preludes to themselves. Schumann described them as 'sketches, beginnings of *études*, or, so to speak, even ruins, a single eagle wing, all colourful and in wild confusion'. These pieces might end on a dominant chord that sounded like the preparation for another movement, or might begin in an ambiguous key that seemed to come out of nothing. Fragments were soon everywhere.

'Symphilosophy is our connection's true name'
Summer 1798: A Vacation in Dresden
and Schelling Arrives

B Y THE START of July 1798, most of the Jena Set were in Dresden. With the second issue of the *Athenaeum* published, it was time for a change of scenery and glorious Dresden was the perfect place for a vacation. Sometimes called the 'Florence of the North' or 'Florence upon Elbe' after the river which flows through it, Dresden was one of the most dazzling cities in the German territories. Situated a little more than one hundred miles to the east of Jena, Dresden had some sixty thousand inhabitants and was a popular tourist destination. Tall, richly ornamented baroque buildings lined shaded boulevards and the Lutheran Frauenkirche, one of Europe's largest churches, dominated the city's skyline. An elegant promenade built on top of the city's fortifications stretched high above the Elbe. Spanning the river itself was an enormous sandstone bridge, over four hundred yards long and more than ten yards wide. On a still day, when the water was calm, the river mirrored the city's spectacular silhouette. Everything in Dresden exuded grandeur.

Dresden was the capital of Saxony and the royal seat of the Saxon Elector Friedrich August.* Much of the city had been built in the early eighteenth century during the reign of August the Strong, a ruler said to have snapped horseshoes in half with his bare hands. He had an equally strong love of the arts, having returned from a grand tour of France and Italy with a burning desire to make his palace the equal of Versailles. He had filled his city with one of the finest collections of paintings, prints, sculpture and porcelain in Europe. With much of August's art now on display in Dresden's public

---

* The Saxon Elector Friedrich August was a relative of Duke Carl August of Saxe-Weimar.

museums and galleries, tourists flocked in from all over Europe to see the greatest collection of ancient Greek and Roman sculpture in the German territories, works by German masters such as the Cranachs and Dürer, and paintings and engravings by Rubens, Rembrandt, Titian, Goya, Velázquez, Veronese and Correggio. The city's most famous exhibit was Raphael's *Sistine Madonna*.

Caroline Schlegel and thirteen-year-old Auguste had gone ahead, arriving in mid-May. August Wilhelm and Friedrich Schlegel came from Berlin at the end of June. The four stayed in the large house of the brothers' older sister, Charlotte Ernst, whose husband was a court official. Charlotte was sociable, kept an open house and was as witty as her brothers. The day after the Schlegel brothers had arrived from Berlin, Caroline wrote to Novalis at the mining academy in Freiberg that everybody was longing to see him. 'Come soon, old friend – don't make us wait long,' Friedrich Schlegel added in a postscript. They were looking forward to a summer of 'symphilosophising'.

Novalis rode the twenty-five miles from Freiberg to Dresden as often as his studies allowed. He was a passionate horseman and never minded the long hours on horseback. He had changed since Sophie's death, the friends thought. Though his physique was still lean and delicate, his face seemed different. His eyes were now those of a 'Ghost-Seer', Friedrich Schlegel noted – almost colourless but piercing – and his ideas were becoming increasingly obscure. Among the bulbous glass bottles and vials in the chemical laboratory at the mining academy in Freiberg, Novalis had begun mixing powders and liquids in an attempt to concoct an elixir which would allow him to transcend his body. Ever since reading Fichte, Novalis had been interested in the concepts of mind and body. But could he make his body disappear and become spirit alone? Friedrich Schlegel was thrilled by the idea. 'He is seeking – on the path of chemistry, too – for a drug to cure physicality (via ecstasy),' Friedrich wrote in excitement. In a way, this was just another attempt to liberate the mind. Freed from the constraints of the body, Novalis believed, the mind might do anything.

As they strolled through Dresden's streets, or at dinner in the evenings, Novalis tried to elaborate his ideas. Couldn't they see how important it was to transcend the boundaries between the body and mind? Forget Fichte's eternally divided Ich and non-Ich. What Novalis wanted was 'to touch his own mind' – though Friedrich Schlegel had to admit that he had no idea what that really meant or how it was going to work. But he was too excited to consider practicalities. There was so much to do. The air, Novalis said, was 'full of the seeds of all things'. Fichte, who had spent the summer with his wife Johanne in Goethe's favourite spa town Karlsbad, in western Bohemia, also stopped in Dresden for a few days to see his Jena friends.

~

The friends couldn't wait to explore. Dresden was dominated by history and culture. In Jena, people met in taverns and parlours to discuss revolutionary ideas, whereas in Dresden the focus was on operas, concerts and exhibitions. In Jena the friends often went on long walks along the Saale, but here they admired architecture, paintings and sculpture. They spent most of their waking hours together. When artists, poets and thinkers came together like a family, Friedrich Schlegel would soon write in the *Athenaeum*, it was an '*ur*-assembly of humanity'. They went on walks along the boulevards, talking, gesticulating and laughing. Surrounded by a gaggle of younger poets, thinkers and philosophers, Caroline was in her element. Thirteen-year-old Auguste, who had inherited her mother's wit and spirit, tagged along. Never daunted by this fiery group, Auguste joked, discussed and formed her own opinions. Everybody thought her delightful.

Caroline, who had explored the city with Auguste during the six weeks before the rest of the group arrived, became their leader, guiding them through the galleries. There was the Japanisches Palais – the Japanese Palace – which didn't look Japanese at all but was a large baroque building set in beautiful gardens on the other side of the Elbe. It housed the famous Gallery of Ancient and Modern Statues, the royal library as well as the magnificent porcelain and coin collections that August the Strong had assembled. Standing in front of the Japanisches Palais, the friends would have seen high above them, emblazoned in golden letters on the architrave of the entrance, the words *Museum usui publico patens* – 'a museum open to public use'. Inside, and spread across ten large rooms on the ground floor, were three hundred sculptures and busts, as well as vases, an Etruscan altar, a Roman sarcophagus and even a few mummies.

Another museum where the friends spent many hours was the spectacular Gemäldegalerie – the famous picture gallery which was located in an elegant sixteenth-century building at the Neumarkt, a large public square just a block south of the river near the Frauenkirche. Here tourists could admire some fourteen hundred paintings and eight hundred plaster casts of ancient Greek and Roman sculpture – one the greatest art collections in Europe. But instead of hushed veneration, the friends burst into the galleries where others were quietly admiring or sketching. They argued and discussed, walking up and down in front of the art to observe it from all angles, raising their voices in excitement, ignoring or simply not noticing other visitors. Every morning 'they took possession of the galleries', one onlooker complained. In the manner of the time, the walls of the Gemäldegalerie were tightly hung with paintings often several rows high, the entire space filled with a riot of colours and gilded frames as portraits, landscapes and religious subjects vied for attention. Over the weeks that followed they moved from one artwork to the next, noisily debating and conferring. Novalis called the galleries 'a repository of all kinds of stimulation for the poet'.

They particularly admired Raphael's early sixteenth-century *Sistine Madonna* – a huge oil painting almost two metres by three, which depicts a tender Madonna with her child. Dressed in a floating cloak and suspended over swirling clouds, she is flanked by two saints and two cherubs as she carries her child into the world, down from the heavens. Commissioned by Pope Julius II in 1512, this artwork was more than a religious painting. For many, it united the earthly and the heavenly realms – the Madonna being a vision that appeared to the saints but also to the observer as she brought Christ to Earth.

This masterpiece became a favourite. Intoxicated by the Madonna's beauty, the young Romantics saw the painting as the perfect example of the merging of sensuality, religion and art. The Madonna's allure and grace could not be expressed in words, Caroline explained to her friends, for it 'goes straight from the eye into the soul'. For them, religious art had left the church and become poetic – an increasingly important subject of discussion in the year that followed.

One day, Caroline guided them to three different paintings of the *Penitent Magdalene*.* This was Mary Magdalene, who had long

---

* Two of the three paintings of the *Penitent Magdalene* were by Italian artists Franceschini (*c.* 1677/8) and Pompeo Batoni (*c.* 1742), while one was attributed to Correggio (painted in the first half of the sixteenth century).

A view of Jena from the south with the Church of St Michael at the centre and the Saale River in the foreground. The Jenzig and Hausberg mountains are to the right with fields on the slopes. The trees in front of the town are part of the Paradise.

A contemporary engraving of the imposing fortress of Königstein where Caroline was imprisoned in 1793.

Caroline Michaelis-Böhmer-Schlegel-Schelling in 1798.

Auguste Böhmer
shortly before her
death in 1800.

August Wilhelm
Schlegel in 1793.

Johann Wolfgang
von Goethe in Italy.

Johann Gottlieb Fichte
in Berlin in 1800.

Friedrich Schiller in
the early 1790s.

Jena's market square viewed from the south. The town hall is the building with the white tower to the left.

A popular promenade, Fürstengraben marked the northern border of the town. This contemporary view shows the street looking west to east. Goethe's botanical garden was situated along this street and the large round tower, front right, is one of the medieval towers of the old town walls. The ancient and empty moat is in front of the tower and the crumbling walls. In the background, at the end of Fürstengraben, the Old Castle is just about visible to the right.

Alexander von Humboldt
in South America.

Caroline Dacheröden–von
Humboldt in *c.*1810.

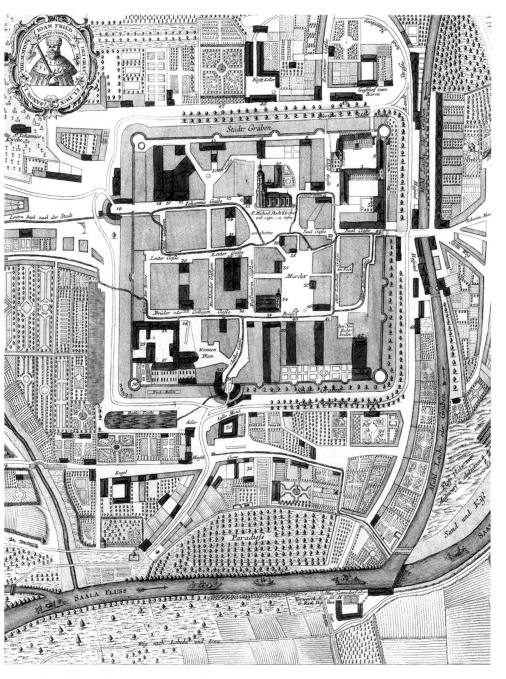

A mid-eighteenth-century map of Jena with the Church of St Michael at the centre. The Old Castle is in the top right-hand corner and the university in the left-hand bottom corner. The red parts of the map depict the town within the medieval walls. Beyond the walls are houses with large gardens, such as Schiller's Garden House. The Saale skirts the town at the bottom, with the Paradise situated adjacent to the river.

Novalis (Friedrich von Hardenberg) in 1799.

The courtyard at Leutragasse 5 where the Schlegels lived from 1796, as depicted in a photograph from around 1910. The house was destroyed in 1945.

been described as a sinner, as a loose woman and sometimes as a prostitute. Yet it was she who had stayed with Jesus at his crucifixion. How, Caroline asked as she examined the first image, could one hold her youthful sins against her? Didn't Mary Magdalene have the right to be happy? Wasn't it as if Mary Magdalene was saying, 'Can't you help me out of this labyrinth?' Or look at this depiction, Caroline said as she moved on to another *Penitent Magdalene*. There was no reason for her penance, Caroline declared. Why should she have to repent? Ushering her friends on to the third Mary Magdalene, Caroline explained that her pure soul could not be 'disfigured by a chance mistake from her youth'. Could Caroline have been thinking about herself? There certainly were echoes of her own life here.

As they walked on, the friends argued and debated. How do we understand art? How do we talk about it? Was art a representation of nature? How important was it? Were there rules? How was art to be judged? Was this objective or subjective? What was more important, sculpture or painting? Portrait or landscape? Caroline caught these discussions in an essay, 'Paintings. A Conversation', which was published in the *Athenaeum* a few months later.* Written as a dialogue, Caroline's piece allowed her to explore the different schools of thought without delivering a dry art historical treatise. It was learned yet easy to understand in its conversational tone.

Everybody enjoyed the lively conversations in the galleries; only Fichte, who knew little about art, was for once outside his comfort zone. A painter and family friend wrote to Charlotte Schiller from Dresden after bumping into the group in the Gemäldegalerie, knowing that she always enjoyed gossip about them. 'You would have laughed, dear Lotte,' the friend reported, 'had you seen the Schlegels with him [Fichte], dragging him around and pelting him with their latest beliefs.'

Only Dorothea Veit was missing in Dresden. Although she had yet to meet August Wilhelm and Caroline Schlegel, Friedrich had failed to persuade his older sister to allow Dorothea to stay at her house. His sister had made the situation clear: her husband

---

* Caroline was the main author of 'Paintings. A Conversation', but it was as always published under her husband's name. August Wilhelm Schlegel sent it to Goethe with a note that most had been written by his wife.

was part of the Saxon court, and under no circumstances could Friedrich conduct an affair with a married woman under her roof. The other reason was money, because on entering Dresden Dorothea would have had to pay a so-called 'Jew toll' – a tax levied on Jews travelling from one German territory to the next. Not only was it expensive, it was insulting and humiliating as it was also imposed on livestock. Some twenty years earlier, Dorothea's father, the philosopher Moses Mendelssohn, had complained that he had been tariffed 'like a Polish ox', on entering Dresden. Prussia had abolished the toll a decade earlier, but Saxony had not. But with Dorothea stuck in Berlin, Friedrich had his portrait painted in Dresden so she wouldn't forget him.

Nonetheless, Friedrich Schlegel was having fun. They drank good wine, ate well, feasted their eyes and fed their imaginations. Sometimes, in the late evening, as the sun's low rays haloed the yellowed stone of the Frauenkirche's magnificent stone dome, they set out again to Neumarkt. When the last light of the day dipped into the river, they climbed up the stairs to the entrance of the Gemäldegalerie. Here guides waited with burning torches, and for a small fee they took the friends through the deserted plastercast collections on the ground floor.

As they followed the flickering warm lights through the dark sculpture exhibition, the contours of the cold plastercast bodies softened in the theatrical play of light and shade. Except for the torches' moving light, the rooms were shrouded in total darkness. How different the space looked at night – empty, quiet and magical, like Novalis's celebration of darkness but writ in three dimensions. If imagination was like a building with many different rooms, maybe this was as close as one could get to walking through one's mind. In his laboratory in Freiberg, Novalis had been searching for a way to dissolve the boundaries between the body and the mind. Here, in the darkened galleries, the imagination materialised.

~

Art was not their only subject. They also talked about revolutions and war. Life in Jena had felt safe since the armistice between France and the Holy Roman Empire the previous year. Although the French had invaded Switzerland to help Swiss revolutionaries there proclaim a republic in March 1798, Napoleon was now mainly concentrating on Egypt. He believed that Egypt was the gateway to crushing British dominance in the Mediterranean Sea and weakening their access to the Indian subcontinent. Napoleon had set sail for Egypt with his fleet from Toulon in May 1798, just as Caroline and Auguste had arrived in Dresden. On 2 July, thirty thousand French soldiers had taken Alexandria.

By now many believed Napoleon to be the greatest general since Alexander the Great. Napoleon commanded not just his own army, Fichte said, but also those of his enemies 'because he always knows how to arrange things so that the enemy does exactly what he wants them to do'. Napoleon was in a sense their romantic ideal of a genius – propelled by his own talents and capabilities rather than touched by divine inspiration. For them, the French general embodied a force of nature – strong, majestic and enigmatic. It helped that Napoleon was fuelled as much by revolutionary passion as he was by a deep interest in the sciences, the arts, antiquity and literature – so much so that he had almost two hundred scholars join his army in Egypt. Their brief was to collect all the available knowledge in what was regarded as the cradle of civilisation.

As the French armies had marched through Europe in the previous years, they had also plundered private and religious collections. Carts and ships piled high with crates of paintings, sculptures and books arrived in Paris to fill the Louvre with treasures. Hundreds of old masters – more than fifty Rubens and a dozen Rembrandts among them – had been stolen from the Netherlands alone. Magnificent altarpieces, glowing still lifes and historical paintings, as well as natural history objects and entire libraries of rare books and manuscripts were packed up and dispatched to France. At times it seemed as though the army was directed by the locations of the greatest masterpieces rather than political motives.

'Above all,' Napoleon had demanded of the French envoy in Genoa two years before, in 1796, 'send me a list of the pictures, statues, cabinets and curiosities at Milan, Parma, Piacenza, Modena and Bologna.' The campaigns in Italy in 1796 had brought a particularly rich bounty as Napoleon confiscated tens of thousands of items ranging from Renaissance art and murals to Roman coins and bronze busts. As more cities and regions fell into French hands, the Italians were forced to hand over Raphaels, Correggios, valuable manuscripts and prized antiquities.

Priding himself on being cultured and learned, Napoleon always took his large and well-thumbed library on his military campaigns. So great was his love of the arts and sciences that he seemed prouder of having been elected as a member of the Institut National des Sciences et des Arts* than of being the commander-in-chief. In Egypt, he signed his letters 'Membre de l'Institut National, Général en Chef', placing his scholarly title before his military role. When Wilhelm von Humboldt saw Napoleon at the end of 1797 in Paris, he had described a lean and simply dressed man who looked intellectual, serious and thoughtful – a man who he could imagine writing at a desk, reading a book or experimenting in a laboratory but not on a battlefield. The friends' admiration was so great that they even bought busts of the French general to take home. And with all the battles taking place so far from Jena, war didn't quite feel real.

~

In Dresden the friends received some news that excited them greatly: one of Germany's greatest young minds was going to join them in Jena. Twenty-three-year-old Friedrich Schelling had been appointed the university's youngest ever professor of philosophy. They had all read Schelling's books, and August Wilhelm Schlegel, Fichte and Novalis had met him. Schelling radiated infinity, Novalis said, and had the potential to surpass them all. Fichte shared the general delight, too – not least because he believed that Schelling's publications were 'entirely commentaries on mine'. And August Wilhelm liked the young philosopher so much that he invited him to Dresden. When Schelling arrived in mid-August 1798, he was quickly adopted as a new member of the group.

Born in 1775, in a small town not far from Tübingen, in the Duchy of Württemberg, Schelling had been raised by kind and patient parents. His bookish and learned theologian father had co-incidentally studied under Caroline's father in Göttingen. Schelling had always done things young. He was bright and his father had taught him well. Aged eleven, Schelling had informed his teachers

* After the Revolution, the Académie des Sciences was incorporated into the Institut National des Sciences et des Arts. In 1816 it once again became the Académie des Sciences – and part of the Institut de France.

that they had nothing new to teach him. Fluent in Latin and ancient Greek, he was years ahead of his peers. Yet despite his precociousness, he was also sociable and easily made friends.

In 1790, aged fifteen, Schelling had been enrolled at the local university, a Protestant seminary known as the Tübinger Stift, despite being three years younger than the other students. It had been his father's decision that he should be a clergyman, although Schelling had no interest in theology. Nonetheless, his time at the Tübinger Stift had a profound impact on his life. Schelling soon found himself sharing a room with Friedrich Hölderlin and Georg Wilhelm Friedrich Hegel, both deep thinkers who, like Schelling, would become famous too.

The Tübinger Stift was a huge stone building perched high above the Neckar River. Plain interiors gave it a monastic feel. The young students slept in cold rooms, their rigid daily routines supervised by monks. Discipline was strict. The chancellor of the university made it perfectly clear that he wanted to break his students' wills while they were still young. They were not allowed to smoke, dance, visit taverns or even ride. They were forced to have the same haircut and had to wear a uniform – a long black coat that looked similar to a cassock, adorned only with a clerical white collar. Every aspect of their lives was controlled, and punishment was enforced in the seminary's own jail. Students said they felt like rowers in a war galley or like 'a miserable cog in a slave machine'.

They were bored and uninspired by their mediocre professors. Schelling felt stifled by the conservative intellectual conventions. At first obedient, he soon began to rebel. He skipped lessons and church services – and was punished for his disobedience. Nonetheless, his grades never slipped. Instead of following the rules, Schelling and his two friends, Hölderlin and Hegel, celebrated the French Revolution, sang the Marseillaise, read Schiller's *Robbers*, studied Kant and admired Fichte's new philosophy. They also secretly read French newspapers, and with Tübingen closer to France than most other German cities, they could almost smell the incendiary ideas from across the border.

Having been raised in the Duchy of Württemberg – under the same absolute ruler who had made Schiller's early life miserable – Schelling was desperate for the moment 'when I will breathe free air'. A political revolution alone, he believed, was not enough. It wasn't just the state that needed reforming, the mind also had to change radically. They had to go further than Kant had ever dared, Schelling had told Hölderlin and Hegel. Everything had to be shattered and rebuilt. Young men like them had to unite.

The result had been a one-page resolution, which despite its brevity was so radical and visionary that it covered everything that would come to drive the Jena Set's thinking.* It fizzed with new ideas. Unite what had been kept apart, it dictated. Tear down all divisions. Philosophy should be sensual, mythology should be philosophical, and poetry should be 'humanity's teacher'. As Novalis and the Schlegels had demanded, they also wanted to poeticise the sciences, to 'give physics wings again'. Much like Schiller's 1795 *Letters on the Aesthetic Education of Man*, this short manifesto saw beauty as the key to unifying everything. And, of course, there was the Ich again, proclaiming its power:

> The first idea is naturally the conception *of my self* as an absolutely free being. Along with the free, self-conscious being an entire *world* emerges simultaneously out of nothingness.

Brought up against the backdrop of the French Revolution, Schelling, Hölderlin and Hegel had witnessed such seismic political shifts that the prospect of a free will seemed for the first time truly possible. 'The Alpha and Omega of all philosophy is – freedom!' twenty-year-old Schelling had declared in his first full-length book, *Of the I as the Principle of Philosophy*, published in 1795, the year that he left the Tübinger Stift. The title revealed his intellectual debt. When Schelling had heard Fichte lecture in Tübingen, he had told Hegel that 'the age of philosophical darkness is now over'.

∼

Like Fichte, Schelling wrote about the Ich and its relationship to the external world, but soon diverged on one crucial point. Unlike Fichte, Schelling did not declare the external world simply as a

---

* This is the so-called 'The Oldest System-Programme of German Idealism' – a title it only received in the early twentieth century. Today, there is much debate about who actually wrote the manifesto. Found in Hegel's papers, it was transcribed in his handwriting. It was first published in 1917, and scholars have variously named Schelling, Hegel and Hölderlin as the author – with the majority claiming it was Schelling. It was probably written at the end of 1796 or the beginning of 1797.

non-Ich. Instead, he explained that nature and the Ich were an interconnected whole. This was Schelling's so-called *Naturphilosophie* – his 'nature-philosophy' – and the subject of the three books he had published in the previous three years. Though the books made him famous, he still had to make a living. Like Fichte and August Wilhelm Schlegel in their time, and now Hölderlin and Hegel, so Schelling worked as a private tutor for a wealthy family. But at least his pupils were older, and in 1796 he had accompanied them to Leipzig where they studied. It had been there that he had first met August Wilhelm and Novalis.

Schiller had also been impressed by the work of the young philosopher, and had talked to Goethe about finding him a position at the university in Jena. Initially, Goethe had been reluctant. Another Ich-philosopher? Another idealist? Goethe had always called himself 'a rigid realist', but, since meeting Schiller and Fichte, he had begun to appreciate some aspects of Idealism – a school of thought which insisted that reality was inseparable from our minds and our perception.* Gone were the times when Goethe, as one acquaintance remarked, was 'drowning in matter', but he wasn't fully convinced. He placed himself somewhere *between* the realists and the idealists. Schiller may have shown him a path away from 'an unnecessarily strict examination of external things', Goethe said, but he liked his place in the middle.

Now, though, having spent four years surrounded by his new friends, Goethe felt that one couldn't know nature purely through observation. One made sense of the external world through the categories of the mind, he admitted, but that didn't mean the idealists were right either. Fichte objected to this view. Never someone who inhabited the middle ground, Fichte argued vehemently against those thinkers who based their knowledge on experience and observation. How could they claim to know what a tree is, for example, just by looking at it? How could they 'possibly know, the very first time they saw a tree, that it was a tree and not their nose'? It was not our experience, Fichte believed, but the Ich which created our knowledge of the tree. The tree was simply in our mind.

---

* Some commentators and philosophers have suggested that 'Idea-ism' would be a more useful term than 'Idealism' since idealists believe that 'ideas' or the mind, not material things, constitute and determine our reality.

Goethe disagreed. Why should Fichte think his the only correct way to understand nature? What about Goethe's own studies? What he had learned through his investigations in comparative anatomy, for example, illustrated that animals were shaped by their environment and not by the observer's mind or imagination. A fish's body was adapted to its watery habitat, much as the giraffe's neck was adapted to the high foliage of the trees in the African savannah and the wings of a bird to its life in the air. Climate, altitude, temperature, water, air and more, Goethe believed, were the factors that determined how animals developed.

How could the Ich-philosophers explain that? Did they really believe the Ich just posited itself and that that very act then brought the non-Ich, or at least the knowledge of the non-Ich, into existence? 'Well, until the philosophers come to some kind of agreement about how to reunify what they've divided,' Goethe joked, he would enjoy his 'undivided existence'. He wasn't sure if Schelling would be able to provide answers but he was intrigued enough to invite him to Jena.

∼

In May 1798, Schelling had travelled the sixty-five miles from Leipzig to Jena to meet Goethe. The poet had asked the young philosopher to come to his rooms in the Old Castle, and there Schelling found him surrounded by books, papers and scientific instruments. During Schelling's four-day visit, they also saw Schiller three times and Fichte one evening. Goethe liked Schelling. It helped that, unlike Fichte, Schelling was deeply interested in the natural sciences.

Two days after Schelling's arrival, Goethe wrote in his capacity as privy councillor to Minister Voigt, his colleague in the Weimar administration, suggesting that the university in Jena should make an offer. Schelling was brilliant and learned, Goethe wrote. He would make the university proud and be a great addition to the 'Jena circle'. The university's administration deliberated and a few weeks later, on 5 July 1798, Goethe was able to inform Schelling that he was expected in Jena in early October. Schelling then formally requested permission to leave for Jena from his ruler, the autocratic Duke of Württemberg, and gave notice to his employers when it was granted. He packed his belongings and asked his parents to send some bedding to Jena – to avoid 'sleeping in a rented bed, when God knows who has slept in it before'. Then, on 18 August, he had arrived in Dresden to enjoy, as he told his father, 'a few months of freedom'.

Schelling spent the next six weeks with the Jena Set. They all liked him. 'He seems to have a very poetic mind,' Novalis said – his greatest compliment. Schelling's appearance mirrored the strength and energy of his mind. Broad-shouldered and compact, the handsome twenty-three-year-old had incredibly clear blue eyes, which beamed with certainty. He looked as young as he was. He had thick curls, wide cheekbones, full lips and a slightly upturned nose. Schelling looked 'strong, stubborn, tough, and noble, through and through' – more a French general than a lecturer, Dorothea Veit thought when she later met him. Caroline Schlegel saw him simply as 'the kind of man who bursts through barriers'.

In Dresden, Schelling spent almost every day with his new friends, even though he couldn't always follow their jokes. A quiet and earnest young man, he was largely incapable of small talk and rarely talked about his feelings. If he had nothing interesting or important to say, he kept silent – but in Dresden he came alive, happily explaining his philosophical ideas. In return, the friends introduced him to their great romantic project of poeticising the world.

Schelling was impressed by everything. The art was divine, the ancient sculptures alive, the architecture imposing, the countryside glorious, but most of all he was enthralled by this group of people. He was so captivated that he forgot everything around him. 'Go ahead and be angry!' he wrote to his parents at the end of September, acknowledging that he had not written from Dresden. He had been too busy. There was no time to send them a colourful account, he wrote, they would simply have to wait until he visited them next year. 'What's a year?' Schelling scribbled; 'only 365 days.' He was happier than he had been for a long time.

But then, as summer turned to autumn, it was time to leave. Novalis returned to the mining academy in Freiberg and Friedrich Schlegel to Dorothea in Berlin. As always, Friedrich had run out of money. Where to live cheaply? How to earn more? Where to work? 'And so the ideal is bound up with the real,' he warned his friend Schleiermacher. Fichte, who had left early, set his pride aside and paid a surprise visit to Schiller on his return to Jena – the first step towards a reconciliation after their falling out over Fichte's essay for *Horen* three years earlier. Because Fichte had made the first step,

Schiller told Goethe, he would play along, regardless of the fact that they would never agree on philosophical matters. August Wilhelm Schlegel, Caroline and Auguste stayed on in Dresden until the beginning of October, when they too travelled back to Jena.

Schelling set off at the same time with an acquaintance he had met in Dresden, but travelled a different route because he wanted to stop off in Freiberg. Having met Novalis in Dresden, he was keen to see the mines, the dark shafts that led into another world – the 'dark tempting lap of Nature', as Novalis later described it. Annoyingly, Novalis wasn't in Freiberg on the day Schelling visited, but another student showed him around.

As they climbed down the steep, almost vertical, wooden ladders, and the last blue of the sky disappeared above, they entered a cold darkness. They crawled along narrow damp tunnels barely illuminated by the weak light of their lamps. It was eerily quiet down here, the only sound the muffled clank of the miners' distant pickaxes and the constant drip of water into puddles on the ground. Schelling's travelling companion was so spooked that he fled back to the daylight. Schelling, though, didn't mind. This was Novalis's magical world of darkness and wonder.

PART III

Connections

The consoling word, as you put it, affects me much more deeply: Love, you say. What kind of love? Where? In heaven or on earth? . . . You know how much love for you we have here, so there is no kind of love you should feel you can't speak of with us.

Caroline Schlegel to Novalis, 4 February 1799

'To be one with everything living' Autumn 1798–Spring 1799: Schelling's *Naturphilosophie*

WHILE THE FRIENDS had been enjoying their summer in Dresden, Goethe and Schiller had been distracted by masons, carpenters and painters. Schiller had added a small building at the end of his garden to house a kitchen and a separate two-storey pavilion with a bath on the ground floor and a study above. Meanwhile, Goethe had been working on a grander scale, supervising the renovations of the theatre in Weimar. Whereas Goethe enjoyed the creative process of building and renovating almost as much as he did composing a poem, Schiller hated the disruption and dust. Goethe, though, had objections to Schiller's home improvements. Why had Schiller placed the new kitchen so close to the charming bower in which they usually sat at the back of the garden? Clouds of smoke mixed with the smells of burned fat, boiled cabbage and fried meat – basically the entire dinner menu – now drifted through the flowers and shrubs to the stone table where they would talk on warm summer evenings. Schiller may have been a great poet and playwright, Goethe thought as he tried to avoid breathing in, but his architectural skills were not impressive.

Whenever there had been time that busy summer of 1798, Goethe rode to Jena. There he experimented with magnetism, inspected the botanical garden, and saw Schiller almost every day. During those weeks Goethe had discussed with Schiller the possibility of turning Schelling's new philosophy into a poem and also dusted off his 1790 essay *Metamorphosis of Plants* to rewrite it in verse. Like the younger generation, Goethe liked the idea of blurring the boundaries between the sciences and art.

He walked through life with the curiosity of a scientist. He prodded, questioned, and noted the smallest occurrences. One day at the end of July 1798, for example, while strolling through his garden in Weimar, he had noticed that all the flies seemed to be buzzing around one particular flower. When he took a closer look, he realised that no bees or beetles were anywhere near the plant. Why was only one insect species attracted to this plant, he wondered, making a note in his diary to investigate other flowers. 'The Wicked Angel of Empiricism', he joked with Schiller, 'continues to pummel me.'

~

When Schelling arrived in Jena on 5 October 1798, he immediately visited Schiller, finding him preoccupied with the imminent premiere of the first part of his *Wallenstein* trilogy. Goethe, Schelling learned, had left four days earlier to prepare the newly renovated Weimar theatre for the staging of this tragedy about Albrecht von Wallenstein, the most notorious warlord during the Thirty Years War. Having worked sporadically on the drama for years, Schiller had been encouraged by Goethe to pick it up again and had been working on *Wallenstein* in earnest since late 1796. The play marked a renewed focus on drama for Schiller, but it was decidedly different from the emotional register of his earlier plays such as *The Robbers*. By contrast, *Wallenstein* is a cynical and pessimistic play about the tension between personal interest and political allegiance, between individuality and moral duty. Today it is regarded as one of Schiller's most important works.

Goethe had read every scene of *Wallenstein* while Schiller worked on it, and had convinced his friend that the play should open the Weimar theatre's winter season. Schiller, though, continued to tinker with the text. He couldn't let go. With the date of the premiere rapidly approaching, Goethe had to pull the manuscript out of Schiller's hands. As rehearsals began, Schiller continued to rewrite, with the actors despairing that the lines were changing before their eyes. Still he would not stop, and with each passing day a delivery maid carried yet more edits from Jena to Weimar. On 9 October, just three days before the opening night, Schiller was still sending new verses and lines.

August Wilhelm Schlegel was also busy. While in Dresden, he had received the news that he too had been made a professor. Finally, he could supplement his income from writing by teaching at the university in Jena. He was soon completely overworked, juggling his lecture commitments with translating, reviewing, editing his poems and supplying content for the *Athenaeum*. Obsessed with detail to the point of fastidiousness, August Wilhelm had a talent for making unnecessary work for himself. When Christian Gottfried Schütz, one of the editors of the *Allgemeine Literatur-Zeitung*, made a minor editorial change to one of his reviews, for example, August Wilhelm dashed off a letter of complaint. Schütz calmly replied that even August Wilhelm Schlegel's writing was not 'unimprovable'. Though they lived in the same town and saw each other often at dinners or parties, August Wilhelm then responded with an eight-page letter listing his objections to the change. His attention to detail was time-consuming and exhausting. At thirty-one, he had begun to look older, his face tired and strained by exertion.

Caroline's workload increased in tandem. She was rarely able to leave her husband's study, she told Novalis, but she spent what little free time she had with the new Jena resident, the 'stubborn Schelling'. Twelve years younger than the thirty-five-year-old Caroline, Schelling had all the elan and energy the exhausted August Wilhelm lacked. He soon became a regular visitor. It was a short walk to Leutragasse from Schelling's lodgings outside the old walls, just opposite the western gate tower. And as his lecture requirements were not too onerous, Schelling often joined the Schlegels for lunch, parties and other social gatherings.

Then, in mid-October, soon after they had all arrived from Dresden, the Schlegels, Fichte, Schelling and some other friends went to Weimar to see the premiere of Schiller's *Wallenstein* – though for once they left Auguste in Jena because the tickets were too expensive. Whenever they went as a group to Weimar, they rented a carriage, but when the men went on their own they often walked to save money. This time there were enough people to justify the transport cost,* and they were looking forward to seeing the newly renovated theatre.

Goethe had been the theatre's director for several years, somehow managing to add yet another role to his numerous other duties. In charge of the performances and set designs, he had also overseen the remodelling of the interior. The result, as Caroline described,

---

* At the end of the eighteenth century the cost for a carriage from Jena to Weimar was 2½ thalers while a horse was 1 thaler for half a day.

was a 'shining fairy palace'. When they arrived that evening, they found that he had installed new balconies and horseshoe-shaped galleries. The columns were painted to resemble yellow marble and curtains were decorated with Greek allegories. Every surface had been freshly painted and gilded, and a huge new chandelier with a circle of oil lamps in the latest London fashion illuminated the room. Goethe had been childlike in his excitement, Caroline wrote to Friedrich Schlegel in Berlin the next day, and had even worked side by side with the carpenters and painters. Everything had to be perfect for the opening night and Goethe had been involved in every detail. The large background canvas of the stage set, depicting Wallenstein's military camp in the Thirty Years War, for example, had been modelled on a scene Goethe had seen painted on an old stove in one of Jena's taverns. Goethe had 'kidnapped' the stove and taken it to Weimar for the artist to copy.

Goethe loved the theatre. Here he was the maestro who conjured up stories and put his audience under a spell. He was also a great host, always bringing food and wine to his box to pass around. He chatted with friends and acquaintances as they walked in, leaning over his box to see who was entering his auditorium as a Roman emperor might watch his gladiators in the arena.

Caroline always enjoyed the theatre and opening nights particularly. The first performance, she said, was like the 'first glass from a bottle of champagne'. This evening was a special treat. Goethe was there, the theatre shone and Schelling had accompanied them. But she didn't like the play. Ever since their falling out more than a year earlier, the Schlegels had kept their distance and become increasingly critical of Schiller's writing, no matter how influential his earlier work had been for them. 'Schiller took years to produce what Goethe could probably have written . . . in an afternoon,' Caroline now said. The costumes were nice though, she wrote to Friedrich Schlegel, and the actors performed well, injecting a lively enthusiasm that compensated for Schiller's dry prose.

After the performance August Wilhelm stayed in Weimar for a meeting with Goethe the next day while Schelling escorted Caroline back to Jena the same night. It was a good three-hour carriage ride from Weimar to Jena, exhausting enough by daylight but at night in mid-October it could be very cold and hazardous. The first part of the journey was through farmland where harsh winds often blasted across open fields in late autumn, but more concerning were the thick forest and steep winding road that followed. This area was known for its highway robbers, and it was pitch dark along the route except for the lanterns fastened to the carriage. But Caroline was in high spirits.

The evening had been fun and she was a little giddy after the four glasses of champagne which Fichte had forced on her at the theatre. In the past Caroline had enjoyed the frisson of danger, whether witnessing the revolution in Mainz or embarking on an illicit affair with a French officer. It had never stopped her. And three hours in a dark bumpy carriage along a deserted road also meant sitting next to Schelling for the entire time. The temptations were as delicious as they were risky.

When the second part of the *Wallenstein* trilogy was performed a few weeks later, Caroline decided not to go with the others but stayed behind in Jena. She hadn't enjoyed the first part, she told her husband, so why should she endure the second? Conveniently, Schelling also remained in Jena, pleading work commitments. No one suspected a thing.

Caroline was alone in her criticism of *Wallenstein*. The play was a huge success and audiences fought for tickets. Schiller had turned a corner. For days nobody talked about anything else, he proudly wrote to his old friend Körner in Dresden. In fact the printed *Wallenstein* sold so well that Schiller's publisher, Johann Friedrich Cotta, began worrying about his valuable author's safety. One day, shortly after a visit to Schiller, Cotta was surprised by a sudden thunderstorm. As violent lightning sliced the sky, he had found himself thinking about Schiller's Garden House, which stood on its own, exposed to the elements, on the outskirts of Jena. The next day Cotta wrote to Schiller, insisting on paying for the installation of a lightning rod.

～

Slowly autumn was replaced by winter. In mid-November 1798, Goethe returned to Jena with the first snow, and as the sound of sleigh bells filled the frosty air, the hardest and longest winter of the century began. Seven watchmen had frozen to death in a single night, Friedrich Schlegel wrote from Berlin, and across the German territories everybody complained about the Arctic temperatures. 'It was so cold – very cold – shocking Cold – never felt so cold in my life,' the English poet Samuel Taylor Coleridge wrote to his wife from Göttingen four months later, in March, after a bitterly cold six-day coach ride from Ratzeburg.

Wrapped in his fur coat with his belly strapped in by the thickest of his stripy waistcoats, Goethe enjoyed Jena's white winter dress. Snow crunched under shoes and sleigh runners, and glistening icicles lined the roofs. The stove kept his rooms in the Old Castle warm and he was able to concentrate. Nine days after his arrival, he dispatched a note to Christiane in Weimar, informing her that she would have to wait a little longer for his return because he needed more time to finish his projects.

In Jena, he worked on his colour theory, continued to study Schelling's *Naturphilosophie* and saw his friends. There were quiet evenings at Schiller's apartment but also dinners with the Schlegels at their house in Leutragasse, as well as large private parties and gatherings at the Professors' Club at the Zur Rose. As Goethe flitted from one party to the next, Schiller stayed at home, sometimes spending the evening playing cards with Schelling. Once again Goethe was inspired by Jena's intellectual buzz – 'I always find all this busy-ness contagious,' he wrote to an old friend on 28 November 1798. And for once not even Schiller was depressed by the long dark nights but rather cheered by the clear skies and glittering cold. 'Today's winter day, interrupted by sleighbells throughout, was not unpleasant,' he wrote to Goethe at the end of November. The weeks Goethe spent in Jena were always Schiller's favourites. Goethe's arrival every evening 'wound up the clock of my thoughts'.

But even when he wasn't in town, Goethe remained part of his friends' lives. Twice a week, letters and borrowed books but also sausages, fruit, wine, tea and other groceries bumped along the winding road between Weimar and Jena. Sometimes Goethe just sent short notes which accompanied manuscripts, other times he suggested books to review or asked for information. Taken together, the knowledge available in the minds of those who lived in Jena was like a great living encyclopaedia covering a vast range of subjects from antiquity to comparative anatomy, from electricity to Spanish literature, from philosophy to poetry, from history to botany – quite the opposite of the conversations Goethe had with the courtiers in Weimar.

~

By the beginning of 1799, three months after moving to Jena, Schelling was eating most meals at the Schlegels' house, and on 27 January he celebrated his twenty-fourth birthday with the couple and Auguste. Occasionally, he and Caroline went out for long walks, leaving August Wilhelm in his study.

Caroline was captivated. She couldn't be in a room with Schelling for more than a few minutes without having an argument, she told Novalis, but 'he is by far the most interesting person I've ever met'. Yet he was still the son of a Swabian pastor and he couldn't quite handle her humour, Caroline laughed, nor the habitual 'irony of the Schlegel family'. Schelling was earnest and could happily discourse about philosophy, nature, the self and science, but he was at a loss whenever the conversation turned to something more light-hearted.

He was stuck 'in a kind of perpetual state of tension', Caroline observed, 'and I haven't yet found the secret to making him relax'. Brash and easily angered when criticised, he was still young, Caroline said, and he had time to calm down. She couldn't stop talking about him. If Schelling were a mineral, she wrote to Friedrich Schlegel, he'd be 'genuine granite'. To which Friedrich pointedly replied: 'But where will Schelling, our Mr Granite find a Mrs Granite?' August Wilhelm didn't seem to notice Caroline's infatuation, or perhaps he didn't care. After all, he had openly flirted with the actress Friederike Unzelmann in Berlin the previous year. He had had his fun, so why shouldn't Caroline have hers?

Meanwhile Schelling's fame continued to spread and his lectures drew an increasing number of international students. Whereas August Wilhelm Schlegel struggled to attract more than five students, Schelling became so popular that people in Jena could tell when his lectures were about to start by the large number of young men rushing across the market square. At no other time of the day was it as busy. Younger than many of his students, Schelling enthralled them all. With an authority that belied his age, his presence at the lectern was determined and commanding. His face and piercing eyes beamed with energy.

He also knew how to stage himself. During those long winter months the clear skies of November were replaced by a leaden grey that weighed on people's moods. For weeks it never seemed to get properly light. As darkness settled over Jena in the late afternoons, Schelling entered the auditorium and carefully placed his notes in front of him. Slowly and deliberately, he lit two candles on the lectern while the rest of the room remained in shadow. It was so dark that he couldn't make out the students' faces, but they saw him wreathed in light. It was quiet, except for an occasional suppressed cough or the creak of a bench. No one said a word until Schelling began.

As a student in Tübingen, Schelling had been inspired by Fichte's work but had then forged his own path. He entered realms where Fichte never strayed, exploring the external world and nature. Where Fichte's Ich was shaped by its opposition to the non-Ich, Schelling believed that the self and nature were identical.* Instead of dividing the world into mind and matter, as philosophers had for centuries – most famously the seventeenth-century French philosopher René Descartes – Schelling now insisted that everything was one. There was a 'secret bond connecting our mind with nature', he told his students.

As he stood at the lectern, Schelling had something 'wonderful, magical' about him, one student said. It was as if reality disappeared. Another student compared him to a courageous general ready to fight the enemy army. Quills ready to scribble down his every word, the young men knew that they were hearing and seeing something momentous. Unlike other professors who taught the works of dead thinkers from Aristotle to Leibniz, Schelling gave his students a glimpse of the future, not an interpretation of the past.

Schelling's new universe was alive. Instead of a fragmented, mechanistic world where humans were little more than cogs in a machine, Schelling conjured up a world of oneness. The living and non-living worlds, he explained, were ruled by the same underlying principles. Everything – from frogs to trees, stones to insects, rivers to humans – was 'linked together, forming one universal organism'. Unlike Kant, who had shown the limits of knowledge by explaining that we can only know things-as-they-appear-to-us but never the thing-in-itself, Schelling revealed a world that was intuitively knowable. Why? Because the system of nature was also the system of our mind. As

---

* Schelling explained this by looking at the moment when the Ich becomes aware of the external world. 'At the first moment when I am conscious of the external world, the consciousness of my self is there as well, and vice versa – at my first moment of self-awareness, the real world rises up before me . . .'

Schelling put it: 'Mind is invisible nature, while nature is visible mind.' If mind and nature really were one, it meant that we must have direct access to and understanding of the workings of nature.

Schelling placed humans firmly *within* nature, both at one with and part of nature. 'As long as I myself am identical with nature,' Schelling told his students, 'I understand what living nature is as well as I understand myself.' Being in nature – walking, exploring, thinking – was therefore always also a self-discovery. It was a thrilling idea.

For millennia, thinkers had turned to their gods to understand their place and purpose in the unknowable divine plan. Then, in the late seventeenth century, a scientific revolution began to illuminate the world. Scientists had peered through microscopes into the minutiae of life or lifted new telescopes to the skies to discover Earth's place in the universe. They had dissected human hearts to learn how the body functioned and classified plants, animals and minerals in neat categories to impose order on the world in which they lived. They had calculated the distance between the Sun and Earth, described how blood circulated through the body, and sailed to Australia, a 'new' continent some ten thousand miles away on the other side of the world. They had discovered oxygen and used mathematics to define the laws of planetary motion and gravity.

The Enlightenment had truly enlightened. But this new rational approach had also created a certain distancing from nature and excluded the roles of feeling and beauty. Nature had become something that was investigated from a so-called objective perspective. Light, for example, was no longer appreciated for its kaleidoscopic play of iridescent colours, Novalis said, but for its refraction and 'mathematical obedience': hence its elevation to the term 'Enlightenment' itself. This was why Schelling's students fell for their young professor. He reunited what the scientific revolution had separated: nature and humankind. No matter how much scientists observed, calculated and experimented, there was something emotional, something visceral and perhaps inexplicable about humanity's connection to nature. However we feel it, nature can soothe, heal or simply fill us with joy. Schelling gave us the philosophical explanation.

And by doing so, his philosophy of oneness became the heartbeat of Romanticism.

Contemporary travel accounts illustrate these changes. Most

eighteenth-century travellers described a village, a city, a landscape or a country as detached observers – as someone watching from a distance. They saw the countryside through the windows of their carriages, and described art and architecture through the prism of their learning and books. Then, in the early nineteenth century, as Schelling's ideas spread, the young Romantics began to feel a deep sense of connection to the world around them. They wanted to see the world through the lens of their own selves. Instead of just visiting museums and cities, this new generation scrambled into caves, slept in forests and hiked up mountains to be in nature. They wanted to *feel* rather than observe what they were seeing. They wanted to discover themselves in nature and 'to be one with everything living', as Schelling's friend, Friedrich Hölderlin, wrote in his novel *Hyperion*.

Standing in the packed auditorium in Jena, Schelling cast a spell. 'I was in a state of rapture,' one student explained, while another wanted to throw himself into Schelling's arms, and some even cried. Their letters home and to friends described an almost religious epiphany. His words were carried by a 'heavenly power', they exulted, and, instead of cold reasoning, Schelling's new world was filled with a 'new, warm, glowing life'. This was the opposite of Newton's automata-like universe that was ruled by natural laws. 'Philosophy applied to nature', Schelling said, 'has to raise it up out of the dead mechanistic world it appears to be caught in.' The natural world was no longer God's well-ordered clockwork or a piece of divine artistry – it was alive.

~

In the first six months of 1799, as winter folded into spring and then summer, a constant stream of visitors arrived at the Schlegels' house in Leutragasse. Family and friends came to stay, some for a few days, others for several weeks, piling into the spare rooms and beds. In May, Caroline organised a dance in her spacious parlour. Novalis came for a visit, as did the group's newest additions, the young couple Ludwig and Amalie Tieck. Friedrich Schlegel had met the twenty-six-year-old novelist and playwright Ludwig Tieck in Berlin and immediately recognised a kindred spirit. 'You fill the space around you like a scent spreading over everything,' Novalis had told Tieck when they first met at Caroline's table.

Like Schelling and Fichte, Tieck had been a child prodigy, able to recite the Bible at the age of four and Goethe's drama *Götz von Berlichingen* at ten. He wrote novels, comedies, plays and poems, as well as translating English and Spanish literature, including Cervantes' *Don Quixote* – constantly moving between different genres and styles. In his comedy *Puss in Boots*, Tieck had created a play within the play. An audience on stage commented on the play, its author had discussions with a fictitious theatre crew, and actors in the stalls shouted at the performance. It was as if Tieck was holding a mirror up to a mirror, creating a series of self-reflecting stories. This was Friedrich Schlegel's dizzying and forever evolving romantic poetry.

There was a feverish quality to Tieck's productivity to which they could all relate. One balmy night after a long wine-fuelled dinner, they decided to hike up a nearby hill. As the moon lit their path, they scrambled to the top, where Tieck declared that he would finish his latest novella on their return to Leutragasse. They all laughed. But back home, when everybody had crawled drunk and exhausted into bed, Tieck stayed up. By the time they woke the next morning, he had completed the last pages.

Although Friedrich Schlegel was still in Berlin, he was with them in spirit. He and Auguste continued their correspondence. She had grown into a charming yet headstrong fourteen-year-old, and in Jena she was thriving. She was clever and pretty. Her hair was curly, like her mother's, and her high-arched eyebrows framed her wide eyes. Blessed with a beautiful voice, she often sang and played the piano at their evening gatherings. Comfortable in adult company and surrounded by the brightest minds of the age, Auguste absorbed knowledge easily. Unlike other girls her age, nothing seemed to have been hidden from her. Auguste teased Friedrich about the flirtatious wife of his publisher who had bombarded him with love letters, and she knew about Dorothea. She wrote him witty rhymes and begged him to come back to Jena. She was very much her mother's daughter.

Caroline remained the centre of what Novalis called 'our splendid circle'. She was writing reviews and had taken over Shakespeare's *As You Like It*. 'I'm translating', she told Novalis, 'iambic pentameter, prose, even rhymes.' Soon she also found herself providing lunch for at least a dozen guests every day. Once in a while, Goethe pulled himself away from Schiller and walked the few hundred yards across the market square to Leutragasse to join the sociable gatherings or to discuss poetry with August Wilhelm. 'He's always here,' Caroline wrote to Novalis; 'yesterday I had supper with him, today I will have supper with him again, and soon I'll be throwing a party for him.'

In the evenings they went to parties or to the popular concerts in the Zur Rose. Though there were often several hundred people listening to the music, Caroline always stood out. She radiated confidence and the young students admired her from afar. If the friends didn't go out, they met in Caroline's parlour, where they read, talked and laughed. The night crept on and the candles burned low, and no one went to bed early. When Caroline's oldest friend Luise Gotter had visited for a few weeks the previous winter, she joked that though having the reputation of being always the first to bed, she never grew tired of the invigorating conversations. In Caroline's house, Luise wrote to her daughter, they always stayed up at least until midnight.

No wonder Novalis declared Caroline the heart of the Jena Set. She was in her element. 'You must stay in the magical atmosphere that surrounds you,' he wrote to her in early 1799. It was Caroline, he believed, who shielded their wonderful 'family of kindred spirits' from the dark clouds and storms rolling in from all sides.

'Idol worshippers, atheists, liars'
1799: Scandals Part One. Fichte's Dismissal

DUKE CARL AUGUST was furious with Johann Gottlieb Fichte. The Ich-philosopher always seemed to attract complaints. In previous years, the duke had heard of fathers grumbling about Fichte's influence on their impressionable sons and of the pious men of Jena opposing the Sunday morning lectures. This time the objection came from none other than the duke's powerful neighbour, Friedrich August, the elector of Saxony. And this was serious. Fichte was being accused of atheism. The reason for the elector's complaint was Fichte's 'On the Ground of our Belief in a Divine World-Governance', an article in a journal which the authorities in Saxony had already confiscated.

In the offending piece, Fichte explained that his God had very little to do with the Christian God. According to Fichte, a belief in God was essentially a belief in a moral world, nothing more. God wasn't a separate entity from us. God was within us and was expressed in our ability to decide whether to act altruistically or selfishly. The 'living and active moral order is itself God', Fichte wrote, because 'we require no other God and we can grasp no other'.

Unsurprisingly, these statements had caused consternation in Saxony, the cradle of Protestantism and Martin Luther's home state. An anonymously published pamphlet had then accused Fichte of atheism as well as of inciting rebellion and subverting the young students in Jena. When someone from the Dresden High Consistory – the body that governed church matters in Saxony – read the pamphlet, it was passed on to the elector. However, with no jurisdiction in the Duchy of Saxe-Weimar, the elector now insisted that Duke Carl August punish Fichte himself. And with this, the dispute was elevated to another realm. What could have been a public row about religion between thinkers and philosophers now became a serious matter involving the authorities of two states.

Carl August's orders to the university in Jena were swift and unambiguous. He demanded that the case be investigated and that Fichte be 'severely punished'. In another letter addressed to his ministers, Voigt and Goethe, the duke fumed that Fichte would ruin the reputation of the university because of an incomprehensible philosophy that was simply a 'mental illness'.

~

With Jena famed for its liberal attitude, it hadn't occurred to Fichte that his article might incur his ruler's wrath. Censorship might be a worry elsewhere, but not in the Duchy of Saxe-Weimar. In fact, Fichte was one of several professors who were given 'freedom from censorship'. What this meant was that as a representative of the university, and thus a representative of the state, Fichte had been entrusted by the administration of the duchy to censor his own work.

Laws in other European countries were far stricter. In Britain, prime minister William Pitt the Younger, for example, had just introduced a series of repressive parliamentary acts to control radical thought. The British government now had the power to deem revolutionary writings and public speeches as well as meetings as 'treason'.* In addition, Pitt had raised taxes on printed materials and ordered that printing presses must be registered – all measures that made the dissemination of incendiary ideas in England more expensive and more difficult.

This was a time when monarchs across Europe worried that the ideas of the French Revolution might infect their subjects. Countries with centralised governments, such as Britain or France, found it easier to control dissent, but in the jigsaw of the German territories censorship was haphazard and difficult to enforce. Concerned about increasingly political writings, the late Prussian king, Friedrich Wilhelm II, had issued the Censorship Edict in 1788. All printed texts – pamphlets, books, newspapers and other treatises – had to be submitted for inspection. As a result a couple of newspapers had had to relocate to other states, one in fact to the Duchy of Saxe-Weimar, and Immanuel Kant had been forced to publish one work outside Prussia. In reality, though, enforcement even in Prussia was

---

* These were the controversial 1795 Seditious Meetings Act and Treasonable Practices Act, as well as the suspension of habeas corpus, which allowed the English government to arrest people based on suspicion only and without a trial.

relatively light because many civil servants continued to believe in the Enlightenment ideals of tolerance and free thinking which had directed Friedrich the Great in the mid-eighteenth century. And if it came to a conflict, writers could always print their works in other German states. In fact, when the elector of Saxony requested that the Prussian administration confiscate Fichte's pamphlet, the civil servants in Berlin refused. It would give Fichte's work more importance than it actually had, they explained, and 'in so doing make the damage we're trying to prevent even worse'.

In Jena, though, the elector of Saxony's complaint about Fichte had hit a nerve. Carl August's letter to his ministers Voigt and Goethe was, in his own words, an 'explosion', with years of pent-up resentment about Fichte's revolutionary ideas pouring onto the page. Carl August loathed Fichte and the 'bric-a-brac sophistry wrapped in incomprehensible words and phrases' with which he seduced the young students.

Goethe urged calm. Maybe, he suggested, it would be advisable to listen to Fichte's defence first and only then judge the case. Everything could be sorted to everybody's satisfaction. This was the idea: the duke would write to the university demanding that the matter be investigated and that Fichte be punished, in the hope of placating the elector of Saxony. He would then officially reprimand Fichte but without further retribution, thereby demonstrating his authority yet also his enlightened rule. Fichte would accept the warning, and perhaps issue an apology, before continuing his work at the university. It was a simple plan, but Voigt and Goethe had forgotten Fichte's volatile temperament and they had underestimated the duke's fury.

～

Far from appeasing his accusers, Fichte launched a counterattack in a new pamphlet, *Appeal to the Public*, which inflamed the already difficult situation. Let the public judge, Fichte said, because he would not go down without a fight. He was speaking up, he wrote with melodramatic swagger, before they had a chance to finish building the pyre on which they planned to burn him. The *Appeal to the Public* was not so much a defence as an onslaught. He was not an atheist, Fichte declared, but his adversaries were 'idol worshippers, atheists, liars, merciless persecutors, creators of false idols'. Banning his work was nothing less than a wicked plan by the opponents of free speech – his enemies weren't afraid of atheism but of radical change. Confiscating Fichte's article was only the first step in their attempt to undermine the unstoppable march of the philosophy of freedom – his Ich-philosophy.

There was a reason why people described him as the 'mighty Fichte who thundered down on all and sundry with his Ich'. Once upset, little could stop him. Charming and funny at parties, Fichte's mood could easily change to fury. It was as if his strength awakened when he felt attacked, one acquaintance said, 'and since he doesn't know his own strength, he tears his opponent to pieces'. His three-year-old son had inherited the same traits, Johanne Fichte said. Little Immanuel Hartmann was kind and lovely but when angry he turned into a 'little lion'.

Friedrich Schiller felt he should weigh in. Duke Carl August and the university, Schiller wrote to Fichte, were not really trying to limit his freedom to write. The problem was that Fichte had gone to press with the *Appeal to the Public*. Why hadn't he written an essay about religion without involving the government? And why not argue in a more measured manner?

But this had never really been about religion. Not even the duke believed that Fichte was an atheist. What concerned him were the philosopher's revolutionary leanings. Fichte was 'a whole new species of heretic', Carl August warned. The duke would never have agreed to the appointment of a 'publicly confessed revolutionary' to Jena, he now said, but he had been away fighting the French back in 1793 when the decision had been made.

Why, the duke thundered, hadn't Goethe used his influence in Jena to stop Fichte's abominations? Why was Goethe so careless when it came to university matters? Why didn't Goethe report on the troublemakers? Why didn't he steer the young people in the right direction? Why didn't Goethe reprimand them? And why, instead of helping, did Goethe find 'those disreputable people charming'? Carl August now seemed more upset with Goethe than with Fichte. He couldn't even talk to Goethe in person about it. Whenever he had tried, Carl August wrote in another letter to Voigt, Goethe had repeated Fichte's incomprehensible philosophical concepts. The duke had lost patience and Goethe his clarity of thought. It was all Fichte's fault. 'I simply can't stop talking about these things,' the duke ended his letter to Voigt, but 'luckily the page is full'.

～

The duke insisted on an official investigation and word of the dispute between Fichte and the Weimar authorities spread fast. The first five thousand copies of Fichte's pamphlet *Appeal to the Public* sold out within two weeks, quickly followed by another five thousand. As newspapers across the German territories reported the scandal on an almost daily basis – even the *St James's Chronicle* in London recorded it – the discussion also raged on in hundreds of letters. Schiller asked Körner what people in Dresden were saying about it, Friedrich Schlegel wrote from Berlin to his brother in Jena, Caroline Schlegel to Novalis in Freiberg. Everybody was talking about it.

When some forty pamphlets were printed in response, most of them critical of Fichte, the younger generation was shocked. 'Brave Fichte is actually fighting for us all,' August Wilhelm Schlegel wrote to Novalis, 'and if he is vanquished, they will be lighting fires around our feet.' If Jena's university – the one place in the German-speaking states famed for its open-minded attitude – was to charge Fichte, they were all in trouble. Everybody seemed to have an opinion, Johanne Fichte complained, and the whole affair 'caused such a scandal that the tailors, the shoemakers, even the beggarwomen give their judgement on it'. She was worried, tired and frustrated. Why was her husband always caught up in disputes?

After several weeks of public rancour, Fichte became so frustrated at waiting for the result of the official investigation that he wrote a long letter to Minister Voigt in which he explained that he wouldn't accept any form of 'public and legal reprehension'. His honour was at stake, Fichte warned, and should the Weimar authorities choose to reprimand him, he would have to hand in his resignation. And why, while he was on the subject, hadn't Johann Gottfried Herder, the man in charge of the duchy's church matters, been accused of atheism? After all, an essay Herder had written on God and Spinoza* was far more offensive than his, Fichte alleged. In fact Herder's essay and atheism 'were as much alike as two peas in a pod'. In a final insult, Fichte also threatened that other professors would leave with him, in solidarity, to establish a new university elsewhere. 'They gave me their word,' Fichte told Voigt.

---

* In *God: Some Conversations about Spinoza's System* (1787), Herder had defended the seventeenth-century Dutch philosopher Spinoza, who had been accused of pantheism for his belief in God as an all-encompassing principle in nature. Spinoza had said that nature, the universe, and God were one.

And then it all went wrong. Three days later, on 25 March 1799, Voigt replied that the duke had in fact decided to issue an official rebuke, and Fichte's resignation had therefore been accepted. Fichte's bluff had backfired spectacularly. Though Fichte had never intended to relinquish his position at the university, Voigt had twisted the content of the letter, treating it as an actual resignation. Almost exactly five years after he had taken up his post, Fichte's career in Jena was over. The letter had presented the duke and the Weimar authorities with the perfect opportunity to get rid of the inconvenient and outspoken professor.

Goethe regretted that 'we had to lose him, and that his foolish arrogance made him lose his job', but he had also been dismayed at Fichte's threat to the authorities. For years Goethe had defended Fichte. This time, though, the philosopher had gone too far. The duke was furious and Fichte disrespectful. Fichte might be one of the cleverest thinkers he had ever met, Goethe said, but 'I would have voted against my own son, had he permitted himself such language against a government'.

~

In Berlin, Friedrich Schlegel worked himself into a rage. Everything that happened to Fichte, he wrote to August Wilhelm, was important to them. The most immediate consequence would be that 'Jena will sink into the chaos of universal banality', but the long-term consequences were more serious. What was at stake was their freedom to think. Caroline echoed Friedrich's concerns when she described Fichte's dismissal to her old friend Luise Gotter at the end of April 1799. The situation was terrible for all those who spoke their mind, she wrote. If Fichte was censored and ousted for what he had published, what would this mean for everybody else? Would they now face restrictions? What was to become of their Jena? And for once even the judicious August Wilhelm was ready to fight. 'Schlegel is hatching wicked plans,' Caroline told a friend. Schelling offered to write a public defence but none of the obvious journals dared to publish it.

It didn't help that many of Fichte's colleagues were jealous of him. Four hundred paying students had attended Fichte's lectures the previous winter, more than any other. No one resigned in solidarity. In updates to friends, Caroline recounted the behaviour of fellow professors who now accused Fichte of impulsiveness and indiscretion. Fichte is 'abandoned and shunned', she wrote, but 'we are sticking together in these bad times'. At least the students were fighting for Fichte's reinstatement, delivering two petitions with several hundred signatures to the court in Weimar. 'Fichte's celebrity', the students declared, had been the main reason for them to come to Jena – with him gone, they would lose their master. The whole affair, they said, was an 'attack against the spirit of free thinking'. Carl August rejected the petitions.

The atheism scandal hit at the height of Fichte's success. Even Karl Leonhard Reinhold, one of Fichte's most outspoken adversaries and his predecessor in Jena, had publicly declared himself a 'Fichtian' – an admission that had caused a sensation. But it was all too late. The 'great Jena Ich', as the Weimar poet Wieland called Fichte, was forced to leave. 'One star sets, and another rises,' Goethe coolly observed, predicting that Schelling would assume his mentor's place.

Closely following these developments from Berlin, Friedrich Schlegel bombarded Caroline with questions. What did Goethe have to say about Fichte? Where was Fichte going to go and when? Would Schelling leave too? How should they show their loyalty? He was going to compose a public defence of Fichte, Friedrich now announced: 'I've moved into a wholly revolutionary state too.' He partly kept his word. Although he did write a piece in which he accused the German public of devouring the Fichte scandal like a cockfight in the streets, Friedrich Schlegel never published it. He wanted to keep his options open for a possible return to Jena.

～

Meanwhile Fichte's prospects were looking increasingly grim. With no paid position in Jena, he desperately needed to find an income. At home, Johanne had had enough. 'You're very proud,' she told her husband; 'I think it's that pride, which no one can stand, which is the real reason for all these disasters we're facing.' But there was not much she could do. Humility, her husband declared, was not a trait he admired, and he was proud of his pride. He would never be 'a dirty little courtier and lickspittle' like the other professors. His time in Jena was over.

But where to go? Johanne's family home in Zurich was now off limits, with the region caught up in the Austrian and Russian battles with the French. Since the peace treaties of April and October 1797, Europe had been relatively calm until spring 1799 when the former allies – including Austria, Russia, Great Britain and several German states – had formed another coalition against France. Prussia, though, retained its neutrality and stayed out of the conflict, and the fighting was concentrated in Switzerland, Italy, Austria and the southern German territories. It would be better for the Fichtes to find something in the northern states, away from the battlefields.

Fichte contacted rulers and universities but no offers arrived. He asked a Danish acquaintance about Copenhagen and another about the university in Mainz. No one seemed keen to employ a professor who had managed to offend the famously lenient Duke Carl August. The University of Göttingen, for example, was instructed by its government to turn Fichte away if he applied. Why encourage a philosopher 'whose writings contain so much poison', wrote the Duke of Braunschweig, another ruler who prided himself on supporting the arts and the sciences. Similarly, when Fichte enquired at the small state of Schwarzburg-Rudolstadt, just twenty miles from Jena, he was rebuffed. Why should the principality's Prince Ludwig Friedrich II give Fichte public protection, Schiller said, and thereby compromise his own reputation and risk upsetting other rulers by supporting a revolutionary?

With one rejection after another, Fichte wrote to Friedrich Schlegel in mid-June 1799, three months after his dismissal, enquiring about Berlin. Friedrich replied immediately. If Fichte pretended to be a passing visitor, the Prussian authorities would be unlikely to question or expel him. Friedrich would be happy to organise lodgings for Fichte but advised him to keep a low profile while in Berlin. Over the previous three years, the two men had become friends. Friedrich admired Fichte's philosophy and, unlike others, he didn't mind Fichte's brusque personality. 'His sharp edges and hard corners never bothered me,' Friedrich Schlegel said – polished and refined people were generally far too smooth for his taste.

With no other options, Fichte packed his bags and reached Berlin in early July 1799. Johanne stayed behind because their young son was ill and too weak to travel. In Berlin, Fichte initially rented a room in a tavern and spent most of his days with Friedrich Schlegel. He enjoyed Friedrich's company but he didn't like Berlin, and he wasn't alone in regarding the city as a cultural and intellectual wasteland. Goethe disliked Berlin so much that he refused to visit at all, and Alexander von Humboldt, who had grown up there, considered it a 'dancing carnivalesque necropolis'.

With only 170,000 inhabitants, Berlin felt provincial compared to other European capitals: London had a population of 1 million and Paris 650,000. Berlin may have been the capital of Prussia, one of the most powerful German states, but it was no sparkling metropolis. Unlike Dresden, no art was on public display and there wasn't even a university. What little culture there was, was limited to the literary salons, a couple of renowned theatres and a thriving publishing industry.

Instead, Berlin had a decidedly military character, with sentries stationed outside most public buildings and visitors remarking on the perpetual drumming and parading of soldiers. In the mid-eighteenth century Friedrich the Great had turned Prussia into a powerful military force with Berlin as its centre. In the morning people were woken up by the synchronised steps of orderly regiments passing their houses, and with almost thirty thousand military personnel in town there sometimes seemed to be more soldiers than civilians. Tourists noted the 'endless display of uniforms of all sorts, in all public places'. It didn't help that the people of Berlin had a reputation for being snobby and superficial, and that the countryside around the city was flat, dull and sandy.

It was a hot and dry summer. As the dust swirled through the streets, Fichte complained to Johanne that Berlin's 'sandy deserts' resembled those in Arabia. Fichte was unhappy. The only people he saw were Friedrich Schlegel, Dorothea Veit and their few loyal friends, such as the theologian Friedrich Schleiermacher. 'Even halfway intelligent people are rather thin on the ground here,' Fichte wrote to Schelling. Yes, there were the literary salons, but Fichte never particularly enjoyed them. He preferred a real audience, not a party. In Jena, he had taught every day, giving lectures from three in the afternoon until seven in the evening. There had never been enough time to write, but suddenly he had nothing. He had thrived in his auditorium, often developing his ideas as he presented them. Fichte realised that he needed his students. 'He lost his Samson's locks,' Caroline later observed, 'when he lost his lectern.'

~

Nothing seemed easy that year, and Fichte's troubles continued. At the end of August 1799, the *Allgemeine Literatur-Zeitung* published a long and scathing statement by the seventy-five-year-old Immanuel

Kant in which the philosopher stated: 'I consider Fichte's *Wissenschaftslehre* an entirely untenable system.' The man who had inspired the Ich-philosophy and who had lifted Fichte out of obscurity, had taken against him. What Kant despised most was the arrogant assumption that his own philosophy should be seen as some kind of introductory work to Fichte's system. How dare Fichte insinuate such a thing? His *Critiques*, Kant concluded, didn't need to be corrected or developed as Fichte seemed to think. In fact, Kant's philosophical system was complete and nothing less than indispensable for the future of humankind.

At first shocked, Fichte quickly turned his anger into retaliation. Conveniently, he had kept a letter Kant had sent him almost two years earlier – a letter in which the philosopher had admitted being too old to keep up with any of the new ideas. Fichte asked Johanne to retrieve it from the box where he kept his correspondence. Less than three weeks later it was published in the *Allgemeine Literatur-Zeitung*. This would suffice as Fichte's response. What could be stronger than Kant's own admission of 'the weakness of my old age'?

Kant's philosophy was, in fact, a preliminary work to the Ich-philosophy, Fichte wrote in the same week to Schelling. Clearly Kant didn't even understand his own *Critiques*. The former philosopher-king, Fichte now boldly claimed, 'had never been particularly familiar with his own philosophy'. Schelling agreed. Let Kant 'drag the dead plaster casts of his *Critiques* around after him', Schelling replied. The old man had not realised that the time for regurgitating his ideas was long over. Kant should gracefully bow out and leave the throne to the next generation.

Their students' enthusiasm was proof enough that Fichte and Schelling were already wearing Kant's crown. They would lead humankind into a new world of freedom and self-determination. Their own lives illustrated how an empowered Ich could steer its destiny. Hadn't Fichte, the son of a poor ribbon weaver, transcended his background to become a celebrated philosopher? Hadn't Schelling walked away from a preordained path as a theologian? Hadn't both men left their home states to forge new lives elsewhere? Fichte had outdone Kant at his own game and twenty-four-year-old Schelling was already famous. Both men had shrugged off the straitjacket of social expectation, and so could their followers. Their Ichs and their philosophy could change the world.

13

'You lose yourself in a dizzy whirl'
1799: Scandals Part Two.
Divorce, Women and Sex

A T THE SAME time as Fichte's atheism dispute began, Friedrich Schlegel and Dorothea Veit were engulfed by their own scandal. In January 1799, just as Fichte published his angry *Appeal to the Public*, Dorothea and her husband Simon Veit were divorced in a Jewish court in Berlin. The proceedings had been initiated by Dorothea who had been deeply unhappy in her loveless marriage. An accomplished and intelligent woman, Dorothea had nothing in common with her banker husband. 'It is simply inexpressible, how banal and empty and hard-hearted he is,' Wilhelm von Humboldt had remarked a few years earlier, having known the Veits from the Jewish salons. Simon Veit was more interested in numbers than in poetry or literature, and Dorothea was deeply in love with Friedrich Schlegel.

There was scandal enough in an open affair, but in seeking and obtaining a divorce Dorothea ignored all the conventions and morals of both Prussian and Jewish society. Only five years previously, in 1794, the new General State Laws for the Prussian States had for the first time laid out the legal parameters for a divorce, but obtaining one was a difficult undertaking. Few reasons were acceptable: threats to life, for example, as well as sodomy, madness, lack of children and 'failure to fulfil marital duties'. Plain dislike or open violence was not enough, unless in very rare circumstances when a judge could be convinced that 'the mutual aversion was so strong and deep-rooted' that there was no hope of reconciliation. But even if a divorce was granted, divorcees were ostracised.

Simon Veit couldn't understand what was happening. Hadn't he looked after Dorothea? Wasn't he a kind husband? Surely his wife's affair with Friedrich Schlegel was just a phase? The divorce proceedings had been painful. Veit had delayed, pleaded and argued, but

Dorothea never gave in. In the end it had taken the intervention of one of her oldest friends to persuade Veit to consent. Dorothea knew that she was gambling her financial security and her social standing. Worse, no eighteenth-century law permitted an adulteress to keep her children. Dorothea's husband had the right to custody of their two young sons, eight-year-old Jonas and five-year-old Philipp.

After months of negotiations, the divorce was finally granted in January 1799. Dorothea felt free for the first time in her life. Thankfully, Simon Veit proved to be more generous than the law. Though he didn't return Dorothea's dowry, nor the inheritance she had received when her father Moses Mendelssohn died – which was now legally his – Simon Veit did grant his ex-wife a small annual income and invested the rest of her former estate in the name of their sons. Their older son Jonas would stay with his father, but Dorothea would be allowed to see him regularly. Veit agreed that their younger son Philipp should live with his mother until his tenth birthday, but only if Dorothea didn't remarry.

This prohibition suited Friedrich Schlegel, who had long made clear his opposition to the institution of marriage. Besides, while their age difference didn't matter now, the twenty-six-year-old Friedrich told Caroline, in later years Dorothea, who was more than seven years his senior, might feel too old for the physical consummation of their union and 'to be his wife in that sense'. Though Dorothea was the love of his life, she was probably not going to be the last woman in his life, he noted.

The moment the divorce became public, an avalanche of outrage hit Dorothea Veit. Old friends and acquaintances turned away, the husband of her best friend prohibited any contact – an injunction the friend ignored – and many were too embarrassed to be seen with Dorothea in public. People behaved like 'a rag-tag pack of dogs', Friedrich complained. A woman did not take control of her life, nor abandon her husband. In so doing, Dorothea had sullied her respected father's name and the standing of Berlin's Jewish community as a whole. It was all a little hypocritical, not least because several other women in Dorothea's more open-minded Berlin salon circles filed for divorce before and after; but no one else was the late, great Moses Mendelssohn's daughter. The additional disgrace was that Dorothea had chosen to conduct an open affair with an impoverished intellectual. If only she had legalised their union, or had at least married a Prussian aristocrat.

Although she had lost almost everything, Dorothea told a friend, 'I can't tell you how much I have *rid myself of* in return.' Independent for the first time in her life, she finally 'belonged to herself'. Philosophers like Fichte and Schelling may have been writing about a powerful self, about the self-determining Ich, but Dorothea was experiencing it at the very core of her being. Who cared that she had few possessions left. She was permitted to see her older son Jonas and had kept custody of her younger son Philipp. And she would never have to endure another unpleasant conversation or any 'demoralising crudeness' from her tedious husband. She was finally in control. 'I am happy now,' she wrote three weeks after the divorce, 'I can live in peace.'

Dorothea moved into a small apartment on the northern outskirts of Berlin, opposite a limestone factory and the barracks of the artillery regiment. Her new neighbours were a cattle farmer, a distillery owner and a fisherman. But she liked it because it was hers. There was little furniture but she had managed to bring her beautiful and much-treasured desk. Friedrich kept his own lodgings with the theologian Schleiermacher, a short fifteen-minute walk away, but spent every day with Dorothea. Gone were the stolen moments and secret rendezvous. Here in Dorothea's new apartment, they made love as long and as passionately as they liked. Their hands fumbled with buttons, belts and ribbons. Corsets were loosened, shirts taken off, and trousers dropped. When their skin finally touched, Friedrich said, their blood boiled and they became one.

Dorothea had been married for sixteen years, but she had never felt this. She was loved, desired and alive. 'You are the fixed point where my spirit finds its peace,' she said. After making love, Friedrich watched as the candlelight stroked Dorothea's smooth skin and flickered over her curves. As she lay with her hair loose, the long dark curls tumbling over her voluptuous chest, he dropped his head into the softness of her bosom and listened to her heart beating. He couldn't stop kissing her. 'You are the priestess of the night,' he declared.

It wasn't all sex and passion. Dorothea was lover, mother, muse, collaborator and friend. Friedrich had never been interested in blushing adolescent girls. He loved Dorothea's maturity and experience, her full plump shape and her strong features but most of all her mind. They worked together, and Friedrich did most of his writing in Dorothea's company. They discussed literature, wrote, edited and commented. And much like Caroline with August Wilhelm, Dorothea became an indispensable collaborator.

He was happy, Friedrich Schlegel wrote to Caroline. Dorothea gave him purpose and made him feel alive. He was humbled by her enormous sacrifice. And thanks to Simon Veit even the delicate issue of finances had been resolved. Dorothea's small divorce settlement would keep them afloat for now. He felt grounded for the first time in his life, ready for 'extraordinary things'. Dorothea was so besotted that she would follow him into death, he told Novalis, who of course appreciated such melodrama. 'If she were to lose me,' Friedrich bragged, 'she would, in Indian fashion, follow me.'

The letters that zigzagged between Berlin, Jena and the mining academy in Freiberg in those early months of 1799 were filled with the joy of their friendship. The last breath and thought before closing a letter, Dorothea said, was sealed between the pages and belonged to the recipient. Sometimes there were complaints if someone didn't write often enough. What was Novalis doing, Friedrich Schlegel asked Caroline, and fired off a dozen questions. Why was Novalis not replying? Why was he not sending more fragments? Who did he love? Did he still love them? What did he say about Fichte's dismissal from the university? How was his silence possible?

Letters connected them and were part of their communal thinking, their 'symphilosophising'. They also used them to develop ideas. Novalis thought their correspondence essential for getting into the mindset of writing a novel – '*Letters* in the evening – light, free, romantic, diverse – Preparatory work for the novel,' he wrote in his notebook. Playful, teasing and encouraging, these notes also contained plans to meet soon. Maybe Caroline and August Wilhelm could come to Berlin? After all, Caroline had never met Dorothea. But where would they stay? With Dorothea, or rent a room elsewhere? When would Novalis next pass through Jena? Maybe Schelling would visit Berlin? Or should Friedrich and Dorothea move to Jena? Or maybe not?

~

It wasn't just Novalis who had begun thinking about novels. During those early months of 1799 Friedrich Schlegel was also finishing his first novel, *Lucinde*. 'You will see,' he told Caroline and August Wilhelm, 'I will become properly practical and useful.' How practical, though, was uncertain, because when *Lucinde* was published, in May 1799, it turned out to be an explicitly erotic novel that thinly disguised Friedrich and Dorothea's own love story.

Friedrich Schlegel believed that the novel was the genre best suited to expressing the spirit of the modern age. Novalis agreed and even spoke about spending his entire life working on *one* novel – never completed, forever being written, infinitely evolving and thereby filling a library with what would be the ultimate romantic project. Most importantly, they wanted to provoke the literary establishment.

Novels were still seen as an inferior literary form. Some thought them shallow and sentimental, worrying that women in particular were in danger of being seduced to irrationality or even immorality. Others believed that libraries which stocked them were harmful to society. Novels evoked a dream world so removed from reality, one critic warned, that young people risked being drawn to dangerously idealistic and revolutionary ideas. That was precisely Friedrich Schlegel's intention. 'I want there to be a real revolution in my writing,' he told Caroline.

Lucinde told the story of the sexual awakening of male protagonist Julius and his relationship with his eponymous lover. The forensic detail of the erotic scenes shocked society, although it wasn't pornographic as such. *Lucinde* was published by a respectable publisher in Berlin and it even passed the censorship bureau. There was a market for erotic literature at the time, but its authors remained anonymous and were not literary critics like Friedrich Schlegel. Most outrageous was that everyone knew the novel to be autobiographical.

Friedrich Schlegel invited his readers into his bedroom to watch him and Dorothea make love. As they turned the pages, readers saw the lovers tear off their clothes and overheard them begging each other to 'be insatiable'. They stood next to Friedrich when he described how the 'wild blood rages in my swollen veins' and how 'my mouth thirsts for union'. Readers glimpsed Dorothea's white hips gleaming in the red light of drawn curtains and watched Friedrich cooling his lips 'in the snow of your breasts'.

Equally disquieting for most readers was that they also observed the lovers swapping roles when making love – with Lucinde/ Dorothea taking the dominant role, and Julius/Friedrich becoming submissive. For Friedrich, this was more than sexual role play: *Lucinde* was an allegory of the equality of men and women. Encouraged by Caroline, he had studied ideas of femininity in antiquity, learning about female heroes and female poets.* *Lucinde* was a celebration of sexual, spiritual and intellectual love between men and women as equal partners. Men and women were as equal as the 'petals of a single flower', Friedrich Schlegel wrote, a sentiment that was quite the opposite of the prevailing image of soft, malleable, gentle and quiet women who lived according to their fathers' and husbands' wishes. He believed that society's strong emphasis on the differences between men and women created the 'most dangerous obstacles to humanity'.

How unusual Friedrich Schlegel's thinking was becomes even more obvious when compared to his contemporaries. Fichte, for example, seemed to forget his celebration of free will when it came to women. His self-determined and powerful Ich was only male. According to Fichte, women had to submit completely to their husbands. Marriage meant that a wife had to give up her estate, money, civic rights and freedom. 'She has ceased to live the life of an individual; her life has become a part of his,' the liberator of the Ich wrote, adding that a wife had no will beyond her husband's.

Although Johanne Fichte was intelligent and spoke her mind, Fichte would reprimand her when she criticised him. He didn't mind when she gave her opinions on domestic matters – the home was her sphere, after all – but under no circumstances was she allowed to comment, for example, on his troubles with the university. His reason was simple: 'you're not a man'. Similarly, Immanuel Kant had claimed that a woman's only purpose was the 'preservation of the species' and to entertain her husband. Though Kant had never married, he believed in what he called the 'natural superiority of the husband'. Schiller also subscribed to this idea of the compliant wife – beautiful outside, gracious within – who enhanced her husband's life. In poems such as 'The Dignity of Women' he idealised them:

> *All honour to women! They're roses celestial*
> *Twining and weaving in lives terrestrial,*

---

* Caroline had also suggested that Friedrich Schlegel read the works of the mathematician and French revolutionary Condorcet, one of the few thinkers to advocate equal rights for women and their right to vote in France.

Weaving the bond of the most blessed love,
Veiled in the Graces' most modest attire
Nourish they watchful the e'erlasting fire
Of lovely feelings with hand from above.

'The Dignity of Women' was the poem Friedrich Schlegel had thought so boring that he had advised reading it backwards. Schiller's view of women, Friedrich believed, was ridiculous. Encouraged by Caroline, August Wilhelm Schlegel wrote a parody of the poem, and although he refrained from publishing it until after Schiller's and Goethe's deaths, he read it to his friends at home in Leutragasse. August Wilhelm's verse began with the same words as Schiller's poem but described the daily drudgery women had to endure much more realistically:

All honour to women! They darn the socks
All woolly and warm, to wade through the bogs.
They mend torn pants as good as new
And cook their husbands hearty stew,
Clean the children's pretty dolls,
Keep house with a stingy weekly allowance.

One of Schiller's most famous poems, 'Song of the Bell', has been memorised by generations of German schoolchildren. Published the same year as Schlegel's *Lucinde*, its verses brought all the gendered clichés together:

The man must go out
In hostile life living,
Be working and striving
And planting and making,
Be scheming and taking,
Through hazard and daring,
His fortune ensnaring.
. . .
The housewife so modest,
The mother of children,
And governs wisely
In matters of family,
And maidens she traineth
And boys she restraineth,
And goes without ending

Her diligent handling,
And gains increase hence
With ordering sense.
And treasure on sweet-smelling presses is spreading,
And turns 'round the tightening spindle the threading,
And gathers in chests polished cleanly and bright
The shimmering wool, and the linen snow-white,
And joins to the goods, both their splendour and shimmer,
And resteth never.

But it wasn't just Friedrich Schlegel's attitude to women that made him different. *Lucinde* was a daring project on many levels – from its approach to femininity and its explicit sexual content to its structure. Nor was it an easy read because Friedrich had deconstructed the traditional framework of a novel. With little story line or chronology, *Lucinde* was a patchwork of literary genres, ranging from letters and philosophical detours to psychological observations and allegories – and of course Friedrich's beloved fragments. This purposefully 'chaotic structure', he claimed, was the essential trait of a novel. And as he jumped from one scene to another, from one idea to the next, large parts of the book read more like an unconscious stream of thought than a coherent narrative.

Most obviously, *Lucinde* was about Friedrich Schlegel himself. 'Confessions belong in Romantic novels,' he explained. Novels had to be shocking and revolutionary, Friedrich said, adding that 'only a genius can write a real novel'. The friends were certainly surprised. When Caroline forwarded the unpublished manuscript to Novalis, he read the 'bizarre Lucinde' in one sitting. One thing was clear, Novalis replied, Friedrich was present on every page. Friedrich's innermost thoughts dissolved and transformed like chemical reactions, Novalis said, to the extent that 'you lose yourself in a dizzy whirl'. The world was not ready for *Lucinde*, he and Caroline agreed, and Novalis worried that they would be 'expected to hold the lamp to light his orgies'. Yet the friends all stood behind Friedrich when the attacks started.

And they came in multitudes. Friedrich Schlegel was accused of 'shameless sensuality', of an obscene imagination and salaciousness. In Jena, the arbiter of literary taste, the *Allgemeine Literatur-Zeitung*, described him as lewd, vain, and a 'sick mind'. More abuse than review, the *Allgemeine Literatur-Zeitung* demolished every aspect of the novel. 'Empty jibber-jabber', 'endless bookishness', 'disgust' and 'intentional mystifications' were just a few of the comments, while the author was described as 'an empty head enthusing around in a state of insanity'. Another critic ridiculed *Lucinde*'s 'metaphysics of the sex act'.

Unsurprisingly, Schiller loathed *Lucinde*, elaborating his dislike in a long letter to Goethe. The novel was an aberration, Schiller said, and he couldn't face reading the whole book in all its fragmented chaos. It was 'empty nonsense'. Diplomatic as always, Goethe replied that even though 'everybody reads it, everybody scolds it', he hadn't read it himself; but added, 'if it falls into my hands, I'll take a look.' Friedrich Schlegel didn't care too much about the critics but he was anxious to know from Caroline what their friends thought. How did Novalis react? With whom did Caroline talk about it? And most importantly, 'doesn't anyone know what Goethe thinks of it?'

Whatever the others thought, it was Dorothea who suffered the most. In the storm caused by *Lucinde*, she was again torn apart, described as a 'common, ugly Jewish woman' and as a hunchbacked and cross-eyed whore. She was mortified. 'I keep feeling burning hot, and then cold around my heart,' she wrote to a friend, 'seeing the innermost things turned inside out like this.' Everything sacred was now out in the open. Even then, though, Dorothea couldn't help feeling that *Lucinde* was also the greatest declaration of love.

When Fichte read *Lucinde*, he chose to ignore the radical views on women and declared it the product of a genius. Friedrich Schlegel and Dorothea Veit were his only friends in Berlin, and for once he was careful not to complicate his life. Though he had rented his own rooms on Friedrichstrasse in the city centre, he spent much of his time with Friedrich at Dorothea's apartment across the river. Fichte's routine was the same every day. He rose early and spent his mornings writing. At noon, a servant helped him powder his hair and dress – 'yes, yes, getting my hair done', he told his wife, who must have wondered why her husband, who had never cared about such things, was suddenly paying attention to his appearance. Every day at one o'clock Fichte walked the ten minutes from his lodgings to Dorothea's. From Friedrichstrasse, he crossed the famous Unter den Linden boulevard and headed towards the new drawbridge on the Spree River. There he would sometimes have to wait while the bridge was opened to allow large sailing boats through, but having crossed the river and passed the army barracks, all he had to do was turn right into Ziegelstrasse where Dorothea lived. Here he joined his friends for lunch, though he complained that 'the portions are so stingy that no one leaves full'.

The afternoons were spent working on their own projects or reading, and in the early evening they put aside their papers and walked back to Unter den Linden. There, they promenaded in the shade of the great lime trees. They were perhaps not the most elegant trio, with Friedrich Schlegel in his old rhubarb-coloured coat next to Dorothea, who couldn't afford nice dresses any more, and Fichte, who had never cared for fashion but who for once had neatly coiffed hair. Their conversation, though, was always lively and they enjoyed each other's company. 'After all,' Friedrich Schlegel wrote to Jena, 'we're all part of the same family of magnificent outlaws.' By ten or eleven o'clock in the evening, Fichte was tucked up in bed after a light dinner and a glass or two of Medoc.

The arrangement worked well. Friedrich Schlegel was happy to have the celebrated thinker at his disposal and Fichte was grateful for their hospitality. He grew fond of Dorothea. She was intelligent and learned, Fichte wrote home, while reassuring his wife that Dorothea had 'few, or more precisely no, physical charms'. Tender to Friedrich, hospitable to Fichte and good-natured in general, Dorothea enjoyed what she called their 'philosophers' convent'. At first scared of the famous Fichte, she was soon completely at ease with him. 'I cannot write another word,' Dorothea wrote shortly after Fichte's arrival in Berlin, 'I am getting dizzy from my philosophers pacing up and down here.'

But, as the *Lucinde* scandal hit and the gossip became increasingly vicious, Friedrich and Dorothea began thinking about moving to Jena. Fichte tried his best to dissuade them because otherwise 'I will be utterly abandoned'. Why didn't they instead all live in Berlin, Fichte now suggested – all of them: Schelling, Friedrich and Dorothea as well as Caroline and August Wilhelm? If Fichte couldn't be in Jena, why not establish a 'Jena Colony' in Berlin? 'We will be a single family, rent a big house, keep a cook, etc.,' Fichte wrote to Johanne, asking her to do what she could to convince Caroline Schlegel. Fichte seemed oblivious to the fact that Johanne had for the past five years remained an outsider in Jena. Considered odd and unsociable, she was also thought so frugal that she was called 'stinginess and envy personified'. Caroline, who dreaded their encounters, called her a 'silly goose'. Nonetheless, Fichte urged his wife, 'don't be intimidated by Madame Schlegel'. But Johanne Fichte was not stupid. Caroline Schlegel had made no effort to be her friend. Under no circumstances, Johanne told her husband, would she live with her in one house.

Over the next weeks the friends endlessly discussed their options. Schelling was happy to move to Berlin if they all went together, Friedrich Schlegel told his brother, but what about August Wilhelm and Caroline? Friedrich would have preferred to live in Jena, but if they all came to Berlin, he would stay. In all the back and forth, Dorothea became confused. Were they moving to Jena or remaining in Berlin? She would be content either way, she wrote to Caroline, but she needed to inform her landlady. 'Write to me', Dorothea scribbled in a note to Caroline, 'immediately, as soon as possible.' Meanwhile, Schelling tried to persuade August Wilhelm Schlegel, but he wouldn't budge – he liked it in Jena. In the middle of August, Schelling informed Fichte that the plan for a 'house of Jena colonists' had failed.

～

In the end, Friedrich Schlegel and Dorothea Veit decided to move to Jena in the autumn of 1799, where they would live with Caroline and August Wilhelm. Two years had passed since Friedrich's break with Schiller, long enough for everybody to have calmed down. However, Dorothea was nervous about moving to Jena and into the house of the formidable Caroline Schlegel. Although they would all be living under one roof and would share the expenses, this was Caroline's household. Dorothea might have been strong-willed and independent, but Caroline was the unchallenged centre of the Jena Set. Worse, Dorothea knew that Caroline had been Friedrich's first great love. With his characteristic, almost childlike ignorance, Friedrich was unconcerned. 'It's impossible to imagine', he had written in his *Athenaeum* fragments, 'what fundamental objections one might have to a marriage *à quatre.*'

14

'The Schlegel clique'
Autumn 1799: Work and Play

FRIEDRICH SCHLEGEL ARRIVED in Jena in early September 1799, marching into Caroline's parlour in Leutragasse with a big smile on his face, gnarled walking stick in hand and a small knapsack on his back. He was glad to be back. Despite their differences in temperament and character, the brothers were close. Though Friedrich could be unreliable and impulsive, he was also energetic and always fizzing with new ideas. They needed each other, the younger brother pushing the older out of his comfort zone and August Wilhelm urging Friedrich to calm down a little.

Caroline too was looking forward to having her brother-in-law live with them once again. She and her maid had spent days preparing for Friedrich's arrival, washing and hanging twenty curtains, scrubbing wooden floors with sand and redecorating rooms for their new living arrangements. Sofas, beds, tables and chairs had been carried up and down the stairs as furniture was rearranged and the vases had been filled with sweet-smelling flowers.

Everybody was to have their own realm. Dorothea and Philipp, her six-year-old son, would follow Friedrich from Berlin in a month or so. She was to live on the ground floor, which had until now been reserved for guests. There was a small parlour for Dorothea, with a sofa and an adjacent sleeping alcove, and Philipp would have the room next door. One floor up was August Wilhelm's study, with the couple's bedroom to one side and Auguste's room to the other. And Friedrich would be back in his old attic rooms. The largest room was Caroline's parlour on the ground floor, its five large windows overlooking the courtyard at the back. It was here, in this open sun-lit room, where everybody met and ate.

That summer the house had been filled with guests, some staying for weeks, others for just a night or two. Family and friends had visited, often arriving with their children and servants in tow. The crowded rooms had echoed with the sounds of laughter and loud debates and banter. Every day the table was laid for a dozen or more guests to eat and drink. Caroline's personality determined the rhythm and tempo of their discussions. If they were an orchestra, she was the conductor who brought the score alive. She listened, objected and steered the conversations. She demanded to hear their opinions and encouraged serious debates, but also easily switched to more light-hearted topics. Caroline was so self-assured, Dorothea later noted in her diary, because 'she thinks everyone is stupider than she is'. Friends and guests loved her hospitality as much as her intellectual contributions. She was always 'extremely intelligent', one admirer said, and when she talked, she was so animated that wisps of brown curls escaped from the pins. The slight squint of her blue eyes, Ludwig Tieck said, gave Caroline such an intense expression that it was impossible to escape her spell. They were all drawn into this 'magic circle'.

~

The town still exerted a pull. Johanne Fichte, who had remained in Jena to nurse her sick son, tried to persuade her husband to return. Fichte had left three months previously but had still not found a paid position. Writing books as an independent scholar in Berlin seemed his only option, but he was not to be rushed. 'I'm always working,' he told his publisher, 'but not like a factory; things are finished when they're finished.' Johanne had different ideas. If Fichte could only set aside his pride and apologise, she was certain he would regain the goodwill of the Weimar authorities. But Fichte could not be persuaded. 'How can you think', he wrote, 'that I would ever want to live among such a ragtag bunch again?'

Novalis rode regularly over from Weißenfels. He was Caroline's favourite visitor and one day, she hoped, they would all be united under '*one* roof'. When apart, they wrote long letters to each other, and when he left Novalis missed his friends. But he was happy again because he had fallen in love with Julie von Charpentier, the twenty-two-year-old daughter of one of his old professors in Freiberg. This was a quieter sort of love. Over a period of several months, rather than minutes, he had slowly opened his heart to Julie's soft features and melancholy eyes. She was beautiful, affectionate, gentle, caring and would make the perfect wife, Novalis thought. 'Love. What kind? Where? In heaven or on earth?' Caroline asked, when the letter with the news had arrived. She was relieved that Novalis was finally finding happiness in the real world.

Having completed his studies in Freiberg, Novalis was now working with his father at the salt mines, and was also employed by the elector of Saxony to inspect other mines in the state. This meant travelling a lot to investigate sites, explore possible coal seams and compile data and reports. He enjoyed the technical and practical side of his life, but it also seeped into his writing. An entire chapter of *Heinrich von Ofterdingen*, the novel which he had begun earlier that year, glorified miners as 'subterranean heroes' who discovered nature's secrets.

Shouldn't they all turn their lives into a novel, he wrote to Caroline. Earlier that year, he had encouraged her to work on a novel herself, a suggestion Friedrich Schlegel had also made many times. She liked the idea but in the midst of all her work with August Wilhelm and the endless stream of visitors, she never managed more than a short synopsis. This outline, though, reveals that Caroline also used her own life as a gateway into the story. In the brief sketch she describes her protagonist as an independently minded, charming and clever woman who could be reckless and passionate but was always self-reliant. Even the scholarly philologist father was modelled on Caroline's.

Dorothea was also writing a novel and turned to herself for inspiration. The protagonist of her *Florentin* was based on the lover she had had in Berlin before meeting Friedrich. The similarities were striking: an aristocratic adventurer from Italy who had been brought up in a monastery and who was wandering across Europe in search of love, friendship and freedom.

Novalis, Friedrich, Caroline and Dorothea believed that their personal experiences were reflections of a wider world. Their private lives and feelings were important enough to resonate on a more universal level. Like a beam of light that refracted through a prism into a spectrum of colours, so their tight focus on the self was refracted through their writings onto broader perspectives. In *Lucinde*, for example, Friedrich had used his love affair with Dorothea to explore the equality of men and women, while Novalis had dealt with his grief for Sophie von Kühn in his *Hymns to the Night* to explore love, death, the self and the divine. 'We have to build a poetic world out of ourselves,' Novalis told Caroline, but she simply didn't have the time. Caroline never returned to her novel.

∼

It was always busy in Leutragasse. The Schlegel household 'went beyond every possible creative chaos', one guest remarked, but life there was always entertaining and animated. It may not have been tidy, but guests loved the lively intellectual atmosphere. That summer, though, Caroline and August Wilhelm had begun to argue. The heaps of luggage, clothes and laundry brought in by the many visitors began to irritate the fastidious August Wilhelm. Another reason for the sharpening tone between the couple was that August Wilhelm had fallen for a celebrated beauty, Elisa van Nuys, who was spending her summer in Jena. Usually so tolerant, Caroline was soon annoyed. Never too concerned about her husband's short-lived dalliances, she disliked his 'serious affairs' and this particular infatuation seemed to be developing in that direction. A surprised August Wilhelm suddenly found himself struggling with his wife's anger. This time he had underestimated Caroline. Yes, they had agreed to the 'freedom existing between us', but he didn't have to flaunt his new obsession. These open affairs, she later said, undermined their marriage.

Caroline herself had been discreet. She and Schelling had fallen in love. Although Schelling came every day for lunch and spent much of his time at Leutragasse, Caroline had made such an effort to be tactful that not even Friedrich Schlegel had noted anything suspicious despite living with them. But when August Wilhelm took to flirting openly with his new mistress, Caroline dropped all caution, unable to hide the way her eyes followed Schelling's every move. The guests noticed that August Wilhelm was tense and moody while Caroline became frosty and exasperated in any company other than Schelling's.

Auguste, now fourteen, was closer in age to the twenty-four-year-old Schelling than he to her thirty-six-year-old mother. The affair upset her. She loved her stepfather and when Schelling tried to be particularly kind to her, Auguste rebuffed him. Blinded by passion, Caroline scolded her daughter harshly. Her manners were 'tart as a crabapple', she told Auguste, and if she continued to be so rude to Schelling, 'I'll start believing that you're jealous of your dear Mama.' In the end, Caroline sent Auguste away to friends in Dessau, some ninety miles to the north, ostensibly to work on her singing with a music tutor. Always so close to her mother, Auguste suddenly found herself separated from her for the first time in her life.

Only Schelling seemed impervious to the atmosphere. Caroline was his muse and his love, and he couldn't imagine life without her. Her intensity matched his own. That she was twelve years older and the wife of his friend didn't matter. Her words inspired him, her intellect excited him and her vivaciousness lured him out of his natural reserve. Only Caroline truly understood him. She was, he wrote in a poem that year, the 'Love of my Life'. Caroline united strength and clarity of thought, he later explained, with the tenderness of the most loving heart. Much like Friedrich Schlegel six years previously, Schelling was captivated by Caroline's seemingly contradictory qualities – her sensitivity and tenacity, her refinement and courage, her sharp mind and gentle soul. She was a 'magnificent woman', he said, a 'masterpiece of the gods'.

As a token of his love, he gave her a black feather, which she wore on her hat every day, and composed a poem that couldn't have been clearer:

> *When in those consecrated early hours*
> *I freely chose to strive for what is holy,*
> *A god forever wed you to my soul,*
> *In a solemn bond of everlasting beauty.*
> *And though the sweetest tidings of our love*
> *No gentle song will tell the future world,*
> *Yet from this poem's obscure hieroglyphic*
> *The riddle of our love will be deciphered.*

Soon the whole of Jena was talking about the affair, with Johanne Fichte reporting every detail to her husband in Berlin. Schelling 'worships Madame Schlegel', she wrote, and they were 'intimate in an inappropriate way'. Fichte was shocked. What was happening in Jena? Were they all out of their minds? Why did August Wilhelm not end all this? Fichte became so concerned that the affair might somehow rub off on his wife that he wrote, 'as far as Schelling and Madame Schlegel are concerned, be on your guard! I beg you, for our love's sake.' Friedrich Schlegel wasn't pleased either. Normally happy to break conventions, he was concerned that Caroline and Schelling's affair might complicate matters. Would he have to choose sides? Which one? His brother's, or that of the woman he had once loved? For now, though, Friedrich held his tongue and watched the situation unfold.

~

Although Schiller had long withdrawn from the Schlegels, Goethe still saw them. Being with them and their friends was like a 'true fairytale', he said, because they were 'in continuous fermentation and conflict'. Their energy was invigorating. 'If I were twenty years younger,' he said just a few days after his fiftieth birthday that September, 'I'd certainly be taking lively part.'

It was as if Goethe breathed in their youth. 'Now that we're older it's always hard to meet young people,' he had said five years before, and he had no intention of giving them up because Schiller disliked them or people gossiped about their unconventional love lives. In any case, he could hardly be appalled by Schelling's and Caroline's affair, having had his own fair share of passionate entanglements. More than once Goethe had been tempted by the beautiful young actresses at the Weimar theatre, and he still hadn't married Christiane Vulpius.

That summer, though, Goethe had found himself stuck in Weimar, overseeing building works at the duke's castle. Instead of seeing his Jena friends, he was dealing with the architect, the duke and 160 workers − craftsmen, builders, gilders, sculptors and labourers − and all this in addition to his usual ministerial tasks, royal visitors and duties at the theatre. At the end of July 1799 he had written to Schiller that he was too busy to come to Jena: 'My business affairs here are like polyps: cut them into a hundred pieces and every last one comes back to life.'

Schiller was in a bad mood and found it hard to concentrate. He was working on a new play − *Maria Stuart* − but the Schillers had house guests who distracted him and it was too hot. The heat was so oppressive and the summer so dry that the lawns at his Garden House were scorched. Schiller yearned for Goethe's company. 'Because of your long absence, I have almost no contact with the outside world,' Schiller told his friend, convinced that he couldn't write a word 'until we've seen each other again and had a good long chat'. Schiller also realised that nothing bound him to Jena any more. He had no teaching commitments at the university, he never went out to socialise and he avoided the Schlegels. 'He hated them,' Goethe told a friend decades later, adding that he had tried as much as he could to encourage some sort of rapprochement. But whenever someone mentioned the Schlegel brothers, Goethe said, Schiller became visibly upset.

During those long lonely summer months of 1799, Schiller began to think seriously about moving to Weimar. The year before he had spent several weeks there, overseeing the rehearsals of his *Wallenstein* trilogy. The plays had been a huge success, both critically and financially, and were now being performed across the German states. Each time a new theatre staged them, they paid Schiller a fee. Perpetually worried about money, he decided to concentrate on writing drama for the foreseeable future. If he lived in Weimar, he could stage them at the town's theatre, but most importantly he would be close to Goethe – and away from the Schlegels.

Schiller began to enquire about suitable accommodation and at the beginning of September 1799, just when Friedrich Schlegel had returned to Jena, Goethe signed a tenancy agreement for an apartment in Weimar on his friend's behalf. The building was only a three-minute walk from Goethe's house and Schiller's plan was to move in late October or early November. Everything was in place 'for our transplantation to Weimar', Schiller said.

Meanwhile, Goethe had escaped to his Garden House by the Ilm River outside Weimar's old walls. This small, cosy building, which was only a ten-minute walk from his main house in the town centre, had been his first home in Weimar. With the 'Jena solitude' out of reach because of work, Goethe stayed here for six weeks. Garlanded with vines and sweet-scented honeysuckle, the Garden House was located in a large park that Goethe had designed for the duke. There were vegetable plots, a meadow with fruit trees and a long path lined with Goethe's beloved hollyhocks. The views from his study stretched across the meadows and groves of the park. As much as he adored it, he hadn't spent much time here over the past few years.

While Goethe stayed at the Garden House, he oversaw the building works at the castle as well as editing a collection of his poems for publication. The seclusion suited him. There were no noisy neighbours or carts rattling along cobblestones, just birdsong and the sound of wind rustling the leaves. On clear and warm nights, he set up his new telescope for a 'visit to the moon', he told Schiller, his gaze wandering over deserted lunar craters and mountains. The clarity of the images captivated him. And since he couldn't get away from Weimar, he sent Christiane and their son August to Jena – 'because that's how it is – without absolute solitude I can't manage to write the least little thing'.

~

Goethe finally returned to Jena on 15 September 1799, after an unusually long absence of almost four months. Schiller was still there and Goethe's days were packed, as his diary made clear: 'A little work on *Faust*. Schelling's *Naturphilosophie. Voyage de Constantinople*. In the evening to Schiller's, read first about magnetism, then about the relationship between empiricism and transcendental philosophy, then the first act of *Maria* [*Stuart*]. Talked over dinner about *Theory of Colours*, especially the historical part.' Goethe worked, socialised and went on walks during the day, and visited Schiller almost every evening. As if to make up for his summer absence, he spent more time in Jena over the next few months than at home. He finally read *Lucinde* and studied Schelling's latest book. He also saw the Schlegel brothers and Schelling most days – just not together with Schiller.

But Goethe continued to mediate between Schiller and August Wilhelm. 'Have you definitively banished him for the future as well?' Goethe asked Schiller. Might there be a reconciliation? Once in a while Schiller gave in and half-heartedly asked August Wilhelm for a contribution for his journal *Musen-Almanach*. But he did it so unenthusiastically, August Wilhelm complained to Goethe, that 'I can hardly make myself think that he means it'. For his part, Schiller didn't want to look keen, he told Goethe, because the last thing he needed was Caroline Schlegel telling everyone that he was desperate for her husband's work. The Schlegels had treated him so dishonourably that Schiller had no interest in being nice to them.

Goethe often defended the Schlegel brothers. Yes, they did sometimes go too far, but he preferred their blunt honesty to the hypocrisy of the literary establishment. But Goethe was also protective of Schiller. On one occasion, for example, when he heard that some of the professors and their wives were staging a parody in which they made fun of Schiller's plays, Goethe told them to choose another victim. 'We'd much rather leave our good friend Schiller out of the play,' he gently explained, leaving no doubt as to how serious he was.

It was easier to avoid the quarrels altogether. Fichte's atheism scandal had been too much for him. The friends were sometimes a little too self-absorbed for his taste. 'These gentlemen', Goethe wrote to Wilhelm von Humboldt, 'chew the cud of their Ich's', and he was not taking sides. The group respected Goethe's stance. As long as everybody pretended to be civil and kept Goethe out of their petty fights, the peace held. Goethe never told Schiller that he had read *Lucinde*, and Schiller and his wife never admitted that they called Caroline 'Madame Lucifer'. Caroline, for her part, didn't tell Goethe that they parodied Schiller's poems in Leutragasse.

And so Goethe continued to be part of all their lives. 'The way the Schlegels are courting Goethe is just astounding,' Johanne Fichte reported to her husband in Berlin in mid-October; 'every day one of them visits him.' Over the past years, Goethe had used August Wilhelm Schlegel almost like an encyclopaedia for ancient Greek literature, as well as perusing the well-stocked library in the Schlegel house in Leutragasse. Goethe's letters from Weimar to August Wilhelm were peppered with requests for books and information. August Wilhelm was something like an 'intellectual neighbour', Goethe told him, as if they 'were living together in a kind of colony'.

They often went for long walks. August Wilhelm made the perfect companion – erudite yet fit enough to keep up with Goethe's fast pace. They discussed poetry and Goethe sought August Wilhelm's advice on metric pattern and verse. They had gone on so many walks that August Wilhelm felt he would 'end up walking his legs off'. It can't have been easy for Schiller to watch his trusted friend and collaborator seeking poetical advice from his nemesis. Occasionally Schiller's frustration emerged, and he would lash out. That autumn, for example, he told Goethe that August Wilhelm's latest Shakespeare translation made for 'more turgid reading than the earlier volumes'. Goethe chose to ignore the comment.

With Schelling Goethe discussed philosophy. Together they read Schelling's latest book, *Introduction to the Sketch of a System of Nature-Philosophy*, with Schelling patiently responding to Goethe's questions. Goethe had always believed that the process of gaining knowledge – *Erkenntnis** – came through direct observation. Most idealists, including Fichte, rejected this idea and insisted that all knowledge of reality originated in the mind. But not Schelling. He was an idealist who believed that 'absolutely all of our knowledge originates in experience'.

Schelling's understanding had evolved. No longer a pure idealist, he was also not a realist for whom the external world was the source of all knowledge. 'Every experiment is a question posed to nature,' Schelling had written in his latest book, 'which it is forced to answer.' This appealed to Goethe, who believed that experiments and scientific observations were important tools for making sense of the world.

---

* The German word *Erkenntnis* is often translated as 'knowledge'; however, this doesn't quite capture its meaning. *Erkenntnis* is a *process* of gaining knowledge and understanding.

But he also understood the limitations. 'Categorising and counting are not in my nature,' he would later explain. Or as he had Faust say:

> *We snatch in vain at Nature's veil,*
> *She is mysterious in broad daylight,*
> *No screws or levers can compel her to reveal*
> *The secrets she has hidden from our sight.*

Schelling was moving against the tide. At the very moment when scientists were beginning to specialise in ever-narrowing disciplines, Schelling's *Naturphilosophie* had opened a door to a world in which everything – from gravity, magnetism and light to plants, animals and humans – was connected. His holistic approach would favour the interdisciplinary collaborations that are at the forefront of research and discovery today.

It was a long journey on the stagecoach from Berlin to Jena. The direct route was around one hundred and fifty miles but the postal route extended the distance to two hundred miles as it went via Halle, Leipzig and other towns. And with all the different stops, it took several days. By early October, the summer's warmth had long evaporated and persistent rain had turned the roads muddy. Water dripped in ever-changing patterns down the carriage window. As the days passed, Dorothea Veit worried about her new life. She had missed Friedrich. After five weeks apart, she couldn't wait to be in his arms, but having heard so much about Caroline, Dorothea was unsure of what to expect in Jena. Anyone who met Caroline praised her wit and grace but also remarked on her sharp mind and quick judgements. By contrast, Dorothea often felt awkward when meeting people for the first time. She had even felt too shy to call on Novalis, her lover's best friend, when the carriage had stopped for a few hours in Weißenfels. 'Only beautiful women have such imperious audacity,' she explained.

For the last part of the journey, Dorothea had rented a carriage because the stagecoach had been delayed. It had all taken much longer than she had anticipated. Finally, on 6 October 1799, Dorothea saw for the first time the low mountains that hugged Jena, and her heart pounded. They were almost there. As the carriage passed through the ancient gate in the town walls, the horses' iron-shod hooves clanked on the cobblestones and her heart raced faster and faster. They turned into Leutragasse and stopped. There was the house. This was her new home. As she climbed down the carriage steps, she looked around but no one was there. Then, the door opened and Friedrich Schlegel slowly walked down the stairs towards her, followed by Caroline.

After a friendly welcome, the two women glanced at each other, sizing each other up. Dorothea was not particularly pretty, Caroline wrote that afternoon to Auguste in Dessau. She was about Caroline's height but heavier and broader. Her eyes were fiery and her voice was gentle. 'I have no doubt whatsoever that I will like her.' Meanwhile, Dorothea noted how beautifully dressed and groomed Caroline was. She looked elegant and much younger than her age, Dorothea thought. Caroline's face was lit up with an open smile, and Dorothea relaxed a little. Friedrich was glad to have her back, August Wilhelm was cordial as always, and Caroline made an effort to make her feel at home.

'It looks as if it's going to be an extremely entertaining winter,' Dorothea happily reported to a friend in Berlin the next day. Caroline was much friendlier than expected. True, Caroline was opinionated and could be judgemental, but she was also charming and not as arrogant as some people had said. There was something candid and straightforward about Caroline that Dorothea rather liked. With no pretence or affected pleasantries, Caroline quickly revealed what she liked or what interested her. She was neither timid nor insecure and she enjoyed being the centre of attention.

Received with warmth, Dorothea quickly fell into the rhythm of the Schlegel household. During the morning everybody worked in their own rooms, with a leisurely break for lunch. Unlike Auguste, who as a girl had been home-schooled, Dorothea's young son Philipp went to school every day and had weekly drawing lessons. Caroline liked him. He was like a little page boy, she told Auguste, and a delightful little rascal. After lunch the adults resumed their projects before taking long walks in the afternoon that sometimes lasted several hours. They reconvened in the evenings in Caroline's parlour for Italian lessons and to read Dante's *Divine Comedy* in the original. Schelling was thinking of turning his philosophy into one great poem – an idea that excited everybody – and he wanted to study Dante's verse scheme. There was an industrious air to the household.

Friedrich Schlegel was trying to finish a sequel to *Lucinde*. Dorothea was writing her novel *Florentin*,* and despite their quarrels Caroline

---

* Dorothea's novel was published under Friedrich Schlegel's name in 1801.

continued to work with August Wilhelm. In just four years they had translated ten Shakespeare plays, including *Hamlet*, *As You Like It* and *The Tempest*. The most recent volume, which presented *Richard II* and *King John* to the German public, had just been published, and they were now translating *Henry IV* as well as preparing the publication of August Wilhelm's collected poems and writing reviews and essays. Dorothea noted how much August Wilhelm depended on his wife's assistance.

Dorothea quietly watched the family dynamics. Maybe it wasn't as perfect as it looked from the outside. Sometimes, when unobserved, Caroline's cheerful facade slipped and she seemed sad. The couple was bickering, and Caroline was clearly more interested in Schelling. The Schlegels' marriage, Dorothea thought, seemed like an alliance between good friends. 'There's not much evidence of the sacrament,' she wrote to Schleiermacher in Berlin, certain that Caroline didn't love her husband.

~

During those autumn weeks in 1799, Schelling prepared his new lecture series for the winter semester. Inspired by the many discussions in Caroline's parlour, art and poetry had become his new focus. Published a few months later as the *System of Transcendental Idealism*, Schelling's lectures introduced aesthetics and the arts as the tools that reveal the union between the subjective world of the self and the objective world of nature.

Schelling explained that it was the unconscious self which brought the external world into existence, and through this act it became the conscious Ich. 'The objective world', Schelling believed, 'is merely the original, still-unconscious poetry of the mind.' But what did art have to do with this? Wasn't art just something beautiful or decorative? A carefully rendered landscape painting, for example, or an exquisitely chiselled marble bust. Or maybe an elegant piece of music or even a rousing drama performed on a stage. No, Schelling said, art was so much more. Because we're part of nature, an artwork produced by us is actually a reflection of nature.

An artwork – a painting, a sculpture, a poem – was therefore the expression of the union between the self and nature. Whatever an artist produced was created by nature through him or her. Nature – the unconscious product of the self – and the conscious self came together in the artistic creation. Art was therefore essential in order to make sense of the world, Schelling declared. Neither rational thought nor the most accurate scientific instruments held the key to understanding the world. Art was the finite or concrete representation of the infinite. Art opened 'the holiest of holies', Schelling wrote. It was the revelation of the universe through the creative production of an artist.*

Schelling's students declared the *System of Transcendental Idealism* a masterpiece and the most important philosophical work of the age. If Schelling was right, scientists needed artistic sensibilities to make sense of nature. Genius was no longer confined to the artistic realm, and reason was not the only arbiter of truth.

Schelling was building on ideas that his Jena friends had discussed over the past two years. Back in 1797, for example, Friedrich Schlegel had demanded that 'all art should become science and all science art', and Novalis had explained that 'science in its perfected form must be poetic'. In aligning his philosophy with these ideas, Schelling framed his friends' thoughts within a complex theoretical structure which he elaborated over almost five hundred pages. By giving art a leading role, Schelling's *System of Transcendental Idealism* became the philosophical underpinning of Romanticism.

Schelling had published five books in as many years. Each book pushed his philosophy further and took it in a different direction. Like Fichte, who had long seen his own *Wissenschaftslehre* as a continuously developing doctrine, Schelling too was constantly changing and shaping his ideas. Whereas some might have seen this evolution as a weakness, the friends regarded a willingness to adapt and overturn one's views as a sign of an active mind. Their works might be short-lived and 'already withered' by the time they were published, Novalis said, but who cared. Didn't a time of upheaval and revolution demand this kind of fluidity of thought? Everything was in flux, and that was a 'modern phenomenon'. Philosophy was not so much a discipline as an activity.

---

* Schelling continued exploring these ideas in his lecture series 'Philosophy of Art' and in his 1807 speech 'On the Relationship of the Fine Arts to Nature' given at the Munich Academy of Fine Arts. He declared art to be the bond uniting the soul and nature. The speech became a key text for the next generation of Romantics.

15

'Solemnly calling a new confederation of minds' November 1799: A Meeting in Leutragasse

NEWS OF NAPOLEON'S coup reached Jena in mid-November 1799. When the French army had suffered embarrassing defeats at the hands of the Austrian army in the southern German territories, Napoleon had rushed home from Egypt. In Paris, he had not only taken control of the French war effort but on 9 November had also overthrown the government in an act that would eventually make him ruler of France. 'Oh child,' Caroline wrote to Auguste, who was still in Dessau, 'just tell yourself "all will be well again".' The Russians had been driven out of Switzerland by Napoleon's army, the English were bound to capitulate in Holland, and the French were marching into Swabia from the south. 'Be happy too,' Caroline wrote, 'otherwise I will think all you are doing is whiling away your time without a single intelligent thought in your head.'

Caroline's revolutionary leanings had not been expunged by her imprisonment six years earlier, nor was she alone in her admiration for Napoleon. With powerful Prussia still respecting the neutrality terms it had agreed in the 1795 Peace of Basel, life in the allied Duchy of Saxe-Weimar felt safe. No one in Jena feared the looting soldiers and food shortages affecting so much of Europe. It was easy for the friends to support the French and watch from a distance.

Johanne Fichte, for one, was pleased with the way Napoleon was tidying up Europe: finally, the Russians would no longer be a threat to her home town of Zurich. 'What a convergence of happy news,' she wrote to her husband in Berlin. His predictions about French success had been correct. 'What in the world do you think of Buonaparte!' Dorothea Veit asked Schleiermacher in Berlin. Wasn't he a 'truly great man'?

~

On 11 November, just as news of Napoleon's coup was being reported, Novalis arrived in Jena. The friends had long wanted to be together in one place, and with Novalis's visit the 'alliance of the chosen ones' – the Schlegel brothers, Caroline, Dorothea, Schelling, Novalis and their new friend Ludwig Tieck – was finally complete. Each would remember the next four days as some of the most extraordinary and creative of their lives. Working together at the Schlegel house in Leutragasse, they composed poems, drafted philosophical treatises, edited essays, set up scientific experiments and translated passages from Cervantes' *Don Quixote* and Shakespeare. During mealtimes the atmosphere became heated as they discussed religion, philosophy and poetry, but then lightened when they threw themselves into a 'rage and blaze of stanzas', composing the wittiest rhymes and poems. 'Wilhelm writes verses,' Friedrich Schlegel wrote to Auguste in Dessau, 'I read some, Madame Veit listens to some, your Mama thinks some, Tieck does everything at once.'

It was never quiet or boring. Their days consisted of a vertiginous bouncing between poetry, art, science, philosophy and religion. No one held back. They agreed that they never had to agree because there was nothing more dull than 'flat uniformity of opinion'. Novalis had always enjoyed their symphilosophising because he needed 'people who can *electrify* me'. Finding himself inspired and exhilarated by this communal way of working, he announced: 'I produce best in dialogue.'

Friedrich Schlegel was working on an article for the *Athenaeum* based on their heated discussions on poetry. Written as a conversation between four men and two women, the piece evoked their long afternoons and evenings in Leutragasse. Can you learn and teach poetry? Should there be a theory of poetry? Wasn't it impossible to classify poetry? Why not? How do you talk about poetry? Was drama applied poetry? Shouldn't philosophy be poetry? Was everything poetry then? And what about love? Shouldn't the spirit of love 'float everywhere, invisibly visible, in romantic poetry'?

Friedrich delighted in these discussions. Known for his theatrical delivery, he would lean back in his armchair while pressing his temples with his index fingers and thumbs, slowly moving his fingers in circular movements towards the middle of his forehead until they met. It was as if he were massaging the thoughts from his mind. Sliding his fingers down along the narrow bridge of his small nose, he would finally begin to talk.

Ludwig Tieck had also joined them for the four-day gathering. His long visit to Leutragasse in the summer had been so inspiring – an endless 'party of wit, high spirits, and philosophy', he said – that he had packed up his belongings and family in Berlin and moved to Jena in October. Twenty-six years old, with a thick mop of dark hair, Tieck was sturdily built and energetic. He was also a gifted actor who entertained the group for hours by reading plays aloud – a 'reading machine' who never seemed to tire, Caroline said. Book in hand, he assumed every role, shifting effortlessly between different voices, accents and facial expressions. High-pitched female characters, loud bellowing farmers, gentle lovers, aristocratic rulers – whatever a play demanded Tieck could bring alive – even once an orang-utan.

Tieck was happy. In Jena, with his new friends, he felt as if the 'breath of kindred souls poured into me'. They adored him, but they weren't so sure about Amalie Tieck. 'Oh, that wife! that wife!' Friedrich Schlegel commented to Caroline. Amalie was quiet and timid, and not interested in literature, regularly falling asleep during her husband's readings. Shy as she was, Amalie was probably also overwhelmed. The others were too witty and literary for her, and she was terrified of Caroline's sharp tongue. Mostly, though, Amalie worried about the effect Caroline had on men, her husband included. After their visit in the summer, she had confided her fears to her sister-in-law, Sophie Bernhardi, who had nothing better to do than inform an old friend, who happened to be Dorothea. Amalie needn't be jealous, Dorothea replied to Sophie Bernhardi in Berlin, because 'Caroline is very busy with Schelling'. Caroline had no time for other flirtations. Only Novalis liked the gentle Amalie – so much so that Caroline noticed. 'I'm sure', she wrote to Auguste, 'that he prefers Madame Tieck over me.'

A few others joined the friends during those days in November 1799 – Novalis's younger brother Karl von Hardenberg as well as Henrik Steffens, one of Schelling's students, and the twenty-two-year-old scientist Johann Wilhelm Ritter. Brilliant but perpetually broke and living in squalor in a tiny room on the outskirts of Jena, Ritter had been quickly embraced by the friends. Like Alexander von Humboldt, Ritter was obsessed with Galvanism – experiments that involved electricity, animals, metals and chemicals. Sometimes Ritter brought his equipment to Leutragasse, along with freshly caught frogs. There, he set up his apparatus, attached wires and chemicals to the frogs, and applied metals and magnets. When he succeeded in producing electrical currents in organic *and* inorganic matter, he seemed to prove Schelling's concept of nature as one organism. If both animate and inanimate matter – frog muscle and metal – reacted to electricity, didn't that mean there was an underlying connection? What difference was there between an animal, a plant, a piece of metal or a stone? Were they not all part of the same organic universe? The friends were fascinated by these ideas, Novalis wrote in one of his notebooks, because Ritter was searching for the 'real soul of the world'. Dorothea simply called him an 'electrical machine'.

Only Auguste was missing – 'my darling *Hühnchen*', her little chick, as Caroline sometimes called her. She had been sent to Dessau in mid-September, but during those long weeks away Caroline updated her daughter with gossip and family news – 'I looked daringly pretty in my dress' and 'Friedrich and I got drunk'. Auguste, though, felt homesick, begging her mother to let her come home. Caroline's playful tone changed when she received her daughter's pleas. Life was not just about amusement, she scolded her daughter, adding that they must have spoiled her in the past. After years of treating her as one of the adults, Caroline had suddenly drawn boundaries. Auguste was to stay in Dessau to continue her singing lessons, no matter how much she longed to return.

~

By now the friends were so famous – or notorious – that they were criticised from many sides. Instead of becoming more careful, though, it put them in combative mood. Friedrich and August Wilhelm Schlegel had just returned from the autumn Leipzig Book Fair where all the talk had been about a hugely successful satirical play that attacked the brothers. The author, August von Kotzebue, was one of Germany's most popular playwrights and a declared enemy of the new 'romantic' school. Himself the subject of press attention as the result of a mistaken arrest as a spy while travelling in Russia, Kotzebue had modelled the main protagonist on Friedrich Schlegel – depicting him as a carelessly dressed young man who had been committed to a madhouse by his ruler and who only spoke in quotations from the brothers' published fragments in the *Athenaeum* and Friedrich's *Lucinde*. Having seen a performance in Leipzig, Friedrich was rather pleased by the attention. A famous playwright had written an entire play about him and everybody was talking about it. How bad could that be? Who cared that it ridiculed him? His revolution was succeeding.

August Wilhelm Schlegel was less delighted. 'When dealing with ignorant writings and people,' he said, 'mockery is the only weapon.' And so he returned the favour by writing a short play about Kotzebue as well as a skit on the Lord's Prayer that made fun of the playwright's recent arrest in Siberia.

> Our Father Who Art in Siberia, applauded be Thy name. Thy theatre come, Thy humour work in Germany as it does in Britain. Give us this day our everyday role, and forgive us our boringness, as we forgive those who bore us. Lead us not into poetry but deliver us from *Gustav Wasa*.* For Thine is the theatre and the crowds and the popularity, from now until the new age. Amen.

Caroline had her own way of dealing with critical reviews and comments: she used the pages on which they were printed 'as paper rolls to curl my hair'. But no matter what weapons they wielded, the friends were in a quarrelsome mood. Nor were they without cause, because the onslaughts came from all corners.

From its nearby office, the *Allgemeine Literatur-Zeitung* had just published two negative reviews of Schelling's *Naturphilosophie*. Schelling was infuriated. And when he felt attacked, he showed it, swearing and stamping about, and describing his adversaries as 'dead dogs', as one of Caroline's old Göttingen friends later recalled. Schelling sent the editors a petulant letter, demanding to be allowed to review his *own* work. Who better than himself, Schelling asked, to assess the work? Unsurprisingly, the *Allgemeine Literatur-Zeitung* didn't take up his offer.

Less understandable was their persistent refusal to review the *Athenaeum*. For more than a year, August Wilhelm Schlegel had asked and nudged, at first in a friendly way but then with increasing irritation, but the editors had ignored his pleas. He didn't understand why. For four years, he had been one of the *Allgemeine Literatur-Zeitung's* most regular contributors, writing and publishing almost three hundred reviews with Caroline's help. And one of the two

---

* *Gustav Wasa* was one of Kotzebue's plays.

editors, Gottlieb Hufeland, was their neighbour at Leutragasse, living just across the courtyard. The Hufelands and the Schlegels met at parties and other social gatherings, and their relationship was cordial. But Hufeland could not be persuaded.

There was more trouble. Fichte wrote from Berlin to report that a journalist there was ridiculing Tieck's latest play as well as spreading false rumours that the Duke of Saxe-Weimar had reprimanded the Schlegels for one of their pieces in the *Athenaeum*. The friends wrote satirical poems in retaliation. As they threw lines and rhymes around the parlour, August Wilhelm Schlegel's and Ludwig Tieck's brown eyes flashed sparks across the room, Caroline wrote to Auguste. Everyone laughed so hard they were almost rolling on the floor.

The friends felt invincible. They believed themselves cleverer, wittier and more poetic than anyone else. They criticised the literary establishment and joked about Schiller's poems. The only voice of caution came from August Wilhelm, who now and again advised against too many 'deviltries'. Treat Schiller too harshly, he warned, and 'we'll spoil our personal relationship with Goethe'.

～

Schiller, though, had more pressing worries. After giving birth to their third child in mid-October, Charlotte Schiller had become so gravely ill that their physician, Dr Stark, diagnosed a 'nervous fever'. The typical symptoms were fevers, loss of appetite, nausea, chills, general weakness, irregular pulse and insomnia, but disturbingly Charlotte also suffered bouts of insanity. Instead of happily packing his belongings to move to Weimar as planned, Schiller had watched his beloved Lolo spiral into some kind of madness. For weeks Charlotte didn't sleep. His wife couldn't be left alone and her screams, Schiller admitted to Goethe, 'pierce my heart'. Although Charlotte's mother arrived to help, Schiller didn't dare leave his wife's bedside, even at night.

Dr Stark tried the full range of his medicine cabinet, but Schiller worried that the doctor's inventiveness had come to an end. Over a period of several weeks, Schiller told Goethe, Dr Stark had prescribed musk against the nervous fever, opium to calm her nerves, henbane against irritability, quinine to bring down her temperature, camphor to induce sweating and zinc oxide against nerve pain. The physician also tried a course of blistering to purify the body, mixing an irritant powder into a poultice and applying it to Charlotte's skin to raise blisters. Once filled with liquid or pus, the blisters were sliced open. Nothing had helped, Schiller wrote at the beginning of November, but 'today they're going to try out belladonna'.

Three weeks into her illness the fever finally subsided and Dr Stark promised that Charlotte would survive. But she was still delirious and often unconscious. Schiller, never strong himself, was shaken by worry and lack of sleep. When Dr Stark tried cold ammonia head compresses, Charlotte's ravings stopped but she fell into a silent stupor and listless lethargy. Schiller feared she would never recover.

Everybody in Jena knew. Johanne Fichte reported to her husband in Berlin that Charlotte Schiller had been deranged for weeks. The playwright couldn't work or think, Johanne wrote, and the Schillers could not move to Weimar as planned. Schiller was so devastated by Charlotte's suffering that he needed a few hours with Goethe in Weimar 'to distract myself'. He took his six-year-old son Karl along and left him in Goethe's care. Goethe's lover Christiane Vulpius looked after the boy during those weeks. Initially homesick at bedtime, little Karl quickly became devoted to 'his dear Damela' – his way of pronouncing 'Demoiselle'* – trailing behind Christiane all day.

And although everyone in the Schlegel house knew about Charlotte's illness, no one walked over to the Schillers' apartment to offer help or condolences. The rift was too deep. 'We don't make enemies,' August Wilhelm Schlegel simply said, 'we already have them.'

~

They were hated because they rattled the very foundations of the literary establishment. He, his brother, Tieck, Schelling and a few others, August Wilhelm declared, were the most radical contributors to the revolution of German literature and philosophy. To show their intentions, they had filled the latest issue of the *Athenaeum* with so many harsh attacks aimed at their adversaries that Caroline, who rarely avoided a fight, couldn't bring herself to read it. Whenever she saw the journal lying around, August Wilhelm said, she 'held her head in her hands'.

---

* 'Demoiselle' was derived from the French *Mademoiselle* and was used for unmarried women, which Christiane Vulpius still was.

Their reputation as radical thinkers and critics had even reached the Prussian court. The previous year, when Novalis published *Faith and Love* – an essay in which he suggested that a state should be led by the universal language of feeling and love rather than be managed, like a factory – the Prussian king had been so confused that he couldn't work out whether or not to censor it. Defeated by the text, he had passed it on from one minister to the next. They too found it impossible to understand but were certain about one thing: the essay must have been written by one of the Schlegels. 'If someone doesn't understand something,' Friedrich Schlegel joked to Novalis, 'then a Schlegel wrote it.'

On 14 November 1799, the third day of their gathering, the discussions became even more heated when Novalis read his new essay *Europe** to the group. In *Europe* he called for a new religion based on feeling, beauty and love rather than doctrines or an insti-tutionalised church. For Novalis, the Reformation was not the beginning of the democratisation of religion but had heralded the destruction of a Europe that had once been unified by *one* faith. Luther and the advent of Protestantism had driven a wedge into the union, Novalis argued, because 'they separated the inseparable' and drained Christianity of the 'great and marvellous religious miracles'.

Though he criticised the Reformation, Novalis didn't advocate a conversion to the Catholic Church. Instead he turned against the modern age – an age that, according to him, had sucked the sublime and the holiness out of religion, as well as beauty, kindness and humanity. As he read on, Novalis evoked the Middle Ages, a time, he said, when the Church had been a mysterious place filled with colourful paintings, sweet scents and heavenly music.

As the blood of tens of thousands manured the fields of an embattled Europe, Novalis spoke of a future of unity. 'Once, there was a brilliant age,' he began, ironically evoking what so many believed to be the so-called Dark Ages with a metaphor of light. Ignoring the Inquisition's brutal history of systematic torture, rape and witch hunts, Novalis idealised a spiritual community 'which paid no attention to national borders' and one which would bring eternal peace to Europe. Let's come together for 'a great feast of

---

* Novalis called his essay *Europe* but it was never printed during his lifetime. It was first published in 1826 under the title *Christianity or Europe: A Fragment*.

love', he said, and a 'festival of peace'. His new religion was 'solemnly calling for a new confederation of minds'.

The Enlightenment, with its focus on rational thought, Novalis explained in *Europe*, had stripped the world of spirituality. Why was religious enthusiasm now equated with fanaticism, he asked, and imagination and feelings branded the new heretics? The world had become a materialistic machine, a gigantic millwheel, endlessly turning and thereby grinding itself to dust. With their talk of reason, productivity and utility, the scientists and philosophers of the Enlightenment had tried to erase all wonder and awe from nature.

'The gentlemen are a bit crazy,' Dorothea observed, as arguments erupted the minute Novalis finished reading the essay. How could Novalis create a future by turning to the past, some asked. Wasn't he going backwards? But Novalis didn't want to go back. He wanted to create a *new* religion. The French Revolution had prepared the ground, he said. It was time to sow the newly ploughed field. Something new would sprout from the chaos. 'True anarchy is what gives rise to religion,' Novalis said.

Couldn't they feel the 'powerful fermentation' underway in the arts and sciences, he asked. Wasn't there an almighty creative power everywhere? An infinite variety of thought? A limitless imagination? For Novalis, his Christ was a 'true genius' who could be inhaled like air, embraced like a lover, heard in songs, experienced in love, death and heavenly lust, consumed as bread and wine, and felt inside one's body. 'Have patience,' Novalis ended his essay, 'it will come, it must come – the sacred age of eternal peace.'

All the friends were thinking about religion. Those days in Jena, Ludwig Tieck later said, were inspired by a 'longing for religious things'. But why the sudden enthusiasm? Where was this coming from? They were certainly not suddenly turning into regular church-goers, nor were they discussing religion as an institution. Rather, they embraced spirituality as part of the greater romantic project. Their new interest was about injecting feelings, imagination and beauty into an increasingly materialistic world. This was not a search for God but a search for themselves as part of the universe.

Religion was also at the heart of Tieck's new play *Life and Death of St Genoveva*, a tragedy set in the Middle Ages which he also read to the friends during those inspiring days in November. Similarly, Friedrich Schlegel was working on a new collection of religious fragments, and even August Wilhelm, never prone to melodramatic outbursts, joined in with his long poem *The Bond of the Church with the Arts*.

Like Novalis, August Wilhelm believed that the Reformation had robbed them of colours and stories, of paintings and poetry. Martin Luther might have brought the Bible to the masses, but in doing so, they believed, he had eradicated the world's magic. The arts had literally been whitewashed off the Church's walls. The religion of the Medieval Church, August Wilhelm later explained, was 'majestically clad in festive attire, not shrouded in the monotonous mourning dress of the Protestant Church'. In his poem, August Wilhelm conjured up a church decorated with alabaster sculptures, gem-encrusted ceilings and glorious paintings – a place where sublime hymns filled the air and sacred stories were told. This was their new Romantic Church. 'Christianity is the order of the day here,' Dorothea wrote to their friend Friedrich Schleiermacher, in Berlin.

～

Schleiermacher – 'Schleier' as the friends called him – was one of the reasons for their recent interest. A few months previously, in the early summer, the theologian and chaplain had anonymously published a book entitled *On Religion: Speeches to Its Cultured Despisers*. When Friedrich Schlegel returned to Jena in September, he had brought several copies. Schelling read it, as did Caroline, and Novalis had dispatched a courier to Jena to get his copy. Religion, Schleiermacher argued, was simply the 'contemplation of the universe' – there was no need for a personal God, for doctrine or for liturgy. Religion was in nature and in us.

Taking his cue from Schelling's concept of unity and Spinoza's idea that God *is* nature, Schleiermacher defined a new kind of religion. 'Considering every finite thing as part of the larger whole: that is religion,' he explained. This was a radical approach, especially as it came from a chaplain and theologian. Having spent the previous two years in the company of Friedrich Schlegel in Berlin, the significance of the Ich had rubbed off on Schleiermacher. His new religion was personal and intimate, only to be found within oneself. It was the wonder of connecting with the infinite directly and intuitively. To have religion, Schleiermacher wrote, was to 'drink in the beauty of the world'. His religion was a 'sacred music' that accompanied humanity. Neither priests nor rationality nor moral arguments paved the way to faith. All that was needed was imagination.

If ever a religion would appeal to the young Romantics, it was one based on imagination. 'Religion is all poetry,' Friedrich Schlegel said, declaring with his usual bravado that he wanted to write a new bible, establish a new religion and follow in Mohammed's and Luther's footsteps. Like Mohammed, Friedrich would use the 'flaming sword of the word' to conquer the world of the mind. Like Christ, he was prepared to die for it. As the new messiah, Friedrich was ready to proclaim his new religion, with artists and poets as his priests. 'The new religion must be entirely *magic*,' Friedrich had written to Novalis when they had first begun to talk about the subject, in the previous year. No, they were not joking, Friedrich Schlegel had replied when his incredulous older brother had asked what was going on. It was one thing to let the arts sing and shine again, August Wilhelm thought, but for Friedrich to declare himself a prophet was preposterous.

As ever, August Wilhelm was careful. When Friedrich suggested publishing Novalis's essay *Europe* in the *Athenaeum*, he disagreed. Philosophers should leave religion to the theologians, he believed. Hadn't the atheism scandal and Fichte's dismissal been proof enough? Maybe Novalis and Friedrich had taken their new enthusiasm too far? Caroline was also unsure. For her, religion was like antiquity and philosophy, Friedrich explained to Novalis, because 'she has always enjoyed marvelling at these things', but that was where her interest ended. Schelling agreed, and as the arguments flew back and forth in Caroline's parlour, he composed a long, sceptical poem on the spot, including these lines:

> *Oh let my one religion be*
> *To love a shapely, pretty knee*
> *And breasts so full and hips so slim*
> *And flowers sweet with scents within,*
> *All pleasures full of sustenance,*
> *All love's sweetest acquiescence.*

Even better, thought Friedrich Schlegel, why not publish Schelling's poem and Novalis's essay together? August Wilhelm remained cautious, as did Dorothea, but the others wanted to include both contributions. Maybe if they added an editorial comment, August

Wilhelm Schlegel suggested, but Schelling refused to have his verses moderated – the works should speak for themselves. They couldn't agree.

It was time to clear their heads with a long walk in the Paradise. It was unseasonably warm for a day in mid-November, only the yellowed leaves on the ground along the river reminding them that winter had arrived. As the Schlegels, Dorothea, Schelling and Novalis meandered along the paths, arms linked, they saw Goethe approaching and stopped for a chat. Goethe had just arrived in Jena and Dorothea had yet to meet him. Since moving to Jena a few weeks before, she had been keen to get to know 'the divine old excellency'.

August Wilhelm introduced Dorothea, and Goethe politely turned around to walk with the friends. Nervous, and desperate to make a good impression, Dorothea couldn't think of a topic that wouldn't bore Goethe. The silence was awkward. Then, as she looked around, she saw the river and blurted out a question about the Saale's fast currents. When Goethe cordially replied, Dorothea was so starstruck she could only stare. But as they walked on, she was lulled by Goethe's friendly manner, and soon recovered. It was one of the best days of her life, she wrote to her friends in Berlin.

And who better to ask whether to publish Novalis's essay on religion, the Schlegel brothers decided. Older, less impetuous and more careful, Goethe became their 'referee'. Over the next few days he met Schelling and the Schlegel brothers individually to discuss the situation in detail. Never rash, Goethe took his time and in the end advised against publication. After the Fichte debacle earlier that year, Goethe had no interest in another provocative religious treatise, and certainly not one that attacked the Reformation in the heartland of the Protestant faith. There was a difference, he told August Wilhelm Schlegel, between what could be thought privately and what could be published. Sometimes it was better to hold back.

Novalis said nothing. Unlike Schelling or Fichte, he never had a problem with criticism or disagreements. It didn't matter. Sooner or later, his religion of love would succeed, of that he was certain.

PART IV

Fragmentation

Listen, this good old Jena really is a den of murderers after all. You have no idea how everyone gossips about everything behind your back, even the people you wouldn't expect.

Caroline Schlegel to August Wilhelm Schlegel,
5 May 1801

'The republic of despots'
Winter 1799–Summer 1800: Estrangements

THE SCHLEGEL HOUSEHOLD was becoming isolated. Yes, their spare rooms were full of guests and the table was still laid for a dozen people, but they were seeing only intimate friends. By the end of November 1799, people were talking about the 'members of the Schlegel clique', and, as Dorothea Veit noted, they now rarely went out to public gatherings, concerts and clubs. The change happened slowly, and almost without realising, the friends withdrew. Their joy of taking part in Jena's social life had been eroded for several reasons: the quarrel with Schiller, Fichte's dismissal, the *Lucinde* scandal and the ongoing fight with the Jena-based *Allgemeine Literatur-Zeitung*. People gossiped so much that it was easier to stay at home.

The trouble with the *Allgemeine Literatur-Zeitung* was particularly infuriating. Schelling was still incensed about the journal's two critical reviews, and August Wilhelm remained annoyed about its refusal to review the *Athenaeum*. Earlier that year, August Wilhelm had warned one of the two editors, their neighbour Gottlieb Hufeland, that he would not write for them any more until they published a review of the *Athenaeum*. But Hufeland was not to be persuaded. It wasn't their fault, he replied, because they had tried to commission someone but no one *wanted* to write about the *Athenaeum*.

The situation deteriorated further when the Schlegels heard that the other editor of the *Allgemeine Literatur-Zeitung*, Christian Gottfried Schütz, had ridiculed the *Athenaeum* in an amateur theatre performance at his house. August Wilhelm usually remained calm, generally favouring a more balanced approach. He was slow to anger, but once roused, little could stop him. The editors had gone too far. He felt like a 'roaring lion', August Wilhelm said, 'looking for something to rip to pieces'. He now demanded to see the text of the play that had been performed in Schütz's house and threatened legal action against the *Allgemeine Literatur-Zeitung*. Why on earth was

August Wilhelm writing letters like a lawyer, Schütz fired back, surely he was allowed to perform whatever he wanted in the privacy of his own home?

Finally, in mid-November, August Wilhelm Schlegel told the editors that he would never write for the *Allgemeine Literatur-Zeitung* again. Rather than bow out quietly, he announced his reasons publicly. His had been the only significant reviews in the entire journal, August Wilhelm insisted, and he was leaving because it was simply too embarrassing to write alongside so many inferior contributors. In an equally long and equally public refutation, the *Allgemeine Literatur-Zeitung* replied that all their reviews were anonymous. How could the public judge August Wilhelm Schlegel's preposterous statement, the editors asked, when no one knew who had written what? They promised their contributors anonymity to ensure honest reviews, and they were not willing to expose their identities for the sake of August Wilhelm Schlegel's vendetta.*

Taking on the *Allgemeine Literatur-Zeitung* was a bold move. Praise on its pages could bring fame, as Fichte had experienced at the beginning of his career. But Fichte cheered on his friends from Berlin. The editors of the *Allgemeine Literatur-Zeitung* were incompetent dilettantes, he told Schelling, who 'need to be personally attacked'. With the atmosphere increasingly tense, Johanne Fichte wrote to her husband, 'there's squabbling here like never before.' Difficult as it was to avoid neighbours and colleagues in a small town like Jena, the offended parties kept out of each other's way. 'We hardly see anyone outside our little group,' Caroline Schlegel wrote to a friend in Göttingen.

Then, out of the blue, the *Allgemeine Literatur-Zeitung* finally published a review of the *Athenaeum* at the end of November 1799. It was brutal — and all the more hurtful because the friends soon discovered that it had been written by an old acquaintance from Caroline's time in Mainz, Ludwig Ferdinand Huber. Caroline was furious, not least because Huber's wife Therese was an old friend from Göttingen and Mainz. Caroline picked up her quill and wrote

---

* Meticulous as always, August Wilhelm Schlegel sorted through his files and counted every single review he had ever submitted to the *Allgemeine Literatur-Zeitung*, printing a conclusive list of almost three hundred titles and corresponding issue numbers in the next issue of the *Athenaeum*.

a long and angry letter to Huber, following it with a second long note two days later. Why had he accepted the commission in the first place? How dare he stab his friends in the back at such a moment? Had he no loyalty? And in any case, he had no understanding of the subjects that were covered in the *Athenaeum*, Caroline fumed. Huber had no knowledge of philosophy, he was confused about the arts, and he was certainly no expert in poetry. 'So since you're lacking all of that,' she wrote, 'why did you take on the job?' He would regret his actions, she predicted, because he had clearly chosen the wrong side in this 'universal battle of good against evil'.

'Caroline wrote, shouted, and hurled insults,' Therese Huber later wrote. Her revolutionary disposition, Caroline warned Huber, had been reignited by receiving the news of Napoleon's coup. Like Napoleon, she was ready to fight. In order to enjoy a dance, Caroline wrote, explaining her combativeness to another friend, you had to stand in the middle of the dance floor and 'get swept up in the whirl of the music'. And that was where she was standing right now – in the very centre as the music reached its climax. She could never forgive Huber, Caroline declared, and she was not going to shy away from a battle.

The fierce opposition to their work, August Wilhelm Schlegel wrote in yet another long letter to Huber, was a sign of how effective they had been. 'People hate us – good! They curse us – even better! They make the sign of the cross to ward us off like blasphemers, Jacobins, and corrupters of youth – God be praised!' In Berlin, Schleiermacher was delighted when August Wilhelm sent him copies of their correspondence with Huber. They were now surrounded by such a 'blaze of hellfire', the theologian quipped, that he could only worship the 'devil', and that devil was August Wilhelm.

~

At the end of November 1799, Charlotte Schiller finally began to feel better. Impatient to leave Jena, Schiller began to organise their move to Weimar. Two weeks later their furniture was packed up and moved to their new home in Windischengasse, a short walk from Goethe's house. The apartment was on the second floor but had additional garret rooms where Schiller could work away from the family bustle. For the first two weeks in Weimar, Charlotte stayed with friends so that she could rest while her husband dealt with the

chaos of the move, decorators and the children. 'Leave all the memories of the last two months behind in the Jena valley,' Schiller told
her at the beginning of December, 'we want to begin a new and
happy life here.' In the weeks that followed, Charlotte slowly regained
her strength and Schiller also felt better than he had for years – he
even went for walks and attended parties and the theatre. 'I have the
feeling that I've changed a lot,' he admitted.

In Weimar, Schiller and Goethe's voluminous literary correspondence trickled down to short notes. 'You are most cordially invited,'
Goethe wrote to Schiller, 'you will find here heated, well-lit rooms
. . . and a glass of punch', and urging him, 'I wonder if you would
care to pay me a little visit today?' Mostly Goethe went to Schiller's
apartment, but Schiller also came – if he felt weak, he called for
porters, who would carry him over to his friend's or to the theatre
in a sedan chair. Every day maids delivered notes between the two
houses. 'Are you going to the opera? Perhaps I can see you there?'
Schiller asked when the theatre in Weimar put on a special performance, and received a reply the same day saying, 'I'll certainly
look out for you at the opera.' There was a kind of breathlessness
in the brief invitations, with both men excited that they were finally
able to see each other all the time. 'Do let me know if I will see
you today and where and when?' Schiller asked Goethe, who replied
impatiently the next day: 'It is three o'clock already and I still have
no word from you.'

'Jena was no longer the place for me,' Schiller explained to his
old friend Körner in Dresden a few weeks after the move. And
although the fifteen miles between him and the Schlegels were a
relief, it didn't end the animosity. Schiller claimed never to finish
any of their publications, because 'I find all that individuality shimmering on every page so repulsive'. To his mind, the Schlegels
had sullied the concept of a self-determined Ich with their self-
absorption and arrogance.

∼

After an unusually warm November, the winter of 1799 became so
exceptionally cold that the friends huddled indoors in front of their
fireplaces and stoves, layered in shawls and blankets. As the icy nights
dragged on, wood supplies ran low and their spirits fell even lower.
Cooped up, with no outside distraction, everyone grew irritable. At

one point, Friedrich Schlegel shouted at Dorothea so fiercely for not immediately understanding the deeper meaning of some new poems he had written that she confessed, 'I almost died of fear.' Friedrich was also in a foul mood because he had once again run out of money. How was he supposed to concentrate on his work?

The atmosphere at Leutragasse was so dark that even seeing Fichte didn't cheer up the friends. Fichte arrived for a visit in early December. He hadn't seen his wife and son for five months. Lonely in Berlin, he had looked forward to reconnecting with his friends in Jena, but soon felt excluded. He joined a couple of dinners in Leutragasse but the atmosphere was tense. Fichte could sense that his friends also disapproved of his continuing friendship with the editors of the *Allgemeine Literatur-Zeitung*. He felt under pressure. Why couldn't they believe in his loyalty? And why did Caroline and Schelling have to conduct their affair in broad daylight? Fichte was uncomfortable watching the lovers flirt openly. He had never embraced his friends' convention-defying free love. Fichte's philosophy might have been revolutionary but his attitude to marriage was resoundingly traditional.

It was all rather inconvenient. Fichte wanted to see Schelling to talk about philosophy and coordinate their responses to those who disliked their work. But whenever Fichte went to Schelling's lodgings, his friend was with Caroline in Leutragasse. Hurt, Fichte said nothing, swallowing his frustration and withdrawing. 'I couldn't,' Fichte told Schelling many months later, 'and didn't want to, go looking for you where you were spending all your time – for very good reasons.'

Fichte's dreams of a Jena Colony were over. Gone were the days of symphilosophising. Instead of fighting the literary establishment and a world devoid of imagination, they fought among themselves. House-bound by ice and snow, everybody quarrelled like schoolboys, Dorothea told Schleiermacher.

After weeks of suppressing his frustration about the affair with Schelling, Friedrich Schlegel now openly turned against Caroline who had for so long been his friend and collaborator. He had once loved her but, tormented by unrequited love, had bowed out for his brother. Maybe it was too painful for Friedrich to watch as Schelling did what he would like to have done years ago. Maybe he now regretted that he hadn't pursued her. Or maybe he feared that the affair would herald the end of Caroline and August Wilhelm's marriage, and with that their communal working. Whatever his reasons, Friedrich's feelings for Caroline turned from love to rejection and eventually to raw hate. He declared that he would always take his brother's side, regardless of whether August Wilhelm asked for it. Either way, Friedrich stopped talking to Caroline and Schelling. There was no longer any pretence of friendship or civility. It made for uncomfortable living. Even Auguste, who had finally returned from her Dessau exile at the end of November, tiptoed through the house. Only August Wilhelm didn't seem to mind that his wife flirted with her lover in front of him.

After her ten weeks in Dessau, Auguste tried her best to make everybody happy. She sang, laughed and did all she could to please her mother. Now kind to Schelling, she told a friend she found him 'much more likeable'. But the once congenial atmosphere had turned sour. Even their new friend Ludwig Tieck turned against them. As the cold set in, Tieck began to suffer from such bad gout in his knees that he could hardly walk. In constant agony, his cheerful disposition metamorphosed into a bitter crankiness. Under such physical duress, he felt uncomfortable among the squabbling Schlegels. The endless discussions about the *Allgemeine Literatur-Zeitung* and their other enemies were unbearably boring.

Tieck also had more personal misgivings. Dorothea was harsh, unkind and far too opinionated – a 'monster' – he now wrote to his sister Sophie Bernhardi in Berlin. Caroline fared no better. Only a few weeks earlier Tieck had been charmed, admiring Caroline's brilliant mind and poetic understanding, but now her erudition struck him as too manly. How could a woman be so confident and intellectual? Suddenly and out of the blue he described Caroline as a 'hermaphrodite' to his sister. Everything was out of control, Tieck continued, because Caroline was having an affair with Schelling, while Schelling somehow remained close to August Wilhelm Schlegel, who himself did nothing. Furthermore, *Lucinde* had revealed far more than anyone wanted to know about Friedrich's and Dorothea's relationship, and it wouldn't have surprised him, Tieck wrote, to discover that Dorothea was trying to have an affair with August Wilhelm. The household was 'like a big farm full of pigs'. Everyone in Jena hated them. If they hadn't been his friends, he would have based a satire on their lives.

In return, the Schlegels gossiped about the Tiecks. 'With Tieck you just talk and talk yourself to death through a whole winter,' Friedrich wrote to a friend in Berlin, while Caroline thought that Tieck's imagination just fluttered and flapped its wings but never quite took off. And once again, Amalie Tieck was attacked. She just didn't fit in, Dorothea wrote to Ludwig Tieck's sister Sophie Bernhardi, who must have wondered exactly what was going on in Jena. Yet none of this stopped Tieck's visits to Leutragasse, not even the pain which prevented him from walking alone. So, several times a week, Friedrich or August Wilhelm would put on their warmest clothes and face the icy wind that whipped through Jena's narrow alleys. They trudged through the snow and skidded over the icy cobblestones across town to collect the invalid from his lodgings, just outside the medieval walls. As Tieck leaned on their arms, everybody pretended that nothing had changed since the autumn.

Caroline was to blame, Tieck told his sister, she was 'the true cause of all the fighting'. By taking Schelling as her lover, she had poisoned the well of friendship. And once Friedrich Schlegel had declared war on his sister-in-law, Dorothea's own misgivings were finally cut loose. Ever since their first exchange of letters in March 1799, Dorothea had tried to charm Caroline to please her beloved Friedrich, but there was no longer any need. From the moment of her arrival in Jena, Dorothea had felt overshadowed by Caroline's personality. Caroline was more beautiful, looked younger, was better dressed and had the ability to charm everybody. In reality, though, Dorothea wrote to an old friend in Berlin, Caroline was 'hard, hard as stone'.

August Wilhelm remained calm throughout those cold winter weeks, telling an exasperated Dorothea that he didn't care what other people thought. Perhaps he didn't, or perhaps Caroline's behaviour gave him the licence to pursue his own adventures. His summer love interest, Elisa van Nuys, had long departed Jena, but there would be others. Whatever his reasons, he didn't turn against his wife's young lover, instead joking that Caroline would in time move on to even younger men: she 'isn't done yet – her next lover is still wearing a little sailor suit!'

Novalis too kept his distance from Caroline. Their relationship had begun to cool the previous autumn when her affair with Schelling became public knowledge. 'I didn't like him this time,' Caroline had told Auguste after one of his visits, but Novalis remained unaware of how acrimonious the atmosphere in Leutragasse had since become. He was too busy at the salt mines* and with his literary work – 'my head is swimming with ideas for novels and comedies,' he told Tieck and Friedrich Schlegel. Whenever he wrote, he sent greetings to the rest of 'the whole poetic family'.

~

That same frosty winter Goethe received some news he had longed for. It came from Madrid, where Wilhelm von Humboldt was on an extended vacation. Alexander had made it to South America, Wilhelm wrote. After a sea voyage of forty-one days, his brother had disembarked in July 1799 in Cumaná, on the coast of New Andalusia.† Within four months, he had experienced his first earthquake and observed a solar eclipse and a spectacular meteor shower. Since then, Alexander had experimented with electric eels – strange five-foot fish that could deliver electric shocks of more than 600 volts – and embarked on a daring adventure deep into the rainforest. It was dangerous, Alexander had told his brother, but he had never been happier and healthier.

While his old friends in Jena tried to keep warm in front of their stoves, Alexander von Humboldt endured the sweltering humidity of the tropical rainforest. As they wrapped blankets around their shoulders and put their cold hands in fur muffs, Alexander encountered beautifully spotted jaguars, observed motionless crocodiles next to his canoe, swam with huge boa constrictors and was relentlessly attacked by swarms of mosquitoes. He and his small team paddled along the Orinoco and the surrounding river networks for fourteen hundred miles. While Goethe, Schiller and the Schlegels heard the sound of passing sleigh bells, Alexander listened to the deafening bellows of howler monkeys and the snoring sounds of river dolphins. Smells and colours assaulted his senses – there were so many new animals, insects and plants, Alexander wrote to his brother, that 'we run around like fools'. It was a world pulsating with life, a network

---

* On 7 December 1799 Novalis had been promoted to assessor of the salt mines, and with this new responsibility his workload increased substantially. After the November meeting, he only briefly stopped in Jena, in April 1800.
† New Andalusia was part of the Spanish Empire and Cumaná is on the coast of what is today Venezuela.

of 'active, organic powers' – one great organism in which everything was connected.

Meanwhile in Madrid, far removed from all the infighting in Jena, Wilhelm von Humboldt continued to read the works of his old acquaintances. Both Fichte and Friedrich Schlegel were 'extraordinary minds', he thought, and their effect on the literary world was much like fermented yeast in sourdough. 'If I wasn't afraid that you would laugh at me for being a missionary,' he told Goethe, he would admit that he had been proselytising their new philosophy in Spain.

∽

As winter stuttered towards spring, Caroline Schlegel buckled. In early March 1800, the fierce headaches and coughs from which she had been suffering developed into a fever. Bed-bound for weeks, she felt as if she had to crawl out of a deep well. August Wilhelm feared for her life, confessing his worries to Goethe. Her physician, Dr Christoph Wilhelm Hufeland (a cousin of their neighbour, Gottlieb Hufeland), diagnosed a 'nervous fever' – the same illness that had almost killed Charlotte Schiller. Dr Hufeland had seen so many cases that he had recently published a book about the disease. Caroline's condition was serious but Dr Hufeland reassured the family that he knew exactly what to do. He prescribed a regime of hot baths, enemas and poultices.

The whole household in Leutragasse was suddenly busy caring for Caroline. Medicines had to be prepared, potions administered and endless buckets of water were carried from the well to the house and then heated for the baths which Caroline was made to take twice a day. But she remained restless and couldn't sleep. When the fevers finally went down, Dr Hufeland prescribed a 'mustard plaster'. He ground 30 grams of mustard seed into a fine powder which he mixed into a paste with a tablespoon of horseradish, sourdough and vinegar. Spreading this concoction onto a piece of linen, he placed it on Caroline's calf for several hours. The burning sensation she felt, he explained, was part of the remedy. But when they removed the mustard plaster, they discovered that Caroline's leg had become inflamed. Worse, her fevers returned with a vengeance, this time accompanied by painful cramps.

Auguste looked after her mother, scuttling up and down the stairs day and night to nurse her. If her mother didn't improve soon, an exhausted Auguste confessed after four weeks, 'we will all die together'. At night, when Caroline couldn't sleep, the maid or Auguste would light the fire in the kitchen to boil water for yet another bath. She was fed a strong broth every day and was taking quinine, musk and laudanum. Caroline was also drinking so much Hungarian wine – which Dr Hufeland believed would strengthen her – that she soon exhausted Jena's supplies and August Wilhelm had to ask Goethe to send more over from Weimar. In the end, Dr Hufeland decided the only way Caroline would recover fully was a cure at a spa town.

Caroline was not alone in her battle against illness. Everybody seemed to be sick. Ludwig Tieck was still experiencing severe gout attacks, and their neighbour Wilhelmine Hufeland, the wife of the *Allgemeine Literatur-Zeitung*'s editor, was incubating a tapeworm. In Weimar, Schiller too was seriously ill, suffering fevers and excruciating cramps. In mid-February his physician, Dr Stark, had prescribed a course of bloodletting which only made Schiller worse. Dr Stark had little hope for his weakened patient. Desperate to get his affairs in order before he died, Schiller asked for strong stimulants so that he could survive a few more days. Fearing the worst, Goethe sat at his bedside. But to everybody's surprise, Schiller pulled through and was back at his desk by the end of March – although still coughing violently. He was so frail that he struggled to walk up the stairs to his study and his hand shook when he wrote his first letters after six weeks.

As Schiller recovered, Goethe began to worry about the French troops marching into the southern German territories. Though the enemy was still several hundred miles away, Goethe feared the reach of Napoleon's ambitions. Now First Consul and effectively France's ruler, Napoleon was intent upon consolidating power domestically but also in Europe. And sure enough, in April 1800, French troops crossed the Rhine and approached the Duchy of Württemberg from the south. Another army under Napoleon's direct command was fighting in Italy. 'The evil news', Goethe wrote, 'gives me, too, cause for concern, even so far away.'

At least the sun was finally shining over the Saale valley, as a spectacular spring hatched from the long winter. By the end of April, almost two months after she first fell ill, a weakened Caroline had recovered enough to venture out for short carriage rides with Schelling and Auguste. The fresh green meadows outside the town

walls were carpeted with purple violets and bright yellow primroses.
Along the Saale, graceful willows dangled branches flushed with new
leaves into the river and lilacs prepared to spread their sweet scent.

Meanwhile Dorothea's patience had run out. With everybody
fussing over Caroline, she had been unable to work on her novel
and she was counting down the days until the invalid left town.
Agitated and always prone to migraines, Dorothea now upped her
medication and took a daily dose of quinine and valerian to calm
her nerves. She also sent a steady flow of long querulous letters to
Schleiermacher in Berlin. Why was everybody still praising Caroline's
'magic and the genius of her mind'? Where was her famous wit,
brilliant mind and sense of poetry? Weren't Caroline's judgements
just shallow and calculated? And her opinions prejudiced? Where
was her acclaimed grace? There was nothing remotely likeable about
Caroline, Dorothea insisted, and 'even her tone of voice slices right
through you'.

Even though she admitted that Caroline had been the first to
invite her into her house and to acknowledge her publicly after her
scandalous divorce, Dorothea continued her attacks. Caroline was
selfish, Schelling was 'a vain stubborn braggart' and August Wilhelm
was just too naïve to deal with the situation. How could August
Wilhelm allow Caroline to rule, dominate and ridicule him? Couldn't
he see how everybody was laughing at him? How could he still
have feelings for Caroline when she had never loved him? And how
could Caroline mistake young Schelling's passion for true love?

~

By now, the only people still talking were August Wilhelm, Caroline
and Schelling. Between them, they decided that it would be best for
Schelling to accompany Caroline to Bamberg, some one hundred
miles south-west of Jena, where she wanted to consult a famous
doctor, and then on to the spa town of Bocklet, where she planned
to recuperate. Auguste would also join them but August Wilhelm
wouldn't. In an attempt to allay the increasingly vicious rumours,
they agreed that it would be better for Schelling to leave Jena a little
earlier and to meet Caroline and Auguste somewhere on the road.
An open flirtation was scandalous enough, but to spend several weeks
travelling with the wife of another man was altogether another matter.

At the beginning of May, when Caroline had recovered enough

to face the exertions of a long journey, Schelling left Jena alone and travelled to Saalfeld, a small town some thirty miles to the south. Caroline, Auguste and August Wilhelm Schlegel followed shortly afterwards to meet him. From Saalfeld August Wilhelm made his way to the Leipzig Book Fair, stopping off at Weißenfels to see Novalis, while Schelling, Caroline and Auguste travelled on to Bamberg. Though carefully thought through, their plan didn't quite work out. It was all too obvious, Dorothea noted, and everybody knew that August Wilhelm Schlegel would 'hand her over to him'.

With Caroline away, Dorothea's accusations grew ever more spiteful. Not even young Auguste was spared. Dorothea now gossiped that Auguste had believed Schelling was courting her and not her mother, which would have made the 'marriage *en quatre* complete'. There was no reason to turn against Auguste, but she couldn't stop herself. The fifteen-year-old was already completely ruined by her mother, Dorothea said – like Caroline, Auguste was an attention-seeking flirt who was only interested in her appearance. Poor August Wilhelm was blinded by his love for mother and daughter. How could he have been so dazzled by Auguste as to claim that she understood Goethe's poetry, Shakespeare and antiquity? It was just absurd, Dorothea thought, and nothing could be further from the truth. Auguste 'borrowed the filthiest pile of books from the library', the starring character in *Lucinde* alleged. Even Friedrich, who had always adored Auguste, now accused Caroline of plotting to marry Auguste to Schelling so that she could be near her lover.

Caroline, Auguste and Schelling remained blissfully unaware. Planning ahead, Schelling had booked several rooms on the same floor of their accommodation in Bamberg – two for Caroline, one for Auguste, one for the maid, and two for himself. They needn't be large but they had to be pleasant, he instructed, requesting a comfortable sofa, a few mirrors, tables, chairs and a writing desk for Caroline's parlour, as well as a small room next door with a bed.

Schelling couldn't believe that the magnificent Caroline was really his. 'You know that I'll follow you wherever you want,' she had told him, but it was Schelling who did exactly that. Seeing his devotion, Auguste teased him and made her mother happy by telling her 'how much he loves you'. Away from Jena, Caroline's health finally began to improve. Then, in mid-June, after six weeks in Bamberg, they travelled on to the spa town of Bocklet, sixty miles to the north-west

– just in time, too, for the French were dangerously close. Only a few days later, the French army would defeat the Austrian forces and take Höchstadt, a town fifteen miles south of Bamberg, before turning south again towards Munich.

In Jena, the gossip continued. At the very moment that forty thousand of Napoleon's soldiers were crossing the snow-covered Alps into the Po valley, in northern Italy, to attack the Austrians, Friedrich Schlegel could still only think about their domestic battles. As he accused Schelling of being 'just a tool in Caroline's hands', Dorothea said she didn't know whether to 'curse, laugh or cry' when she thought of August Wilhelm's refusal to be upset.

~

Goethe still came to Jena, albeit less often – and not once during Schiller's first few months in Weimar. The old friends visited him in Weimar, but mostly to say their goodbyes. The first to leave had been Fichte, who finally severed all ties with Jena when he took his family back to Berlin with him in March 1800. Schelling had come in April before his departure to Bamberg, and in mid-June Ludwig and Amelie Tieck called when they moved back to Berlin. Tieck had had enough of the petty fights, and the Schlegels had made their dislike clear. 'In the republic of despots, the Tiecks are the outlaws,' Dorothea had told Schleiermacher a few months previously.

In the first half of 1800, as the exodus continued, August Wilhelm Schlegel became Goethe's most reliable visitor and correspondent from Jena. Schiller couldn't understand why Goethe was still seeing the Schlegels. 'You have to wonder', Schiller wrote to a friend, 'how he can possibly maintain his connection with people like the Schlegel brothers.' The answer was simple. Goethe genuinely liked them and their youthful enthusiasm; but he also used them. August Wilhelm Schlegel assisted with verse composition, translations and queries on antiquity, and Friedrich Schlegel was so well read that he could answer almost any question. In return Goethe counselled August Wilhelm on his ongoing feuds with the *Allgemeine Literatur-Zeitung*.*

---

* August Wilhelm wanted to take legal action against the *Allgemeine Literatur-Zeitung* and sent his files and documentation to Goethe. Rather than take the matter to the courts, Goethe suggested simply lodging a complaint with the Academic Senate of the university. He even drafted a short missive for August Wilhelm.

Then, in July 1800, after an absence of seven months, Goethe spontaneously decided to visit Jena. He couldn't get any work done in Weimar, he told Schiller, 'I just can't ever concentrate here.' Having been busy the whole year with building works at the castle and his court duties, it was time to escape. Goethe packed and left that same afternoon. Schiller missed him but also understood. Everything that Goethe had produced in the past four or five years, Schiller told his old friend Körner, was created in Jena.

August Wilhelm Schlegel warned Goethe that it was quiet in Jena. His brother and Dorothea were still there but with everyone else gone, August Wilhelm spent much of the time at his desk, trying to reduce the ever-increasing pile of work without the help of Caroline. Instead of going away for the summer, he had decided to stay in Jena, hunker down and write.

~

And then everything changed. After weeks of caring for her mother, Auguste suddenly fell ill, suffering from fever, diarrhoea and painful stomach cramps. On 6 July, Schelling wrote from Bocklet to August Wilhelm Schlegel that Caroline was much better but that Auguste was sick. Nothing serious, Schelling reassured him, and Auguste would be fine soon. The local doctor in Bocklet administered opium mixed with gum arabic, as well as a rhubarb tincture, both of which acted as laxatives – perhaps the worst medical intervention for her symptoms, but common at the time. Schelling, who had met several progressive clinicians in Bamberg before coming to Bocklet, was troubled by the prescription but believed the physician's optimistic diagnosis. Caroline, less certain, refused to leave her daughter's room. Auguste's fever continued as did her diarrhoea, exacerbated by the doctor's medication. She was suffering from dysentery.

There was not much that Caroline could do except gently dry her daughter's clammy skin, stroke her damp hair and help her with the chamber pot. When the fever escalated, Caroline might have changed Auguste's nightdress and held her head so she could drink to replenish the lost fluids. Perhaps Caroline read to Auguste in her soothing voice, or just held her hand. The roles of patient and carer were reversed. They had already been through so much together. In prison in Königstein, seven years previously, it had been her daughter's sunny personality that had kept Caroline going. They needed each other. Everybody noticed how much Auguste adored Caroline. Even Dorothea could see how she 'clings to her mother with the deepest love'. Whatever had happened in the past, mother and daughter had always had each other.

As the days passed, Auguste weakened and Schelling was certain that she was being treated incorrectly. He became so concerned that he suggested administering pure opium rather than mixing it with the laxatives. His interest in the latest medical advances was one of the reasons why they had stopped in Bamberg on their way to Bocklet. The doctors in Bamberg were practising so-called Brownism or Brunonianism, a new medical approach which regarded the body as an organism that had to be kept in balance. In their opinion, medical intervention should be designed to help boost the body's defence system. Illnesses that weakened the body, for example, had to be cured with strengthening methods such as warmth, nutritious food and opiates. Physicians following the Brunonian doctrine largely gave up on vomitives, purgatives, laxatives and bloodletting, the staples of eighteenth-century practice up to that point.

But no matter what Schelling said, the doctor in Bocklet refused to take any advice from a philosophy professor, and Auguste continued to decline. Schelling and Caroline finally sent an express messenger to ride the sixty miles to Bamberg to fetch the doctor who had treated Caroline a few weeks before. Normally it was a two-day coach ride between Bocklet and Bamberg, but even a fast rider would not have been able to reduce the trip to less than a day in each direction. It would have taken the doctor at least two days to arrive.

Then the unimaginable happened. On 12 July, eight days after Auguste had become ill, she closed her eyes and never woke again. When the doctor from Bamberg finally arrived, Auguste was already cold. Darkness enveloped Caroline. How would she, how could she, survive without her beloved Auguste? 'The light of my life is gone,' she despaired, and then fell silent. She didn't write, she didn't talk.

Blaming himself for not summoning the doctor from Bamberg earlier, Schelling too fell into a deep depression. When the news reached August Wilhelm, in Jena, he couldn't stop crying. He was 'utterly shattered', he told Caroline's old friend Luise Gotter. He felt as if he was going mad. He had loved Auguste as his own child. He left Jena immediately for Bamberg, where Schelling had taken

Caroline. 'With my broken heart I can write you only a few lines,' August Wilhelm wrote to Goethe; 'my daughter who I loved so unspeakably much has died of dysentery.' He feared the worst for her weakened mother. How was Caroline to survive?

'O what a black fog'
Summer 1800–Spring 1801: Darkness Falls

O N 24 JULY 1800, two days after leaving Jena, August Wilhelm Schlegel embraced his inconsolable wife. For the next seven months he did not leave her side. Only they could comfort each other. Caroline Schlegel remained sleepless, weeping every night for her child.

'I'm only half alive,' she said many weeks later, 'I wander this earth like a shadow.' Caroline couldn't bring herself to write a single letter, but August Wilhelm wrote obsessively. 'It's as if I had saved up all my tears for just this,' he told Ludwig Tieck. With each letter, August Wilhelm conjured Auguste onto the page, describing her personality and his great love for her. When he could no longer bear the pain, he travelled from Bamberg to Bocklet to visit Auguste's grave. The small simple village cemetery was nestled in a low hollow and surrounded by open countryside. It was a hot summer and the nearby meadows were parched. It was peaceful, yet the dark soil of Auguste's fresh grave was a visceral reminder of their loss. A single wilted wreath lay on the ground. August Wilhelm knelt down and cried.

Friedrich Schlegel was devastated too. 'I am with you in my thoughts on your sad journey,' he wrote to his brother. Despite his recent bitterness and anger, Friedrich had loved Auguste – his 'sweet little heart' – like a naughty younger sister. He had always treated her as a fully formed human being, not like a child. Friedrich had taught her ancient Greek and arithmetic but also imparted grown-up gossip. And he had been surprisingly straightforward about adult subjects. On her twelfth birthday he had described her mother's nature to her as 'politico-erotic' and a few months later joked about August Wilhelm's rumoured affair with a neighbour.

After months of petty fighting, Friedrich now brushed aside their disputes and promised to look after August Wilhelm's affairs and correspondence in Jena. 'The house is an empty wasteland,' he wrote to August Wilhelm at the end of July. Dorothea, though, still seemed crazed. Less than two weeks after Auguste's death, she told a friend that a 'misfortune always has a good side, too; like a proper thunderstorm that purifies the atmosphere'. Nor was Dorothea alone in her attacks – even Novalis now condemned Caroline. By putting her love for Schelling above all else, Novalis claimed, Caroline had abandoned her daughter.

But why did Novalis turn against Caroline? So similar in temperament and in taste, each had adored the other from the moment they met. One reason was Novalis's aristocratic roots. On some fundamental level, Novalis respected social expectation and boundaries. Though often regarded as the most romantic of the young Romantics, he was much more traditional than the others when it came to marriage and women. From a young age, Novalis had yearned for 'quiet domestic happiness'. The previous year, he had reprimanded Friedrich Schlegel and Dorothea several times for not marrying. Novalis's sense of freedom lay within him, not without – and certainly not in the breaking of conventions.

Caroline's affair with Schelling was morally unacceptable to him and it had damaged their unique alliance. Novalis now blamed Caroline for all the tensions within their group. He also blamed August Wilhelm for deserting his stepdaughter when he accepted Schelling as his wife's lover. Oh, beautiful, charming Auguste, Novalis exclaimed, commenting that her fair complexion and slender frame 'no doubt foreshadowed her early demise' – suddenly casting the energetic and opinionated teenager as fragile and delicate. Her death should be a warning for Caroline. Let us be happy for Auguste, Novalis wrote to Friedrich Schlegel, for she had escaped a 'dark fate' and entered a better world.

Others were kinder. Fichte sent condolences from Berlin, and for a heartbroken Ludwig Tieck all the disagreements of previous months were forgotten. Auguste's death put everything into perspective. How was Caroline? And August Wilhelm? 'If only I could do something to comfort you!' Tieck wrote to August Wilhelm. Death recalibrated the past, and they had wasted their precious time. As a friend, Tieck felt, he hadn't been good enough. 'Time is too fleeting,' he insisted, 'we have to make it last longer.'

Their circle of friends and acquaintances was shocked. 'That magnificent girl – I can't believe she's dead,' wrote one friend. Surely the lively and spirited Auguste couldn't be gone – 'so much life, such blossoming – and now dead'. Others worried about Caroline's well-being. 'Oh God, my dear Madame Schlegel, there is nothing I can say to you,' wrote the wife of a painter who had stayed with them the previous summer. To console them, she sent a pencil drawing of Auguste – a portrait of the 'heavenly girl'. It was the only likeness Caroline had of her daughter. But it wasn't enough and August Wilhelm made plans to commission a monument for the graveyard in Bocklet.

As Caroline tumbled into darkness, August Wilhelm feared that she might never resurface. How could she recover? Watching this 'total collapse of her strength', all August Wilhelm could do was be with her. He asked his brother to dispatch clothes and books from Jena because he had decided to stay with Caroline as long as was needed. Nothing else counted. Caroline cried and cried but August Wilhelm knew 'there is no way she could ever cry this pain out'. She was with her child in heaven, Caroline later said, and her own body was just an empty shell that remained in this world.

Schelling, who had stayed in Bamberg with Caroline and August Wilhelm, began to talk of suicide. Consumed by an increasing sense of guilt, he became unable to see Caroline's pain. Withdrawing, he left her in the care of her husband.

In Jena, Dorothea was sounding more and more deranged, telling anyone who would listen that Auguste had not died of dysentery at all. Over the years the poor girl had suffered so much emotional upheaval that it wasn't surprising she had died. It had been a mistake to treat Auguste like an adult, Dorothea said, and it was no wonder that 'of course, given her peculiar early maturity, she had to die young as well'. But there was more. Dorothea also blamed Schelling for Auguste's death. Friends from Jena who had been in Bocklet at the time had told her that Schelling had overruled the local doctor's medical advice and prescribed the wrong remedies. Feeding Schelling's sense of guilt, Dorothea accused him and Caroline of not calling on an experienced doctor from Bamberg until Auguste was half dead – 'until she was cold from the waist down'. Caroline was also relent-lessly attacked. 'And now this ostentatious mourning!' Dorothea continued. Without having seen or spoken to her, she declared Caroline too healthy and too composed to be truly mourning her child.

~

Meanwhile, Friedrich Schlegel took advantage of Schelling's prolonged absence from Jena and announced a series of lectures on transcendental philosophy for the upcoming winter semester. He desperately needed the money. When August Wilhelm advised him not to, Friedrich was confused. Why not, he asked his brother in early August 1800, 'have you heard that Schelling is coming back or something?' He urgently needed to know, Friedrich wrote. Even the self-confident Friedrich Schlegel had to admit that he would never be able to lure students away from the university's most popular lecturer if he was also in Jena. Why was nobody telling him about their plans? Was anybody coming back? What about Caroline? And August Wilhelm? Friedrich had no idea who was returning and who wasn't. None the wiser a month later, he continued to urge his brother to send 'any news of Schelling's return'.

To distract himself, Friedrich began to flirt with Sophie Mereau, the novelist and poet who was still stuck in a loveless marriage and entangled in numerous love affairs. In the past they had met at parties and dinners, and Friedrich had always been attracted to her. He admired her beauty, poetic sensibility and visceral sexuality. He praised her writing but also asked her to 'think of me with or without clothes on', and signed off one passionate love letter, 'Your burning Friedrich'.

No matter what Dorothea had given up for him, no matter how much he had ostracised Caroline for her affair with Schelling, and no matter how much he advocated the equality of women in his writings, all Friedrich Schlegel now wanted was to hold the slender Sophie Mereau in his arms. 'Stay light-hearted, get lusty, and be lewd,' he demanded. Within a few weeks, Sophie had had enough of Friedrich's advances. She kept her distance. Dorothea suspected nothing. The affair, if it could even be called that, was over almost as quickly as it had begun. Later that year, though, Friedrich embarked on a short dalliance with Karoline Paulus, the wife of one of Jena's professors and a friend of Dorothea's. Thirty-six-year-old Dorothea retaliated with a brief affair with the twenty-three-year-old scientist Johann Wilhelm Ritter. Years later a friend said that Dorothea had 'offered him [Ritter] sex as a formal initiation into the clique'.*

~

* This was Clemens Brentano, who also gossiped that Ritter 'had slept with Madame Veit every day for two months'.

Having spent no time at all in Jena during the first six months of the year, Goethe made up for his absence in the second half of 1800. Finally, he could concentrate on his own work, and as always he embarked on numerous projects at once, translating a Voltaire play, studying botanical classification and insect anatomy, and dissecting an amputated human foot with the professor of anatomy. He also picked up his *Faust* manuscript again – 'I solved a little puzzle in Faust today,' he wrote to Schiller in August.

With everybody else away, Goethe turned to the younger Schlegel brother for assistance. He needed help with the verse metre for one of the *Faust* scenes. Mostly, though, they discussed philosophy. Poetry was once again demoted, Goethe admitted to Schiller, but 'I can't blame anyone but myself'. Whenever he felt like company, Goethe dispatched a short note to Friedrich Schlegel, asking to meet for a walk or dinner. Initially, Friedrich had been thrilled by the attention but, unlike his diligent brother, he soon became irritated by the regular summons. Flattering as Goethe's interest was, it was just too time-consuming. 'I've already got what I can from him,' Friedrich bragged, and in any case, he felt that Goethe would never quite understand his thinking.

Novalis also visited that autumn. Coughing blood, short of breath and suffering violent stomach cramps, he came to consult Dr Stark. In an attempt to get better, he had already radically changed his diet: he drank very little wine, ate hardly any meat and essentially lived off milk and vegetables. Friedrich Schlegel and Dorothea were shocked at how frail their friend looked. 'We thought he looked miserable,' they reported to August Wilhelm in September 1800.

~

In October 1800, a little more than three months after Auguste's death, Schelling, August Wilhelm and Caroline Schlegel left Bamberg. Schelling went to Jena while August Wilhelm took Caroline to her mother and her sister Luise, who still lived in Braunschweig. Within days of their arrival, Caroline once again lapsed into a nervous fever, becoming so weak that she rarely left her room. August Wilhelm delayed his planned departure to Jena. He couldn't leave her. For the next four months the couple lived together in Braunschweig with Caroline's sister and mother. Slowly, as Caroline emerged from her grief, August Wilhelm enticed her into working on another

Shakespeare translation. They fell into their old rhythm, but with more tenderness and kindness. 'I can live without love,' Caroline had said many years earlier, 'but taking friendship away from me takes away everything that makes me love life.'

Now back in Jena, Schelling reclaimed the students who had subscribed to Friedrich Schlegel's philosophy classes. It had been easy because Friedrich was a terrible teacher – his only incentive had been money, but he had quickly become bored. The students were 'unspeakably stupid', Friedrich told his brother two weeks after his first lecture, while they in turn found him incomprehensible.

Equipped with only a few notes scribbled on a single sheet of paper – just '+ = φ ∩ and other such scribbles', Dorothea explained to August Wilhelm – Friedrich Schlegel's approach to teaching was careless and arrogant. Unlike Fichte or Schelling, who spent weeks preparing their lectures, Friedrich believed in improvisation. Surely, a lectern wasn't that different from expounding his theories to his friends from an armchair at home? Unsurprisingly, the students understood little and returned to Schelling's auditorium. Friedrich Schlegel was 'dead and now buried', Schelling declared.

For all his bravado, though, Schelling was lonely and miserable – riven by guilt about Auguste's death and desperately missing Caroline. But, instead of consoling Caroline or offering a word of comfort, he curled deeper into himself, nursing his grief and still tormented by thoughts of suicide.

～

In Braunschweig, Caroline was slowly returning to the world of the living. Auguste's death had been the darkest moment of her life, and nothing would ever replace the halo of light and happiness that her daughter had carried; but that didn't mean there was no hope. Caroline had always been able to find joy in the smallest things. When her three other children had died; when she had discovered her pregnancy during her imprisonment in Königstein; when she had been treated like an outcast afterwards; when Friedrich Schlegel and Dorothea had turned against her – Caroline had always found something to make her heart sing. A book, a flower, a smile, or the rain drumming against the window while she sat at her table writing. All her life those small moments had provided the strength to turn pain into light. They would do so again.

She had a core of steel which could not be destroyed by trauma or despair. It was as if she had internalised the Ich-philosophy. And though she didn't write theoretical treatises or essays, she lived and breathed the new philosophical ideas. Caroline was the embodiment of the empowered free self. Life had placed hurdles before her at every step but she never gave up. She had always taken control of her own destiny. 'In spite of God and man I want to be happy,' she had once said. She would not succumb to bitterness.

From Braunschweig, Caroline dispatched consoling letters to Schelling. 'My heart, my life – I love you with all my being. Have no doubt about that.' How she wished that she could blow away the 'black fog' that enveloped him. Yes, all seemed dark now, she told him, but one day they would see the blue sky again and feel the golden sun on their faces. If he truly loved her, he would have to stop talking about death in his letters. At Christmas, she sent him a coat – 'I gave it strict orders to hold you tight and keep you warm' – and he sent her a ring. It was 'my first, my only true wedding ring', she told him.

Deeply worried, Caroline lifted herself out of her long silence and wrote to Goethe in late November 1800, asking him to look after her lover. Schelling had plunged into 'a state of mind that is likely to break him', she wrote, and only Goethe would be able to help him. The older poet and the young philosopher had become close over the past two years, with Schelling trusting Goethe almost like a father. She herself was too weary and ill, Caroline explained, but Goethe was like a ray of sunshine that could disperse the darkness that entrapped Schelling. Caroline urged Goethe to look beyond the brash behaviour and iron armour.

And so, when Goethe left Jena after a two-week visit at the end of December, he invited Schelling to join him. When Schelling accepted and stayed for more than a week, he was even persuaded to attend an elegant masked ball at the Weimar court on New Year's Eve. In his role as the ball's impresario, Goethe had excelled himself. The rooms where the guests danced and drank were illuminated with hundreds of candles. As the music played and the guests chatted, only Schelling remained quiet. After the midnight bell rang, Goethe ushered his young friend and Schiller into a small parlour, away from the party. The table was laden with bottles, and with a never-ending flow of champagne. Goethe became jovial while Schiller grew increasingly serious, delivering a long speech on aesthetics. Once in a while,

Goethe tried to interrupt his earnest friend, joking and teasing him, but Schiller refused to be distracted and continued his dry lecture. Schelling said nothing.

In Braunschweig, the New Year celebrations were subdued. Caroline and August Wilhelm Schlegel stayed in. Not feeling well, August Wilhelm slept the whole evening on the sofa in Caroline's room while she was downstairs in the parlour. When the clock struck midnight, she went upstairs to wake August Wilhelm only to find him on his way down to her. 'So we encountered each other on the stairs like the two centuries,'* she wrote to Schelling. Her soul, though, was with her lover, and his ring was on her finger.

~

Just a few days after the lavish celebrations in Weimar, Goethe suddenly fell so ill that everybody feared for his life. With high fevers, violent coughing fits and a painful outbreak of large blisters in his mouth and throat, he could hardly breathe and felt he was suffocating. His left eye became so infected that it bulged from its socket, dripping pus onto his cheek. When his glands, head and neck swelled up too, a red rash spread over his face and he became so delirious that he didn't recognise anyone. Dr Stark rushed from Jena to Weimar and prescribed a course of bloodletting and footbaths. Christiane fussed over him, his son August was hushed, and Schiller came every day to sit at his friend's bedside.

During the nights Goethe fell into vivid, feverish dreams. Amazingly, the main subject of these nightly ravings was Schelling's *Naturphilosophie*, a surprised Schiller informed the young philosopher. Goethe seemed to have internalised Schelling's ideas so deeply that they had come to occupy his unconscious mind. And by doing so, he later joked, he almost lost himself. As he slowly recovered, Goethe repeatedly mentioned his 're-entry into life'. The greatest relief, he wrote to a friend afterwards, was 'that the moment I returned to consciousness I was back in my own self'. What did he mean? That he was once again in control of his own thoughts? Or that he had left the dizzying dangers of an unconstrained self?

---

* There was a heated debate at the time as to whether the new century had begun on 1 January 1800 or 1 January 1801. Caroline's comment illustrates that she believed the latter.

Friedrich Schlegel in *c.*1790.

Dorothea Mendelssohn–
Veit–Schlegel in 1798.

The Jena Set spent the summer of 1798 in Dresden. This is an engraving of Canaletto's view of the Neumarkt in the eighteenth century – to the left is the picture gallery (Gemäldegalerie) where the friends spent many hours discussing art, and the magnificent domed Frauenkirche is at the centre.

Berlin's famous boulevard Unter den Linden where Friedrich Schlegel, Dorothea Veit and Johann Gottlieb Fichte liked to promenade in 1799.

Friedrich Wilhelm Joseph Schelling in 1801.

Georg Friedrich Wilhelm Hegel in his late fifties.

Goethe's house in Weimar.

A contemporary engraving of the rugged landscape and mountains along the last part of the road from Weimar to Jena.

A sketch of Goethe and Schiller in 1804 – the playwright towering over the older poet.

Schiller's Garden House outside Jena's old walls. The windows of Schiller's study in the attic rooms are just visible behind the tree to the left.

Contemporary view of Jena from the north.

To the south of the town, just beyond the medieval walls, was the Paradise – a popular park where Jena's inhabitants enjoyed walking and boating.

This wintry scene from the 1790s depicts people skating on Ratsteich, one of the town's ponds, just outside the old walls. The building behind the wall on the left is the university library.

The Battle of Jena, 14 October 1806, with Napoleon and his officers in the foreground, looking across the battlefield.

Several of the town's houses burned during the Battle of Jena.

Note the injured man being carried on a stretcher and the French soldier banging on a door with his rifle.

The delirium triggered something that made him think again about *Faust*, the play he had been writing on and off for three decades. He had written some of it in the early 1770s and then continued in the late 1780s. In 1790 he had published a few scenes as *Faust. A Fragment*, but had only revisited the material shortly after Alexander von Humboldt's long stay in Jena in 1797. Since then, encouraged by Schiller, Goethe had occasionally worked on the play, but only for a few days at a time.

When Goethe recovered, at the beginning of February 1801, he immediately took out the *Faust* manuscript. For the next four weeks he worked on it almost every day. He began to compose the scenes he called the 'great gap', bridging the beginning and the later sections he had already finished. These missing scenes had stalled his progress for the past two years. One was the all-important pact between Faust and Mephistopheles. A central part of the play, the scene is peppered with allusions to Schelling's *Naturphilosophie* and Idealism.

Here is Goethe's Faust, for example, cursing his inability to grasp the thing-in-itself, the real world, because his mind is blinded and confused by things-as-they-appear-to-us:

> *Cursed be illusion, fraud and dream,*
> *That flatter our guileless sense . . .*

or, a few lines on, a chorus of spirits accusing Faust of having destroyed the world and then demanding that he rebuild it inside his mind:

> *More splendidly, let it come to birth*
> *Again, within you!*

In one of the scenes which Goethe wrote after his illness, Faust tries to make sense of everything. How did the world begin? he asks. 'In the beginning was the *Word*,' Faust suggests, but then discards the idea. 'In the beginning was the *Thought*,' he continues, but again he rejects it. He then wonders if 'In the beginning was the *Power*' would work. Again he dismisses it, but finally a spirit leads him to an answer straight out of Fichte's Ich-philosophy and Schelling's *Naturphilosophie*: 'In the beginning was the *Act*' – the first act that creates the universe or the original act of the Ich as it posits itself.

Schelling would later call *Faust* the 'deepest, purest quintessence of our age'. It was a play into which Goethe wove many of the themes that occupied him and the Jena Set, including the fusion of art and science, the pitfalls of rationalism, the unity of man and nature, and, of course, the self and subjectivity. At its heart is the relationship between humankind and nature – with Faust desperately trying to understand nature as an interconnected whole, declaring in the first scene:

> *How it all lives and moves and weaves*
> *Into a whole! Each part gives and receives.*

~

As Goethe raved about Schelling's *Naturphilosophie* in his feverish dreams, the young philosopher was dealing with his own demons. He felt torn. In one letter, he showered Caroline with passionate declarations, while the next insinuated he might kill himself. Sometimes he accused her of not loving him, only then to threaten that he might leave her. Schelling's mood swings were so extreme that Caroline was at a loss. Despite her own pain, she tried to assure him of her love and commitment. When she reminded him of her own grief, Schelling insisted that they didn't deserve each other after what had happened to Auguste.

Until now, Schelling had been accustomed to success. He had been a bright student who often outdid his peers. He had published his first book at the age of twenty, while still a student at the Tübinger Stift, and had been made professor at one of the finest universities in the German territories only three years later. He was part of a group of men and women who believed that they had incited a revolution of the mind. He was admired by Goethe, the greatest German poet, and inspired a new generation of students. He was loved by a brilliant and strong woman who had made him feel alive. Schelling was not used to trauma and darkness. So when grief swallowed him, he didn't know what to do. Instead of opening his heart to Caroline, he attacked her.

'Don't leave me, I love you,' Caroline implored. 'Oh, don't interrupt my gentle sorrow, my dear Schelling, by making me shed bitter tears over you as well.' If she had found the power to survive, why couldn't he? Soon, she promised, she would be in Jena. She read his letters again and again, despairing when he didn't write. Another time, Schelling alleged that she might one day be unfaithful. Had she not betrayed her own husband for him? 'Don't mock me,' she replied; 'being true to myself means being true to you.'

If he wanted to condemn her, she warned, it would be kinder to abandon her rather than torture her with accusations. Mostly, though, her letters were filled with tender love. They belonged together, she promised, and she would never leave 'my all and everything'. Caroline trusted Schelling, as he should trust her. 'Love me,' she urged, asking, 'but why are you so sad?' His melancholy tore her apart. If she were to translate his mood into geography, he was the dark stormy North, she wrote, 'so come and stay in my South, come, you most, most beloved man.'

~

In early January 1801, Schelling's old room-mate from Tübingen, Georg Wilhelm Friedrich Hegel, arrived in Jena. Known as Wilhelm to his family, thirty-year-old Hegel was almost five years older than Schelling and had the same thick Swabian dialect. Even as a student, Hegel had seemed older than his contemporaries. Friends at the Tübinger Stift had made fun of the studious Hegel by sketching him stooped and bald, calling him 'the old man'. His face was dominated by earnest and heavy-lidded blue eyes. While young Schelling had written one book after another, Hegel had pondered, read and taken his time. But Hegel was no introverted misanthrope; quite the opposite, he was sociable, jovial and enjoyed flirting. He loved wine and played cards whenever there was an opportunity, but he wasn't a wild dreamer. He was level-headed, grounded and rarely spoke about his feelings. On a trip through the Alps, for example, he had been unmoved by the majestic snow-capped peaks. Nature didn't speak to him. Instead, Hegel had been interested in the technical aspects of Swiss cheese making. He was thorough and not prone to rapturous declarations.

Like so many young scholars without a private income, Hegel had worked as a private tutor after he left the Tübinger Stift, in 1793. While Schelling was making history as Jena's youngest philosophy professor, Hegel had first been employed by a wealthy family in Switzerland and then moved on to another in Frankfurt. There had been little time for his own writing. In Switzerland, Hegel had felt isolated and detached from the latest philosophical ideas, and he had been glad to leave for Frankfurt in 1797 when his other old Tübingen room-mate, the poet Friedrich Hölderlin, found him a position as a tutor there. It had been Hölderlin who pulled Hegel into the world of Fichte's Ich-philosophy and the concept of free will.

Then, in January 1799, Hegel's father died, leaving his son just enough money to become an independent scholar for a few years. Never particularly assertive or decisive, Hegel had then waited for almost two years before handing in his notice in Frankfurt. Everything in his life had to be deliberated, little by little, and then gradually changed. But Hegel had long been certain about wanting to live in Jena, the centre of the new philosophy, near his famous friend Schelling. First, though, he wondered whether it might be sensible to go to another university town for a test run, so he had written to Schelling, 'before I dare to entrust myself to the literary whirlwind of Jena'.

Yet, by the time Hegel had made up his mind and arrived in Jena, the literary whirlwind had almost blown itself out. Fichte was in Berlin as was Ludwig Tieck, Novalis was still too ill to visit, August Wilhelm and Caroline Schlegel were in Braunschweig, Schiller had moved to Weimar and the only people left – Schelling and Friedrich Schlegel – were not talking.

Schelling, though, was delighted to have his old friend in town. He needed a philosophical sparring partner. Goethe had become a trusted friend and mentor, but when it came to philosophy Schelling had always been the teacher. Schelling also felt that he had come to a dead end. Grief-stricken, exhausted and drained, he felt Jena was waning and sensed an end coming soon. The old friends had fallen out, Caroline's sparkling thirst for life had been dimmed by the loss of Auguste, and, worse, she hadn't returned from Braunschweig.

The world was changing. Even the war with France was over. After Napoleon's daring crossing of the Alps into Italy in May 1800, more French victories had followed; and not just in Italy, but also in the southern German territories and Austria. The French campaigns had been so successful and decisive that in early February 1801 – just a month after Hegel's arrival in Jena – Napoleon would force the Holy Roman Empire to sign the Treaty of Lunéville. The German territories west of the Rhine were ceded to France, as were parts of the Netherlands and large areas of northern and central Italy. Only the British continued to fight the French.

~

As the French Republic and the Holy Roman Empire signed their peace treaty, August Wilhelm Schlegel and Caroline agreed the new terms of their relationship. After seven months of caring for Caroline, August Wilhelm felt he had fulfilled his duty. He couldn't look after Caroline forever. It was obvious how much she loved Schelling and it was time to take care of himself. August Wilhelm didn't want to return to the wreckage of their old life in Jena. In the five years of their marriage, Caroline had been his most trusted friend, but she was no longer his lover. So the couple agreed that August Wilhelm would leave Braunschweig at the end of February 1801, to travel to Berlin.

There, he rushed back into the arms of his old mistress, the famous actress Friederike Unzelmann. Beautiful and unhappily married, she had brightened his time in Berlin in 1798, before the friends' summer vacation in Dresden. It was time to enjoy life again. But even then, August Wilhelm and Caroline continued to correspond, regularly exchanging letters. How was the accommodation in Berlin? Caroline asked. Was he well? Did he sleep soundly? And how was 'your little Unzeline'? How was his work going? Did he need help?

As she came back to life, Caroline's letters began to fill again with sage advice, news and gossip. His more restrained responses were packed with literary news and comments about his work. August Wilhelm shouldn't write reviews any more but concentrate on his poetry instead, Caroline insisted, because 'when the world goes up in flames like a scrap of paper, works of art will be the last living sparks'. And he should ignore annoying critics. She missed her husband. 'Please do write often,' she urged. By way of distraction, she translated into German parts of the Italian writer Boccaccio's fourteenth-century book *The Decameron*, but the work wasn't the same without him. She had always enjoyed collaborating with August Wilhelm.

Then tragedy hit again. In Braunschweig at the beginning of March, shortly after August Wilhelm's departure, Caroline's sister Luise lost her baby son to a short and sudden illness. The baby had been a lively, happy boy. One week he was wriggling so furiously in Caroline's arms that she could barely hold him, the next he was dead. She cradled the little body as he turned cold. Her heart shattered when his eyes closed for the last time. In the face of Luise's grief, Caroline found herself spiralling back into darkness. The baby had followed Auguste, she wrote to August Wilhelm in a long emotional letter, 'and in the middle of the night I pressed a kiss to his lips for him to take to her'. Auguste was everywhere. It was time to leave Braunschweig and return to Jena.

~

At the end of March 1801, as Caroline prepared for her departure, Friedrich Schlegel galloped the thirty miles from Jena to Weißenfels. It was a race against time. Novalis had been ill for nine months, coughing blood, suffering excruciating abdominal pain and finding it difficult to breath. Novalis had tuberculosis and his doctors had given him a few days at most. But he was at peace, and with the little energy that remained he had dictated a letter to Friedrich Schlegel, asking him to visit one last time.

In September 1800, when Novalis had last seen Dr Stark in Jena, his treatments had had no effect. A month later, Novalis's parents had taken him to the best doctors in Dresden. Two of his brothers joined them, along with Julie von Charpentier, his fiancée. Still there in November, they had received the awful news that their youngest son and brother, thirteen-year-old Bernhard, had drowned in the Saale at Weißenfels. Shocked, Novalis experienced such a violent haemorrhage that he never really recovered. In Dresden, during the cold winter days of December and January, the doctor had prescribed daily four-hour excursions in an open carriage to clear Novalis's chest and breathing, but nothing helped. After weeks of being purged and hypnotised, swallowing vast amounts of quinine and drinking nothing but donkey milk, Novalis felt worse than ever. Emaciated and frail, he continued to cough blood.

Charlotte Ernst, Friedrich and August Wilhelm Schlegel's older sister, still lived in Dresden and saw Novalis almost daily. She updated her brothers regularly. Novalis was a shadow of his former self, almost unrecognisable, she reported in January 1801, and his condition was so desperate that his fiancée, Julie, was crumbling, perpetually fighting back tears. Where his words had once poured out so quickly that it was difficult to follow his thoughts, he now hardly spoke. He lay on the sofa, often falling asleep as others talked. He looked 'like a dead person', Charlotte wrote. 'It pains me that I mustn't speak,' Novalis had written to Ludwig Tieck in early January, 'when speaking is practically indispensable to my thinking.'

In mid-January, when the doctors agreed that nothing more could be done, Novalis's father had brought his son home to Weißenfels. There he began to feel a little better. He became hopeful again, telling his brother Karl that once he had recovered, 'you'll hear what real poetry is — I have magnificent poems and songs in my head.' But then, on 19 March 1801, the fourth anniversary of Sophie von Kühn's death, Novalis rapidly deteriorated. The news flew across the country. Friedrich Schlegel updated his brother in Berlin, who then informed Caroline in Braunschweig. Ludwig Tieck couldn't bear the thought of losing Novalis. 'The good people die,' he wrote from Berlin to Friedrich Schlegel in Jena, 'and the villains live, to spite God and the Devil.'

When Caroline Schlegel heard about Novalis's illness, she envied him for soon being reunited in heaven with his first fiancée, Sophie von Kühn. She too would have preferred to follow Auguste. But Caroline still couldn't forgive Novalis for blaming her for Auguste's death, writing: 'I won't be sorry when he's gone.'

When Friedrich Schlegel arrived at Weißenfels, on 23 March 1801, he was shocked. Though warned by his sister, Friedrich hadn't been able to imagine Novalis drained of all energy and life. His feet were swollen, as was his once handsome face. He looked disfigured, Friedrich wrote to August Wilhelm in Berlin. For two long days, Friedrich sat at Novalis's bedside. When Novalis woke, they talked with Friedrich telling him about his latest work and ideas.

On 25 March, after a restful night, Novalis read a little and even had some breakfast. But at eight in the morning the physician examined him and warned everybody that it might be his last day. Shortly afterwards, Novalis asked his brother to play the piano, and as the music filled the air, Novalis closed his eyes. Sometimes he skipped a breath or two, sometimes he woke and spoke incoherently. Friedrich Schlegel listened to the rasping of his best friend's breath. Just after noon, Novalis quietly stopped breathing. He was twenty-eight years old.

Novalis even died well. 'Really it's almost impossible to believe what a gentle, beautiful death it was,' Friedrich Schlegel wrote to his brother two days later. He was too upset to write more but glad he had seen his best friend one more time. As the devastating news rippled through the group, it became clear how much had changed. Novalis's death felt like an amputation, Ludwig Tieck wrote to

Friedrich Schlegel. 'Our life is shared, as all lives must be,' Tieck ended his letter, 'but now the unity has been split apart in the cruellest way possible.' The void that Novalis left, Friedrich Schlegel agreed, could probably never be filled. Novalis was nothing less than 'divine'. There had always been something almost mythical and other-worldly about him. Tieck now confessed he had had a premonition that Novalis would die young. 'I had seen him as a dead man,' he wrote. Shortly after Sophie's death, Novalis himself had said, almost prophetically, 'in the full flower of youth I will have to leave everything.'

Yet, his work survived. There was *Pollen*, his fragment collection, along with his magnificent immortalisation of Sophie in *Hymns to the Night*. Thereafter, Novalis had written novels. 'Philosophy is now just resting peacefully on my bookshelves,' he had said. He had worked on *Heinrich of Ofterdingen*, a novel set in the Middle Ages in which the poet protagonist searches for an elusive 'Blue Flower' – a symbol of longing for eternal love, self-discovery and the lost unity with nature. Once again, Novalis had played with the tension between reality and fantasy by including dreams, fairy tales and songs. Like Friedrich Schlegel's *Lucinde*, his *Heinrich of Ofterdingen* also followed disjointed plot lines and was fragmentary by choice. 'Shouldn't a novel include all sorts of styles, bound together in a varying order, and animated by a common spirit?' Novalis had asked. When Friedrich Schlegel and Ludwig Tieck had read the draft of the first part of the novel the year before, they loved it. But that was all Novalis had written. Nonetheless, the novel had to be published, the friends agreed. The only question was how?

August Wilhelm Schlegel suggested that Ludwig Tieck should complete the book. After all, Tieck was both a novelist and had been a close friend. Hearing this, Friedrich Schlegel exploded. The thought was preposterous, he wrote to his brother and Tieck in April 1801, only three weeks after Novalis's death. The idea that anyone else should complete Novalis's exquisite work was 'sacrilegious, heinous, godless, unholy'. Had they lost all respect and reverence? How could anyone else finish such a glorious beginning? The heart and soul of the novel was 'far far removed from anything that Tieck says or can say', and no one was going to touch Novalis's 'divine fragment'. Yes, it had to be published, but no one was allowed to add a word.

'When philosophers start eating one another like starving rats' Spring 1801–Spring 1803: Separations

AFTER SIX MONTHS in Braunschweig, Caroline left on 21 April 1801. It took three days to travel the one hundred and seventy miles to Jena, and as her destination approached she grew anxious. With August Wilhelm Schlegel in Berlin, and Schelling's letters still morose and dark, she was unsure what to expect. Although Friedrich Schlegel and Dorothea Veit had moved out of the house in Leutragasse into their own apartment, they were still just around the corner, and Jena was small. Most of all Caroline feared returning to the rooms where everything would remind her of Auguste.

On 23 April 1801, as dusk settled over Jena, Caroline arrived home. It had been almost exactly a year since she and Auguste had left Jena to travel to Bamberg and then Bocklet. Exhausted by the long journey, Caroline stepped into her eerily quiet house. As she walked through the rooms she found a trail of squalor and neglect. Not only had Friedrich and Dorothea taken her piano to their new apartment, but bedsteads were missing and much of her precious porcelain and glass was broken. 'I will spare you all the details,' Caroline immediately wrote to August Wilhelm. But it wasn't just the missing items – fire tongs, tables, bed covers, linen and so much more – the house itself was devoid of laughter and conversation. Shocked and tired, Caroline didn't even tell Schelling that she had arrived until the next day.

In the next few weeks, Caroline and Friedrich Schlegel stumbled from one row to another. Friedrich emphasised the rift by using the formal 'Frau Schlegel' in the terse notes that shuttled between their houses. When Caroline demanded her property back, Friedrich reluctantly dropped some of the items off. Caroline sent long lists of complaints to August Wilhelm in Berlin: Friedrich and Dorothea had wrecked the house by hosting wild parties, the returned piano was stained and dirty, the bookshelves looked suspiciously empty, and they continued to gossip about her and Schelling. Dorothea had cracked her good porcelain using it to warm food on the stove, and Caroline was outraged to learn from her maid that Friedrich had used her private parlour as his bedroom, ruining her sofa by sleeping on it. It was awful, Caroline complained; 'this good old Jena really is a den of murderers after all.' She wished August Wilhelm was there. 'Don't stay away long,' she pleaded with him.

Caroline and Friedrich's fight placed August Wilhelm in an awkward position. At first he tried to be neutral because he hated conflict. 'I truly don't like to take sides,' he told Ludwig Tieck a few days after Caroline's arrival in Jena, but his brother's and Dorothea's behaviour was simply not acceptable. And so August Wilhelm sided with Caroline.

～

Schelling was relieved to have Caroline back in Jena, even if he couldn't live with her in Leutragasse. Though August Wilhelm was in Berlin and everyone knew about the affair, Caroline was still married. As long as that remained the case, Schelling could never truly be with her. They could meet for meals, go for walks and spend their days and evenings together, but Schelling could not move in. At least, though, Caroline was home.

And as if life wasn't difficult enough, Schelling also found himself embroiled in a bitter fight with his old friend Johann Gottlieb Fichte. The problems had begun the previous autumn when Friedrich Schlegel had told him that Fichte had criticised the *Naturphilosophie* behind his back. Hurt and furious, Schelling had dashed off an angry letter accusing Fichte of spreading falsehoods. This unleashed Fichte's infamous temper and a heated argument developed, played out in an increasingly angry exchange of letters.

Even the Schlegel brothers, until then close friends of Fichte's, had been drawn in. Feeling betrayed by Friedrich Schlegel's gossip, Fichte thought that the brothers had revealed themselves to be 'liars and blackhearted traitors'. Why did Schelling believe Friedrich Schlegel? Fichte asked. He also cautioned Ludwig Tieck about Friedrich. He had loved Friedrich once, Fichte said, but he ended his letter saying, 'as a friend it is my duty to warn against those who are not true friends.'

The fight had escalated when Fichte described Schelling as his collaborator, rather than as an independent philosopher, in a newspaper in early 1801. While Goethe was amused, the thin-skinned Schelling was not, and Caroline cheered her lover into the attack. Fichte had tried to 'make you and your *Naturphilosophie* a subfield of his own', she told Schelling. Yes, Fichte had an extraordinary conceptual mind and sharp deductive powers, Caroline admitted, but there was nothing poetic about his thinking. 'He has light, in its most dazzling brightness,' she told Schelling, 'but you have warmth, too.'

How dare Fichte treat Schelling like this, Caroline wrote to August Wilhelm in Berlin. His thinking might be revolutionary but his behaviour was unacceptable and his writing was impenetrable. Fichte's latest work, *A Report Clear as Daylight*,* had been intended to clarify the *Wissenschaftslehre* but was precisely the opposite of what its title promised. Even Goethe, normally so diplomatic, joked that he had bought it 'to let Fichte torture me for a few hours'.

Caroline was biased, of course. Both Schelling and Fichte's writings equally abounded with convoluted sentences and complex ideas. It didn't help that both were in a continuous philosophical dialogue with themselves, constantly revising their own theories as well as attacking each other's. Fichte insisted that the Ich created all knowledge of the external world. 'Are you actually of the opinion', an incredulous Schelling asked Fichte, 'that there is light only so that rational beings can see one another when they talk to each other?' Didn't this view amount to an 'annihilation of nature'? Fichte was incensed and accused Schelling of not understanding him.

Their philosophies were dynamic – almost like living creatures, hydras with so many heads it was often confusing to follow their thinking in all its intricacies over the years. It was a shame, Goethe thought, that the two men couldn't work together; their philosophical concepts were complicated enough, but it was almost impossible to follow their ever-changing arguments. Goethe had a point.

In the past, Schelling and Fichte had explored different avenues. Schelling had long talked about nature and the self as one organism,

---

* The full title was *A Report Clear as Daylight to the Public at Large Concerning the Actual Character of the Latest Philosophy: An Attempt to Force the Reader to Understand.*

but this had not answered the question of where the self-conscious self originated in the first place. What came before the Ich?

Schelling now drew inspiration from the seventeenth-century Dutch philosopher Spinoza, who had declared that there was *one* all-encompassing substance or principle in the universe. This substance was the origin of everything and the essence from which everything derived. It could not be produced by anything else. According to Spinoza, this substance was God but also nature, because for him God was nature and nature was God, the two were one and the same. Schelling applied the same principle to his philosophy and called this first original substance the 'Absolute'. According to Schelling, the Absolute contained all ideas, concepts, bodies, souls, individuals, objects and so on. It united the ideal and the real. It was the One or the unity, before it divided into the self-conscious self and external nature.

Schelling's Absolute was the '*Urbild*' – a term he used to expand on Goethe's concept of the *Urform* or the 'archetype' – which was 'uncreated and truly immortal'. The Absolute came before everything else, but it also contained everything already. This was the last step that severed Schelling's philosophy from that of Fichte, who had given the Ich the role of founding the external world. Fichte's philosophy was an 'Idealism of the Ich', Schelling explained, while his system was an 'Idealism of Nature'.

As the attacks and heated explanations went back and forth, there were some attempts at reconciliation, although Fichte made it very clear that he believed Schelling's philosophy only existed within the framework of his own. Like a condescending schoolmaster, he continued to treat Schelling as his pupil. Hegel came to Schelling's defence in a pamphlet, *The Difference between Fichte's and Schelling's Systems of Philosophy*, in which he adopted a partisan position, explaining in a matter-of-fact way the limitations of the *Wissenschaftslehre*. Like Schelling, Hegel disagreed with Fichte that the Ich created all knowledge of the world. There was something before the Ich that was neither subjective nor objective, and that was the Absolute, the unity of subject and object. The allegiances were settled – or so Schelling thought.

Focused on Fichte, Schelling had failed to notice the more subtle undercurrents that were eroding his friendship with Hegel. Since Hegel's arrival in Jena earlier that year, the two old friends had worked closely together. They had founded a new journal, the *Critical Journal of Philosophy*, and even shared an apartment for a while. As the bright sun in the philosophical firmament, Schelling was in charge. Much as Fichte saw Schelling, Schelling regarded the older Hegel as his disciple. It certainly looked that way, and Hegel's university seminars attracted few students. Hegel had started with eleven and later worked up to almost thirty, but would never get close to Schelling's numbers. No great orator, Hegel's lectures were sometimes painful to attend, because he faltered, hesitated, spoke slowly and was often interrupted by long and loud coughing fits. 'Every word, every syllable,' one student later said, 'emerged only reluctantly.' Few of Hegel's students returned or signed up for the next semester.

Schelling seemed oblivious to Hegel's philosophical development. For his part, Hegel was at first glad of his association with his famous friend, but soon began to dislike being regarded as 'Schelling's squire'. Almost unseen, Hegel was quietly working on his own ideas. Where Schelling and Fichte's ideas gushed out onto the page – often raw and unfinished – Hegel's thoughts formed unhurriedly. He shaped and carved until everything was perfect. For the next six years he kept silent, but when his *Phenomenology of Spirit* was published in 1807 it would be a reckoning.

The thermometer refused to rise during the early summer months after Caroline's return, and they were still lighting fires in June. Caroline's health remained fragile and she often suffered from head-aches and fevers. 'Mostly, I'm as stationary as a plant,' she wrote to August Wilhelm, 'and from the outside probably no one can see me breathe, live, love.'

Worried, Caroline's trusted childhood friend Luise Gotter sent her daughter Julie to Jena to keep her company for the next nine months. Seventeen-year-old Julie slept in Dorothea's old rooms downstairs, and every morning she went up to Caroline's bedroom to join her for breakfast. Julie helped with domestic chores, enter-tained Caroline and played the piano. She became a shadow daughter. Also at Leutragasse was Caroline's younger sister Luise, who had come from Braunschweig to stay after the loss of her baby son earlier that year. Schelling visited every day and joined them for meals. In the afternoons, the women wrapped themselves in warm shawls and walked to Schelling's new lodgings in one of the garden villas on Jena's outskirts, for a stroll along the Saale.

Caroline desperately missed her husband. She continued to address him as 'my darling' and 'my dear heart'. He could bring his lover Friederike Unzelmann to Jena, Caroline told him. She wouldn't mind. She needed August Wilhelm as an ally and friend. 'I am sick from all the sorrowful tears,' she told him, because Auguste was everywhere and 'wherever I go, I see traces of her and can't help hopelessly sobbing'. Where should she hang Auguste's portrait? When was he coming? Why was he still in Berlin? 'My best dear good handsome Wilhelm,' she cajoled. He was her rock. If he would only return, all would be well. Together they would construct a little hut 'under the rubble of the old splendour'.

Her long letters to August Wilhelm Schlegel were filled with gossip about the neighbours, news from friends and her frustration with Friedrich and Dorothea, as well as household matters ranging from a tea recipe to outstanding bills. She embroidered his shirts – 'with my eyes' last strength', she told him – but mostly, she wrote about literary matters. She filled pages and pages with detailed advice: 'I am absolutely certain about the superfluous stanza: you need to cut it', for example, or she urged him not to quarrel with Ludwig Tieck about his poems. When August Wilhelm was experiencing problems with the publisher of their Shakespeare translations, she cautioned him to remain calm and 'stand very very firm'.* She discussed poems, plays, and offered editorial comments on his work. And with every letter she asked him to come to Jena – work would also be much easier to discuss in person.

August Wilhelm Schlegel, though, was enjoying his freedom in Berlin. After his affair with the actress Friederike Unzelmann, he had fallen in love with Ludwig Tieck's unhappily married sister, the twenty-six-year-old novelist Sophie Bernhardi. Conveniently, August Wilhelm was living in the Bernhardis' house when they began their passionate affair – unbeknown to Sophie's husband and despite her

---

* Their publisher had reprinted the first volume of the Shakespeare translation without informing them or paying them a fee. Ultimately, August Wilhelm Schlegel filed a lawsuit, and as a result he found himself without a contract for the continuation of the Shakespeare project.

well-advanced pregnancy (she gave birth to a son during the first week of July 1801). 'I have never loved the way I do now,' Sophie Bernhardi told August Wilhelm, and he declared their love to be the 'first great event of my life'. For once August Wilhelm ignored Caroline's wishes. But he remained worried, and dispatched a note to Schelling – 'tell me your sense of Caroline's health' – trying to find out how Caroline really was. Schelling obliged, reassuring him that she was holding up. She was fragile, but all she needed was peace and quiet.

～

After six months in Berlin, August Wilhelm Schlegel tore himself from Sophie Bernhardi's arms and finally returned to Jena in mid-August 1801. He was shocked to see how unwell Caroline was and how poisonous the town's atmosphere had become. It was terrible, Caroline said, 'how everyone gossips about everything behind your back'. Friedrich Schlegel and Dorothea Veit kept their distance, and the neighbours were whispering. August Wilhelm quietly slipped back into the rhythm of the house, ensuring that Caroline was comfortable. In the mornings he worked and in the afternoons he went for long walks. After so many months in Braunschweig and then Berlin, it was a joy to climb along mountain streams outside Jena again. Mealtimes may have been quieter than they had been only two years before, but in the evenings August Wilhelm read to everybody, as he had so often done before.

As the weeks went by, though, the tension between Friedrich and August Wilhelm Schlegel grew. Maids carried letters between Leutragasse and Friedrich and Dorothea's new apartment, just across the market square. As the letters shuttled back and forth, the arguments became increasingly petty. Soon the brothers avoided all contact. Friedrich couldn't forgive his older brother for choosing to side with Caroline.

They all needed a break. At the end of September 1801 the whole Schlegel household, including Julie Gotter and Caroline's sister as well as Schelling, decamped to Weimar for eleven days. August Wilhelm wanted to watch his former lover Friederike Unzelmann perform at the Weimar theatre and Caroline had arranged to see her best friend Luise Gotter – Julie's mother – who came to Weimar from Gotha, some thirty miles to the west. Everyone had a glorious

time. They stayed at Der Erbprinz on the market square, one of
Weimar's only two decent inns. They saw Goethe almost every
evening, at the theatre and for meals, and watched the artist Friedrich
Tieck – Sophie Bernhardi and Ludwick Tieck's younger brother –
sketching Goethe. For a brief moment it felt like old times, but the
vacation was over as quickly as it had begun.

~

During those weeks in Jena August Wilhelm desperately missed
Sophie Bernhardi, who was in Berlin with her husband and new-born
baby. It was 'all just too lonely and miserable', he told her, promising
to return soon. August Wilhelm, who according to Caroline had
never been capable of wild passions, had allowed himself to fall into
a turbulent affair. His feelings tumbled onto the pages of his letters
to Sophie – 'I will not rest until I can see that my love will make
you happy,' he wrote, 'you need to know that I want to live solely
for you'; 'I lie at your feet'. This was still not enough for Sophie
Bernhardi. 'My burning desire is eating me alive,' she told him, but
soon she was accusing August Wilhelm of cooling towards her. 'I'm
yours,' he replied, 'entirely yours, for ever.'

August Wilhelm also insisted that Caroline made no claims on
him. She was and would always be interested in his life. They had
a 'friendly, tender relationship', but that was all. In fact, Caroline
had always been his most trusted friend and he wished he could tell
her about his feelings for Sophie. 'It's painful that I can't make her
my confidante,' he admitted. In the past he had loved Caroline as
he now loved Sophie, he clumsily explained, but his feelings had
never been reciprocated by his wife. No matter how inept, August
Wilhelm's reassurances worked. 'Your kisses give me such blissful
happiness,' Sophie wrote on 14 October 1801, 'just come, oh, come
to me.' Three weeks later, he was on his way to Berlin. He had spent
less than three months in Jena.

~

A month after August Wilhelm departed, Friedrich Schlegel also bid
his goodbyes and travelled to Berlin, leaving Dorothea behind. He
too had had enough. His lectures at the university had been poorly
attended and with Schelling back in town, he didn't stand a chance.
Dorothea was often ill, old friends had become enemies and he had

run out of money. All the fun had gone. At least in Berlin he would be distracted. In Jena, Dorothea waited patiently for her lover to make a decision as to where they should live. 'It all comes down to Friedrich,' she wrote to Ludwig Tieck, '*I* am perfectly ready to move, and I can't wait to get away from here.' The more Friedrich Schlegel kept his distance, the more obsequious Dorothea became. The woman who had dared to divorce, who had truly lived Fichte's empowered Ich, seemed to have become completely subservient. 'How I worship this Friedrich,' she wrote to a friend.

It was miserable in Jena. Lonely and ill, Dorothea found that no one talked to her – no one, that is, except for the never-ending stream of tradesmen who knocked on the door to claim payment for outstanding bills. It was all too overwhelming, and at some point she even asked her eight-year-old son Philipp to notify Friedrich Schlegel that a lawyer had turned up at the apartment to demand money for unpaid furniture and other items. Sometimes these debtors called on Caroline in Leutragasse to collect the outstanding sums – innkeepers, tailors, wine merchants and cobblers. 'Everyone knows how lazy or unable to work he is, and what a glutton,' Caroline told August Wilhelm. In one tavern alone, Friedrich had run up a debt of 55 thalers and the wine merchant was asking for 70 thalers (at a time when a Jena student needed just 200 thalers a year to live and study comfortably). 'He must have drunk an incredible amount,' Caroline said, unsurprised that he was getting so fat.

In Berlin, Friedrich Schlegel wrote desperate letters to his publisher begging for advance payments for four dramas. He received the money eventually, but never delivered the plays, seemingly so preoccupied with his problems that even his loyal friend Schleiermacher became exasperated. Friedrich Schlegel's only real interest was Friedrich himself. Though he never cared much about his literary adversaries, he wanted to be loved, admired and idolised by his friends. 'It does me good', he told Schleiermacher, when they 'compete over how much they love me'. Though struggling to make a living himself, Schleiermacher footed most of Friedrich's expenses in Berlin. Schleiermacher had hoped to resume their old living and working arrangements, but Friedrich had other ideas and flitted around the salons. Friedrich was 'rather spoiled and rich in little needs, to his great misfortune', Schleiermacher complained to his sister.

Finally, after almost two months in Berlin, Friedrich Schlegel made up his mind and notified Dorothea that they were moving to Dresden. To save money, Friedrich had decided to stay with his sister Charlotte Ernst, but Dorothea would have to rent a room next door. Once again Charlotte bailed out her brother, but she remained adamant that the unmarried lovers could not live together in her house. At the end of January 1802, Dorothea departed Jena.

Only Caroline and Schelling remained. One by one, the friends had left. Caroline hardly saw anyone. 'You can imagine how hermit-like we live here,' she wrote to August Wilhelm. She felt like a ship, 'still at anchor, in a dead calm, with the ship refusing to move forwards or backwards'.

~

During those winter months at the end of 1801 and the beginning of 1802, the fight between Schelling and Fichte rumbled on. Enraged, Fichte had written to one of the Jena professors threatening 'to expose every last flaw' in Schelling's thinking and declaring that the young philosopher had never understood the *Wissenschaftslehre*. Schelling was never meant to see this letter, but Jena was too small for secrets. On 25 January 1802, just as Dorothea Veit was leaving town, Schelling wrote one final letter to Fichte and after that the two men stopped corresponding.

In the same month, Schelling published an article in which he explained that his own system was a 'philosophy whole and entire' – not a part of, not a sub-category of, and certainly not an explan-ation of the *Wissenschaftslehre*. It was an alternative. And with this, their fight moved to the public arena of journals and pamphlets. Their old adversaries enjoyed the mauling – 'all we can do is let them go at each other's throats and flail away until they topple,' one wrote. Wasn't it fun, another said, 'when philosophers start eating one another like starving rats'. What a spectacle it was to watch pupils eating their teachers, protégés their mentors, and 'every crea-ture his own creator'.

At twenty-seven, though, Schelling was at the height of his fame. He had liberated himself from Fichte, his publications were read across Europe, he attracted international students, and his lectures were packed. 'Many foreigners come to hear me now – graduates, military men and other people of rank, Englishmen too,' he proudly told his father. There was even a wealthy Hungarian baron who paid handsomely for private tutorials, 'filling my pockets with money and cellar with Tokay wine'.

The auditorium was so full that the broad-shouldered Schelling often had problems getting through the crowd to his lectern. Every seat was taken and so many students stood in the aisles, in the doorway and in the corridors that there was no room. 'His lecture hall can't hold the audience any more,' Caroline told Julie Gotter, who had returned home after her nine months in Jena.

Schelling was giving a series of lectures on the 'Philosophy of Art', in which he united his ideas about the importance of art, previously presented in his *System of Transcendental Idealism*, with his concept of the Absolute as the underlying principle of the universe. 'Every artwork is the expression . . . of the Absolute itself,' Schelling told his students in 1802. Art was the intersection between the ideal and the real. The 'Philosophy of Art', Schelling said, was nothing less than the study of how art represents the universe. Music, for example, was according to Schelling the original rhythm of nature itself, while sculpture was the realised *Urform* of organic nature. Humans could only truly comprehend nature through the creative output of artists, not by reading scientific treatises or theories.

The students were spellbound by this 'poetry of the universe', as they called Schelling's philosophy. Some of the English students, however, were less euphoric about Schelling's professed dislike of English thinkers. How could one expect anything scholarly from a 'country that values the Mathematics only as it helps to make Spinning Jennies & Stocking-weaving machines'? Schelling asked his students. The English might be famous for their manufacturing, production methods and profitable efficiency, but where was the poetry in that? Even the term 'philosophy' had been sullied by this English fashion for utility – so overused and misapplied that there would undoubtedly soon be 'a Philosophy of Transport and a Philosophy of Cooking'.

~

Back in Berlin, August Wilhelm Schlegel was also giving lectures, focusing on the arts and literature. With no university in the Prussian capital, many scholars rented private rooms or lecture halls to give public talks. Though August Wilhelm had nowhere near the audience numbers of Schelling, his lectures were a success. Aimed at a general

audience, the doors were open to women too. Unlike most men of
his age, August Wilhelm had always admired intelligent women, and
he made a point of inviting women since they were not allowed to
attend university and were often excluded from public lectures. The
famous Jewish hostesses attended, bringing their salon friends. Soon,
Prussian princes, Polish counts, Austrian diplomats, civil servants,
merchants and more came to hear August Wilhelm.

He gave two seminars a week in which he presented the ideas
that had been developed by the Jena Set, ranging from an analysis of
the Romantic project to a survey of the arts from antiquity to the
present. Unlike Enlightenment thinkers, for whom 'progress' and
'future' had been the watchwords, August Wilhelm Schlegel investigated the past in order to make sense of the present. He sought
similarities in different eras, disciplines and art forms. In much the
same way that Alexander von Humboldt began to look at nature on
a global scale – by comparing plants from the Andes, say, with those
from the Alps and the Pyrenees – August Wilhelm Schlegel synthe-
sised culture across the disciplines of sculpture, literature and painting.

To that end August Wilhelm ranged from the ancient Greeks to
the Middle Ages, and from Indian culture to the history of Europe.
Just as Alexander von Humboldt went beyond the narrow bounds
of taxonomy, so August Wilhelm cast aside conventional and narrow
aesthetic classifications and described new connections: architecture,
he said, combined geometrical forms with art; dance brought together
poetry and music; sculpture united fluidity with solidity; poetry fused
philosophy, mythology and imagination. His lectures, August Wilhelm
proudly told Goethe in January 1802, 'made quite a splash'. He
seemed happy. He was in Berlin, he was working and he was with
his lover Sophie Bernhardi.

～

Gradually, during the early months of 1802, the tone of Caroline
and August Wilhelm's letters changed. What had been a charming
gossipy correspondence became peppered with complaints. In
mid-January Caroline sent a long letter to Berlin, vehemently
defending herself against August Wilhelm's accusation that she was
spending too much. His deficit, she calmly noted, was due to *his*
lack of income rather than an increase in *her* expenditures. She had
not cost him anything. Quite the opposite, she wrote; she had used

the capital from her small inheritance and had given him money in Bamberg and Braunschweig. There was humour in her defence, but she made it clear that he had treated her unfairly.

August Wilhelm hated discussing money. Five days later, Caroline received a sharp reply from her usually good-natured husband. Since he never wrote down what he spent or earned, he told her, he didn't know who owed whom or how much, but he would repay his debt to her. If she could once and for all calculate how much she needed, August Wilhelm continued, he would be able to work out what he had to earn. But, he emphasised, she would have to make adjustments.

Despite this shift in tone, Caroline began to prepare for a long-planned visit to Berlin. Her sister Luise made her a fur coat as well as a dozen bonnets and hats. Schelling gave her a pair of fur-lined shoes, which she intended to wear at the theatre. She compiled a list of books to take for August Wilhelm and she requested the names of inns outside Berlin from where he might collect her. Finally, on 19 March, Caroline left for Berlin.

In the previous weeks, August Wilhelm had several times insinuated that he would have preferred her not to come, but Caroline had ignored the hints. In any event, she would be staying with acquaintances while August Wilhelm lived about a mile away with Sophie Bernhardi and her cuckolded husband. The mood was dark. Sophie had just lost her eight-month-old baby but now found herself pregnant again with what August Wilhelm believed to be his child. Enveloped in grief and weakened by pregnancy, Sophie was depressed and ill. Seeing her, Caroline's old wounds re-opened. Whenever she heard that a child had died, she cried so much that her 'tears felt like tears of blood', she later said. When August Wilhelm had written with news of the death of Sophie's baby, just a few days before her arrival in Berlin, Caroline had been glad that she wasn't in town at the time. She would have felt like an 'angel of death'.

There was little joy during those long dark weeks in Berlin. Everything was laden with sadness. City life was tiring, and although Schelling had promised to join her, he was still not in Berlin at the end of April. When he did arrive, in May, for a two-week break, they all went to the theatre and saw friends and acquaintances; but then something happened that ended Caroline and August Wilhelm's deep friendship.

During Caroline's last few days in Berlin a quick exchange of notes precipitated this break. Caroline accused August Wilhelm of reneging on his promise to pay for her trip to Berlin. In a furious response, her husband admitted that he had agreed to cover the costs, but added that he no longer felt bound by his assurances. Wasn't it understandable, he asked her, 'that I feel released from my obligations by what's happened during your stay here'?

It's unclear precisely what happened, but there are many potential causes – August Wilhelm's refusal to return to Jena, his affair with the pregnant Sophie Bernhardi, Schelling's arrival and their financial disputes. Whatever the reason – singular or plural – Caroline returned to Jena towards the end of May 1802 with the intention of legalising their separation. 'In Berlin, where I disliked everything and Schlegel wanted to stay anyway,' Caroline later explained, 'I came to my decision.' The only option, the couple agreed, was divorce.

~

Caroline and Schelling left Berlin on 19 May 1802. Five days later they arrived in Jena and Caroline immediately moved out of her home in Leutragasse. With August Wilhelm settled in Berlin, the house was far too big and expensive for her. The new apartment she found was at the north-eastern corner of town, just outside the old walls, next to the Zum Schwarzen Bären. Smaller and cheaper than her old home, it could be noisy when guests and students stumbled drunkenly into the street, and sometimes the pungent smells of the tanner's shop on the ground floor wafted up to her windows. Nonetheless, Caroline liked it. She was relieved not to be in Berlin. 'Every day I thank my lucky stars that I'm back here,' she said.

From the windows at the back, she could see the hills that surrounded the town and across the fields of cereals and vegetables which furrowed in orderly rows up the lower slopes to the edge of the forest. There was even a small garden. At her request, the landlord papered the parlour blue and she brought her furniture from Leutragasse – sofas, chairs, tables and beds – and quickly made it her home. The windows at the front faced Jena and received the full midday sun. And since the building was set slightly higher than most in town, she could see out over the roofs under which they had all lived, argued and written not that long ago.

Caroline's new lodgings on the town's periphery seemed symbolic.

She saw Schelling every day but few others, venturing out for long walks by the Saale River but not to parties or dinners. She had always found solace in nature. Wrapped in her dark grey cashmere coat, she braved gusty winds. Since Auguste's death, the veil of sadness that had dropped over her never quite lifted, but here she was at least content.

It was quiet in Jena but also in the rest of Europe. In early February 1801 France and the Holy Roman Empire had signed a peace treaty, and a year later, in spring 1802, Great Britain, Spain and the Netherlands followed with the Treaty of Amiens. After its many victories, France had been in a strong position to negotiate, and the terms of the treaty had favoured them. They kept control of the Netherlands, parts of Italy and the territories along the west bank of the Rhine, while Britain agreed to leave Egypt and surrendered its claims to the Dutch colony at the Cape of Good Hope. In return, the Dutch ceded Sri Lanka to Britain and the Spanish accepted British rule in their former colony of Trinidad. And for the first time since the French Revolution, the British officially recognised the French Republic as a country.

Soldiers went home, cannons were dismantled and uniforms stored in trunks. For the first time in almost a decade there was peace in Europe. As travelling became less dangerous, those who could afford it made plans for long vacations and trips abroad. Italy, Switzerland, France and Spain were reachable again. The English, who had not been able to cross the Channel for almost a decade, flocked to the Continent and to Paris in particular. Everybody wanted to see the treasures Napoleon had pillaged while on his military campaigns – a vast collection of priceless art ranging from Roman statues and Renaissance portraits to Dutch landscape paintings and Egyptian artefacts. Painters arrived in Paris to fill their sketchbooks with copies of Italian masters and ancient sculpture. What had been spread out across Europe, and previously accessible only to those who could afford an expensive grand tour, was now assembled in one place and on show at the Louvre.

Scientists came too, hoping to discuss their latest discoveries and research. The Paris Natural History Museum had similarly been filled with collections that Napoleon's troops had looted from across Europe – plant specimens, stuffed animals and fossils. And at the menagerie of the Jardin des Plantes there were even two living elephants from

Holland. No other city was as steeped in the sciences as Paris. The reach of the Catholic Church had been curtailed by the French Revolution, and scientists in France now found themselves freed from orthodox beliefs. They could question anything and everything. Artists, writers, poets and scholars went to Paris to meet, work and have fun. One was Friedrich Schlegel.

As Caroline moved into her new apartment in Jena, Friedrich Schlegel and Dorothea Veit had packed up in Dresden. Once again Friedrich had changed his mind. Germany, he decided, was not the solution to his financial woes. He and Dorothea would try their luck in Paris. He would teach the French about Germany's new romantic literature and the Germans about France, and he would publish yet another magazine. He would call it *Europe* and intended to report on Paris – a city which exuded scholarship, art and intellectual discourse – and its treasures. The idea was to sell the journal everywhere, from Frankfurt, London and Copenhagen to St Petersburg and Stockholm.

Friedrich wanted to address the question of whether the many countries that made up Europe could be understood as one nation. Was there unity in diversity? European literature, for example, was multifaceted, he explained, but also an 'interconnected whole' in which nothing developed in isolation. Wasn't Europe a similar construct? Shouldn't the Continent's countries also be regarded as 'a whole'?

As so often, Friedrich Schlegel thought that running away would solve his problems. He didn't care what people said, he told the surprised Schleiermacher, not even 'if they think I'm crazy'. Friedrich needed a new venture. He and Ludwig Tieck had just finished editing the first volume of Novalis's collected works.* It was a project that felt like a capstone on their time in Jena and Friedrich was ready to move on.

It was a time for endings. Friedrich Schlegel and Dorothea Veit were leaving Germany. Novalis's work was posthumously published.

---

* The first volume was published in June and the second in December 1802. It included Novalis's *Hymns to the Night* and the fragment collection *Pollen* as well as his novel *Heinrich von Ofterdingen*, which Friedrich Schlegel and Ludwig Tieck had decided to leave unfinished after all. These two volumes would make Novalis famous in Europe but also in the United States. Editing the work had been difficult, Tieck admitted. 'It always feels so petty to make these little corrections when you're overwhelmed by the beauty of the whole,' he had told Friedrich Schlegel.

Schiller severed his last connection with Jena when he sold his beloved Garden House in June 1802, in order to use the money to buy a house in Weimar. Caroline's voluminous correspondence with August Wilhelm had trickled to a few short notes about bills and financial matters. At the end of June 1802 she posted the final accounts. 'If you have no general objections to my calculations, I would ask you to spare me any remarks about the details,' she wrote, adding that anything else would have to be settled in their divorce proceedings. It was time to file their divorce petition.

~

They should never have married, Caroline believed, 'Schlegel and I should only ever have been friends.' Only children would have made their alliance 'indissoluble'. With Auguste dead, Caroline had lost her family and now she sought tranquillity. Too much had happened. August Wilhelm had begun a new life in Berlin and, aged thirty-four, he was in the prime of his life. He could start again, perhaps with a new wife and children. For her part, she was ready to leave Jena and stay by Schelling's side. Schelling was so excited about the possibility that Caroline might at last be free that he finally dared to tell his parents about her. 'She has been my closest friend for many years,' he wrote, informing them that they would soon visit. Under no circumstances, Schelling said, could he come on his own because it would be too painful to leave her behind.

In September 1802, three months after she had left Berlin, Caroline wrote one last letter to her husband. Using the formal pronoun *Sie* for the first time, she informed August Wilhelm that she had asked Goethe for help because the divorce itself was proving a complicated process that involved obtaining the permission of Duke Carl August. Schelling would coordinate everything with Goethe. 'Please stay on good terms with him [Schelling],' Caroline's last sentence to her husband read, 'I am stepping aside entirely.'

Amazingly, the relationship between Schelling and August Wilhelm Schlegel had remained amicable over the past years. The two men had regularly written to each other about literary and philosophical matters as well as about Caroline's health and well-being. They had helped each other professionally, conveyed messages to Caroline and exchanged news. So, with August Wilhelm in Berlin, it seemed natural that Schelling would take over.

As a testament to their enduring friendship, August Wilhelm also stepped in to defend Schelling in yet another fight with the *Allgemeine Literatur-Zeitung*. In a scathing review of *In Praise of the Latest Philosophy* – a pamphlet that lauded Schelling's ideas – the *Allgemeine Literatur-Zeitung* had taken the extraordinary step of accusing Schelling of having caused Auguste's death by recommending the wrong medical treatment. The anonymous reviewer joked that one could only hope that no other idealists had the misfortune to 'take the people they had healed in ideal terms and kill them in reality'. Nothing but malice could have led the paper to make such a vicious attack now, exactly two years after Auguste's death. Schelling, Caroline and August Wilhelm were shocked.

Caroline was abruptly thrust back into her grief. Reading the review made her relive the pain. August Wilhelm was so enraged that he could think of little else. Honest and impartial to a fault, he insisted that Schelling had done nothing wrong. And so August Wilhelm took it upon himself, as he explained to the editors of the *Allgemeine Literatur-Zeitung*, to 'defend Professor Schelling's rights in this matter'. August Wilhelm also published an account of the last days of Auguste's life in which he accused the 'disgraceful knaves' at the *Allgemeine Literatur-Zeitung* of having sullied his stepdaughter's sacred memory. Auguste, he wrote, had been used as a 'pawn in a game of petty revenge and truly wretched overzealousness'. The *Allgemeine Literatur-Zeitung* then printed a half-hearted correction in which the anonymous reviewer explained that he was only referring to gossip and had never himself said that Schelling was responsible for Auguste's death.

During those months Schelling also travelled between Jena and Weimar to consult Goethe on the divorce proceedings. The negotiations were tortuous. The fact that the novelist Sophie Mereau had been divorced the previous year was, as Caroline pointed out, not helpful, because the duke would want to ensure that 'the exception wouldn't turn into a rule'. A consortium of councillors in Weimar would have to decide the formalities – and to make matters even more complicated, most of them disliked the Schlegels, including Johann Gottfried Herder, who was serving as president. Everybody talked about the divorce. Herder's wife, for example, was outraged that Schelling 'is living in Jena with Schlegel's wife as though she were his own'.

Neither Caroline nor August Wilhelm wanted to give their adversaries the pleasure of appearing in front of the court in person. They even discussed, but decided against, bribing some members of the consortium. It was a stressful few months. What if the consortium decided against them? What if it turned into even more of a public spectacle than it already was? Goethe advised and amended the draft petition before enlisting his court connections. In mid-October 1802 Schelling sent the signed divorce petition to Goethe, who delivered the papers to the appropriate officials in Weimar. Goethe also helped the couple avoid the dreaded appearance in front of the consortium. They had only to follow his instructions, he said, 'and I'll take care of the rest'.

Over the next few weeks and months Schelling regularly updated August Wilhelm Schlegel about the proceedings, writing more than two dozen letters to Goethe and August Wilhelm, passing on information, enquiring and clarifying. Finally, nine months later, on 17 May 1803, the divorce was granted. Goethe was in Jena when the news arrived. The ornate Weimar court script decreed that it was 'most mercifully resolved that both spouses were to be entirely divorced from their marriage'. Caroline and August Wilhelm were at last free.

Three days later, on 20 May, while frantically packing, Schelling wrote a final note to August Wilhelm. They were leaving soon, Schelling explained, but he wanted to let him know that Caroline had just spent a few days in Weimar, where she had advised the sculptor Friedrich Tieck on a bust she had commissioned of Auguste. The likeness was better than they had dared hope. That evening Schelling joined Goethe for dinner. They would never see each other again.

At three o'clock in the morning of 21 May, Caroline and Schelling stepped into a carriage and left Jena forever. 'I will look after Caroline in every way and try my best to preserve her health like a precious sacred treasure,' Schelling promised a mutual friend. She would soon turn forty and Schelling was twenty-eight. Five years after first setting eyes on each other, they could finally be together. Schelling couldn't believe his luck that this glorious woman – this 'divine creature' – loved him. They belonged together, and he felt that their lives were interwoven by a thousand roots.

For the first time since Auguste had died almost three years previously, Caroline was feeling better. 'I am almost happy,' she admitted, and even her health was improving. It didn't matter how many malicious lies and slanderous rumours would be spread about her. She had made her peace and she was with Schelling. Nothing else was important. A month later they married. It was Caroline's third marriage. She was now Caroline Schelling.

19

'The current exodus'
1804–1805: Jena Abandoned

S O MUCH HAD changed since Goethe and Schiller had first spoken after the meeting of Jena's Natural History Society on that hot July day in 1794. Goethe had watched everybody leave: first Fichte, in 1799, then the Schlegel brothers, and finally Schelling and Caroline, in 1803. They were not alone. The 'current exodus', as Goethe described it, continued with the departure of several other professors, many of them following Schelling, who had accepted a well-paid position at the University of Würzburg, in Bavaria.* As Goethe told Duke Carl August, even he hadn't been able to stop the 'emigrating professors'.

As news spread that 'Jena was no longer what it once was', the students began to vanish. Some sixty young men followed Schelling to Würzburg. It was a vicious circle. Professors were paid directly by their students, and as numbers dwindled so did their potential income. 'I'm afraid our academy in Jena is drawing to a close now,' Schiller wrote to Wilhelm von Humboldt from Weimar; 'the exodus of philosophy is complete, with Schelling's departure.' Everybody talked about the decline. 'Jena now seems to be on the brink of Ruin,' Henry Crabb Robinson, one of the English students, reported – why study here when all the great professors were leaving? As quickly as Jena had risen, it seemed to tumble. Its beating heart, fuelled by the enthusiasm of the visionary young thinkers, simply stopped. The 'Kingdom of Philosophy', as Caroline had called the small town, had ceased to exist.

---

* As part of the negotiations with France, the previously ecclesiastical Prince-Bishopric of Würzburg had been ceded to Bavaria in 1803, and in due course the Bavarian ruler wanted to restructure and secularise the former Catholic university in Würzburg. Hence the reason they were poaching professors from other universities by offering very generous salaries.

Hegel, though, remained. Never quick to make decisions, he simply watched the others pack and leave. Goethe saw him occasionally. 'He is an admirable, splendid person,' Goethe commented, but not a great conversationalist or lecturer. Goethe even wondered if someone might teach Hegel 'techniques in the art of public speaking'. The philosopher was a deep and thorough thinker who couldn't articulate his thoughts, Goethe told Schiller. Meanwhile, Hegel felt as if he had been left on a sinking ship. Except for an occasional dinner and his lectures, he stayed at home and worked on his philosophical ideas.

Even Schiller yearned for the old Jena. Though the previous five years had been marked by professional and financial success – his plays were staged to great acclaim all over Germany – he missed spending long evenings in his parlour discussing ideas, plays, poetry and philosophy. It seemed a lifetime ago, he wrote to Wilhelm von Humboldt, who was now Prussian Minister at the Vatican, in Rome, 'that we philosophised together in Jena and were electrified by our intellectual friction'.

Schiller now lived in an elegant house on Weimar's fashionable tree-lined promenade. Duke Carl August had also ennobled him, so he was now Friedrich *von* Schiller. He purported not to care about this elevation, but his aristocratic wife Charlotte did. 'Lolo is really in her element,' Schiller teased, 'peacocking around at court.' He was celebrated, his hugely popular plays received standing ovations, he was handsomely paid, and he didn't have to worry any more; but the intellectual thrill they had all felt during those early days in Jena had disappeared. 'My life is so monotonous and empty,' Schiller wrote as an excuse for the brevity of his letters. There was nothing exciting to report.

~

By 1804 the old friends had scattered across Germany and Europe – from Jena to Rome and Würzburg, from Berlin to Switzerland, from Paris to Cologne. Fichte was still in Berlin where he continued to work on his *Wissenschaftslehre*, revising, explaining and clarifying his original idea of the Ich and the non-Ich. He worked hard – too hard, Johanne Fichte thought – usually writing until mid-afternoon when he gave private lectures to wealthy students and aristocrats. With almost one hundred and fifty paying guests, his Sunday lectures were particularly popular. Princes, diplomats, dukes, scholars and professors were among the audience, Johanne proudly informed her cousin. But their circle of friends was small, and they lived a quiet life. Largely happy, Fichte's biggest complaint was that his disciples spread inaccurate accounts of his philosophical ideas. One day, he hoped, he would establish a true 'School for Philosophers', an academy that would train older and wiser men who were truly able to understand his work.

Meanwhile, Schelling and Caroline settled into their new life in Würzburg. Schelling enjoyed teaching but told Hegel that the intellectual spirit was 'still far behind what held sway in Jena'. Caroline relished being the wife of the most important professor at the university and the foremost philosopher in Germany. After years of living frugally in Jena, they now had a spacious and elegant apartment and Caroline went on a shopping spree. She bought rugs, hand-painted fire screens and ottomans, as well as beautiful dresses.

She also quickly fell out with the wives of Schelling's colleagues. Some were old Jena adversaries, and others didn't like Caroline's confidence. Having never played the role of a demure wife, Caroline didn't hide her eloquence, nor her knowledge. She refused to engage in any of the domestic tittle-tattle, and it didn't help that she described one academic's wife as a 'Swabian scullery maid'. Caroline soon wrote that 'our good friends from Jena are as backstabbing here as they were there'. But she was happy: married to the love of her life, intellectually stimulated and continuing to work and write reviews. They belonged together, Schelling said, because they were 'united by the most sacred bonds'.

Then, in early May 1804, exactly one year after their divorce, Caroline received a surprise visitor. August Wilhelm Schlegel, in town for one night, had arranged to see Schelling in a tavern, thinking that meeting Caroline might be too awkward. The new husband, though, had different ideas and like an excited puppy dragged August Wilhelm to his apartment. At eleven o'clock at night, the two men stormed into Caroline's parlour. Luckily, she was awake.

It was a tender encounter. Caroline looked healthier than she had during their last months together in Jena, August Wilhelm thought, and was dressed flatteringly, as always. They talked until one o'clock in the morning. Sitting under the portrait of their beloved Auguste, they felt the bond of their old friendship and were glad to see each other. Very early the next day, August Wilhelm came back for a final farewell. They embraced and said their goodbyes, not knowing if they would ever see each other again. Caroline 'was touched when I left her', August Wilhelm recalled. By eight o'clock he was on the road to Switzerland in the company of another formidable woman: Germaine de Staël-Holstein, otherwise known as Madame de Staël. Their destination was her family chateau at Coppet, on Lake Geneva.

~

August Wilhelm Schlegel had been glad to leave Berlin. Though his lectures had been a success, his personal life was a mess. When Sophie Bernhardi had given birth seventeen months earlier to a son, August Wilhelm had believed himself the father. He had scraped together what funds he had to help his mistress escape her unhappy marriage, only to discover that the baby was the child of a third man. Sophie had not only cheated on her husband but also on him. August Wilhelm was tired. He looked exhausted. He couldn't wait to see the Swiss Alps and to hike, swim and write.

He was travelling with the thirty-eight-year-old French writer Madame de Staël. Brilliant and phenomenally rich, Madame de Staël had inherited a fortune from her banker father, the late French king's finance minister. She had lived in Paris for most of her life, surrounded by the greatest thinkers. Famed across Europe, she was known as much for her wit and writing as she was for her unconventional love life and idiosyncratic wardrobe that often revealed more than it hid. Having married and separated, she had enjoyed numerous affairs and had borne four children – but only one had been fathered by her husband.* She was also demanding. As one long-term lover observed, everybody had to be at her disposal at every minute of the day 'or else there is an explosion like all thunderstorms and earthquakes put together'. Her temper and sharp mind later led the English poet Lord Byron to describe her as being as 'frightful as a precipice'.

A fervent supporter of the French Revolution, Madame de Staël had turned against Napoleon when he made himself First Consul

---

* Madame de Staël had a daughter in 1787 who died in infancy, two sons by her lover Louis de Narbonne born in 1790 and 1792, and a daughter in 1797 by her subsequent lover Benjamin Constant. In 1812, aged forty-five, she would have another son by Jean-Michel de Rocca.

for life. As punishment, Napoleon banished her from Paris. Exiled, she had set off to meet Germany's greatest thinkers and writers, to research a book about the new German philosophy and literature that had come out of Jena. If the French Revolution had led to Napoleon, she believed, then something had gone wrong. It was time to search for answers elsewhere. The French were too rational, she thought, and the English too empirical. But the Germans had come up with a new way of understanding the world. Madame de Staël wanted to know everything about their self-determined Ich.

At the end of 1803, she had travelled to the Duchy of Saxe-Weimar to learn more about this new philosophy. She paid Henry Crabb Robinson, one of Schelling's former English students, to instruct her, and pressed Schiller and Goethe for explanations. Madame de Staël talked and questioned relentlessly but was surprised to discover that neither Goethe nor Schiller read political newspapers. German poets didn't seem to talk about politics, she noted. Instead, people followed Schelling's philosophy and preferred 'the Ideal' to reality. Maybe, she mused, Germans escaped to this 'ideal' world because their real world was so unsophisticated and restricted: the climate was harsh, the food was terrible and they were still ruled by monarchs, princes and dukes instead of by elected governments. Germans were living in their minds and found there what 'their limited destiny denies them on earth', she would write in *Germany*, an international bestseller that brought the ideas of the Jena Set into the parlours of Europe and the United States.

Madame de Staël was like a firework that exploded over Weimar. Goethe and Schiller liked her but she exhausted them. When she finally left for Berlin, after eleven weeks, Schiller confessed that he felt 'as if I had survived a serious illness'. Goethe had given her a letter of introduction to August Wilhelm Schlegel because no one knew more about the Jena Set's ideas. Madame de Staël liked August Wilhelm immediately. He had more 'knowledge and wit in literary matters than anyone I know', she said. She also met Fichte. Although she couldn't speak German and Fichte's French was poor, Madame de Staël nonetheless demanded that he summarise his *Wissenschaftslehre* in fifteen minutes. After ten minutes, she interrupted him: 'Ah! That's enough, I understand, I understand you perfectly well, Monsieur Fichté.'

August Wilhelm Schlegel delighted her. He spoke English like an

Englishman and French like a Frenchman, she said. In Berlin, they saw each other almost every day, and she had attended his lectures. In a few hours of listening to him, she later said, 'we reap the fruit of the labour of a lifetime'. In turn, August Wilhelm was dazzled by her mind, personality and wealth – and she soon persuaded him to accompany her to Switzerland by offering him a job teaching her thirteen- and eleven-year-old sons. His commitments would not be onerous, she promised, but he would also have to instruct her in all German literary matters.

Her offer gave him financial independence, liberating him from the demands of publishers and magazine editors, and from his lecturing commitments. Once the children were grown, he could stay on and receive the same salary and a lifelong pension. August Wilhelm didn't hesitate. He couldn't wait to travel to Switzerland, he told her, and begin 'our great project'.

～

Meanwhile, in Paris, Friedrich Schlegel's latest money-making projects were not going to plan. His new journal *Europe* only had around three hundred subscribers and his lectures drew barely twenty people. Confident that the French would welcome him as the great critical mind of the young Romantics, he had quickly discovered that the Parisians had no interest in learning anything about German literature. This was not how he had imagined his life. 'Paris has one flaw,' Friedrich Schlegel soon said; 'there are rather too many Frenchmen here.'

Since meeting Caroline back in 1793, Friedrich had been a supporter of the French Revolution, but the France he encountered was very different from what he had thought it would be. As Napoleon seized more and more power, the old ideals seemed to disappear just as the painted words *liberté*, *égalité* and *fraternité* faded from the walls of Paris. Churches reopened and after a ten-year silence the bells of Notre-Dame were allowed to ring again. The sounds of workmen echoed through the streets of the capital as Napoleon razed timber-framed medieval houses to make space for a modern city with grand boulevards, canals and water reservoirs, public parks and fountains. The First Consul took charge of every aspect of life: newspapers were run by loyal editors, and he established both a national police force and a national bank, the Banque of France. Then, in late spring

1804, Napoleon announced his coronation as Emperor of France later that year. All powers would be held by him, and he would be able to pass them on to his heirs. Napoleon intended to found a dynasty.

Disillusioned, Friedrich Schlegel abandoned his idea of a united Europe with Paris at the centre. 'I've never been more stubbornly and idiotically German,' he confessed. That didn't mean that he wasn't working. He was. Friedrich being Friedrich, he had found a new subject. Making use of Persian and Indian manuscripts the French had plundered from libraries and private collections while on their warpath across Europe, Friedrich Schlegel now began to study Persian and Sanskrit. 'I feel unbelievably drawn to Oriental things,' he wrote to Ludwig Tieck, buzzing with new ideas about the importance of Sanskrit as 'the root of all language' and its influence on Greek, Latin and the Germanic languages. He was so obsessed with the subject that he published the first comprehensive study of Sanskrit in Germany in 1808, *On the Language and Wisdom of the Indians*, which also included translations of ancient texts. None of this put any money in his pocket, however, and to supplement their income Dorothea translated French texts and novels into German, as well as renting out rooms in their apartment, at the foot of Montmartre.

They felt isolated in Paris. It didn't help that France was yet again at war. After the short-lived Peace of Amiens of 1802, Britain had declared war on France in May 1803. Sidelined by French dominance in Europe, Britain was increasingly worried about Napoleon's colonial intentions. His ambitions seemed insatiable. He continued to interfere in Swiss politics and Italian affairs, and, in any event, few believed any of the parties involved would keep to the agreed terms of the treaty.

Friedrich Schlegel wanted to leave France. But where to go? Maybe the university in Würzburg could offer him a position? Why had no one asked him? Wasn't it strange, he asked, considering that people seemed to have been 'sent out along all the country lanes and hedgerows in search of professors and scholars to invite to Würzburg and Munich'? But despite enquiries, no job offer came. Dorothea couldn't understand why. Why didn't rulers and governments appreciate her wonderful Friedrich? Why didn't they seek his advice? If they did, 'the world would be so much better!'

When their German lodgers, who came from Cologne, suggested

that they might be able to find a teaching position for Friedrich in their home town, he decided to move once again. But Cologne was a staunchly Catholic city where he could never have succeeded without legalising his relationship with Dorothea. And so, with only the vaguest prospect of a position, Dorothea gave up her Jewish faith and was baptised. The lovers married in a Protestant church in April 1804.* They left Paris shortly afterwards and moved to Cologne.

~

They missed an old friend from Jena by just a couple of months. After almost five years in South America, Alexander von Humboldt arrived in Paris in early August 1804, his trunks filled with hundreds of sketches and tens of thousands of astronomical, geological and meteorological observations and calculations. The thirty-four-year-old scientist had returned with rocks, insects and stuffed animals as well as some sixty thousand plant specimens. No one had ever assembled more, he boasted.

Alexander von Humboldt and his travelling companion, the French botanist Aimé Bonpland, had covered thousands of miles. They had paddled along the Orinoco, deep into the rainforest, and crossed the Andes from Bogotá to Lima – some two and a half thousand miles along the longest mountain range on the planet. Accompanied by huge Andean condors gliding in the sky, they had traipsed up and down snow-capped mountains and valleys, battling through blizzards, rain and thunderstorms at high altitudes before descending into the heavy heat of tropical forests.

On the way they had climbed every reachable volcano and pushed to heights where they could hardly breathe. The crown of Humboldt's obsession was Chimborazo, an inactive volcano some one hundred miles south of Quito, in today's Ecuador. At almost twenty-one thousand feet, it was then believed to be the highest mountain in the world. Despite thick snow and fog, they almost reached the summit. Further south, on their way to Lima, Alexander von

---

* According to the terms of Dorothea's divorce settlement, her ex-husband had a right to custody of their son Philipp when he turned ten or if she remarried. But as Simon Veit had not claimed Philipp on his tenth birthday, the previous year, it was unlikely that he would do so now. A few months after the wedding, Dorothea thanked Simon Veit for his generosity. 'I will be grateful for your goodness as long as I live,' she wrote to him on 5 January 1805.

Humboldt had sketched and admired Inca ruins and met many of the indigenous tribes. They had also spent a year in Mexico where he had become fascinated by Aztec culture.

As he traversed the continent, Alexander von Humboldt stayed true to the spirit of Jena. That nature and imagination were so closely interwoven in his work, he told Goethe later, was due to the 'influence of your writings'. To show his appreciation, Humboldt dedicated the first book he published after his return to his old friend. Goethe had equipped him with 'new senses', and it was with those new senses that Alexander von Humboldt had explored South America. And though he had travelled with forty-two scientific instruments, he wasn't just interested in empirical data. Like his old Jena friends, he believed that feelings and imagination were essential tools for making sense of the external world. With his books he wanted to feed 'the desire for knowledge and the powers of imagination at the same time'.

Goethe was excited by his friend's safe return. Alexander had been away for so long, Goethe said, that it felt as if he 'had risen from the dead'. Yet, when Schiller heard the news of Humboldt's arrival, his old jealousy surfaced again. He immediately wrote to his publisher, Johann Friedrich Cotta, advising him not to commission Alexander von Humboldt's travel journals. Everybody would want them, Schiller said, 'but Herr von Humboldt is not a gifted writer'. One of the most respected figures in the publishing world, Cotta had Goethe and Schiller on his books as well as Schelling, Fichte, August Wilhelm Schlegel and the poet Friedrich Hölderlin.

Alexander von Humboldt believed that he belonged in that company. 'Who indeed would be better to work with than you,' he wrote to Cotta, 'the friend of my friends?' An astute businessman as well as a patron of the arts, Cotta ignored Schiller's advice. He was not going to lose the story of the greatest exploration of the age. In fact, he would match any offer Alexander von Humboldt received from other publishers.

And so the old friends from Jena were reunited in the pages of Cotta's catalogue. They may have moved or fallen out, but their words were published by Cotta, and his books carried their ideas into the world. In the past decade they had turned everything upside down, redefining the relationship between the self and the world. They had founded a literary and philosophical movement that prom-ised freedom and original thinking. Just as the French Revolution had been no simple linear trajectory, so too their revolution. The path may have looped and zigzagged but the direction had been forward, towards a self-determined life. They had no intention of stopping. In time their works would influence some of the greatest writers and thinkers across Europe and the United States.

~

On the first day of 1805 Goethe awoke with the premonition that either he or Schiller would die that year. Two weeks later, both men were unwell. A skin infection that had previously caused Goethe problems flared up again, followed by fever and pneumonia. By the beginning of February his doctor feared the worst. The prospect of losing his friend shocked Schiller so much that he was himself hit by fever cramps that same night.

It had been a long, cold winter in which deep snow had covered the Duchy of Saxe-Weimar for months. 'This Jena winter simply refuses to end,' Hegel wrote to a friend at the beginning of March 1805, worrying, like everybody else, about Goethe and Schiller. Bed-bound, the two men sent each other letters and books. On 1 March, Schiller had recovered enough to visit his convalescing friend. They embraced, holding each other tightly, and smiled. They had survived. Or so they thought. Less than a week later, Goethe collapsed again, this time suffering from a kidney infection or renal colic. As he slowly recovered, Schiller got worse again. No one was allowed to mention Schiller's illness in Goethe's house: it was as if silence was a remedy. Over the weeks that followed the two old friends seesawed between recovery and fever. Whenever they felt a little better, they tried to work and exchanged manuscripts.

'I have to force myself,' Schiller told Goethe on 27 March, after spending a few hours writing, 'but I'm back underway.' Slowly, though, they seemed to improve. A month later, at the end of April, Goethe felt strong enough to visit his friend, and a week after that Schiller even ventured out to the theatre. On his way he bumped into Goethe and they had a brief chat, but that night Schiller went to bed shivering and soon developed another high fever.

Three days later, on 4 May, he dragged himself to his desk to work on his new drama, *Demetrius*, but the next day he was back in bed with a high temperature again. On the morning of 9 May the doctor ordered a bath and a glass of champagne to get his patient's circulation going – probably not the best treatment for a man who had suffered chronic illnesses for more than a decade. Schiller fainted several times and couldn't speak. By late afternoon he was dead. Schiller was forty-five years old.

In the previous fourteen years, Schiller had suffered so many debilitating illnesses that most of his organs were almost completely destroyed. It was a surprise, the autopsy report stated, that he had managed to live so long. Schiller really didn't have a heart, Friedrich Schlegel drily commented after hearing that the doctor had found only 'a kind of hard, petrified sponge'. Schiller's left lung had collapsed, his heart was deformed, his liver resembled dry paper and his intestines were constricted. The complaints of ill health that had littered his many letters to friends and family were not those of a hypochondriac but rather of a man who had produced some of his best work by pushing his weakened body to the limit.

When the news reached Goethe's house, in the early evening of 9 May, no one dared say anything. His secretary rushed out without even saying good night. Everybody was so quiet that Goethe sensed something. As he wept in bed, fearing the worst, Christiane pretended to be asleep. 'Schiller was very sick yesterday, wasn't he?' he asked her the next morning, and she broke down, unable to lie to him. 'Is he dead?' he said. 'He's dead!' Goethe locked himself away in his study. The theatre remained closed the next day, and on 12 May Schiller was buried in the graveyard of Weimar's St Jakobskirche, a short fifteen-minute walk from Goethe's house. Feigning illness, Goethe didn't attend the funeral. He couldn't. 'I lose a friend and, with him, half of my own life,' he said, mourning 'my irreplaceable Schiller'.

Everybody feared for Goethe. 'I'm afraid the old man will turn entirely to stone now,' Friedrich Schlegel wrote from Cologne to his brother in Switzerland. Weakened both by illness and the loss of Schiller, Goethe was closely watched by Christiane and his friends. In his study at the back of his house, overlooking his garden, Goethe tried to ignore reality by working. He didn't mention Schiller, and no one else dared. But his friend was with him. On Goethe's desk was a pile of papers covered in Schiller's handwriting – his unfinished *Demetrius*. They had discussed the play in so much detail that Goethe said, 'I could write the rest of his Demetrius myself.'

He was determined to complete the work, 'to spite Death', as he wrote. Doing so would unite them again. Even if only in Goethe's own mind, they could still work together, argue and write. When performed on German stages, the play would resurrect his friend and their mutual love of theatre. So, as summer unfurled the flowers in the garden beyond his windows, Goethe stayed in his study. He tried. And he tried again. Nothing came. He couldn't do it. He missed Schiller too much.

When he finally put away the manuscript, it was as if Schiller had died a second time. He was distraught and lonely. The pages of Goethe's diary during those weeks after Schiller's death are blank – the expression, he later said, of his 'hollowed condition'.

20

'The French are in town!'
October 1806: The Battle of Jena

IN THE AUTUMN of 1806 more than a hundred thousand Prussian soldiers and their Saxon allies were waiting for the French in and around Jena. Napoleon and his grand army of more than one hundred and fifty thousand soldiers were marching from southern Germany towards Berlin, the Prussian capital. The small Duchy of Saxe-Weimar lay directly in their path.

The Prussian and Saxon troops had arrived in Jena at the end of September 1806, setting up a huge camp in the Paradise, the parkland by the Saale River where the Jena Set had so often walked. Endless rows of white tents dotted the meadows and thousands of thin smoke trails curled up from the campfires. As horses stood in orderly lines drinking from the river, the smell of bread drifted from a large field bakery across the meadows. Soldiers had butchered every cow and ox for miles around, and felled hundreds of trees to fuel their fires. They had emptied the grain stores, and food prices in Jena were increasing daily.

Jena's streets were now crowded with Prussian and Saxon military personnel dressed in colourful uniforms. Wherever the people of Jena now looked, they saw silver trim, lace edgings, fur linings, buttons in all colours, red and blue piping, long double-breasted coats, short tailored jackets and embroidered lapels. Sashes were worn around the waist or crisscrossed over the breast, while bicorne hats displayed a vast collection of large plumes, trims, embroidery and tassels. The heels of polished boots clacked on cobblestones. Soldiers carrying curved sabres, lances, muskets with bayonets, pistols and swords filled the market square with cannons, ammunition and other artillery equipment.

The generals were easy to identify, their jackets richly decorated with tassels, golden epaulettes, medals and embroidered stars, their swords swinging as they strutted across town. Officers wore hats with large white feathers which bounced over the heads of the crowd.

Most impressive of all were the feared 'Death's Head Regiment' – moustachioed Prussian hussars mounted on fast greys with saddlecloths made of black sheepskin trimmed in poppy red. These cavalrymen wore short black jackets and black hats emblazoned with the skull and crossbones. To the residents of Jena, the Prussian army and their Saxon allies exuded strength and confidence.

It was the first time since the Seven Years War, more than four decades earlier, that Jena had faced an enemy army. Even during the previous fourteen years, when much of Europe had been at war, the battlefields and soldiers had been far enough away for the town to feel safe for most of the time. The closest the French had come had been some one hundred and forty miles to the south-west in the summer of 1800 when Auguste had died. But war had resumed after the short-lived Treaty of Amiens, and Napoleon was now moving north from Würzburg and Bamberg, coming dangerously close.

As the French had collected one victory after another over the course of the past decade, the Holy Roman Empire had begun to crumble. In the summer of 1806, time was finally called on its thousand-year rule when Napoleon replaced it with the so-called Confederation of the Rhine, an alliance of sixteen German states with Napoleon as their 'protector'. Those German states not part of the Confederation of the Rhine were promptly declared France's enemies, and as Napoleon marched through Europe he swallowed them up.

'Napoleon with his sharp teeth is grazing through one country after another,' Caroline had written in March 1806, from Würzburg, now part of the Confederation of the Rhine. Schelling scoured the news with excited anticipation, hoping that the old monarchies and their despotic systems might finally be swept away. 'Finally, the revolution has started in Germany,' he wrote; 'at last there will be space for a new world.'

For more than a decade, Prussia had kept clear of the Napoleonic Wars, staying determinedly neutral. The stance had gained the Prussian king, Friedrich Wilhelm III, no popularity among the European nations fighting against France, and many regarded it as weakness. Then, in late summer 1806, after some border skirmishes and French provocations over territorial rights to Hanover, Friedrich Wilhelm III had begun to mobilise his army. At the end of September, he had dispatched an ultimatum to Napoleon, demanding that French troops be removed from Prussian territory. Ignoring the ultimatum, Napoleon declared war in early October 1806. With the Confederation of the Rhine siding with Napoleon and effectively under his control, Prussia suddenly found itself at war with France, with only the Electorate of Saxony and the smaller Saxon dukedoms as allies.

~

Goethe tried to ignore the outside world. He had been ill on and off since Schiller's death the previous year, but a summer vacation at his favourite spa town, Karlsbad, had renewed his spirits. It helped that no soldiers were to be seen in Karlsbad and that no one had talked about politics. But as the threat of the French army grew, Goethe had once again found comfort in the study of nature, resuming his still unpublished work on colour theory and cataloguing his growing rock collection.

He went to Jena to work on his projects. Here Goethe read and discussed the latest philosophical publications with Hegel. When he sent rock samples to the University of Göttingen, the professor who received them expressed surprise that Goethe had nothing more important to do as the army prepared for war. Goethe had, of course, not been able to neglect his ministerial duties, which included provisioning the Prussian and Saxon troops. So when the generals and soldiers arrived in Jena, he reluctantly closed his notebooks and took out his court dress. He put on his black silk breeches and richly embroidered waistcoat and coat. He rolled up his white stockings, powdered his hair, cinched his sword belt under his bulging belly, and then went to meet the Prussian generals who were lodging in the Old Castle. Vacating his rooms for them, he moved into a side wing.

As everybody talked about Napoleon, war and politics, Goethe listened politely and said little. On his last day in Jena, on 6 October, he walked to the town's highest point, on the northern edge near the old medieval moat. There, not far from the entrance to his beloved botanical garden, he looked down over the angled roofs and let his thoughts drift. He could see the tall spire of the Church of St Michael and the distant tower of the university to the south. He felt lonely. Most of his friends were gone. Some were dead, others had left, and only a few continued to write. And now this small town, the crucible of so many inspiring ideas, faced the French army.

There was a glimmer in the sky, Goethe noted, that reminded him of the dancing air above hot coals. It felt like an omen. It was time to return to his family in Weimar. Goethe left Jena that day, not knowing that it would be seven months before he returned.

～

Five days later, in the early hours of 11 October 1806, news arrived that only thirty miles south of Jena some Prussian regiments had been defeated by the French. Shouts echoed through the streets: 'The French are in town!' And Jena's inhabitants rushed to buy provisions and harvest the remaining vegetables from their plots, stocking their larders. Others dug holes under the trees and shrubs in their gardens to hide valuables, burying jewellery, coins and important papers in trunks and small boxes.

There was an air of panic. At one point, a group of Prussian soldiers pushed their heavy cannons so quickly over the cobblestones that the wheels were crushed under the weight and the valuable artillery became stuck. The situation became so confusing that regiments barred each other's way. When one Saxon regiment lost all its luggage and provisions in the commotion, its soldiers had to sleep hungry and under the cold autumn sky in a field outside town. The Prussian campsite on the banks of the Saale was hurriedly packed up, the troops rushing out of town along the road to Weimar to get into position in the surrounding fields – the thousands of yellowed grass squares where their tents had stood left a ghostly reminder of their presence. Fires had been extinguished but the ash was still warm. It took almost two days for the Prussians and their allies to leave. Then all went quiet. Everybody stayed at home, not knowing what else to do.

On the morning of 13 October the first French troops arrived. With the Prussian regiments preparing for a French attack in the villages beyond Jena, Napoleon's soldiers simply marched through the unmanned town gates. At midday Jena was overrun with looting French soldiers. Soldiers banged against doors with the butts of muskets and charged into homes. 'They stormed the houses like devils,' one professor later wrote to Goethe. Women were searched, jewellery was ripped from their necks and watches were taken. Drawers were opened, desks ransacked and trunks overturned and emptied.

Jena's inhabitants were terrified. Some set up tables with food in front of their houses to feed the invading army, hoping it afforded them some protection. But the soldiers were merciless. They grabbed purses filled with money, carried wine in buckets out of cellars, took bedding, clothes and food. Bayonets pressed against the chests of frightened residents, the French stripped local men of hats and boots, leaving them shoeless in the streets. Some were even forced to take off their trousers. By evening, thousands of French soldiers were camping in the market square, their officers billeted in private residences. A French tailor set up shop in the Zum Schwarzen Bären, next to Caroline's last apartment. Any blue material, whether ladies' coats or peasants' capes, was seized and turned into breeches for the French soldiers. Napoleon's troops were waiting for reinforcements to arrive so that they could destroy the Prussian army.

~

Hegel was also still in town, desperately trying to finish the *Phenomenology of Spirit*, the book he had been working on for five years. He had dispatched parts of the manuscript a few days earlier, but his publisher in Bamberg would only pay Hegel once he had received the complete manuscript, and the deadline was 18 October. Having rationed his small inheritance over the past seven years, Hegel had finally run out of money. He desperately needed the honorarium.

On 13 October, despite the French marching through the streets, Hegel wrapped the final part of the manuscript and ran to the market square to deliver his parcel to the last stagecoach leaving town. As the coachman took the reins and spurred the horses forward, Hegel watched the carriage drive away. 'God knows my dark forebodings as I ventured to send off these pages,' he wrote to a friend. It was his only copy, and for days he had tightly clutched his satchel containing the manuscript at all times. He had been right to worry because later that day his rooms were ransacked by the French. The chances the manuscript would survive the crossfire were slim.

Barring a few articles and the 1801 pamphlet in which he had explained the differences between Fichte and Schelling's philosophy,*

* Schelling and Hegel only published two volumes of the *Critical Journal of Philosophy*. Their collaboration ended in 1803 when Schelling moved away from Jena.

Hegel had published nothing in his almost six years in Jena. Work on the *Phenomenology of Spirit* had been painfully slow, and wrestling with his ideas had made Hegel melancholic. His studies, he later explained, had led him along labyrinthine paths to the deep recesses of his mind, to 'dark domains where nothing is stable and definite and certain'. But the more he descended into this darkness, the more Hegel worked. The result was a new system of philosophy – one, he believed, that would change everything.

Building on Schelling's work, Hegel had set out to explain how the mind appeared to itself and how, in so doing, it developed an understanding both of itself and of reality – a process that moved from consciousness to self-consciousness and then to what Hegel defined as 'absolute knowing'. What interested Hegel was the development of the mind, or what he called 'the process of its own becoming'. His 'absolute knowing' had nothing to do with an objective truth nor with Kant's unknowable thing-in-itself – concepts that fundamentally assumed a division between mind and matter. 'It is the spirit knowing itself in the shape of spirit,' Hegel explained in the concluding chapter – the last stage of the evolution of the mind, when it realises that reality is its own creation and therefore can be known directly. Hegel's 'absolute knowledge' is the mind watching itself constructing reality.

In time, *Phenomenology of Spirit* would make Hegel the most famous philosopher of his age, dethroning Fichte and Schelling. It was also the book that triggered his break with Schelling. But for now Hegel's only concern was that his manuscript reached the printer in Bamberg, so that he could be paid. The prospect of losing the product of years of work was unimaginable.

In the early afternoon that day, as Hegel rushed through the crowded streets, he suddenly saw Napoleon. Hegel was enthralled. 'I saw the Emperor – this world soul – ride out through the city on reconnaissance,' he wrote to a friend; 'it is truly a marvellous sensation to see such an individual, who, concentrated here at a single point, seated on a horse, reaches out across the world and dominates it.'

Hegel was not alone in his admiration but Napoleon divided the Germans. Some thought him a genius, others a tyrant. Some believed he had betrayed the ideals of 1789 by crowning himself emperor in 1804, while others hoped he would restore order to France and

Europe so that those ideals could finally unfold. Caroline simply called him 'destiny personified . . . which I do not hate, and do not love, I merely wait and see where it will take the world'. When Goethe met Napoleon two years after the Battle of Jena, he too was in awe. As Hegel later explained, Goethe admired Napoleon's genius and strength, not the brutal military man or the politician. For Goethe, Napoleon had the same creative energy and productivity as an artistic genius. The difference was that his mode of expression was action, not poetry. The French emperor had ended the turmoil of the French Revolution, Goethe believed, and reinstated law and order.

Napoleon was, as Hegel had written on the very pages he had just dispatched to Bamberg, the executor of the ideals of the French Revolution and the incarnation of spirit. He was the 'world soul'. To Hegel's mind, Napoleon was a step on the way to 'absolute knowledge'. And although his lodgings had been plundered and though he feared for his manuscript, Hegel, like so many others in Jena and Germany, wanted the French to win. 'Now everyone is hoping for the success of the French army,' he wrote to a friend that evening, 'as I have already been doing for a while.' The original intentions of the French Revolution might have been diluted over the past seventeen years, but what had happened in France was still better than the injustices, inequalities and oppressions enacted by the rulers of the German states.

None of this made the immediate situation in Jena any less dangerous. Grabbing what he could, Hegel fled his lodgings and went to friends who lived in a large house on Fürstengraben, the tree-lined promenade at the northern edge of the town. By evening, around one hundred and thirty people had crowded in, including seventy to eighty French officers. That night, everybody in Jena went to bed fully dressed, prepared to flee at any moment. The plundering continued. Intoxicated by the rich spoils from Jena's well-stocked wine cellars, soldiers broke doors and windows. The dreaded call 'Ouvrez la porte!' – 'Open the door!' – echoed through the streets that night.

Those who fled their houses and couldn't find temporary protection with friends and neighbours wandered the streets, carrying what they could and dragging their crying children along. One man pulled a large trunk on ropes behind him, another wore one boot, one slipper and his torn nightgown. A half-dressed woman had inexplicably rescued her two finest hats but no other clothes, and others wore so many layers that they could barely move. They slept outside, in the fields and in gardens beyond the medieval walls, or hid behind the gravestones in the cemetery and in ditches. A thick fog crept in across the mirrored surface of the Saale and over the undulating hills. It was freezing – the first night that winter on which ice laced the windows and icicles like stiff tassels ribboned the roofs.

At three o'clock in the morning the fire bell rang. 'Fire!' people shouted as flames illuminated the night sky. 'Fire!' The row of houses between the Schlegels' old house in Leutragasse and the street one block north was burning. Before the sun rose, twenty homes had been destroyed. Luckily there was no wind that night, and the rest of the town was spared.

~

That same night Napoleon ordered his troops to move the cannons and ammunition up a steep hill less than a mile to the north-west of the town. The hill was just north of the road that led from Jena to Weimar, and in the darkness the French soldiers struggled to heave the heavy artillery along a narrow holloway. The men were exhausted. Over the previous twenty-four hours they had marched towards Jena, relentlessly harried by their generals. Now they shoved, pushed and pulled wagons and cannons up over jagged stones and boulders. Higher up, where the path narrowed further, the first wagon became stuck, with two hundred more piling up behind. It was pitch dark. Then, as some of the men looked up, they saw Napoleon himself standing ahead of them. Holding a torch in his hand, he began to instruct the men where to widen the path with axes and shovels. Napoleon stayed with his soldiers until the slow line started to move again. They reached the top in the middle of the night.

A few hours later, at six o'clock on the morning of 14 October 1806, Napoleon stood with his troops on the crest of the hill they had climbed. Jena's valley was behind them and ahead lay the open expansive plateau. From it rose the Dornberg hill, the highest eleva-tion in the area, where a small part of the Prussian army had bivouacked. In pre-dawn darkness and enveloped in thick fog, some twenty-two thousand French soldiers attacked the eight thousand

Prussians. Three hours later Napoleon had captured the Dornberg, from where he directed his army for the rest of the day.

Over the preceding days the French regiments had marched quickly in three separate columns from southern Germany before converging on Jena. They had advanced so rapidly that the Prussians had been unsure of when and where to expect them, and were completely unprepared for a French strike that day. With their regiments camped at different sites around the local villages and fields, it was only when the Prussians heard the cannon fire and gun shots echoing through the fog from the Dornberg that they realised the French were attacking. Tens of thousands of Prussian soldiers were woken up by the noise, hurriedly dressing before stumbling out of their tents to get into position.

By the time the Prussian and Saxon generals had brought their men into long linear formations, more French troops were following the rolling advance. The French pressed forward, driving back the Prussians, who tried to send their cavalry into the French lines, only to be forced back. Two miles away, in Jena, the constant refrain of cannon fire reverberated through the streets. 'All the thunder in the world', one said, 'doesn't roar as frightfully as the cannons on the hills shook our town during that day.'

On the battlefields, dense smoke replaced the morning fog. In the hours that followed more French regiments arrived, and wave after wave of soldiers who had marched all night went straight into battle. Retreating, the famously orderly lines of the Prussian army descended into chaos. A thin three-kilometre-long line of Prussians stood unprotected against the lead force of guns and cannons. Riding his horse behind his troops, Napoleon oversaw large sections of the battlefields from his elevated position on the Dornberg. As his men fell, he replenished them with new troops from behind. Riders galloped back and forth with orders for the French generals to coordinate their attacks.

In the chaos of smoke and bullet fire, it took the Prussians a while to realise that they were facing the full might of the French army. Men and horses fell, blood stained the soil, guns were dropped, and screams filled the air. As the German soldiers turned to flee from the French advance, they ran into other Prussian and Saxon regiments moving forward. As their officers were killed, the German troops found themselves without orders, and soon regiments didn't know what they were supposed to do or where they should go. The Prussians panicked and ran. Worse, another Prussian army of sixty thousand men was annihilated by a French force half the size only a few kilometres to the north of Jena. Within hours, the once formidable Prussian army had been entirely crushed to the driving rhythm of French drums. By four o'clock that afternoon the battles were over.

Tens of thousands of Prussians were taken prisoner and many thousands died on the battlefield, but there were no civilian casualties.* The wounded were brought to Jena's most prominent landmark, the imposing Church of St Michael, which was turned into a hospital. Pews were ripped out and the floor was covered with straw to bed the soldiers. The injuries were horrific. Hands, arms, feet and legs were missing, skin was burned and organs ripped apart. Some men were unconscious. Others screamed. Dr Stark, the physician who had operated on Sophie von Kühn, Novalis's fiancée, a decade earlier, amputated, operated and stitched so many wounds that he could barely move his fingers for days afterwards. Soon there was no room left in the church for the injured who were still being brought in, and they were taken to the university, the town hall, the Old Castle and to inns and taverns, as well as to private houses.

Wounded soldiers were even treated in Leutragasse 5 where the friends had once worked, laughed, eaten and argued in Caroline's beautifully furnished rooms. The auditorium where Fichte had liberated the Ich in his inaugural lecture twelve years previously filled with dying men. There seemed to be no end to the stream of soldiers in torn and bloodied uniforms. It was a gruesome orchestra composed of the groans of the wounded, the ringing of the fire bell, the wails of inhabitants, shots from the battlefield and the sound of hurried boots on cobblestones. As the afternoon sun dipped low, both victors and the defeated streamed into town.

That night more houses burned and the looting continued. French soldiers cooked their meals on open fires in the streets and squares where philosophers and poets had once met. Chickens were plucked and roasted as soldiers sang and drank. When Napoleon returned from the battlefield, he stayed in the rooms at the Old Castle where Goethe had spent so much time and had written some of his most

---

* The numbers killed can only be estimated. Around eight to nine thousand French died on 14 October 1806, and around twenty thousand Prussians and Saxons.

famous work. In the evening, Napoleon could be seen pacing back and forth in front of the window as he dictated letters to his secretary. That night, the Emperor of France slept in Goethe's bed.

~

The week before, when Goethe had returned to Weimar from Jena, he had found the town in turmoil. People were shouting, trunks were being loaded onto carriages and, with each passing day, the disorder increased. For a man who was easily irritated by a barking dog or the distant rattle of a loom, the situation had become unbearable. Worse, drunken Prussian soldiers had smashed windows and furniture at Goethe's beloved Garden House, in the park just outside Weimar. Stoically, Goethe pretended nothing was happening. Even when messengers reported the imminent arrival of tens of thousands of French soldiers, he was undeterred, insisting on opening Weimar's theatre. On the evening before the Battle of Jena, while others hid their valuables or sang patriotic songs, Goethe arranged for a performance of a light-hearted operetta called *Fanchon, the Hurdy-Gurdy Girl*. The lead actress was furious. 'We should be praying,' she said, 'and we have to perform a comedy.'

Goethe's diary entry for 14 October 1806, the day of the Battle of Jena, was brief: 'Five in the afternoon: cannonballs flying through the roofs. At five-thirty, the chasseurs entered the town. Seven o'clock: fire, plunder, a terrible night. Only fortitude and luck saved our house.' He was terrified. Dozens of people had been billeted with him and several panicked neighbours stayed in his house. Late that evening, French soldiers burst into the house and Goethe's bedroom, their bayonets drawn. Dressed only in his voluminous nightgown – his 'prophet's mantle', as he called it – Goethe felt paralysed. It fell to Christiane to rescue the situation. Screaming, shouting and kicking, she and some of the neighbours who had taken refuge in the house chased the soldiers out of the room and locked the door. They were lucky not to lose anything more than some food, wine and money.

Over the next few days there was no word from his Jena friends. Worried, Goethe dispatched a courier on 18 October with a list of all their names and addresses, asking them each to write a word or two to reassure him about their safety. They all did. 'God knows what I'm supposed to live on this winter,' one friend wrote. The students had also been plundered and most had fled town, another reported. 'I and wife and children are still alive,' one short note read, but his wife had been beaten so brutally by the soldiers that they feared long-term damage to her health. Most had not slept for days and one professor, having lost everything, had decided to leave Jena for good. They worried about the future of the university, and desperately needed financial support from the administration in Weimar – 'otherwise we are totally ruined'.

During those first days after the battle, Goethe also wrote to assure friends across the German territories of his safety. 'We're alive!' was the first sentence in many of his letters. The invasion marked a turning point for Goethe. Though he had escaped relatively unscathed, the intrusion into his home had rattled him more than he at first admitted. 'I've been suffering from something since 14 October,' he later wrote to Duke Carl August, 'something physical too, but I'm still too close to it to put it into words.'

Five days after the battle, he married Christiane with only August, their sixteen-year-old son, and Goethe's secretary as witnesses. Significantly, the date he had engraved in their wedding rings was '14 October 1806', the day of the battle. In times of peace, Goethe explained, one can ignore conventions and etiquette, but 'in times like these we have to honour them'. It was as if Goethe needed to tighten the bonds, Caroline wrote when she heard about the wedding, just as everything else was falling apart.

Unsurprisingly, Weimar's high society was displeased. By making Christiane his wife, Goethe had altered the town's social dynamic. Now, they couldn't ignore her. They would have to invite Christiane to their events and she would even be admitted at court. Charlotte Schiller refused to congratulate her old friend. 'What right does he have', another friend complained, 'to force us to meet her and socialise with her as if she were worthy of us?' Only Johanna Schopenhauer, the mother of the philosopher Arthur Schopenhauer and a recent arrival in Weimar, invited Christiane to her salon. 'I think that if Goethe gives her his name,' she wrote to her son five days after the wedding, 'we can give her a cup of tea.'

~

Once the news of the Battle of Jena rolled out across the German states and Europe, the letters came pouring in. 'I can't tell you how

worried I am about the fate of our poor Jena,' Schelling wrote from
Munich, where he and Caroline had moved earlier that year. Only
now did Schelling realise how precious Jena was to him, commenting
that its fate affected him 'as that of my true fatherland'. Caroline
and Schelling couldn't bear the thought of a devastated Jena and
simply couldn't imagine how a quarter of a million soldiers had
descended on the small town and the surrounding villages. They
read every newspaper they could get their hands on to glean more
details.

They were most concerned about Goethe. 'Our hearts tremble,'
Schelling wrote to him a week after the battle. But still they didn't
hate the French. Like Hegel, who had been awed to see Napoleon
riding through Jena on the eve of the battle, so Caroline, Schelling
and many others welcomed the French victory. Her heart bled for
Jena, Caroline said, but it had been time for change. 'That's how it
was and how it had to be, and what can last no longer must perish,'
she wrote to her old childhood friend Luise Gotter. Schelling agreed.
The destruction of Jena was tragic for those who lived there but it
had been necessary, he told a friend, because despotic governments
and monarchies had to fall. What did it matter that Europe was once
again sliced and divided up, Caroline said, 'because really, none of
those defeated rulers are any great loss; countries can always get new
ones just like the old ones.'

Jena itself was devastated, the blackened ruins of the burned houses
standing like sentinels of death. The passage of two such huge armies
had been too much for the small town to bear. When the French
troops moved on, there was no food or drink left. The wine stores
had been emptied, every animal had been slaughtered and not a
crumb of bread could be found. When they had exhausted the town's
stores of firewood, the soldiers had burned chairs, tables, beds,
cupboards and other furniture. Farmers couldn't work their fields
because all their horses had been stolen and their oxen eaten. Even
water was scarce, because the wells and fountains ran dry when heavy
French artillery had smashed the pipes. There were piles of broken
doors, windows and furniture on every street.

After the battle, the university sent a delegation to Napoleon,
pleading with him not to shut down the 'nursery where the greatest
scholars flourished'. Their wish was granted, but the winter semester's
intake was meagre, with only a little over one hundred students

returning and a paltry thirty-one newly enrolling. The university's professors were also shocked to discover that their books and manuscripts had been used to heat ovens and fireplaces. Some lost all their belongings. 'No bread, robbed, not a penny left, billeting, more fear than you can imagine,' wrote one professor to Goethe, 'oh, God have mercy on my family! . . . My tears don't let me write any more.' The glasses and vials of the anatomy collection in the Old Castle had been smashed, although Goethe's botanical garden had been miraculously spared except for some uprooted plants and a few broken greenhouse windowpanes.

The botany professor who also ran the botanical garden had fared worse. He had been forced to watch as his apartment had been ransacked, his collections scattered across the floor and his valuable herbarium completely destroyed when French soldiers emptied the botany cabinet to use as a wardrobe. Precious specimens were 'lying around on the ground in the dirt and the water', he wrote in despair to Goethe, and his rare botanical books had been used for kindling.

With everybody gone, he wasn't sure who was in charge. Would there be lectures? Or even students? And who would pay him? As his remaining possessions now fitted into one suitcase, he told Goethe that he had accepted a French general's offer to accompany him as a private physician. But in any case, someone should be sent over from Weimar 'because the authorities here have completely lost their minds'. Goethe sent money, provisions, clothes and reassurance. Don't be afraid, he told one terrified professor, 'when the storm is past, we can bring everything back to normal'.

For those who lived in Jena, it didn't seem that way. Wherever one looked, there were signs of horror. In the Saale River, dead horses, bloodied uniforms and severed arms and legs floated by – some still with boots on. As corpses began to rot in the streets, residents feared an epidemic. With around six thousand wounded soldiers, the makeshift hospitals remained full for weeks and it would be over six months before services resumed in the Church of St Michael. Every morning, at nine o'clock, 'the death cart rattled up gruesomely punctual', one of Auguste's old friends recounted. The farm cart stopped at the hospitals to collect those who had died the night before. Covered only with straw, the heads, arms and legs of corpses often poked out as the wheels bumped along the cobbled streets.

'We just drag ourselves along from day to day,' a friend wrote to Goethe two months after the battle. Goethe couldn't face seeing his beloved Jena in its destroyed state. 'All these upheavals affect me too deeply,' he confessed to the duke at the end of December, and he avoided Jena until the early summer of the next year.

⁓

As a result of the Battle of Jena, Prussia lost half its territory to the French. On 27 October 1806, Napoleon took Berlin and rode on a white horse through the Brandenburg Gate. Dominique-Vivant Denon, the director of the Louvre, arrived the same day to assess and carry away the royal art collections. As Napoleon's troops marched through Prussia over the ensuing months, cities and fortresses capitulated and fell into French hands. Following the army closely, Denon was packing up sculptures, medals, antiquities and more than one thousand paintings. Exactly a year after the Battle of Jena, they were on show in the Louvre. Prussia was no longer a major European power, its economy brought to a standstill by the immense reparations the French imposed as part of their peace treaty.

In December 1806, two months after the Battle of Jena, France also signed a peace treaty with Saxony and the smaller Saxon dukedoms in which they joined Napoleon's Confederation of the Rhine. The Duchy of Saxe-Weimar had to pay France two million francs – an impossibility, Goethe's colleague, Minister Voigt, pointed out, since the small state's entire annual income was only 150,000 francs.

A French commander was stationed in Jena, leading to great confusion as few could speak French well enough to communicate with the new administration. Books and newspapers were now printed under the supervision of the French authorities. Letters were opened by French censors, and those who criticised the French government or army were punished. The people turned inwards.

Jena's exhilarating intellectual atmosphere had disappeared. 'The scholarly exchange that existed when you were here is absolutely gone,' one young professor wrote to Schelling, reporting how he ate alone at home and that there were no social gatherings. When student numbers dropped from almost nine hundred in the 1790s to less than two hundred in 1806, the town's tradesmen lost their customers and shops closed. Almost every profession struggled. Carpenters, bakers, butchers, milliners and tailors went out of business and food became expensive as the price of grain rose sevenfold. Over the next few years the university – and with it Jena – stagnated and declined. There was not much hope 'for its rebirth', a friend wrote to Goethe, for 'we have no saviour to reawaken the dead'.

Even Hegel finally moved away. With so few students in town, he couldn't earn any money. After the director of the botanical garden fled Jena, a desperate Hegel had applied for his position, but someone else had snapped it up. Hegel had also tried the universities in Heidelberg and Würzburg without success. The only option left was an offer to be the editor of a newspaper in Bamberg. So, in late February 1807, four months after the battle, Hegel hurriedly packed his possessions and climbed into a stagecoach bound for southern Germany. He had no money, he was exhausted, and he was also fleeing fatherhood, for his illegitimate son had been born just a few days earlier. The mother was Hegel's landlady, a married woman who had already been abandoned by her husband. Hegel felt guilty at leaving her, but not guilty enough. It would be nine years before he accepted responsibility for his son.

The only good news was that the manuscript of Hegel's *Phenomenology of Spirit* had survived its hazardous journey through enemy lines. Published five months after the Battle of Jena, in March 1807, it became Hegel's most influential work. In it, he explained how humanity had progressed through a series of stages, moving from feudal systems to democratic societies. The end of this process, he believed, would be the moment when humankind lived in a society ruled by the universal right to freedom. For Hegel, Napoleon's victory on the battlefields of Jena was that moment – nothing less than the 'end of History', the end of the long evolution of human society itself and the beginning of an epoch of freedom.

Epilogue

Alas, everyone who once came together in our little Jena circle is now scattered across the world ... My only regret is that they're no longer making poetry together – we at least don't hear anything of their songs.

Caroline Schlegel to Luise Gotter,
4 January 1807

Part I: After Jena

ON A COLD Sunday in December 1807, a little more than a year after Napoleon's victory at Jena, Johann Gottlieb Fichte began a lecture series entitled 'Addresses to the German Nation' at the Prussian Academy of Sciences in Berlin. Despite defeat by the French, he told his audience, and the many state boundaries dividing the German territories, the Germans constituted a nation. Were they not all part of a greater entity based on a shared language and culture? Unlike languages such as French or Italian which had been grafted on to a dead and foreign Latin root, German was a living language that had been spoken by Germans from the very beginning. Their language connected them 'to a single shared understanding'. It linked them to their roots and to each other.*

It seemed that Fichte had become interested in what he called the 'national self'. Until France's decisive victory, the Ich-experience

---

* This approach was founded in Johann Gottfried Herder's writings. 'Every nation speaks according to the way it thinks and thinks according to the way it speaks,' Herder had written already in 1768. The truest expression of this, he said, was the poetry of old folk tales and songs, which he collected and published. But unlike Fichte, who elevated the German language to the true one, Herder didn't judge if a particular language or a people were better than any other.

had been the lens through which the friends in Jena had experienced reality. Now, Fichte also paved the way for a bigger Ich – the Ich of a nation. This was a dangerous idea, and one that would be exploited in Germany in the future.

Fichte remained in Berlin for the rest of his life. In 1808, he became so seriously ill that his left arm and leg remained partially paralysed, but even then he could not be stopped. He was finally back at a university lectern in 1810 when he was made the first professor of philosophy at the new university in Berlin which Wilhelm von Humboldt had founded the previous year. In 1811, Fichte's colleagues elected him rector. Soon, though, his combative nature led him into disputes with students and colleagues, and Fichte was forced to resign less than a year later. He continued to revise his *Wissenschaftslehre* and gave private lectures, but age didn't calm his temper.

With Berlin under occupation by the French, Fichte turned his anger against Napoleon, who he believed had betrayed the ideals of the French Revolution. When a militia formed in Berlin in the summer of 1813, Fichte was seen strutting through the streets with a long dagger and shield. Not long afterwards, though, on 29 January 1814, he suddenly died after contracting typhus from his wife Johanne who had been nursing wounded soldiers. Fichte was fifty-one. Newspapers across the German territories reported his death, and at his funeral many hundreds of students walked behind his coffin. 'The eye of Germany has closed,' Rahel Levin, one of Berlin's most famous literary hostesses said. There was no doubt how important Fichte's contributions had been. His Ich-philosophy had been the starting point from which the Jena Set had developed their ideas and theories.

~

Caroline finally found happiness in her third marriage. In spring 1806, just a few months before the Battle of Jena, the couple had moved to Munich when the Bavarian Academy of Sciences and Humanities offered Schelling a well-paid position. The mountain air made her strong again and she was healthier than she had felt in years. Caroline liked living in the shadow of the magnificent Alps, she told her old friend Luise Gotter, but at the age of forty-three she had also finally realised that she didn't want to put down roots. She embraced transience. 'I don't want to settle down anywhere again,' she said, 'I want to take the fact that we are all just wanderers on earth entirely literally.'

She wrote reviews, went to the theatre and worked with Schelling, but she remained nostalgic for the old Jena. 'What I miss, and Schelling too, is how every night the door would open and we would see a couple of familiar faces,' she said. And though a part of her longed for that past, nothing was more important than her present with the man she loved. The couple couldn't bear being parted. All her life Caroline had enjoyed the company of other people. She had organised parties and lively gatherings in her parlour – the more, the merrier. In Munich, though, their circle of friends was small, she told Luise, and she wouldn't have wanted it any other way. Caroline had Schelling, and he had her, and that was enough.

Schelling was happy, too. With no teaching obligations at the Academy of Sciences and Humanities, he could concentrate on his philosophical work. He became interested in religion and began exploring a synthesis of faith and science. He had time to write, was well paid and he was married to the woman he had adored and admired for so long. He loved everything about Caroline – her brilliant mind, energy, grace and the melody of her voice.

But then the unthinkable happened and everything stopped. In September 1809, only six years after their wedding and a few days after her forty-sixth birthday, Caroline suddenly died during a visit to Schelling's parents, who lived in a little village some one hundred and fifty miles from Munich. She had been unusually quiet one day and had come down with a fever, cramps and diarrhoea that evening. Doctors were called and administered their medicines. Schelling sat at her bedside but over the following days she rapidly declined. Caroline had contracted dysentery, the same disease that had taken Auguste.

On the morning of 7 September, Caroline fell asleep and never woke. Schelling collapsed beside her, holding her slender body. How could she still look so alive and graceful? 'I stood there in shock, crushed to the depths of my soul and unable even to grasp my grief,' he wrote to Luise Gotter two weeks later. How was he to survive? It was unbearable. 'All that remains for me is pain and sorrow, to be ended by nothing but death,' he cried. He buried her two days later and placed a large obelisk on her grave with the words: 'GOD gave Her to me / Death cannot take Her from me'.

Caroline had known that she was dying, Schelling told Luise, but she had been content during those last days. Hers was a life lived to the full. She had taken risks, made mistakes and also suffered great pain, but, unlike most women, she had lived *her* life – determined, confident and in control of her own destiny. She had also been part of something bigger than an individual life. Caroline had been the heart of the Jena Set. Muse, collaborator, writer and lover, she had been the conductor of their great symphony.

Still only thirty-four years old, Schelling spiralled into depression. Many feared he would lose his mind. Caroline had been everything to him. No one was like her, he cried, for she was in a category all by herself. 'This masterpiece of the minds' had gone forever, Schelling wrote shortly after her death. 'Oh, none like her will ever return!' He withdrew from friends and lived quietly. Only in solitude, Schelling explained, could he find solace. There were rumours that he still had the table laid for her when he ate, hanging her dressing gown over the chair so that he could pretend she was still with him.

Yet, even after her death, there was gossip. In early October 1809, less than a month after Caroline died, Hegel, who had seemingly never liked his old friend's wife, wrote to one of their former philosophy colleagues from Jena. He and his friends, Hegel said, had 'proposed the hypothesis that the devil had come and taken her'. Meanwhile, Charlotte Schiller told publisher Johann Friedrich Cotta that Caroline's death had finally freed Schelling, while Friedrich Schlegel pretended not to care. 'What effect does this news have on me? I have to think about it,' he told Dorothea; 'obviously she has been dead to me for a long time.'

A little less than three years later, in June 1812, Schelling emerged from the darkness and married twenty-five-year-old Pauline Gotter, the daughter of Caroline's oldest childhood friend Luise and the sister of Julie, who had spent several months in Jena after Auguste's death. They had six children and named their first-born daughter Caroline. Schelling never loved Pauline as passionately as he had Caroline but she created a peaceful home. He taught at the university in Munich and later in Berlin but published little up to his death, in 1854, just a few months short of his eightieth birthday. In the intervening years, as his work turned darker, moving into religious and mythical domains, Schelling had to cope with the bitter realisation that Hegel had become far more famous than him. He had been overshadowed by his old friend.

~

August Wilhelm Schlegel stayed with Madame de Staël from 1804 until her death, in 1817. He assisted with her book *Germany*. He advised, explained and above all steered her towards the works and ideas that he and his friends had developed in Jena. She paid him handsomely but demanded unwavering devotion. He had vowed to be loyal to the grave, and August Wilhelm was not a man to renege on his promises. 'I am proud to be your property,' he had written shortly after his arrival at her chateau Coppet in Switzerland; 'I hereby declare that you have every right over me, and I none over you.' They had never been lovers, but Madame de Staël wanted nothing less than total submission.

Life with Madame de Staël was turbulent. Though she demanded August Wilhelm Schlegel's loyalty, she herself tumbled from one love affair to the next. Two weeks before her forty-sixth birthday, she had another child, this time by a lover who was twenty-two years younger than her and only two years older than her eldest son. She was so unpredictable that August Wilhelm felt punished by what he described as her 'sudden crazed mood swings'. One minute she was charming and delightful, the next she would accuse August Wilhelm of being complicated, glum and generally intolerable. 'I bear wounds in my heart that will not heal – and you have inflicted one,' he retorted in a rare moment of courage. Another wound had been inflicted by Caroline, his best friend who had never truly loved him. 'My youth is gone, my life has been a waste, and here I am, alone, on the shadow side of existence,' he said in 1813.

Worse was to come. In 1818, the year after Madame de Staël's death, fifty-year-old August Wilhelm Schlegel married again. Half his age, his second wife, Sophie Paulus, was the daughter of an old colleague from Jena. Although no one knows exactly what happened, the marriage lasted less than two weeks. Sophie's parents apparently accused August Wilhelm of debauchery and impotence, and he in turn blamed Sophie's mother, Karoline Paulus, for refusing to let her daughter go. He never married again.

August Wilhelm Schlegel did what he did best – he threw himself into his work. 'After all, one can only try to leave behind a shining trace of one's dark life on this earth,' he had said. Still fascinated by languages, he took the baton from his brother Friedrich, who had long moved on from his Sanskrit studies, and began to study non-European cultures. Always a gifted linguist, August Wilhelm Schlegel was soon translating important Hindu works. He became the first professor of Indology at the University of Bonn, where he moved after Madame de Staël's death. Following the Romantic spirit of bringing together the sciences, art and poetry, his lectures in Bonn encompassed a wide range of subjects from art history to philology, ranging over vast geographical regions and long time periods.

August Wilhelm Schlegel remained one of Germany's foremost intellectuals and linguists. With age, though, he became more and more pompous. He had always been impeccably groomed and well dressed, but as he grew older his vanity increased too. Dressed in embroidered waistcoats and silk breeches tailored according to the latest Parisian fashion, he would appear in the auditorium heavily perfumed and wearing white leather gloves. A uniformed servant followed him everywhere, often standing next to the lectern, polishing the silver candlesticks that illuminated his lecture notes or filling a glass with sweetened water for him. The students were awestruck by his mind and erudition. He died in 1845 in Bonn, aged seventy-seven.

~

Dorothea was deeply unhappy in Cologne. Friedrich Schlegel continued to be unpredictable and unreliable, often disappearing for weeks or months at a time under the pretence of research. They were poor and jobless, and Dorothea was desperately lonely. Shortly after his thirteenth birthday, her son Philipp returned to his father in Berlin in 1806. As a Jewish divorcee who had converted to Protestantism, Dorothea found herself doubly ostracised in Catholic Cologne. She missed Jena. 'Yes, I do often think back with real longing,' she wrote to an old Jena friend. Dorothea's hair may have turned white with sadness, but nothing was ever Friedrich's fault. It didn't matter that he seemed perpetually to change his mind, nor that he was unable to earn any kind of income, nor indeed that he had grown fat and curmudgeonly. Friedrich Schlegel, some friends said, played with Dorothea 'like a bulldog with a little lapdog'.

Then after four years in Cologne, Friedrich and Dorothea converted to Catholicism in April 1808. Though surprising at first, the seeds of this step had been germinating for some time. Seven years earlier, in November 1799, during the inspiring four-day meeting in Jena, when the friends had met in Caroline's parlour to work together, they had talked about founding a new religion – a religion filled with feeling and imagination. Having failed to do so, Friedrich had then looked backwards to find spirituality in the medieval world of the Catholic Church. It was a step that also mirrored his increasingly conservative attitudes. Friedrich Schlegel discarded his youthful ideas and anyone associated with the Jena Set. Deeply religious, he now insisted that Fichte's philosophy was just 'idolising the *Ich* and the *self*'. Fichte, Friedrich wrote, had confused the self with the divine. Fichte, Schelling and Hegel were all entangled in 'dead abstractions'.

In a remarkable U-turn, Friedrich now even declared a dislike of Goethe, describing him as 'this old worn-out demigod'. Friedrich was offended that Goethe never mentioned him publicly. Hadn't it been the Schlegel brothers' praise in their many publications, reviews and essays that had made Goethe's work from the 1790s famous, Friedrich now asked? Never short of confidence, he believed it was he who had lifted Goethe to the literary Mount Olympus. 'The old man', Friedrich Schlegel wrote to a friend, 'is really starting to get on my nerves.'

After their conversion, the couple lived in Vienna – another Catholic city – where they moved eight times in the first two years, from one damp apartment to the next. Friedrich edited journals, including one decidedly anti-Napoleonic magazine, as well as lecturing on art, literature, history and philosophy. Dorothea supplemented his irregular income by translating historical texts, myths and novels from French into German, including one book by Madame de Staël. As before, Dorothea's work was published under Friedrich's name.

In 1809, with the help of his brother and the well-connected Madame de Staël, Friedrich eventually found employment as a court secretary in the Austrian civil service. He joined the Austrian diplomatic corps, which, given his personality, was never likely to be the most suitable career. By 1816 he had angered so many people that he was moved to a role at the state archives, but even there he created tension and two years later his employment was terminated. He continued to lecture and travel. As he grew older, the once handsome

Friedrich became hugely obese, and in 1829 he died suddenly of a stroke during a visit to Dresden, aged fifty-six. Dorothea received the news in Vienna three days after his funeral. She was shocked. They had been together for thirty years and, being almost eight years older, she had always assumed she would be the first to die.

He bequeathed her a mountain of debt and trunks full of unpublished notes and manuscripts. Dorothea moved to Frankfurt to be near her son Philipp and his family. She died ten years later, in her mid-seventies. Friedrich Schlegel's true intellectual accomplishments were only fully acknowledged when, more than a century later, a critical edition made his previously unpublished papers available, revealing him as one of the great thinkers of the first generation of Romantics.

~

After his return from South America in 1804, Alexander von Humboldt lived in Paris and Berlin. He became so famous that cab drivers didn't need an address to know where to take visitors, 'Chez Monsieur de Humboldt' would do. He wrote dozens of books – many of which became international bestsellers – and stayed in contact with most of the old Jena friends. He saw the Schlegel brothers, was Fichte's neighbour in Berlin for a while, and remained close to Goethe who described meeting Alexander as one of the 'brightest points in my life'.

Alexander von Humboldt also corresponded with Schelling. The *Naturphilosophie*, he wrote to Schelling a few months after his return from South America, was nothing less than 'revolutionary' and a rejection of the sciences as a 'dry piling up of facts'. Though Alexander von Humboldt never turned away from rational methods, he quietly opened the door to subjectivity.* Instruments, measurements, data and rigorous observation alone were not enough, he said, because 'what speaks to the soul, escapes our measurements'. He wrote books that wove together lively prose and rich descriptions of the landscape with scientific observation. So evocative was Humboldt's new nature writing that 'you believe you are riding the waves with him', the

---

* In *Cosmos*, Alexander von Humboldt also acknowledged his debt to Schelling, who had described nature as 'the sacred, eternally creative, originary power of the world, which brings forth all things'.

French Romantic writer François-René de Chateaubriand said, 'losing yourself with him in the depths of the woods'.

Alexander von Humboldt described Earth as an organism pulsating with life. 'Nature is a living whole,' he wrote in his international bestseller *Cosmos* in 1845, 'not a dead aggregate.' It was an interconnected whole where everything was entangled in 'a wonderful web of organic life' – a concept of nature that still shapes our thinking today. By the time he died, in 1859, a few months before his ninetieth birthday, he was the most famous scientist of his age. Thomas Jefferson pronounced Humboldt 'the most scientific man of his age', Ralph Waldo Emerson described him as 'one of those wonders of the world' and Charles Darwin said that Humboldt was the reason he boarded the *Beagle* to sail across the world. Humboldt was the 'Shakespeare of the Sciences'.

~

Wilhelm von Humboldt founded Berlin's first university which today is named after him and his brother. As the new Prussian education minister, Wilhelm set out to reform the nation's education system. Instead of the technical and vocational training which turned the sons of carpenters into carpenters, he wanted to turn 'children into people'. Learning, Wilhelm von Humboldt insisted, was less about subject matter than it was about instilling the ability to think. Higher education, he explained, was a process of self-emancipation. Shaped by his time in Jena and by the concept of a self-determined Ich, he insisted that education should enable students to think independently and creatively. He advocated a holistic approach, combining teaching and research as well as the arts and the sciences. Today, his model is followed by universities worldwide.

In later years Wilhelm von Humboldt worked as a Prussian diplomat in Vienna and London before moving back to Tegel, the family estate just outside Berlin, in 1819. In retirement, he found time for his language studies, further developing Herder's and Fichte's ideas about the connection between language and nationhood. He studied Sanskrit, Chinese and Japanese as well as Polynesian and Malay, looking at languages through their wider cultural, geographic and demographic contexts. 'Every language contains its own world view,' he explained, asserting that 'in this sense each nation is a mental whole, a particular form of humanity characterised by a specific language.'

Caroline von Humboldt remained at her husband's side. Wherever they lived, she opened their doors to artists, poets, thinkers and writers. She wrote about art, supported artists and continued to have affairs. Wilhelm von Humboldt's love for her never wavered. 'I implore you once again, enjoy it, however you want, and don't let anything limit you,' he told her. No one else, friends commented, lived in a relationship that 'gives and takes such complete freedom'.

Then, at the end of 1828, Caroline became so ill that her doctors gave up all hope. Watching his beloved wife decline, Wilhelm couldn't bear the thought that he was going to survive her. Their love was the foundation of his existence, Wilhelm wrote to Goethe in February 1829. What was he to do without her? 'Love is the purpose of our life,' she wrote in one of her last letters, 'and robs Death of its bitterness.' A month after her sixty-third birthday, Caroline died in Tegel in the early morning of 26 March 1829. They had been married for almost forty years. Wilhelm von Humboldt followed her six lonely years later, at the age of sixty-seven, having fallen ill after visiting her grave one cold wet day in spring 1835.

～

After witnessing the Battle of Jena and the long shadow it cast over the small town on the banks of the Saale, Hegel left for Bamberg, where he worked as a newspaper editor and where his *Phenomenology of Spirit* was published. The book was Hegel's reckoning with Schelling's philosophy and his overexcited, zealous disciples. Schelling's approach, Hegel wrote, lacked logic and intellectual rigour. Instead of imagination, Hegel demanded scientific methods. 'Today people try to replace slow hard work with ingenuity,' he complained, but philosophy wasn't meant to be fun. It was 'serious business'. The celebration of the artist and genius as the harbinger of knowledge was nonsense, Hegel wrote, and Schelling's elevation of art was simply wrong. It was time to rid philosophy of enthusiasm, imagination and feeling: Hegel wanted to put science and logic back into the discourse. With the *Phenomenology of Spirit*, a contemporary writer observed, Hegel freed himself from Schelling.

Today one of the most famous philosophical texts, *Phenomenology of Spirit* was largely ignored when it was published in spring 1807. As usual, nothing happened quickly in Hegel's life, and the first review took two years to appear. But fame did come eventually. In

1818, more than a decade after his departure from Jena, Hegel accepted Fichte's vacant chair in philosophy in Berlin, and later became the university's rector.

By the time Hegel died, aged sixty-one, in 1831, he had long overtaken Schelling. He had become so worshipped that his followers were known as 'Hegelians'. Unsurprisingly, Schelling was not happy to have been relegated to the sidelines. 'If it weren't for me there would be no Hegel and no Hegelians,' he grumbled, but no one listened. Today, Hegel is regarded as one of the most important thinkers in Western philosophy.

~

After Novalis's death, in 1801, at the age of twenty-eight, Friedrich Schlegel and Ludwig Tieck edited and published his work. They chopped, reordered and shortened his fragments, suppressed his political essays and ignored his scientific work. In doing so they disconnected the poet from his practical, scientific and theoretical interests. Had they included that material, Friedrich Schlegel told Tieck in 1801, it would have been 'misleading as to the character of the author'.

They shaped his legacy by creating a myth, and in due course the young poet posthumously became the figurehead of the young Romantics. Friedrich Schlegel and Ludwig Tieck turned Novalis's love for Sophie, her death, and *Hymns to the Night* into the kernel of that myth. Sophie became an 'otherworldly creature' – too ethereal for this world – and Novalis, her poet. And so the young man who had worked in the mines, and who had filled his diary with descriptions of his sexual urges, was transformed into something akin to a patron saint of the Romantics. After his death, his poems and fragments were read like 'meaningful oracles' and he became a Christlike figure for the movement. Novalis continued to have an intangible presence in their lives, old friends and acquaintances said, like a melody that always accompanied them.

Unlike the others, Novalis hadn't lived long enough to see Napoleon crowned emperor, nor to see France's descent into reactionary politics. Where Friedrich Schlegel, Schelling and Fichte became religious, conservative and nationalistic, Novalis would forever remain the young inspired poet they had known during their Jena years. As the others grew older, it was Novalis – frozen in time and youth – who became the embodiment of the 'First Romantic'. This image appealed to poets, artists and readers across the world: the forlorn lover who experienced the 'sacred power of pain', the mythical poet who celebrated darkness. Even Novalis's appearance – his delicate features, his deep eyes, his long hair – was part of the myth. He had been a genius who experienced 'even everyday life as a marvellous fairy-tale', Ludwig Tieck wrote in his introduction to Novalis's work.

~

Ironically, the unsung hero of the Jena Set was Friedrich Schiller – the man who had brought everyone to the small town in the Duchy of Saxe-Weimar. He had been the reason why Goethe had spent many weeks and often months each year away from Weimar, and why Novalis had studied in Jena as an eighteen-year-old. Schiller, Novalis said, was the 'idol of the most sacred moments of my boyhood years'. Even before they had all lived in Jena, Schiller had united the friends on the pages of his journal *Horen* – Fichte, the Humboldt brothers, Goethe and August Wilhelm Schlegel. Though he rarely left his house, the playwright had been a magnet for the younger generation.

It was Schiller who had invited August Wilhelm Schlegel to Jena, and paid him generously for his contributions to *Horen*. Had August Wilhelm not moved, neither Caroline nor Friedrich Schlegel nor Dorothea would have followed. Schiller had also been instrumental in bringing Schelling to the town. Astute and keenly aware of the latest philosophical ideas, Schiller had encouraged Goethe to find a position for the young philosopher at the university. Schiller may not have joined the others in Caroline's salon, but he had made their 'Alliance of Minds' possible.

Although the Schlegels turned against Schiller and ignored his literary contributions in their later lectures and publications, his 1795 *Letters on the Aesthetic Education of Man* in *Horen* had inspired them. His celebration of imagination and the elevation of art as the force unifying reason and feeling were at the core of their beliefs. Schiller was closer in age to August Wilhelm Schlegel, Caroline and Fichte than he was to Goethe, yet it sometimes felt as if he was much older than the impetuous group at Leutragasse. Schiller himself summed up the situation when he told Fichte that history might judge them as allies although in reality they had shared few beliefs. 'We lived in the same age, and posterity will turn us from contemporaries into neighbours,' Schiller said, 'although we actually had so little in common.'

~

Johann Wolfgang von Goethe never moved away from the small Duchy of Saxe-Weimar. He remained Duke Carl August's privy councillor, but he disliked the new and decidedly emotional nationalism that emerged after the Battle of Jena. Having been part of the Weimar administration for thirty years, Goethe was a *realpolitiker*. During his lifetime he had seen how alliances had shifted during wars – whether the Seven Years War of 1756–63 or the French Revolutionary Wars. Today's allies easily became tomorrow's enemies. Cooperation rather than resistance had always been his motto. As a child, when the French had occupied his family's house in Frankfurt, Goethe had reacted by learning French. What was the point in fighting against the French? For the sake of peace and order, he accepted Napoleon's power, and even called him 'my Emperor'.

Goethe met Napoleon two years after the Battle of Jena, in Erfurt, not far from Weimar, where the French Emperor invited the rulers of the Confederation of the Rhine and their courtiers to consolidate the alliance. Napoleon had specifically asked to meet Germany's most famous poet, and the two men talked for an hour about the theatre and *The Sorrows of Young Werther*. Napoleon also awarded Goethe the Legion of Honour, which he wore proudly.

In the end, Napoleon's onward rush through Europe was stalled. In 1812 he lost almost half a million troops in Russia and in the following year a coalition of Austrian, Russian, Swedish and Prussian armies decisively defeated the French at the Battle of Leipzig. Napoleon was exiled to Elba, a small island in the Mediterranean. Within a year, though, he had escaped back to Paris, assembling another army of two hundred thousand men. This was a last, desperate attempt to bring Europe back under his control. A few weeks later, in June 1815, Napoleon was beaten by the British and the Prussians at the Battle of Waterloo. Goethe was exhausted just trying to follow the events in the papers, but his fascination remained. 'He strode through life like a demigod,' Goethe said, years after Napoleon had died in exile on the remote island of St Helena.

Goethe continued to write and experiment for the rest of his life. In spring 1808, aged fifty-eight, he finally published the first part of

Faust. Schelling hailed the play as the essence of the age, Samuel Taylor Coleridge was so enraptured that he began to translate it into English, and Madame de Staël dedicated a long chapter in *Germany* to it, writing, 'Faust astonishes, moves, and melts us.'

In June 1816, Christiane died after a long illness at the age of fifty-one. As with Schiller, Goethe refused to engage with his wife's death. He didn't talk about it and he didn't attend her funeral. It was as if he believed that, by ignoring it, it would go away. They had been together for twenty-eight years. 'Emptiness and deathly silence, within me and without,' he wrote in his diary. Goethe turned inwards and worked.

Feeling increasingly removed from the world, he too missed the lively exchanges he had had with the friends of the Jena Set. Unlike in Paris, Goethe complained, where French thinkers congregated in one great city, in Germany everybody lived apart. With one person in Berlin, the next in Munich and yet another in Bonn, the exchange of ideas was stifled by distance. How different life would be, Goethe thought after his old friend Alexander von Humboldt visited him at the end of 1826, if they could all live close together again.

As he grew older, Goethe began to look back on his life. He started (but never finished) an autobiography, pulling together materials from his past – recollections, letters and other manuscripts. 'I seem more and more historical, even to myself,' he wrote to Wilhelm von Humboldt. He also edited and published an eagerly awaited volume of his correspondence with Schiller. When August Wilhelm Schlegel read these letters, he was shocked to discover how viciously Schiller had talked about him. That Schiller had disliked them, he had known, but not that his 'implacable hatred' had been so bitter, August Wilhelm wrote to Ludwig Tieck.

Goethe died in March 1832 at the age of eighty-two. A month earlier, he had told a young scholar: 'I took in and used whatever came before my eyes, my ears, my senses. Thousands of individuals contributed to the creation of my works – wise people and fools, intellectuals and idiots, children, men in their prime, and old people . . . I often reaped what others had sown. My life's work is that of a collective.'

Part II: Influence

The first book to spread the Jena Set's ideas across Europe was pulped before it could be distributed. When Madame de Staël's *Germany* was published in Paris in 1810, Napoleon ordered the destruction of the entire first edition of 10,000 copies, including the original printing plates. Reading Madame de Staël's description of Germany as a nation of poets and thinkers, Napoleon was outraged. How could ideas and works originating in Germany be superior to the finest French philosophers and literature? Germany would never soar over France, either politically or economically, and certainly not intellectually.

Madame de Staël disagreed. The French might be witty but they were also frivolous, materialistic and superficial. Germans, by contrast, were deep thinkers, profound and serious. 'A Frenchman can speak, even without ideas,' she observed, but 'a German has always more in his head than he is able to express.' While France's intellectual ambitions had stagnated after the Revolution, Madame de Staël explained, Germans had discovered the power of a free self. Fine conversations and elegant fashion might make for entertaining dinner parties, but they were also the breeding grounds for shallow people who only cared what others thought of them. This had resulted in a general conformity in France, whereas the Germans had discovered the power of individuality.

Even during the Revolution, Madame de Staël wrote in *Germany*, the French had simply followed the general will. As the people had risen up, others had blindly marched along. 'The French are all-powerful only *en masse*', while the Germans celebrated a self-determined Ich and free-thinking. France should learn from Germany, 'the native land of thought', she told readers. Napoleon was not pleased. France had been at war with the German states for almost two decades, his minister of police told Madame de Staël, so why would she write a book that praised the Germans above all other nations?

As punishment, Napoleon issued an order confining her to a five-mile radius of chateau Coppet, on Lake Geneva, effectively putting her under house arrest. But Madame de Staël was not intimidated. She had no intention of being imprisoned, nor of allowing her work to be suppressed. With all copies of *Germany* destroyed by

Napoleon's censors, she smuggled the original proofs out of Coppet and escaped with the help of August Wilhelm Schlegel. They then spent months wandering through Europe and Russia before the three volumes were finally published in English in London in October 1813.*

The first edition sold out within three days and *Germany* became an international bestseller. Ranging from German manners to literature, art and philosophy, Madame de Staël wrote about particular works such as Goethe's *Faust* and Schiller's various plays, about poetry and novels, but also about individual writers and thinkers. Given August Wilhelm Schlegel's presence in her life, the 'new philosophy' of the Jena Set was unsurprisingly her particular interest. 'With the torch of genius', she wrote, they 'penetrate into the interior of the soul'. Madame de Staël's *Germany* defined and promoted Romanticism across the world and introduced an international readership to the ideas of the Jena Set.

In Jena, Madame de Staël wrote, 'there seemed to be collected together all the astonishing lights of the human understanding.' August Wilhelm's influence was all over the pages, so much so that Goethe called it 'the Staël-Schlegel book'. The term '*romantique*', one newspaper reported, 'is a word that, since Schlegel and Madame de Staël, everyone in France is pronouncing'. The term that the friends had first used in the *Athenaeum* back in 1798 had gone mainstream.

~

The Jena Set's ideas rippled out from the small town in the Duchy of Saxe-Weimar to the wider world. Their emphasis on individual experience, their description of nature as a living organism, their rejection of rigorous rules in poetry, and their insistence that art was the unifying bond between mind and the external world became popular themes in the works of artists, writers, poets and musicians across Europe and the United States. And at the core of Romanticism was their concept of the unity of humankind and nature.

The Ich was identical with nature, Schelling had said, which meant that being in nature – be it in a forest or on a mountain, walking

---

* Madame de Staël's *Germany* was printed and distributed by John Murray, in London, who also published Lord Byron, Goethe, Coleridge and later Alexander von Humboldt's books.

along a path or looking at the sky – was always a journey into oneself. The sentiment appealed to poets and artists everywhere. The German painter Caspar David Friedrich, for one, translated the new ideas onto canvases. His lonely figures, which were often self-portraits, are depicted in vast, deserted landscapes, contemplating nature. 'The painter should not only paint what he sees,' Friedrich said, 'but also what he sees within him.' Inspired by the Jena Set's writings, the artist explored the relationship between the self and the external world.

The founders of the Romantic movement in England, William Wordsworth and Samuel Taylor Coleridge, had a similar approach. They were 'walking poets' who not only needed to be in nature but also wrote outdoors. There they found their voices and them-selves. Wordsworth's famous poem 'Tintern Abbey', for example, stands in sharp contrast to the detached descriptions of nature that had been so typical of earlier eighteenth-century poetry. It shows Wordsworth's own emotional response to nature:

> . . . *well pleased to recognise*
> *In nature and the language of the sense*
> *The anchor of my purest thoughts, the nurse,*
> *The guide, the guardian of my heart, and soul*
> *Of all my moral being.*

That Schelling's impact on Coleridge's thinking was profound is graphically illustrated by the changes he made to 'The Eolian Harp', a poem he had written back in 1795. Twenty-two years later, after plunging deep into the *Naturphilosophie*, Coleridge republished the poem in 1817, adding these new lines to the second verse:

> *O! the one Life within us and abroad,*
> *Which meets all motion and becomes its soul,*
> *A light in sound, a sound-like power in light,*
> *Rhythm in all thought . . .*

This was Schelling's *Naturphilosophie* writ in verse.

Coleridge was deeply influenced by the ideas that had emerged from the small town on the Saale. Though he never made it to Jena to meet his heroes, he did learn German and read their works. In 1814, when caught in the vortex of his opium addiction, he explained that he held tight to their ideas like ivy twisted round an oak tree for support. For him, Schelling was 'a great and original genius' who unlocked a new way of thinking about poetry. Coleridge was a 'Schellingianer', his friend Henry Crabb Robinson observed, who 'metaphysicised *à la* Schelling'.

Following Schelling's lead, Coleridge wrote about the unity between the internal and the external world, and declared art to be the 'mediatress between, and reconciler of, nature and man'. So obsessed was Coleridge that he inserted whole pages and long passages by Schelling in his work. Sentence by sentence, paragraph by paragraph, Coleridge translated Schelling's words and passed them on as his own. When his literary autobiography *Biographia Literaria* was published, his friend and fellow writer Thomas de Quincey accused him of 'bare-faced plagiarism', claiming that 'the entire essay from the first word to the last is a verbatim translation from Schelling'.

Though this was a bit of an exaggeration, there was some truth in it. Famed for his addiction memoir *Confessions of an English Opium Eater*, De Quincey was able to recognise the borrowing as he too had devoured the works of the Jena Set. Their books were like an inexhaustible 'El Dorado', he said, and 'my library was rich with the wickedest of German speculations'. The vitality of youth and an instinct for truth jumped off the pages, he wrote.

As the Jena Set's fame spread, their works were read by the next generation of Romantics. The English poet Lord Byron met August Wilhelm Schlegel in 1816, in the company of Madame de Staël, in Switzerland, and found him in 'high force'. That same summer the young writer Mary Shelley wrote her famous novel *Frankenstein* in the company of Lord Byron in a villa just across Lake Geneva, opposite Madame de Staël's chateau Coppet. The novel had been influenced by ideas that had occupied the friends during the late 1790s, such as the electrical experiments that Alexander von Humboldt and Johann Wilhelm Ritter had conducted. In *Frankenstein*, Victor Frankenstein creates a monster from body parts and then animates the lifeless matter with a galvanic electrical spark. Ritter and Humboldt were most likely the 'physiological writers of Germany' mentioned in the very first sentence of *Frankenstein*'s preface.

Two years later, in March 1818, Mary Shelley was once again travelling from England to the Continent to meet Lord Byron. Shortly after landing in Calais, her husband, the Romantic poet Percy Bysshe Shelley, opened a copy of the English edition of August

Wilhelm Schlegel's popular *Lectures on Dramatic Art and Literature*. For six long days, as they rattled along the bumpy roads from Reims to Lyons, Shelley read the book aloud to Mary and the other passengers. Romantic poetry, August Wilhelm Schlegel argued in his book, was 'the expression of the secret attraction to a chaos . . . which is perpetually striving after new and wonderful births'. The sentiment appealed to all of them.

～

When the Jena Set's ideas grew popular in the United States, studying and learning German became the rage. Reading lists included Goethe, Kant, Fichte, Schelling and later Novalis and Alexander von Humboldt – these 'deep mighty thinkers', as the Transcendentalists called them. This group of American writers and thinkers, who gathered in the small Massachusetts town of Concord in the 1830s and 1840s, would go on to define Americans' relationship with nature. They bought the Jena Set's books or borrowed them from the libraries in nearby Boston and Harvard, as well as writing and reading reviews, essays and translations in American magazines.

If they couldn't read German writers in the original, Americans learned about their work by way of Madame de Staël's English edition of *Germany* and Coleridge's theoretical writings, in particular his *Biographia Literaria*. There were other sources too. The Scotsman Thomas Carlyle, for example, popularised their work in Britain and the United States with his widely read essays, reviews and translations in *Foreign Review* and other journals. As a result the Transcendentalists were inspired by Schelling's unity of mind and matter, by Alexander von Humboldt's concept of nature as a living organism, and by Novalis's evocation of awe and wonder in nature – themes that both informed their own writing and would make them famous.

Among those thinkers was one of America's most beloved nature writers, Henry David Thoreau, a man who spent his life walking, observing and investigating what he called the 'mysterious relation between myself and these things'. Born in 1817, Thoreau had been a shy boy who preferred the company of animals to that of other children. Aged sixteen he had enrolled at Harvard where he studied Greek, Latin and German as well as maths, history and philosophy, but he spent as much time as possible outdoors. Some thought him cantankerous, while others described him as 'somewhat rustic' – and with ill-fitting clothes, straggly beard and ruddy complexion, his appearance matched his character.

He was certainly more at ease with nature and words than with people. Squirrels ran towards him, birds perched on his shoulders, mice ran along his arms and snakes coiled around his legs. He filled his journal with observations about the songs of birds, the chirping of crickets, the scarlet dye of autumn leaves and the first delicate blooms of the year, and there was a visceral sense of his synchrony with nature and the changing seasons. At one with nature, he felt the unity the Jena Set had described.

In the mid-1840s Thoreau spent two years in a cabin at Walden Pond, to live simply, as he put it, and face the essential facts of life. When he returned to Concord he sat down to capture the experience in a book, but struggled to align his passion for detailed observations of nature with his love of poetry. 'With all your science can you tell how it is', he asked despairingly, 'that light comes into the soul?' Then Thoreau read Alexander von Humboldt's books and everything changed. Nature, Humboldt explained, should be described with scientific accuracy but without being 'deprived thereby of the vivifying breath of imagination'. Humboldt poeticised the sciences and showed Thoreau how to weave together the empirical and the wonderful, the particular and the whole. His books provided an answer to Thoreau's difficulties in finding a balance between meticulous scientific enquiry and poetry. After studying Humboldt's books, Thoreau began to 'look at Nature with new eyes' and completely rewrote his manuscript for *Walden*.

Thoreau's friend and mentor Ralph Waldo Emerson was even more immersed in the Jena Set's writings. Emerson's elder brother had impelled him to 'learn German as fast as you can', and eventually his library was packed with books by Goethe, Schiller, Novalis, Alexander von Humboldt, Fichte and the Schlegel brothers as well as the collected works of Schelling. 'Some minds think about things; others think the things themselves,' Emerson wrote about Schelling, scribbling the sentence under the heading 'Genius' in his notebook. Just like the Jena Set, he celebrated the power of the self-reliant individual.

In January 1836, with the snow piling up high in what was the coldest winter on record in New England, Emerson wrote *Nature*, the Transcendentalists' manifesto on the relationship between nature and the mind. Only a few weeks previously, he had read one of the chapters in Coleridge's *Biographia Literaria* which so generously borrowed from Schelling. It's perhaps not surprising therefore that *Nature* introduced the idea of oneness, of the unity of the self and nature, to many Americans. Each leaf, crystal or animal was part of the whole, Emerson explained, 'each particle is a microcosm, and faithfully renders the likeness of the world'. We *are* nature, Emerson wrote, because 'the mind is a part of the nature of things'.* Or as Thoreau put it: 'Am I not partly leaves and vegetable mould myself?'

The poet Walt Whitman was another American writer who breathed the ideas that were coming out of Jena. Though he had left school at the age of eleven, Whitman was a ravenous reader and autodidact. Before he published his famous poetry collection, *Leaves of Grass*, in 1855, he had worked as clerk, printer, teacher and journalist. Never hurried, he deliberated and admitted to having 'an unusual capacity for standing still'. He thought, procrastinated and followed the path of the 'illustrious four' – Kant, Fichte, Schelling and Hegel – 'from a poet's point of view'.

Whitman too felt at one with nature, and especially when naked. 'Never before did I get so close to Nature; never before did she come so close to me,' he wrote as an old man, after a long hot summer of nude swimming and sunbathing. This 'theory that the human mind and external nature are essentially one', Whitman jotted in his notebook in the mid-nineteenth century, was 'beautiful and majestic'. *Leaves of Grass*, he said, was a poetic distillation of what he called the 'great System of Idealistic Philosophy in Germany'. His poem 'Song of Myself', for example, was about the relationship between humankind, the self and nature. It begins:

> *I celebrate myself,*
> *And what I assume you shall assume,*
> *For every atom belonging to me as good belongs to you.*

When he first published *Leaves of Grass*, Whitman didn't include his name on the title page. Instead, he placed a portrait of himself as frontispiece. The engraving shows a handsome young man wearing a plain shirt and crumpled work trousers – right hand on hip, left

---

* Emerson's nature was also God. 'The currents of the Universal Being circulate through me,' he wrote in *Nature*, 'I am part or parcel of God.'

in his trouser pockets, head cocked. It was only on page 29 that a line revealed the name of the author: 'Walt Whitman, an American, one of the roughs, a kosmos'* – perhaps a nod to Alexander von Humboldt's *Cosmos* which the poet kept on his desk as he composed.

The Jena Set's writings permeated the North American literary world. Besides Whitman, Thoreau and Emerson, numerous other nineteenth-century writers read their works, among them Nathaniel Hawthorne, Edgar Allan Poe and Herman Melville. Melville, for example, gleaned much of his knowledge from Coleridge's *Biographia Literaria* but he also recounted whisky-filled late-night discussions with German scholars about Hegel, Friedrich Schlegel, Kant and the concept of 'Free-Will' during an ocean crossing in 1849.

The Americans' admiration went so far that Edgar Allan Poe even accused Nathaniel Hawthorne of copying so much of Ludwig Tieck's work that 'he is not original in any sense'. This was a sin Poe may have recognised, for he had himself lifted several pages from August Wilhelm Schlegel's *Lectures on Dramatic Art and Literature* and published them under his own name.

～

International students who had attended the university in Jena also spread the Romantic gospel. One was Henry Crabb Robinson, the English student who had taught Madame de Staël about Schelling's philosophy during her stay in Weimar at the beginning of 1804. Enthralled by his time in Jena, Crabb Robinson said: 'I have seen too a galaxy of literary talents & genius, which future ages will honour as the poetical ornaments of the 18th Century.' Or the Norwegian Henrik Steffens, one of Schelling's most devoted students and an admirer who described Caroline as this 'first-rate and highly intelligent woman'. Steffens introduced Scandinavia to Schelling's *Naturphilosophie* when he began to lecture and publish in Copenhagen.

The Jena Set's ideas emerged in Italy, France, Russia, Spain and Poland. The Polish pianist and writer Maurycy Mochnacki was profoundly influenced by August Wilhelm Schlegel and Schelling,

---

* 'Kosmos' is the only word that didn't change in the various versions of Whitman's famous self-identification in the different editions of *Leaves of Grass*. It began as 'Walt Whitman, an American, one of the roughs, a kosmos' in 1855 and became 'Walt Whitman, a kosmos, of Manhattan the son' in the last edition in 1892.

for example, and became one of the founders of Polish Romanticism. 'If we cannot be original,' he wrote, 'then we better imitate the great Romantic poetry of the Germans and decisively reject French models.' They were all suffering from 'Germanomania', Adam Mickiewicz, one of Poland's leading poets, said.

Similarly, at the University of Uppsala a group of young Swedish Romantics established an association inspired by the Jena Set.* And after meeting Schelling in Munich in the late 1820s, the Russian Romantic poet Fyodor Tyutchev wrote poems that incorporated the *Naturphilosophie* concept of the unity of mind and matter. 'All is in me – I in all!' Tyutchev wrote in one poem in the early 1830s, and 'Seek out that world within your soul' in another.

Later in the nineteenth century and the early twentieth, in Vienna, Sigmund Freud referred back to the Jena Set's works. Freud's library contained many of their books, and he counted Goethe, Schiller and Schelling among his few great influences. The Jena Set's ideas on the centrality of self-consciousness helped to pave the way for modern psychology and psychoanalysis. In 1930, Freud even talked about 'Goethe's connection to psychoanalysis' and ventured that the poet might have liked it. Hadn't Goethe said, 'Look within yourselves and you will find everything'? There are numerous parallels between Freud's theories and the ideas that came out of Jena, including the unity of self and nature, the concept of the unconscious self, and the importance of imagination.

Perhaps more than any other modern writer, the Irish novelist James Joyce took some of the Jena Set's ideas to their logical conclusion – in particular, their definition of Romantic poetry as inherently incomplete. Like so many others in the English-speaking world, Joyce had read about the Jena Set's works in Coleridge's *Biographia Literaria*, although he might also have studied other translations and critical essays.

Romantic poetry was forever evolving, Friedrich Schlegel had written in the *Athenaeum*, 'it should forever be becoming, never perfected'. Like Friedrich Schlegel's *Lucinde*, Joyce's novel *Finnegans Wake* has a fragmentary structure and dissolved chronology and timelines. In it, Joyce fused poetry and prose, transcending genres.

---

* One of them was the Swedish poet Per Atterbom, who had met Schelling and Fichte in Dresden. He became Schelling's friend.

Finnegans Wake was 'Schlegelian', one critic wrote, because there was no obvious order to what happened, why, when, where and to whom. This was the unruliness and anarchy in the arts that the Jena Set had demanded – the 'chaos . . . from which a world can spring'. A novel should defy all classifications, Friedrich Schlegel had written, and include everything from fairy tales and dreams to fragments, letters, songs and confessions. 'The essence of a novel is its chaotic structure,' he had said. Even Joyce, the most modern of the Modernists, was grounded in the ideas that had evolved in Jena.

Part III: The Art of Being Selfish

The Jena Set changed our world. They did so irrevocably. It is impossible to imagine our lives, thoughts and way of understanding the world without the foundation of their ground-breaking ideas.

'Perhaps Jena was the last truly vital occurrence of its type for centuries to come?' Schiller wrote to Wilhelm von Humboldt in 1803. He had a point. We might have forgotten this small town in the Duchy of Saxe-Weimar, and its short intellectual reign, but the friends did something utterly new when they boldly placed the self and free will centre stage. Their ideas are ingrained in us. Fichte put the Ich at the nexus of his philosophy, and it has stayed there ever since.

This revolution of the mind shifted not just our perspective of who we are and what we can do but also our place in the world. We have internalised Fichte's Ich, though we may not have heard of the man himself. We believe we are self-determined – at least, those of us lucky enough to live in democratic states. Yet this freedom brings with it both responsibilities and dangers. The friends in Jena struggled with that, just as we do today.

From the moment this seismic shift rippled out of Jena, people have had to deal with the perils of this new emboldened self. But while some of the Jena Set's critics described Fichte's philosophy as 'Ich-fetishism' and as 'metaphysical egotism', Fichte never intended his ideas to be a narcissistic celebration of the self. Instead, he always insisted that our freedom was tightly interwoven with our moral obligations. 'Only those are *free*', he told students during his first lecture series, in 1794, 'who will try to make everyone around them free.' Freedom gives us the choice as to how to act and behave, and elevates us above base instincts such as greed, hunger or fear. Freedom always brings along its twin: moral duty.

The choice remains with us. Life is a negotiation between our rights as an individual and our role as a member of a community, including our responsibilities towards future generations who will inhabit this planet. How can we live a meaningful life in which we determine the direction of our path while also being a morally good person? How do we reconcile personal liberty with the demands of society? Are we selfish? Are we pursuing our dreams? Are we treading on someone else's liberty? Are we looking only after ourselves? Or others? Or both? We have entered a social contract with each other and with our governments, agreeing to abide by laws and conventions – yet this only works if we are free and trust one another at the same time.

The Jena Set believed that we have to be conscious of our selves – to be 'selfish' in the sense of being aware of and in control of our own being and free will. Today, when we talk about selfishness, we mean a person obsessed with their own pleasure and profit, concerned only with their own advantage. But seen in its historical context and original conception, the 'Art of being Selfish' liberated the Ich with the intention of creating a better society: a society that was founded on individuals who were no longer chained by monarchs and rulers to a predestined place and path but who were in control of their own destiny and identity.

The 'Art of being Selfish', in the context of Schelling's *Naturphilosophie*, also means understanding one's place in this great interconnected living organism that is nature. 'Since we find nature in the self,' one of Schelling's students concluded, 'we must also find the self in nature.' Being selfish in that sense means comprehending and recognising the concept of unity with the universe. Not harming the planet therefore means not harming yourself. The 'age of Introversion', Ralph Waldo Emerson said in 1837, referring to the new focus of the Ich, was easily criticised, but it was 'a very good one, if we but know what to do with it'.

'The most wonderful phenomenon, the eternal fact, is *our own existence*,' Novalis wrote in 1797. Life's most important task was to grasp the self because 'without perfect self-understanding we will never learn truly to understand others'. Let Novalis's sentence roll in your mind for a moment. What he meant was that we are morally obliged to turn inwards in order to be good members of society. Only if we are fully aware of ourselves – of our needs, our wishes, and of our thoughts – can we truly embrace the other. This emphasis on the Ich means being 'self aware' as the prerequisite for 'being aware and concerned for the other'. Only through self-awareness can we feel empathy with others. Only through self-reflection can we question our behaviour towards others. Self-examination in that sense is for the greater good – for us, for our wider community, for society in general and for our planet.

The Jena Set gave wings to our minds. How we use them is entirely up to us.

Acknowledgements

A LARGE PART OF this book was written during the pandemic, but luckily I had done most of my research before everything shut down. Over the past twenty years the Internet has made research so much easier. Many original letters, manuscripts and illustrations are now available online (and are actually easier to read since you can zoom in); likewise, a great number of eighteenth- and nineteenth-century books. I don't know what I would have done without the vast collection of scanned books on the Internet Archive website and many of the German digital libraries, such as the one at the Sächsische Landesbibliothek – Staats- und Universitätsbibliothek Dresden (SLUB Dresden), the Münchener Digitalisierungs Zentrum and the works by German writers at Zeno.org, among many others. During the pandemic the wonderful team at the London Library dispatched much-needed books and emergency scans of letters – I have always loved the London Library, but now even more.

But I missed the people who I normally meet in archives and libraries. In that sense writing *Magnificent Rebels* was the opposite of *Invention of Nature*, for which I travelled the world, encountering the most wonderful people. Somehow, as if the subject of the book determined the way I researched, I travelled inside rather than outside. So, in a way, this has been a lonely book to write. When the real world became too dark and depressing, I entered late eighteenth-century Jena. When libraries closed, I opened the books my protagonists had read and written, and when restaurants and bars shut their doors, I met the Jena Set in their parlours and around their dining table. In this sense, the making of *Magnificent Rebels* has been unlike anything I have ever written, but this doesn't mean it was done without help. There are always wonderful, clever and generous people – old friends and kind strangers alike. My deepest thanks go out to all of them – for reading, for listening, for sharing their research and knowledge, for their time and recommendations, and for sending books, chapters and scans. You all brought the wider world to my little cottage in the middle of nowhere. You have been my saviours.

Thank you (in alphabetical order) to Jerry Brotton, Jennifer Croft, Tom Holland, Leo Hollis, Jeanette Lamble at the Staatsbibliothek zu Berlin, Vicki Müller-Lüneschloß at the Schelling Edition and Archive at the Bayerische Akademie der Wissenschaften, Ulrich Päßler, Ingo Schwarz and Wiebke Witzel at the Berlin-Brandenburgischen Akademie der Wissenschaften, Günther Queisser at the Museum 1806 in Jena, Regan Ralph, Kerstin Schellbach at SLUB Dresden, Robert Rowland Smith, Doug Stott at www.carolineschelling.com (whose references, editorial notes and accompanying contemporary illustrations were an invaluable resource at a time when archives and libraries were closed), and James Vigus at Queen Mary, University of London. And thanks to everybody at the Santa Fe Institute for creating such an inspiring place and for awarding me the generous Miller Scholarship: in particular to David Krakauer, Tim Taylor and Caroline Seigel, librarian extraordinaire who dug up the most obscure German publications from the inter-library loan system and sent scans, ebooks and articles across the Atlantic during the pandemic.

A big fat thank you to Paul Hamilton at Queen Mary, University of London, who answered the email of a complete stranger and then agreed to read an early draft of the entire manuscript, sending sage comments and queries – thank you for being so generous with your time and knowledge. Similarly, to Robert J. Richards at the University of Chicago, who wrote a book that helped me to understand the world of Schelling's *Naturphilosophie* more than any other – thank you for writing *The Romantic Conception of Life* and for reading and commenting on earlier draft chapters. A huge thank you to Damion Searls for insightful, beautiful and pitch-perfect translations of hundreds of German quotations and numerous poems. And after months of circular discussions brilliant Kirsty Lang finally came up with the greatest of titles – thank you for rescuing me. Special thanks go to Heidrun Gebhart at C. Bertelsmann, who helped me to come up with the idea for this book by asking the right questions when I didn't know how ever to find a new subject after Alexander von Humboldt. Thank you!

My grateful thanks to my mother Brigitte Wulf for her skill in deciphering eighteenth-century German letters written in Sütterlin, and to Trixi Wulf for long days marching up and down Jena's streets – again and again. And to my wise and wonderful daughter Linnéa for letting me grow up with her. A big thank you to Reiner Bauer for finding me in the humid wilderness of South America and taking me to the wide horizons and solitude of northern Germany, where I could finally finish this book (and for so much more).

I am a very lucky person to have the smartest and most insightful people in my life – people who are willing to spend hours, days, weeks reading and rereading every single line of the manuscript – they are my first editors, my wise and discerning advisers. This book would be very different without them. Thank you to my magnificent rebel friend Julia-Niharika Sen, who laboured through the very first draft, word for word and line for line, no matter how busy she was – for all those nights, going through this book page by page, dissecting and suggesting: I love you and owe you so much. And thank you to my father Herbert Wulf, the most avid of readers who commented on several drafts – still sharp as a razor. Also to my remarkable friend Misha Glenny, who still surprises me on a regular basis with his deep knowledge of German history – thank you for reading, listening and discussing this book from its very beginning. To my generous friend Victoria Johnson for reading every page and for many sage suggestions (as well as emergency research on eighteenth-century medicine) – thank you so much. Last but not least, thank you to Patrick Walsh, the best of friends and the best of agents – what would I do without you? I can't tell you how deeply grateful I am for your marvellous edits, wisdom, generosity, dinners, laughter and friendship.

And a big thank you to Patrick's incredible team at PEW Literary, in particular John Ash and Margaret Halton. I am also grateful to the wonderful team at Knopf and in particular my trusted editor Edward Kastenmeier. And at John Murray I would like to thank Georgina Laycock, Nick Davies and Caroline Westmore for their continued support, Sara Marafini for the evocative and stunning cover and Hilary Hammond for her copy-edit.

This book is dedicated to Saskia 'Robinson-Nixdorf-Manners' (almost keeping up with Caroline), who knows all too well why she's my mothership. Thank you for being in my life.

Picture Credits

Page 1: Jena from the south, circa 1790, Johann Lorenz Julius von Gerstenberg © Stadtmuseum Jena. Page 2 above: Königstein Fortress, 1793, Johann Christian Berndt © Freies Deutsches Hochstift/ Frankfurter Goethe-Museum; below: Caroline Michaelis-Böhmer-Schlegel-Schelling, 1798, Johann Friedrich August Tischbein © Städtische Museen Jena. Page 3 above: Auguste Böhmer, circa 1800, Johann Friedrich August Tischbein, Wieneke 1914; below: August Wilhelm Schlegel, 1793, Johann Friedrich August Tischbein, Freies Deutsches Hochstift/Frankfurter Goethe-Museum. Foto © Ursula Edelmann – Artothek. Page 4 above: Johann Wolfgang von Goethe, 1787, after Johann Heinrich Wilhelm Tischbein © Wellcome Collection; centre: Johann Gottlieb Fichte, 1800, Friedrich Bury, Wahl and Kippenberg 1932; below: Friedrich Schiller, 1791, after Anton Graff © Wellcome Collection. Page 5 above: Market square, Jena, 1812, Ludwig Hess © Städtische Museen Jena; below: Fürstengraben, Jena, circa 1791, Carl Benjamin Schwarz, SLUB Dresden/Deutsche Fotothek. Page 6 above: Alexander von Humboldt, 1806, after Friedrich Weitsch © Wellcome Collection; below: Caroline Dacheröden-von Humboldt, circa 1810, after Gottlieb Schick, Oeser 1932. Page 7: Map of Jena, circa 1750, Matthäus Seutter, SLUB Dresden/Deutsche Fotothek. Page 8 above: Novalis (Friedrich von Hardenberg), 1799, after Franz Gareis, Oeser 1932; below: Leutragasse 5, Jena, 1910, unknown photographer © Städtische Museen Jena. Page 9 above: Friedrich Schlegel, circa 1790, Caroline Rehberg, Wieneke 1914; below: Dorothea Mendelssohn-Veit-Schlegel, 1798, unknown artist, Wieneke 1914. Page 10 above: View of Neumarkt in Dresden, 1744, after Canaletto, SLUB Dresden/Deutsche Fotothek; below: Berlin, Unter den Linden, Granville 1829 © Wellcome Collection. Page 11 above: Friedrich Wilhelm Joseph Schelling, 1801, Friedrich Tieck, Wahl and Kippenberg 1932; below: Georg Friedrich

Wilhelm Hegel, 1828, after Julius Ludwig Sebbers © Städtische Museen Jena. Page 12 above: Goethe's House, Weimar, Granville 1829 © Wellcome Collection; below: Mühlenthal near Jena, circa 1801, Georg Melchior Kraus, SLUB Dresden/Deutsche Fotothek. Page 13 above: Goethe and Schiller, attributed to Johann Christian Reinhart or Johann Gottfried Schadow, 1804, Oeser 1932; below: Schiller's Garden House, Jena, circa 1857, unknown artist, SLUB Dresden/ Deutsche Fotothek. Page 14: View of Jena, circa 1800, Georg Melchior Kraus, SLUB Dresden/Deutsche Fotothek. Page 15 above: Paradise, Jena, 1780, Christian Gotthilf Immanuel Oehme, SLUB Dresden/ Deutsche Fotothek; below: Teichgraben (Ratsteich), Jena, 1792, Ernst Friedrich Ulrich Schenk © Städtische Museen Jena. Page 16 above: Battle of Jena, 14 October 1806, after Jacques François Joseph Swebach-Desfontaines, SLUB Dresden/Deutsche Fotothek; centre and below: Johannisstrasse, Jena, 14 October 1806, Johann Christian Schnorr © Städtische Museen Jena.

Notes

In order to avoid making the endnotes even longer than they are, I have shortened references to letters written by the main protagonists to the name of the sender, addressee and date. Those letters can all be found in the published letter editions or digital collections which are listed in the bibliography. To avoid confusion, names of women who were married or divorced are always the same in the references – for example, Caroline is always referenced as Caroline Schlegel (CS) in the notes although she was Caroline Michaelis, Caroline Böhmer and Caroline Schelling in some of the letters.

Names have been abbreviated as follows:

AH: Alexander von Humboldt
AWS: August Wilhelm Schlegel
CH: Caroline von Humboldt
CS: Caroline Michaelis-Böhmer-Schlegel-Schelling
DV: Dorothea Mendelssohn-Veit-Schlegel
FS: Friedrich Schlegel
WH: Wilhelm von Humboldt

Abbreviations have also been used for the following sources:

ALZ: *Allgemeine Literatur-Zeitung*
AWS SW: August Wilhelm Schlegel, *August Wilhelm von Schlegel's Sämmtliche Werke*, ed. Eduard Böcking, Leipzig: Weidmann'sche Buchhandlung, 1846–7
BBAW: Brandenburgische Akademie der Wissenschaften
CS Letters: Caroline Schlegel-Schelling, *Caroline: Briefe aus der Frühromantik*, ed. Erich Schmidt, Leipzig: Insel Verlag, 1913
Fichte GA: Johann Gottlieb Fichte, *Johann Gottlieb Fichte: Gesamtausgabe der Bayerischen Akademie der Wissenschaften*, ed. Reinhard Lauth et al., Stuttgart: Frommann Holzboog Verlag, 1964–2005
Fichte Gespräch: Erich Fuchs (ed.), *J. G. Fichte im Gespräch: Berichte der Zeitgenossen*, Stuttgart: Frommann Holzboog Verlag, 1978–92
Fichte SW: Johann Gottlieb Fichte, *Johann Gottlieb Fichte's Sämmtliche Werke*, ed. I. H. Fichte, Berlin: Veit & Comp., 1845–6
FS KA: Friedrich Schlegel, *Kritische Friedrich-Schlegel-Ausgabe*, ed. Ernst Behler, Munich: F. Schöningh, 1958–2006

Goethe Diaries: Johann Wolfgang von Goethe, *Tagebücher*, in *Goethes Werke*, Part III, published on behalf of Grand Duchess Sophie of Saxe-Weimar-Eisenach, Weimar: Herman Böhlau, 1887–1919

Hegel Werke: Georg Wilhelm Friedrich Hegel, *Werke*, ed. Eva Moldenhauer and Karl Markus Michel, Frankfurt: Suhrkamp, 1986

Novalis Schriften: Novalis, *Schriften: Die Werke Friedrich von Hardenbergs*, ed. Paul Kluckhohn et al., Stuttgart: Kohlhammer, 1960–2006

Schelling SW: Friedrich Wilhelm Joseph Schelling, *Sämmtliche Werke*, ed. K. F. A. Schelling, Stuttgart and Augsburg: J. G. Cotta'scher Verlag, 1856–61

SLUB: Sächsische Landesbibliothek – Staats- und Universitätsbibliothek Dresden

Prologue

4 'A person should be': Fichte, *Einige Vorlesungen über die Bestimmung des Gelehrten*, 1794, Lecture 1, Fichte SW, vol. 6, p. 297.

5 CS's arrest: Caroline left Mainz on 30 March 1793 but was stopped in Oppenheim some ten miles south of Mainz. She was then taken to Frankfurt which was about thirty miles from Oppenheim. CS to F. L. W. Meyer, 15 June 1793; S. T. Sömmerring to C. G. Heyne, 6, 8 and 13 April 1793, Forster 1877, pp. 614–18, 620–1; Therese Huber to Therese Forster, 17–25 July 1803, Huber 1999, vol. 1, p. 422.

5 CS's imprisonment: CS to F. L. W. Meyer, 15 June 1793; S. T. Sömmerring to C. G. Heyne, 6, 8 and 13 April 1793, Forster 1877, pp. 614–18, 620–1; Therese Huber to Therese Forster, 17–25 July 1803, Huber 1999, vol. 1, p. 422.

5 'made a great editor': S. T. Sömmerring to C. G. Heyne, 6 April 1793, Forster 1877, p. 615.

5 journey from Frankfurt to Königstein: S. T. Sömmerring to C. G. Heyne, 8 and 13 April 1793, Forster 1877, pp. 616–17, 620–1; Liebeskind 1795, pp. 34–40.

6 CS in Königstein: CS to F. W. Gotter, 28 April 1793 and 15 June 1793; CS to Luise Gotter, 19 April 1793; for conditions in Königstein, see Liebeskind 1795, pp. 41–88.

6 CS's upbringing: Roßbeck 2008, p. 17ff.

6 Guests at CS's house: CS to Luise Gotter, 30 September 1783; Appel 2013, pp. 15–16.

6 'a little wild': H. C. Boie about CS in 1779, quoted in Appel 2013, p. 19.

6 'I never flatter': CS to Juliana Studnitz, 28 September 1778.

6 CS's appearance: painter Friedrich August Tischbein about CS, CS Letters, vol. 1, p. 742; C. G. Körner to Schiller, 17 April 1797; Caroline Tischbein-Wilken, 1799, Stoll 1923, p. 110; Ludwig Tieck about CS, CS Letters, vol. 1, p. 748; see also portraits of CS.

7 'Vivre libre ou': CS to F. L. W. Meyer, 27 October 1792; for cockade, see 6 October 1792.

7 events in France: CS to Lotte Michaelis, October 1789.

7 'Let the wealthy': CS to F. L. W. Meyer, 1 March 1789.

7 'After all, we are': CS to Luise Gotter, 20 April 1792.

7 'Who knows when': CS to F. L. W. Meyer, 17 December 1792.

7 CS in Mainz: CS to Luise Gotter, 20 April 1792; CS to F. L. W. Meyer, 29 July 1793; see also CS Letters, vol. 1, pp. 692–6.

7 Tree of Liberty: Damn 2005, p. 33.

7 CS's affairs: FS to AWS, 3 April 1793; J. G. L. Möller to AWS, 16 May 1793; S. T. Sömmerring to C. G. Heyne, 6 April 1793, Forster 1877, p. 616; Therese Huber to Therese Forster, 17–25 July 1803, Huber 1999, vol. 1, p. 422.

8 French more handsome: CS to Luise Gotter, 20 April 1792.

8 CS's pregnancy: CS to F. L. W. Meyer, 30 July 1793; Therese Huber to Therese Forster, 17–25 July 1803 and 3 September 1803, Huber 1999, vol. 1, pp. 422, 428.

8 'Vive la nation!': CS to Luise Gotter, 24 January 1793; for Marseillaise, see FS to AWS, 30 January 1796.

8 'A long imprisonment': CS to F. W. Gotter, 1 May 1793.

8 frozen grapes: Goethe to Christiane Vulpius, 3 July 1793.

9 CS's health declining: CS to F. W. Gotter, 28 April 1793 and 15 June 1793.

9 CS heard cannons: CS to F. W. Gotter, 12 May 1793.

9 prisoners beaten: CS to F. W. Gotter, 15 June 1793.

9 'how desperately I need': CS to F. W. Gotter, 12 May 1793.

9 friends turning away: ibid.

9 AWS helped: J. G. L. Möller to AWS, 16 May 1793; WH to AWS, 25 May 1793.

9 FS told AWS about affair: FS to AWS, 3 April 1793.

9 poison for CS: CS to F. L. W. Meyer, 30 July 1793; Therese Huber to Therese Forster, 17–25 July 1803, Huber 1999, vol. 1, p. 422.

9 mistress of the Prussian king: Friedrich Wilhelm II to Gottfried Philipp Michaelis, 4 July 1793, in Kleßmann 2008, p. 200; see also Wiedemann 1929, pp. 81–2; CS to Luise and F. W. Gotter, 30 June 1793 and 13 July 1793.

11 rulers in Germany: Brunschwig 1975, pp. 77–9.

11 by special dispensation: Allgemeines Landrecht für die Preußischen Staaten, 2. Part, 1. Titel, § 30–2 (General State Laws for the Prussian States).

11 'Things are becoming reality': Novalis to FS, 1 August 1794.

11 'We have to believe': FS KA, vol. 18, no. 776; see also FS, 'Über die Philosophie: An Dorothea', Athenaeum, vol. 2, 1799, p. 3.

11 'writers ruled the world': Henriette Hoven to Charlotte Schiller, 4 April 1803, C. Schiller 1862, vol. 3, p. 273.

11 'French Revolution seems': Fichte, Beitrag zur Berichtigung der Urtheile des Publikums über die französische Revolution, 1793, Fichte SW, vol. 6, p. 39; for singing Marseillaise, see K. F. A. Schelling in Hegel 1970, p. 14.

12 a person 'should be': Fichte, Einige Vorlesungen über die Bestimmung des Gelehrten, 1794, Lecture 1, Fichte SW, vol. 6, p. 297.

12 'revolution brought about': Schelling to Hegel, 21 January 1795.

12 'Everything is useful': Hegel Werke, vol. 3, p. 415.

13 'Nature has been reduced': Novalis, Lehrlinge zu Sais, Novalis Schriften, vol. 1, p. 99.

13 'the eternally creative music': Novalis, *Die Christenheit oder Europa*, Novalis 2018, p. 77.

13 four and a half thousand inhabitants: Ziolkowski 1998, p. 24.

13 university library: Henry Crabb Robinson to Thomas Crabb Robinson, 1 June 1802, Robinson 1929, p. 125.

13 two per cent illegitimate: Deinhardt 2007, pp. 39–40.

13 dominated by its university: ibid., pp. 79ff., 112ff.

14 food in Jena: J. G. Rist, end 1795/spring 1796, Rist 1880, p. 52; Anonymous 1798, p. 72; Ziolkowski 1998, pp. 28–30.

14 'Here the torches': Anonymous 1798, p. 31.

14 libraries and bookstores: Alt 2004, vol. 1, p. 597.

14 poetry, philosophy and music: DV to Rahel Levin, 2 June 1800.

14 bottles of beer: Steffens 1841, vol. 4, p. 25.

14 few other distractions: A. G. F. Rebmann 1787–1789, Rebmann 1994, pp. 72, 89.

14 flowers in spring: DV to Rahel Levin, 28 April 1800; Ziolkowski 1998, p. 33; for beer gardens, see Anonymous 1798, p. 88.

14 Goethe skating: J. G. Rist, end 1795/spring 1796, Rist 1880, p. 67.

15 'Kingdom of Philosophy': CS to Luise Michaelis Wiedemann, 19 June 1803. '

15 more than fifteen hundred states: Wehler 1989, vol. 1, p. 47.

15 censorship: Watson 2010, p. 55.

15 universities in Germany: Boyle 1992, p. 19.

15 literacy rates: Watson 2010, pp. 55–6.

15 'In no country is': ibid., p. 56.

15 'Age of Paper': *Intelligenzblatt*, ALZ, 20 June 1798, no. 88; for German book trade: Boyle 1992, p. 20.

16 Schiller about Jena: Schiller to C. G. Körner, 6 April 1795; see also 29 August 1787.

16 Jena university: Ziolkowski 1998, p. 19.

16 ALZ and Kant: Steffens 1841, vol. 4, p. 143.

16 'Dare to know': Kant, 'An Answer to the Question. What is Enlightenment', 1784, Kant used the Latin 'Sapere Aude!'

16 'most fashionable seat': Henry Crabb Robinson, 1801, Stelzig 2010, p. 59; see also A. G. F. Rebmann 1787–9, Rebmann 1994, p. 53; see also Watson 2010, p. 147.

16 'man's emergence from': Kant, 'An Answer to the Question. What is Enlightenment', 1784.

17 'The professors in Jena': Schiller to C. G. Körner, 29 August 1787.

17 'here we have complete': Kühn 2012, p. 210.

17 'foolish obsession with liberty': ibid., p. 211.

17 'Jacobins of poetry': FS KA, vol. 18, no. 1524, p. 319.

17 'we are called to': Novalis, 'Blüthenstaub' ('Pollen'), no. 32, Novalis Schriften, vol. 2, p. 426.

18 AWS about Romanticism: AWS 1815, vol. 2, p. 99; AWS 1846, vol. 6, pt. 2, pp. 161–2.

18 'is the beginning': Hölderlin, *Hyperion*, Hölderlin 2020, p. 90.

18 'Speak nothing but German': S. T. Coleridge to Thomas Poole, 8 October 1798, Sandford 1888, vol. 1, p. 279.

19 Coleridge and Jena Set's work: Holmes 1998, vol. 2, pp. 398–402.

19 'this admirable Schelling': R. W. Emerson to James Cabot, September 1845, Vogel 1970, p. 108.

19 'this strange genial': Emerson's Journal, 1846, Emerson 1960–92, vol. 9, p. 359.

19 'great thinkers of the': Parker, Theodore, 'German Literature', *The Dial*, January 1841, p. 324.

Chapter 1: 'A happy event' – Summer 1794: Goethe and Schiller

23 fruits and wine autumn 1794: Goethe, 1794, Goethe 1994b, p. 33.

23 'the Snail': Koch 1939, pp. 214–15.

23 'little Switzerland': Anonymous 1798, p. 87.

24 Goethe learned French: Goethe 1949–60, vol. 9, p. 90.

24 'I withdraw into myself': Goethe 1787, p. 17.

24 Werther fever: Friedenthal 2003, p. 137.

24 duke in Werther uniform: Merseburger 2009, p. 67.

24 'has put more individuals': Lord Byron to Goethe, 14 October 1820.

24 Goethe's arrival in Weimar: Merseburger 2009, p. 67.

24 duke and Goethe in Weimar: ibid., pp. 67–9; Boyle 1992, pp. 202ff., 243; Safranski 2017, p. 173ff.

25 a hundred thousand inhabitants: Preisendörfer 2018, p. 482; five million in Prussia: Brunschwig 1975, p. 189.

25 duchy of Saxe-Weimar: Boyle 1992, pp. 233, 236.

25 rural Weimar: Alt 2004, vol. 1, pp. 531–4.

25 Duke did nothing without Goethe: K. A. Böttiger, October 1791, Böttiger 1998, p. 33.

25 'I never smoked': Goethe, recounted by J. S. Grüner, 21 August 1822.

25 Goethe's appearance: Marie Körner to Weber, August 1796; David Veit to Rahel Levin, 20 March 1793; K. A. Böttiger about Goethe, mid-1790s; Charlotte von Stein to Fritz von Stein, 25 February 1796, Goethe 1982–96, vol. 3, pp. 235, 354, 447, 464.

25 'a woman in the last': Botting 1973, p. 38.

25 Goethe's clothes: Goethe to Christiane Vulpius, 27 November 1797; Schnorr von Carolsfeld about Goethe, April/May 1800, in Goethe 1982–96, vol. 4, p. 114.

25 Goethe's hair: Schnorr von Carolsfeld about Goethe, April/May 1800, Goethe 1982–96, vol. 4, p. 114.

26 Goethe properly dressed: Goethe to Christiane Vulpius, 2 May 1800.

26 Goethe hated noise: K. A. Böttiger, 6 November 1800, Böttiger 1998, p. 98; skittle alley, Preisendörfer 2018, p. 44.

26 'problem child': Alt 2004, vol. 2, p. 156.

26 Goethe and botanical garden: Goethe 1994b, p. 32.

27 Jena . . . flair of a city: Schiller to C. G. Körner, 29 August 1787.

27 stream flushed: Anonymous 1798, p. 9.

27 trades in Jena: Deinhardt 2007, pp. 374–9.

27 Jena at night: ibid.; J. G. Rist, end 1795/spring 1796, Rist 1880, p. 56.

27 'Professors' Club' and taverns: Anonymous 1798, pp. 77, 80, 83–5; for reading Fichte see Ernst Moritz Arndt, in 1840 about his time in Jena in 1794, Fichte Gespräch, vol. 1, p. 128.

28 'source of all reality': Fichte, *Grundlage der gesammten Wissenschaftslehre*, 1794/5, Fichte SW, vol. 1, p. 134.

28 Goethe suggested Fichte: Goethe to Voigt, 27 July 1793.

28 people promenading: Anonymous 1798, p. 9.

28 first meeting: Goethe, *Glückliches Ereignis*, 1817, Goethe 1887–1919, pt 2, vol. 11, pp. 16–18; see also Goethe 1965–2000, vol. 4, pp. 84–6.

28 Duke Karl Eugen: Alt 2004, vol. 1, p. 28ff.

29 Schiller at military academy: Safranski 2009a, p. 23ff.

29 *The Robbers*: Alt 2004, vol. 1, p. 276.

29 'theatre was like a madhouse': ibid., p. 282.

29 'My God! . . . who is': S. T. Coleridge to Robert Southey, 3 November 1794, Coleridge 1956–71, vol. 1, p. 67.

29 Schiller arrested: Alt 2004, vol. 1, pp. 303–5.

30 Goethe avoided Schiller: Goethe, *Glückliches Ereignis*, 1817, Goethe 1887–1919, pt 2, vol. 11, p. 15.

30 Goethe arrogant: Friedrich Hölderlin to C. L. Neuffer, 19 January 1795; Jean Paul to Otto, 18 June 1796, Goethe 1982–96, vol. 3, pp. 356, 474.

30 'cold, monosyllabic god': Jean Paul Richter to Christian Otto, 1796, quoted in Klauss 1991, p. 14.

30 'greatest egoist': C. M. Wieland, 10 November 1794, recounted by K. A. Böttiger, Böttiger 1998, p. 134

30 Goethe and *The Robbers*: Goethe, *Glückliches Ereignis*, 1817, Goethe 1887–1919, pt 2, vol. 11, p. 14; Goethe to J. S. Grüner, 19 August 1822, Goethe 1889–96, vol. 4, pp. 195–6.

30 like seducing a prude: Schiller to C. G. Körner, 2 February 1789.

30 Schiller's different financial position: Schiller to C. G. Körner, 12 September 1788.

30 Goethe's life a reminder: Schiller to C. G. Körner, 9 March 1789.

30 Schiller and Goethe's finances: Alt 2004, vol. 1, p. 649; see also Schiller to C. G. Körner, 24 December 1789.

30 Goethe's high fees: Boyle 2000, p. 215.

31 'could kiss my ass': Schiller to C. G. Körner, 9 March 1789.

31 Schiller always indoors: Schiller to Goethe, 19 February 1795; Schiller to C. G. Körner, 17 August 1795.

31 'Winter . . . such a gloomy': Schiller to C. G. Körner, 4 January 1804.

31 Schiller's erratic hours: Schiller to Goethe, 7 September 1794 and 8 December 1795; see also Petersen 1909, vol. 3, pp. 45, 67.

31 neighbours saw Schiller: Petersen 1909, vol. 3, p. 67.

31 *Wallenstein* and imagination: Schiller to C. G. Körner, 12 September 1794.

31 philosophy and poetry: Schiller to C. G. Körner, 4 September 1794.

31 'Imagination disturbs my': Schiller to Goethe, 31 August 1794.

31 Goethe and Schiller's first meeting: Goethe, *Glückliches Ereignis*, 1817, Goethe

1887–1919, pt 2, vol. II, pp. 16–18; see also Goethe 1965–2000, vol. 4, pp. 84–6 and 'Erste Bekanntschaft mit Schiller', Goethe 1982–96, vol. 3, pp. 320–1.

31 'fragmentary way of looking': Goethe, *Glückliches Ereignis*, 1817, in Goethe 1887–1919, pt 2, vol. II, p. 17; see also Goethe, 'Erste Bekanntschaft mit Schiller', Goethe 1982–96, vol. 3, pp. 320–1; Goethe 1965–2000, vol. 4, pp. 84–6.

32 Goethe's height: 5 feet 9¼ inches or 1 m 76 cm.

32 primordial form: Goethe had explained this in his 1790 work *Versuch die Metamorphose der Pflanzen zu erklären*.

32 'Forwards and backwards': Goethe, 17 May 1787, Goethe 1949–60, vol. II, p. 375.

32 'an idea': Goethe, *Glückliches Ereignis*, 1817, Goethe 1887–1919, pt 2, vol. II, p. 17.

32 hard-headed realist: Goethe, *Glückliches Ereignis*, 1817, Goethe 1887–1919, pt 2, vol. II, p. 18; see also Goethe 1965–2000, vol. 4, 1980, p. 85.

32 Schiller was 'idealist': Schiller to WH, 9 January 1796.

32 'gets too much': Schiller to C. G. Körner, 1 November 1790.

32 'intellectual pleasure': C. G. Körner to Schiller, 10 September 1794; for competition between realism and idealism, see Goethe, *Glückliches Ereignis*, 1817, Goethe 1887–1919, pt 2, vol. II, p. 19.

33 'Each of us was': Schiller to C. G. Körner, 1 September 1794.

33 'most beneficial event': Schiller to Charlotte von Schimmelmann, 23 November 1800.

33 'a second youth': Goethe to Schiller, 6 January 1798.

33 'force himself to': Goethe, January 1794, quoted in Boyle 2000, p. 215.

33 felt like a new spring: Goethe, *Glückliches Ereignis*, 1817, Goethe 1887–1919, pt 2, vol. II, p. 19; see also Goethe, 1794, Goethe 1994b, p. 38.

33 Goethe increasingly disillusioned: Goethe to J. P. Eckermann, 18 May 1825.

33 'Robespierre's atrocities': Goethe, 1794, Goethe 1994b, p. 27.

33 Goethe and French Revolution: Goethe 1982–96, vol. 3, p. 323; see also Goethe, 1794, Goethe 1994b, pp. 26–9.

33 Goethe in Mainz: Goethe was away from Weimar to join the Duke from 12 May to 23 August 1793. See letters: Goethe to Christiane Vulpius, 29 May 1793 and 3 July 1793; Goethe to Herder, 15 June 1793; Goethe to C. G. Voigt, 3 July 1793; Goethe to J. H. Meyer, 10 July 1793.

33 Goethe worked in tent: Goethe 1982–96, vol. 3, p. 256; Goethe to Herder, 15 June 1793.

34 money for plants instead of cannons: Goethe to C. G. Voigt, 14 June 1793.

34 'objects of thought': Goethe to Karl von Knebel, 2 July 1793.

34 Goethe saw injured: Goethe to Christiane Vulpius, 29 May 1793.

34 'mind had come': Goethe to C. G. Voigt, 3 July 1793.

34 'destruction and misery': Goethe to J. H. Meyer, 10 July 1793.

34 'plank in a shipwreck': Goethe, 1793, Goethe 1994b, p. 25.

34 Goethe and botanical garden and optics: Goethe to Duke Carl August, 11 February 1794, and Goethe's letters to A. J. Batsch in spring 1794; see also Boyle 2000, pp. 205–6; Goethe to S. T. Sömmerring, 16 July 1794.

34 Goethe invited Schiller: Goethe to Schiller, 4 September 1794.

34 Schiller cautioned: Schiller to Goethe, 7 September 1794.

35 'a kind of darkness': Goethe to Schiller, 27 August 1794.

35 Goethe's house: the duke had bought the house for Goethe in 1792 but only formally transferred the deeds in June 1794.

35 interior of Goethe's house: K. Morgenstein, 25 April 1798, Goethe 1965–2000, vol. 4, p. 413; David Veit to Rahel Levin, 20 March 1793, Goethe 1982–96, vol. 3, p. 235.

35 Goethe's new study: Goethe to J. H. Meyer, 15 May 1794.

35 'makes it impossible': Goethe to J. P. Eckermann, 25 March 1831.

35 fourteen days in Weimar: Schiller to Charlotte Schiller, 16, 20 and 24 September 1794; Goethe to J. H. Meyer, 22 September 1794.

35 'my sluggish thoughts': Goethe to J. H. Meyer, 22 September 1794; for Schiller's nights, see Schiller to Charlotte Schiller, 24 September 1794.

35 Schiller in Weimar: Schiller to Charlotte Schiller, 20 September 1794.

36 'But at the love-god's behest': Goethe, *Roman Elegies*, 1795, Elegie no. 7 (trans. David Luke), Goethe 1988, pp. 48–9.

36 *Roman Elegies*: Alt 2004, vol. 2, p. 47.

36 'Erotica': Ziolkowski 1998, p. 231.

36 'admittedly risqué': Schiller to Charlotte Schiller, 20 September 1794.

36 Christiane Vulpius: Goethe and Christiane met on 12 July 1788, Boyle 1992, pp. 537ff., 579ff.

37 'a pig with a': C. M. Wieland, 26 March 1797, recounted by K. A. Böttiger, Böttiger 1998, p. 221.

37 Schiller had gossiped: Schiller to C. G. Körner, 1 November 1790; he continued to criticise the relationship in private, see Schiller to Charlotte von Schimmelmann, 23 November 1800.

37 Schiller and Charlotte and Caroline von Lengefeld: Alt 2004, vol. 1, p. 633ff.

37 Schiller's letters: for example Schiller to Charlotte von Lengefeld and Caroline von Beulwitz, 15 and 30 November 1798.

37 'managed the household': Kratzsch 2009, p. 127; see also Goethe's letters to Christiane Vulpius, August–September 1792.

37 'What you do is easy': Christiane Vulpius to Goethe, 30 May 1798.

37 'your dear bedfellow': C. E. Goethe to Goethe, 24 September 1795.

38 'dear little one': Goethe to Christiane Vulpius, 21, 25 August 1792, 14 November 1792, 22 June 1793 and 10 August 1794.

38 'darling sweetheart': Christiane Vulpius to Goethe, 22 May 1798.

38 'The wood gathered': Goethe to Schiller, 15 December 1795.

38 'because the quiet castle': Goethe to Christiane Vulpius, 9 November 1795.

38 Goethe in bed, dictating: Goethe to F. H. Jacobi, 2 February 1795.

38 Goethe and dog: Luise Seidler, Goethe 1982–96, vol. 3, p. 354.

38 Goethe at Schiller's apartment: K. W. F. von Funck to C. G. Körner, 17 January 1796, Petersen 1909, vol. 3, pp. 34–5.

38 talked through the night: Goethe to Christiane Vulpius, 9 November 1795; Schiller to WH, 9 November 1795; Schiller's dressing gown and slippers, see J. D. Sander to his wife, 1797, Petersen 1909, vol. 3, p. 69.

38 tea, wine and liquor: K. W. F. von Funck to C. G. Körner, 17 January 1796, Petersen 1909, vol. 3, p. 34.

39 'how the mind tyrannised': ibid., p. 35.

39 'I would add another verse': Goethe to Schiller, 23 August 1797.

39 'vivid longing': Goethe to Schiller, 11 March 1795.

39 'quick ride to see': ibid.

39 Goethe from Weimar to Leipzig: Boyle 1992, p. 303.

39 Goethe was intuitive: Schiller to Goethe, 31 August 1794.

39 Schiller pushed frail body: Schiller to C. M. Wieland, see Alt 2004, vol. 2, p. 54; see also W. F. T. von Burgsdorff to K. G. von Brinkman, 12 December 1796, Burgsdorff 1907, p. 59.

39 Schiller pressured himself: Schiller to Charlotte Schiller, 10 March 1801.

39 'as if I'm hanging': Schiller to Goethe, 19 March 1799.

39 fear of not being able to produce: Schiller to Goethe, 19 March 1799 and Schiller to C. G. Körner, 27 April 1801.

40 'has only to shake': Schiller to J. H. Meyer, 21 July 1797.

40 no one since Shakespeare: Schiller to Charlotte von Schimmelmann, 23 November 1800.

40 Schiller began with the general: Schiller to Goethe, 18 June 1797.

40 'Your close observation': Schiller to Goethe, 23 August 1794.

40 Goethe pulled cerebral Schiller: K. W. F. von Funck to C. G. Körner, 17 January 1796, Petersen 1909, vol. 3, p. 36.

40 food for heart and mind: Schiller to Goethe, 7 January 1795.

40 'art, nature and': Goethe, 16 March 1797, Goethe Diaries, vol. 2, p. 61.

40 'new era': Goethe to Charlotte von Kalb, 28 June 1794; see also Schiller to C. G. Körner, 31 August 1798.

40 'demi-god': Sophie Tischbein to AWS, 14 December 1795.

Chapter 2: 'I am a priest of truth'
Summer 1794: Fichte's Ich-philosophy

41 Fichte's inaugural lecture: Fichte to Johanne Fichte, 26 May 1794; see also J. W. Camerer, 27 June 1794, Fichte Gespräch, vol. 6.1, pp. 56–7.

41 jostling for seats: Schiller to J. B. Erhard, 26 May 1794.

41 description of Fichte: J. R. Rahn to J. H. Rahn, c. 19 June 1794; Anonymous to Heinrich Laube, 1794/5; F. K. Forberg to unknown, 27 January 1795; Heinrich Schmidt, summer 1798, Fichte Gespräch, vol. 1, pp. 136, 234, 504, vol. 6.1, p. 53; Steffens 1841, vol. 4, p. 79.

41 'Bonaparte of Philosophy': J. G. Rist, end 1795/spring 1796, Rist 1880, p. 70; see also Anonymous to Heinrich Laube, 1794/5, Fichte Gespräch, vol. 1, p. 136.

41 importance of philosophy: Ziolkowski 1998, p. 49.

41 'I am a priest': Fichte, Einige Vorlesungen über die Bestimmung des Gelehrten, 1794, Lecture 4, Fichte SW, vol. 6, p. 333.

41 Fichte's childhood and studies: I. H. Fichte, 1830, Fichte Gespräch, vol. 1, p. 7ff.; see also Fichte Gespräch, vol. 6.1, p. 1 and Kühn 2012, p. 17ff.

42 Fichte as tutor: Antonius Ott to J. J. Hess, 20 April 1788, Fichte Gespräch, vol. 1, p. 22 and Kühn 2012, p. 102.

42 Fichte had no money: Kühn 2012, p. 110 and Fichte's letters to Johanne Fichte in 1790 and 1791.

42 work, walks and booze: Fichte to Johanne Fichte, 4 June 1793; Anonymous to Heinrich Laube, 1794/5, Fichte Gespräch, vol. 1, p. 137.

42 dropped Saxon accent: Fichte to S. G. Fichte, 24 June 1794.

42 Johanne's description of herself: Johanne Fichte to S. G. Fichte, 27 December 1794, Fichte GA III, vol. 2, p. 243.

42 'Ever since I've read': Fichte to F. A. Weißhuhn, 1 August 1790; see also Fichte to Johanne Fichte, 5 September 1790 and Fichte to H. N. Achelis, 1 November 1790.

44 'intellectual rebirth': Arthur Schopenhauer, quoted in Pikulik 1992, p. 36.

44 revolution of his thinking: Fichte to H. N. Achelis, 1 November 1790.

44 broke off engagement: Johanne Fichte to Fichte, 11 December 1792 (referring to his letter from 1 March 1791).

44 'clip his wings': Fichte to S. G. Fichte, 1 March 1791.

44 Fichte tried to impress Kant: Fichte, diary, 10 July 1791, Fichte GA II, vol. 1, p. 415; Fichte to F. A. Weißhuhn, 11 October 1791.

44 Fichte's manuscript on religion: Fichte to F. A. Weißhuhn, 11 October 1791; Fichte to Kant, 18 August 1791.

44 Fichte went to Kant: Fichte, diary, 23 August 1791, Fichte GA II, vol. 1, p. 415.

44 'His weak body': Fichte to C. F. G. Wenzel, 1 July 1791; see also Fichte, diary, 4 July 1791, Fichte GA II, vol. 1, p. 415 and a drawing 'Immanuel Kant, Senf zubereitend' by Friedrich Hagemann, 1801.

45 'is beginning to lose': Fichte to C. F. G. Wenzel, 1 July 1791.

45 Kant read and advised: Fichte, diary, 6 September 1791, Fichte GA II, vol. 1, p. 418; Fichte to F. A. Weißhuhn, 11 October 1791.

45 'Can it be true?': Fichte, diary, 6 September 1791, Fichte GA II, vol. 1, p. 418.

45 *Attempt at a Critique:* Fichte, *Versuch einer Kritik aller Offenbarung,* 1792.

45 missing name on cover: Fichte to F. A. Weißhuhn, 11 October 1791.

45 two different cover pages: Theodor von Schön, summer 1791, Fichte Gespräch, vol. 1, p. 31; see also Fichte GA I, vol. 1, p. 10.

45 review of *Critique of All Revelation*: ALZ, 30 June 1792, Fichte GA I, vol. 1, pp. 10–11; see also J. B. Erhard to K. L. Reinhold, 30 June 1792, Fichte Gespräch, vol. 1, p. 38; Kühn 2012, p. 157.

45 eight Kant experts: Gottlieb Hufeland to Fichte, 14 November 1792.

45 'the great Master': K. L. Reinhold to J. I. Baggesen, 22 June 1792, Fichte Gespräch, vol. 1, p. 35.

46 'Read it and': ibid.

46 'I have not contributed': Kant to ALZ, 31 July 1792, published in ALZ on 22 August 1792, Fichte Gespräch, vol. 1, p. 39.

46 better endorsement: Theodor von Schön to Fichte, 5 September 1792.

46 'third sun in the': J. I. Baggesen to K. L. Reinhold, 11 September 1792, Fichte Gespräch, vol. 1, p. 44.

46 'It's the same with Kantian': Goethe to C. G. Voigt, 27 July 1793.

46 job offer for Fichte: C. G. Voigt to Fichte, 26 December 1793 (asking Fichte to begin at Easter 1794).

46 travels by foot: Fichte to Johanne Fichte, 20 May 1794.

46 'My will alone': Fichte, *Einige Vorlesungen über die Bestimmung des Gelehrten*, 1794, Lecture 3, Fichte SW, vol. 6, p. 323.

46 students electrified: Friedrich Karl von Savigny, summer 1799, Stoll 1891, p. 18.

47 'Act! Act! That's': Fichte, *Einige Vorlesungen über die Bestimmung des Gelehrten*, 1794, Lecture 5, Fichte SW, vol. 6, p. 345.

47 'like a triumphant': Anonymous to Heinrich Laube, 1794/95, Fichte Gespräch, vol. 1, p. 137.

47 nothing gentle about Fichte: F. K. Forberg to unknown, 27 January 1795, Fichte Gespräch, vol. 1, p. 234; see also J. G. Rist, end 1795/spring 1796, Rist 1880, p. 70 and Kühn 2012, p. 105.

47 Fichte ate snuff: Anonymous to Heinrich Laube, 1794/5, Fichte Gespräch, vol. 1, p. 138.

47 'I haven't written my': ibid.

47 'filthy and disgusting': ibid.

47 'rooted firmly in': J. G. Rist, end 1795/spring 1796, Rist 1880, p. 70.

47 'originally and unconditionally posits': Fichte, *Grundlage der Wissenschaftslehre*, 1794, Fichte SW, vol. 1, p. 98. I'm using Boyle's translation here as it is better than Seidel 1993, p. 38; Boyle 2000, p. 209.

47 'which is different from': Fichte, *Einige Vorlesungen über die Bestimmung des Gelehrten*, 1794, Lecture 1, Fichte SW, vol. 6, p. 295.

48 freedom was a spark: Fichte, 'Über Belebung und Erhöhung des reinen Interesse für Wahrheit', 1795, Fichte SW, vol. 8, p. 343.

48 Schiller arrested: Alt 2004, vol. 1, pp. 303–5.

48 'Your Serene Royal': Schelling to Duke of Württemberg, 8 August 1798.

48 rules in Duchy of Saxe-Weimar: Goethe to C. G. Voigt, 3 July 1793 and Henriette Schütz to Goethe, 3 December 1800; Goethe to Henriette Schütz, 22 December 1800.

48 'Temple of Reason': Boyle 2000, p. 185.

49 Fichte's two pamphlets: *Zurückforderung der Denkfreiheit von den Fürsten Europens* and *Beitrag zur Berichtigung der Urtheile des Publicums über die französische Revolution* (both published 1793).

49 'breaking dawn': Fichte, *Beitrag zur Berichtigung der Urtheile des Publicums über die französische Revolution,* 1793, Fichte SW, vol. 6, p. 45.

49 *idea* of a state: Rosenkranz 1844, p. 32.

49 'My system is from': Fichte to K. L. Reinhold, 8 January 1800.

49 'Gentlemen, go into': Henrik Steffens, 'Fact and Feelings from the Life of Steffens', 1799, *Foreign Quarterly Review*, vol. 31, 1843, p. 139.

49 'hubris' and 'pomposity': Ziolkowski 1998, p. 59.

50 Fichte on freedom and morality: Fichte to H. N. Achelis, 1 November 1790; and Fichte, *Einige Vorlesungen über die Bestimmung des Gelehrten*, 1794, Lecture 2, Fichte SW, vol. 6, p. 309.

50 'moral ennobling of mankind': Fichte, *Einige Vorlesungen über die Bestimmung des Gelehrten*, 1794, Lecture 4, Fichte SW, vol. 6, p. 332.

50 'morally the best person': ibid., p. 333.

50 students talking about equality: Anonymous, 1794/5 and C. M. Wieland to K. L. Reinhold, 27 June 1794, Fichte Gespräch, vol. 1, pp. 126, 190.

50 'Only when he abandons': C. M. Wieland, 28–30 December 1797, recounted by K. A. Böttiger, Böttiger 1998, p. 232.

50 'Anyone who can't learn': J. R. Steck to Zehender, mid-January 1796, Fichte Gespräch, vol. 6.1, p. 190.

50 Fichte was students' idol: Anonymous to Heinrich Laube, 1794/5, Fichte Gespräch, vol. 1, p. 138; see also Ziolkowski 1998, p. 58.

50 foreign students: Heinrich Schmidt about summer 1798; J. R. Steck to M. M. Steck, 23 October 1795, Fichte Gespräch, vol. 1, p. 504 and vol. 6.1, p. 181.

51 'My celebrity': Fichte to Johanne Fichte, 26 May 1794.

51 'great things could be': Schiller to C. G. Körner, 12 June 1794; see also 4 July 1794 and Schiller to J. B. Erhard, 26 May 1794.

51 end of Kant's era: J. I. Baggesen to K. L. Reinhold, 4 September 1794, Fichte Gespräch, vol. 1, p. 143.

51 Goethe reconciled with philosophy: Goethe to Fichte, 24 June 1794.

51 'a strange fellow': Goethe to F. H. Jacobi, 2 February 1795.

51 Fichte visited Goethe: F. W. Riemer, c.1840 about May 1794, Fichte Gespräch, vol. 6.1, p. 47; see also Boyle 2000, p. 207.

51 Goethe's colour theory: Goethe 1840, Part 3, 'Chemische Farben' § 502, p. 206.

52 Fichte's importance for Goethe's work: Boyle 2000, p. 213ff.

52 Goethe struggled to understand Fichte: Goethe to F. H. Jacobi, 8 September 1794.

52 Listen to Fichte: Goethe to Charlotte von Kalb, 28 June 1794.

52 'Dear *non-Ich*': Goethe to F. H. Jacobi, 23 May 1794.

52 'lawless capriciousness': Jean Paul quoted in Safranski 2009a, p. 390.

52 'This preacher of freedom': Basilius von Ramdohr to C. G. Schütz, 20 February 1795, Fichte Gespräch, vol. 1, p. 250; see also C. M. Wieland to K. L. Reinhold, 31 December 1794, Fichte GA III, vol. 2, p. 245.

52 Fn. Kant had reviewed: Goethe 1982–96, vol. 3, p. 355.

52 'disgustingly playing with': J. G. Herder quoted in Kühn 2012, p. 271.

52 Fichte's temper: F. K. Forberg to unknown, 27 January 1795, Fichte Gespräch, vol. 1, p. 235; see also Kühn 2012, p. 170.

52 war on non-Ich: J. G. Rist, end 1795/spring 1796, Rist 1880, p. 70.

52 'wicked Jacobin': C. G. Voigt to Goethe, 15 June 1794.

53 'It is the purpose': Fichte, *Einige Vorlesungen über die Bestimmung des Gelehrten*, 1794, Lecture 2, Fichte SW, vol. 6, p. 306.

53 'My system is the': Fichte to J. I. Baggesen, 14 April 1795 (trans. in Boyle 2000, p. 35).

53 kings and princes: C. G. Voigt to Goethe, 15 June 1794; see also Duke Carl August to Goethe, 7 June 1794.

53 Carl August's admiration for Friedrich the Great: Safranski 2017, p. 173.

53 'the first servant of': Friedrich the Great, quoted in Brunschwig 1975, p. 27.

53 'he wanted no thinkers': Ernst August I, quoted ibid., p. 183.

53 imprisonment of the mind: Fichte, *Zurückforderung der Denkfreiheit von den Fürsten Europens*, 1793, Fichte SW, vol. 6, p. 26; see also pp. 6–7.

54 'Prince, you have no': ibid., p. 28.

54 Duke sent Goethe to Jena: Boyle 2000, p. 207; see also Carl August to Goethe, 7 June 1794.

54 'one of the most competent': Goethe, quoted in Boyle 2000, p. 207; see also Fichte to Goethe, 24 June 1794.

54 sheepish letter: Fichte to Johanne Fichte, end November/beginning December 1792 – this letter is lost but Johanne replied on 11 December 1792; see also 5 March 1793.

54 'abandoned by all': J. G. Rist, end of 1795/spring 1796, Rist 1880, p. 70.

54 Johanne's description of herself: Johanne Fichte to S. G. Fichte, 27 December 1794.

54 Johanne and parsimonious: Jakob Horner to Kaspar Horner, 20 April 1795, Fichte Gespräch, vol. 1, p. 269.

54 Johanne's calming temper: Fichte to Johanne Fichte, 12 June 1793.

54 'took up only fleeting': Anonymous to Heinrich Laube, 1794/5, Fichte Gespräch, vol. 1, p. 137.

54 'where nothing will disturb': Fichte to Johanne Fichte, 21 July 1794.

55 gossip about Johanne: Jakob Horner to Kaspar Horner, 20 April 1795; see also J. R. Rahn to J. H. Rahn, 30 May 1795 and 31 August 1797, Fichte Gespräch, vol. 1, p. 269; vol. 6.1, pp. 67, 149.

55 fashion in Jena: Fichte to Johanne Fichte, 14 June 1794.

55 'Goddess of Abundance': Dora Stock to Charlotte Schiller, 24 October 1798, C. Schiller 1862, vol. 3, p. 24.

55 help with wardrobe: Anonymous to Heinrich Laube, 1794/95, Fichte Gespräch, vol. 1, pp. 139–40.

55 people pointing at Johanne: J. R. Rahn to J. H. Rahn, 30 May 1795, Fichte Gespräch, vol. 6.1, p. 149.

55 lecture schedule: Ziolkowski 1998, p. 161.

56 'with the listeners': Fichte to J. K. Lavater, 1 February 1794.

56 'Society of Free': Fichte GA III, vol. 2, p. 255.

56 reading Fichte in taverns: Ernst Moritz Arndt in 1840 about his time in Jena in 1794, Fichte Gespräch, vol. 1, p. 128.

56 feeling obsolete: F. K. Forberg about Fichte, 1794/5, Fichte Gespräch, vol. 1, p. 103.

56 swept and carried away: F. K. Forberg to unknown, 27 January 1795, Fichte Gespräch, vol. 1, p. 234.

56 became 'unbearable': F. K. Forberg about Fichte, 1794/5, Fichte Gespräch, vol. 1, p. 103.

Chapter 3: 'The nation's finest minds'
Winter 1794–Spring 1795: Where All Paths Lead

58 'People always want me': Friedrich Förster quoting Goethe, 4 August 1831.

58 'these knavish executioners': Schiller to C. G. Körner, 8 February 1793.

58 Schiller more aristocratic: Goethe to J. P. Eckermann, 4 January 1824.

58 'wild animals': Schiller to Duke Friedrich Christian von Augustenburg, 13 July 1793.

59 'happy distraction': Schiller, *Horen*, Announcement, 10 December 1794.

59 'The German Reich': Schiller, *Deutsche Größe*, draft fragment of a poem.

59 'Spit out the water': J. G. Herder quoted in Ferber 2010, p. 102.

59 'A people of a language': J. G. Herder, 'Briefe zur Beförderung der Humanität', 1793–7, Herder 1877–99, vol. 17, p. 287.

59 Schiller stayed at home: Schiller to Goethe, 19 February 1795.

59 'literary society': Schiller to Goethe, 13 June 1794.

59 'the nation's finest minds': Schiller to J. B. Erhard, 26 May 1794.

60 Fn. AWS later explained: AWS to Tieck, 3 September 1803.

60 too salacious: Goethe to Schiller, 12 May 1795; see also Schiller to C. G. Körner, 10 July 1795.

60 'How can a woman embrace': Goethe, *Roman Elegies*, no. 3 (unpublished), 1795 (trans. David Luke), Goethe 1988, pp. 40–1.

60 'all respectable women': K. A. Böttiger, Goethe 1979, vol. 2, p. 41; K. A. Böttiger to Schulz, 27 July 1795, Ziolkowski 1998, p. 233.

60 *Horen* and *Huren*: J. G. Herder, Goethe 1979, vol. 2, p. 4.

60 'in *Horen* the great men': C. M. Wieland about *Horen*, 8 November 1795, recounted by K. A. Böttiger, Böttiger 1998, p. 164.

60 'divine Elegies': FS to AWS, 31 July 1795; for AWS's comment see AWS to Schiller, 13 October 1795.

60 Schiller's *Aesthetic Education*: Schiller, *Über die ästhetische Erziehung des Menschen in einer Reihe von Briefen, 1795*; see also Alt 2004, vol. 2, pp. 111–53; Ziolkowski 1998, pp. 118–26, 240–7; Schiller to Duke Friedrich Christian von Augustenburg, 13 July 1793.

61 'Utility is the great idol': Schiller, *Über die ästhetische Erziehung des Menschen*, Letter 2, Schiller 1962, vol. 5, p. 572.

61 feeling, reason and art: Schiller, *Über die ästhetische Erziehung des Menschen*, Letter 9, Schiller 1962, vol. 5, p. 592ff.

61 Kant and imagination: Kaag 2014, pp. 27–8, 37ff.

61 unite sensual and rational sides: Schiller, *Über die ästhetische Erziehung des Menschen*, Letters 12 and 19, Schiller 1962, vol. 5, pp. 588ff., 626ff.

61 'just as unreliable': Schiller to Duke Friedrich Christian von Augustenburg, 13 July 1793.

61 'art is a daughter': Schiller, *Über die ästhetische Erziehung des Menschen*, Letter 2, Schiller 1962, vol. 5, p. 572.

61 'it is through beauty': ibid., p. 573.

61 'masterpiece': Hegel to Schelling, 16 April 1795.

62 *Horen* was widely read: Schiller to Goethe, 25 January 1795; see also Alt 2004, vol. 2, p. 205.

62 'people tear the issues': Goethe to Schiller, 18 March 1795.

62 'so many excellent people': Schiller to C. G. Voigt, 6 April 1795.

62 university's governance: Friedrich Gedike's 1789 report to King Friedrich Wilhelm II, quoted in Ziolkowski 1999, pp. 234–5.

62 freedom to teach: A. G. F. Rebmann 1787–9, Rebmann 1994, p. 66.

62 universities in France and England: Ziolkowski 1999, pp. 221–2.

63 'Professors in all the': Henry Crabb Robinson, quoted in ibid., p. 235.

63 WH and CH's apartment: Wilhelm and Caroline von Humboldt had

moved to Jena in February 1794 but had lived just outside the old town walls on the northern edge. They moved to their apartment at Unterm Markt in October 1794.

63 WH and CH's previous visits: Alt 2004, vol. 2, p. 176.

63 'die Wunderäugige': Rahel Levin about CH, quoted in Gersdorff 2013, p. 12.

63 lonely childhoods: WH to CH, April 1790 and 9 October 1818.

64 'but to know you': CH to WH, 13 October 1790.

64 club and concerts in Jena: Anonymous 1798, pp. 84–5; Ziolkowski 1998, p. 32.

64 Schiller didn't like travelling: Schiller to C. G. Körner, 20 July 1794.

64 'great bustling oceans': Schiller to Caroline von Beulwitz, 27 November 1788.

64 Schiller read travel accounts: W. F. T. von Burgsdorff to K. A. von Brinkman, 12 December 1796, Burgsdorff 1907, p. 59.

64 happy only at home: Schiller to C. G. Körner, 20 July 1794.

64 'all my ideas develop': Schiller to C. G. Körner, 18 May 1794.

64 Schiller's thoughts on WH: ibid. and 21 November 1794 and 6 August 1797.

65 'study himself to death': AH to W. G. Wegener, 27 February 1789, Humboldt 1973, p. 44.

65 'from within': Schiller to C. G. Körner, 19 February 1793; see also 4 July 1794.

65 'individual perfection': Schiller to WH, 22 July 1796; see also Schiller to C. G. Körner, 6 August 1797.

65 'I really fear that': Schiller to C. G. Körner, 7 November 1794.

65 Schiller took the lead: Alt 2004, vol. 2, p. 178.

65 Goethe enjoyed their debates: Goethe to F. H. Jacobi, 31 October 1794 and 2 February 1795.

65 no politics: Goethe to Friedrich von Stein, 28 August 1794; see also Goethe to F. H. Jacobi, 31 October 1794.

65 'three-leaf clover': Schiller to C. G. Körner, 20 October 1797.

65 'social thinking': WH to Schiller, 4 August 1795.

65 'food for the soul': Goethe to Schiller, 12 May 1795.

65 meetings were electrifying: Schiller to WH, 17 February 1803.

65 bound to nature: Schiller to Goethe, 27 February 1795.

65 'never trade Jena': Schiller to C. G. Körner, 5 April 1795.

66 'fichticising': FS to Novalis, 5 May 1797 and 8 June 1797.

66 'But the non-Ich': Fichte, *Grundlage der gesammten Wissenschaftslehre*, 1794/5, in Fichte SW, vol. 1, p. 106; trans. Seidel 1993, p. 56 (I have changed Seidel's 'not-self' to 'non-Ich').

66 'Sparks of ideas': Fichte to K. L. Reinhold, 21 March 1797.

66 not understanding everything: Schiller to J. B. Erhard, 8 September 1794 and Goethe to F. H. Jacobi, 8 September 1794.

66 Hölderlin on Fichte's lectures: Hölderlin to J. C. Gok, 17 November 1794, Hölderlin 1943–85, vol. 6.1, p. 142.

66 'Titan fighting for': Hegel to Schelling, end January 1795.

66 'soul of Jena': Hölderlin to C. L. Neuffer, November 1794, Hölderlin 1943–85, vol. 6.1, p. 139.

66 500 students: Fichte to C. G. Voigt, 18 November 1794.

66 'church service of Reason': Anonymous, 1794/5, Fichte Gespräch, vol. 1, p. 181.

66 'temple of Reason': ibid., p. 185.

66 had to stop Sunday lectures: J. W. Schmid to Fichte, 23 November 1794.

66 'full stomach': Fichte to C. G. Voigt, 18 November 1794.

67 resumed Sunday lectures: Kühn 2012, p. 272.

67 fraternities in Jena: Fichte to Duke Carl August, 18 December 1794; see also Fichte GA III, vol. 2, p. 255.

67 stone-throwing: the first attack happened on 31 December 1794, Kühn 2012, p. 277ff.; Fichte to C. G. Voigt, 16 February 1795; Fichte to J. H. Voigt, 21 February 1795; J. R. Rahn to J. H. Rahn, c.8 May 1795, Fichte Gespräch, vol. 6.1, p. 147.

67 Colleagues laughing: Fichte to C. G. Voigt, 16 February 1795; Jakob Horner to Kasper Horner, 20 April 1795, Fichte Gespräch, vol. 1, p. 269.

67 shouted obscenities at Johanne: Fichte to C. G. Voigt, 16 February 1795.

67 'living skeleton': J. R. Rahn to J. H. Rahn, 30 May 1795, Fichte Gespräch, vol. 6.1, p. 149.

67 attacks on 9 April: Fichte, 'Rechenschaft an das Publikum über seine Entfernung von Jena in dem Sommerhalbjahr 1795'; A. von Gohren's protocol of Fichte's landlord Müller's testimony, 10 April 1795; J. R. Rahn to J. H. Rahn, c.8 May 1795, Fichte Gespräch, vol. 1, pp. 284–5 and vol. 6.1, pp. 143, 147.

67 'What do you want?' and following quotes: Fichte, 'Rechenschaft an das Publikum über seine Entfernung von Jena in dem Sommerhalbjahr 1795', Fichte Gespräch, vol. 1, pp. 284–5.

68 'Have him move out': ibid., p. 285.

68 take some time off: C. G. Voigt to Goethe, 9 April 1795.

68 Fichte to Oßmannstedt: Fichte stayed in Oßmannstedt from the end of April to early October 1795.

68 'most disagreeable way': Goethe, 1795, Goethe 1994b, p. 46; see also Goethe to C. G. Voigt, 10 April 1795.

68 'Fichte's supreme genius': Schiller to F. W. von Hoven, 22 November 1794.

68 'this path goes towards': Schiller to J. B. Erhard, 8 September 1794.

68 world like a ball: Schiller to Goethe, 28 October 1794.

69 'About Mind and Letters': Fichte, 'Über Geist und Buchstab in der Philosophie'; Fichte to Schiller, 21 June 1795.

69 'dry, cumbersome, and': Schiller to Fichte, 23 June 1795, 1st draft.

69 'shapeless length': Schiller to Fichte, 24 June 1795, 4th draft.

69 'salto mortale': ibid.

69 'the most abstruse': ibid.

69 'You're expecting me': ibid.

69 'most confused of all': Fichte to Schiller, 27 June 1795.

70 Goethe asked Schiller for advice: Schiller to Fichte, 3 August 1795, 1st draft.

70 'like an old woman': WH to Schiller, 17 July 1795.

70 Fichte couldn't let it go: Fichte's letter is lost but Schiller's reply sheds light on the content.

70 readers should not decide: Schiller to Fichte, 4 August 1795, 3rd draft.

70 'We are of two very': ibid.

Chapter 4: 'Electrified by our intellectual friction' 1795–1796: Love, Life and Literature

71 long and uncomfortable journey: J. C. F. Schlegel and Julie Schlegel to AWS, 13 August 1795; for hazardous travelling see also CS to Luise Gotter, 16 April 1795.

71 average travel speed: Preisendörfer 2018, p. 58.

71 inspections at borders: Steffens 1841, vol. 4, p. 171.

72 war was one of the reasons to resign: AWS to C. G. Heyne, 24 September 1795.

72 marriage proposal: FS to AWS, 5 December 1791 and January 1792.

72 'Schlegel and me!': CS to Lotte Michaelis Wiedemann, 1789.

72 AWS's childhood: Paulin 2016, pp. 20–30.

72 AWS was meticulous: Schelling to Fichte, 5 September 1800.

72 AWS's articles for *Horen*: in 1795 AWS contributed a four-part translation of Dante and an essay about poetry 'Briefe über Poesie, Silbenmaas und Sprache' ('Letters on Poetry, Metre and Language').

72 CS teased impeccably dressed AWS: Appel 2013, p. 132; Roßbeck 2008, p. 69.

73 stopped in Hanover: FS to AWS, 4 July 1795.

73 Mother Schlegel's warnings: J. C. E. Schlegel to AWS, early summer 1793 and 2 August 1795.

73 AWS arrived in Braunschweig: FS to AWS, 31 July 1795; AWS had seen CS last in Leipzig in July 1793, FS KA, vol. 23, p. xlii.

73 'great Ich in Oßmannstädt': Schiller to Goethe, 6 July 1795; see also Goethe to Schiller, 19 July 1795; WH to Schiller, 17 July 1795.

73 CS's appearance: painter Friedrich August Tischbein about CS, in CS Letters, vol. 1, p. 742; C. G. Körner to Schiller, 17 April 1797; Caroline Tischbein-Wilken, 1799, Stoll 1923, p. 110; see also CS's portraits.

73 CS's upbringing and education: Roßbeck 2008, p. 17ff.

73 'contest of wit': K. G. von Brinckmann to Rahel Levin, 29 March 1799, quoted in Oellers 1990, p. 130.

73 'I'll teach him': CS to FS, August 1795.

74 CS's first marriage: Roßbeck 2008, p. 44ff.

74 'prisoner in a dungeon': CS to F. L. W. Meyer, 14 October 1789.

74 CS escaped into books: CS to Luise Michaelis Wiedemann, 1785.

74 CS's children died: her son Wilhelm died on 20 July 1788 and her daughter Therese (who she called Röschen) died on 17 December 1789; Roßbeck 2008, pp. 64, 72.

74 CS's admirers: Roßbeck 2008, pp. 65, 74, 81.

74 CS no interest in remarrying: CS to Luise Gotter, 31 October 1791, see also CS to F. L. W. Meyer, 29 October 1792.

74 'overenthusiastic ideas': Luise Gotter to CS, 10 November 1791.

74 live with the consequences: CS to F. L. W. Meyer, 29 October 1792.

74 'loves freedom and not': Luise Michaelis Wiedemann to AWS, 7 May 1793.

74 'I wouldn't leave here': CS to Luise Gotter, 20 April 1792.

74 CS released from Königstein: CS to Luise and F. W. Gotter, 30 June 1793 and 13 July 1793.

75 AWS helped: AWS to Luise Michaelis Wiedemann, 18 June 1793; CS to F. L. W. Meyer, 30 July 1793; FS KA, vol. 23, p. xlii; see also CS Letters, vol. 1, pp. 702–3.

75 rumours that AWS was father of child: FS KA, vol. 23, p. xlii; FS to AWS, 21 August 1793.

75 CS's baby: Wilhelm Julius Krantz was born on 3 November 1793; FS KA, vol. 23, p. xlii.

75 'so that you won't heap': FS to AWS, 4 November 1793.

75 CS bribed priest: ibid.

75 'revolutionary whore': Roßbeck 2008, p. 120.

75 'one little foolishness': CS to F. L. W. Meyer, 30 July 1793.

75 'I'm an outcast': CS to F. L. W. Meyer, 20 February 1794.

76 Luise's reputation suffered: ibid.

76 'Berlin is big enough': CS to F. L. W. Meyer, 30 July 1793.

76 'respectable families': Reskript des Hannoverschen Universitätskuratoriums, Verbot des Aufenhalts in Göttingen, 16 August 1794, CS Letters, vol. 1, p. 346; for authorities in Dresden see FS to AWS, 27 October 1794.

76 'My life in Germany is': CS to F. L. W. Meyer, 15 June 1793; see also 16 March 1794.

76 only marriage could save her: CS to Julie Gotter, 18 February 1803.

76 'Were I to be my own': CS to Luise Gotter, 1 November 1781.

76 marrying AWS: CS to Julie Gotter, 18 February 1803; for governess position, see CS to G. J. Göschen, January 1796.

76 CS about AWS: CS to FS, before 28 August 1793 quoted in FS to AWS, 28 August 1793; CS to G. J. Göschen, January 1796.

76 friendship and love: CS to Luise Gotter, 1 November 1781.

76 new name: FS to AWS, 27 October 1794.

76 CS enjoyed male attention: FS to AWS, 13 April 1792.

77 CS arrival in Braunschweig: CS arrived in April 1795, FS KA, vol. 23, p. xlii; see also CS to Luise Gotter, 16 April 1795.

77 CS's baby died: FS to AWS, 20 May 1795.

77 'this child of my heart': CS to Luise Gotter, February 1794.

77 Auguste Böhmer: CS to Luise Gotter, February 1794; CS to F. L. W. Meyer, 16 March 1794.

77 'I can make happiness': CS to F. L. W. Meyer, 12 August 1792; see also CS to Schelling, 18 November 1800.

77 'I'm sure you can calm': FS to AWS, 20 May 1795.

77 don't wait: FS to AWS, 4 July 1795.

77 FS criticised AWS for his affair: FS to AWS, 16 June 1795.

77 AWS's affair in Amsterdam: FS to AWS, 4, 28 July 1792, 10 March 1793, 28 August 1793, 30 October 1793.

78 where to go?: for Holland see FS to AWS, 27 October 1794; for Rome see FS to AWS, 7 April 1795.

78 'Apart from the freedom': FS to AWS, 20 May 1795.

78 CS loved quick decisions: CS to F. L. W. Meyer, 10 May 1794.

78 AWS distant at first: CS to FS, August 1795.

78 'is truly a consolation': AWS and CS to G. J. Göschen, after 6 August 1795.

78 AWS and CS adding postscripts: AWS and CS to G. J. Göschen, after 6 August 1795; CS and AWS to Luise Gotter, autumn 1795.

78 'your Caroline': J. C. E. Schlegel to AWS, 1 November 1795.

78 'Böhmer': J. C. E. Schlegel to AWS, 2 August 1795.

78 'So I am more or less': Schiller to C. G. Körner, 4 July 1795; see also 17 August 1795.

79 'Lord help me': Schiller to C. G. Körner, 29 December 1794.

79 'from whom I can expect': Schiller to WH, 9 November 1795; see also Schiller to C. G. Körner, 19 January 1795 and 23 February 1795.

79 too much abstract material: Schiller to Goethe, 15 May 1795.

79 'let's just continue': Goethe to Schiller, 15 May 1795.

79 Schiller felt like giving up: Schiller to WH, 21 August 1795.

79 Humboldt's advice: WH to Schiller, 31 August 1795.

79 'watery soups': Schiller to J. F. Cotta, 3 September 1795.

79 'heavy cavalry': Schiller to Goethe, 1 November 1795.

79 review of *Horen*: Nicolai 1796, vol. 11, p. 181.

80 'The insect just couldn't': Schiller to Goethe, 16 October 1796.

80 'We really and truly': Schiller to Goethe, 1 November 1795; see also Schiller to Goethe, 27 January 1796.

80 AWS to review *Horen* in ALZ: Schiller to AWS, 29 October 1795.

80 'in the hands of': Goethe to Schiller, 26 December 1795.

80 AWS's *Horen* contributions: AWS's Dante translation was published in *Horen*, nos 3, 4, 7 and 8; the essay 'Briefe über Poesie, Silbenmaaß und Sprache' was published in issue no. 11.

80 'Send us whatever': Schiller to AWS, 12 June 1795; see also 14 September 1795 and 5 October 1795.

80 AWS's doubts about literary talent: FS to AWS, 11 February 1792.

80 AWS in love with CS: WH to Schiller, 25 August 1795.

80 letters to WH to help CS: WH to AWS, 25 May 1793.

80 'had a decisive influence': WH to Schiller, 25 August 1795.

80 luring AWS to Jena: WH to Schiller, 30 October 1795.

81 AWS's plans: Schiller to AWS, 5 October 1795.

81 CS scanning verses: FS to AWS, 30 January 1796; for CS's contribution, see Roßbeck 2008, pp. 128, 145–7; see also AWS and CS's manuscript for the translation of *Romeo and Juliet*, SLUB, Mscr.Dresden.e.90, xxii, 10.

81 Shakespeare prose translations: Schiller to AWS, 11 March 1796. This related to previous translations by J. J. Eschenberg, C. M. Wieland and G. A. Bürger.

81 'The recurring rhythm': AWS quoted in Schulz 2000, p. 559.

81 'don't fit the verse metre': AWS to Schiller, 1 March 1796.

81 published in *Horen*: Schiller to AWS, 11 March 1796.

81 Shakespeare publication dates: Bernays 1872, p. 4.

81 'to see how much he': AWS to Tieck, 3 September 1837.

82 CS shaped AWS's thinking: WH to Schiller, 25 August 1795; for CS's influence see also FS to AWS, 9 October 1793.

82 CS's contributions to essays and reviews: AWS 1828, vol. 2, contents page (CS's contributions marked with an asterisk); see also Roßbeck 2008, p. 128; Reulecke 2020, pp. 372–4; SLUB Mscr. Dresd. App. 2712, A7 and https://www.carolineschelling.com/carolines-literary-reviews-vol-1/#back*.

82 CS's voice: FS to AWS, 27 February 1794; Schelling to Luise Gotter, 24 September 1809.

82 '. . . Oh, should you wish': J. D. Gries, 'An Aug. Wilh. Schlegel. Bei Zurücksendung seiner Lebensmelodien', 1798, Gries 1829, vol. 2, p. 11 (trans. Damion Searls).

82 CS became indispensable: CS to Luise Gotter, 7 September 1797.

82 'Why can't you live': Schiller to AWS, 10 December 1795.

82 'pilgrimage' to Jena: AWS to Schiller, 18 December 1795.

82 Schiller was delighted: Schiller to AWS, 9 January 1796.

82 'Letters on Poetry, Metre': AWS, 'Briefe über Poesie, Silbenmaaß und Sprache', Horen, 1796, no. 11.

83 'Once you're here': Schiller to AWS, 9 January 1796.

83 'close up the philosophical': Schiller to Goethe, 17 December 1795.

83 Horen and poems: see in particular Horen, 1795, no. 9.

83 Schiller's first poem: this was Schiller's 'Poesie des Lebens', June 1795, Goethe 1982–96, vol. 3, p. 393.

83 Schiller's philosophy was too poetic: Schiller to Goethe, 31 August 1794.

83 philosophy and poetry: Schiller to WH, 5 October 1795; Schiller to Charlotte von Schimmelmann, 4 November 1795; Schiller to Goethe, 17 December 1795; Schiller to C. G. Körner, 18 January 1796.

83 'muses suck a person': Schiller to Goethe, 29 August 1795.

83 'a poetic oaf compared': Schiller to C. G. Körner, 27 June 1796.

83 'restless activity': WH to Schiller, 4 August 1795.

83 editing Wilhelm Meister: Goethe to Schiller, 18 June 1795.

83 'I cannot express how': Goethe to Schiller, 20 May 1796.

83 administrative tasks in Jena: for gardener's salary see Goethe to Duke Carl August, 11 February 1794; for flood defences see Goethe to C. G. Voigt, 28 April 1796.

84 billiard table: Goethe to C. G. Voigt, 13 March 1796.

84 'my novel is like': Goethe to J. H. Meyer, 30 December 1795.

84 'Only the absolute silence': Goethe to Schiller, 17 March 1798.

84 'this lovely crazy': Goethe to K. F. Zelter, 16 February 1818.

84 more days in Jena: for example during the first half of 1796, Goethe stayed in Jena on 3–17 January, 16 February–16 March and 28 April–8 June.

84 Goethe different in Jena: Charlotte Schiller to Charlotte von Stein, 1 October 1797, Goethe 1965–2000, vol. 4, p. 320; see also DV to Sophie Bernhardi, 7 October 1799.

84 Goethe's clothing: K. A. Böttiger, 1795, Böttiger 1998, p. 67.

84 daily walks: Goethe to Christiane Vulpius, 8 January 1796.

84 walking helped digestion: K. A. Böttiger, November 1798, Böttiger 1998, p. 92.

84 Schiller's new apartment: in April 1795 Schiller had moved to the Griesbach house at Löbdergraben 15a, next to the auditorium where he had given his inaugural lecture.

84 stayed until midnight: Schiller to WH, 9 November 1795.

84 'without it he couldn't live': Goethe to J. P. Eckermann, 8 October 1827.

85 Goethe's instructions: Goethe to Christiane Vulpius, 20 February 1796 and 14 April 1796.

85 How was August: Goethe to Christiane Vulpius, 9 November 1795.

85 fruits for August: Goethe to Christiane Vulpius, 6 June 1797; August Goethe to Goethe, 26 September 1798.

85 Christiane disliked his absences: Christiane Vulpius to Goethe, 9 April 1795, 20 February 1796 and many more letters; Goethe to Schiller, 3 August 1799.

85 'don't make eyes': Christiane Vulpius to Goethe, 11 April 1795.

85 Christiane's life in Weimar: Christiane Vulpius to Goethe, 27 February 1796, 2 March 1796, 21 February 1797.

85 Christiane's parties and dancing: Christiane Vulpius to Goethe, 2 March 1796, 22 November 1798, 27 March 1799.

85 'My dear child': Goethe to Christiane Vulpius, 9 September 1796.

85 'Before I go': Goethe to Christiane Vulpius, 2 July 1795.

85 'I'm sick of working': Goethe to Christiane Vulpius, 7 March 1796.

85 room in Zum Schwarzen Bären: ibid.

85 Goethe played with August: Luise Seidler, Goethe 1982–96, vol. 3, pp. 354–5; see also K. A. Böttiger, 1795, Böttiger 1998, p. 67; for pumpkin see August Goethe to Goethe, 26 September 1798.

86 caught frogs with August: Goethe, 30 May 1796, Goethe Diaries, vol. 2, p. 44.

86 August's notes to Goethe: August Goethe to Goethe, 7 June 1797, 28 March 1798, 30 May 1798, 8 June 1798.

86 Goethe skating: J. G. Rist, end 1795/spring 1796, Rist 1880, p. 67; see also J. I. Weitzel, Goethe 1982–96, vol. 3, p. 450.

86 Schiller as father: Heinrich Voß to Christian Niemeyer, April 1804, Petersen 1909, vol. 3, pp. 95–6.

86 children a part of their lives: Goethe to Christiane Vulpius, 1 November 1796; Schiller to J. C. and E. D. Schiller, 21 November 1794; for breast-feeding, see Schiller to Goethe, 12 July 1796. Breastfeeding had become so acceptable that the recently codified *Allgemeines Landrecht für die Preußischen Staaten* stipulated that mothers should breastfeed their children – though fathers decided the duration (2. Part, 2. Titel, §§ 67–8).

86 'Love childhood' and following quote: Rousseau 1965, pp. 33, 39.

87 'Golden Boy': Schiller to J. C. and E. D. Schiller, 21 November 1794; for Karl Schiller and whip, see K. W. F von Funck to C. G. Körner, 17 January 1796, Petersen 1909, vol. 3, p. 35.

87 'August is looking': Goethe to Schiller, 20 May 1796; see also Charlotte von Stein to Fritz von Stein, 14 April 1796, Goethe 1982–96, vol. 3, p. 458.

87 united by a family bond: Schiller to Goethe, 26 October 1795.

87 Schiller had to have a girl: Goethe to Schiller, 1 November 1795.

87 Goethe's children: unnamed, October 1791; Caroline Goethe, 21 November 1793–4 December 1793; Karl Goethe, 30 October 1795–18 November 1795; Kathinka Goethe, 18 December 1802–21 December 1802.

87 Goethe mourned their deaths: J. H. Meyer about Goethe, December 1793, Goethe 1965–2000, vol. 4, p. 47.

87 Goethe distracted himself: Goethe to Schiller, 21 November 1795.

87 concealed authorship: Schiller to WH, 1 February 1796.

87 *Xenien* his bastard children: Schiller to C. G. Körner, 1 February 1796.

87 laughter and *Xenien*: Maria Körner, about April/May 1796, Goethe 1965–2000, vol. 4, p. 222; they had begun composing the *Xenien* in late December 1795, see Goethe to Schiller, 23 December 1795 and Schiller to Goethe, 29 December 1795.

87 'around with a flyswatter': CS to Luise Gotter, 4 September 1796.

88 'I am I, and I posit': Goethe and Schiller, *Xenien*, in *Musen-Almanach für das Jahr 1797*, p. 294.

88 *Xenien* and Friedrich Reichardt: Goethe to Schiller, 30 January 1796; see for example *Xenien*, no. 30.

88 'Here are another few': Schiller to Goethe, 27 January 1796.

88 'But here fluttering': Goethe and Schiller, *Xenien*, in *Musen-Almanach für das Jahr 1797*, p. 218; CS sent a letter to Luise Gotter with a key on which verse was addressed at whom, CS to Luise Gotter, 22 (?) October 1796.

88 'Almanac of the Furies': Schiller to Goethe, 28 October 1796.

88 *Musen-Almanach* sold out: Schiller to J. F. Cotta, 31 October 1796.

88 'To a certain extent': Schiller to C. G. Körner, 10 April 1796 (this was Goethe's *Egmont*).

88 'This year': Schiller to WH, 4 January 1796.

89 CS's story or novella: AWS to Schiller, 28 June 1796.

89 Goethe approved translation: AWS to G. J. Göschen, 24 June 1796.

89 Goethe remembered CS: AWS to Schiller, 28 June 1796.

89 'democratic tendencies': Goethe to J. H. Meyer, 20 May 1796.

89 discussions entertaining with AWS: Goethe to WH, 27 May 1796.

89 'You are now': K. A. M. Schlegel to AWS, 1 July 1796.

89 AWS got soaked: AWS to Schiller, 28 June 1796.

89 future with CS in Jena: AWS to G. J. Göschen, 24 June 1796.

89 'His literary fame': Therese Huber to Therese Forster, 17–25 July 1803, Huber 1999, vol. 1, p. 423.

89 'new generation': Goethe to Schiller, 26 December 1795.

Chapter 5: 'Philosophy is originally a feeling'
Summer 1796: Novalis in Love

90 Sophie's surgery: Jeannette Danscour to Novalis, 8 July 1796.

90 surgical instruments: Savigny 1800.

90 Sophie's illness: Jeannette Danscour to Novalis, 7 March 1795 and 8 July 1796; Novalis to Karl von Hardenberg, 20 November 1795.

90 common eighteenth-century treatments: Stark 1799, pp. 207, 216–18; Tsouyopoulos 1990, p. 102.

90 leeches: Stark 1799, p. 207.

90 Dr Stark: Hesse 2004, p. 73ff.

91 Sophie's surgery: Jeannette Danscour to Novalis, 8 July 1796; for contemporary surgeries in general, see Richter 1794, pp. 32–3, 249ff.

91 cloth over face: Hesse 2004, p. 75.

91 'how much stuff': Jeannette Danscour to Novalis, 8 July 1796.

91 Dr Stark's doubts: Novalis to Wilhelmine von Thümmel, 18 July 1796.

91 Novalis in Jena: ibid.

92 Fn. De Novali: Novalis to AWS, 24 February 1798.

92 Novalis's childhood sickness: A. C. Just, 'Friedrich von Hardenberg', 1805 and Ludwig Tieck about Novalis, 1815, Novalis Schriften, vol. 4, pp. 538, 552.

92 'foolish, crazy acts': Novalis to K. L. Reinhold, 5 October 1791.

92 'worth more than': ibid.

92 Novalis's appearance and character: Steffens 1841, vol. 4, pp. 320–3; A. C. Just, 'Friedrich von Hardenberg', 1805 and Ludwig Tieck about Novalis, 1815, Novalis Schriften, vol. 4, pp. 540, 549, 558ff.; see also FS to AWS, January 1792, 11 February 1792 and 13 April 1792; FS to Novalis, end of May 1793; Erasmus von Hardenberg to Novalis, 6 December 1794.

93 Novalis's voice: Steffens 1841, vol. 4, p. 321.

93 'electrified me': Henriette Mendelssohn to DV, 19 April 1799.

93 'few people in my': Steffens 1841, vol. 4, p. 323.

93 five-hour ride to Jena: Novalis to Wilhelmine von Thümmel, 19 September 1796.

93 Novalis's visit in Jena: Novalis saw Fichte at Professor Niethammer's house, together with Hölderlin, on 28 May 1795. F. I. Niethammer, 28 May 1795, diary, Fichte Gespräch, vol. 1, p. 284.

93 'first electric sparks': A. C. Just, 'Friedrich von Hardenberg', 1805, Novalis vol. 4, p. 539.

93 'dreadful loops of': Novalis to FS, 14 June 1797; Novalis's Fichte studies comprise of around five hundred MS pages written from winter 1795 to autumn 1796, see Novalis, 'Fichte Studies', Novalis Schriften, vol. 2, pp. 104–296 and Novalis 2003 (for English translation); see also Hädecke 2011, pp. 116–24.

93 'fichticising than Fichte': Novalis, 'Logologische Fragmente', no. 1, Novalis Schriften, vol. 2, p. 524.

93 'the one who woke': Novalis to FS, 8 July 1796; for Fichte as second Copernicus, see Novalis, 'Allgemeine Brouillon', no. 460, Novalis Schriften, vol. 3, p. 335; Novalis 2007, p. 77.

94 'practise slowness': Novalis, 'Fichte Studies', no. 407, Novalis Schriften, vol. 2, p. 234; Novalis 2003, p. 133.

94 'if one only wills': Novalis, 'Fichte Studies', no. 420, Novalis Schriften, vol. 2, p. 235; Novalis 2003, p. 134.

94 'Where do I exit': Novalis, 'Fichte Studies', no. 372, Novalis Schriften, vol. 2, p. 231; Novalis 2003, p. 129.

94 'From where do': Novalis, 'Fichte Studies', no. 567, Novalis Schriften, vol. 2, p. 271; Novalis 2003, pp. 168–9.

94 'Fichtean philosophy': Novalis, 'Fichte Studies', no. 567, Novalis Schriften, vol. 2, p. 271; Novalis 2003, p. 168.

94 questions about origin of Ich: Novalis, 'Fichte Studies', no. 14, Novalis Schriften, vol. 2, p. 112; Novalis 2003, p. 12; see also Pikulik 1992, p. 40 and Uerlings 1991, p. 115.

94 'Philosophy is originally': Novalis, 'Fichte Studies', no. 15, Novalis Schriften, vol. 2, p. 113; Novalis 2003, p. 13.

94 why had Fichte ignored love?: Novalis to FS, 8 July 1796.

94 'Freedom and love': Novalis, 'Allgemeine Brouillon', no. 717, Novalis Schriften, vol. 3. p. 406; Novalis 2007, p. 132; see also Ludwig Tieck about Novalis, 1815, Novalis Schriften, vol. 4, p. 559.

94 child was love made visible: Novalis, 'Allgemeine Brouillon', no. 79, Novalis Schriften, vol. 3. p. 253; Novalis 2007, p. 79.

94 'synthesising force': Novalis, 'Fichte Studies', no. 651, Novalis Schriften, vol. 2, p. 292.

94 Ich became 'You': Novalis, 'Allgemeine Brouillon', no. 820, Novalis Schriften, vol. 3. p. 430; Novalis 2007, p. 151.

94 theory of love: Novalis, 'Allgemeine Brouillon', no. 79, Novalis Schriften, vol. 3. p. 253; Novalis 2007, p. 12.

95 'The sciences and love': Novalis to Caroline Just, 10 April 1796.

95 'To what we love': Erasmus von Hardenberg to Novalis, 4 September 1795; see also J. R. von Rockenthien to Novalis, 10 February 1796.

95 Novalis's father: Köpke 1855, vol. 1, p. 249.

95 Sophie's jolly family: Karl von Hardenberg to Erasmus von Hardenberg, 16 December 1795, Novalis Schriften, vol. 4, p. 590.

95 topics avoided at home: Köpke 1855, vol. 1, p. 249.

95 'blind religious zeal': Erasmus von Hardenberg to Novalis, 6 December 1794.

95 Novalis loved Sophie's family: Novalis to Wilhelmine von Thümmel, February 1796; Karl von Hardenberg to Erasmus von Hardenberg, 4 March 1796, Novalis Schriften, vol. 4, p. 594.

95 seeing Sophie for fifteen minutes: Erasmus von Hardenberg to Novalis, 28 November 1794.

95 'Again nothing happened': Sophie von Kühn, diary, 1 January–14 March 1795, Novalis Schriften, vol. 4, p. 586ff.

95 Sophie stood up to Novalis: Erasmus von Hardenberg to Novalis, 4 September 1795.

96 'when I remember to': Sophie von Kühn and other family members to Novalis, 26 March 1795.

96 Novalis fell in love easily: Erasmus von Hardenberg to Novalis, 28 November 1794 and 24 September 1795; Karl von Hardenberg to Erasmus von Hardenberg, 18 September 1794, Novalis Schriften, vol. 4, p. 578.

96 'sensual again this': Novalis, diary, 7 May 1797, Novalis Schriften, vol. 4, p. 34.

96 'lewdness raged from': Novalis, diary, 12 May 1797, ibid., p. 35.

96 'much lewdness': Novalis, diary, 14 May 1797, ibid., p. 36.

96 'took lewdness a little': Novalis, diary, 21 May 1797, ibid., p. 38.

96 'this morning's lewd': Novalis, diary, 9 June 1797, ibid., p. 45.

96 'I was rather': Novalis, diary, 24 April 1797, ibid., p. 30.

96 'We kiss and kiss': Novalis Schriften, vol. 6.1, p. 249; see also pp. 121, 184, 249, 527 (trans. Damion Searls).

96 'Rosy silk wreathed': Novalis Schriften, vol. 6.1, p. 527 (trans. Damion Searls).

96 'preferred inspecting': Karl von Hardenberg and Novalis to C. F. Brachmann, 15 September 1794, Novalis Schriften, vol. 4, p. 141.

96 'In the end I avoided': Novalis to Erasmus von Hardenberg, early November 1794.

96 'Devil of Lewdness': Novalis to C. F. Brachmann, 16 November 1794.

97 Sophie too young to be seductive: O'Brien 1995, p. 39ff.; see also Erasmus von Hardenberg to Novalis, 28 November 1794.

97 secret engagement: Novalis to H. U. E. von Hardenberg, mid-June 1796.

97 family first reluctant: ibid.; see also Novalis to J. W. Oppel, late January 1800.

97 FS suggested to visit: Novalis to FS, 8 July 1796.

97 'as long as you like': ibid.

97 FS's journey to Weißenfels: FS to AWS, 28 July 1796; FS to Novalis, 23 July 1796; FS left Dresden on 21 July and Leipzig on 29 July 1796.

97 FS's and Novalis's friendship: FS to AWS, 11 February 1792, 13 April 1792 and 21 November 1792; FS to Novalis, mid-May 1793.

97 FS as mentor: FS to AWS, 13 April 1792.

98 'he can do anything': FS to AWS, 11 February 1792; see also FS to AWS, January 1792.

98 Novalis's fire: FS to AWS, January 1792.

98 'a sensual pleasure': FS to Novalis, end of May 1793.

98 'You introduced me to Heaven': Novalis to FS, first half of August 1793.

98 'high priest': ibid.

98 Friedrich's 'prophet': FS to Novalis, mid-August 1793.

98 'shackle myself': FS to AWS, 2 June 1793

98 'wedding night, marriage': Novalis to FS, 1 August 1794.

98 Novalis in Jena: Novalis to Wilhelmine von Thümmel, 18 July 1796 (Novalis had returned on 18 July 1796 and went back to Jena on 23 July, just before FS's arrival); meeting Novalis on the road: FS to AWS, 28 July 1796; FS to CS, 2 August 1796.

98 Weißenfels: Bach 2003, p. 176ff.

99 'I'm not in such a hurry': Novalis to FS, 8 July 1796.

99 'Sophie is her name': ibid.

99 'are integrated halves': Novalis, 'Logologische Fragmente', no. 115, Novalis Schriften, vol. 2, p. 548.

99 'catch sight of ourselves': Novalis, 'Allgemeine Brouillon', no. 820, Novalis Schriften, vol. 3, p. 429; Novalis 2007, p. 151.

99 'back and forth': Novalis, 'Fichte Studies', no. 19, Novalis Schriften, vol. 2, p. 117.

99 philosophy had to be contradictory: FS KA, vol. 18, p. 407; see also Endres 2017, p. 47.

99 philosophy a never-ending process: Pikulik 1992, pp. 57, 59; Hädecke 2011, pp. 121–2.

100 FS and CS met first: FS to AWS, 2 August 1793; CS had arrived in Leipzig on 20 July 1793.

100 'Imagine that I'm': FS to CS, 2 August 1796.

100 'Very early on': FS to AWS, 21 August 1793; for CS's influence on FS, see also FS to AWS, 29 September 1793 and 11 December 1793, 27 February 1794 and 9 May 1794; CS to FS, June 1795.

100 'She made me a better': FS to AWS, 11 December 1793.

100 FS, CS and French Revolution: Zimmermann 2009, p. 88.

100 nation as the greater Ich: ibid.

100 'You have to not just carry': ibid., p. 87.

100 AWS worried about CS's influence: FS to AWS, 11 December 1793.

100 'also thinking somewhat': CS to FS, August 1795.

100 'A word of command': Novalis, 'Blüthenstaub' ('Pollen'), no. 2, Novalis Schriften, vol. 2, p. 413; Novalis 1991, p. 383.

101 like an expectant father: FS to AWS, 4 November 1793.

101 'his passion raged': FS, Lucinde, 1799, F. Schlegel 1999, pp. 70–1; see also Roßbeck 2008, p. 113.

101 FS left for Jena: FS arrived in Jena 6 August 1796, FS KA, vol. 23, p. 508.

101 FS's critical review: AWS to J. F. Reichardt, 20 June 1796; FS to AWS, 28 July 1796; FS's review was published at the end of July 1796.

101 FS asked Körner for help: C. G. Körner to Schiller, 22 July 1796.

101 FS asked AWS for help: FS to AWS, 28 July 1796.

Chapter 6: 'Our splendid circle'
Summer–Winter 1796: The Schlegels Arrive

102 AWS's appearance: Appel 2013, p. 132; Roßbeck 2008, p. 69, AWS portrait by Johann Friedrich August Tischbein, 1793; Paulin 2016, pp. 246, 307.

102 CS's clothes: CS portrait by Johann Friedrich August Tischbein, 1798; see also DV to Schleiermacher, 11 October 1799; for CS as seamstress, see Roßbeck 2008, p. 26.

102 description of fashion: Fashion plates in Journal des Luxus und der Moden (Journal for Luxury and Fashions), vol. 11, January–December 1796.

102 fashion during CS's youth: see silhouette of Caroline, her sister Luise and her mother, c. 1780–90, anonymous, private collection Martin Reulecke, printed in Bamberg and Ilbrig 2018, p. 89.

103 'bold mixture of such': FS, Lucinde, 1799, F. Schlegel 1999, p. 71.

103 'One look is all it': FS, Lucinde, 1799, F. Schlegel 1999, p. 70.

103 intellectual duel with CS: K. G. von Brinckmann to Rahel Levin, 29 March 1799, Oellers 1990, p. 130.

103 'a firm, almost instinctive': CS to F. L. W. Meyer, 15 June 1793; for CS and other women, see gossip in Würzburg in 1804 in letters from Karoline Paulus, Rosine Eleanore Niethammer and Henriette Hoven to Charlotte Schiller, in C. Schiller 1862, vol. 3.

103 AWS and CS visited Schillers: CS to Luise Gotter, 11 July 1796; see also Schiller to Goethe, 9 July 1796. They arrived in Jena on 8 July but it was too late to visit the Schillers. They visited the next day, on 9 July, and then again on 11 July.

103 AWS and CS's second visit to Schiller: CS to Luise Gotter, 11 July 1796; see also Schiller to Goethe, 11 July 1796.

103 'some kind of thorn': Schiller to WH, 22 July 1796.

103 Goethe looked forward to meeting Schlegels: Goethe to Schiller, 12 July 1796.

104 Goethe in Jena: CS to Luise Gotter, 17–20 July 1796; Goethe, 16–18 July 1796, Goethe Diaries, vol. 2, p. 45; see also Goethe to Schiller, 7 July 1796.

104 Schlegels' garden villa: for the location see Kösling 2010, pp. 18–19.

104 CS and Goethe in Göttingen and Mainz: CS to Luise Gotter, 30 September 1783; Karl and Julie Schlegel, 18 July 1796; see also AWS to Schiller, 28 June 1796.

104 CS hardly recognised Goethe: CS to Luise Gotter, 17–20 July 1796; CS and AWS to Karl and Julie Schlegel, 18 July 1796.

104 CS undressing in heat: CS to Luise Gotter, 17–20 July 1796.

104 Goethe and CS reminisced: CS to Karl and Julie Schlegel, 18 July 1796; see also AWS to Schiller, 28 June 1796.

104 Goethe and CS's imprisonment: Goethe to F. H. Jacobi, 7 July 1793.

104 Goethe 'threatened': CS to Luise Gotter, 17–20 July 1796.

104 CS and AWS in Jena: CS to Luise Gotter, 17–20 July 1796; CS and AWS to Karl and Julie Schlegel, 18 July 1796.

104 concerts and amateur plays: CS to Luise Gotter, 12 December 1796; see also Sophie Mereau's diary for 1796–7, Mereau-Brentano 1996, pp. 22–3, 27.

104 'a short, stocky': CS to Karl and Julie Schlegel, 18 July 1796.

104 son named Immanuel: CS to Luise Gotter, 17–20 July 1796.

104 Schiller rarely left house: J. G. Rist, end 1795/spring 1796, Rist 1880, p. 68.

104 'armies of young believers': Anonymous, summer 1798, Fichte Gespräch, vol. 1, p. 501; for resumption of lectures, see J. G. Rist, end 1795/spring 1796, Rist 1880, p. 62.

104 three hundred students: A. F. May, diary, 19/20 July 1796, Fichte Gespräch, vol. 1, p. 364.

105 Schiller's family ill and French advances: Schiller to C. G. Körner, 23 May 1796; Schiller to J. F. Cotta, 13 July 1796.

105 people 'trembled': CS to Luise Gotter, 17–20 July 1796.

105 'For whom do you fight': H. C. Boie, quoted in Brunschwig 1975, p. 278.

105 green-and-yellow uniforms: Boyle 2000, p. 392.

105 Fn. Schiller's parents: Christophine Reinwald to Schiller, 20 July 1796.

106 French and Schiller family: Christophine Reinwald to Schiller, 20 July 1796; for Goethe dispatching news, see Goethe to Schiller, 22 July 1796.

106 'Political matters, which': Schiller to Goethe, 25 July 1796.

106 Schiller feared the French: Schiller to J. F. Cotta, 1 August 1796.

106 Horen delayed: J. F. Cotta to Schiller, 5 August 1796.

106 Goethe's mother in Frankfurt: C. E. Goethe to Goethe, 22 July 1796 and 1 August 1796.

106 Goethe's mother playing piano: C. E. Goethe to Goethe, 1 August 1796.

106 'mountains that otherwise': Goethe to Schiller, 30 July 1796.

106 safe-keeping in Weimar: see for example Goethe to C. E. Polex, 23 December 1796, Goethe 1982–96, vol. 3, p. 526.

106 Goethe cancelled vacation: Goethe to WH, 27 May 1796.

106 FS arrived in Jena: FS arrived on 6 August 1796, FS KA, vol. 23, p. 508.

106 FS's first forty-eight hours: FS to Novalis, 9 August 1796.

106 Schiller about FS: Schiller to WH, 7 August 1796 and Schiller to Goethe, 7 August 1796.

107 FS worried his parents: for example J. C. E. Schlegel to AWS, early summer 1793.

107 FS's studies in Leipzig: Zimmermann 2009, pp. 28–30.

107 thinkers stunted by convention: FS to AWS, 19 June 1793.

107 'My goal is to live': FS to AWS, 2 June 1793; see also FS to AWS, end of May 1793.

107 FS's character: FS to AWS, 21 November 1792; WH to F. H. Jacobi, 23 January 1797.

107 FS's appearance: Caroline Tischbein-Wilken, 1799, Stoll 1923, p. 114; Schleiermacher to Charlotte Schleiermacher, 31 December 1797, Schleiermacher 1988, Part 5, vol. 2, p. 220; WH to F. H. Jacobi, 23 January 1797.

107 'People prefer to': FS to AWS, 21 November 1792.

107 FS suicidal: FS to AWS, 21 November 1792; Novalis to FS, 15 August 1793.

107 'For several days': FS to AWS, 19 June 1793 and Zimmermann 2009, p. 31.

107 FS had no money: FS to AWS, 21 November 1792; 1 August 1792; FS to Novalis, 15 July 1793.

107 'Fritz is bankrupting us': J. C. E. Schlegel to AWS, beginning April 1793.

107 'give him some good': J. C. E. Schlegel to AWS, early summer 1793.

108 Schlegels' house in Jena: Kösling 2010, pp. 18–19, 55; Luise Gotter to Julie Gotter, 14 January 1798, BBAW Nachlass Schelling, no. 936; DV to Schleiermacher, 11 October 1799; CS to Auguste, 30 September 1799; CS to Luise Gotter, 5 October 1799; CS to J. D. Gries, 27 December 1799.

108 jokes about windows: CS to Luise Gotter, 4 September 1796.

108 'he isn't one': CS to Luise Gotter, 15 October 1796; see also AWS to G. J. Göschen, 17 October 1796.

108 Humboldts returned to Jena: Schiller to Goethe, 2 November 1796; see also Gall 2011, pp. 82–4.

108 Goethe couldn't leave Schiller: Goethe to C. G. Voigt, 20 September 1796.

108 'It was impossible to get': Goethe to C. G. Voigt, 20 September 1796.

108 'he seems to have arrived': CH to K. G. von Brinckmann, 3 December 1796; for WH and AWS reconnecting, see WH to AWS, 23 July 1796.

109 Burgsdorff in Jena: see his letters to Rahel Levin, October 1796–summer 1797, Burgsdorff 1907, pp. 17–100.

109 '27 July in Spa': WH, diary, July–August 1789, Berglar 1970, p. 39.

109 to live free of all constraints: Gersdorff 2013, pp. 29, 58.

109 'I found what I': WH, quoted in ibid., pp. 62–3.

109 'All this racket': CH to WH, 19 December 1790.

109 'When you forgo': WH quoted in Gersdorff 2013, p. 58.

109 Burgsdorff accompanied them: W. F. T. von Burgsdorff to Rahel Levin, 21 November 1796 and 28 November 1796, W. F. T. von Burgsdorff to K. G. von Brinckmann, 12 December 1796, Burgsdorff 1907, pp. 49–51, 53, 58–9; CH to K. G. von Brinckmann, 3 December 1797; Goethe to Schiller, 30 November 1796.

109 CH rested in the afternoons: CH to K. G. von Brinckmann, 3 December 1797.

109 'my dear, my great': W. F. T. von Burgsdorff to Rahel Levin, 28 December 1797, Burgsdorff 1907, p. 63.

109 CH pouring tea: W. F. T. von Burgsdorff to Rahel Levin, 21 November 1796, ibid., p. 49.

109 'She is the noblest': W. F. T. von Burgsdorff to Rahel Levin, 26 February 1798, ibid., p. 85.

109 WH travelling: W. F. T. von Burgsdorff to Rahel Levin, 28 November 1796 and 7 April 1797, ibid., pp. 52, 91.

110 'they run around': WH to CH, 28 April 1797.

110 'I want to do everything': WH to CH, 6 May 1797.

110 WH completely open with: WH to CH, 16 May 1797.

110 'Decide for yourself': WH to CH, 6 April 1797.

110 Burgsdorff and CH's affair: W. F. T. von Burgsdorff to K. G. Brinckmann, 30 August 1797 and 28 January 1798, Burgsdorff 1907, pp. 108, 123.

110 'an alliance that': CS to Julie Gotter, 18 February 1803.

110 CS in amateur play: CS to Luise Gotter, 12 December 1796; this was the role of Cäcilie in Goethe's *Stella: Ein Schauspiel für Liebende*.

110 life of unmarried women: Bake and Kiupel 1996, p. 157.

110 assets signed over to husband: *Allgemeines Landrecht für die Preußischen Staaten*, 2. Part, 1. Titel, § 205ff.

111 'The man is the head': ibid., § 184.

111 wife like ivy: Joachim Heinrich Campe's *Vätherlicher Rath für meine Tochter*, Preisendörfer 2018, p. 392.

111 'she has the same organs': Rousseau 2010, p. 531.

111 'to bear a husband's': ibid., p. 546.

111 illegitimate children: a quarter of children born in Jena at the time were born out of wedlock, compared to 2 per cent elsewhere. Deinhardt 2007, pp. 39–40.

111 'to have slept': FS to AWS, 27 May 1796.

111 'tiny beauty': Goethe to Schiller, 15 October 1796.

111 Sophie Mereau: for Fichte's lectures and Schiller see Gersdorff 1990, pp. 57ff., 100ff.

111 'adorable Miniature-Grace': Jean Paul Richter to Christian Otto, 30 November 1798, Mereau-Brentano 1996, p. 48; for admirers see J. G. Rist, end 1795/spring 1796, Rist 1880, p. 68.

111 'an enchanting bedfellow': FS to AWS, 27 May 1796; for FS falling for

Sophie, see FS to Sophie Mereau, 8, 30 August, 15 September 1800; Sophie Mereau, diary, August 1800, Mereau-Brentano 1996, p. 73.

112 'most scandalous bosom': CS to Luise Gotter, October/November 1796; for rumours about Fichte and Anna Henriette Schütz, see Johanne Fichte to Fichte, 26 June 1794; J. R. Rahn to J. H. Rahn, *c.* 19 June 1794, Fichte Gespräch, vol. 6.1, p. 53.

112 Karoline Paulus's reputation: she had a brief fling with FS and most likely also with AWS. FS to Auguste Böhmer, 15 July 1797; DV to Schleiermacher, 16 June 1800; FS to Karoline Paulus, late 1800.

112 'trampled all propriety': Charlotte Schiller to Schiller, 25 March 1801.

112 CS's walk through Jena: please refer to the map of Jena in this book.

112 Zum Schwarzen Bären: Anonymous 1798, p. 70.

114 ferry at Saale: ibid., p. 9.

114 Saxe-Weimar allied with Prussia: Boyle 2000, p. 395; for Jena feeling safe, see Goethe to J. H. Meyer, 12 October 1796.

114 'The French Storm': Goethe to Schiller, 30 July 1796.

114 'Here she's allowed': CS to Luise Gotter, 15–17 October 1796.

114 food served in Leutragasse: Caroline Tischbein-Wilken, 1799, Stoll 1923, p. 112.

114 capable cook: CS to Luise Gotter, 6 June 1799.

115 intellectual menu: Caroline Tischbein-Wilken, 1799, Stoll 1923, p. 112.

115 'intelligent god': K. G. von Brinckmann to Rahel Levin, 29 March 1799, Oellers 1990, p. 130; see also Steffens 1841, vol. 4, p. 75.

115 'big and entirely literary': Goethe to Schiller, 21 December 1796; CS and AWS went to Weimar from 17–19 December 1796.

115 Goethe and yellow paint: Goethe 1810, p. 290.

115 Goethe serving food: CS to Luise Gotter, 25 December 1796.

115 people in Weimar liked CS: CS to Luise Gotter, 3 October 1796.

115 'high-priestess': K. A. Böttiger to AWS, 27 July 1796.

115 'delightful wife': J. D. Falk to AWS, December 1796.

115 'didn't he just bring back': CS to Luise Gotter, 25 December 1796.

115 Novalis's visits to Jena: he came six times in six months, Kösling 2010, p. 39; see also Novalis's letters for the period.

115 Sophie's illness: Hädecke 2011, pp. 137–42; Friederike von Mandelsloh to Novalis, 8 July 1796 and 5 September 1796; Novalis to Wilhelmine von Thümmel, 24 August 1796 and 19 September 1796.

115 Dr Stark reassured Novalis: Dr Stark to Novalis, 23 November 1796.

115 FS and Novalis in Jena: FS to Novalis, 5 May 1797 and 8 June 1797.

115 'I like him very much': FS to Novalis, 24 May 1797; see also 10 March 1797 and 26 May 1797.

116 article about republicanism: FS, 'Versuch über den Begriff des Republikanismus', 1796.

116 Revolutions his greatest passion: FS to AWS, 27 May 1796.

116 'When something inside me': FS to AWS, 15 January 1796.

116 'Dictator-Critic': FS to AWS, 31 October 1797; see also FS to C. G. Körner, 21 September 1796.

116 pen as a guillotine: FS, 'Der Epitaphios des Lysias', 1796, FS KA, vol. 1, p. 159.

116 'geographical cabinet': FS, *Über das Studium der griechischen Poesie*, 1795–7, FS KA, vol. 1, p. 222.

116 FS vain and spiteful: WH to F. H. Jacobi, 23 January 1797.

116 friends and Schiller about FS: Steffens 1841, vol. 4, p. 304; Schiller to C. G. Körner, 4 July 1795; Schiller to WH, 17 December 1795.

116 'It's strange': Goethe to Schiller, 28 April 1797.

116 'I can talk daggers': FS to AWS, 21 June 1792.

116 poem best read backwards: Schiller, 'Die Würde der Frauen', 1796 in FS's review of *Musen-Almanach 1796* in Friedrich Reichardt's *Deutschland*, FS KA, vol. 2, p. 6.

116 Goethe a genius: ibid., pp. 7–9.

117 'pump out his thoughts': FS to AWS, 17 August 1795.

117 'I am merely waiting': FS to AWS, 23 December 1795.

117 AWS tried to help FS: AWS to Schiller, 23 April 1796.

117 'so childishly thin-skinned': FS to C. G. Körner, 21 September 1796.

117 'very much entertains': CS to Luise Gotter, 4 September 1796.

117 CS happy in Jena: CS to Luise Gotter, 11 July 1796 and 4 September 1796.

117 CS glad for Auguste: CS to F. L. W. Meyer, 10 May 1794.

117 'female Odysseus': FS to CS, 12 December 1797.

117 Auguste's education: Auguste Böhmer to Cäcilie Gotter, 24 October 1796, CS Letters, vol. 1, p. 761; FS to Auguste Böhmer, 15 July 1797, 25 July 1797, 26 August 1797 and mid-September 1797.

117 'unfolding of inborn': CS to Luise Gotter, 8 March 1789.

117 'a strategy of doing nothing': ibid.

117 Auguste and FS: FS to Auguste Böhmer, 25 July 1797.

117 'Father' and 'Uncle Fritz': Auguste Böhmer to Cäcilie Gotter, 24 October 1796, CS Letters, vol. 1, p. 761.

118 'little sweetheart': FS to Auguste Böhmer, 28 April 1797.

118 'at a distance from': CS to Luise Gotter, early 1797; Auguste's friend was Luise Seidler, who would become a painter.

118 'Gusteline': FS to AWS, 10 November 1793.

118 'Can you believe how': FS to Novalis, 26 September 1797.

118 'my Caroline': AWS to G. J. Göschen, 25 November 1797; AWS to K. A. Böttiger, 5 January 1797.

118 working on Shakespeare: Roßbeck 2008, pp. 128, 145–7; AWS to G. J. Göschen, 7 November 1796; see for example AWS and CS's manuscript of *Romeo and Juliet*, SLUB Dresden, Mscr.Dresd.e.90, xxii, 10; *Hamlet*, SLUB Dresden, Mscr.Dresd.e.90, xxii, 1; and *Midsummer Night's Dream*, SLUB Dresden, Mscr.Dresd.e.90, xxii, 11.

118 FS watching CS: FS to AWS, 30 January 1796.

118 'You wouldn't believe': CS to Luise Gotter, 7 September 1797.

119 AWS copied passages: AWS (and CS), 'Romeo und Julia', *Horen*, vol. 10, 1797, CS to AWS, 1797 (?), CS Letters, vol. 1, p. 426ff.

119 female authors in *Horen*: see in particular *Horen* in 1797.

119 'No one notices *me*': Schiller, 'Die berühmte Frau', 1788 (trans. Damion Searls).

119 'to shine as a writer': AWS 1828, vol. 2, p. xviii.

119 AWS listened to CS's advice: Tieck, 'Eine Sommerreise', Tieck 1838–42, vol. 5, p. 164.

120 '*esprit de* Caroline': FS to AWS, 13 April 1798.

Chapter 7: 'Our little academy'
Spring 1797: Goethe and Alexander von Humboldt

123 AH in anatomy theatre: A. Humboldt 1797, vol. 1, p. 76ff.

123 'breathing life into': ibid., p. 79.

124 AH and web of life: A. Humboldt 1845–52, vol. 1, p. 21; A. Humboldt 1845–50, vol. 1, p. 21.

124 'animal electricity' and experiments: AH to Friedrich von Schuckmann, 14 May 1797; AH to Carl Freiesleben, 18 April 1797.

124 AH in Jena: 6–10 March 1794, 15–16 April 1794, 14–19 December 1794, 16–20 April 1795, April 1796, January 1797, 1 March–30 or 31 May 1797.

124 experiments on himself: AH to J. F. Blumenbach, 17 November 1793 and June 1795.

124 experiments in Jena: AH to Friedrich von Schuckmann, 14 May 1797.

124 'I can't live': ibid.

124 'You can't get as': Goethe to Duke Carl August, early March 1797.

124 Goethe and AH introduced: Goethe 1982–96, vol. 3, p. 303.

125 AH and WH different: WH to CH, 9 October 1804.

125 AH and WH's childhood: AH to Carl Freiesleben, 5 June 1792; WH to CH, April 1790 and 9 October 1818; see also Wulf 2015, pp. 13–16.

125 'the little apothecary': Bruhns 1873, vol. 1, p. 20.

125 AH's appearance: AH's 1798 passport, Bruhns 1873, vol. 1, p. 394; Karoline Bauer, 1876, Clark and Lubrich 2012b, p. 199.

125 AH torn: WH to CH, 6 November 1790.

125 'The poor boy is': WH to CH, 2 April 1790; see also WH to CH, 6 November 1790 and 3 June 1791.

125 '10,000 pigs': AH to David Friedländer, 11 April 1799.

125 AH talked incessantly: WH to CH, 30 November 1815; Ludwig Börne, 12 October 1830, Clark and Lubrich 2012b, p. 82; see also Wulf 2015, pp. 139, 237–8.

126 'overcharged instrument': Heinrich Laube, Laube 1875, p. 334; for AH like a meteor, see K. A. Varnhagen von Ensen, 1810, Varnhagen 1987, vol. 2, p. 139; WH to CH, 25 December 1825.

126 'There is a drive': AH to W. G. Wegener, 23 September 1790.

126 AH might 'snap': CH to WH, 22 January 1791.

126 'eight legs and four hands': AH to Carl Freiesleben, 19 July 1793.

126 WH glad about mother's death: W. F. T. von Burgsdorff to Rahel Levin, 21 November 1796, Burgsdorff 1907, p. 51.

126 'great voyage': AH to A. G. Werner, 21 December 1796; for AH's relief about his mother's death, see Carl Freiesleben to AH, 20 December 1796.

126 'all forces of nature': AH to David Friedländer, 11 April 1799; see also AH to K. M. E. von Moll, 5 June 1799.

126 Goethe and science: Goethe 1994b, pp. 18–19, 23, 25, 32, 40–1, 51, 55, 59.

126 'I never observed': Goethe to J. P. Eckermann, 18 January 1827.

127 Goethe's butterflies and moths: Goethe, *Naturwissenschaftliche Schriften*, Goethe 1887–1919, Part 2, vol. 6, pp. 416–17; see also Goethe to Schiller, 8 February 1797.

127 'most beautiful phenomenon': Goethe to Schiller, 6 August 1796.

127 prepared specimens: Goethe, *Naturwissenschaftliche Schriften*, Goethe 1887–1919, Part 2, vol. 6, pp. 401–2, 417–19.

127 'caterpillar near metamorphosis': and following quotes, ibid., pp. 401–2.

127 Goethe's dissections: for hawk moth, snail and frog, ibid., pp. 401–5; for catching frogs, see Goethe, 30 May 1796, Goethe Diaries, vol. 2, p. 44.

127 'March 30th: still': Goethe, *Naturwissenschaftliche Schriften*, Goethe 1887–1919, Part 2, vol. 6, p. 403.

127 'he devotes himself': CS to Luise Gotter, 4 September 1796.

128 urge to talk about science: Goethe to Salomon Maimon, 16 October 1794.

128 'my recent dissections': Goethe to Schiller, 21 December 1796.

128 'I've started examining': Goethe to Schiller, 26 October 1796.

128 'My scientific studies': Goethe to Schiller, 26 April 1797.

128 AH's publications: *Mineralogische Beobachtungen über einige Basalte am Rhein* (1790) and *Florae Fribergensis specimen* (1793); for his articles see A. Humboldt 2018, vol. 1, pp. 573–83.

128 AH's inventions: A. Humboldt 1799, plate 3; AH to Carl Freiesleben, 20 January 1794, 5 October 1796; for Goethe's interest in mining see Goethe to C. G. Voigt, 4 May 1797.

128 AH in Jena: AH to Carl von Freiesleben, 18 April 1797; AH to Friedrich von Schuckmann, 14 May 1797; Goethe, March–May 1797, Goethe Diaries, vol. 2, pp. 58–71.

128 Duke met AH in Jena: Duke Carl August to Goethe, 4 and 7 March 1797; C. G. Voigt to Goethe, 15 March 1797.

128 he 'forced us': Goethe, 17–19 December 1794, Goethe 1965–2000, vol. 4, p. 116.

128 Napoleon at Battle of Arcole: Scurr 2021, p. 51.

129 'We do not march': Saltzman 2021, p. 12; see also p. 15.

129 'Now I can hardly': Goethe to J. I. Gerning, 28 April 1797.

129 encouraged by AH: Goethe dictated his *First Sketch of a General Introduction to Comparative Anatomy* in early 1795 to Max Jacobi during a visit to Jena. Goethe to F. H. Jacobi, 2 February 1795; CH to WH, 1 May 1797; Goethe 1994b, p. 41.

129 Goethe and *Urform*: Richards 2002, p. 445ff.

129 Goethe swinging his arms: K. A. Böttiger about Goethe in 1795, Böttiger 1998, p. 69.

129 'Our little academy': Goethe to Duke Carl August, 14 March 1797; for daily meetings, see Goethe, 1 March–31 May 1797, Goethe Diaries, vol. 2, pp. 58–71.

130 concert in Jena: J. F. Fries to Karl von Zezschwitz, 23 May 1797, Fichte Gespräch, vol. 1, p. 436.

130 star-struck at party: Ehrenfried von Willich to Charlotte Pritzbauer, 9 January 1797, Fichte Gespräch, vol. 1, pp. 397–8.

130 'was at the height': Goethe in 1797, Goethe 1994b, p. 59.

130 days in middle of March: Goethe, 12–28 March 1797, Goethe Diaries, vol. 2, pp. 60–3.

130 FS's book: *Die Griechen und Römer: Historische und kritische Versuche über das Klassische Alterthum*, 1797.

130 'like a rock crashing': Goethe to J. H. Meyer, 18 March 1797.

130 'that you sometimes': Goethe to Karl von Knebel, 28 March 1797; see also Goethe to J. F. Unger, 28 March 1797.

130 'Morning: revised poem': Goethe, 19 March 1797, Goethe Diaries, vol. 2, p. 61.

131 'chemical experiments': Goethe, 1 March 1797, Goethe Diaries, vol. 2, p. 58.

131 'frog anatomy': Goethe, 9 March 1797, Goethe Diaries, vol. 2, p. 59.

131 'early morning snail': Goethe, 11 May 1797, Goethe Diaries, vol. 2, p. 67.

131 'earthworms anatomised': Goethe, 12 May 1797, Goethe Diaries, vol. 2, p. 67.

131 Goethe was exhausted: Goethe to Karl von Knebel, 28 March 1797.

131 Goethe asked AH: Goethe to AH, 14 April 1797.

131 AH in Weimar: Goethe, 19–25 April 1797, Goethe Diaries, vol. 2, pp. 65–6. Goethe returned to Jena on 29 April.

131 'Peace has been': Goethe to Schiller, 26 April 1797.

131 'greatest antagonists': Goethe 1987, p. 458.

131 idealist in *Faust*: Goethe, *Faust Part One*, ll. 4347–51 (trans. David Luke), Goethe 2008, p. 138.

131 'all Nature's hidden': Goethe, *Faust Part One*, l. 441 (trans. Walter Kaufmann), Goethe 1961, p. 99.

131 'That I may detect': ibid., l. 382–3, p. 95.

132 *Elective Affinities*: Goethe, *Die Wahlverwandschaften*, 1809.

132 'affected me powerfully': AH to Goethe, 14 May 1806.

132 'Nature must be': AH to Goethe, 3 January 1810.

132 'the external world': A. Humboldt 1845–52, vol. 1, p. 64; A. Humboldt 1845–50, vol. 1, pp. 69–70.

132 'melt into each other': ibid.

132 'influence of your': AH to Goethe, 3 February 1810.

132 'new senses': AH to Caroline von Wolzogen, 14 May 1806, Goethe 1876, p. 407.

132 *Essay on the Geography*: AH, *Ideen zu einer Geographie der Pflanzen*, 1807.

132 'How I would like': Goethe 2002, p. 222.

132 'the more the frontiers': Schiller, *Über die ästhetische Erziehung des Menschen*, Letter 2, Schiller 1962, vol. 5, p. 572.

133 'naked, analytical reason': Schiller to C. G. Körner, 6 August 1797.

133 'to see chains of': WH to K. G. von Brinckmann, 18 March 1793.

133 'never create, only': Schiller to C. G. Körner, 6 August 1797.

133 proofs of *Wilhelm Meister*: Schiller to Goethe, 11 October 1796.

133 'having lived several': Goethe to J. P. Eckermann, 12 December 1828.

133 'Garden House': Schiller to Goethe, 17 February 1797; see also Schiller to Goethe, 2 May 1797; Goethe, 18 March 1797, Goethe Diaries, vol. 2,

p. 61; for change of scenery and exercise, see Schiller to Goethe, 11 January 1797; Schiller to C. G. Körner, 7 February 1797; Charlotte Schiller to Fritz von Stein, 3 March 1797, Petersen 1909, vol. 3, p. 64.

133 'It's all very awkward': Goethe to Christiane Vulpius, 28 May 1797; see also 25 May 1798.

134 Goethe visited Schiller: Goethe, 19, 20, 21, 22, 24, 26, 27, 29, 30 May 1797, Goethe Diaries, vol. 2, pp. 68–71.

134 arbour at back: Goethe to J. P. Eckermann, 8 October 1827; for glorious weather, see Schiller to Goethe, 2 May 1797.

134 big guns: FS to C. G. Körner, 30 January 1797.

134 FS's review of Horen: published in 1796 in Reichardt's Deutschland, FS KA, vol. 2, p. 47.

134 'great piece of deviltry': FS to Novalis, late February 1797.

134 'I like it when': FS to C. G. Körner, 30 January 1797.

134 'This Herr Friedrich': Schiller to Goethe, 16 May 1797; see also Goethe 1982–96, vol. 3, p. 586.

134 Goethe talked to FS: Goethe, 26 May 1797, Goethe Diaries, vol. 2, p. 79.

135 Goethe talked to all parties: Goethe, 30 May 1797, Goethe Diaries, vol. 2, p. 80.

135 would prefer to be in Weimar: Goethe to Christiane, 28 May 1797.

135 'It was a pleasure': Schiller to AWS, 31 May 1797.

135 'Indeed, I would': AWS and CS to Schiller, 1 June 1797.

135 'We sincerely admire': ibid.

135 AWS to see Goethe: Goethe, 2 June 1797, Goethe Diaries, vol. 2, pp. 71–2.

135 Goethe saw AWS and Schiller: Goethe, 3 June 1797, Goethe Diaries, vol. 2, p. 72.

135 'an unpleasant necessity': Schiller to AWS, 1 June 1797.

135 AH left Jena: Goethe, 30 May 1797, Goethe Diaries, vol. 2, p. 71.

135 Inheritance and sale of Tegel: WH's letters to CH from April to June 1797.

136 Fn. Burgsdorff's movements: W. F. T. von Burgsdorff to Rahel Levin, 7 April 1797, Burgsdorff 1907, p. 91; CH to WH, 1 May 1797; for Burgsdorff in Dresden, see CH to WH, 1 May 1797; see also W. F. T. von Burgsdorff to Rahel Levin, 4 March 1797, Burgsdorff 1907, p. 87.

136 CH's health: W. F. T. von Burgsdorff to K. G. von Brinckmann, 2 January 1797; W. F. T. von Burgsdorff to Rahel Levin, 3 and 26 February 1797, Burgsdorff 1907, pp. 68, 74, 84.

136 AH's plans and preparations: AH to Friedrich von Schuckmann, 14 May 1797; AH to Goethe, 16 July 1795.

136 'I'm leaving this': AH to Friedrich von Schuckmann, 14 May 1797, A. Humboldt 1973, p. 580.

136 Goethe saw AWS and Schiller: Goethe, 2–8 June 1797, Goethe Diaries, vol. 2, pp. 71–2.

137 Goethe and AWS's essay: Goethe, 8 June 1797, ibid., p. 72; Goethe to Schiller, 10 June 1797; Goethe to AWS, 14 June 1797.

137 too self-centred and highly strung: Schiller to Goethe, 30 June 1797.

137 accusations of plagiarism: FS's review of Horen 1796 in Reichardt's Deutschland, FS KA, vol. 2, p. 47; see also FS to Novalis, 26 May 1797.

137 'impertinent lie': K. L. von Woltmann in ALZ, 20 May 1797, Borcherdt 1948, p. 530.

137 advised FS to leave: Goethe, 10 June 1797, Goethe Diaries, vol. 2, p. 73.

137 FS to Berlin: FS to Novalis, 8 June 1797; FS left on 3 July 1797 and on his way to Berlin he stopped in Weißenfels, see also FS to Novalis, 29 June 1797.

137 *Horen*'s subscriptions declined: Alt 2004, vol. 2, p. 205; see also Schiller to J. F. Cotta, 5 January 1798; Schiller to Goethe, 26 January 1798.

137 'of somehow being': FS to Novalis, 21 June 1797.

137 gossip in Dresden: C. G. Körner to Schiller, 10 June 1797.

137 Körner turned against Schlegels: C. G. Körner to Schiller, 29 May 1797.

137 CS corrupted brothers: C. G. Körner to Schiller, 10 June 1797.

137 'as ugly': CS to Luise Gotter, 13 February 1797.

137 'I'm glad you're': CH to Charlotte Schiller, 29 September 1797, C. Schiller 1862, vol. 2, p. 173.

138 Charlotte Schiller's character: Alt 2004, vol. 1, pp. 645–6.

138 'The minute she's': R. E. Niethammer to F. I. Niethammer, before October 1797, quoted in Kleßmann 2008, p. 234.

138 weather: Goethe to Schiller, 10 June 1797; Goethe to Duke Carl August, 12 June 1797.

138 'the desire to look': Goethe to Duke Carl August, 6 June 1797.

138 duke granted permission: Boyle 2000, p. 506.

138 unpacked *Faust*: Goethe, 23–27 June 1797, Goethe Diaries, vol. 2, pp. 74–5.

138 'work that's well suited': Goethe to Duke Carl August, 29 June 1797.

139 parcel that held *Faust* imprisoned: Goethe to Schiller, 2 December 1794.

139 'feverish unrest': Goethe, *Faust Part One*, l. 435 (trans. Walter Kaufmann), Goethe 1961, p. 99.

139 'so you can tell me': Goethe to Schiller, 22 June 1797.

139 'vain attempt to unite': Schiller to Goethe, 23 June 1797; see also 26 June 1797.

139 'but I've long since': Schiller to Goethe, 23 June 1797.

139 'I'm quite lonely': Schiller to C. G. Körner, 3 June 1797.

139 Schiller in Weimar: 11–18 July 1797, Wais 2005, p. 235.

139 'The Cranes of Ibycus': Schiller, 'Die Kraniche des Ibycus', 1797; Schiller wrote the ballad in August 1797, Wais 2005, pp. 235–7; see also Goethe to Schiller, 23 August 1797.

139 something of Goethe: Schiller to Goethe, 21 July 1797.

139 AWS to contribute to *Musen-Almanach*: AWS to Goethe, 16 July 1797.

139 AWS sent a poem: AWS, 'Prometheus', 1797; see also Goethe to Schiller, 18 July 1797.

139 Goethe read poem: Goethe to AWS, 19 July 1797.

140 'it seems that the': Goethe to Schiller, 22 July 1797.

140 Schiller's edits of poem: Schiller to AWS, 21 Aug 1797.

140 AWS's reply to edits: AWS to Schiller, 28 July 1797.

140 Schiller accepted poem: Schiller to AWS, 27 July 1797 and 21 August 1797.

140 'Arion. A Romance': AWS, 'Arion. Romanze', 1797.

140 AWS's letter to Goethe: AWS to Goethe, 24 September 1797; Goethe had left Weimar on 30 July 1797, see Goethe, 30 July 1797, Goethe Diaries, vol. 2, p. 76.

140 'cold, dry, and of': Schiller to Goethe, 7 September 1797.

140 'hadn't stolen them': AWS Schiller to C. G. Körner, 20 October 1797.

140 'If we treat Schiller': AWS to Schleiermacher, 1 November 1799.

140 'His attentive consideration': AWS in 1837, Borcherdt 1948, p. 452.

Chapter 8: 'Grasp, then, a handful of darkness'
Summer–Winter 1797: Novalis's Death Wish

141 Novalis in Sophie's room: Friederike von Mandelsloh, 1846, about Novalis after Sophie's death, Novalis Schriften, vol. 4, p. 605; see also Novalis to Caroline Just, 28 March 1797.

141 'Without her there': Novalis, 20 May 1797, diary, Novalis Schriften, vol. 4, p. 38.

141 Sophie's death and surgeries: Novalis, 19 March 1797, ibid., p. 27; Novalis to Wilhelmine von Thümmel, 19 September 1796.

141 'heavenly creature': Novalis to K. L. von Woltmann, 22 March 1797; for Novalis's last visit, see Novalis, 10 March 1797, diary, Novalis Schriften, vol. 4, p. 27.

141 'penchant for childish' and following descriptions: Novalis, August or September 1796, Novalis Schriften, vol. 4, pp. 24–5.

142 his 'non-Ich': Friederike von Mandelsloh to Novalis, 22 September 1796.

142 Novalis wanted to marry: Novalis to FS, 1 August 1794; A. C. Just, 'Friedrich von Hardenberg', 1805, Novalis Schriften, vol. 4, p. 541.

142 'a busy, fretful joy': FS to AWS, 13 April 1792; see also Novalis to A. B. von Hardenberg, June 1793.

142 'you live, the others': FS to Novalis, late May 1793.

142 his 'Sichselbstfindung': Novalis, 'Blüthenstaub' ('Pollen'), no. 22, Novalis Schriften, vol. 2, p. 421.

142 Erasmus died: Erasmus von Hardenberg died on 14 April 1797.

142 'Nachsterben': Novalis to Caroline Just, 28 March 1797.

142 his death was a wedding night: Novalis, July 1798 (?), Novalis Schriften, vol. 4, p. 50.

142 'incessant thinking about': Novalis, 25 May 1797, diary, Novalis Schriften, vol. 4, p. 40.

143 'Grasp, then': Novalis, 'Fichte Studies', no. 3, Novalis Schriften, vol. 2, p. 106; for Novalis's return to Fichte's writings, see Novalis, 21, 26, 29–30 May 1797, diary, Novalis Schriften, vol. 4, pp. 38, 41, 42.

143 regrow amputated arm: Novalis, 'Miscellaneous Fragments', no. 247, Novalis Schriften, vol. 2, p. 583.

143 'kill oneself by': ibid.; see also Pikulik 1992, p. 40.

143 'My petrification proceeds': Novalis to Caroline Just, 24 March 1797.

143 Novalis stayed near Grüningen: Novalis arrived in Tennstedt on 18 April 1797; see Novalis, 18 April 1797, diary, Novalis Schriften, vol. 4, p. 29.

143 'stranger on Earth': Karl von Hardenberg, 'Biographie seines Bruders', 1802, Novalis Schriften, vol. 4, p. 533.

143 Sophie's grave: Novalis to K. L. von Woltmann, 3 May 1797; Novalis to FS, 13 April 1797; Novalis, May–June 1797, diary, Novalis Schriften, vol. 4, p. 34ff.

143 'my sacred shrine': Novalis to FS, 3 May 1797.

143 'I walked to the': Novalis, 21 May 1797, diary, Novalis Schriften, vol. 4, p. 39.

143 'I feel unspeakably': Novalis, 19 May 1797, diary, ibid., p. 38.

143 'flashing moments': Novalis, 13 May 1797, diary, ibid., p. 36.

143 'I blew the grave': Novalis, 13 May 1797, diary, ibid., p. 36; Novalis 1988, p. 17 (trans. based on O'Brien 1995), p. 264.

144 love as uniting: Novalis, 'Fichte Studies', no. 651, Novalis Schriften, vol. 2, p. 292.

144 'wavered and faltered': Novalis, 19 April 1797, diary, Novalis Schriften, vol. 4, p. 29.

144 'steadfast again': Novalis, 16 May 1797, diary, ibid., p. 37.

144 'Very lustful': Novalis, 13 May 1797, diary, ibid., p. 35.

144 'much lewdness': Novalis, 14 May 1797, diary, ibid., p. 36.

144 'the beginning – she will': Novalis to Wilhelmine von Thümmel, 13 April 1797.

144 Sophie laughed at Novalis: Jeannette Danscour to Novalis, 6 July 1795.

144 'as if she did not belong': Novalis to Caroline Just, 24 March 1797.

144 'true self-sacrifice': Novalis, 26 May 1797, diary, Novalis Schriften, vol. 4, p. 41.

144 'Death is self-conquest': Novalis, 'Blüthenstaub' ('Pollen'), no. 11, Novalis Schriften, vol. 2, p. 414; Novalis 1991, p. 384.

145 'it is obvious': Novalis to FS, 13 April 1797.

145 Novalis's love for Sophie: ibid.

145 'you can count on me': FS to Novalis, 5 May 1797.

145 'my insides are crumbling': Novalis to Caroline Just, 24 March 1797.

145 FS almost jealous: FS to Novalis, 5 May 1797.

145 'I have boundless respect': Novalis to FS, 15 August 1793; for FS being suicidal, see FS to AWS, 21 November 1792.

145 'I think you'll be': FS to Novalis, 7 May 1797; see also Novalis, 13 May 1797, diary, Novalis Schriften, vol. 4, p. 35.

145 Novalis and Shakespeare: Novalis to FS, 25 May 1797.

145 'German Shakespeare': Novalis to AWS, 30 November 1797.

145 Hölderlin and suicide: Martens 1996, p. 94.

146 'artistic understanding': FS to Novalis, beginning March 1799.

146 resolve not strong enough: for example, Novalis, 14–15 May, 14, 16–29 June 1797, diary, Novalis Schriften, vol. 4, pp. 36, 46, 48.

146 'May God preserve': Novalis, 6 June 1797, diary, ibid., p. 44.

146 'Christ and Sophie': Novalis, 16–29 June 1797, diary, ibid., p. 48; see also O'Brien 1995, p. 65 for the concept of this being an epitaph. Sophie and Christ also become interwoven in the 4th hymn in Hymns to the Night.

146 'I have religion for': Novalis, 'Fragmentblatt', no. 56, Novalis Schriften, vol. 2, p. 395.

146 Novalis returned to reality: Novalis, 16–29 June 1797, diary, Novalis Schriften, vol. 4, p. 47.

146 'He thinks elemental': FS to AWS, March 1798.

146 FS in Weißenfels: FS to Auguste Böhmer, 15 July 1797.

146 'This way of life': Novalis, 3 July 1797, diary, Novalis Schriften, vol. 4, p. 49.

146 stopped dating diary: 6 July 1797, diary, Novalis, ibid.; O'Brien 1995, p. 65.

146 'beware when dealing': Novalis, 16–29 June 1797, diary, Novalis Schriften, vol. 4, p. 48.

146 Novalis in Jena: Novalis to FS, 5 September 1797.

147 'natural genius': Bate 1986, p. 6.

147 'The poet's eye': Novalis to FS, 25 May 1797.

147 quotation used by English Romantics: Bate 1986, pp. 11, 171–2.

147 'closer to the secret': A. W. Schlegel 1815, vol. 2, p. 99; AWS SW, vol. 6, pt 2, p. 161.

147 'original love': ibid.

147 Shakespeare disordered and vulgar: A. W. Schlegel 1815, vol. 2, p. 109; AWS SW, vol. 6, pt 2, p. 167.

147 'drunken savage': A. W. Schlegel 1815, vol. 2, p. 106; AWS SW, vol. 6, pt 2, p. 168.

147 master of emotions and against rules: A. W. Schlegel 1815, vol. 2, pp. 109, 128; AWS SW, vol. 6, pt 2, p. 170, 186.

148 'the spirit of romantic': A. W. Schlegel 1815, vol. 2, p. 98; AWS SW, vol. 6, pt 2, p. 160.

148 British writers: Mary Shelley, 16–21 March 1816, diary, Shelley 1987, vol. 1, pp. 198–9; William Hazlitt's review of AWS's *Lectures on Dramatic Art and Literature*, Paulin 1998, p. 203; Bate 1986, pp. 8–9.

148 S. T. Coleridge and AWS: Holmes 1998b, p. 278ff.

148 'a German critic first taught': S. T. Coleridge to William Mudford, 1818, quoted in Haney 1906, p. 33.

148 'discoverer of Shakespeare': *Analectic*, 1818, Pochmann 1978, p. 485.

148 'Few are more alive': Novalis to FS, 5 September 1797.

148 Novalis more productive: ibid.

148 'his melancholy has': AWS to Goethe, 24 September 1797.

148 'that you're so busy': FS to Novalis, 26 September 1797.

148 Novalis's arrival in Freiberg: Hädecke 2011, p. 160; Novalis to G. J. Göschen, 7 December 1797.

148 A. G. Werner: Watson 2010, pp. 169–70.

149 Description of Freiberg mine: Steffens 1841, vol. 4, p. 219ff.

149 'path into the hidden': Novalis, *Heinrich von Ofterdingen*, Novalis Schriften, vol. 1, p. 242.

149 Novalis in Freiberg: Novalis to FS, 11 May 1798; Ludwig Tieck to F. W. Riemer, 3 July 1841, Novalis Schriften, vol. 4, p. 560.

149 'an all-consuming fire': H. G. von Carlowitz to Monsieur Bouc, 29 April 1798, Novalis Schriften, vol. 4, p. 616.

149 'the electricity I feel': Novalis to AWS, 24 February 1798.

149 'wonderful healing powers' . . . 'opiates': Novalis to Erasmus von

Hardenberg, 26 February 1797; see also Novalis to AWS, 12 January 1798.

150 'Laboratories will be': Novalis, *Die Lehrlinge zu Sais*, Novalis Schriften, vol. 1, p. 105.

150 'encyclopaedia' and *Encyclopédie*: Novalis 2007, p. xxv.

150 'theory of the future' . . . 'theory of excitation': Novalis, 'Allgemeine Brouillon', nos 78, 387, 435, 72, 333, Novalis Schriften, vol. 3, pp. 253, 311, 321, 252, 299.

150 'absolute universal body': Novalis, 'Allgemeine Brouillon', no. 333, Novalis Schriften, vol. 3, p. 299; for living scientific system, see Novalis to FS, early November 1798.

150 mind was like refracted light: Novalis, *Lehrlinge zu Sais*, Novalis Schriften, vol. 1, p. 82.

150 'seed of all books': Novalis, 'Allgemeine Brouillon', no. 557, Novalis Schriften, vol. 3, p. 363.

150 'The sciences must': Novalis to AWS, 24 February 1798.

150 'what I really want': FS to Schleiermacher, July 1798.

150 poets rather than scientists: Novalis, 'Allgemeine Brouillon', no. 1093, Novalis Schriften, vol. 3, p. 468.

151 'Poetry is true': Novalis, 'Über Goethe', no. 473, Novalis Schriften, vol. 2, p. 647.

151 Fn. Coleridge and Davy: S. T. Coleridge, *The Friend*, 1810, Harman 2009, p. 320; Holmes 1998b, p. 288.

151 'my Magical Idealism': Novalis, 'Allgemeine Brouillon', no. 399, Novalis Schriften, vol. 3, p. 315.

151 'magical, powerful faculty': Novalis, 'Allgemeine Brouillon', no. 1075, Novalis Schriften, vol. 3, p. 466; Novalis 2007, p. 181; see also nos 338, 642, 826, pp. 301, 385, 430.

151 thoughts became objects: Novalis, 'Allgemeine Brouillon', no. 338, Novalis Schriften, vol. 3, p. 301.

151 '1 foot long': Linnaeus 2003, p. 170.

152 'The more poetical': Novalis, 'Über Goethe', no. 473, see also 'Allgemeine Brouillon', no. 717, Novalis Schriften, vol. 2, pp. 647, 406.

152 'Downwards I turn': Novalis 1988, p. 11 (translation changed).

152 'Down into the': ibid., p. 39 (translation changed).

152 'quiet messenger of': ibid., p. 15.

152 'Doesn't all that inspires': ibid., p. 21.

153 'inwards runs the': Novalis, 'Blüthenstaub' ('Pollen'), no. 16, Novalis Schriften, vol. 2, p. 418; Novalis 1991, p. 385.

153 'And you are Death': Novalis 1988, p. 30 (translation changed).

153 'lovely Sun of': ibid., p. 12.

153 'poppies' brown juice': ibid., p. 15.

153 'longing for death': ibid., p. 39.

153 'The world becomes': Novalis, *Heinrich von Ofterdingen*, Novalis Schriften, vol. 1, p. 319.

153 'mechanical administration': Novalis, 'Glauben und Liebe', no. 36, Novalis Schriften, vol. 2, p. 494.

153 the point of riches: ibid.

153 to romanticise the world: Novalis, 'Logologische Fragmente', no. 105, Novalis Schriften, vol. 2, p. 545.

Chapter 9: 'Sublime impertinence'
Winter 1797–Spring 1798: The Dawn of Romanticism

154 FS in Berlin salons and clothes: Schleiermacher to Charlotte Schleiermacher, 22 October and 31 December 1797, Schleiermacher 1988, Part 5, vol. 2, pp. 177, 220; FS to AWS, 31 October 1797; see also Ziolkowski 2006, p. 18ff.; Caroline Tischbein-Wilken, 1799, Stoll 1923, p. 114; DV to Clemens Brentano, mid-November 1800.

154 'aesthetic anarchy': FS, *Ueber das Studium der griechischen Poesie*, 1795–7, FS KA, vol. 1, p. 224.

154 'in analogy of his': Schleiermacher to Charlotte Schleiermacher, 31 December 1797, Schleiermacher 1988, Part 5, vol. 2, p. 220.

154 'My acquaintances multiply': FS to AWS, 19 September 1797; see also AWS to Goethe, 24 September 1797.

154 Schleiermacher's moral compass: FS to AWS and CS, 28 November 1797.

154 'unstoppable flood of': Schleiermacher to Charlotte Schleiermacher, 22 October 1797, Schleiermacher 1988, Part 5, vol. 2, p. 177.

155 FS and Schleiermacher's daily routine: Schleiermacher to Charlotte Schleiermacher, 31 December 1797, Schleiermacher 1988, Part 5, vol. 2, pp. 217–19.

155 Fn. DV's name change: Frank 1988, p. 55.

155 'Jewish Socrates': Clark 2007, p. 75.

155 DV's upbringing: Fürst 1858, p. 111ff.

155 DV not beautiful: ibid., p. 116; DV looked like her father, Frank 1988, p. 211.

155 DV and Simon Veit: Horn 2013, p. 44.

155 'unspeakably unhappy': WH to CH, 26 June 1790.

156 DV's lover: this was Eduard d'Alton, Stern 1994, pp. 75–7.

156 Berlin Jewish salons: Fürst 1858, pp. 130ff.

156 'Castle Boredom': ibid., p. 129.

156 'The mind is a powerful': ibid., p. 130.

156 FS liked bold fonts and personalities: Schleiermacher to Charlotte Schleiermacher, 31 December 1797, Schleiermacher 1988, Part 5, vol. 2, p. 220.

156 'In daintiness she': FS to Novalis, 17 December 1798.

156 'She's only a sketch': ibid.

156 FS about DV: FS to CS, mid-February 1798.

156 DV fell for FS: Stern 1994, p. 81.

156 'eternal union of': FS, *Lucinde*, 1799, F. Schlegel 1999, p. 17; F. Schlegel 1971, p. 48.

157 'The Magnificent One': DV to Schleiermacher, March 1799.

157 'I'm expecting' . . . 'volcanic matter': FS to Novalis, 26 September 1797.

157 adultery punishable: Allgemeines Landrecht für die Preußischen Staaten, 2. Part, 20. Titel, §§ 1063, 1064.

157 'Either great or small': DV to Rahel Levin, 6 June 1793.
157 'The letter is the': FS to Novalis, 2 December 1798; see also FS, 'Über die Philosophie: An Dorothea', *Athenaeum*, vol. 2, 1799, p. 3.
157 'great plan': FS to AWS, 31 October 1797.
157 'prostitution': FS to AWS, 2 November 1797.
157 'sublime impertinence': ibid.
158 her brothers were vain: Charlotte Ernst to Novalis, 1 February 1799.
158 FS hoped for CS's contribution: FS to AWS, 31 October 1797.
158 *Herkules*: ibid.
158 FS's letters: FS to AWS, 31 October, early November, before 28 November, 28 November, *c.* 1 December, 5, 12, 18 and 28 December 1797.
158 'How impatiently – yes': FS to AWS, CS, and Auguste Böhmer, early November 1797.
158 FS couldn't concentrate: FS to AWS, November 1797.
158 called it *Athenaeum*: FS to AWS, *c.* 1 December 1797; FS to AWS, 28 December 1798; FS to AWS, 15 January 1798.
158 rumours of affair: K. A. Varnhagen von Ense to Rahel Levin, 21 September 1808, Varnhagen 1874–5, vol. 1, p. 40. See also FS's letters from the time, mentioning Friederike Unger.
159 'a great philosophical': FS to CS, 12 December 1797.
159 infinite supply of fragments: FS to AWS, 31 October 1797.
159 'My whole self': FS to AWS, 18 December 1797.
159 'my nature consists': Novalis to Erasmus von Hardenberg, August 1793.
159 'historian is a prophet': FS, '*Athenaeum* Fragmente', no. 80, FS KA, vol. 2, p. 176; F. Schlegel 1971, p. 170.
159 'publishing is to thinking': FS, '*Athenaeum* Fragmente', no. 62, FS KA, vol. 2, p. 174; F. Schlegel 1971, p. 169.
159 'women are treated': FS, '*Athenaeum* Fragmente', no. 49, FS KA, vol. 2, p. 172; F. Schlegel 1971, p. 167.
159 'so-called religion': Novalis, 'Blüthenstaub' ('Pollen'), no. 77, Novalis Schriften, vol. 2, p. 447; Novalis 1991, p. 396.
159 compose fragments together: FS to AWS, 31 October 1797.
159 'marginalia on the': FS, '*Athenaeum* Fragmente', no. 259, FS KA, vol. 2, p. 209.
159 'spoiled children': FS to AWS, 31 October 1797.
159 'literary seeds': Novalis, 'Blüthenstaub' ('Pollen'), no. 114, Novalis Schriften, vol. 2, p. 463.
159 'if you only write for': FS to AWS, 19 January 1796.
160 'Friends, the soil': Novalis, 'Blüthenstaub' ('Pollen'), epigram, Novalis Schriften, vol. 2, p. 413; Novalis 1991, p. 383.
160 'giant symphonising': FS to AWS, 25 March 1798; see also FS, '*Athenaeum* Fragmente', no. 125, FS KA, vol. 2, p. 185.
160 FS was relentless: FS to AWS, 5 December 1797.
160 'stubborn little girl': FS to Auguste Böhmer, 15 July 1797.
160 Auguste's education: Auguste to Cäcilie Gotter, 24 October 1796, CS Letters, vol. 1, p. 761; FS to Auguste Böhmer, 25 July 1797 and 26 August 1797.

160 'Äffchen Augustchen': FS to Auguste Böhmer, 26 August 1797.

160 'Farewell, sweet child': FS to Auguste Böhmer, 15 July 1797; for FS's requests, see FS to Auguste Böhmer, mid-September 1797 and 2 November 1798.

160 gossip from Jena: FS to Auguste Böhmer, c. 24 October 1797; for FS's love affair, see FS to Auguste Böhmer, 26 August 1797.

160 Auguste a child and woman: FS to Auguste Böhmer, 26 August 1797.

160 'Won't Auguste contribute': FS to AWS, 5 December 1797.

161 AWS woke CS: FS to AWS, 18 December 1797.

161 CS sent household out: CS to Luise Gotter, 3 December 1797.

161 'from hers, yours, mine': FS to AWS, 18 December 1797.

161 'Like a truffle dog': Schleiermacher and FS to AWS, 15 January 1798.

161 CS and *Wilhelm Meister*: ibid.; for following requests by FS, see FS to AWS, 13 April 1798 and Schleiermacher and FS to AWS, 15 January 1798.

161 'Won't that be': FS to AWS, 15 January 1798.

161 CS as editor: FS to AWS, 5 December 1797, 6 March 1798, 28 March 1798.

161 Caroline as a river: I 'stole' this image from the last paragraph of *Middlemarch* where George Eliot describes her protagonist Dorothea Brooke as being like a river that runs in many channels.

162 *Hamlet* in Berlin: CS to Luise Gotter, early July 1798.

162 'strange fairy child': AWS, 'Das Feenkind', AWS SW, vol. 1, p. 235.

162 'even by actresses': CS to Luise Gotter, early July 1798.

162 'republicanised through the': AWS, '*Athenaeum* Fragmente', no. 209, FS KA, vol. 2, p. 197.

162 *terroriste* and other new words: Leclercq 1989, pp. 286, 290.

162 'omnipotent alphabet': FS, 'Ideen Fragmente', no. 61, FS KA, vol. 2, p. 262; see also Schnyder 1990, pp. 43–5.

163 *Pollen*: Novalis, *Blüthenstaub*, 1798.

163 *Fragments* in *Athenaeum*: as Caroline never published under her name, we don't know how many fragments she contributed in the end, but August Wilhelm Schlegel wrote at least eighty-six fragments, Schleiermacher provided twenty-eight and Novalis wrote thirteen, see Endres 2017, p. 147.

163 'our first symphony': AWS to Schleiermacher, 22 January 1798.

163 German word *romantisch*: Pikulik 1993, p. 74ff.

163 two thousand pages long: FS to AWS, c. 1 December 1797; FS wrote of '125 sheets' – one sheet was sixteen printed pages in octavo format – so, 125 sheets are 2,000 printed pages.

163 'Romantic poetry is a': FS, '*Athenaeum* Fragmente', no. 116, FS KA, vol. 2, p. 182; F. Schlegel 1971, p. 175.

164 Romantic poetry: Novalis to AWS, 24 February 1798; Novalis, 'Logologische Fragmente', nos 17, 42 and 'Anekdoten', no. 280, Novalis Schriften, vol. 2, pp. 527, 535, 590.

164 'By giving': Novalis, 'Logologische Fragmente', no. 105, Novalis Schriften, vol. 2, p. 545; see also Novalis, 'Fragmente und Studien, 1799–1800', no. 671, Novalis Schriften, vol. 3, p. 685.

164 'living organism': Novalis to AWS, 12 January 1798; see also Novalis,

'Blüthenstaub' ('Pollen'), no. 70 and Novalis, 'Logologische Fragmente', no. 43, Novalis Schriften, vol. 2, pp. 440, 535.

164 'that it should forever': FS, 'Athenaeum Fragmente', no. 116, FS KA, vol. 2, p. 182; F. Schlegel 1971, p. 175.

164 left room for the imagination: Heiner Voß about Goethe, November/ December 1803, Goethe 1982–96, vol. 4. p. 423.

164 open system: Novalis, 'Fichte Studies', no. 648, Novalis Schriften vol. 2, p. 289.

164 poiëtikós and romantic poetry: Beiser 2003, p. 16.

165 'possesses an invisible': FS, 'Gespräch über Poesie', 1800, FS KA, vol. 2, p. 304.

165 poetry within us: ibid., p. 285.

165 'to poeticise is to': Novalis, 'Logologische Fragmente', no. 36, Novalis Schriften, vol. 2, p. 534; for AWS on poetry, see Beiser 2003, p. 16.

165 'Annotations to a poem': AWS, 'Athenaeum Fragmente', no. 40, FS KA, vol. 2, p. 171; F. Schlegel 1971, p. 166.

165 'had destroyed all': John Keats, 28 December 1817, recounted by Benjamin Robert Haydon, Haydon 1960–3, vol. 2, p. 173.

165 logic was mechanical thinking: Novalis, 'Logologische Fragmente', no. 16, Novalis Schriften, vol. 2, p. 526.

165 'rational chaos': Novalis, 'Allgemeine Brouillon', no. 234, Novalis, vol. 3, p. 281, Novalis 2007, p. 34.

165 'poet is but the': Novalis, 'Allgemeine Brouillon', no. 717, Novalis, vol. 3, p. 406; Novalis 2007, p. 132.

165 'most prominent feature': Novalis to A. C. Just, 26 December 1798; see also Novalis, 'Fichte Studies', no. 578, Novalis Schriften, vol. 2, p. 275; Novalis 2013, p. 174.

165 Plato and imagination: Kaag 2014, p. 26.

165 'a licentious and': Samuel Johnson, Rambler, quoted in Bate 1986, p. 10.

165 'men are mightily': Costelloe 2018, p. 23.

166 Kant and imagination: Kaag 2014, p. 27ff.

166 Fichte and imagination: Pikulik 1992, pp. 37–9; Fichte, Grundlagen der Gesammten Wissenschaftslehre, 1794/5, Fichte SW, vol. 1, p. 216.

166 'Imagination alone is': Fichte, Wissenschaftslehre nova methodo, 1798/9, Fichte 1982, p. 208.

166 'we write the world': FS, 'Lecture on Transcendental Philosophy', 1800/1, FS KA, vol. 12, p. 105.

166 Fichte didn't go far enough: Pikulik 1992, p. 38.

166 'a balm of miraculous': AH, 22 November 1799–7 February 1800, diary, A. Humboldt 2000, p. 179.

166 Fn. Heine on Goethe and Schlegels: Heinrich Heine, Die Romantische Schule, Richards 2002, p. 462.

166 'Goethe is presently': Novalis, 'Blüthenstaub' ('Pollen'), no. 118, Novalis Schriften, vol. 2, p. 466; Novalis 1991, p. 402.

166 'now is the time': Novalis, 'Blüthenstaub' ('Pollen'), no. 120, Novalis Schriften, vol. 2, p. 466; Novalis 1991, p. 402.

167 'Once over thirty': Goethe, Faust Part Two, ll. 6787–9 (trans. David Luke), Goethe 1994a.

167 'not Greek, but': FS to AWS, mid-March 1798.

167 'degree of passion': CS to FS, August 1795.

167 wild Dionysian element: Zimmermann 2009, pp. 45–6.

167 'poetry of the frenzied': FS, *Geschichte der Poesie der Griechen und Römer*, 1798, FS KA, vol. 1, p. 404.

167 'crooked line': Novalis, 'Fichte Studies', no. 485, Novalis Schriften, vol. 2, p. 257; Novalis 2013, p. 154.

167 prefix *sym*: FS to Novalis, 26 September 1797; Novalis to CS Schlegel, 9 September 1798; FS to Novalis, November 1798; FS, '*Athenaeum* Fragmente', no. 125, FS KA, vol. 2, p. 185.

167 'Symphilosophy is our': FS to Novalis, 26 September 1797.

168 'a strange phenomenon': C. M. Wieland to K. A. Böttiger, 28 May 1798, Novalis Schriften, vol. 4, p. 617.

168 'how brazen we are': FS to CS, 20 October 1798.

168 'The Schlegels': Therese Huber to Therese Forster, 17–25 July 1803; Huber 1999, vol. 1, p. 423.

168 'You just have to accept': Goethe, 6 February 1799, Goethe 1982–96, vol. 3, p. 21.

168 discussing first issue: Goethe to AWS, 18 June 1798.

168 'This know-it-all': Schiller to Goethe, 23 July 1798.

168 Schlegels' influence: Schiller to Goethe, 8 May 1798.

168 'wasps' nest': Goethe to Schiller, 25 July 1798.

168 Schlegel brothers: Schiller to Goethe, 27 July 1798.

168 mentally deranged: Charlotte Schiller to Fritz von Stein, 2 January 1802, Wais 2005, p. 300.

168 Schlegels at war: CS to FS, 14–15 October 1798.

168 *Athenaeum* sales: Endres 2017, p. 293.

169 'my German expedition': S. T. Coleridge to Thomas Poole, 16 June 1798, Coleridge 1956–71, vol. 1, p. 250; for Coleridge in Germany see also Holmes 1998a, pp. 205–37.

169 'frightened at the expences': S. T. Coleridge, 22 September 1798, notebooks, Coleridge 1958–2002, vol. 1, p. 341; see also S. T. Coleridge to Sara Coleridge, 28 September 1798, Coleridge 1956–71, vol. 1, p. 254.

169 pronunciation was 'hideous': S. T. Coleridge to Josiah Wedgewood, 21 May 1799, Coleridge 1956–71, vol. 1, p. 283.

169 bag full of philosophical books: ibid., p. 284.

169 mind of philosopher: Haney 1906, p. 39.

169 'No man was ever': S. T. Coleridge, quoted in Bate 1986, p. 20.

169 'There is no doubt': Henry Crabb Robinson to Mrs Clarkson, 29 November 1811, Robinson 1869, vol. 1, p. 226.

169 'the spontaneous overflow': William Wordsworth, *Lyrical Ballads*, Preface, 1800.

170 Coleridge and imagination: Holmes 1998b, p. 394.

170 'sketchy work': Delacroix, quoted in Ferber 2010, p. 127.

170 'sketches, beginnings of': Robert Schumann's review of Chopin's preludes, *Neue Zeitschrift für Musik*, vol. 11, November 1839, pp. 19, 163.

Chapter 10: 'Symphilosophy is our connection's true name'
Summer 1798: A Vacation in Dresden and Schelling Arrives

171 'Florence of the': J. G. Herder, 1802, quoted in Alt 2004, vol. 1, p. 409.

171 elegant promenade: this was Brühl's Terrace.

171 river reflection: CS and AWS, 'Die Gemählde. Gespräch', *Athenaeum*, vol. 2, 1799, p. 54.

172 Dresden's museums: Boller 2015, pp. 196–230; Pilz 2015, pp. 240–75.

172 CS travelled to Dresden: AWS to Goethe, 9 May 1798; Gries 1855, p. 25.

172 lived with Charlotte: CS to Luise Gotter, early July 1798; see also Henriette Mendelssohn to DV, 19 April 1799.

172 'Come soon, old': Caroline, AWS and FS to Novalis, 1 July 1798.

172 'symphilosophising': FS to Schleiermacher, 3 July 1798; Novalis to CS, 9 September 1798.

172 passionate horseman: Ludwig Tieck to F. W. Riemer, 3 July 1841, Novalis Schriften, vol. 4, p. 560.

172 'Ghost-Seer': FS to Schleiermacher, July 1798.

172 'He is seeking': ibid.

172 'to touch his own': ibid.

173 'full of the seeds': ibid.

173 Fichte in Dresden: Dora Stock to Charlotte Schiller, 24 October 1798, C. Schiller 1862, vol. 3, p. 25.

173 'ur-assembly of': FS, 'Ideen Fragmente', no. 122, FS KA, vol. 2, p. 268.

173 everybody loved Auguste: Caroline Tischbein-Wilken, 1799, Stoll 1923, p. 109.

173 Japanisches Palais: Boller 2015, p. 209.

173 Gemäldegalerie: Pilz 2015, p. 240.

174 'they took possession': Dora Stock to Charlotte Schiller, 24 October 1798, C. Schiller 1862, vol. 3, p. 25.

174 'a repository of': Novalis, 'Studien zur Bildenden Kunst', no. 476, Novalis Schriften, vol. 2, p. 648.

174 'goes straight from': CS and AWS, 'Die Gemählde. Gespräch', *Athenaeum*, vol. 2, 1799, p. 125.

175 'Can't you help me': CS and AWS, ibid., p. 88.

175 'disfigured by a chance': CS and AWS, ibid., p. 92.

175 Fn. 'Paintings' essay: AWS to Goethe, 8 March 1799.

175 'You would have': Dora Stock to Charlotte Schiller, 24 October 1798, C. Schiller 1862, vol. 3, p. 25.

176 'Jew toll': FS to Schleiermacher, 5 May 1800; CS to AWS, 8 March 1802.

176 'like a Polish ox': Moses Mendelssohn, quoted in FS KA, vol. 25, p. 452.

176 FS's portrait for DV: FS to Schleiermacher, mid-July 1798.

176 their evenings in Dresden: P. D. A. Atterbom to E. G. Geijer, 24 January 1818 (about summer 1798), Fichte Gespräch, vol. 2, p. 4.

176 with torches in gallery: Novalis to H. U. E. von Hardenberg, 1 September 1798; Jean Paul Richter, 1798, Grabowski 1861, vol. 3, p. 138.

176 armistice: this was the Treaty of Leoben, April 1797.

177 'because he always': F. K. Forberg recounting Fichte, April 1797, Fichte Gespräch, vol. 1, p. 418.

177 Napoleon as force of nature: Steffens 1841, vol. 4, p. 57.

177 'Above all, send': Napoleon to Guillaume Faipoult, 1 May 1796, quoted in Saltzman 2012, p. 11.

178 'Membre de l'Institut': Scurr 2021, p. 62.

178 WH's description of Napoleon: WH, 26 December 1797, diary, W. Humboldt 1903–36, vol. 14, pp. 376–7.

178 Napoleon busts: Kleßmann 2008, p. 242.

178 news about Schelling: AWS, FS, CS to F. I. Niethammer, 6 July 1798.

178 meeting Schelling: AWS to Gottlieb Hufeland, 15 July 1798; Schelling to F. I. Niethammer, 23. October 1797; Schelling met AWS at the end of May 1798 in Leipzig, Schelling 1962–75, vol. 1, p. 76.

178 Novalis on Schelling: Novalis to FS, 14 June and 26 December 1797.

178 'entirely commentaries on': Fichte to K. L. Reinhold, 2 July 1795.

178 AWS invited Schelling: AWS to Gottlieb Hufeland, 15 July 1798; Schelling 1962–75, vol. 1, p. 76.

178 Schelling's childhood: Jaspers 1955, p. 15; Tilliette 2004, pp. 11–15.

178 Schelling's father studied under CS's father: Tilliette 2004, p. 12.

179 Life at Tübinger Stift: Schelling 1962–75, vol. 1, pp. 9–18; Tilliette 2004, p. 16ff.; Klaube 2020, p. 42; Pinkard 2001, p. 21; Vieweg 2020, p. 59ff.

179 'a miserable cog': K. P. Conz (and also Georg Kerner), quoted in Vieweg 2020, pp. 62–3.

179 Schelling rebelled: Tilliette 2004, pp. 26–7.

179 'when I will breathe': Schelling to Hegel, January 1796.

180 philosophical revolution: Schelling to Hegel, 6 January 1795 and 21 July 1795.

180 Fn. one-page manifesto: Schelling 1962–75, vol. 1, pp. 57–8; Tilliette 2004, p. 45ff.

180 'humanity's teacher': Anonymous, 'Das älteste Systemprogramm des deutschen Idealismus', c. 1796/7.

180 'give physics wings': ibid.

180 'The first idea is': ibid. (trans. Behler 1987), p. 161.

180 'The Alpha': Schelling, Vom Ich als Prinzip der Philosophie, 1795, Schelling SW, vol. 1, p. 177; see also Schelling to Hegel, 4 February 1795.

180 'the age of philosophical': Schelling to Hegel, 6 January 1795.

181 Schelling's books: his first book was Of the I as the Principle of Philosophy or on the Unconditional in Human Knowledge in 1795, followed by Ideas Concerning a Philosophy of Nature in 1797 and About the World Soul in 1798.

181 Schiller impressed by Schelling: Schiller to Goethe, 10 April 1798; see also letters between Schiller and Goethe in January 1798.

181 'a rigid realist': Goethe to F. H. Jacobi, 17 October 1796.

181 'drowning in matter': Countess Görtz about Goethe, Boyle 2000, p. 222.

181 between realists and idealists: Goethe to Schiller, 30 June 1798.

181 'an unnecessarily strict': Goethe to Schiller, 6 January 1798.

181 'possibly know, the': Fichte, Privatissimum für G. D., April 1803, Fichte GA II, vol. 6, p. 331.

182 animals and environment: Goethe, *Erster Entwurf einer Allgemeinen Einleitung in die Vergleichende Anatomie*, 1795.

182 'Well, until the philosophers': Goethe to Schiller, 6 January 1798.

182 Schelling to Jena: Goethe, 28–30 May 1798, Goethe Diaries, vol. 2, p. 209.

182 'Jena circle': Goethe to C. G. Voigt, 29 May 1798 and 21 June 1798; see also C. G. Voigt to Goethe, 16 July 1798, and for Fichte's recommendation, Fichte Gespräch, vol. 1, p. 526.

182 job offered to Schelling: Goethe to Schelling, 5 July 1798.

182 requested permission to resign: Schelling to Duke of Württemberg, 8 August 1798.

182 'sleeping in a rented bed': Schelling to J. F. Schelling, 6 August 1798.

183 'a few months of': Schelling to J. F. Schelling, 25 June 1798.

183 'He seems to have': Novalis to FS, 26 December 1797.

183 Schelling's appearance: Gries 1855, p. 28; F. K. von Savigny, 30 July–2 August 1799, Stoll 1891, p. 14; Steffens 1841, vol. 2, pp. 75–6; Garlieb Merkel, 1799, and Henry Crabb Robinson, 1802, diary, in Tilliette 1974, pp. 41, 102.

183 'strong, stubborn, tough': DV to Schleiermacher, 28 October 1799.

183 'the kind of man who': CS to FS, 14–15 October 1797.

183 Schelling quiet and no jokes: CS to Novalis, 4 February 1799; Schiller to Goethe, 21 December 1798.

183 Schelling enthralled: Schelling to J. F. Schelling, 20 September 1798.

183 'Go ahead and': ibid.

183 'What's a year?': ibid.

183 'And so the ideal is': FS to Schleiermacher, before mid-August 1798.

183 Fichte and Schiller: Schiller to Goethe, 28 August 1798.

184 Schelling to Freiberg's mines: Gries 1855, p. 30.

184 'dark tempting lap': Novalis, *Lehrlinge zu Sais*, Novalis Schriften, vol. 1, p. 104.

184 another student: this was J. G. Herder's son August Herder, Gries 1855, p. 30.

184 descriptions of mines in Freiberg: Steffens 1841, vol. 4, p. 219ff.

184 travel companion spooked: Gries 1855, p. 30.

Chapter 11: 'To be one with everything living'
Autumn 1798–Spring 1799: Schelling's *Naturphilosophie*

187 Schiller and Goethe's building works: Schiller to Wilhelm Reinwald, 19 July 1798, and Goethe, July, August and September 1798, Goethe Diaries, vol. 2, pp. 213–20.

187 Schiller and Goethe on building works: Schiller to Goethe, 20 July 1798; Goethe to Schiller, 21 July 1798.

187 kitchen smells: Goethe to J. H. Meyer, 8 June 1798.

187 Goethe in Jena: Goethe spent almost three weeks in Jena in June, three days in July, and another two weeks in August; see Goethe, June–August 1797, Goethe Diaries, vol. 2, pp. 210–17.

187 Schelling's philosophy and *Metamorphosis of Plants*: Goethe, 17 and 18 June 1798, Goethe Diaries, vol. 2, p. 212.

188 Goethe, flies and flower: Goethe, 29 July 1798, Goethe Diaries, vol. 2, p. 216.

188 'The Wicked Angel': Goethe to Schiller, 14 July 1798.

188 Schelling saw Schiller: Schiller to Goethe, 5 October 1798.

188 Schiller and *Wallenstein*: Schiller to C. G. Körner, 25 May 1792, 12 September 1794, 27 December 1796, 23 January 1797 and 20 November 1797; Schiller to Goethe, 18 March 1796 and 23 October 1796; Goethe to Karl von Knebel, 28 March 1797.

188 *Wallenstein* at Weimar theatre: Goethe, 13 September 1798, Goethe Diaries, vol. 2, p. 218; Schiller to C. G. Körner, 30 September 1798.

188 Schiller tinkered with the text: Goethe to J. H. Meyer, 26 September 1798; Goethe to Schiller, 7 October 1798; Schiller to Goethe, 9 October 1798.

188 AWS became professor: AWS to Goethe, 18 July 1798.

188 AWS overworked: CS to Novalis, 15 November 1798.

189 not 'unimprovable': C. G. Schütz to AWS, beginning December 1797.

189 eight-page reply: AWS to C. G. Schütz, 10 December 1797.

189 AWS looking old: F. K. von Savigny, 30 July–2 August 1799, Stoll 1891, p. 15.

189 'stubborn Schelling': CS to Novalis, 15 November 1798; see also Steffens 1841, vol. 4, p. 75; for CS in AWS's study, see CS to Novalis, 4 February 1799.

189 Schelling's lecture requirements: Schelling to J. F. and G. M. Schelling, 12 November 1798.

189 leaving Auguste behind: CS to FS, 14–15 October 1798.

189 Fn. transport costs: A. G. F. Rebmann 1787–9, Rebmann 1994, p. 87.

189 theatre director: Goethe became director in 1791.

190 'shining fairy palace', and following descriptions of the theatre: CS to FS, 14–15 October 1798.

190 'kidnapped': Anton Genast, before 12 October 1798, Goethe 1982–96, vol. 3, p. 769.

190 Goethe in his theatre box: M. W. G. Müller, 26 February 1800, Goethe 1982–96, vol. 4, p. 95.

190 'first glass from': CS to Luise Gotter, early 1799.

190 'Schiller took years': CS to FS, 14–15 October 1798.

190 CS returned with Schelling: ibid.

191 four glasses of champagne: ibid.

191 CS and Schelling remained in Jena: Steffens 1841, vol. 4, p. 108.

191 everybody talked about *Wallenstein*: Schiller to C. G. Körner, 8 May 1799.

191 lightning rod: J. F. Cotta to Schiller, 20 May 1798.

191 longest winter: Boyle 2000, p. 631.

191 seven watchmen froze: FS to CS, mid-December 1798.

191 'It was so cold': S. T. Coleridge to Sara Coleridge, 10 March 1799, Coleridge 1956–71, vol. 1, p. 272; Coleridge travelled from 6 to 12 February 1799.

192 stripy waistcoat: Goethe to Christiane Vulpius, 27 November 1798.

192 Goethe stayed longer in Jena: Goethe to Christiane Vulpius, 20 November 1798.

192 Goethe in Jena: Goethe, 11–29 November 1798, Goethe Diaries, vol. 2, pp. 222–5.

192 Schiller and Schelling: Schiller to Goethe, 24 November 1798.

192 'I always find all': Goethe to Karl von Knebel, 28 November 1798.

192 'Today's winter day': Schiller to Goethe, 24 November 1798 and 22 December 1798.

192 'wound up the': Schiller to Goethe, 30 November 1798.

193 Schelling's birthday: Roßbeck 2008, p. 165.

193 'he is by far the most': CS to Novalis, 4 February 1799.

193 'irony of the Schlegel': ibid.

193 'and I haven't yet found': ibid.

193 'genuine granite': CS to FS, 14–15 October 1798.

193 'But where will': FS to CS, 29 October 1798.

193 AWS and Friederike Unzelmann: CS to Luise Gotter, early July 1798.

193 AWS's students: F. K. von Savigny, 30 July–2 August 1799, Stoll 1891, p. 14; for Schelling's students at market square, G. H. Schubett, 1801, Tilliette 1974, p. 69.

193 Schelling's lectures: Steffens 1841, vol. 4, pp. 75–6; F. K. von Savigny, 30 July–2 August 1799, Stoll 1891, p. 14; Rudolf Abeken, c. autumn 1799, and G. H. Schubett, 1801, Tilliette 1974, pp. 35, 37–8.

194 Fn. Schelling and the self: Schelling, *Ideen zu einer Philosophie der Natur*, 1797, Schelling SW, vol. 2, pp. 217–18.

194 'secret bond connecting': ibid., p. 55.

194 'wonderful, magical': Rudolf Abeken, c. autumn 1799, Tilliette 1974, p. 38.

194 Schelling like a general: Steffens 1841, vol. 4, p. 77.

194 Schelling's universe was alive: ibid., p. 128.

194 'linked together, forming one': Schelling, *Von der Weltseele*, 1798, Schelling SW, vol. 2, p. 569; for Schelling and nature as organism, see also Richards 2002, p. 129ff.

194 nature and mind: Schelling, *Ideen zu einer Philosophie der Natur*, 1797, Schelling SW, vol. 2, p. 39.

195 'Mind is invisible': ibid., p. 56.

195 'As long as I myself': ibid., p. 47 (trans. Richards 2002, p. 134).

195 self-discovery in nature: Henrik Steffens to Schelling, 1 September 1800.

195 'mathematical obedience': Novalis 2018, p. 78.

196 'to be one with everything': Hölderlin, *Hyperion*, 1797 and 1799.

196 'I was in a state': Steffens 1841, vol. 4, p. 76; for students crying, see Friedrich Muhrbeck to Hölderlin, September 1799, Hölderlin 1943–85, vol. 7, pt 1, p. 144.

196 'heavenly power': G. H. Schubert, 1801, Tilliette 1974, p. 69; see also Anonymous, 1799, ibid., p. 36.

196 'new, warm, glowing life': Steffens 1841, vol. 4, p. 128.

196 'Philosophy applied to': Schelling, *Erster Entwurf eines Systems der Naturphilosophie*, 1799, Schelling SW, vol. 3, p. 13.

196 CS organised ball: Sophie Mereau, 20 May 1799, diary, Mereau-Brentano 1996, p. 58.

196 Tiecks stayed: CS to Luise Gotter, 5 October 1799.

196 'You fill the space': Novalis to Tieck, 6 August 1799.

196 Tieck's youth: Safranski 2009, p. 90.

197 *Puss in Boots*: Tieck, *Der gestiefelte Kater*, 1797.

197 hiking up hills at midnight: and Tieck finishing novella: Köpke 1855, vol. 1, p. 248; the hill they climbed was the Hausberg.

197 Auguste's appearance: Auguste Böhmer's portrait by Johann Friedrich August Tischbein, 1799.

197 Auguste and music: Luise Gotter to Julie Gotter, 14 January 1798, BBAW, NL Schelling, no. 936.

197 Auguste teased FS: Auguste Böhmer to FS, April 1799.

197 'our splendid circle': Novalis to CS, 27 February 1799.

197 'I'm translating': CS to Novalis, 4 February 1799.

197 CS's lunches: CS to Luise Gotter, 6 June 1799; CS to J. D. Gries, 9 June 1799.

197 Goethe and Schlegels: Goethe, 28 and 29 March 1799, Goethe Diaries, vol. 2, p. 239.

197 'He's always here': CS to Novalis, 15 November 1798.

198 concerts at Zur Rose: F. K. von Savigny, 30 July–2 August 1799, Stoll 1891, p. 17.

198 students admired CS: ibid. and K. Morgenstern, end of July 1797, Fichte Gespräch, vol. 6.1, p. 252.

198 stayed up until late: Luise Gotter to Julie Gotter, 14 January 1798, BBAW, NL Schelling, no. 936.

198 CS heart of Jena Set: Novalis, 'Randbemerkungen zu Friedrich Schlegels *Ideen*', 1799, Novalis Schriften, vol. 3, p. 492.

198 'You must stay': Novalis to CS, 20 January 1799.

Chapter 12: 'Idol worshippers, atheists, liars'
1799: Scandals Part One. Fichte's Dismissal

199 elector of Saxony's complaint: Friedrich August III, Elector of Saxony, Saxon Letter of Requisition to the Weimar Court, 18 December 1798, Fichte Gespräch, vol. 2, pp. 25–6; for Fichte and atheism dispute see also Kühn 2012, p. 376ff., Boyle 2000, p. 625ff., and Estes and Bowman 2010.

199 'On the Ground': Fichte, 'On the Ground of our Belief in a Divine World-Governance', Estes and Bowman 2010, pp. 21–9; Fichte, 'Über den Grund unsers Glaubens an eine göttliche Weltregierung', *Philosophisches Journal einer Gesellschaft Teutscher Gelehrten*, 1798, vol. 8, no. 1, Fichte GA I, vol. 5, pp. 347–57.

199 confiscated the journal: 'Confiscation of *Philosophisches Journal einer Gesellschaft Teutscher Gelehrten*', Estes and Bowman 2010, pp. 77–8.

199 'living and active moral': Fichte, 'Über den Grund unsers Glaubens an eine göttliche Weltregierung', Fichte GA I, vol. 5, p. 354; Estes and Bowman 2010, p. 26; see also Kühn 2012, p. 377.

199 pamphlet accused Fichte: Anonymous, 'Schreiben eines Vaters an seinen studierenden Sohn über den Fichtischen und Forbergischen Atheismus', 1798, Fichte GA I, vol. 6, pp. 121–38; Estes and Bowman 2010, pp. 57–75.

200 'severely punished': Duke Carl August to University of Jena, 27 December 1798, Fichte Gespräch, vol. 6.1, p. 316.

200 'mental illness': Duke Carl August to C. G. Voigt (with request to share the letter with Goethe), 26 December 1798, Fichte GA III, vol. 3, p. 179.

200 'freedom from censorship': Fichte, 'Gerichtliche Verantwortungsschriften', 1799, Fichte GA I, vol. 6, p. 37; Estes and Bowman 2010, p. 166 and see also p. 147.

200 laws in Great Britain: Briggs 2000, p. 118.

200 censorship in Prussia: Brunschwig 1976, p. 273.

201 'in so doing make': Auswärtige Departement to Kurfürstlich-Sächsischen Geheimen Räte, Berlin, 16 April 1799, Fichte Gespräch, vol. 6.1, p. 410.

201 'explosion': Duke Carl August to C. G. Voigt (with request to share the letter with Goethe), 26 December 1798, Fichte GA III, vol. 3, p. 179.

201 'bric-a-brac sophistry': ibid.

201 Goethe urged calm: Goethe to C. G. Voigt, 26(?) December 1798; see also C. G. Voigt to Goethe, 25 December 1798; Boyle 2000, p. 626ff.; Estes and Bowman 2010, p. 82.

201 *Appeal to the Public*: Fichte, *Appellation an das Publikum*, 1799, Fichte GA I, vol. 5, pp. 415–53; Estes and Bowman 2010, pp. 85–125.

201 not going down without a fight: Fichte, *Appellation an das Publikum*, 1799, Fichte GA I, vol. 5, p. 418; Estes and Bowman 2010, p. 95; see also Fichte to Schiller, 18 January 1799.

201 'idol worshippers, atheists': J. K. Lavater to Fichte, 7–12 February 1799.

201 wicked plan by his opponents: Fichte, *Appellation an das Publikum*, 1799, Fichte GA I, vol. 5, p. 417; Estes and Bowman 2010, p. 94.

202 'mighty Fichte who': C. S. L. Reimarus to J. C. Frommann, 21 March 1798, Fichte Gespräch, vol. 1, p. 485.

202 'and since he doesn't': Anonymous to J. G. Herder, 1799, Fichte Gespräch, vol. 2, p. 97.

202 'little lion': Johanne Fichte to Fichte, 1 November 1799.

202 Schiller explained situation: Schiller to Fichte, 26 January 1799.

202 'a whole new species': Duke Carl August to J. G. Herder, 24 January 1799, Fichte Gespräch, vol. 2, p. 43.

202 'publicly confessed revolutionary': Duke Carl August to C. G. Voigt (with request to be shared with Goethe), 26 December 1798, Fichte GA III, vol. 3, p. 179.

202 'those disreputable people': Duke Carl August to C. G. Voigt (second letter), 26 December 1798, Fichte GA III, vol. 3, p. 180.

202 'I simply can't stop': ibid.

203 print run of *Appeal*: Boyle 2000, p. 627; Estes and Bowman 2010, p. 85.

203 *St James's Chronicle*: *St James's Chronicle*, 5 February 1799, Fichte Gespräch, vol. 6.1, p. 335.

203 everybody talking about it: Schiller to C. G. Körner, 10 February 1799; FS to AWS, 5 February 1799; CS to Novalis, 4 February 1799; for more letters, see Fichte Gespräch, vol. 6.1.

203 forty pamphlets in response: Boyle 2000, p. 627.

203 'Brave Fichte is': AWS to Novalis, 12 January 1799.

203 'caused such a scandal': Johanne Fichte to J. J. Wagner, 20 March 1799.

203 'public or legal reprehension': Fichte to C. G. Voigt, 22 March 1799.

203 'were as much alike': ibid.

203 'They gave me': ibid.

204 Fichte's resignation accepted: C. G. Voigt to Fichte, 25 March 1799; see also C. G. Voigt to Goethe, 7 April 1799 and Fichte to C. G. Voigt, 3 April 1799.

204 'we had to lose him': Goethe to J. G. Schlosser, 30 August 1799.

204 'I would have voted': ibid.

204 'Jena will sink into': FS to AWS, April 1799.

204 Fichte's dismissal: CS to Luise Gotter, 24 April 1799.

204 'Schlegel is hatching': CS to J. D. Gries, 9 June 1799; see also FS to AWS, April 1799.

204 Schelling offered public defence: G. Hufeland to Schelling, c. 20 January 1799, Fichte Gespräch, vol. 6.1, p. 324.

205 'abandoned and shunned': CS to Luise Gotter, 24 April 1799.

205 'we are sticking together': CS to J. D. Gries, 9 June 1799.

205 student petitions: Steffens 1841, vol. 4, p. 154ff.

205 'Fichte's celebrity': ibid., p. 154.

205 'attack against the': ibid., p. 153.

205 'Fichtian': K. L. Reinhold to W. J. Kalmann, 26 March 1797; see also K. L. Reinhold to J. I. Baggesen, 3 February 1797, Fichte Gespräch, vol. 1, pp. 402 and 416, and FS to Novalis, 10 March 1797.

205 'great Jena Ich': C. M. Wieland to Heinrich Gessner, 21 February 1797, Fichte Gespräch, vol. 1, p. 417.

205 'One star sets': I. H. Fichte quoting Goethe, March 1799, Fichte Gespräch, vol. 6.1, p. 371.

205 what did Goethe say: FS to CS, late April 1799 and May 1799.

205 'I've moved into a': FS to CS, late April 1799; see also FS to Fichte, May 1799.

205 FS's defence of Fichte: FS, 'Für Fichte. An die Deutschen', FS KA, vol. 1, p. 522.

205 possible return to Jena: FS to AWS, early April 1799.

205 'You're very proud': Johanne Fichte to Fichte, 27 September 1799.

205 no humility: Fichte to Johanne Fichte, 20 September 1799.

205 'a dirty little courtier': Fichte to Johanne Fichte, 5 October 1799.

205 war in Zurich: FS to CS, late April 1799; Johanne Fichte to Fichte, 16 August 1799.

206 Fichte job-hunting: Henrik Steffens to Schelling, September 1799 and Fichte to Wilhelm Jung, 10 May 1799.

206 University of Göttingen and Fichte: Government of Braunschweig-Lüneburg to C. Meiners, 24 April 1799, Fichte Gespräch, vol. 6.1, p. 442.

206 'whose writings contain': Duke of Braunschweig, 1799, recounted by K. A. Böttiger, 10 August 1799, Fichte Gespräch, vol. 2, p. 219.

206 Schwarzburg-Rudolstadt and Fichte: Schiller to Goethe, 14 June 1799.

206 Berlin and Fichte: FS to Fichte, before 24 June 1799.

206 'His sharp edges': FS to C. G. Körner, 30 January 1797.

206 Fichte's son ill: CS to J. D. Gries, 9 June 1799.

206 Fichte's life in Berlin: Fichte to Johanne Fichte, 6 and 20 July 1799.

206 Goethe and Berlin: Steffens 1841, vol. 4, p. 151.

206 'dancing carnivalesque': AH to H. C. Schumacher, 2 March 1836.

207 population of London and Paris: the first reliable census in London was taken in 1801 – it counted 1,096,784 people; for Paris see Preisendörfer 2018, p. 482.

207 military character of Berlin: Henry Crabb Robinson to Thomas Crabb Robinson, 13 April 1803, Robinson 1929, p. 121; DV to Rahel Levin, 2 June 1800; Steffens 1841, vol. 4, pp. 151–2, 185; in 1798, Berlin had 169,019 inhabitants of whom 26,920 were military personnel, see Loewenthal 1895, pt 4, p. 183.

207 'endless display of': A. B. Granville, October 1827, Granville 1829, vol. 1, p. 332.

207 'sandy deserts': Fichte to Johanne Fichte, 6 July 1799.

207 'Even halfway intelligent': Fichte to Schelling, 20 July 1799.

207 lecture schedule in Jena: Fichte to J. E. C. Schmidt, 17 March 1799.

207 'He lost his Samson's': CS to AWS, 27 July 1801.

208 'I consider Fichte's': Kant, *Intelligenzblatt*, ALZ, no. 109, 28 August 1799.

208 Fichte shocked: Fichte to K. L. Reinhold, 15 September 1799.

208 Kant's letter to Fichte: Kant to Fichte, December 1797, published in *Intelligenzblatt*, ALZ, no. 122, 28 September 1799; see also Fichte to Johanne Fichte, 8 September 1799; Fichte to Schelling, *c.* 12 September 1799; Schelling to Fichte, 12 and 16 September 1799.

208 Kant's letter published: *Intelligenzblatt*, ALZ, no. 122, 28 September 1799.

208 'the weakness of my': ibid., Kant to Fichte, December 1797.

208 'had never been particularly': Fichte to Schelling, 20 September 1799.

208 'drag the dead plaster': Schelling to Fichte, 12 September 1799.

Chapter 13: 'You lose yourself in a dizzy whirl'
1799: Scandals Part Two. Divorce, Women and Sex

209 DV's divorce: the divorce was on 11 January 1799, Stern 1994, p. 97.

209 DV unhappy: Fürst 1858, pp. 112–13.

209 'It is simply inexpressible': WH to CH, 26 June 1790.

209 'failure to fulfil': Allgemeines Landrecht für die Preußischen Staaten, Part 2, 1. Titel, § 694.

209 'the mutual aversion': ibid., §§ 718, 717.

210 intervention of DV's friend: Fürst 1858, p. 114.

210 DV felt free: DV to K. G. von Brinckmann, 2 February 1799.

210 Simon Veit more generous: DV received 400 thalers annually and a one-off payment of 1,100 thalers; FS to Novalis, 17 December 1798; see also FS to CS, 27 November 1798, and Stern 1994, pp. 99–100.

210 DV visited Jonas: DV to CS, 3 August 1799.

210 conditions of divorce: FS to Novalis, 17 December 1798; DV to Schleiermacher, 11 April 1800.

210 FS's opposition to marriage: FS to CS, 27 November 1798.

210 'to be his wife in': ibid.

210 avalanche of outrage: FS to CS and AWS, 22 December 1798; DV to K. G. von Brinckmann, 2 February 1799.

210 husband prohibited contact: Fürst 1858, p. 115.

210 'a rag-tag pack': FS to CS and AWS, 22 December 1798.

211 'I can't tell you': DV to K. G. von Brinckmann, 2 February 1799.

211 'belonged to herself'': ibid.

211 'demoralising crudeness': ibid.

211 'I am happy now': ibid.

211 DV's apartment: Fürst 1858, p. 114.

211 DV's desk: DV to K. G. von Brinckmann, 2 February 1799.

211 FS spent days with DV: Fürst 1858, p. 114.

211 FS and DV making love: FS, *Lucinde*, 1799, F. Schlegel 1999, pp. 16, 43, 45, 79, 81; F. Schlegel 1971, pp. 47, 68–70, 98, 100. I've based the following scene on *Lucinde* because FS and DV admitted that much of the novel was autobiographical. Sometimes even exact phrases from FS's letters appear in *Lucinde*, such as his description of DV following him onto the funeral pyre, like Indian widows, or finding his youth in her arms. (FS to Novalis, 17 December 1798; FS to CS, mid-February 1798: FS, *Lucinde*, 1799, F. Schlegel 1999, pp. 17, 81; F. Schlegel 1971, p. 48, 100.)

211 'You are the fixed': FS, *Lucinde*, 1799, F. Schlegel 1999, p. 115; F. Schlegel 1971, p. 127.

211 'You are the priestess': FS, *Lucinde*, 1799, F. Schlegel 1999, p. 114; F. Schlegel 1971, p. 126.

211 DV not just lover: FS, *Lucinde*, 1799, F. Schlegel 1999, pp. 12, 82–3; F. Schlegel 1971, p. 101.

211 FS loved DV's maturity: FS, *Lucinde*, 1799, F. Schlegel 1999, p. 81; F. Schlegel 1971, p. 100.

212 DV gave FS purpose: FS to CS, mid-February 1798 and 15 December 1798.

212 finances: FS to Novalis, 17 December 1798.

212 'extraordinary things': FS to CS, 15 December 1798.

212 'If she were to': FS to Novalis, 17 December 1798.

212 last breath in letter: DV to Schleiermacher, March 1799.

212 FS bombarded CS with questions: FS to CS, July 1799 and *c.* 1 August 1799.

212 '*Letters* in the evening': Novalis, 'Allgemeine Brouillon', no. 373, Novalis Schriften, vol. 3, p. 308; Novalis 2007, p. 56.

213 'You will see': FS to CS and AWS, 22 December 1798; FS mentioned *Lucinde* already on 20 October 1798 in a letter to Novalis.

213 FS and Novalis on novels: FS KA, vol. 11, p. 160; Novalis to CS, 27 February 1799; Endres 2017, p. 329.

213 danger of novels: F. C. Laukhard, 1792, quoted in Maier 2004, p. 209.

213 'I want there to be': FS to CS, *c.* 20 November 1798.

213 'be insatiable': FS, *Lucinde*, 1799, F. Schlegel 1999, p. 12; F. Schlegel 1971, p. 44.

213 'wild blood rages': FS, *Lucinde*, 1799, F. Schlegel 1999, p. 16; F. Schlegel 1971, p. 47.

213 'in the snow of': FS, *Lucinde*, 1799, F. Schlegel 1999, p. 45; F. Schlegel 1971, p. 70.

213 swapping roles: FS, *Lucinde*, 1799, F. Schlegel 1999, p. 19; F. Schlegel 1971, p. 49.

214 Fn. CS suggested Condorcet: CS to FS, June 1795.

214 'petals of a single': FS, *Lucinde*, 1799, F. Schlegel 1999, p. 18; F. Schlegel 1971, pp. 48–9.

214 'most dangerous obstacles': FS, 'Über die Philosophie: An Dorothea', *Athenaeum*, vol. 2, 1799, p. 8.

214 'She has ceased': Fichte, *Erster Anhang des Naturrecht. Grundriss des Familienrechts*, Fichte SW, vol. 3, pp. 313–14; Fichte gave lectures on this topic in 1795/6.

214 'you're not a man': Fichte to Johanne Fichte, 29 August 1795.

214 'preservation of the': Zimmermann 2009, p. 140; see also Bake and Kiupel 1996, p. 41.

214 'natural superiority': Kant, 'Rechtslehre' § 26, Kant 1991, p. 98.

214 'All honour to women!': Schiller, 'Würde der Frauen', 1796, trans. Marianna Wertz, https://archive.schillerinstitute.com/fid_91-96/933_dig_women.html

215 'All honour to women!': AWS, 'Schillers Lob der Frauen: Parodie', AWS SW, vol. 2, 1846, p. 172 (trans. Damion Searls).

215 'The man must go': Schiller, 'Die Gocke', 1799 (trans. Marianna Wertz, https://archive.schillerinstitute.com/transl/trans_schil_1poems.html#song _bell).

216 'chaotic structure': FS, 'Fragmente zur Poesie und Litteratur', no. 274, FS KA, vol. 16, p. 276.

216 'Confessions belong in': FS, 'Charakteristiken und Kritiken', no. 1339, FS KA, vol. 2, p. 338.

216 'only a genius can': FS, 'Fragmente zur Poesie und Litteratur', no. 582, FS KA, vol. 16, p. 134.

216 'bizarre Lucinde': Novalis to CS, 27 February 1799.

216 'you lose yourself': ibid.

216 'expected to hold': ibid.; see also CS to L. F. Huber, 22 November 1799.

216 reviews about *Lucinde*: Zimmermann 2009, p. 146.

216 'sick mind': and following quotes, L. F. Huber, *Lucinde* Review, ALZ, no. 130, 7 May 1800.

217 'metaphysics of the': Jenisch 1799, p. 363.

217 'empty nonsense': Schiller to Goethe, 19 July 1799.

217 'everybody reads it': Goethe to Schiller, 20 July 1799.

217 'doesn't anyone know': FS to CS, *c.* 1 August 1799.

217 'common, ugly Jewish': Stern 1994, p. 126; see also Daniel Jenisch to K. A. Böttiger, June 1799, Zimmermann 2009, p. 147.

217 'I keep feeling burning': DV to Schleiermacher, 8 April 1799; see also Fürst 1858, p. 116.

217 Fichte reading *Lucinde*: Fichte to Johanne Fichte, 8–10 September 1799.

217 'yes, yes, getting': and his routine, Fichte to Johanne Fichte, 20 July 1799.

217 Fichte lived in Friedrichstrasse: Fichte to Johanne Fichte, 17 August 1799.

218 'the portions are so': Fichte to Johanne Fichte, 17 August 1799.

218 FS, DV and Fichte's appearance: Fichte to Johanne Fichte, 20 July 1799; there are numerous accounts mentioning FS's shabby clothes, see for example: Caroline Tischbein-Wilken, 1799, Stoll 1923, p. 114; DV to Clemens Brentano, mid-November 1800.

218 'After all . . . we're all': FS to CS, July 1799.

218 'few, or more precisely': Fichte to Johanne Fichte, 13 September 1799.

218 'philosophers' convent': DV to CS, July 1799.

218 'I am getting dizzy': ibid.

218 'I will be utterly': Fichte to Johanne Fichte, 2 August 1799; see also FS to CS, *c.* 1 August 1799.

218 'Jena Colony': Schelling to Fichte, 1 November 1799; see also Fichte to Schelling, 9 August 1799.

218 'We will be a single': Fichte to Johanne Fichte, 2 August 1799.

219 'stinginess and envy personified': K.U. Boehlendorf to Anna Noltenius, 10 February 1803, Fichte Gespräch, vol. 3, p. 150.

219 'silly goose': CS to AWS, 15 February 1802, see also CS to Auguste Böhmer, 14 October 1799.

219 'don't be intimidated': Fichte to Johanne Fichte, 2 August 1799.

219 Friedrich preferred Jena: FS to AWS, 10 August 1799.

219 'Write to me': DV to CS, 3 August 1799.

219 'house of Jena': Schelling to Fichte, 9 August 1799.

219 DV nervous: DS to Schleiermacher, 11 October 1799.

219 'what fundamental objections': FS, '*Athenaeum* Fragment', no. 34, FS KA, vol. 2, p. 170.

Chapter 14: 'The Schlegel clique' – Autumn 1799: Work and Play

220 FS's arrival: Caroline Tischbein-Wilken, 1799, Stoll 1923, p. 114.

220 preparing the house: CS to Auguste Böhmer, 16 and 30 September 1799.

220 rooms in Leutragasse: Luise Gotter to Julie Gotter, 14 January 1798, BBAW, NL Schelling, no. 936; DV to Schleiermacher, 11 October 1799; see also Kösling 2010, p. 55; CS to Auguste Böhmer, 30 September 1799; CS to Luise Gotter, 5 October 1799; CS to J. D. Gries, 27 December 1799.

221 lunches: CS to Luise Gotter, 5 October 1799.

221 CS demanding opinions: Steffens 1841, vol. 4, p. 113.

221 'she thinks everyone': DV, diary, no date, D. Schlegel 1881, vol. 1, p. 93.

221 'extremely intelligent': Steffens 1841, vol. 4, p. 82.

221 CS's squint: Ludwig Tieck about CS, CS Letters, vol. 1, p. 748.

221 'magic circle': Steffens 1841, vol. 4, p. 83.

221 tried to persuade Fichte: Johanne Fichte to Fichte, 27 September 1799 and 1 November 1799; Fichte to Johanne Fichte, 5 October 1799.

221 'I'm always working': Fichte to J. F. Cotta, 13 January 1800.

221 'How can you think': Fichte to Johanne Fichte, 23 October 1799.

221 '*one* roof': CS to Novalis, 20 February 1799.

221 Novalis missed them: Novalis to FS, 31 January 1800.

221 Julie von Charpentier: Novalis to Caroline Just, 5 February 1798; Novalis to FS, 20 January 1799; Novalis to J. W. Oppel, late January 1800; Steffens 1841, vol. 4, p. 217; Sidonie von Hardenberg to Wilhelmine Thielmann, 9 May 1799, Novalis Schriften, vol. 4, p. 627.

221 Julie perfect wife: Novalis to J. W. Oppel, late January 1800.

221 'Love. What kind?': CS to Novalis, 4 February 1799.

222 Novalis's employment: Hädecke 2011, pp. 224–9.

222 'subterranean heroes': Novalis, *Heinrich von Ofterdingen*, Novalis Schriften, vol. 1, p. 241.

222 turn life into novel: Novalis to CS, 27 February 1799.

222 encouraged CS to write novel: ibid.; FS to CS, 20 and 29 October 1798; FS to Auguste Böhmer, November 1798.

222 CS's brief synopsis: CS Letters, vol. 1, pp. 662–4.

222 protagonist in *Florentin*: this was DV's previous lover Eduard d'Alton. CS to AWS, 10 and 27 July 1801; see also Stern 1994, pp. 75–7, 206–8.

222 'We have to build': Novalis to CS, 20 January 1799.

223 'went beyond every': Caroline Tischbein-Wilken, 1799, Stoll 1923, p. 109.

223 CS and AWS argued: ibid., pp. 112–13.

223 AWS's affair: AWS to Elisa van Nuys, 13 September 1799.

223 'serious affairs': CS to AWS, 16 March 1801.

223 'freedom existing': CS to Julie Gotter, 18 February 1803.

223 not even FS noted anything: FS to Schleiermacher, mid-September 1801.

223 AWS and CS in bad mood: Caroline Tischbein-Wilken, 1799, Stoll 1923, pp. 112–14; DV to Schleiermacher, 11 October 1799.

223 Auguste irritated: Caroline Tischbein-Wilken, 1799, Stoll 1923, p. 114.

223 'tart as a crabapple': CS to Auguste Böhmer, 14 October 1799.

223 only Schelling was impervious: Caroline Tischbein-Wilken, 1799, Stoll 1923, p. 114.

224 Schelling about CS: Schelling to Martin Wagner, 5 October 1809; Schelling to F. I. Niethammer, 2 October 1809; Schelling to Philipp Michaelis, 29 November 1809.

224 'Love of my Life': Schelling's poem to Caroline, Christmas 1799, Schelling 1869–70, vol. 1, p. 290.

224 CS united strength and tenderness: Schelling to Philipp Michaelis, 29 November 1809.

224 'magnificent woman': Schelling to Niethammer, 2 October 1809.

224 'masterpiece of the gods': Schelling to Philipp Michaelis, 29 November 1809.

224 black feather: CS to Auguste Böhmer, 14 October 1799.

224 'When in those consecrated': Schelling's poem to Caroline, Christmas 1799, Schelling 1869–70, vol. 1, p. 292 (trans. Damion Searls).

224 'worships Madame Schlegel': Johanne Fichte to Fichte, 16 October 1799.

224 'as far as Schelling': Fichte to Johanne Fichte, 23 October 1799.

224 FS not pleased: FS to Schleiermacher, 14 February 1800 and 15 September 1801.

224 'true fairytale': Goethe to J. G. Schlosser, 30 August 1799.

225 'If I were twenty': Goethe to WH, 16 September 1799.

225 'Now that we're': Goethe to F. H. Jacobi, 27 December 1794.

225 beautiful actresses: Goethe to J. P. Eckermann, 22 March 1825.

225 building works and other duties: Goethe to Schiller, 10 August 1799; Goethe, summer 1799, Goethe Diaries, vol. 2, pp. 255–7.

225 'My business affairs': Goethe to Schiller, 27 July 1799.

225 Schiller in bad mood and scorched lawn: Schiller to Goethe, 25 June 1799 and 5, 9 July 1799.

225 'Because of your long': Schiller to Goethe, 15 July 1799.

225 'He hated them': Goethe to K. F. Zelter, 20 October 1831.

225 Schiller upset about Schlegels: Goethe to Adele Schopenhauer, 16 January 1830.

225 moving to Weimar: Schiller to Goethe, 12 August 1799.

226 Schiller's fees: Schiller to C. G. Körner, 6 August 1799.

226 tenancy agreement: Goethe to Schiller, 4 September 1799.

226 'for our transplantation': Schiller to Goethe, 16 August 1799.

226 Goethe to Garden House: Goethe, 31 July–15 September 1799, Goethe Diaries, vol. 2, pp. 256–8.

226 'Jena solitude': Goethe to Schiller, 1 January 1797.

226 Goethe's work: Goethe to Schiller, 3 August 1799.

226 'visit to the moon': Goethe to Schiller, 10 August 1799.

226 'because that's how': Goethe to Schiller, 7 August 1799; Christiane and August came back from Jena on 9 August 1799, Goethe, 9 August 1799, Goethe Diaries, vol. 2, p. 257.

226 Goethe to Jena: Goethe, 15 September 1799, Goethe Diaries, vol. 2, p. 258.

226 'A little work on': Goethe, 19 September 1799, ibid., pp. 259–60.

227 Goethe in Jena: Goethe, 16 September–14 October 1799, 10 November–8 December 1799, ibid., pp. 259–65, 269–74.

227 *Lucinde* and Schelling's book: Goethe, 15 September 1799, ibid., p. 258; this was Schelling's *Einleitung zu dem Entwurf eines Systems der Naturphilosophie*, 1799.

227 'Have you definitively': Goethe to Schiller, 4 April 1798.

227 'I can hardly make': AWS to Goethe, 10 June 1798.

227 Schiller and Schlegels: Schiller to Goethe, 28 June 1798.

227 preferred their honesty: Goethe to Schiller, 17 August 1799.

227 'We'd much rather': Steffens 1841, vol. 4, p. 100.

227 'These gentlemen': Goethe to WH, 16 September 1799.

227 'Madame Lucifer': Karoline Paulus to Charlotte Schiller, 11 March 1804, Henriette Hoven to Charlotte Schiller, 4 August 1804; R. E. Niethammer to Charlotte Schiller, 25 October 1804, C. Schiller 1862, vol. 3, pp. 182, 187, 275; for Goethe and *Lucinde*, see Goethe, 15 September 1799, Goethe 1982–96, p. 63.

228 made fun of Schiller's poems: CS to Auguste Böhmer, 21 October 1799.

228 'The way the Schlegels': Johanne Fichte to Fichte, 16 October 1799.

228 request for books: see for example Goethe to AWS, 26 March 1799 and 16 October 1799.

228 'intellectual neighbour': Goethe to AWS, 18 June 1798.

228 walks with AWS: Goethe, September 1799, Goethe Diaries, vol. 2, pp. 261–2.

228 'end up walking': CS to Auguste Böhmer, 30 September 1799.

228 'more turgid reading': Schiller to Goethe, 22 October 1799.

228 Goethe and Schelling: Goethe, 15 September–13 October 1799, Goethe Diaries, vol. 2, pp. 258–65; see also Schelling to Carus (?), 9 November 1799; for Goethe, Schelling and *Naturphilosophie*, see Richards 2002, p. 463ff.

228 *Introduction to the*: Schelling, *Einleitung zu dem Entwurf eines Systems der Naturphilosophie*, 1799.

228 'absolutely all of our': ibid., Schelling SW, vol. 3, p. 278; see also Richards 2002, p. 143.

228 neither idealist, nor realist: K. A. von Wangenheim to King Friedrich von Württemberg, 15 November 1811, Tilliette 1974, p. 211.

228 'Every experiment is': Schelling, *Einleitung zu dem Entwurf eines Systems der Naturphilosophie*, 1799, Schelling SW, vol. 3, p. 276.

228 Goethe and *Naturphilosophie*: FS to AWS, 26 July 1800; Goethe to Henrik Steffens, 29 May 1801; see also Richards 2002, p. 463ff.; Vater and Woods 2012, p. 137.

229 'Categorising and counting': Goethe, *Morphologie*, 1817, Goethe 1949–60, vol. 13, p. 155.

229 'We snatch in vain': Goethe, *Faust Part One*, ll. 672–5 (trans. David Luke), Goethe 2008, p. 23.

229 DV's journey to Jena: DV to Schleiermacher, 11 October 1799.

229 DV worried about CS: ibid.; DV to Rahel Levin, 18 November 1799.

229 'Only beautiful women': DV to Schleiermacher, 28 October 1799.

229 DV rented carriage: DV to Schleiermacher, 11 October 1799.

229 DV's heart pounded: ibid.

230 CS's appearance: ibid.; see also DV to Rahel Levin, 18 November 1799.

230 'I have no doubt': CS to Auguste Böhmer, 6 October 1799.

230 DV commenting on CS's appearance: DV to Schleiermacher, 11 October 1799.

230 'It looks like': DV to Sophie Bernhardi, 7 October 1799.

230 DV about CS: DV to Schleiermacher, 11 October 1799; DV to Rahel Levin, 18 November 1799.

230 daily life in Leutragasse: CS to Auguste Böhmer, 14 October 1799; DV to Sophie Bernhardi, 7 October 1799; DV to Schleiermacher, 11 October 1799.

230 Philipp Veit's schooling: DV to Schleiermacher, 11 October 1799; CS to Auguste Böhmer, 14 October 1799.

230 CS about Philipp Veit: CS to Auguste Böhmer, 6 October 1799.

230 long walks: CS to Auguste Böhmer, 30 September 1799.

230 Italian lessons and Dante: DV to Schleiermacher, 11 October 1799; CS to Auguste Böhmer, 14 October 1799.

230 Schelling's poem: Friedrich to Schleiermacher, 6 January 1800.

230 sequel to *Lucinde*: DV to Schleiermacher, 28 October 1799.

231 CS working with AWS: DV to Karoline Paulus, 3/4 June 1805; AWS to J. F. Cotta, 4 October 1799; for recent Shakespeare translations, see AWS to Goethe, 22 October 1799; AWS to A. F. Bernhardi, 30 September 1799.

231 AWS depended on CS: DV to Schleiermacher, 11 October 1799.

231 DV watched family dynamics: DV to Schleiermacher, 11 and 28 October 1799; DV to Sophie Bernhardi, 7 October 1799.

231 'There's not much': DV to Schleiermacher, 11 October 1799; see also DV to Rahel Levin, 18 November 1799.

231 *System of Transcendental*: Schelling, *System des transzendentalen Idealismus*, 1800.

231 Schelling introduced aesthetics: on Schelling and Transcendental Idealism, see Richards 2002, p. 151ff.

231 'The objective world': Schelling, *System des transzendentalen Idealismus*, 1800, Schelling SW, vol. 3, p. 349; see also Richards 2002, p. 470.

231 nature, self and art: Richards 2002, pp. 161–2.

232 finite representation of infinity: Schelling, *System des transzendentalen Idealismus*, 1800, Schelling SW, vol. 3, p. 620.

232 'the holiest of holies': ibid., p. 628.

232 most important philosophical work: Henrik Steffens to Schelling, 1 September 1800.

232 'all art should become': FS, 'Kritische Fragmente', no. 115, FS KA, vol. 2, p. 161.

232 'science in its': Novalis, 'Logologische Fragmente', no. 17, Novalis Schriften, vol. 2, p. 527.

232 'already withered': Novalis to FS, November 1798.

232 'modern phenomenon': ibid.

Chapter 15: 'Solemnly calling a new confederation of minds' November 1799: A Meeting in Leutragasse

233 'Oh child': CS to Auguste Böhmer, 28 October 1799.

233 'Be happy too': ibid.

233 'What a convergence': Johanne Fichte to Fichte, 22 October 1799; see also Johanne Fichte to Fichte, 1 November 1799.

233 'What in the world': DV to Schleiermacher, 28 October 1799.

234 'alliance of the': F. Schlegel 1846, vol. 1, p. 115.

234 working together in Leutragasse: AWS to Goethe, 7 January 1800.

234 'rage and blaze': DV to Schleiermacher, 6 January 1800.

234 'Wilhelm writes verses': FS to Auguste Böhmer, 17 October 1799.

234 vertiginous flitting between subjects: DV to Rahel Levin, 23 January 1800.

234 'flat uniformity of': AWS and FS, 'Vorerinnerung', *Athenaeum*, vol. 1, 1798, p. iv.

234 'people who can': Novalis to AWS, 24 February 1798.

234 'I produce best': ibid.

234 'float everywhere': FS, 'Gespräch über die Poesie', FS KA, vol. 2, pp. 333–4.

234 FS's manners while thinking: Steffens 1841, vol. 4, p. 303.

235 'party of wit': Tieck 1828–54, vol. 5, dedication page.

235 'reading machine': CS to Auguste Böhmer, 4 November 1799.

235 Tieck brought protagonists alive: Steffens 1841, vol. 4, p. 115.

235 'breath of kindred': Tieck to FS, 23 April 1801.

235 'Oh, that wife!': FS to CS, July 1799; see also DV to Schleiermacher, 28 October 1799.

235 Amalie fell asleep: CS to Auguste Böhmer, 21 October 1799; FS to Auguste Böhmer, October 1798.

235 Amalie jealous: DV to Sophie Bernhardi, 7 October 1799.

235 'Caroline is very busy': ibid.

235 'that he prefers': CS to Auguste Böhmer, 30 September 1799.

235 J. W. Ritter: FS to Schleiermacher, 15 November 1799; J. W. Ritter about Novalis, 1810, Novalis Schriften, vol. 4, p. 650.

235 Ritter brought frogs: CS to Novalis, 4 February 1799.

236 part of same organic universe: Ritter 1798, p. 171; see also Wetzels 1990, p. 203.

236 'real soul of': Novalis, 'Fragmente und Studien 1799–1800', no. 584, Novalis Schriften, vol. 3, p. 655.

236 'electrical machine': DV to Schleiermacher, 17 November 1800.

236 'my darling *Hühnchen*': CS to Auguste Böhmer, 14 October 1799.

236 'I looked daringly pretty': ibid. (Auguste was in Dessau from 14 September to 26 November 1799.)

236 Auguste wanted to come home: CS to Auguste Böhmer, 6 October 1799.

236 CS scolded Auguste: CS to Auguste Böhmer, 17 October 1799.

236 satirical play in Leipzig: CS to Auguste Böhmer, 21 October 1799; Kotzebue's play *Der hyperboreeische Esel* premiered in Leipzig in October 1799; see Zimmermann 2009, p. 147; for Schlegel brothers at book fair, see AWS to Goethe, 22 October 1799.

237 FS and *Der hyperboreeische Esel*: CS to Auguste Böhmer, 21 October 1799; Zimmermann 2009, p. 147.

237 'When dealing with': AWS to Elisa van Nuys, 13 September 1799.

237 short play on Kotzebue: AWS, *Ehrenpforte und Triumphbogen für den Theater-Präsidenten von Kotzebue*, 1801.

237 'Our Father Who Art': AWS to Schleiermacher, 22 December 1800 (trans. Damion Searls).

237 'as paper rolls': CS to AWS, 8 March 1802.

237 bad reviews in ALZ: These were reviews of Schelling's *Ideen zu einer Philosophie der Natur* in ALZ, nos 316 and 317, 3 and 4 October 1799.

237 'dead dogs': Therese Huber to Therese Forster, 17–25 July 1803; Huber 1999, vol. 1, p. 424.

237 Schelling's letter to ALZ: Schelling to editors of ALZ, 6 October 1799, printed in *Intelligenzblatt*, ALZ, no. 142, 2 November 1799.

238 Fichte reported from Berlin: Fichte to Schelling, 22 October 1799.

238 laughing so much: CS to Auguste Böhmer, 28 October 1799, DV to Schleiermacher, 28 October 1799.

238 they felt invincible: Steffens 1841, vol. 4, p. 137.

238 'deviltries' . . . 'we'll spoil': AWS to Schleiermacher, 1 November 1799.

238 'nervous fever': Schiller to Goethe, 25 October 1799; Charlotte was ill from 23 October 1799; see also Schiller to Goethe, 28 October 1799, 1, 4, 8 and 19 November 1799.

238 'pierce my heart': Schiller to Goethe, 25 October 1799.

238 Dr Stark's prescriptions: Schiller to Goethe, 4 November 1799.

239 'today they're going': ibid.

239 Charlotte delirious, then silent stupor: Schiller to Goethe, 30 October 1799, 1 and 4 November 1799.

239 Johanne about Charlotte's illness: Johanne Fichte to Fichte, 18 November 1799.

239 'to distract myself': Schiller to Goethe, 4 November 1799.

239 Karl stayed in Weimar: Goethe to Schiller, 8 November 1799.

239 'his dear Damela': Christiane Vulpius to Goethe, 20 November 1799; see also Boyle 2000, vol. 2, p. 646.

239 'We don't make enemies': AWS to Elisa van Nuys, 13 September 1799.

239 most radical revolutionaries: ibid.

239 'held her head': AWS to Tieck, 16 August 1799; the attacks were printed as 'Litterarischer Reichsanzeiger oder Archiv der Zeit und ihres Geschmacks', *Athenaeum*, vol. 2, 1799, pp. 328–40.

240 *Faith and Love*: Novalis, *Glauben und Liebe*, 1798.

240 'If someone doesn't': FS to Novalis, late July 1798.

240 'they separated the': Novalis 2018, p. 72.

240 'great and marvellous': ibid., p. 74.

240 the Church as mysterious place: ibid., p. 68.

240 'Once, there was': ibid., p. 67; for metaphor of light see O'Brien 1995, p. 232.

240 'which paid no attention': Novalis 2018, p. 88.

240 'a great feast of': ibid., p. 87.

241 'solemnly calling for a new': ibid., pp. 84–5.

241 Novalis on Enlightenment: ibid., p. 85.

241 religious enthusiasm: ibid., p. 77.

241 world was like millwheel: ibid.

241 erasing wonder from nature: ibid., p. 79.

241 'The gentlemen are': DV to Schleiermacher, 15 November 1799.

241 'True anarchy is': Novalis 2018, p. 80.

241 'powerful fermentation': ibid., p. 82.

241 'true genius': ibid., p. 83.

241 'Have patience': ibid., p. 89.

241 'longing for religious': Tieck quoted in Stockinger 2015, p. 113.

241 Tieck read *Genoveva*: FS to Schleiermacher, 15 November 1799; Tieck 1820, p. 4; see also Ziolkowski 2006, p. 156ff.

242 '*The Bond of*': AWS, 'Bund der Kirche mit den Künsten', 1800, AWS SW, vol. 1, pp. 86–96; FS had been working on this collection throughout the summer months of 1799, FS to AWS, 10 August 1799. They were published under the title 'Ideen' in *Athenaeum,* vol. 3, 1800.

242 'majestically clad in': AWS to A. I. G. de Broglie, 13 August 1838.

242 'Christianity is the': DV to Schleiermacher, 15 November 1799.

242 'Schleier': Ziolkowski 2006, p. 22.

242 *On Religion*: Schleiermacher, *Über die Religion: Reden an die Gebildeten unter ihren Verächtern*, 1799.

242 reading *On Religion*: FS to Schleiermacher, 16 and 20 September 1799.

242 'contemplation of the': Schleiermacher 1958, pp. 66, 71.

242 Schleiermacher and Spinoza: ibid., p. 31.

242 'Considering every finite': ibid., p. 32.

242 'drink in the beauty': ibid., p. 67.

242 'sacred music': ibid., p. 38.

243 imagination and religion: Novalis to A. C. Just, 26 December 1798.

243 'Religion is all': FS, summer 1798, Novalis Schriften, vol. 4, p. 621; for FS's new religion, see FS to Novalis, 20 October 1798 and 2 December 1798.

243 'flaming sword': FS to Novalis, 2 December 1798.

243 'The new religion': ibid.

243 not joking about religion: FS to AWS, 7 May 1799.

243 publishing Novalis's *Europe:* FS to Schleiermacher, 15 November 1799; AWS to Schleiermacher, 16 December 1799.

243 leave religion to theologians: AWS to J. D. Gries, 10 May 1799.

243 'she has always enjoyed': FS to Novalis, 28 May 1798.

243 'Oh let my one': Schelling, 'Epikurisch Glaubensbekenntniss Heinz Widerporstens', Schelling 1962–75, vol. 2, p. 207 (trans. Damion Searls but based on trans. Daniel Whistler and Judith Kahl, https://www.caroline-schelling.com/appendices/volume-1/sup-ap-schelling-widerporst/#*).

243 AWS and DV against publication: DV to Schleiermacher, 9 December 1799; AWS to Schleiermacher, 16 December 1799.

243 AWS suggested editorial note: DV to Schleiermacher, 9 December 1799.

244 unseasonably warm: Goethe, 13 and 14 November 1799, Goethe Diaries, vol. 2, pp. 269–70.

244 meeting Goethe in the Paradise: DV to Schleiermacher, 15 November 1799; DV to Rahel Levin, 18 November 1799.

244 'divine old excellency': DV to Schleiermacher, 15 November 1799.

244 DV and Goethe: ibid.; DV to Rahel Levin, 18 November 1799.

244 'referee': DV to Schleiermacher, 9 December 1799.

244 Goethe met Schelling, FS and AWS: Goethe, 23, 26, 27 November 1799 and 7 December 1799, Goethe Diaries, vol. 2, pp. 271, 274.

244 Goethe advised against publication: FS to Schleiermacher, 9 December 1799; AWS to Schleiermacher, 16 December 1799.

244 difference between private and public: Goethe, 7 December 1799, Goethe Diaries, vol. 2, p. 274.

244 Novalis didn't mind criticism: A. C. Just about Novalis, 1805, Novalis Schriften, vol. 4, p. 549; see also Novalis to FS, 31 January 1800.

Chapter 16: 'The republic of despots'
Winter 1799–Summer 1800: Estrangements

247 'members of the Schlegel': J. D. Sander to K. A. Böttiger, 23 November 1799, Fichte Gespräch, vol. 2, p. 258; for staying at home, see DV to Schleiermacher, 11 October 1799.

247 AWS and ALZ: AWS to G. Hufeland, late April 1799, and G. Hufeland to AWS, 2 May 1799.

247 'roaring lion': AWS to Schleiermacher, 22 December 1800; see also FS to AWS and CS, 7 May 1799.

247 threatened legal action: AWS to C. G. Schütz, 20 October 1799.

248 Schütz fired back: C. G. Schütz to AWS, 20 October 1799.

248 AWS's resignation from ALZ: *Intelligenzblatt*, ALZ, no. 145, 13 November 1799.

248 ALZ's reply to AWS: Editors of ALZ, 'Erläuterungen über den vorstehenden Abschied', *Intelligenzblatt*, ALZ, no. 145, 13 November 1799.

248 Fn. AWS's reviews for *ALZ: Athenaeum*, vol. 3, 1800, insert after p. 164.

248 influence of ALZ: Steffens 1841, vol. 4, p. 147.

248 'need to be personally': Fichte to Schelling, 19 November 1799.

248 'there's squabbling': Johanne Fichte to Fichte, 18 November 1799.

248 'We hardly see anyone': CS to J. D. Gries, 27 December 1799.

248 *Athenaeum* review in ALZ: L. F. Huber in ALZ, no. 372, 21 November 1799.

249 'So since you're lacking': CS to L. F. Huber, 24 November 1799.

249 'universal battle of good': CS to L. F. Huber, 22 November 1799.

249 'Caroline wrote, shouted': Therese Huber to Therese Forster, 17–25 July 1803, Huber 1999, vol. 1, p. 423.

249 CS's revolutionary disposition: CS to L. F. Huber, 22 November 1799.

249 'get swept up': CS to J. D. Gries, 27 December 1799.

249 'People hate us – good!': AWS to L. F. Huber, 28 December 1799.

249 'blaze of hellfire': Schleiermacher to AWS, 18 January 1800.

249 Charlotte Schiller felt better: Schiller, 21 November 1799, Wais 2005, p. 270.

249 Schiller dealt with move: Schiller to Luise von Lengefeld, 8 December 1799; Schiller to Charlotte Schiller, 15 December 1799.

250 'Leave all the memories': Schiller to Charlotte Schiller, 4 December 1799.

250 'I have the feeling': Schiller to C. G. Körner, 16 June 1800.

250 'You are most': Goethe to Schiller, 17 December 1799.

250 'you will find here': Goethe to Schiller, 23 December 1799.

250 'I wonder if you': Goethe to Schiller, 29 December 1799.

250 sedan chair: ibid.; Schiller to Goethe, 3 January 1800.

250 'Are you . . .?': Schiller to Goethe, 1 January 1800.

250 'I'll certainly look': Goethe to Schiller, 1 January 1800.

250 'Do let me know': Schiller to Goethe, 5 January 1800.

250 'It is three o'clock': Goethe to Schiller, 6 January 1800.

250 'Jena was no': Schiller to C. G. Körner, 5 January 1800.

250 'I find all that': Schiller to C. G. Körner, 28 December 1801.

250 cold winter: CS to J. D. Gries, 27 December 1799.

251 'I almost died': DV to Schleiermacher, 16 January 1800.

251 FS run out of money: DV to Schleiermacher, 9 December 1799; FS to Schleiermacher, 28 March 1800.

251 Fichte came for dinner: DV to Schleiermacher, 14 February 1800.

251 Fichte felt criticised: Fichte to Schelling, 2 October 1800, 1st draft.

251 'and didn't want to': Fichte to Schelling, 3 October 1800.

251 quarrelling: DV to Schleiermacher, 16 January 1800.

251 FS enraged about CS and Schelling: FS to Schleiermacher, 14 February 1800; DV to Schleiermacher, 14 February 1800; FS to Schleiermacher, mid-September 1801.

252 FS taking AWS's side: FS to Schleiermacher, 14 February 1800; DV to Schleiermacher, 14 February 1800; FS to Schleiermacher, mid-September 1801.

252 Auguste back: CS to L. F. Huber, 24 November 1799.

252 'much more likeable': Caroline Tischbein to Auguste Böhmer, 16 December 1799, CS Letters, vol. 1, p. 756.

252 sour atmosphere: DV to Schleiermacher, 14 February 1800.

252 Tieck's gout: CS to J. D. Gries, 27 December 1799; AWS to Goethe, 28 February 1800.

252 'monster': Tieck to Sophie Bernhardi, 6 December 1800.

252 Tieck had admired CS: Tieck, in CS Letters, vol. 1, p. 748; Tieck, 'Eine Sommerreise', Tieck 1838–42, vol. 5, p. 164.

252 'hermaphrodite': Tieck to Sophie Bernhardi, 6 December 1800.

252 'like a big farm': ibid.

253 'With Tieck you': FS to Rahel Levin, 2 June 1800; for CS about Tieck, see CS to FS, 14–15 October 1798.

253 DV about Amalie: DV to Sophie Bernhardi, 16 January 1800.

253 AWS and FS collecting Tieck: AWS to J. D. Gries, 16 March 1800; CS to J. D. Gries, 27 December 1799.

253 'the true cause': Tieck to Sophie Bernhardi, 6 December 1800; see also FS to Schleiermacher, mid-September 1801.

253 'hard, hard as stone': DV to Rahel Levin, 23 January 1800.

253 AWS didn't care: DV to Schleiermacher, 15 May 1800.

253 'isn't done yet': DV to Karoline Paulus, 4 June 1805.

253 'I didn't like him': CS to Auguste Böhmer, 30 September 1799.

254 Fn. Novalis busy: Ziolkowski 2006, p. 199.

254 'my head is swimming': Novalis to Tieck, 23 February 1800; see also Novalis to FS, 31 January 1800.

254 'the whole poetic': Novalis to FS, 31 January 1800.

254 news from WH and AH: WH to Goethe, 28 November 1799.

254 AH in Cumaná and earthquakes: Wulf 2015, pp. 58–9.

254 electric eels: ibid., pp. 62–4.

254 AH happy: AH to WH, 16 July 1799.

254 AH along Orinoco: Wulf 2015, pp. 65–73.

254 'we run around': AH to WH, 16 July 1799.

255 'active, organic powers': A. Humboldt 2014, p. 147; A. Humboldt 1849a, vol. 1, p. 337.

255 'extraordinary minds': WH to Christiane Reinhard, 26 May 1800, Fichte Gespräch, vol. 2, p. 343.

255 'If I wasn't afraid': WH to Goethe, 28 November 1799.

255 CS in a deep well: CS to Luise Michaelis Wiedemann, 31 January 1807.

255 AWS's concerns: AWS to Goethe, 8 March 1800.

255 'nervous fever': AWS to J. D. Gries, 16 March 1800.

255 Hufeland's book: Hufeland, *Bemerkungen über das Nervenfieber und seine Complicationen, in den Jahren 1796, 1797 u. 1798, Jena, 1799*.

255 nervous fever: Hufeland 1799, pp. 10–15.

255 CS's illness and baths: Auguste Böhmer to Luise Michaelis Wiedemann, 30 March 1800, Olshausen 1927, p. 351; Auguste Böhmer to Luise Gotter, 31 March 1800, CS Letters, vol. 1, p. 595.

255 'mustard plaster': AWS to J. D. Gries, 16 March 1800; DV to Schleiermacher, 17 March 1800.

255 Hufeland's recipe for mustard plaster: Krünitz 1773–1858, vol. 153, p. 217.

255 fever and cramps: AWS to J. D. Gries, 16 March 1800; FS and DV to Schleiermacher, 18 March 1800; AWS to Goethe, 23 March 1800; Auguste Böhmer to Luise Gotter, 31 March 1800, CS Letters, vol. 1, p. 595.

256 'we will all die': Auguste Böhmer to Luise Michaelis Wiedemann, 30 March 1800, Olshausen 1927, p. 351.

256 remedies: AWS to Goethe, 23 March 1800; FS and DV to Schleiermacher, 18 March 1800; see also Hufeland 1799, pp. 21, 23.

256 Goethe sent wine: AWS to Goethe, 23 March 1800.

256 everybody sick: AWS to J. D. Gries, 16 March 1800.

256 Schiller's illness: ibid.; see also Schiller to J. C. Mellish, 16 March 1800; Goethe, 15 February 1800, Goethe Diaries, vol. 2, p. 283.

256 Goethe feared worst: Goethe, February and March 1800, Goethe Diaries, vol. 2, pp. 283–6; Goethe to C. G. Voigt, 25 February 1800.

256 Schiller still frail: Schiller to C. G. Körner, 24 March 1800.

256 'The evil news': Goethe to G. H. Rapp, 2 April 1800.

256 spring in Jena: DV to Rahel Levin, 28 April 1800.

256 CS ventured out: DV to Schleiermacher, 28–30 April 1800.

257 DV ran out of patience: DV to Schleiermacher, 4 April 1800; DV to Rahel Levin, 10 April 1800.

257 DV's medication: DV to Schleiermacher, 14 February 1800; about migraines see DV to Schleiermacher, 28 October 1799.

257 'magic and the': DV to Schleiermacher, 28–30 April 1800.

257 'even her tone': ibid.

257 DV continued attacks: DV to Schleiermacher, 4 April 1800.

257 'a vain stubborn': DV to Schleiermacher, 28 April 1800.

257 AWS dominated by CS: DV to Schleiermacher, 15 May 1800.

258 meeting in Saalfeld: AWS to Goethe, 4 May 1800.

258 AWS in Weißenfels: Luise Brachmann to AWS, 28 May 1800.

258 'hand her over': DV to Schleiermacher, 15 May 1800.

258 'marriage *en quatre*': ibid.

258 'borrowed the filthiest': ibid.

258 FS accused CS: FS to Schleiermacher, mid-September 1801.

258 Schelling booked rooms: Schelling to A. F. Marcus (?), 3 May 1800.

258 'You know that': CS to Schelling, 9 June 1800.

258 'how much he': Auguste Böhmer to Schelling, 4–5 June 1800, CS Letters, vol. 1, p. 599.

258 CS to Bocklet: CS went to Bocklet on 12 June 1800. CS to Schelling, 9 June 1800; Schelling had travelled from Bamberg to his parents in Schorndorf because his brother had died, but returned soon to Bocklet.

259 'just a tool in': FS to Schleiermacher, late May 1800.

259 'curse, laugh or cry': DV to Rahel Levin, 2 June 1800.

259 Fichte saw Goethe: Fichte to Goethe, 10 March 1800; Goethe to C. G. Voigt, 12 March 1800.

259 Schelling and Tieck saw Goethe: Schelling to Schiller, 16 April 1800; Schelling to Goethe, 16 April 1800; Goethe to Schelling, 19 April 1800; Goethe, 11 June 1800, Goethe Diaries, vol. 2, p. 298.

259 'In the republic': DV to Schleiermacher, 10 March 1800.

259 AWS and Goethe: see Goethe's Diaries for April, May and June 1800 for visits in Weimar, but AWS also saw Goethe in Leipzig in May 1800.

259 'You have to wonder': Schiller to Charlotte von Schimmelmann, 23 November 1800.

259 Fn. AWS and legal action: AWS to Goethe, 30 May 1800, 6, 13 June 1800

and 11 July 1800; AWS to Schelling, 31 May 1800; Goethe to AWS, 10 June 1800.

260 'I just can't ever': Goethe to Schiller, 22 July 1800.

260 Goethe creative in Jena: Schiller to C. G. Körner, 3 September 1800.

260 quiet in Jena: AWS to Goethe, 11 July 1800.

260 AWS decided to stay in Jena: AWS to J. D. Gries, 7 July 1800.

260 Auguste's illness: Schelling to AWS, 6 July 1800 and 3 September 1802; see also Wiesing 1989, pp. 275–95.

260 prescriptions for Auguste: Schelling to AWS, 3 September 1802.

261 'clings to her mother': DV to Schleiermacher, 15 May 1800.

261 Schelling's prescription: Schelling to AWS, 3 September 1802.

261 express messenger: Wiesing 1989, p. 278.

261 'The life of my': CS to Julie Gotter, 18 February 1803.

261 Schelling depressed: Schelling to AWS, 3 September 1802.

261 'utterly shattered': AWS to Luise Gotter, 21 August 1800; see also AWS to Ludwig Tieck, 14 September 1800.

262 'With my broken': AWS to Goethe, 20 July 1800.

Chapter 17: 'O what a black fog'
Summer 1800–Spring 1801: Darkness Falls

263 AWS to Bamberg: AWS left Jena on 21 July and arrived in Bamberg on 24 July 1800.

263 'I'm only half': CS to Luise Gotter, 18 September 1800; for CS after Auguste's death, see AWS to Luise Gotter, 21 August 1800.

263 'It's as if I had': AWS to Ludwig Tieck, 14 September 1800.

263 AWS to Auguste's grave: AWS to Luise Gotter, 21 August 1800.

263 wilted wreath and tears: AWS, 'Todten-Opfer für Augusta Böhmer', AWS SW, vol. 1, p. 132.

263 'I am with you': FS to AWS, after 21 July 1800.

263 'sweet little heart': FS to Auguste Böhmer, 28 April 1797.

263 'politico-erotic': ibid.; for AWS's rumoured affair, see FS to Auguste Böhmer, 15 July 1797.

263 'The house is an': FS to AWS, after 21 July 1800.

264 'misfortune always has': DV to Clemens Brentano, 25 July 1800.

264 CS abandoned Auguste: Novalis to FS, 28 July 1800.

264 'quiet domestic happiness': A. C. Just, 'Friedrich von Hardenberg', 1805, Novalis Schriften, vol. 4, p. 541.

264 Novalis insisted on marriage: Novalis to FS, 20 January 1799; DV to Schleiermacher, 11 April 1800.

264 'no doubt foreshadowed': Novalis to FS, 28 July 1800.

264 'dark fate': ibid.

264 Fichte's condolences: Fichte to AWS, 6 September 1800.

264 'If only I could': Tieck to AWS, 27 August 1800.

264 'Time is too fleeting': ibid.

264 'That magnificent girl': Henrik Steffens to Schelling, 8 August 1800.

265 'so much life': ibid.

265 'Oh God, my': Sophie Tischbein to CS, 28 August 1800.

265 'heavenly girl': ibid., this was a pencil drawing by Auguste's friend Caroline Tischbein, her father the painter J. F. A. Tischbein also painted a portrait of Auguste.

265 monument to Auguste: AWS to Luise Gotter, 21 August 1800; AWS to Schleiermacher, 20 August 1800.

265 'total collapse of': AWS to Luise Gotter, 21 August 1800; see also AWS to Tieck, 14 September 1800.

265 FS dispatched books etc: FS to AWS, 26 July 1800.

265 'there is no way': AWS to Luise Gotter, 21 August 1800.

265 body empty shell: CS to Julie Gotter, 17 October 1802.

265 Schelling suicidal: CS to Schelling, 18 November 1800.

265 'of course, given': DV to Schleiermacher, 22 August 1800.

265 DV blamed Schelling: ibid.

265 'until she was cold': ibid.

265 'And now this': ibid.

265 CS too healthy: DV to Schleiermacher, 28 July 1800; see also 17 January 1801.

266 'have you heard that': FS to AWS, 6 August 1800.

266 'any news of Schelling's': FS to AWS, 12 September 1800.

266 FS's affair with Sophie Mereau: see FS's letters to Sophie Mereau in August and September 1800; see Sophie Mereau's diaries for August to October 1800, Mereau-Brentano 1996, pp. 73–6.

266 'think of me': FS to Sophie Mereau, 30 August 1800.

266 'Your burning Friedrich': FS to Sophie Mereau, c. 8 August 1800.

266 'Stay light-hearted': FS to Sophie Mereau, 30 August 1800.

266 FS's dalliance with Karoline Paulus: FS to Karoline Paulus, November/ December 1800.

266 DV's affair with Ritter: DV to Schleiermacher, 31 October 1800.

266 'offered him [Ritter]': Clemens Brentano to F. K. von Savigny, 14 June 1803, FS KA, vol. 25, p. 536.

266 Fn. DV and Ritter: Clemens Brentano to F. K. von Savigny, 4 June 1803, FS KA, vol. 25, p. 536.

267 Goethe in Jena: Goethe, 22 July–4 August 1800, 3 September–4 October 1800, 14–25 November 1800, 12–26 December 1800, Goethe Diaries, vol. 2, pp. 302–9, 312–15.

267 'I solved a little': Goethe to Schiller, 1 August 1800; see also Goethe to Schiller, 29 July 1800.

267 *Faust* scenes: Goethe to Schiller, 12 September 1800; Goethe, 12–14, 22–26 September 1800, Goethe Diaries, vol. 2, pp. 305–7.

267 'I can't blame': Goethe to Schiller, 18 November 1800; see also Goethe to Schiller, 30 September 1800.

267 FS and Goethe: Goethe, 5, 20, 25 and 30 September 1800 and 3 October 1800, Goethe Diaries, vol. 2, pp. 304–9; DV and FS to AWS, 30 September 1800.

267 'I've already gotten': FS to Schleiermacher, 17 November 1800.

267 consulted Dr Stark: DV to AWS, 23 September 1800; Novalis ill: Novalis to Tieck, 1 January 1801; Ludwig Tieck about Novalis, 1815, Novalis Schriften, vol. 4, p. 556.

267 'We thought he': DV to AWS, 23 September 1800.

267 AWS and CS to Braunschweig: they left Bamberg on 1 October 1800 and travelled via Gotha (where CS's friend Luise Gotter lived) and then Göttingen in order to deal with Auguste's estate. AWS continued to Hanover to visit his parents and then on to Braunschweig, to be with CS.

267 CS ill again: CS to Luise Gotter, 24 November 1800.

267 AWS delayed departure to Jena: AWS to Schleiermacher, 5 October 1800.

267 CS and AWS in Braunschweig: Wiedemann 1929, p. 84.

268 Shakespeare translation: CS to Schelling, 25 January 1801.

268 'I can live without': CS, quoted in Damm 2005, p. 53.

268 'unspeakably stupid': FS to AWS, 10 November 1800; see also FS to Schleiermacher, 23 January 1801; for FS and students, see DV to AWS, 28 October 1800; Schelling to Fichte, 31 October 1800.

268 '+ = φ ∩': DV to AWS, 28 October 1800.

268 students understood little: Friedrich Muhrbeck to Hölderlin, September 1799, Hölderlin 1943–85, vol. 7, pt 1, p. 142.

268 'dead and now': Schelling to Fichte, 31 October 1800.

268 Schelling suicidal: CS to Schelling, 18 November 1800; CS to Goethe, 26 November 1800.

268 CS's joy in small things: CS to F. L. W. Meyer, 12 August 1792; CS to Schelling, 18 November 1800.

269 'In spite of God': CS to F. L. W. Meyer, 11 July 1791.

269 'My heart, my life': CS to Schelling, October 1800.

269 'black fog': CS to Schelling, 18 November 1800.

269 see blue sky again: CS to Schelling, 27 December 1800.

269 'I gave it strict': CS to Schelling, 20 December 1800.

269 'my first, my only': CS to Schelling, late December 1800.

269 'a state of mind': CS to Goethe, 26 November 1800.

269 Christmas with Goethe: Goethe, 26 December 1800, Goethe Diaries, vol. 2, p. 315.

269 masked ball: Steffens 1841, vol. 4, p. 408ff.

269 New Year in Weimar: ibid., pp. 411–12.

270 'So we encountered': CS to Schelling, 2 January 1801.

270 Goethe's illness: Boyle 2000, p. 695; Caroline Herder to Karl von Knebel, 22 January 1801, Knebel 1858, vol. 2, pp. 1–2; Schiller to C. G. Körner, 5 January 1801; Goethe 1982–96, vol. 4, p. 167; Goethe to J. F. Reichardt, 5 February 1801; Steffens, vol. 4, p. 412; CS to Schelling, January 1801. Goethe was suffering from erysipelas, a common bacterial infection that is very treatable today but without antibiotics could be potentially fatal.

270 Christiane, August and Schiller: Goethe to K. E. Goethe, 1 February 1801; Schiller to C. G. Körner, 17 January 1801.

270 Goethe's nightly ravings: CS to AWS, 27 February 1801.

270 Goethe almost lost himself: Goethe to Elisa Gore, 17 January 1801.

270 're-entry into life': Goethe to K. E. Goethe, 1 February 1801.

270 'that the moment': Goethe to J. F. Reichardt, 5 February 1801.

271 Goethe working on Faust: Goethe, 7 February–12 March 1801, Goethe Diaries, vol. 3, pp. 5–9; see also Boyle 2000, pp. 758–71.

271 'great gap': Goethe to Schiller, 6 April 1801.

271 'Cursed be illusion': Goethe, *Faust Part One*, ll. 1593–4 (trans. Walter Kaufmann), Goethe 1961, p. 177.

271 chorus of spirits: Goethe, *Faust Part One*, l. 1609 (trans. David Luke), Goethe 2008, p. 49.

271 'More splendidly': Goethe, *Faust Part One*, ll. 1620–1 (trans. David Luke), Goethe 2008, p. 50.

271 'In the beginning' . . . 'was the *Power*': Goethe, *Faust Part One*, ll. 1224–37 (trans. David Luke), Goethe 2008, p. 39, with some changes by me: the German original is 'im Anfang war der *Sinn*', which Luke translates as 'Mind' and others have translated as 'Intelligence' or 'Thought'; similarly 'im Anfang war die *Tat!*' has been variously translated as 'Deed' or 'Act'.

271 'deepest, purest': Schelling, 'Philosophie der Kunst', 1802, Schelling SW, vol. 5, p. 446.

272 'How it all lives': Goethe, *Faust Part One*, ll. 447–8 (trans. David Luke), Goethe 2008, p. 17.

272 Schelling's behaviour towards CS: None of Schelling's letters survive but his accusations can be deduced from Caroline's replies; see her letters to Schelling in February and March 1801.

272 'Don't leave me': CS to Schelling, 18 November 1800.

272 'Oh, don't interrupt': CS to Schelling, 13 February 1801.

272 despaired when Schelling didn't write: CS to Schelling, 5 and 9 January 1801.

273 'Don't mock me': CS to Schelling, March 1801.

273 kinder to abandon her: CS to Schelling, 17 February 1801.

273 'my all and everything': CS to Schelling, late February 1801.

273 'Love me': CS to Schelling, early February 1801.

273 'but why are you': CS to Schelling, 13 February 1801.

273 tore her apart: CS to Schelling, 6 March 1801.

273 'so come and stay': CS to Schelling, March 1801.

273 Hegel's dialect: Hegel 1970, p. 79; Hegel was called Wilhelm: Kaube 2020, p. 29.

273 'the old man': Kaube 2020, p. 43; Pinkard 2001, p. 26; see also Georg Friedrich Fallot's sketch in Hegel's Stammbuch, Universitätsbibliothek Tübingen.

273 Hegel's character: Gustav Binder and Christoph Theodor Schwab about Hegel in Tübingen, in Hegel 1970, pp. 16, 18; Schelling to G. H. Schubert, 27 May 1809.

273 Hegel in the Alps: Kaube 2020, p. 91.

273 Hegel felt isolated: ibid., p. 106; Pinkard 2001, p. 55ff.

274 Hegel and Hölderlin: Kaube 2020, pp. 110–15; Pinkard 2001, p. 8off.

274 Hegel and inheritance: Schelling 1962–75, vol. 1, p. 453; Kaube 2020, p. 122.

274 'before I dare to': Hegel to Schelling, 2 November 1800.

274 Schelling depressed: Schelling 1962–75, vol. 1, p. 464; Boyle 2000, p. 712.

275 AWS to leave Braunschweig: AWS to Schleiermacher, 9 February 1801.

275 AWS and Friederike Unzelmann: CS to Luise Gotter, July 1798; CS to AWS, 26 March 1801.

275 CS's letters: CS to AWS, 24 and 27 February 1801, 1–2, 5–6, 16, 26–27 March 1801, 4 April 1801.

275 'your little Unzeline': CS to AWS, 26 March 1801.

275 AWS letters: none of AWS's letters to CS from that time survive but her replies illuminate the content and the tone of his letters.

275 'when the world': CS to AWS, 1–2 March 1801.

275 ignore critics: CS to AWS, 5–6 March 1801.

275 'Please do write': CS to AWS, 24 February 1801; see also 1–2 March 1801.

275 CS and *The Decameron*: CS to AWS, 5–6 March 1801; CS to Schelling, 13 February 1801; she translated Boccaccio's *The Tale of Ghismonda and Guiscardo*.

275 death of Luise's baby: CS to AWS, 16 March 1801.

276 'and in the middle': ibid.

276 Novalis's illness: Novalis to Tieck, 1 January 1801; Tieck about Novalis, 1815, Novalis Schriften, vol. 4, p. 556; FS to AWS, 6 and 24 March 1801; for diagnosis, Hädecke 2011, p. 360.

276 Novalis to Dresden: Sidonie von Hardenberg to Wilhelmine von Thümmel, 11 October 1800, Novalis Schriften, vol. 4, p. 665.

276 brother drowned: on 28 October 1800; A. C. Just, 'Friedrich von Hardenberg', 1805, and Tieck about Novalis, 1815, Novalis Schriften, vol. 4, pp. 546, 557.

276 violent haemorrhage: A. C. Just, 'Friedrich von Hardenberg', 1805, Novalis Schriften, vol. 4, p. 546.

276 open carriage rides: FS to AWS, 6 March 1801; H. U. E. von Hardenberg to A. B. von Hardenberg, 14 January 1801, Novalis Schriften, vol. 4, p. 671.

276 hypnotised, quinine and donkey milk: Novalis's doctor in Dresden was Johann Nathanael Petzold, a disciple of Franz Anton Mesmer, who used hypnosis (or 'mesmerism', as it was then called) as a treatment: Hädecke 2011, p. 351; FS to AWS, 6 March 1801; Novalis to A. C. Just, 1 February 1801 and H. U. E. von Hardenberg to A. B. von Hardenberg, 14 January 1801, Novalis Schriften, vol. 4, pp. 344, 672.

276 coughing blood: A. B. von Hardenberg to Sidonie von Hardenberg, 28 November 1800, Novalis Schriften, vol. 4, p. 666.

276 Charlotte Ernst on Novalis: Charlotte Ernst to AWS, mid-January and late January 1801.

276 'like a dead person': Charlotte Ernst to AWS, mid-January 1801.

276 'It pains me': Novalis to Tieck, 1 January 1801.

277 'you'll hear': Karl von Hardenberg, 'Biographie seines Bruders', 1802, Novalis Schriften, vol. 4, p. 535.

277 fourth anniversary: ibid.

277 'The good people': Tieck to FS, mid-March 1801.

277 CS on Novalis: CS to Luise Gotter, 23 January 1801; see also CS to AWS, 10 April 1801.

277 'I won't be': CS to Schelling, 13 February 1801.

277 Novalis looked disfigured: FS to AWS, 24 March 1801.

277 FS at Weißenfels: ibid.; see also A. C. Just, 'Friedrich von Hardenberg', 1805, Novalis Schriften, vol. 4, p. 547.

277 Novalis's last day: Karl von Hardenberg, 'Biographie seines Bruders', 1802; A. C. Just, 'Friedrich von Hardenberg', 1805; Tieck about Novalis, 1815, Novalis Schriften, vol. 4, pp. 535, 547, 556; FS to AWS, 27 March 1801.

277 'Really it's almost': FS to AWS, 27 March 1801.

277 FS too upset: FS to Schleiermacher, 27 March 1801.

278 'Our life is shared': Tieck to FS, 23 April 1801.

278 void never filled: FS to Schleiermacher, 17 April 1801.

278 'divine': FS to CS, 20 November 1798.

278 'I had seen him': Tieck to FS, 23 April 1801.

278 'in the full flower': Novalis, 26 May 1797, diary, Novalis Schriften, vol. 4, p. 41.

278 'Philosophy is now': Novalis to A. C. Just, February 1800.

278 'Shouldn't a novel': Novalis, 'Allgemeine Brouillon', no. 169, Novalis Schriften, vol. 3, p. 271; Novalis 2007, p. 26.

278 read manuscript of *Heinrich von Ofterdingen*: Novalis to FS, 4 April 1800.

278 'sacrilegious, heinous' . . . 'divine fragment': FS to AWS, 17 April 1801.

Chapter 18: 'When philosophers start eating one another like starving rats' − Spring 1801–Spring 1803: Separations

279 CS left Braunschweig: she left on 21 April and arrived in Jena on 23 April 1801; CS to AWS, 20 and 24 April 1801.

279 CS's arrival: CS to AWS, 24 April 1801.

279 missing and broken items: ibid.; CS to AWS, 27 April 1801 and 5 May 1801.

279 'I will spare you': CS to AWS, 24 April 1801; FS to CS, 24 April 1801.

279 CS didn't tell Schelling: CS to AWS, 24 April 1801.

279 'Frau Schlegel': FS to CS, 24 April 1801.

279 dropped off some items: CS to AWS, 5 May 1801; FS to AWS, 27 April 1801.

279 CS's list of complaints: CS to AWS, 24 and 27 April 1801, 7 and 18 May 1801.

280 'this good old': CS to AWS, 5 May 1801.

280 'Don't stay away': ibid.

280 'I truly don't like': AWS to Tieck, 28 April 1801

280 AWS sided with CS: FS to AWS, 18 May 1801.

280 heated Schelling–Fichte exchange: Schelling to Fichte, end of September 1800 (this letter is lost but Fichte defended himself in a letter to Schelling on 3 October 1800 (with a first draft written on 2 October) and quoted Schelling's accusations in a letter to Tieck, c. 22 October 1800; see also Schelling to Fichte, 13 October 1800; Fichte to Schelling, 22 October 1800.

280 'liars and blackhearted': Fichte to Schelling, 22 October 1800; see also Fichte to J. F. Cotta, 18 October 1800.

280 'as a friend': Fichte to Tieck, c. 22 October 1800.

281 Fichte described Schelling as collaborator: Fichte's 'Announcement', Cotta'sche *Allgemeine Zeitung*, 24 January 1801, Schelling 1963–75, vol. 1, p. 223; see also Fichte to Schelling, 31 May 1801 and 15 January 1802.

281 Goethe amused: Goethe to Schelling, 1 February 1801; CS to AWS, 31 May–1 June 1801.

281 'make you and your': CS to Schelling, 1 March 1801.

281 'He has light': ibid.

281 How dare Fichte: CS to AWS, 28 January 1802.

281 Fichte's writing impenetrable: CS to AWS, 18 May 1801.

281 *A Report Clear:* Fichte, *Sonnenklarer Bericht an das größere Publikum*, 1801.

281 'to let Fichte torture': CS to AWS, 31 May–1 June 1801.

281 'Are you actually'. . . .'annihilation of nature': Schelling to Fichte, 3 October 1801.

281 accused Schelling of not understanding: Fichte to Schelling, 8 October 1801.

281 impossible to follow their arguments: Goethe to WH, 19 November 1800.

282 Schelling's new ideas: Richards 2002, pp. 180–6; see also Schelling's *Über den wahren Begriff der Naturphilosophie*, 1801, Schelling SW, vol. 4, p. 80ff.; *Darstellung meines Systems der Philosophie*, 1801, Schelling SW, vol. 4, p. 107ff.

282 Schelling's 'Absolute': Schelling, *Bruno, oder über das göttliche und natürliche Prinzip der Dinge*, 1802, Schelling SW, vol. 4, p. 283.

282 'uncreated and truly': ibid.; see also Richards 2002, p. 186.

282 'Idealism of the Ich': Schelling, *Über den wahren Begriff der Naturphilosophie*, 1801, Schelling SW, vol. 4, p. 84; see also Richards 2002, p. 187.

282 *The Difference between:* Hegel, *Differenz des Fichteschen und Schellingschen Systems der Philosophie*, 1801; see also Pinkard 2001, pp. 153–60.

283 *Critical Journal:* Schelling and Hegel's *Kritisches Journal der Philosophie* (1802–3).

283 Hegel as Schelling's disciple: Pinkard 2001, pp. 110–11.

283 Hegel's students: Rosenkranz 1844, p. 161.

283 'Every word, every': H. G. Hotho, quoted in Preisendörfer 2018, p. 134; for Hegel's coughing attacks, see Alexander Jung about Hegel's lectures, Hegel 1970, p. 532.

283 'Schelling's squire': K. L. Reinhold to C. G. Bardili, 21 December 1801, Fichte Gespräch, vol. 3, p. 91.

283 CS's health: Julie Gotter to Luise Gotter, 29 June 1801, BBAW, NL Schelling, no. 933; CS to AWS, 27 July 1801.

283 'Mostly, I'm as': CS to AWS, 31 May–1 June 1801.

283 Julie in Jena: Julie Gotter arrived on 31 May 1801 and stayed until 6 March 1802; Julie Gotter to Luise Gotter, 26 June 1801, BBAW, NL Schelling, no. 933; see also CS to AWS, 31 May–1 June 1801.

283 Schelling visited and walks: Schelling to AWS, 31 July 1801; CS to AWS, 31 May–1 June 1801; Julie Gotter to Luise Gotter, 8 June 1801, BBAW, NL Schelling, no. 933; Julie Gotter to Cäcilie Gotter, 9 June 1801, BBAW, NL Schelling, no. 931.

284 'my darling': CS to AWS, 7 May 1801.

284 'my dear heart': CS to AWS, 25 May 1801.

284 bring Friederike Unzelmann: CS to AWS, 7 May 1801.

284 'I am sick from': CS to AWS, 5 May 1801; for Auguste's portrait, see CS to AWS, 7 May 1801.

284 'My best dear good': CS to AWS, 27 April 1801.

284 'under the rubble': CS to AWS, 7 May 1801.

284 'with my eyes': CS to AWS, 26 November 1801.

284 'I am absolutely certain': CS to AWS, 5 May 1801; for advice on Tieck, see CS to AWS, 19 July 1801.

284 'stand very very': CS to AWS, 25 May 1801, see also 18 May 1801.

284 asked AWS to return: CS to AWS, 5, 7–8, 18 May 1801 and 19 July 1801.

285 'I have never loved': Sophie Bernhardi to AWS, mid-September 1801.

285 'first great event': AWS to Sophie Bernhardi, 4 September 1801.

285 'tell me your sense': AWS to Schelling, 26 May 1801.

285 CS's health: Schelling to AWS, 31 July 1801.

285 situation in Jena on AWS's return: Julie Gotter to Luise Gotter, 18–21 August 1801, BBAW, NL Schelling, no. 933.

285 'how everyone gossips': CS to AWS, 5 May 1801.

285 AWS's joy in walking: AWS to Sophie Bernhardi, 21 August 1801.

285 tensions between FS and AWS: Julie Gotter to Luise Gotter, 18–21 August 1801, BBAW, NL Schelling, no. 933; AWS to Sophie Bernhardi, 24 August 1801; see also AWS to FS, 14 September 1801.

285 Weimar vacation: 21 September–2 October 1801, AWS to Sophie Bernhardi, 3 October 1801; see also Goethe, 21 September–1 October 1801, Goethe Diaries, vol. 3, pp. 35–6.

286 'all just too lonely': AWS to Sophie Bernhardi, 24 August 1801.

286 'I will not rest' . . . 'your feet': AWS to Sophie Bernhardi, 4 September 1801 and 3 October 1801.

286 'My burning desire': Sophie Bernhardi to AWS, mid-August 1801.

286 'I'm yours' . . . 'for ever': AWS to Sophie Bernhardi, 3 October 1801; see also 4 September 1801.

286 'friendly, tender' . . . 'my confidante': AWS to Sophie Bernhardi, 4 September 1801.

286 'Your kisses give': Sophie Bernhardi to AWS, 14 October 1801; see also 13 October 1801.

286 AWS to Berlin: AWS left on 3 November 1801.

286 FS to Berlin: FS arrived in Berlin on 2 December 1801: Schleiermacher to Charlotte Schleiermacher, 19 January 1802, Dilthey 1858–63, vol. 1, p. 301.

287 'It all comes down': DV to Tieck, 17 December 1801.

287 'How I worship': DV to Rahel Levin, January 1802.

287 DV in Jena: CS to AWS, 11–14, 28 January 1802.

287 Philipp notified FS: Philipp Veit to FS, December 1801.

287 'Everyone knows': CS to AWS, 22 February 1802.

287 'He must have': CS to AWS, 8 March 1802; for FS getting fat, see CS to AWS, 26 November 1801.

287 FS and his publisher: FS to G. A. Reimers, 22 January 1802.

287 'It does me good': FS to Schleiermacher, mid-September 1801.

287 'rather spoiled and': Schleiermacher to Charlotte Schleiermacher, 19 January 1802, Dilthey 1858–63, vol. 1, p. 301.

288 DV and FS in Dresden: FS to Schleiermacher, 4 February 1802; FS to Rahel Levin, 15 February 1802.

288 DV left Jena: CS to AWS, 1 February 1802.

288 'You can imagine' . . . 'or backwards': CS to AWS, 23 November 1801; see also CS to Luise Gotter, late November 1801.

288 'to expose every': Fichte to J. B. Schad, 29 December 1801.

288 Schelling's final letter: Schelling to Fichte, 25 January 1802; see also CS to AWS, 28 January 1802.

288 'philosophy whole and': Schelling, 'Über das Verhältnis der Naturphilosophie zur Philosophie überhaupt', 1802, quoted in Kühn 2012, p. 448.

288 'all we can do': F. H. Jacobi to K. L. Reinhold, 10 August 1802, Fichte Gespräch, vol. 3, p. 130.

288 'when philosophers start': Salat 1803, p. 446.

288 'every creature his': Jean Paul to Karoline Herder, 22 April 1802, Fichte Gespräch, vol. 3, p. 125.

288 'Many foreigners come' . . . 'Tokay wine': Schelling to J. F. Schelling, 6 December 1802.

289 'His lecture hall': CS to Julie Gotter, 29 November 1802.

289 Schelling's 'Philosophy of Art' lectures: Vigus 2010, pp. 74–6. Schelling taught the subject in winter 1799/1800, winter 1800/1 and summer 1801. His formal 'Philosophy of Art' lectures began in 1802.

289 'Every artwork is': Schelling, 'Philosophy of Art', transcribed by Henry Crabb Robinson, 1802–3, in Vigus 2010, pp. 74–6.

289 art represents the universe: Schelling, 'Philosophie der Kunst', 1802, Schelling SW, vol. 5, p. 369.

289 'poetry of the': K. P. Kayser, May 1804, Tilliette 1974, p. 151.

289 'country that values': Henry Crabb Robinson to Thomas Crabb Robinson, 14 November 1802, Robinson 1929, p. 118.

289 'a Philosophy of Transport': K. P. Kayser, May 1804, Tilliette 1974, p. 151; see also Schelling, 'Philosophie der Kunst', 1802, Schelling SW, vol. 5, p. 364.

289 AWS's Berlin lectures: Paulin 2016, pp. 202–20; see also admission tickets for ASW's lectures (held on Wednesdays and Sundays at noon), reprinted in Körner 1969, vol. 3, p. 19; the lectures were published posthumously with one volume covering art, a second dealing with classical literature and a third about romantic literature, see AWS 1884.

290 AH and nature: Wulf 2015, pp. 88–90; A. Humboldt 1814–29, vol. 3, p. 160; A. Humboldt 1845–52, vol. 1, p. xviii; A. Humboldt 1845–50, vol. 1, p. vi.

290 AWS found connections in art forms: Paulin 2016, p. 211.

290 'made quite a splash': AWS to Goethe, 19 January 1802.

290 CS defending her expenses: CS to AWS, 11 January 1802.

291 AWS's snappy reply: AWS to CS, 26 January 1802.

291 CS's preparations for Berlin: CS to AWS, 28 December 1801, 21 January, 15 February 1802.

291 CS left for Berlin: CS to AWS, 18 March 1802.

291 AWS didn't want CS to come: AWS to CS, 17 May 1802.

291 AWS and CS accommodation: CS to Julie Gotter, 24 April 1802; Caroline stayed at Unter den Linden 66 and August Wilhelm at Oberwasserstrasse 10.

291 dark mood in Berlin: CS to Julie Gotter, 24 April 1802, CS to AWS, 8 March 1802. The baby was born in November 1802.

291 'tears felt like': CS to Meta Liebeskind, 19 August 1804.

291 'angel of death': CS to AWS, 8 March 1802.

291 tiring city life: CS to Julie Gotter, 24 April 1802.

291 Schelling in Berlin: on 24 April CS still didn't know when or if Schelling was coming, but they left Berlin together on 19 May and arrived in Jena on 24 May 1802.

292 'that I feel released': AWS to CS, 17 May 1802; see also CS to AWS, 17 and 18 May 1802.

292 'In Berlin, where': CS to Julie Gotter, 18 February 1803.

292 AWS and CS divorce: Friedrich Tieck to Sophie Bernhardi, 15 June 1803; CS to AWS, end of June 1802.

292 CS moved out: Schelling to Hegel, 24 May 1802.

292 description of CS's new apartment: CS to AWS, 10, 20–21, 28 December 1801; Kösling 2010, p. 31. Schelling had previously lived here; see CS to AWS, 20–21 December 1801.

292 'Every day I': CS to Julie Gotter, 15 June 1802.

293 solace in nature: DV to Schleiermacher, 15 May 1800.

293 cashmere coat: CS to Julie Gotter, 17 October 1802.

293 scientists in Paris: A. Humboldt 1987, p. 104.

294 FS and finances in Paris: FS to Rahel Levin, 15 February 1802.

294 FS's *Europe*: Endres 2017, pp. 294–5; Paulin 2016, pp. 195–6; FS to Friedrich Wilmans, 15 April 1803.

294 'interconnected whole' . . . 'a whole': FS, *Über das Studium der griechischen Poesie*, 1795–7, FS KA, vol. 1, p. 225.

294 'if they think': FS to Schleiermacher, 8 February 1802.

294 Fn. Novalis's collected works: Tieck to FS, 10 December 1801.

295 Schiller's Garden House: Goethe to Schiller, 12 February 1802; Schiller sold it in June 1802.

295 CS and AWS's correspondence: CS to AWS, 3, 18, and 21 June 1802.

295 'If you have': CS to AWS, end of June 1802.

295 divorce: CS to AWS, 5 July 1802.

295 'Schlegel and I' and following quote: CS to Julie Gotter, 18 February 1803.

295 'She has been my': Schelling to J. F. Schelling, 28 May 1802.

295 'Please stay on': CS to AWS, after 27 August 1802.

296 'take the people': ALZ, no. 225, 10 August 1802.

296 Schelling and CS shocked: Schelling to AWS, 19 August 1802.

296 AWS enraged: AWS to Schelling, 27 August 1802.

296 'defend Professor Schelling's': AWS to C. G. Schütz, 18 September 1802, Schlegel 1802, p. 21.

296 'disgraceful knaves' . . . 'wretched overzealousness': Schlegel 1802, p. 14.

296 ALZ half-hearted correction: C. G. Schütz to AWS, 24 September 1802; see also *Intelligenzblatt*, no. 173, ALZ, 25 September 1802.

296 'the exception wouldn't': CS to AWS, September 1802; see also C. G. Voigt to Goethe, 13 September 1802.

296 consortium in Weimar: Schelling to AWS, 24 September 1802.

296 'is living in Jena': Karoline Herder to J. G. Müller, March 1803, Herder 1977–2016, vol. 8, p. 538.

297 bribing consortium: Schelling to AWS, 24 September 1802; Goethe to Schelling, 9 October 1802.

297 draft petition: Schelling to Goethe, 2 October 1802; AWS and CS, Divorce Petition to Carl August, Herzog von Sachsen-Weimar, October 1802, CS Letters, vol. 2, p. 342ff.; Goethe to Schelling, 9 October 1802; Schelling to AWS, 11 October 1802.

297 signed divorce petition: Schelling to Goethe, c. 17 October 1802; for Goethe's help with consortium, see J. G. Herder to AWS, 14 December 1802; Schelling to Goethe, 28 December 1802; Schelling to AWS, 21 January 1803; Goethe 1982–96, vol. 4, p. 333.

297 'and I'll take': Goethe to Schelling, 7 January 1803.

297 Schelling's letters concerning divorce: see his correspondence with Goethe and AWS from September 1802 to May 1803.

297 news of divorce: Goethe, 15–29 May 1803, Goethe Diaries, vol. 3, p. 73; Unterberger 2002, p. 247.

297 'most mercifully': Herzogliche Oberconsistorium Weimar, 17 May 1803, SLUB Dresden, Mscr.Dresden.e.90, xix, vol. 22; for an English translation see Doug Stott, https://www.carolineschelling.com/letters/volume-2-index/letter-377g/#★

297 final missive to AWS: Schelling to AWS, 20 May 1803.

297 Goethe and Schelling: Goethe, 20 May 1803, Goethe Diaries, vol. 3, p. 73.

297 three o'clock: Ritter to H. C. Ørsted, 22 May 1803, Ørsted 1920, vol. 2, p. 37.

297 'I will look after': Schelling to Johanna Fromann, 20 or 21 May 1803.

297 'divine creature': Schelling to Luise Gotter, 24 September 1809.

297 a thousand roots: Schelling to F. I. Niethammer, 2 October 1809.

297 'I am almost': CS to Julie Gotter, 18 February 1803.

298 CS and Schelling's marriage: On 26 June 1803, Schelling 1869–70, vol. 1, p. 465.

Chapter 19: 'The current exodus' – 1804–1805: Jena Abandoned

299 'current exodus': Goethe, 28 June 1805, Goethe 1982–96, vol. 4, p. 595.

299 position in Würzburg: CS to Luise Michaelis Wiedemann, 8–17 September 1803.

299 'emigrating professors': Goethe to Duke Carl August, 31 August 1803; see also Hegel to Goethe, 3 August 1803; Goethe 1982–96, vol. 4, p. 387; Goethe, 7–11 August 1803, Goethe Diaries, vol. 3, pp. 76–7.

299 'Jena was no longer': F. W. von Hoven in 1803, Merkel 1840, p. 153.

299 sixty students followed Schelling: K. A. von Wangenheim to King Friedrich von Württemberg, 15 November 1811, Tilliette 1974, p. 210.

299 'I'm afraid our': Schiller to WH, 18 August 1803.

299 'Jena now seems': Henry Crabb Robinson to Thomas Crabb Robinson, 20 September 1803, Robinson 1929, p. 130.

299 'Kingdom of Philosophy': CS to Luise Michaelis Wiedemann, 19 June 1803.

300 Goethe and Hegel: Goethe, 26 November 1803 and 2, 3, 8, 20 December 1803, Goethe Diaries, vol. 3, pp. 88–92.

300 'He is an admirable'. . . .'public speaking': Goethe to Schiller, 27 November 1803.

300 Hegel at home: Hegel to F. I. Niethammer, 10 December 1804.

300 'that we philosophised': Schiller to WH, 17 February 1803.

300 Friedrich *von* Schiller: Schiller was ennobled in November 1802, Wais 2005, p. 312.

300 'Lolo is really': Schiller to WH, 17 February 1803.

300 'My life is so': Schiller to Wilhelm von Wolzogen, 24 November 1803, see also 20 March 1804.

300 Fichte's work and lectures: Johanne Fichte to Charlotte Schiller, 18 July 1804; Johanne Fichte to F. I. Niethammer, 4 April 1803; Johanne Fichte to J. H. Rahn, 25 February 1805; see also handbill to lecture 1804, Fichte GA III, vol. 5, p. 279.

301 small circle of friends: Johanne Fichte to Charlotte Schiller, 18 July 1804.

301 'School for Philosophers': Fichte to F. X. von Moshamm, 18 June 1804.

301 'still far behind': Schelling to Hegel, 3 March 1804.

301 CS's shopping spree: Henriette Hoven to Charlotte Schiller, 4 April 1804, C. Schiller 1862, vol. 3, p. 272.

301 CS's falling out with other wives: Therese Huber to C. G. Heyne, 16 August 1803 and Therese Huber to Therese Forster, 3 September 1803, Huber, vol. 1, pp. 427, 429; Karoline Paulus to Charlotte Schiller, 11 March 1804 and Henriette Hoven to Charlotte Schiller, 4 August 1804, C. Schiller 1862, vol. 3, pp. 187, 276; Oellers 1990, p. 124; F. W. von Hoven, 1803, Merkel 1840, p. 166; CS to Beate Gross, 2 September 1804.

301 'Swabian scullery': Henriette Hoven to Charlotte Schiller, 4 April 1804, C. Schiller 1862, vol. 3, p. 272; see also CS to Beate Gross, 2 September 1804.

301 'our good friends': CS to Julie Gotter, 18 March 1804.

301 CS's reviews: Schelling to H. K. A. Eichstädt, 20 December 1804; H. K. A. Eichstädt to Goethe, 30 December 1804.

301 'united by the': Schelling to Philipp Michaelis, 29 November 1809.

301 AWS visited Würzburg: AWS to Sophie Bernhardi, 15 May 1804.

302 'was touched when': ibid.

302 child of a third man: Paulin 2016, p. 185.

302 AWS exhausted: AWS to Madame de Staël, end of March 1804; AWS to Sophie Bernhardi, 27 May 1804; see also Paulin 2016, p. 240.

302 'or else there is': Benjamin Constant, quoted in Herold 1975, p. 189.

302 'frightful as a precipice': Lord Byron to Henrietta d'Ussières, 8 June 1814, Byron 1982, p. 104.

303 book about new German philosophy: Madame de Staël to F. H. Jacobi, 15 November 1803, Higonnet 1986, p. 163.

303 paid a student: Henry Crabb Robinson to Thomas Crabb Robinson, 20 January 1804 and 29 March 1804, Robinson 1929, pp. 133–5, 139.

303 no newspapers, no politics: Madame de Staël to C. M. Wieland, 1804, Alt 2004, vol. 2, p. 552.

303 'the Ideal': ibid., p. 553.

303 'their limited destiny': Staël 1813, vol. 1, p. 151.

303 Madame de Staël in Weimar: Schiller to Goethe, 30 November 1803; Schiller to C. G. Körner, 4 January 1804; see also Schiller to Goethe, 21 December 1803, and Goethe, 24 December 1803, Goethe 1982–96, vol. 4, p. 433. She arrived in Weimar on 14/15 December 1803 and left on 1 March 1804.

303 'as if I had survived': Schiller to Goethe, early March 1804.

303 letter of introduction: Goethe to AWS, 1 March 1804.

303 'knowledge and wit': Madame de Staël to Jacques Necker, 23 March 1804, Paulin 2016, p. 234.

303 'Ah! That's enough': Madame de Staël, Fichte GA III, vol. 5, p. 234.

303 Madame de Staël in Berlin with AWS: AWS to Caroline de la Motte-Fouqué, 26 March 1804; AWS to C. G. von Brinckmann, 28 March 1804.

304 'we reap the fruit': Staël 1813, vol. 2, p. 376.

304 offered AWS job: Madame de Staël to Jacques Necker, 23 March 1804, Paulin 2016, p. 235.

304 salary and pension: Paulin 2016, p. 239.

304 'our great project': AWS to Madame de Staël, end of March 1804.

304 subscribers and lectures: Endres 2017, p. 294; Stern 1994, p. 186; Zimmermann 2009, p. 184.

304 'Paris has one': FS to Karoline Paulus, 18 September 1804.

305 'I've never been': FS to Karoline Paulus, 27 March 1805.

305 'I feel unbelievably': FS to Tieck, 13 September 1802.

305 'the root of all': FS to Tieck, 15 September 1803.

305 'On the Language': FS, Über die Sprache und Weisheit der Inder, 1808; see also Paulin 2016, pp. 292, 297–8.

305 DV translated and lodgers: Zimmermann 2009, p. 183; FS and DV to Charlotte Ernst, 10 April 1804.

305 isolated in Paris: DV to Charlotte and L. E. Ernst, 6 April 1804.

305 'sent out along': FS to Karoline Paulus, 27 March 1805.

305 'the world would': DV to Karoline Paulus, 3 August 1804.

306 moving to Cologne: FS and DV to Charlotte Ernst, 10 April 1804.

306 Fn. DV thanked Veit: DV to Simon Veit, 5 January 1805, D. V. Schlegel 1881, vol. 1, p. 146.

306 marriage: DV to Charlotte and L. E. Ernst, 6 April 1804.

306 AH's collections: A. Humboldt 2009b, p. 86; A. Humboldt 1987, pp. 103–4.

306 Bogotá to Quito: Wulf 2015, pp. 77–80; A. Humboldt 1814, vol. 1, p. 63ff.; AH, 14 September, 27 November, 22 December 1801, diary, A. Humboldt 2003, vol. 1, pp. 124, 131, 163; AH to WH, 21 September 1801; AH to WH, 25 November 1801; AH to WH, 14 October 1804.

306 AH and Chimborazo: Wulf 2015, pp. 85–8; AH, 23 June 1802, diary, A. Humboldt 2003, vol. 2, pp. 100–9; AH to WH, 25 November 1802.

307 'influence of your': AH to Goethe, 3 January 1810.

307 dedicated first book: A. Humboldt, Ideen zu einer Geographie der Pflanzen, 1807.

307 'new senses': AH to Caroline von Wolzogen, 14 May 1806.

307 AH's instruments: A. Humboldt 1814–29, vol. 1, pp. 33–9.

307 'the desire for': A. Humboldt 1807, p. 41.

307 'had risen from': Goethe to WH, 30 July 1804.

307 'but Herr von Humboldt': Schiller to J. F. Cotta, 31 August 1804.

307 'Who indeed would': AH to J. F. Cotta, 24 January 1805.

307 Cotta's offer to AH: J. F. Cotta to AH, 5 July 1805.

308 Goethe's premonition: Heinrich Voß to Niemeyer, 12 August 1806, Goethe 1982–96, vol. 4, p. 546.

308 Goethe's illness: Goethe 1982–96, vol. 4, p. 556ff.

308 Schiller's illness: ibid. pp. 556–9; Schiller to Goethe, 22 February 1805; Wais 2005, p. 340.

308 'This Jena winter': Hegel to F. I. Niethammer, 4 March 1805.

308 Schiller's visit to Goethe: Heinrich Voß to Niemeyer, 12 August 1806, Goethe 1982–96, vol. 4, p. 562

308 Goethe's kidney infection: 7 March 1805; see August von Goethe to J. H. Meyer, 24 June 1805, Goethe 1982–96, pp. 563, 591.

308 silence: Christiane Vulpius to J. H. Meyer, 20 May 1805, Goethe 1982–96, vol. 4, p. 573.

308 'I have to force': Schiller to Goethe, 27 March 1805.

308 slowly recovering: Schiller to C. G. Körner, 25 April 1805.

308 Schiller bumped into Goethe: Goethe, 1 May 1805, Goethe 1982–96, vol. 4, p. 576.

309 Schiller's last illness: Goethe 1982–96, vol. 4, p. 577; Alt 2004, vol. 2, p. 608.

309 Schiller's autopsy: Goethe 1982–96, vol. 4, p. 579; Henry Crabb Robinson to Thomas Crabb Robinson, 17 June 1805, Robinson 1929, p. 170; Alt 2004, vol. 2, p. 54.

309 'a kind of hard': FS to AWS, 15–16 July 1805.

309 news reached Goethe's house: Heinrich Voß to Niemeyer, 12 August 1806; Heinrich Voß to Solger 22/26 May 1805, Goethe 1982–96, vol. 4, p. 578.

309 'Schiller was very' . . . 'dead!': Heinrich Voß to Niemeyer, 12 August 1806, Goethe 1982–96, vol. 4, p. 578.

309 Schiller's funeral: Goethe 1982–96, vol. 4, p. 579.

309 'I lose a friend': Goethe to K. F. Zelter, 1 June 1805.

309 my irreplaceable Schiller: Goethe, mid-May 1805, Goethe 1982–96, vol. 4, p. 580.

309 'I'm afraid the': FS to AWS, 24 May 1805.

309 not mentioning Schiller: Goethe 1982–96, vol. 4, p. 581.

309 'I could write': Goethe to Förster, 4 August 1831, Goethe 1982–96, vol. 4, p. 574; see also Safranksi 2017, p. 397.

309 'to spite Death': Goethe, mid-May 1805, Goethe 1982–96, vol. 4, p. 581.

310 'hollowed condition': ibid., p. 582.

Chapter 20: 'The French are in town!'
October 1806: The Battle of Jena

311 Soldiers in Jena: Paul 1920, p. 6ff.; Johanna Schopenhauer to Arthur Schopenhauer, 19 October 1806, J. J. Griesbach to his friends, 7 November

1806, in Hellmann 2005, pp. 113, 125; there had been some troops earlier, in 1805, but the main army arrived in autumn 1806.

311 tents and bakery: Paul 1920, p. 9, Danz 1809, p. 20.

311 food prices: Paul 1920, p. 10.

311 uniforms: Based on contemporary engravings and depictions; see also Nowak and Hellmann 2005, pp. 86–8.

311 artillery at market square: Paul 1920, p. 8.

312 first time since Seven Years War: Danz 1809, p. 12.

312 'Napoleon with his sharp': CS to Julie Gotter, 12 March 1806.

312 'Finally, the revolution': Schelling to C. J. Windischmann, 7 January 1807.

313 no soldiers and politics in Karlsbad: Goethe, summer 1806, Goethe 1982–96, vol. 4, p. 715.

313 colour theory and rock collection: Goethe, 9–30 September 1806 and 1–2 October 1806, Goethe Diaries, vol. 3, pp. 169–72.

313 Goethe and Hegel: Goethe 19, 27, 28, 29 August 1806 and 1 October 1806, Goethe Diaries, vol. 3, pp. 160–6, 172.

313 sent rock samples: Goethe to J. F. Blumenbach, 1 October 1806.

313 provisioning troops: Prince Hohenlohe-Ingelfingen, 2 October 1806, Goethe 1982–96, vol. 4, p. 748.

313 Goethe's court dress: ibid.

313 vacating rooms: Goethe, 1 October 1806, Goethe Diaries, vol. 3, p. 172; see also Goethe 1982–96, vol. 4, p. 748.

313 Goethe listened: Johanna Frommann about Goethe, October 1806, Goethe 1982–96, vol. 4, p. 750.

313 Goethe's walk in Jena, 6 October 1806: J. H. Meyer about Goethe, Goethe 1982–96, vol. 4, p. 750.

314 glimmer over hot coals: ibid.

314 Goethe left Jena: Goethe, 6 October 1806; he would be back in May 1807, Goethe, 16–24 May 1807, Goethe Diaries, vol. 3, pp. 173, 209.

314 'The French are': Paul 1920, p. 15.

314 hiding valuables: ibid., p. 19.

314 Saxons lost luggage: Nowak and Hellmann 2005, p. 23.

314 abandoned campsite: Johanna Frommann, 1806, Hellmann 2005, p. 230.

314 events of 13 October 1806: Hegel to F. I. Niethammer, 13 October 1806; Paul 1920, p. 24; Danz 1809, pp. 52–5; J. J. Griesbach to his friends, 7 November 1806, J. K. Wesselhöft, 1806, Johanna Frommann, 1806 and Luise Seidler, 1806, in Hellmann 2005, pp. 115, 224ff., 231ff., 241–2; J. K. Wesselhöft to Coelln, 19 October 1805, Paul 1920, p. 29.

314 'They stormed the': J. G. Lenz to Goethe, 22 October 1805.

314 plundering: J. G. Lenz to Goethe, 22 October 1806; Paul 1920, pp. 30–3; 48–9; J. J. Griesbach to his friends, 7 November 1806 and Johanna Frommann, 1806, in Hellmann 2005, pp. 115, 232ff.

315 French in market square: Paul 1920, p. 37; Danz 1809, pp. 52, 71; Johanna Frommann, 1806, in Hellmann 2005, p. 231ff.

315 French tailor: Paul 1920, p. 66.

315 *Phenomenology of Spirit* MS: Hegel to F. I. Niethammer, 13 October 1806. Hegel had already sent parts on 8 and 10 October 1806.

315 publisher's deadline: Pinkard 2001, p. 227.

315 'God knows my': Hegel to F. I. Niethammer, 13 October 1806.

315 carrying MS: Hegel to F. I. Niethammer, 18 October 1806; see also Vieweg 2020, p. 257.

316 'dark domains where': Hegel to C. J. Windischmann, 27 May 1810.

316 'absolute knowing': Hegel, *Phänomenologie des Geistes*, 1807, Hegel Werke, vol. 3, p. 575; Hegel 2018, p. 454.

316 'the process of its': Hegel, quoted in Watson 2010, p. 242.

316 'It is the spirit': Hegel, *Phänomenologie des Geistes,* 1807, Hegel Werke, vol. 3, p. 582; Hegel 2018, p. 460.

316 'I saw the Emperor': Hegel to F. I. Niethammer, 13 October 1806.

317 'destiny personified': CS to Pauline Gotter, 24 August 1807.

317 Goethe admired Napoleon: Hegel, 'Vorlesungen über die Philosophie der Geschichte', Hegel Werke, vol. 12, p. 339.

317 Napoleon's energy and productivity: Goethe to J. P. Eckermann, 11 March 1828.

317 'Now everyone is': Hegel to F. I. Niethammer, 13 October 1806.

317 Hegel fled: Hegel to F. I. Niethammer, 18 October 1806.

317 one hundred and thirty people: Johanna Frommann, 1806, in Hellmann 2005, p. 232.

317 drunken soldiers: K. Wesselhöft, 1806, in Hellmann 2005, p. 224.

317 'Ouvrez la porte!': Danz 1809, p. 69; Paul 1920, p. 48.

317 people fleeing their houses: Danz 1809, pp. 76–7; Paul 1920, pp. 54, 58.

318 slept outside: Paul 1920, p. 59; Johanna Frommann, 1806, in Hellmann 2005, pp. 232, 234.

318 icicles: F. J. Frommann, 1806, in Hellmann 2005, p. 219.

318 'Fire!': J. J. Griesbach to his friends, 7 November 1806, in Hellmann 2005, p. 117; see also Paul 1920, pp. 55–6; K. F. E. Frommann to Goethe, 19 October 1806; J. F. A. Hertel to Goethe, 20 October 1806.

318 up the hill: this was the so-called 'Steiger', a steep path up the Landgrafen hill. Duke of Rovigo, 13/14 October 1806, Nowak and Hellmann 2005, p. 31; Danz 1809, p. 35ff.; General Savary, 'Bericht über die Schlacht bei Jena', Hellmann 2005, pp. 206–7.

318 marched towards Jena: Nowak and Hellmann 2005, p. 2.

318 battle of 14 October 1806: ibid., pp. 32–42.

319 'All the thunder': Paul 1920, p. 61; see also Johanna Frommann, 1806, in Hellmann 2005, p. 235.

320 Fn. death toll Battle of Jena: Nowak and Hellmann 2005, p. 49.

320 wounded soldiers and hospitals: Nowak and Hellmann 2005, p. 48; Paul 1920, pp. 61–3, 80; Danz 1809, p. 39; J. G. Lenz to Goethe, 24 October 1806; K. Wesselhöft, 1806, in Hellmann 2005, p. 227.

320 Dr Stark: Paul 1920, pp. 132–3.

320 wounded in Leutragasse 5: ibid., p. 62.

320 auditorium as hospital: ibid.; J. J. Griesbach to his friends, 7 November 1806, Hellmann 2005, p. 118.

320 chaos on 14 October: Paul 1920, p. 63; J. J. Griesbach to his friends, 7 November 1806 and Johanna Frommann, 1806, in Hellmann 2005, pp. 116–17, 234.

320 fire and looting: Paul 1920, p. 83; W. C. E. von Reitzenstein, 1806, in Hellmann 2005, p. 255.

320 French soldiers plucking chickens: Luise Seidler, 1806, in Hellmann 2005, p. 241.

320 Napoleon in Goethe's rooms: Karl von Knebel to Goethe, 21 October 1806; Luise Seidler, 1806, in Hellmann 2005, p. 242.

321 chaos in Weimar: Goethe to J. F. Blumenbach, 20 October 1806; see also Goethe 1982–96, vol. 4, p. 751.

321 soldiers at Garden House: J. H. C. Koës, 13 October 1806, diary, Goethe 1965–2000, vol. 6, p. 149.

321 'We should be praying': C. G. M. Lineke, 13 October 1806, diary, Goethe 1965–2000, vol. 6, p. 150.

321 'Five in the afternoon': Goethe, 14 October 1806, Goethe Diaries, vol. 3, p. 174; for 14 October 1806 in Weimar in general, see K. J. R. Ridel to his brother, 3 November 1806, and Johanna Schopenhauer to Arthur Schopenhauer, 19 October 1806, in Hellmann 2005, pp. 120, 132ff.; Goethe 1982–96, vol. 4, pp. 754–5; F. W. Riemer, 14 October 1806, Goethe 1965–2000, vol. 6, p. 153.

321 'prophet's mantle': F.W. Riemer about 14 October 1806, Goethe 1965–2000, vol. 6, p. 153.

321 Christiane chased soldiers: F. W. Riemer about 14 October 1806, see also J. H. C. Koës, 14 October 1806 and J. C. Loder to C. W. Hufeland, 8 April 1807, Goethe 1965–2000, vol. 6, pp. 154–5, 164.

321 Goethe dispatched courier: Goethe to his Jena friends, 18 October 1806.

321 'God knows what': J. G. Lenz to Goethe, 18 October 1806.

322 students fled: J. F. Fuchs to Goethe, 23 October 1806.

322 'I and wife': J. F. A. Hertel to Goethe, 20 October 1806 and Marianne Hertel to Goethe, 20 October 1806.

322 most had not slept: J. N. Trabitius to Goethe, 21 October 1806; for professor leaving Jena, see F. J. Schelver to Goethe, 18 October 1806.

322 'otherwise we are': J. P. Gabler to H. K. A. Eichstädt for Goethe, 19 October 1806; see also H. K. A. Eichstädt to Goethe, 18 October 1806.

322 'We're alive!': Goethe to J. H. Meyer, J. F. Blumenbach and J. F. Cotta, 20 October 1806.

322 'I've been suffering': Goethe to Duke Carl August, 29 December 1806, Goethe 1982–96, vol. 4, p. 792.

322 Goethe's wedding: Goethe to Karl von Knebel, 21 October 1806; Goethe, 19 October 1806, Goethe Diaries, vol. 3, p. 175; Goethe 1982–96, vol. 4, p. 759.

322 'in times like these': Johanna Schopenhauer to Arthur Schopenhauer, 24 October 1806, Goethe 1982–96, vol. 4, p. 760.

322 CS about Goethe's wedding: CS to Luise Michaelis Wiedemann, 30 November 1806.

322 Charlotte Schiller refused: Charlotte Schiller to Fritz von Stein, 24 November 1806, Goethe 1982–96, vol. 4, p. 760.

322 'What right does': F. H. Jacobi to K. F. Zelter, 3 July 1805.

322 'I think that if': Johanna Schopenhauer to Arthur Schopenhauer, 24 October 1806, Goethe 1982–96, vol. 4, p. 761.

322 correspondence about battle: Schelling to H. K. A. Eichstädt, 21 October 1806; Schelling to Goethe, 21 October 1806; CS to Luise Michaelis Wiedemann, 30 November 1806; CS to Luise Gotter, 28 November 1806.

322 'I can't tell you': Schelling to H. K. A. Eichstädt, 21 October 1806.

323 'as that of my true': ibid.

323 a quarter of a million soldiers: Schelling to H. K. A. Eichstädt, 16 November 1806; for reading newspapers: CS to Luise Michaelis Wiedemann, 30 November 1806.

323 'Our hearts tremble': Schelling to Goethe, 21 October 1806.

323 heart bled for Jena: CS to Luise Gotter, 4 January 1807.

323 'That's how it': CS to Luise Gotter, 28 November 1806.

323 destruction necessary: Schelling to C. J. Windischmann, 18 December 1806.

323 'because really, none': CS to Luise Michaelis Wiedemann, 30 November 1806.

323 destruction of Jena: Paul 1920, p. 80; Heinrich Luden, October 1806, in Hellmann 2005, p. 212ff.

323 arrival of huge armies: Paul 1920, pp. 67ff., 117, 130–1.

323 water scarce: Nowak and Hellmann 2005, p. 48; Paul 1920, p. 117; Luise Seidler, 1806, in Hellmann 2005, p. 243.

323 'nursery where the': Gabriel Henry to Napoleon, 15 October 1806, in Paul 1920, p. 120; see also Pinkard 2001, p. 231; H. K. A. Eichstädt to Goethe, 18 October 1806.

323 student numbers: Steinmetz 1958, vol. 1, p. 242.

324 'No bread, robbed': J. G. Lenz to Goethe, 20 October 1806; see also Goethe to C. G. Voigt, 20 October 1806.

324 anatomical collection and botanical garden: J. F. Fuchs and Goethe, 23 October 1806; Paul 1920, p. 75; F. J. Schelver to Goethe, 18 October 1806; Karl von Knebel to Goethe, 26 October 1806.

324 'lying around on': F. J. Schelver to Goethe, 18 October 1806.

324 'because the authorities': ibid.

324 'when the storm': Goethe to J. G. Lenz, 21 October 1806; see also Goethe to C. G. Voigt, 20 October 1806; Goethe to Karl von Knebel, 21, 23 October 1806 and 1 November 1806; Karl von Knebel to Goethe, 24 October 1806; Goethe to J. H. Meyer, 15 or 16 October 1806.

324 boots on legs: Luise Seidler, 1806, in Hellmann 2005, p. 243.

324 epidemic: Paul 1920, p. 134; Nowak and Hellmann 2005, p. 49.

324 six thousand wounded: reports varied between three and a half and nine thousand injured soldiers, Paul 1920, p. 63; first sermon was on 21 June 1807, see ibid., p. 134.

324 'the death cart': Luise Seidler, 1806, in Hellmann 2005, p. 242.

325 'We just drag': Karl von Knebel to Goethe, 5 December 1806.

325 'All these upheavals': Goethe to Duke Carl August, 29 December 1806.

325 Goethe back in Jena: Goethe, 16–24 May 1807, Goethe Diaries, vol. 3, pp. 209–13.

325 Denon in Berlin: Saltzman 2021, p. 179.

325 Napoleon through Prussia: Nowak and Hellmann 2005, p. 53.

325 Denon packed art: Saltzman 2021, p. 184.

325 150,000 francs: Safranski 2017, p. 410.

325 few spoke French: H. K. A. Eichstädt to Goethe, 19 October 1806.

325 French censorship: Paul 1920, p. 138.

325 'The scholarly exchange': Lorenz Oken to Schelling, 3 September 1808.

325 Jena in decline: Deinhardt 2007, pp. 28, 86, 106, 374–6.

326 'for its rebirth': Karl von Knebel to Goethe, 5 December 1806.

326 Hegel applied for position: Hegel to Goethe, end of January 1807.

326 Hegel applied to universities: Hegel to J. H. Voß, May 1805; Hegel to F. I. Niethammer, 14 January 1806.

326 Hegel's son: Ludwig Fischer was born on 5 February 1807; Kaube 2020, p. 183; Pinkard 2001, p. 237.

326 'end of History': Kojève 1969, p. 160, see also p. 44.

Epilogue

327 'Addresses to the': Fichte, *Reden an die deutsche Nation*, 1807–8. Fichte gave fourteen lectures from December 1807 to March 1808.

327 Germans one nation: Fichte, *Reden an die deutsche Nation*, 1807–8, Fichte, SW, vol. 7, p. 314.

327 Fichte and languages: ibid., pp. 311ff., 459ff.

327 'to a single shared': ibid., p. 326.

327 Fn. Herder and language: Herder 1877–99, vol. 2, p. 18; see also Kremer 2016, p. 60.

327 'national self': Fichte, *Reden an die deutsche Nation*, 1807–8, Fichte, SW, vol. 7, p. 274.

328 Fichte paralysed: Fuchs 2014, p. 585.

328 Fichte at Berlin university: Jacobs 2012, pp. 190–8.

328 Fichte with dagger and shield: Bettina von Arnim described Fichte, Safranski 2009b, p. 186; see also Fuchs 2014, p. 598.

328 Fichte's funeral: J. G. Fichte to J. C. L. Fichte and J. E. Fichte, 31 January 1816, Fichte Gespräch, vol. 5, p. 74; for newspaper reports see p. 90ff.

328 'The eye of Germany': Rahel Levin to K. A. Varnhagen von Ense, 14 February 1814, Fichte Gespräch, vol. 5, p. 110.

328 mountain air: Schelling to Luise Gotter, 24 September 1809.

328 'I don't want to': CS to Luise Gotter, 28 November 1806.

329 CS's reviews: these were reviews for Goethe's newly established *Jenaer Allgemeine Literatur-Zeitung*.

329 'What I miss': CS to Luise Michaelis Wiedemann, 31 January 1807.

329 small circle of friends: CS to Luise Gotter, 4 January 1807.

329 Schelling about CS: Schelling to Luise Gotter, 24 September 1809; Schelling to Martin Wagner, 5 October 1809.

329 CS's last illness: Schelling to Luise Gotter, 24 September 1809.

329 'I stood there': ibid.

329 'All that remains': ibid.

329 'GOD gave Her': Schelling 1869–70, vol. 2, p. 168–70.

330 Schelling's depression: Bettina Brentano to Achim von Arnim, September 1809, Steig and Grimm 1894–1904, vol. 2, p. 334; Franz von Baader to Stransky, Baader 1851–60, vol. 15, p. 236.

330 CS unique: Schelling to Philipp Michaelis, 29 November 1809.

330 'This masterpiece': ibid.; see also Schelling to F. I. Niethammer, 2 October 1809; Schelling to Martin Wagner, 5 October 1809.

330 CS's dressing gown: Therese Huber to K. A. Böttiger, 17 October 1811, Huber 1999, vol. 4, p. 482.

330 'proposed the hypothesis': Hegel to F. I. Niethammer, 4 October 1809.

330 Schelling freed: Charlotte Schiller to J. F. Cotta, 27 October 1809, CS Letters, vol. 2, p. 664.

330 'What effect does': FS to DV, late November 1809.

330 Pauline Gotter and Schelling: Tilliette 2004, p. 249; Jaspers 1955, p. 37.

330 first-born daughter: Tilliette 2004, p. 290.

331 'I am proud to': AWS to Madame de Staël, 18 October 1805.

331 Madame de Staël's last child: Appel 2011, pp. 302, 350.

331 'sudden crazed mood': AWS to Madame de Staël, 3 August 1813.

331 'I bear wounds': ibid.

331 'My youth is gone': ibid.

331 AWS's marriage to Sophie Paulus: Paulin 2016, p. 439; AWS to Jakob Lamberz, 10 January 1819.

331 'After all, one': AWS to Madame de Staël, 3 August 1813.

332 AWS's appearance at Bonn lectures: Heinrich Heine, *Die Romantische Schule*, Heine 1972, p. 73.

332 Philipp returned to father: Stern 1994, p. 228.

332 'Yes, I do often' and white hair: DV to Karoline Paulus, 20 September 1804.

332 'like a bulldog': Achim von Arnim to Clemens Brentano, March 1803, Steig and Grimm 1894–1904, vol. 2, p. 67.

332 conversion to Catholicism: Stern 1994, p. 234.

333 FS increasingly conservative: FS to Karoline Paulus, 27 March 1805.

333 'idolising the *Ich*': FS, *Zur Philosophie und Theologie*, 1817, FS KA, vol. 19, p. 327.

333 Fichte confused the self with the divine: FS, 'Philosophie des Lebens, Wiener Vorlesung, 1827', FS KA, vol. 10, p. 16.

333 'dead abstractions': ibid., p. 165.

333 'this old worn-out': FS to Sulpiz Boisserée, 11 December 1811.

333 Goethe famous because of FS: Körner 1924, p. 190.

333 'The old man': FS to Sulpiz Boisserée, 16 January 1813.

333 moved eight times: Frank 1988, p. 210.

333 DV's translations: Stern 1994, pp. 213–14.

333 FS and Austrian civil service: this was in April 1809, Stern 1994, pp. 254–5, 270ff.; Endres 2017, p. 18ff.

333 FS as diplomat: Endres 2017, pp. 23–4.

334 FS's death: ibid., p. 28.

334 DV after FS's death: Stern 1994, pp. 292–3; Frank 1988, pp. 264–5.

334 critical edition: This was Ernst Behler's *Kritische Friedrich-Schlegel-Ausgabe*, 1958–2006.

334 'Chez Monsieur': Bruhns 1873, vol. 2, p. 89.

334 AH and Jena friends: AH saw FS in Paris and AWS in Rome, FS to G. A. Reimers, 16 March 1805; FS to AWS, 15–16 July 1805; Paulin 2016,

p. 253; for AH and Fichte, see Henrik Steffens, about spring 1806, Fichte
Gespräch, vol. 3, p. 401; AH continued to correspond with Goethe and
visited him several times in Weimar, see for example Goethe, 11–13
December 1826 and 26–27 February 1831, Goethe Diaries, vol. 10, pp.
279–81 and vol. 13, pp. 17–18.

334 'brightest points in': Goethe to WH, 18 June 1821.

334 'revolutionary': AH to Schelling, February 1805; see also AH to Schelling, 10
February 1806, and AH's reference to Schelling in A. Humboldt 1807, p. v.

334 'dry piling up': AH to C. C. J. Bunsen, 22 March 1835.

334 Fn. AH's debt to Schelling: Humboldt 1845–50, vol. 1, p. 39; the reference
to Schelling and this sentence is missing in the English edition (Humboldt
1845–52, vol. 1, p. 40); Humboldt quoted Schelling's 1807 speech 'Über
das Verhältnis der bildenden Künste zur Natur'.

334 'what speaks to': A. Humboldt 1814–29, vol. 4, p. 134.

334 AH and new nature writing: Wulf 2015, pp. 132–3.

334 'you believe you are': François-René de Chateaubriand, in Clark and
Lubrich 2012b, p. 29.

335 'Nature is a': A. Humboldt 1845–50, vol. 1, p. 39.

335 'a wonderful web': ibid., p. 21.

335 'the most scientific'; Thomas Jefferson to William Armistead Burwell, 1804,
Fries 1959, p. 181.

335 'one of those wonders': Emerson, 14 September 1869, Emerson 1971–2013,
vol. 11, p. 458.

335 Darwin on *Beagle* because of AH: Charles Darwin to D. T. Gardner, August
1874, published in *New York Times*, 15 September 1874.

335 'Shakespeare of the Sciences': Herman Trautschold, 1869, Roussanova 2013,
p. 45.

335 'children into people': WH quoted in Clark 2007, pp. 331–2.

335 'Every language contains': *Einleitung zum Kawiwerk*, W. Humboldt 1903–36,
vol. 7, pt 1, p. 60.

335 'in this sense': *Über die Verschiedenheiten des menschlichen Sprachbaues*,
W. Humboldt 1903–36, vol. 6, pt 1, p. 125.

336 CH's love affairs: Gersdorff 2013, pp. 109ff., 160ff.

336 'I implore you': WH to CH, 19 June 1804.

336 'gives and takes': K. A. Varnhagen von Ense about Humboldts, Gersdorff
2013, p. 160.

336 CH's last illness: W. and C. Humboldt 1910–16, vol. 7, p. 342.

336 WH couldn't bear: WH to August von Hedemann, 12 December 1828.

336 love was the foundation: WH to Goethe, 12 February 1829.

336 'Love is the purpose': CH in 1829, W. and C. Humboldt 1910–16, vol. 7,
p. 342.

336 WH's death: Gersdorff 2013, p. 258.

336 Hegel's reckoning with Schelling: Schelling 1962–75, vol. 1, pp. 500–19;
see also the preface of Hegel's *Phänomenologie des Geistes*, 1807, Hegel
Werke, vol. 3, pp. 11–67.

336 Schelling lacked logic: Hegel, *Vorlesungen über die Geschichte der Philosophie*,
Schelling 1962–75, vol. 1, p. 506.

336 'Today people try': Hegel, notebooks, 1805/6, Schelling 1962–75, vol. 1, p. 515.

336 'serious business': Hegel, *Phänomenologie des Geistes*, 1807, Hegel Werke, vol. 3, p. 62; Hegel 2018, p. 42.

336 Hegel on Schelling and art: Schelling 1962–75, vol. 1, p. 503.

336 Philosophy has to be science: Hegel, *Phänomenologie des Geistes*, 1807, Hegel Werke, vol. 3, p. 14.

336 Hegel freed of Schelling: Jean Paul Richter to F. H. Jacobi, 6 September 1807, Tilliette 1974, p. 184.

336 first review took two years: Schelling 1962–75, vol. 1, p. 519.

337 'If it weren't': Schelling to K. F. Dorfmüller, 10 September 1841.

337 'misleading as to': FS to Tieck, 5 November 1801.

337 created Novalis myth: O'Brien 1995, pp. 12–25.

337 'otherworldly creature': Ludwig Tieck about Novalis 1815, Novalis Schriften, vol. 4, p. 553.

337 'meaningful oracles' and Christ-like: Steffens 1841, vol. 4, p. 324.

337 Novalis like a melody: ibid.

338 'sacred power of pain': Ludwig Tieck about Novalis, 1815, Novalis Schriften, vol. 4, p. 554.

338 'even everyday life': ibid., p. 559.

338 'idol of the most': Novalis to K. L. Reinhold, 5 October 1791.

338 'Alliance of Minds': Steffens 1841, vol. 4, p. 123.

338 'We lived in': Schiller to Fichte, 3 August 1795.

339 Goethe learned French: Goethe, *Dichtung und Wahrheit*, Goethe 1949–60, vol. 9, p. 90.

339 'my Emperor': WH to CH, 9 January 1809; for accepting Napoleon, see F. W. Riemer, November 1806, Goethe 1995–2000, vol. 6, p. 172.

339 Goethe met Napoleon: Seibt 2008, p. 120ff.

339 Legion of Honour: WH to CH, 9 January 1809.

339 exhausted following campaigns: Goethe to Karl von Knebel, 22 April 1815.

339 'He strode through': Goethe to J. P. Eckermann, 11 March 1828.

340 'Faust astonishes, moves': Staël 1813, vol. 1, p. 390; for Schelling on *Faust*, see Schelling, 'Philosophie der Kunst', 1802, Schelling SW, vol. 5, p. 446; for Coleridge and *Faust*, see Wulf 2015, p. 170.

340 Christiane's death: Damm 1998, pp. 501–2.

340 'Emptiness and deathly': Goethe, 6 June 1816, Goethe Diaries, vol. 5, p. 239.

340 thinkers spread out too far: Goethe to J. P. Eckermann, 3 May 1827.

340 'I seem more and': Goethe to WH, 1 December 1831.

340 'implacable hatred': AWS to Tieck, 15 January 1830.

340 'I took in and used': Goethe recounted by Frédéric Soret, 17 February 1832, Soret 1929, p. 630.

341 Napoleon and *Germany:* Staël 1813, vol. 1, pp. 13–17; Appel 2011, pp. 286–7; Lewis 2001, p. 423.

341 difference between French and Germans: Staël 1813, vol. 1, pp. 70–90.

341 'A Frenchman can': ibid., p. 75.

341 French and French Revolution: ibid., pp. 85–7.

341 German and individuality: ibid., p. 87.

341 blindly followed: ibid., p. 85.

341 'The French are all-powerful': ibid., p. 87.

341 'the native land': ibid., p. 23.

341 Napoleon and *Germany*: ibid., pp. 13–17; Appel 2011, pp. 286–7; Lewis 2001, p. 423.

342 *Germany* London publication: Appel 2011, p. 326.

342 'new philosophy': Staël 1813, vol. 3, p. 136. ·

342 'With the torch': ibid., p. 133.

342 'there seemed to be': Staël 1813, vol. 1, p. 149.

342 'the Staël–Schlegel book': Goethe quoted in Higonnet 1986, p. 161.

342 '*romantique* is a': *Le Globe*, 24 March 1825, quoted in Wilcox 1953, p. 365.

343 Caspar David Friedrich and Jena Set: see Amstutz 2020 for an in-depth study of the Jena Set's influence on the artist.

343 'The painter should': Caspar David Friedrich quoted in ibid., p. 14.

343 ' . . . well pleased to': W. Wordsworth, 'Lines Written a Few Miles above Tintern Abbey', 1798.

343 'O! the one Life': S. T. Coleridge, 'The Eolian Harp', 1817; see also Harman 2009, pp. 319–20.

343 Coleridge in Germany: Holmes 1998a, pp. 205–37.

343 ivy and oak tree: Holmes 1998b, p. 254.

344 'a great and original': S. T. Coleridge, *Biographia Literaria*, quoted in ibid., p. 400.

344 'Schellingianer': Henry Crabb Robinson about Coleridge, quoted in Ashton 1994, p. 53.

344 'metaphysicised *à la*': Henry Crabb Robinson, 3 June 1824, diary, Robinson 1869, vol. 2, p. 273.

344 'mediatress between, and': Coleridge, 'On Poesy or Art', Coleridge 1983, vol. 1, p. cv.

344 Coleridge plagiarised Schelling: Coleridge 1983, vol. 1, pp. cxiv–cxxii; see chapters 5–9 and 12–13 in Coleridge's *Biographia Literaria*.

344 'bare-faced plagiarism': Thomas de Quincey, September 1834, Beach 1942, p. 41.

344 'El Dorado': De Quincey 1896, vol. 2, p. 85.

344 'my library was rich': ibid., vol. 11, p. 370.

344 'high force': Lord Byron to Samuel Rogers, 29 July 1816, Clayden 1889, vol. 1, p. 228.

344 *Frankenstein* and Jena Set: Holmes 2008, pp. 328–30.

344 'physiological writers': Shelley 1998, p. 13.

344 Shelley read AWS's book: Mary Shelley, 16–21 March 1816, diary, Shelley 1987, vol. 1, pp. 198–9.

345 'the expression of': AWS 1815, vol. 2, p. 99; AWS 1846, vol. 6, pt 2, p. 161.

345 'deep mighty thinkers': Parker 1841, p. 324.

345 Jena Set's ideas in US: Vogel 1970, pp. 74–5, 106–7, 172–6; Wellek 1943, p. 41ff.; American journals that published the Jena Set's work were, for example, *The Dial*, *Blackwood's Magazine*, *Harbinger* and *Foreign Quarterly Review*.

345 *Germany* and *Biographia Literaria*: Vogel 1970, p. 106.

345 Carlyle's work: see for example, Carlyle, *The State of German Literature*, 1827 and Carlyle, *German Romance: Specimens of its Chief Authors; with Biographical and Critical Notices*, 1827.

345 'mysterious relation between': Thoreau, 18 April 1852, journal, Thoreau 1981–2002, vol. 4, p. 468.

345 Thoreau as a boy: John Weiss, *Christian Examiner*, 1865, Harding 1989, p. 33; for his studies at Harvard, see Richardson 1986, pp. 12–13.

345 'somewhat rustic': Nathaniel Hawthorne, September 1842, Harding 1989, p. 154; for his appearance see Channing 1873, p. 25.

346 Thoreau and animals: Mary Hosmer Brown, *Memories of Concord*, 1926, Harding 1989, pp. 150–1; Thoreau 1910, pp. 170, 173.

346 Thoreau's time at Walden Pond: Thoreau 1910, p. 118.

346 'With all your science': Thoreau, 16 July 1851, journal, Thoreau 1981–2002, vol. 3, p. 307.

346 Thoreau and AH: Wulf 2015, p. 257ff.; Sattelmeyer 1988, pp. 206–7; see also Thoreau's journals for references to AH, for example: Thoreau, 1 April 1850, 12 May 1850, 27 October 1853, journal, Thoreau 1981–2002, vol. 3, pp. 52, 67–8 and vol. 7, p. 119.

346 'deprived thereby of the': A. Humboldt 1845–52, vol. 2, p. 87; A. Humboldt 1845–50, p. 74.

346 'Look at Nature': Thoreau, 4 December 1856, journal, Thoreau 1981–2002, vol. 9, p. 157; for rewriting Walden see Sattelmeyer 1992, p. 492ff.

346 'learn German as fast': Gura 2008, p. 29; see also Emerson, 4 May 1837, journal, Emerson 1960–92, vol. 5, p. 319; Richardson 1986, p. 20. Emerson owned two hundred volumes that were either original German publications, translations or German-subject books, Vogel 1970, pp. 172–6.

346 'Some minds think': Emerson, 'Encyclopedia Notebook', 1824–36, Emerson 1960–92, vol. 6, p. 195.

346 Emerson writing *Nature* and Coleridge's *Biographia Literaria*: Richardson 1995, p. 218–19.

347 Emerson and Schelling: Labriola 2002, p. 129ff.

347 'each particle is': Emerson, *Nature*, 1836, Emerson 2003, p. 60.

347 'The mind is a part': Emerson, *Nature*, 1836, Emerson 2003, p. 72.

347 Fn. Emerson, nature and God: Emerson, *Nature*, 1836, Emerson 2003, p. 39.

347 'Am I not partly': Thoreau 1910, p. 182.

347 left school at eleven: Callow 1992, p. 26ff.

347 'an unusual capacity': ibid., p. 50.

347 'illustrious four' . . . 'point of view': Whitman's advertisement for *Leaves of Grass*, 1872, Pochmann 1978, p. 469; see also pp. 470, 786.

347 'Never before did': Whitman, 'A Sun–Bath – Nakedness', Whitman 1892, p. 103.

347 'beautiful and majestic': Whitman quoted in Pochmann 1978, pp. 472, 787.

347 'great System of Idealistic': ibid., p. 469.

347 'I celebrate myself': Whitman, *Leaves of Grass*, 1855, p. 13.

348 'Walt Whitman, an American': ibid., p. 29. The word 'kosmos' is the only

one that didn't change in the various versions of Whitman's famous self-identification. It began as 'Walt Whitman, an American, one of the roughs, a kosmos' in the first edition and became 'Walt Whitman, a kosmos, of Manhattan the son' in the last.

348 Whitman and AH's *Cosmos*: Walls 2009, pp. 279–83.

348 Hawthorne, Poe and Melville: Schiffman 2012, p. 42ff; Pochmann 1978, p. 405ff., 436ff.

348 'Free-Will': Melville quoted in Pochmann 1978, p. 43; for Melville reading *Biographia Literaria*, see Marovitz 2008, p. 49.

348 'he is not original': Poe quoted in Schiffman 2012, p. 42; for Edgar Allan Poe plagarising AWS's work, see Pochmann 1978, pp. 405–6.

348 'I have seen too': Henry Crabb Robinson to Thomas Crabb Robinson, 17 June 1805, Robinson 1929, p. 169.

348 'first-rate and': Steffens 1841, vol. 4, p. 82.

348 Steffens in Scandinavia: Müller-Wille 2016, p. 579.

348 Maurycy Mochnacki: Coghen 2016, p. 558.

349 'If we cannot be': Maurycy Mochnacki quoted in Kopij-Weiß 2013.

349 'Germanomania': Adam Mickiewicz quoted in Kopij-Weiß 2013.

349 Fn. Swedish Romantics: P. D. A. Atterbom to E. G. Geijer, 24 January 1818, Fichte Gespräch, vol. 2, p. 4.

349 Uppsala: Müller-Wille 2016, p. 580.

349 Tyutchev and Schelling: Tyutchev 2014, pp. xviii, xxxv–xl.

349 'All is in me': Fyodor Tyutchev, untitled poem, first half of 1830s, Tyutchev 2014, p. 44.

349 'Seek out that': Fyodor Tyutchev, 'Silentium!', second half of 1820s, Tyutchev 2014, p. 30.

349 Freud and Jena Set: Askay and Farquhar 2006, pp. 73–4.

349 'Goethe's connection': Freud quoted in Askay and Farquhar 2006, p. 75.

349 'look within yourselves': Goethe, *Maximen und Reflexionen*, no. 1080.

349 Joyce and Jena Set: Laman 2004, pp. 14, 16, 18.

349 'it should forever': FS, '*Athenaeum* Fragment', no. 116, FS KA, vol. 2, p. 183; Schlegel 1971, p. 175.

349 *Finnegans Wake*: Laman 2004, p. 113ff.

350 'Schlegelian': ibid., p. 117 and see also p. 85.

350 the 'chaos': FS, 'Ideen', no. 71, FS KA, vol. 2, p. 263.

350 novel should defy classifications: FS, 'Gespräch über die Poesie', 1800, FS KA, vol. 2, pp. 336–7.

350 'The essence of a': FS, 'Fragmente zur Poesie und Litteratur', no. 274, FS KA, vol. 16, p. 276.

350 'Perhaps, Jena was': Schiller to WH, 18 August 1803.

350 'Ich-fetishism': Friedrich Bouterwek to F. H. Jacobi, Göttingen, 24 February 1801, Fichte Gespräch, vol. 3, p. 11.

350 'metaphysical egotism': K. L. Reinhold to A. J. Batsch, 3 May 1801, Fichte Gespräch, vol. 3, p. 37.

350 'Only those are *free*': Fichte, *Einige Vorlesungen über die Bestimmung des Gelehrten*, 1794, Lecture 2, Fichtes SW, vol. 6, p. 309.

351 'Since we find nature': Henrik Steffens to Schelling, 1 September 1800.

351 'age of Introversion': Emerson, *The American Scholar*, 1837, Emerson 2003, p. 101.

351 'The most wonderful': Novalis, 'Dialogen und Monolog. 1798/99', Novalis Schriften, vol. 2, p. 362.

351 'without perfect self-understanding': Novalis, 'Blüthenstaub' ('Pollen'), no. 28, Novalis Schriften, vol. 2, p. 424; Novalis 1991, p. 387.

Bibliography and Sources

Bibliography

Most of my research was done before the libraries closed during the pandemic in 2020 and 2021, but when I needed to find additional works and letters during this period, I had to use editions that were available online. For this reason I have sometimes included several editions of the same source in what follows.

Alt, Peter André, *Schiller: Leben – Werk – Zeit: Eine Biographie*, Munich: C. H. Beck, 2004

Ameriks, Karl (ed.), *The Cambridge Companion to German Idealism*, Cambridge: Cambridge University Press, 2017

Amstutz, Nina, *Caspar David Friedrich: Nature and the Self*, New Haven, CT and London: Yale University Press, 2020

Anonymous (Hegel, Hölderlin or Schelling), *Das älteste Systemprogramm des deutschen Idealismus*, n.p., *c.*1796/7

——, *The Oldest System Programme of German Idealism*, trans. Diana I. Behler, in *Philosophy of German Idealism: Fichte, Jacobi and Schelling*, ed. Ernst Behler, New York: Continuum, 1987

Anonymous, *Zeichnung der Universität Jena: Für Jünglinge, welche diese Akademie besuchen wollen*, Leipzig: Friedrich Leopold Gupprian, 1798

Appel, Sabine, *Madame de Staël: Kaiserin des Geistes: Eine Biographie*, Munich: C. H. Beck, 2011

——, *Caroline Schlegel-Schelling: Das Wagnis der Freiheit: Eine Biographie*, Munich: C. H. Beck, 2013

Ashton, Rosemary, *The German Idea: Four English Writers and the Reception of German Thought, 1800–1860*, London: Libris, 1994

Askay, Richard and Jensen Farquhar (eds), *Apprehending the Inaccessible: Freudian Psychoanalysis*, Evanston, IL: North Western University Press, 2006

Baader, Franz von, *Franz von Baader's Sämmtliche Werke*, ed. Franz Hoffmann et al., Leipzig: Herrmann Bethmann Verlag, 1851–60

Bach, Ingo, 'Weißenfels am Ende des 18. Jahrhunderts und das sozial-kulturelle Umfeld der Familie von Hardenberg', in *Bergbau und Dichtung: Friedrich von Hardenberg*, ed. Eleonore Sent, Weimar: Hain Verlag, 2003

Bake, Rita and Birgit Kiupel, *Unordentliche Begierden: Liebe, Sexualität und Ehe im 18. Jahrhundert*, Hamburg: Kabel, 1996

Bamberg, Claudia and Cornelia Ilbrig (eds), *Aufbruch ins romantische Universum: August Wilhelm Schlegel*, Frankfurt: Freies Deutsches Hochstift, 2018

Bate, Jonathan, *Shakespeare and the English Romantic Imagination*, Oxford: Clarendon Press, 1986

Beach, Joseph Warren, 'Coleridge's Borrowings from the German', *English Literary History*, vol. 9, no. 1, 1942

Beck, Adolf (ed.), *Hölderlin: Chronik seines Lebens*, Frankfurt and Leipzig: Insel Verlag, 2003

Beinecke Rare Books and Manuscripts Library, *Goethe: The Scientist*, exhibition catalogue, New Haven, CT and London: Yale University Press, 1999

Beiser, Frederick C., *The Romantic Imperative: The Concept of Early German Romanticism*, Cambridge, MA and London: Harvard University Press, 2003

Behler, Ernst (ed.), *Philosophy of German Idealism: Fichte, Jacobi and Schelling*, New York: Continuum, 1987

Berglar, Peter, *Wilhelm von Humboldt in Selbstzeugnissen und Bilddokumenten*, Reinbek: Rowohlt, 1970

Berlin, Isaiah, *The Roots of Romanticism*, ed. Henry Hardy, London: Pimlico, 2000

Bernays, Michael, *Zur Entstehungsgeschichte des Schlegelschen Shakespeare*, Leipzig: G. Hirzel, 1872

Blanning, Tim, *The Romantic Revolution*, London: Phoenix, 2010

Boller, Hildegard Gabriele, 'Die Dresdener Antikensammlung', in *Tempel der Kunst. Die Geburt des öffentlichen Museums in Deutschland 1701–1815*, ed. Bénédicte Savoy, Cologne, Weimar, Wien: Böhlau Verlag, 2015

Borcherdt, H. H. (ed.), *Schiller und die Romantiker: Briefe und Dokumente*, Stuttgart: J. G. Cotta'sche Buchhandlung, 1948

Böttiger, Karl August, *Literarische Zustände und Zeitgenossen: Begegnungen und Gespräche im klassischen Weimar*, ed. Klaus Gerlach and René Sternke, Berlin: Aufbau-Verlag, 1998

Botting, Douglas, *Humboldt and the Cosmos*, London: Sphere Books, 1973

Boyle, Nicholas, *Goethe: The Poet and the Age*, vol. 1, *The Poetry of Desire: 1749–1790*, Oxford: Clarendon Press, 1992

——, *Goethe: Der Dichter in seiner Zeit, 1791–1803*, trans. Holger Fliessbach, Munich: C. H. Beck, 1999

——, *Goethe: The Poet and the Age*, vol. 2, *Revolution and Renunciation: 1790–1803*, Oxford: Clarendon Press, 2000

Breitenborn, Konrad and Justus H. Ulbricht, *Jena und Auerstedt: Ereignis und Erinnerung in europäischer, nationaler und regionaler Perspektive*, Dößel: Verlag Janos Stekovics, 2006

Breuer, Ulrich and Dirk von Petersdorff (eds), *Das Jenaer Romantikertreffen im November 1799: Ein Romantischer Streitfall*, Athenäum-Jahrbuch der Friedrich Schlegel-Gesellschaft, Paderborn: F. Schöningh, 2015

Briggs, Asa, *The Age of Improvement, 1783–1867*, London: Longman, 2000

Bruhns, Karl (ed.), *Life of Alexander von Humboldt*, London: Longmans, Green & Co., 1873

Brunschwig, Henri, *Gesellschaft und Romantik in Preußen im 18. Jahrhundert*, Frankfurt: Ullstein, 1975

Burgsdorff, Wilhelm von, *Briefe an Brinkman, Henriette v. Finckenstein, Wilhelm v. Humboldt, Rahel, Friedrich Tieck, Ludwig Tieck und Wiesel*, ed. Alfons Fedor Cohn, Berlin: Behr, 1907

Byron, Lord, *Lord Byron: Selected Letters and Journals*, ed. Leslie A. Marchand, London: John Murray, 1982

Callow, Philip, *Walt Whitman: From Noon to Starry Night*, London: Allison & Busby, 1992

Carlyle, Thomas, *German Romance: Specimens of its Chief Authors*, Edinburgh: W. Tait, 1827

——, 'The State of German Literature', *Edinburgh Review*, October 1827

Channing, William Ellery, *Thoreau: The Poet-Naturalist*, Boston, MA: Roberts Brothers, 1873

Clark, Christopher, *Iron Kingdom: The Rise and Downfall of Prussia: 1600–1947*, London: Penguin, 2007

Clark, Rex and Oliver Lubrich (eds), *Cosmos and Colonialism: Alexander von Humboldt in Cultural Criticism*, New York and Oxford: Berghahn Books, 2012a

—— (eds), *Transatlantic Echoes: Alexander von Humboldt in World Literature*, New York and Oxford: Berghahn Books, 2012b

Clayden, P. W., *Rogers and His Contemporaries*, London: Smith, Elder & Co., 1889

Coghen, Monika, 'Polish Romanticism', in *The Oxford Handbook of European Romanticism*, ed. Paul Hamilton, Oxford: Oxford University Press, 2016

Coleridge, Samuel Taylor, *Collected Letters of Samuel Taylor Coleridge*, ed. Earl Leslie Griggs, Oxford: Clarendon Press, 1956–71

——, *The Notebooks of Samuel Taylor Coleridge*, ed. Kathleen Coburn, Princeton, NJ: Princeton University Press, 1958–2002

——, *Collected Works. Biographia Literaria*, ed. James Engell and W. Jackson Bate, London: Routledge & Kegan Paul Ltd, 1983

——, *Lectures 1818–1819 on the History of Philosophy*, ed. J. R. de J. Jackson, Princeton, NJ: Princeton University Press, 2000

Costelloe, Timothy M., *Imagination in Hume's Philosophy: The Canvas of the Mind*, Edinburgh: Edinburgh University Press, 2018

Cunningham, Andrea and Nicholas Jardine (eds), *Romanticism and the Sciences*, Cambridge: Cambridge University Press, 1990

Damm, Sigrid, *Christiane und Goethe: Eine Recherche*, Frankfurt and Leipzig: Insel Verlag, 1998

Damm, Sigrid (ed.), *Caroline Schlegel-Schelling: Die Kunst zu leben*, Frankfurt and Leipzig, Insel Verlag, 2005

Danz, Johann T. L., *Ansicht der Stadt Jena in den Octobertagen 1806*, Jena: Seidler, 1809

Day, Aidon, *Romanticism*, London and New York: Routledge, 1996

De Quincey, Thomas, *The Collected Writings of Thomas De Quincey*, ed. David Masson, Edinburgh: A. & C. Black, 1896

Deinhardt, Katja (ed.), *Stapelstadt des Wissens: Jena als Universitätsstadt zwischen 1770 und 1830*, Cologne: Böhlau Verlag, 2007

Dilthey, Wilhelm, *Aus Schleiermacher's Leben: in Briefen*, Berlin: G. Reimer, 1858–63

Ehrlich, Lothar and Georg Schmidt (eds), *Ereignis Weimar-Jena: Gesellschaft und Kultur um 1800 im internationalen Kontext*, Cologne: Böhlau Verlag, 2008

Ehrlich, Willi, *Goethes Wohnhaus am Frauenplan in Weimar*, Weimar: Nationale Forschungs- und Gedenkstätten der Klassik, 1983

Emerson, Ralph Waldo, *The Journals and Miscellaneous Notebooks of Ralph Waldo Emerson*, ed. William H. Gilman et al., Cambridge, MA: Harvard University Press, 1960–92

——, *The Collected Works of Ralph Waldo Emerson*, ed. Alfred R. Ferguson et al., Cambridge, MA: Harvard University Press, 1971–2013

——, *Nature and Selected Essays*, ed. Larzer Ziff, New York: Penguin, 2003

Endres, Johannes (ed.), *Friedrich Schlegel Handbuch: Leben – Werk – Wirkung*, Stuttgart: J. B. Metzler Springer Verlag, 2017

Estes, Yolanda and Curtis Bowman (eds), *J. G. Fichte and the Atheism Dispute (1798–1800)*, Farnham: Ashgate, 2010

Ferber, Michael, *Romanticism: A Very Short Introduction*, Oxford: Oxford University Press, 2010

Fichte, Johann Gottlieb, *Versuch einer Kritik aller Offenbarung*, 1792, in *Johann Gottlieb Fichte's Sämmtliche Werke*, ed. I. H. Fichte, vol. 5

——, *Beitrag zur Berichtigung der Urtheile des Publikums über die französische Revolution: Zur Beurtheilung ihrer Rechtmäßigkeit*, 1793, in *Johann Gottlieb Fichte's Sämmtliche Werke*, ed. I. H. Fichte, vol. 6

——, *Einige Vorlesungen über die Bestimmung des Gelehrten*, 1794, in *Johann Gottlieb Fichte's Sämmtliche Werke*, ed. I. H. Fichte, vol. 6

——, *Erster Anhang des Naturrecht: Grundriss des Familienrechts*, in *Johann Gottlieb Fichte's Sämmtliche Werke*, ed. I. H. Fichte, vol. 3

——, *Grundlage der gesammten Wissenschaftslehre*, 1794/5, in *Johann Gottlieb Fichte's Sämmtliche Werke*, ed. I. H. Fichte, vol. 1

——, 'Erste Einleitung zur Wissenschaftslehre', 1797, in *Johann Gottlieb Fichte's Sämmtliche Werke*, ed. I. H. Fichte, vol. 1

——, *Reden an die deutsche Nation*, 1807/8, in *Johann Gottlieb Fichte's Sämmtliche Werke*, ed. I. H. Fichte, vol. 7

——, *Johann Gottlieb Fichte's Sämmtliche Werke*, ed. I. H. Fichte, Berlin: Veit & Comp., 1845–6

——, *Johann Gottlieb Fichte: Gesamtausgabe der Bayerischen Akademie der Wissenschaften*, ed. Reinhard Lauth et al., Stuttgart: Frommann Holzboog Verlag, 1964–2005

——, *Wissenschaftslehre nova methodo: Kollegnachschrift K. Chr. Fr. Krause 1798/99*, ed. Erich Fuchs, Hamburg: Meiner, 1982

Forster, Georg, *Georg Forster's Briefwechsel mit S. Th. Sömmerring*, ed. Hermann Hettner, Braunschweig: Friedrich Vieweg, 1877

Frank, Heike, *Die Disharmonie, die mit mir geboren ward, und mich nie verlassen wird: Das Leben der Brendal/Dorothea Mendelssohn-Veit-Schlegel (1764–1839)*, Frankfurt: Peter Lang, 1988

Frank, Manfred, *The Philosophical Foundations of the Early German Romanticism*, Albany, NY: SUNY Press, 2004

Friedenthal, Richard, *Goethe: Sein Leben und seine Zeit*, Munich and Zurich: Piper, 2003

Friis, Herman R.,'Alexander von Humboldts Besuch in den Vereinigten Staaten von Amerika', in *Alexander von Humboldt: Studien zu seiner universalen Geisteshaltung*, ed. Joachim H. Schulze, Berlin: Walter de Gruyter & Co., 1959

Frischmann, Bärbel, 'Friedrich Schlegel und die Revolution', in *Romantik und Revolution: Zum politischen Reformpotential einer unpolitischen Bewegung*, ed. K. Ries, Heidelberg: Universitätsverlag Winter, 2012

Fuchs, Erich, 'Fichte's Final Year', *Rivista de Storia della Filosofia*, vol. 69, no. 4, 2014

——, (ed.), *J. G. Fichte im Gespräch: Berichte der Zeitgenossen*, Stuttgart: Frommann Holzboog Verlag, 1978–92

Fürst, Julius (ed.), *Henriette Herz: Ihr Leben und ihre Erinnerungen*, Berlin: Wilhelm Herz, 1858

Gall, Lothar, *Wilhelm von Humboldt: Ein Preuße von Welt*, Berlin: Propyläen, 2011

Geier, Manfred, *Die Brüder Humboldt: Eine Biographie*, Hamburg: Rowohlt, 2010

Gersdorff, Dagmar von, *Dich zu lieben kann ich nicht verlernen: Das Leben der Sophie Brentano-Mereau*, Frankfurt and Leipzig: Insel Verlag, 1990

——, *Caroline von Humboldt: Eine Biographie*, Berlin: Insel Verlag, 2013

Goethe, Johann Wolfgang von, *Die Leiden des jungen Werthers*, revised edn, Leipzig: Weygandschen Buchhandlung, 1787

——, *Zur Farbenlehre*, Tübingen: J. G. Cotta'scher Buchhandlung, 1810

——, *Theory of Colours*, trans. Charles Lock Eastlake, London: John Murray, 1840

——, *Goethe's Briefwechsel mit den Gebrüdern von Humboldt (1795–1832)*, ed. F. Th. Bratanek, Leipzig: Brockhaus, 1876

——, *Weimar und Jena im Jahre 1806*, ed. Richard and Robert Keil, Leipzig: Verlag Edwin Schloemp, 1886

——, *Goethes Werke*, published on behalf of Grand Duchess Sophie of Saxe-Weimar-Eisenach, Weimar: Herman Böhlau, 1887–1919

——, *Tagebücher*, 1790–1800 and 1801–8, in *Goethes Werke*, Part III, vols 2–3, 1887–1919

——, *Goethes Gespräche*, ed. Woldemar von Biedermann, Leipzig: F. W. Biedermann, 1889–96

——, *Goethes Briefwechsel mit Wilhelm und Alexander v. Humboldt*, ed. Ludwig Geiger, Berlin: H. Bondy, 1909

——, *Goethes Ehe in Briefen*, ed. Hans Gerhard Gräf, Frankfurt: Rütten & Loening, 1921

——, *Goethes Werke*, ed. Herbert von Einem et al., Hamburg: Christian Wegener Verlag, 1949–60

——, *Italienische Reise*, in *Goethes Werke*, ed. Herbert von Einem et al., vol. 11

——, *Faust*, trans. Walter Kaufmann, New York: Doubleday, 1961

——, *Goethe: Begegnungen und Gespräche*, ed. Ernst and Renate Grumach, Berlin and New York: Walter de Gruyter, 1965–2000

——, *Goethes Briefe*, ed. Karl Robert Mandelkrow, Hamburg: Christian Wegener Verlag, 1968–76

——, *Goethe in vertraulichen Briefen seiner Zeitgenossen*, Berlin: Aufbau-Verlag, 1979

——, *Briefe an Goethe, Gesamtausgabe in Regestform*, ed. Karl Heinz Hahn, Weimar: Böhlau, 1980–2000

——, *Goethes Leben von Tag zu Tag: Eine Dokumentarische Chronik*, ed. Robert Steiger, Zurich: Artemis Verlag, 1982–96

——, *Sämtliche Werke: Briefe, Tagebücher und Gespräche*, ed. Hendrik Birus, Frankfurt: Deutscher Klassiker Verlag, 1985–2013

——, *Schriften zur Morphologie*, ed. Dorothea Kuhn, Frankfurt: Deutscher Klassiker Verlag, 1987

——, *Roman Elegies; and the Diary* (in German and English), trans. David Luke, London: Libris, 1988

——, *Schriften zur Allgemeinen Naturlehre, Geologie und Mineralogie*, ed. Wolf von Engelhardt and Manfred Wenzel, Frankfurt: Deutscher Klassiker Verlag, 1989

——, *Faust Part Two*, trans. David Luke, Oxford: Oxford University Press, 1994a

——, *Johann Wolfgang Goethe Tag-und Jahreshefte*, ed. Irmtraut Schmid, Frankfurt: Deutscher Klassiker Verlag, 1994b

——, *Die Wahlverwandschaften*, Frankfurt: Insel Verlag, 2002

——, *Faust Part One*, trans. David Luke, Oxford: Oxford University Press, 2008

Goethe, Johann Wolfgang von and Friedrich Schiller, *Briefwechsel zwischen Schiller und Goethe in den Jahren 1794–1805*, Stuttgart and Augsburg: J. G. Cotta'scher Verlag, 1856

Goldstein, Jürgen, *Georg Forster: Zwischen Freiheit und Naturgewalt*, Berlin: Matthes & Seitz, 2015

Grabowski, Stanislaus, *Vertraute Geschichte der sächsischen Höfe und Staaten seit Beendigung des dreißigjährigen Krieges*, Berlin: Julius Adelsdorff's Verlag, 1861

Granville, A. B., *St. Petersburgh: A Journal of Travels to and from that Capital. Through Flanders, the Rhenich Provinces, Prussia, Russia, Poland, Silesia, Saxony, the Federated States of Germany, and France*, London: Henry Colburn, 1829

Gries, Johann Diedrich, *Gedichte und poetische Übersetzungen*, Stuttgart: F. C. Löflund & Sohn, 1829

——, *Aus dem Leben von Johann Diedrich Gries*, Leipzig: F. A. Brockhaus, 1855

Gura, Philip F., *American Transcendentalism: A History*, New York: Hill & Wang, 2008

Hädecke, Wolfgang, *Novalis Biographie*, Munich: Carl Hanser Verlag, 2011

Hamilton, Paul (ed.), *The Oxford Handbook of European Romanticism*, Oxford: Oxford University Press, 2016

Haney, John Louis, *The German Influence on Samuel Taylor Coleridge*, Philadelphia: University of Pennsylvania Press, 1902

Harding, Walter (ed.), *Thoreau as Seen by His Contemporaries*, New York: Dover Publications and London: Constable, 1989

Harman, P. M., *The Culture of Nature in Britain, 1680–1860*, New Haven, CT and London: Yale University Press, 2009

Haydon, Benjamin Robert, *The Diary of Benjamin Robert Haydon*, ed. Willard Bissell Pope, Cambridge, MA: Harvard University Press, 1960–3

Hegel, Georg Wilhelm Friedrich, *Differenz des Fichteschen und Schellingschen Systems der Philosophie*, Jena: Akademische Buchhandlung, 1801

——, *Phänomenologie des Geistes*, 1807, in *Werke*, ed. Eva Moldenhauer and Karl Markus Michel, vol. 3

——, *Briefe von und an Hegel, 1785–1812*, ed. Johannes Hoffmeister, Hamburg: Felix Meiner Verlag, 1952

——, *Hegel in Berichten seiner Zeitgenossen*, ed. Günther Nicolin, Hamburg: Felix Meiner Verlag, 1970

——, *Werke*, ed. Eva Moldenhauer and Karl Markus Michel, Frankfurt: Suhrkamp, 1986

——, *Phenomenology of Spirit*, trans. Terry Pinkard, Cambridge: Cambridge University Press, 2018

Heine, Heinrich, 'Die Romantische Schule', 1836, in *Werke und Briefe*, vol. 5, ed. Hans Kaufmann, Berlin and Weimar: Aufbau Verlag, 1972

Hellmann, Birgitt, *Wie zwey Enden einer grossen Stadt . . . Die 'Doppelstadt Jena-Weimar' im Spiegel regionaler Künstler*, Jena: Städtische Museen Jena, 1999

Hellmann, Birgitt (ed.), *Bürger, Bauern und Soldaten: Napoleons Krieg in Thüringen 1806 in Selbstzeugnissen: Briefe, Berichte und Erinnerungen*, Weimar: Hain Verlag, 2005

Herder, Johann Gottfried, 'Über die neuere Deutsche Litteratur', 1768, in *Herders Sämmtliche Werke*, ed. Bernhard Suphan et al., Berlin: Weidmann, 1877–99, vol. 2

——, 'Briefe zur Beförderung der Humanität', 1793–7, in *Herders Sämmtliche Werke*, ed. Bernhard Suphan et al., Berlin: Weidmann, 1877–99, vol. 2

——, *Briefe, Gesamtausgabe 1763–1803*, ed. Karl-Heinz Hahn et al., Weimar: Bühlau, 1977–2016

Herold, J. Christopher, *Mistress to an Age: A Life of Madame de Staël*, Westport, CT: Greenwood Press, 1975

Hesse, Volker, 'Johann Christian Stark d. Ältere (1753–1818): Der Arzt Goethes und Schillers', in *Wegbereiter der modernen Medizin: Jenaer Mediziner aus drei Jahrhunderten: von Loder und Hufeland zu Rössle und Brednow*, ed. Christian Fleck et al., Jena and Quedlinburg: Verlag Dr Bussart & Stadler, 2004

Hibbert, Christopher, *The French Revolution*, London: Penguin, 1980

Higonnet, Margaret R., 'Madame de Staël and Schelling', *Comparative Literature*, vol. 38, no. 2, 1986

Hölderlin, Friedrich, *Sämtliche Werke: Große Stuttgarter Ausgabe*, ed. Friedrich Beißner et al., Stuttgart: W. Kohlhammer, 1943–85

——, *Hyperion: Oder der Eremit in Griechenland*, Munich: Anaconda, 2020

Holl, Frank, 'Alexander von Humboldt: Wie der Klimawandel entdeckt wurde', *Die Gazette*, vol. 16, 2007–8

Holmes, Richard, *Coleridge*, vol. 1, *Early Visions*, London: HarperCollins, 1998a

——, *Coleridge*, vol. 2, *Darker Reflections*, London: HarperCollins, 1998b

——, *The Age of Wonder: How the Romantic Generation Discovered the Beauty and Terror of Science*, London: Harper Press, 2008

Horn, Gisela, *Mir kann nicht genügen an dieser bedingten Freiheit: Frauen der Jenaer Romantik*, Jena: DominoPlus, 2013

Horne, Alistair, *Seven Ages of Paris*, New York: Vintage Books, 2004

Huber, Therese, *Briefe*, ed. Magdalene Heuser, Berlin: De Gruyter, 1999

Hufeland, C. W., *Bemerkungen über das Nervenfieber und seine Complicationen, in den Jahren 1796, 1797 u. 1798*, Jena: Akademische Buchhandlung, 1799

Humboldt, Alexander von, *Versuch über die gereizte Muskel- und Nervenfaser*, Berlin: H. A. Rottmann, 1797

——, *Über die unterirdischen Gasarten und die Mittel, ihren Nachteil zu vermindern: Ein Beytrag zur Physik der praktischen Bergbaukunde*, Braunschweig: Vieweg, 1799

——, *Ideen zu einer Geographie der Pflanzen nebst einem Naturgemälde der Tropenländer*, Tübingen: F. G. Cotta and Paris: F. Schoell, 1807

——, *Researches concerning the Institutions & Monuments of the Ancient Inhabitants of America with Descriptions & Views of some of the most Striking Scenes in the Cordilleras!*, London: Longman, Hurst, Rees, Orme, Brown, John Murray, and H. Colburn, 1814

——, *Personal Narrative of Travels to the Equinoctial Regions of the New Continent during the years 1799–1804*, trans. Helen Maria Williams, London: Longman, Hurst, Rees, Orme, Brown and John Murray, 1814–29

——, *Central-Asien: Untersuchungen über die Gebirgsketten und die vergleichende Klimatologie*, Berlin: Carl J. Klemann, 1844

——, *Kosmos: Entwurf einer physischen Weltbeschreibung*, vols 1–3, Stuttgart and Tübingen: J. G. Cotta'scher Verlag, 1845–50

——, *Cosmos: Sketch of a Physical Description of the Universe*, vols 1–3, trans. Elizabeth J. L. Sabine, London: Longman, Brown, Green and Longmans, and John Murray, 1845–52

——, *Ansichten der Natur mit wissenschaftlichen Erläuterungen*, 3rd edn (extended), Stuttgart and Tübingen: J. G. Cotta'scher Verlag, 1849a

——, *Aspects of Nature, in Different Lands and Different Climates, with Scientific Elucidations*, trans. Elizabeth J. L. Sabine, London: Longman, Brown, Green and John Murray, 1849b

——, *Die Jugendbriefe Alexander von Humboldts 1787–1799*, ed. Ilse Jahn and Fritz G. Lange, Berlin: Akademie Verlag, 1973

——, *Aus meinem Leben: Autobiographische Bekenntnisse*, ed. K.-R. Biermann, Munich: C. H. Beck, 1987

——, *Reise durch Venezuela: Auswahl aus den Amerikanischen Reisetagebüchern*, ed. Margot Faak, Berlin: Akademie Verlag, 2000

——, *Reise auf dem Río Magdalena, durch die Anden und Mexico*, ed. Margot Faak, Berlin: Akademie Verlag, 2003

——, *Briefe von Alexander von Humboldt und Christian Carl Josias Bunsen*, ed. Ingo Schwarz, Berlin: Rohrwall Verlag, 2006

——, *Alexander von Humboldt und Cotta: Briefwechsel*, ed. Ulrike Leitner, Berlin: Akademie Verlag 2009a

——, *Essay on the Geography of Plants*, ed. Stephen T. Jackson, Chicago and London: University of Chicago Press, 2009b

——, *Views of Nature*, ed. Stephen T. Jackson and Laura Dassow Walls, Chicago and London: University of Chicago Press, 2014

——, *Sämtliche Schriften: Berner Ausgabe*, ed. Oliver Lubrich and Thomas Nehrlich, Munich: DTV, 2018

Humboldt, Caroline von, *Neue Briefe von Karoline von Humboldt*, ed. Albert Leitzmann, Halle: Max Niemeyer, 1901

Humboldt, Wilhelm von, *Briefe von Wilhelm von Humboldt an Friedrich Heinrich Jacobi*, ed. Albert Leitzmann, Halle: Max Niemeyer, 1892

——, *Gesammelte Schriften*, ed. Albert Leitzmann, Berlin: B. Behr, 1903–36

Humboldt, Wilhelm von and Caroline von Humboldt, *Wilhelm und Caroline von Humboldt in ihren Briefen*, ed. Anna von Sydow, Berlin: Mittler & Sohn, 1910–16

Jacobs, Wilhelm G., *Johann Gottlieb Fichte: Eine Biographie*, Frankfurt and Leipzig: Insel Verlag, 2012

Jaspers, Karl, *Schelling: Größe und Verhängnis*, Munich: Piper, 1955

Jenisch, Daniel, *Diogenes Laterne*, Leipzig: Wilhelm Rein, 1799

Kaag, John, *Thinking through the Imagination: Aesthetics in Human Cognition*, New York: Fordham University Press, 2014

Kant, Immanuel, *The Metaphysics of Morals*, trans. Mary Gregor, Cambridge: Cambridge University Press, 1991

Kaube, Jürgen, *Hegels Welt*, Berlin: Rowohlt, 2020

Klauss, Jochen, *Goethes Wohnhaus in Weimar: Ein Rundgang in Geschichten*, Weimar: Klassikerstätten zu Weimar, 1991

Kleßmann, Eckart, *Universitätsmamsellen: Fünf aufgeklärte Frauen zwischen Rokoko, Revolution und Romantik*, Frankfurt: Eichborn, 2008

Knebel, Karl Ludwig von, *Zur deutschen Literatur und Geschichte: Ungedruckte Briefe aus Knebels Nachlass*, ed. Heinrich Düntzer, Nuremberg: Bauer & Raspe, 1858

Koch, Herbert (ed.), *Altes und Neues aus der Heimat: Sonderdruck der Beilage zum Jenaer Volksblatt, 1909–1920*, Jena: Verlag Bernhard Vopelius, 1939

Kojève, Alexandre, *Introduction to the Reading of Hegel: Lectures on the Phenomenology of Spirit*, ed. Allan Bloom, Ithaca, NY and London: Cornell University Press, 1969

Kopij-Weiß, Marta, 'Der Einfluss der deutschen Literatur der klassisch-romantischen Wende auf die polnische Literatur der Romantik, Bundeszentrale für politische Bildung', 2013, https://www.bpb.de/veranstaltungen/doku mentation/152252/der-einfluss-der-deutschen-literatur-der-klassisch-roman-tischen-wende-auf-die-polnische-literatur-der-romantik?p=all

Köpke, Rudolf (ed.), *Ludwig Tieck: Erinnerungen aus dem Leben des Dichters*, Leipzig: Brockhaus, 1855

Körner, Josef, *Romantiker und Klassiker: die Brüder Schlegel in ihren Beziehungen zu Schiller und Goethe*, Berlin: Askanischer Verlag, 1924

Körner, Josef (ed.), *Krisenjahre der Romantik: Briefe aus dem Schlegelkreis*, Bern and Munich: Francke Verlag, 1969

Kösling, Peer, *Die Familie der herrlichen Verbannten: Die Frühromantiker in Jena*, Jena: Jenzig Verlag, 2010

Kratzsch, Konrad, *Klatschnest Weimar*, Würzburg: Königshausen & Neumann, 2009

Kremer, Arndt, 'Transitions of a Myth? The Idea of a Language-Defined Kulturnation in Germany', *New German Review: A Journal of Germanic Studies*, vol. 27, no. 1, 2016

Krünitz, Johann Georg, *Oeconomische Encyclopädie*, Berlin: Pauli, 1773–1858, vol. 153

Kühn, Manfred, *Kant: Eine Biographie*, Munich: DTV, 2007

——, *Johann Gottlieb Fichte: Ein deutsche Philosoph*, Munich: C. H. Beck, 2012

Labriola, Patrick, 'Germany and the American Transcendentalists: An Intellectual Bridge', *The Concord Saunterer*, vol. 6, 1998

——, 'Ralph Waldo Emerson's "Nature": Puritan Typology and German Idealism', *The Concord Saunterer*, vol. 10, 2002

Laman, Barbara, *James Joyce and German Theory: 'The Romantic School and All That'*, Madison, WI: Fairleigh Dickinson University Press, 2004

Laube, Heinrich, *Erinnerungen: 1810–1840*, Vienna: Wilhelm Braumüller, 1875

Leclercq, Henri, 'New Concepts and Terms during the French Revolution: A Classification of the Neologisms According to their Origin', in *Conceptual and Numerical Analysis of Data*, ed. Otto Optiz, Berlin: Springer Verlag, 1989

Leitner, Ulrike, 'Alexander von Humboldts Schriften – Anregungen und Reflexionen Goethes', *Das Allgemeine und das Einzelne – Johann Wolfgang von Goethe und Alexander von Humboldt im Gespräch*, *Acta Historica Leopoldina*, vol. 38, 2003

Levere, Trevor H., *Poetry Realized in Nature: Samuel Tayler Coleridge and Early Nineteenth-Century Science*, Cambridge: Cambridge University Press, 1981

Lewis, Tess, 'Madame de Staël: The Inveterate Idealist', *Hudson Review*, vol. 54, no. 3, 2001

Liebeskind, Johann Heinrich, *Rükerinnerungen von einer Reise durch einen Theil von Teutschland, Preußen, Kurland und Liefland, während des Aufenthalts der Franzosen in Mainz und der Unruhen in Polen*, Strasburg: n.p., 1795

Lindemann, Mary, *Health & Healing in Eighteenth-Century Germany*, Baltimore, MD: Johns Hopkins University Press, 1996

Linnaeus, Carl, *Philosophia Botanica*, trans. Stephen Freer, Oxford: Oxford University Press, 2003

Loewenthal, W. and S. (eds), *Berliner Adreßbuch für das Jahr 1895*, Berlin: W. & S. Loewenthal, 1895

Mähl, Hans-Joachim, 'Der poetische Staat: Utopie und Utopienreflexion bei den Frühromantikern', in *Utopienforschung: Interdisziplinäre Studien zur neuzeitlichen Utopie*, vol. 3, ed. W. Voßkamp, Stuttgart: J. B. Metzler, 1982

Maier, Heidi-Melanie (ed.), *'Gestern Abend schlief er auf dem Sofa ein': Alltägliches Leben um 1800, Alltag*, Erfurt: Landeszentrale für politische Bildung Thüringen, 2004

Marovitz, Sanford E., 'Melville's Problematic "Being"', in *Hermann Melville: New Edition*, ed. Harold Bloom, New York: Bloom's Literary Criticism, 2008

Martens, Gunter, *Friedrich Hölderlin*, Hamburg: Rowohlt, 1996

Meisner, Heinrich (ed.), *Briefe von Dorothea Schlegel und Friedrich Schleiermacher*, Berlin: Literaturarchiv Gesellschaft, 1913

Mereau-Brentano, Sophie, *Wie sehn' ich mich hinaus in die freie Welt: Tagebücher, Betrachtungen und vermischte Prosa*, ed. Katharina von Hammerstein, Munich: DTV, 1996

Merkel, Andreas, H. (ed.), *Biographie des Doctor Friedrich Wilhelm von Hoven*, Nuremberg: Joh. Leonh. Schrag, 1840

Merseburger, Peter, *Mythos Weimar: Zwischen Geist und Macht*, Munich: DTV, 2009

Müller, Gerhard et al., *Die Universität Jena: Tradition und Innovation um 1800*, Stuttgart: F. Steiner, 2001

Müller-Wille, Klaus, 'Scandinavian Romanticism', in *The Oxford Handbook of European Romanticism*, ed. Paul Hamilton, Oxford: Oxford University Press, 2016

Nicolai, Friedrich, *Beschreibung einer Reise durch Deutschland und die Schweiz im Jahre 1781*, vol. 11, 1796

Nipperdey, Thomas, *Deutsche Geschichte, 1800–1866: Bürgerwelt und starker Staat*, Munich: C. H. Beck, 2013

Novalis, 'Fichte Studies', 1795/6, in *Schriften: Die Werke Friedrich von Hardenbergs*, ed. Paul Kluckhohn et al., vol. 2

——, 'Blüthenstaub', 1798, in *Schriften: Die Werke Friedrich von Hardenbergs*, ed. Paul Kluckhohn et al., vol. 2

——, 'Das Allgemeine Brouillon', 1798/9, in *Schriften: Die Werke Friedrich von Hardenbergs*, ed. Paul Kluckhohn et al., vol. 3

——, 'Heinrich von Ofterdingen', 1802, in *Schriften: Die Werke Friedrich von Hardenbergs*, ed. Paul Kluckhohn et al., vol. 1

——, 'Lehrlinge zu Sais', 1802, in *Schriften: Die Werke Friedrich von Hardenbergs*, ed. Paul Kluckhohn et al., vol. 1

——, 'Tagebücher, Briefwechsel, zeitgenössische Zeugnisse', in *Schriften: Die Werke Friedrich von Hardenbergs*, ed. Paul Kluckhohn et al., vol. 4

——, *Schriften: Die Werke Friedrich von Hardenbergs*, ed. Paul Kluckhohn et al., Stuttgart: Kohlhammer, 1960–2006

——, *Hymns to the Night* (in German and English), trans. Richard C. Higgins, New York: McPherson, 1988

——, 'Miscellaneous Remarks: Original Version of Pollen', trans. Alexander Gelley, *New Literary History*, vol. 22, no. 2, 1991

——, *Novalis: Fichte Studies*, ed. Jane Kneller, Cambridge: Cambridge University, 2003

——, *Notes for a Romantic Encyclopaedia, Das Allgemeine Brouillon*, trans. David W. Woods, Albany, NY: SUNY Press, 2007

——, *Fragmente und Studien: Die Christenheit oder Europa*, ed. Carl Paschek, Stuttgart: Reclam, 2018

Nowak, Holger and Birgitt Hellmann, *Die Schlacht bei Jena und Auerstedt am 14. Oktober 1806*, Jena: Städtische Museen, 2005

O'Brien, William Arctander, *Novalis: Signs of Revolution*, Durham, NC: Duke University Press, 1995

Oellers, Norbert, 'Die Dame Luzifer zwischen Revolution und Literatur', *Deutsche Romantik und Französische Revolution: Internationales Kolloquium, Acta Universitatis Wratislaviensis*, no. 115, *Germanica Wratislaviensia*, vol. 80, 1990

Oergel, Maike, 'Jena 1789–1819: Ideas, Poetry and Politics', in *The Oxford Handbook of European Romanticism*, ed. Paul Hamilton, Oxford: Oxford University Press, 2016

Oeser, Hans Ludwig, *Das Zeitalter Goethes: Menschen und Werke*, Berlin: Deutsche Buch-Gemeinschaft, 1932

Oesterle, Günther, 'Friedrich Schlegel in Paris oder die Romantische Gegenrevolution', in *Les Romantiques allemands et la Révolution française: Die deutsche Romantik und die französische Revolution*, ed. Gonthier-Louis Fink, Strasbourg: Université des Sciences Humaines, 1989

Olshausen, Waldemar von, 'Neues aus dem Caroline-Kreis', *Euphorion*, vol. 28, 1927

Ørsted, Hans Christian, *Correspondance de H. C. Örsted avec divers savants*, ed. M. C. Harding, Copenhagen: H. Aschehoug & Co., 1920

Parker, Theodore, 'German Literature', *The Dial*, vol. 1, January 1841

Paul, Gertrud, *Die Schicksale der Stadt Jena und ihre Umgebung in den Octobertagen 1806*, Jena: Gustav Fischer Verlag, 1920

Paulin, Roger, *The Life of August Wilhelm Schlegel: Cosmopolitan of Art and Poetry*, Cambridge: Open Book Publishers, 2016

Paulin, Tom, *The Day-Star of Liberty: William Hazlitt's Radical Style*, London: Faber & Faber, 1998

Petersen, Julius (ed.), *Schillers Persönlichkeit: Urtheile der Zeitgenossen und Dokumente*, Weimar: Gesellschaft der Bibliophilen, 1909

Pieper, Herbert, 'Alexander von Humboldt: Die Geognosie der Vulkane', *HiN Alexander von Humboldt im Netz VII*, vol. 13, 2006

Pikulik, Lothar, *Frühromantik. Epoche – Werke – Wirkung*, Munich: C. H. Beck, 1992

Pilz, Katharina, 'Die Gemäldegalerie in Dresden unter Berücksichtigung der Mengsschen Abguss-Sammlung', in *Tempel der Kunst: Die Geburt des öffentlichen Museums in Deutschland 1701–1815*, ed. Bénédicte Savoy, Cologne, Weimar, Wien: Böhlau Verlag, 2015

Pinkard, Terry, *Hegel: A Biography*, Cambridge: Cambridge University Press, 2001

Pochmann, Henry A., *German Culture in America: Philosophical and Literary Influences, 1600–1900*, Westport, CT: Greenwood Press, 1978

Porter, Roy (ed.), *Cambridge History of Science*, vol. 4, *Eighteenth-Century Science*, Cambridge: Cambridge University Press, 2003

Preisendörfer, Bruno, *Als Deutschland noch nicht Deutschland war: Reise in die Goethezeit*, Cologne: Kiepenheuer & Witsch, 2018

Rebmann, Georg Friedrich, *Jena fängt an, mir zu gefallen: Stadt und Universität in Schriften und Briefen*, ed. Werner Greiling, Jena: Academica & Studentica Jensensia, 1994

Reulecke, Martin, ' "Eigentümliche Naturformen": Caroline Schlegel-Schelling als Briefkünstlerin und Rezensentin', in *Femmes de lettres – Europäische Autorinnen des 17. und 18. Jahrhunderts*, ed. Marina Ortrud M. Hertrampf, Berlin: Frank & Timme, 2020

Richards, Robert J., *The Romantic Conception of Life: Science and Philosophy in the Age of Goethe*, Chicago: University of Chicago Press, 2002

Richardson, Robert D., *Henry Thoreau: A Life of the Mind*, Berkeley, CA: University of California Press, 1986

——, *Emerson: The Mind on Fire*, Berkeley, CA and London: University of California Press, 1995

Richter, August Gottlieb, *Medical and Surgical Observations*, trans. Thomas Spens, Edinburgh: T. Duncan, 1794

Ries, Klaus (ed.), *Zwischen Universität und Stadt: Aspekte demographischer Entwicklung in Jena um 1800*, Weimar: Hain Verlag, 2004

——, *Romantik und Revolution: Zum politischen Reformpotential einer unpolitischen Bewegung*, Heidelberg: Universitätsverlag Winter, 2012

Rist, Johann Georg, *Johann Georg Rists Lebenserinnerungen*, ed. G. Poel, Gotha: F. A. Berthes, 1880

Ritter, Johann Wilhelm, *Beweis, das ein beständiger Galvanismus den Lebensprocess in dem Thierreich begleite*, Weimar: Industrie-Comptoir, 1798

Robinson, Henry Crabb, *Diary, Reminiscences, and Correspondence of Henry Crabb Robinson*, ed. Thomas Sadler, London: Macmillan & Co., 1869

——, *Crabb Robinson in Germany, 1800–1805: Extracts from His Correspondence*, ed. Edith J. Morley, Oxford: Oxford University Press, 1929

Roßbeck, Brigitte, *Zum Trotz glücklich: Caroline Schlegel-Schelling und die romantische Lebenskunst*, Munich: Siedler, 2008

Rosenkranz, Karl, *Georg Wilhelm Friedrich Hegel's Leben*, Berlin: Duncker & Humblot, 1844

Rosenstrauch, Hazel, *Wahlverwandt und ebenbürtig: Caroline und Wilhelm von Humboldt*, Berlin: Die Andere Bibliothek, 2009

Roussanova, Elena, 'Hermann Trautschold und die Ehrung, Alexander von Humboldts in Russland', *HiN Alexander von Humboldt im Netz XIV*, vol. 27, 2013

Rousseau, Jean-Jacques, *The Emile of Jean-Jacques Rousseau*, trans. William Boyd, New York: Columbia University Press, 1965

——, *Emile, or On Education*, ed. Allan D. Bloom and Christopher Kelley, Hanover, NH: University Press of New England, 2010

Safranski, Rüdiger, *Friedrich Schiller, oder, Die Erfindung des deutschen Idealismus*, Munich: Hanser, 2009a

——, *Romantik. Eine deutsche Affäre*, Frankfurt: Fischer Verlag, 2009b

——, *Goethe: Life as a Work of Art*, New York: Liveright, 2017

Salat, Jakob, *Ueber den Geist der Philosophie*, Munich: Joseph Lentner, 1803

Saltzman, Cynthia, *Napoleon's Plunder and the Theft of Veronese's Feast*, London: Thames & Hudson, 2021

Sandford, Margaret E., *Thomas Poole and His Friends*, London: Macmillan & Co., 1888

Sattelmeyer, Robert, *Thoreau's Reading: A Study in Intellectual History with Bibliographical Catalogue*, Princeton, NJ: Princeton University Press, 1988

——, 'The Remaking of "Walden"', in *'Walden' and 'Resistance to Civil Government': Authoritative Texts, Thoreau's Journal, Reviews and Essays in Criticism*, ed. William Rossi, New York and London: W. W. Norton, 1992

Savigny, J. H., *A Catalogue of Chirurgical Instruments made and sold by J. H. Savigny*, London: Bulmer & Co., 1800

Schiffman, Robyn, 'Novalis and Hawthorne: A New Look at Hawthorne's German Influences', *Nathaniel Hawthorne Review*, vol. 38, no. 1, 2012

Schelling, Friedrich Wilhelm Joseph, 'Ideen zu einer Philosophie der Natur', 1797, in *Sämmtliche Werke*, ed. K. F. A. Schelling, vol. 2

——, *Von der Weltseele*, 1798, in *Sämmtliche Werke*, ed. K. F. A. Schelling, vol. 2

——, *Einleitung zu dem Entwurf eines Systems der Naturphilosophie*, 1799, in *Sämmtliche Werke*, ed. K. F. A. Schelling, vol. 3

——, 'Erster Entwurf eines Systems der Naturphilosophie', 1799, in *Sämmtliche Werke*, ed. K. F. A. Schelling, vol. 3

——, *System des Transzendentalen Idealismus*, 1800, in *Sämmtliche Werke*, ed. K. F. A. Schelling, vol. 3

——, 'Darstellung meines Systems der Philosophie', 1801, in *Sämmtliche Werke*, ed. K. F. A. Schelling, vol. 4

——, 'Über den wahren Begriff der Naturphilosophie', 1801, in *Sämmtliche Werke*, ed. K. F. A. Schelling, vol. 4

——, 'Bruno, oder über das göttliche und natürliche Prinzip der Dinge', 1802, in *Sämmtliche Werke*, ed. K. F. A. Schelling, vol. 4

——, 'Philosophie der Kunst', 1802, in *Sämmtliche Werke*, ed. K. F. A. Schelling, vol. 5

——, *Sämmtliche Werke*, ed. K. F. A. Schelling, Stuttgart and Augsburg: J. G. Cotta'scher Verlag, 1856–61

——, *Aus Schellings Leben: In Briefen*, ed. Gustav L. Plitt, Leipzig: R. Hirzel, 1869–70

——, *Briefe und Dokumente*, ed. Horst Fuhrmans, Bonn: Bouvier Verlag, 1962–75

——, *Historisch-kritische Ausgabe der Bayerischen Akademie der Wissenschaften*, ed. Hans Michael Baumgartner et al., Stuttgart: Frommann-Holzboog, 1976–

Schiller, Charlotte, *Charlotte von Schiller und ihre Freunde*, Stuttgart: J. G. Cotta'scher Verlag, 1862

Schiller, Friedrich, *On the Aesthetic Education of Man*, 1795, trans. Reginald Snell, Mineola, NY: Dover Publications, 2004

——, *Über die ästhetische Erziehung des Menschen in einer Reihe von Briefen*, 1795, in *Sämtliche Werke*, ed. Gerhard Fricke et al., Munich: Hanser, 1962

——, *Schillers Leben: Verfasst aus Erinnerungen der Familie, seinen eignen Briefen und den Nachrichten seines Freundes Körner*, ed. Christian Gottfried Körner and Caroline von Wolzogen, Stuttgart and Tübingen: J. G. Cotta'sche Buchhandlung, 1830

——, *Schillers Werke: Nationalausgabe. Briefwechsel*, ed. Julius Petersen and Gerhard Fricke, Weimar: Herman Böhlaus Nachfolger, 1943–2003

——, *Sämtliche Werke*, ed. Gerhard Fricke et al., Munich: Hanser, 1962

Schiller, Friedrich and Christian Gottfried Körner, *Schillers Briefwechsel mit Körner*, Berlin: Veit & Comp., 1847

Schlegel, August Wilhelm, *An das Publicum: Rüge einer in der Jenaischen Allgemeinen Literatur-Zeitung begangnen Ehrenschädigung*, Tübingen: Cotta, 1802

——, *August Wilhelm Schlegel's Vorlesungen über dramatische Kunst und Litteratur*, 1809–11, in *August Wilhelm von Schlegel's Sämmtliche Werke*, ed. Eduard Böcking, vols 5 and 6

——, *Lectures on Dramatic Art and Literature*, trans. John Black, London: Baldwin, Cradock & Joy, 1815

——, *Kritische Schriften*, Berlin: Reimer, 1828

——, *August Wilhelm von Schlegel's Sämmtliche Werke*, ed. Eduard Böcking, Leipzig: Weidmann'sche Buchhandlung, 1846–7

——, *A. W. Schlegels Vorlesungen über schöne Litteratur und Kunst*, ed. Jakob Minor, Heilbronn: Verlag Gebr. Henniger, 1884

——, *Kritische Schriften und Briefe*, ed. Edgar Lohner, Stuttgart: Kohlhammer, 1962–74

Schlegel, Dorothea, *Dorothea v. Schlegel geb. Mendelssohn und deren Söhne Johannes und Philipp Veit. Briefwechsel*, ed. J. M. Reich, Mainz: Verlag Franz Kirchheim, 1881

Schlegel, Friedrich, 'Über das Studium der griechischen Poesie', 1795–7, in *Kritische Friedrich-Schlegel-Ausgabe*, ed. Ernst Behler, vol. 1

——, 'Kritische Fragmente' (Lyceum-Fragmente), 1797, in *Kritische Friedrich-Schlegel-Ausgabe*, ed. Ernst Behler, vol. 2

——, 'Geschichte der Poesie der Griechen und Römer', 1798, in *Kritische Friedrich-Schlegel-Ausgabe*, ed. Ernst Behler, vol. 1

——, '*Athenaeum* Fragmente', 1798, in *Kritische Friedrich-Schlegel-Ausgabe*, ed. Ernst Behler, vol. 2

——, 'Fragmente zur Poesie und Litteratur', 1798–1801, in *Kritische Friedrich-Schlegel-Ausgabe*, ed. Ernst Behler, vol. 16

——, 'Gespräch über die Poesie', 1800, in *Kritische Friedrich-Schlegel-Ausgabe*, ed. Ernst Behler, vol. 2

——, 'Ideen', 1800', in *Kritische Friedrich-Schlegel-Ausgabe*, ed. Ernst Behler, vol. 2

——, 'Zur Philosophie und Theologie', 1817, in *Kritische Friedrich-Schlegel-Ausgabe*, ed. Ernst Behler, vol. 19

——, 'Philosophie des Lebens', Wiener Vorlesung, 1827, in *Kritische Friedrich-Schlegel-Ausgabe*, ed. Ernst Behler, vol. 10

——, *Sämmtliche Werke*, 2nd edn, Vienna: Ignaz Klang, 1846

——, *Literary Notebooks 1797–1801*, ed. Hans Eichner, London: Athlone Press, 1957

——, *Kritische Friedrich-Schlegel-Ausgabe*, ed. Ernst Behler, Munich: F. Schöningh, 1958–2006

——, *Friedrich Schlegel's Lucinde and the Fragments*, trans. Peter Firchow, Minneapolis: University of Minnesota Press, 1998

——, *Lucinde: Studienausgabe*, ed. Karl Konrad Polheim, Stuttgart: Reclam, 1999

Schlegel, Friedrich and Dorothea, 'Briefe von und an Friedrich und Dorothea Schlegel', in *Kritische Friedrich-Schlegel-Ausgabe*, ed. Ernst Behler, vols 23–32, Munich: F. Schöningh, 1958–2006

Schlegel-Schelling, Caroline, *Caroline: Briefe aus der Frühromantik*, ed. Erich Schmidt, Leipzig: Insel Verlag, 1913

Schlegel-Schelling, Caroline and August Wilhelm Schlegel, 'Die Gemählde. Gespräch', *Athenaeum*, vol. 2, 1799

Schleiermacher, Friedrich, *Über die Religion: Reden an die Gebildeten unter ihren Verächtern (1799)*, Hamburg: Felix Meiner Verlag, 1958

——, *Briefwechsel*, in *Kritische Schleiermacher-Gesamtausgabe*, Part 5, ed. Andreas Arndt et al., Berlin: De Gruyter, 1985–

Schmidt-Dorotić, Carl, *Politische Romantik*, Munich and Leipzig: Duncker & Humblot, 1919

Schnyder, Paul, 'Politik und Sprache in der Frühromantik', *Athenäum,* vol. 9, 1990

Scholl, John William, *Friedrich Schlegel and Goethe, 1790–1802: A Study in Early German Romanticism*, Baltimore, MD: University of Baltimore Press, 1906

Schulz, Gerhard, *Die deutsche Literatur zwischen Französischer Revolution und Restauration*, Munich: C. H. Beck, 2000

Scurr, Ruth, *Napoleon: A Life in Gardens and Shadows*, London: Chatto & Windus, 2021

Seibt, Gustav, *Goethe und Napoleon: Eine historische Begegnung*, Munich: C. H. Beck, 2008

Seidel, George Joseph, *Fichte's Wissenschaftslehre of 1794: A Commentary on Part I* (in German and English), West Lafayette, IN: Purdue University Press, 1993

Seigel, Jerrold, *The Idea of the Self: Thought and Experience in Western Society since the Seventeenth Century*, Cambridge: Cambridge University Press, 2005

Sent, Eleonore, *Bergbau und Dichtung: Friedrich von Hardenberg*, Weimar: Hain Verlag, 2003

Shelley, Mary, *The Journals of Mary Shelley 1814–1844*, ed. P. R. Feldman and D. Scott-Kilvert, Oxford: Clarendon Press, 1987

——, *Frankenstein, or, The Modern Prometheus*, Oxford: Oxford University Press, 1998

Soret, Frédéric, *Zehn Jahre bei Goethe: Erinnerungen an Weimars klassische Zeit 1822–1832*, trans. and ed. H. H. Houben, Leipzig: F. A. Brockhaus, 1929

Staël, Germaine de, *Germany*, London: John Murray, 1813

——, *Deutschland,* Reutlingen: Mäcken'schen Buchhandlung, 1815

Stark, Johann Christian, *Handbuch zur Kentniss und Heilung innerer Krankheiten des menschlichen Körpers*, Jena: J. C. G. Göpferdt, 1799

Steffens, Henrik, *Was ich erlebte: Aus der Erinnerung niedergeschrieben*, vol. 4, Breslau: Verlag Josef Mar & Komp., 1841

——, 'Fact and Feelings from the Life of Steffens, 1799', *Foreign Quarterly Review*, vol. 31, 1843

Steig, Reinhold (ed.), *Achim von Armin und Clemens Brentano*, Stuttgart: J. G. Cotta'sche Buchhandlung, 1894

Steig, Reinhold and Herman Grimm (eds), *Achim von Arnim und die ihm nahe standen*, Stuttgart: J. G. Cotta'sche Buchhandlung, 1894–1904

Steinmetz, Max, *Die Geschichte der Universität Jena 1548/58–1958*, Jena: Gustav Fischer Verlag, 1958

Stelzig, Eugene L., *Henry Crabb Robinson in Germany: A Study in Nineteenth-Century Life Writing*, Lewisburg, PA: Bucknell University Press, 2010

Stern, Carola, *Ich möchte mir Flügel wünschen: Das Leben der Dorothea Schlegel*, Reinbek: Rowohlt, 1994

Stockinger, Claudia, 'Tiecks Genoveva und das Jenaer Romantikertreffen 1799', in *Das Jenaer Romantikertreffen im November 1799: Ein romantischer Streitfall*, Athenäum-Jahrbuch der Friedrich Schlegel-Gesellschaft, ed. Ulrich Breuer and Dirk von Petersdorff, Paderborn: F. Schöningh, 2015

Stokoe, F. W., *German Influence in the English Romantic Period, 1788–1818*, New York: Russell & Russell, 1963

Stoll, Adolf, *Friedrich Karl von Savignys Sächsische Studienreise 1799 und 1800*, Leipzig: n.p., 1891

——, *Der Maler Joh. Friedrich August Tischbein und seine Familie: Ein Lebensbild nach den Aufzeichnungen seiner Tochter Caroline*, Stuttgart: Strecker & Strecker, 1923

Strack, Friedrich (ed.), *Evolution des Geistes: Jena um 1800: Natur und Kunst, Philosophie und Wissenschaft im Spannungsfeld der Geschichte*, Stuttgart: Klett-Cotta, 1994

Strand, Mary R., *I/You: Paradoxical Constructions of Self and Other in Early German Romanticism*, New York: Peter Lang, 1998

Thoreau, Henry David, *Walden*, New York: Thomas Y. Crowell & Co., 1910

——, *The Writings of Henry D. Thoreau: Journal*, ed. Robert Sattelmeyer et al., Princeton, NJ: Princeton University Press, 1981–2002

Tieck, Ludwig, *Leben und Tod der heiligen Genoveva: Ein Trauerspiel*, Berlin: G. Reimer, 1820

——, *Ludwig Tieck's Schriften*, Berlin: G. Reimer, 1828–54

——, 'Eine Sommerreise', in *Ludwig Tieck's gesammelte Novellen: Vermehrt und verbessert*, Breslau: Verlag Josef Mar & Komp., 1838–42

Tilliette, Xavier, *Schelling: Biographie*, Stuttgart: Klett-Cotta, 2004

Tilliette, Xavier (ed.), *Schelling im Spiegel seiner Zeitgenossen*, Torino: Bottega d'Erasmo, 1974

Tsouyopoulos, Nelly, 'Doctors Contra Clysters and Feudalism: The Consequences of a Romantic Revolution', in *Romanticism and the Sciences*, ed. Andreas Cunningham and Nicholas Jardine, Cambridge: Cambridge University Press, 1990

Tyutchev, Fyodor, *Selected Poems*, trans. John Dewey, Gillingham: Brimstone Press, 2014

Uerlings, Herbert, *Friedrich von Hardenberg, genannt Novalis: Werk und Forschung*, Stuttgart: J. B. Metzler, 1991

Unterberger, Rose, *Die Goethe-Chronik*, Frankfurt and Leipzig: Insel Verlag, 2002

Varnhagen, K. A. von Ense, *Aus dem Nachlass Varnhagen's von Ense: Briefwechsel zwischen Varnhagen und Rahel*, Leipzig: Brockhaus, 1874–5

——, *Denkwürdigkeiten des eigenen Lebens*, ed. Konrad Feilchenfeldt, Frankfurt: Deutscher Klassiker Verlag, 1987

Vater, Michael G. and David W. Woods (eds), *J. G. Fichte / F. W. J. Schelling: The Philosophical Rupture between Fichte and Schelling: Selected Texts and Correspondence (1800–1802)*, Albany, NY: SUNY Press, 2012

Vieweg, Klaus, *Hegel: Der Philosoph der Freiheit*, Munich: C. H. Beck, 2020

Vigus, James, *Henry Crabb Robinson: Essays on Kant, Schelling, and German Aesthetics*, MHRA Critical Texts 18, London: Modern Humanities Research Association, 2010

Vogel, Stanley M., *German Literary Influences on the American Transcendentalists*, Hamden, CT: Archon Books, 1970

Wahl, Hans and Anton Kippenberg, *Goethe und seine Welt*, Leipzig: Insel Verlag, 1932

Wais, Karin, *Die Schiller Chronik*, Frankfurt and Leipzig: Insel Verlag, 2005

Walls, Laura Dassow, *Seeing New Worlds: Henry David Thoreau and Nineteenth-Century Natural Science*, Madison, WI: University of Wisconsin Press, 1995

———, *The Passage to Cosmos: Alexander von Humboldt and the Shaping of America*, Chicago and London: University of Chicago Press, 2009

Watson, Peter, *The German Genius: Europe's Third Renaissance, the Second Scientific Revolution, and the Twentieth Century*, London and New York: Simon & Schuster, 2010

Wehler, Hans-Ulrich, *Deutsche Gesellschaftsgeschichte, 1700–1815*, Munich: C. H. Beck, 1989

Wellek, René, 'Emerson and German Philosophy', *New England Quarterly*, vol. 16, no. 1, 1943

———, 'German and English Romanticism: A Confrontation', *Studies in Romanticism*, vol. 4, no. 1, 1964

Wetzels, Walter D., 'Johann Wilhelm Ritter: Romantic Physics in Germany', in *Romanticism and the Sciences*, ed. Andreas Cunningham and Nicholas Jardine, Cambridge: Cambridge University Press, 1990

Whitman, Walt, *Leaves of Grass*, New York, n.p., 1855

———, *Complete Prose Works*, Philadelphia, PA: David McKay, 1892

Wiedemann, Luise, *Erinnerungen von Luise Wiedemann*, ed. Julius Steinberger, Göttingen: Vereinigung Göttinger Bücherfreunde, 1929

Wieneke, Ernst (ed.), *Caroline und Dorothea Schlegel in Briefen*, Weimar: Gustav Kiepenheuer, 1914

Wiesing, Urban, 'Der Tod der Auguste Böhmer: Chronik eines medizinischen Skandals, seine Hintergründe und seine historische Bedeutung', *History and Philosophy of the Life Sciences*, vol. 11, no. 2, 1989

Wilcox, John, 'The Beginnings of l'art pour l'art', *Journal of Aesthetics and Art Criticism*, vol. 11, no. 4, 1953

Wordsworth, William, *Lyrical Ballads, with Other Poems*, London: T. N. Longman and O. Rees, 2nd edn, 1800

Wulf, Andrea, *The Invention of Nature: Alexander von Humboldt's New World*, New York: Knopf, 2015

Zimmermann, Harro, *Friedrich Schlegel, oder die Sehnsucht nach Deutschland*, Paderborn: F. Schöningh, 2009

Ziolkowski, Theodore, *Das Wunderjahr in Jena: Geist und Gesellschaft 1794–1795*, Stuttgart: Klett-Cotta, 1998

———, *German Romanticism and its Institutions*, Princeton, NJ: Princeton University Press, 1999

———, *Vorboten der Moderne: Eine Kulturgeschichte der Frühromantik*, Stuttgart: Klett-Cotta, 2006

———, *Stages of European Romanticism: Cultural Synchronicity Across the Arts, 1798–1848*, Rochester, NY: Camden House, 2018

Online Sources

For those who want to dig deeper into Caroline Schelling's letters and life, Doug Stott has created a fantastic English-language research resource: www. carolineshelling.com. This is the only place where Caroline's letters are available in translation (although the translations in *Magnificent Rebels* are by Damion Searls and me).

Allgemeine Literatur-Zeitung: https://zs.thulb.uni-jena.de/receive/jportal_jpjournal_00000005

August Wilhelm Schlegel's correspondence: https://august-wilhelm-schlegel.de/briefedigital/

Friedrich Schiller's correspondence: https://www.friedrich-schiller-archiv.de/briefe/; http://www.wissen-im-netz.info/literatur/schiller/briefe/index.htm

Schiller's poems in translation: https://archive.schillerinstitute.com/transl/translations_main.html

Goethe's and Schiller's original libraries at Herzogin Amalia Bibliothek: https://haab-digital.klassik-stiftung.de/viewer/browse/

Münchener Digitalisierungs Zentrum: https://www.digitale-sammlungen.de/en/

SLUB Dresden: https://digital.slub-dresden.de/kollektionen

SUB Göttinger Digitalisierungs Zentrum: https://gdz.sub.uni-goettingen.de

Works by German writers, poets and thinkers: http://www.zeno.org/Literatur

Newspapers

Allgemeine Literatur-Zeitung
Athenaeum
Horen
Journal des Luxus und der Moden
Intelligenzblatt der Allgemeine Literatur-Zeitung
Musen-Almanach

Index